North German Opera
in the Age of Goethe

North German Opera in the Age of Goethe

THOMAS BAUMAN

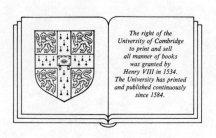

The right of the
University of Cambridge
to print and sell
all manner of books
was granted by
Henry VIII in 1534.
The University has printed
and published continuously
since 1584.

CAMBRIDGE UNIVERSITY PRESS

Cambridge
London   New York   New Rochelle
Melbourne   Sydney

Published by the Press Syndicate of the University of Cambridge
The Pitt Building, Trumpington Street, Cambridge CB2 1RP
32 East 57th Street, New York, NY 10022, USA
10 Stamford Road, Oakleigh, Melbourne 3166, Australia

First published 1985

Printed in Great Britain at
the University Press, Cambridge

Library of Congress catalogue card number: 84-29214

British Library cataloguing in publication data
Bauman, Thomas
North German Opera in the Age of Goethe.
1. Opera – Germany, Northern – History and criticism
I. Title
782.1′0943   ML1729
ISBN 0 521 26027 2

FOR MY PARENTS .

Contents

Illustrations

Figures

Plates

Acknowledgments

I wish to express my thanks to those who have aided me with their assistance and counsel in completing this study. My research in Europe was made possible by a Fellowship for Independent Study and Research from the National Endowment for the Humanities. I also benefited from the help of the staffs at many libraries, but especially the Library of Congress, The British Library, The New York Public Library, the Bayerische Staatsbibliothek, the Staatsbibliothek Preussischer Kulturbesitz, the Herzog-August-Bibliothek, and the Sächsische Landesbibliothek.

Several colleagues have provided me with valuable advice and criticism touching on all or part of this book. For the earlier sections Professors Gary Tomlinson, Daniel Heartz, and particularly Gudrun Busch have offered penetrating and thought-provoking insights. Mr John Warrack has read an early draft of the entire typescript and contributed fundamentally to improving every chapter of this study. My deepest and most inexpressible debt is to my wife Martha Feldman, who has read every word of what follows with care, perspicacity, and vibrant idealism which has brought home to me the lesson that, even in scholarship, everything perishable is but an image of what we strive for.

1

Introduction

We often judge as trivial that for which we have not yet found a context. The historian's duty in approaching neglected terrain lies far less in crying injustice than in seeking to provide such a context. In this spirit we ought to approach the variety of operatic works produced in North Germany during the last third of the eighteenth century. Scarcely a single opera from this time and place is known to any but the specialist by more than its name and certain historical truisms which have lent a few of them an inert, shadowy importance. Having little beyond this to rely on in the way of common ground, the historian faces a considerable gulf between him and his reader, and it is just as well for him to state at the outset how he intends to bridge it.

In his valuable study of Mozart's operas, Edward Dent dismissed the German operas we shall be discussing with sentiments that many other scholars have inclined to share: attempts at serious opera in German he called "abortive," and he saw even less merit in comic opera, "the triviality of which is for the most part beneath contempt."[1] To counter such received ideas by convincing the reader of North German opera's intrinsic importance in the scheme of eighteenth-century opera as a whole would be a hopeless task, as well as a misguided one. German-language opera of all kinds during the Enlightenment, although it absorbed many features from French and Italian opera, did not share in their international currency, but led a wholly insular existence, even after German *belles-lettres* began winning acclaim in other lands during the age of Goethe. Both as literature and as music, German opera – especially in the North – held interest only for a local audience of German theater-goers.

Not surprisingly, standard surveys of operatic history have not taken the music of North German opera very seriously, nor have literary historians taken much notice of its special literary character. Only in the fledgling discipline of theatrical history have scholars attempted to confront North German opera on its own terms – as a special idiom which blended musical and literary values under the compelling imperatives of the region's distinctive theatrical institutions. The present study, too, has taken as its point of departure the belief that a sympathetic and relevant understanding of North German opera is best arrived at if the traditional issues and queries concerning opera raised by literary science and musicology are considered within the

[1] *Mozart's Operas*, 2nd ed. (London, Oxford and New York, 1947), p. 30.

1

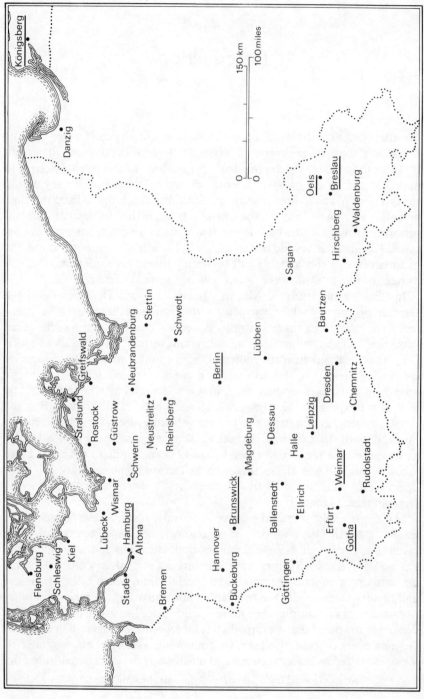

Figure 1 Map showing the location of North German operatic centers

framework of the theatrical world which so decisively shaped operatic activity in North Germany during the last third of the eighteenth century.

North German opera from the end of the Seven Years' War to the Napoleonic era began, but did not end, with the simple, rustic comic operas of Christian Felix Weisse and Johann Adam Hiller. At its very birth the genre embraced far less German musical traditions than it did those of a young, struggling German theater, and this was to be the source of all its diversity and uniqueness. Soon German opera grew from a fairly homogeneous conception – one of rustic comedy or farce peppered with relatively modest musical items – into a multivariate, complex activity. Experimentation and adjustment touched on literary, musical, and dramaturgical aspects. Not only did the weight of each of these vary from work to work or year to year, but in addition each factor absorbed and transformed elements of other traditions.

If we devote some preliminary attention to the environment in which librettists, composers, and performers worked, the recombinant character of North German opera becomes apparent at once. After taking up these three occupations in the following sections, we shall be in a position to grapple with the problem of generic labels for North German opera's many guises in this period, and to offer a brief preliminary survey of the next seven chapters.

But first, what do we mean by "North German"? Culturally and politically we are speaking largely of three areas: (1) Saxony and the Thüringian States, (2) Prussia, including its possessions Silesia and East Prussia, and (3) the kingdom of Hannover and adjacent lands to the north, most in Lower Saxony. In large part we shall be occupied with only a few important cities and courts within this region: Leipzig, Berlin, Hamburg, Weimar, Gotha, Dresden, Breslau, and Königsberg. In these centers the great majority of all the operas we are studying were first produced.

Figure 1 presents a map of the region to which our study has limited itself. It locates all the major and minor operatic centers we shall be discussing in the coming chapters. The physical bounds chosen here do not correspond to the more restricted notion "North German" evokes as a purely geographical concept of, roughly speaking, Berlin and points north. A more accurate designation for our region would have been North and Central Germany and Prussia's eastern possessions, an ungainly label we have streamlined to "North German." Institutional, political, stylistic, and to an extent denominational factors distinguish operatic activity in this area from that in the German-speaking lands we are excluding – Austria, South Germany, and the Rhineland.

Each court or municipality shown in Figure 1 had its own personality in the eighteenth century, with direct and important consequences for the cultivation of opera and drama. A strong university community (as at Göttingen, Halle, or Leipzig) usually offered a hostile interest group, as did a vocal clergy or Pietistic city council. Some courts (notably Weimar, Gotha, and Oels) reflected very faithfully the cultural interests of their sovereigns and their élite coterie of noble advisers and administrators. Those at which Italian opera was strong (Hannover, Brunswick, Berlin, and Dresden) mostly looked on German opera as a concession to a cultural sphere external to the court itself. Commercial interests, particularly at towns such as Leipzig or Hamburg, often proved conducive to the flourishing of theatrical and operatic activity. Yet, in any one of these local environments, the decisive role in theatrical life was played by the organizational system of the theater which served the community's needs.

Theatrical organization in Germany

Throughout the last third of the eighteenth century, three concepts dominated theatrical enterprise in North Germany – patronage, Prinzipalschaft, and the national theater. They are by no means mutually exclusive. The system of pure court patronage, for example, is relatively rare for German opera, though common at courts such as those at Brunswick, Dresden, and Potsdam for Italian opera. More often one finds a court extending its protection or a "privilege" granting exclusive rights to perform within its lands to a private entrepreneur, or Prinzipal, usually with an annual stipend and access to certain court facilities. Let us consider, for example, the Hannoverian court. With only 15,000 inhabitants in the capital city, it could in no way support a standing theater of its own – all the more so since its titular head, King George III of England, was absent. In 1769 the court contracted with the principal Abel Seyler to perform not only at Hannover but at other cities and towns throughout the realm. He was granted 1,000 Reichstaler and free use of the court theater. He also received for his performances at Hannover "free music from the royal Hofkapelle for a douceur to be paid them yearly by Abel Seyler."[2] Contracts with succeeding principals such as Friedrich Ludwig Schröder were similar.

A few courts did establish standing German theaters of their own. They seldom lasted more than a few years, and often had a theater- or opera-loving patron to thank for their existence. An example is the court theater of Duke Friedrich August at Oels in Silesia, where Dittersdorf worked from 1793 until 1797. The court theater at Weimar under Goethe's direction is perhaps the most familiar and long-lived example. The first court theater for German-language productions wholly under the control of the court itself had been established at Gotha in 1775. Four years later, however, Duke Ernst II shut down the enterprise in disgust at the laxity of the court company.

German principals were delighted to be taken under the wing of a court, even if only for a brief series of performances. The best alternative to such an appointment was permission to perform at a major municipality, and if that was not to be had there was nothing to do but to travel from place to place,

[2] Quoted by Heinz Rahlfs, *Die Städtischen Bühnen zu Hannover und ihre Vorläufer in wirtschaftlicher und sozialischer Hinsicht* (Hannover, 1928), p. 5.

staying only as long as repertory and public interest allowed. In many smaller towns such troupes might well be refused permission to perform on the grounds that they were drawing local money away from the town; often the clergy took an active role in condemning the character and morals of itinerant actors. Traveling left little time for preparing new works, and in general it constituted such a hand-to-mouth existence that it is exceptional to find the better performers in such troupes.

But whether established in one or two cities or forced to travel frequently, such companies inevitably had to compete with one another for their survival. Not surprisingly, their mortality rate was high. Even the best, most tenacious troupes had to suffer occasional reorganization and changes of leadership. It was into this situation, more than into the system of court theaters, that German opera first entered with the comic operas of Hiller and Weisse in the 1760s. From then until the end of the century, we witness nearly universal popular preference for German opera (as well as French and Italian operas in translation) over the spoken repertory of many troupes. Schröder twice attempted to eliminate both opera and ballet from his company's repertory at Hamburg, and each time he was forced to reinstate them. The very first German comic operas of 1766 and 1767, as well shall see in the next chapter, rescued the shaky enterprise of Heinrich Gottfried Koch at Leipzig.

The third form of theatrical organization mentioned earlier, the "national theater," placed a public stage in the service of elevating theatrical standards and taste without regard to profit, this by means of court or private subvention. The phenomenon occurs at the beginning of the era with the Hamburg National Theater, immortalized in Lessing's *Hamburgische Dramaturgie*, and in the century's last decade with the national theater instituted at Berlin by Friedrich Wilhelm II. The Hamburg enterprise, which lasted from April 1767 to March 1769, looked with suspicion on opera as a blight on good theatrical taste and practice, and rejected anything but spoken drama from its repertory. Probably this decision played a part in the collapse of the experiment. No such exclusion was entertained by the Berlin National Theater in the later 1780s, which at one point went so far as to engage two music directors to oversee its operatic activities.

The composers

Composers of German opera during the last third of the century show a wide spectrum of experience and inexperience with the stage. Some of North Germany's most prominent composers of the era had literally nothing to do with German opera – Carl Philipp Emanuel Bach is an example. Many others wrote only one or two works, including some which were apparently never performed. Most, however, had some connection with a particular stage, and more often than not this influenced the shape their scores took. The completely untrained singers in Koch's troupe in the 1760s are often cited as a decisive element in Hiller's utterly simple, popular vocal style in his first comic operas. This deficiency of skill was quickly remedied, however, and by the mid-1770s nearly every troupe seriously engaged in performing German opera had at least two or three trained singers, a few of whom yielded to no one in virtuosity.

Germany had no conservatory system such as existed at Naples and Venice, and until German opera became an accepted part of theatrical life, offered little opportunity for composers to serve any kind of meaningful apprenticeship in dramatic composition. The better composers seem to have either served for a time at courts where Italian opera was performed or become attached to theatrical companies as music directors. Dilettante composers were usually blessed with a musical education involving some compositional instruction, and they sometimes gained direct experience with the theater at the courts to which they were attached. Baron von Kospoth, for instance, acted as *maître des plaisirs* at the Prussian court beginning in 1776, journeyed to Italy in 1783, and returned to become music director of the stage at Weimar in 1785. Baron von Lichtenstein managed the theater at Dessau from 1797 on. Karl von Seckendorff, after years in Austria and Sardinia, returned to Weimar as Kammerherr in 1775 and until 1784 was in charge of the Hofkapelle. He collaborated with Goethe on two operas, some occasional pieces with music, and a melodrama.

Travel was a part of the education as well as the administrative duties of many courtier-composers, and opened new musical vistas to them. Most other composers saw no such opportunity come their way, unless they were attached to a court which put sufficient store in the musical advantages to be gained from sending a promising young composer to Italy. Duke Friedrich III of Gotha sent Georg Benda to Italy in 1765 for just such reasons. Johann Gottlieb Naumann took his pupils Joseph Schuster and Franz Seydelmann from Dresden to Italy about the same time (much as Gluck had gone with Dittersdorf in tow in 1763). Anton Schweitzer was sent to Italy by the court at Hildburghausen for three years, but unlike the others mentioned here never wrote an Italian opera, the fruits which the princes funding such trips expected.

Many of the most important composers of German opera, however, learned their trade wholly at home. Johann Friedrich Reichardt as a young man had planned a trip to Italy, but could not carry it out. Johann André was content with the exposure that Frankfurt and Offenbach afforded him to opéra-comique. Hiller was introduced to the beauties of the Italian opera scores of Hasse and Graun at Dresden, and these were all he wanted to know. Johann Kaffka, Christian Gottlob Neefe, Carl David Stegmann, and Ernst Wilhelm Wolf – each of whom contributed importantly to German opera – never left Germany.

Increasingly, major composers of German opera during this period had at least some direct practical contact with a traveling company or a court or municipal stage. Early on, in the 1760s and 1770s, lack of such contact was seldom a significant handicap. Hiller, for example, wrote nearly all of his comic operas before he became attached to the Seyler company briefly in 1776, and his pupil Neefe wrote many of his most popular scores before serving as music director first with Seyler and then with Gustav Friedrich Wilhelm Grossmann. In the last two decades of the century, for reasons which will become clear when we examine the changes in operatic style during these years, an intimate knowledge of the mechanics of operatic dramaturgy became essential.

Several crucial differences between theatrical life in Germany and that in France and Italy made the professional careers of German operatic composers fundamentally different from those of composers abroad. First, the diffuseness of German culture – the so-called Kleinstaaterei – prevented the rise of one or a few urban centers with competing theaters demanding new works each season. Though performances were routinely forbidden during Lent in most places, nothing like the *stagione* system in Italy can be said to have existed anywhere in Germany. Second, competition between rival troupes tended to involve the spoken as much as the musical repertory. In some places, pressure from wandering companies of French and Italian operatists encouraged German troupes to adopt a significant number of foreign musical works, limiting the demand for domestic production. Third, successful older works tended to remain in repertories longer, especially those of companies who moved from place to place. Finally, institutional arrangements did not always favor the production of German opera. A Kapellmeister to a court involved himself with operatic productions as a primary duty only if this were Italian opera (Reichardt at Potsdam, Naumann and others at Dresden, Schwanenberger at Brunswick). Where a German theater was established at a court, it usually had its own music director.

The music director, in fact, represents the German operatic composer in the purest form. This position alone offered a musician the combination of practical dramaturgical experience in selecting, preparing, rehearsing, and conducting opera; of constant contact with new works, both domestic and imported; and of a ready-made forum for his own endeavors.

The librettists

Only a few of the important librettists of German opera were primarily men of the theater and, in line with traditions in other nations, they seldom set great store by their librettos. Nearly all of them wrote for the spoken stage as well – Weisse, Goethe, Kotzebue, Grossmann, Gotter, Schiebeler, Schink, and Wieland, to name the most prominent. A fair number of composers in North Germany wrote or translated many of their own librettos: Kaffka, Dittersdorf, André, Baron von Lichtenstein, Reichardt, Wagenseil, and Hensel.

For nearly all librettists, the production of texts for German operas was a secondary activity at best, although some fairly prolific writers such as Christoph Friedrich Bretzner, Carl Alexander Herklots, and Gottlob Ephraim Heermann are chiefly remembered today as librettists. Several distinguished poets who otherwise were not very active as dramatists lent their skills to opera (Carl Wilhelm Ramler, Johann Georg Jacobi, Johann Benjamin Michaelis). Although most of the librettists had little direct connection with the theater, a few were actors (such as the composer-librettist Kaffka) or were otherwise connected with a stage (Goethe and his brother-in-law Vulpius at Weimar). Early in this period the principal Seyler created a new position in his troupe, that of Theaterdichter, for which he hired Michaelis in 1769. Several other librettists acted in this capacity, which more often involved the writing of poetic speeches to open or close a series of performances than the production of new dramatic works.

Many North German librettos were to some degree translations of French, English, Italian, and occasionally Spanish works.[3] Of Weisse's dozen-odd librettos, for example, only two full-length comic operas are original. The norm in translating or adapting was also to transpose the scene, usually to somewhere in Germany, and with concomitant changes in characterization, tone, and topical references. Such alterations were called "nationalization" at the time, a process already common in translations of spoken drama for the German theater.

The attitude of librettists toward opera and toward their own contributions to the genre changed considerably during the last third of the eighteenth century. Throughout this period, to be sure, librettists were uniformly apologetic about their wares, but the reasons for this shifted as North German opera adopted a less literary and more frankly musical stamp. Early on librettists passed off their texts as harmless depictions of rural life enlivened with simple songs, but later on they pointed to the restrictions of writing for the composer and the singers as handcuffs on any pretensions to literary merit they may have entertained.

The practice of translating Italian and French works with retention of the original music was far less common than in the Rhineland and Southern Germany, where libretto mills for opéra-comique became especially notorious. Some Northern examples of this art - Eschenburg's *Robert und Kalliste*, for instance (based on Guglielmi's setting of *La sposa fedele*) - were praised for their felicity. The efforts of Vulpius for Goethe's stage at Weimar were not so lucky.

There was never a concerted movement to reform the Northern libretto, since literary considerations were seldom thwarted by musical exigencies until late in the era. And, anyway, Italian and Viennese specimens which ever threatened to crowd German operas out of most companies' repertories were

---

[3] In Part II of the Catalogue appended to this study we have attempted to identify as many such dependencies as possible, although of course no claim of completeness can be made for this scantily studied area.

always considered far worse. One of the principal ambitions of many idealistic librettists was to establish wholly composed, serious opera on the German stage, an endeavor which began with Wieland's *Alceste* in 1773 and continued to the end of the century. The Viennese reform operas of Gluck and Calzabigi were both known and admired in the North, but like North German serious operas after *Alceste* they were seldom performed and even then usually only in concert format. Vienna's true legacy to the North, first apparent in the mid-1780s, lay in the overwhelming popularity of the comic operas of Mozart, Dittersdorf, Wranitzky, and Wenzel Müller.

North German librettos enjoyed favor among composers from other German lands. In South Germany and the Rhineland in the last third of the century there were well over fifty settings of Northern librettos, mostly those of the most prominent writers – Weisse, Heermann, Gotter, Goethe, Bretzner, and Kotzebue. At Vienna Bretzner in particular came into vogue in the early 1780s, a phenomenon culminating in Mozart's *Die Entführung aus dem Serail*. This literary commerce tended not to be bilateral: during this period there were few settings by Northern composers of South German, Rhenish, or Austrian librettos.

The problem of genre

A first, sweeping look at German opera from 1766 to 1799 involves us in problems of definition and nomenclature. The reader may perhaps already have wondered why the term "Singspiel" has not yet occurred as even a loose synonym for North German operas. Two strong arguments can be made against its use. First, it had no clear and precise meaning in the eighteenth century, being neither widespread enough to merit the right of universality, nor precise enough to be attached to a specific genre. Second, nineteenth- and twentieth-century scholarship and journalism have invested it with a clear modern meaning, a German comic opera with spoken dialogue – a "play with singing" rather than a "sung play," in other words. Still, we are today reasonably comfortable with the tandem labels in Italian for serious and comic opera in that language, which have just as little contemporary justification in usage (as distinct from practice). Similarly, we usually refer to French opera with spoken dialogue as opéra-comique, although contemporary labels for genres here were even more diverse than in Italy. Why not continue to use "Singspiel"?

The reasons lie squarely in eighteenth-century terminology and the repertory it sought to describe. Table 1.1 lists the common generic descriptions used on the title pages of eighteenth-century North German librettos. While a table such as this cannot show the degree of stylistic unity among works which bear the same designation, it does suggest that librettists tended to prefer four distinct categories.

Table 1.1. Designations in printed North German librettos, 1767–1799

Designation	67-69	70-72	73-75	76-78	79-81	82-84	85-87	88-90	91-93	94-96	97-99	Total
Oper					1					3	4	8
Komische Oper	6	5	9	5	3	2	1		1	4		36
Romantisch–Komische Oper							1	1			2	4
Operette	4	3	5	2	6	3					1	24
Komische Operette	1	1	4		1	2			3			12
Singspiel			1	4		6		6	3	3	5	28
Komisches Singspiel			1						2	5		8
Romantisches Singspiel								1				1
Singeschauspiel				1	1							2
Tragisches Singspiel						1						1
Lustspiel mit Gesang			1	1	1	2	1					6
Trauerspiel mit Gesang				1			1	2				3
Schauspiel mit Gesang			1	3	7	2	2			1		16
Posse mit Gesang				1	1						1	3
Nachspiel mit Gesang				1	1							2
Lyrisches Drama									2	1		3
Lyrische Posse										1		1
SUMMARY:												
Oper	6	5	9	5	4	2	2	1	1	7	6	48
Operette	5	4	9	2	7	5			3		1	36
Singspiel			2	5	1	7		7	5	8	5	40
—— mit Gesang			2	7	10	4	4	2			1	30

The single most popular term throughout the period was "Komische Oper," one that both Weisse and Hiller used for every one of their full-length comic operas. The related labels "Operette" and "Komische Operette" saw much use during the first half of the era, which was dominated by French example, but dropped from favor in the early 1780s, just when Italian and especially Viennese operas initiated a major transformation in North German taste and practice.

In 1773 Wieland introduced the term "Singspiel" as a designation for his recitative opera *Alceste*, and this association of the term with a "dramma per musica" of more or less Italianate stamp remained: ten of the twelve North German recitative operas whose text or music was published after *Alceste* also called themselves "Singspiele."[4] Only in the century's last decade did "Singspiel" acquire currency for all kinds of German opera, serious and comic, with or without recitative. Dittersdorf labeled most of his comic operas written from 1794 to 1797 for the court at Oels "Komische Singspiele."

Finally, in 1775 Goethe employed, apparently for the first time anywhere, the designation "Schauspiel mit Gesang" for his first libretto, *Erwin und Elmire*. Others took it up soon after to describe works which shared the more serious, elevated tone which distinguishes Goethe's text. "Schauspiel" in these cases is an equivalent of the French "drame." The important element in the label, however, is "mit Gesang," which meant that the work, whatever its character, alternated spoken dialogue and set musical numbers.

On this score, at least, eighteenth-century usage is absolutely consistent. No clearer example can be adduced than Goethe's dropping of "Schauspiel mit Gesang" when he revised *Erwin und Elmire* and its companion *Claudine von Villa Bella* during his Italian journey, substituting the designation "Singspiel," in fact, when he revised both works into operas with recitative throughout instead of spoken dialogue. Terms combining a dramatic designation (Lustspiel, Schauspiel, Posse, even Trauerspiel) and "mit Gesang" were used frequently from 1775 to 1790. Their disappearance at that time may be related to the new realities of German opera in the 1790s, which accepted the Italianate subordination of the values of spoken drama, hitherto a distinctive characteristic of North German opera, to those of the music.

In general, except for the unambiguous implication that a work "mit Gesang" is also "mit Dialog," inconsistency played a prominent role in eighteenth-century German usage, probably because the works themselves did not always fall into well-defined categories. Rather than squander a multiplicity of terms to give a proper impression of this diversity, we have chosen the saner if more colorless course of using "German opera" as a term capable of accommodating it.

Even a spectrum needs some limits, and in our case we must still clarify the nature of the repertory we wish to consider from the broad band of music-

---

[4] Herder called his *Brutus* (first produced in 1774) a "Drama zur Musik," apparently a literal translation of Metastasio's "dramma per musica."

theatrical activities in North Germany. Beyond works which are obviously to be classed as "incidental music," we find dramas with all degrees of musical involvement, from those with only a few songs sprinkled here and there to wholly composed works obviously tailored at every turn to musical demands. At what point is the music's contribution to the work sufficient for us to speak of a true collaboration? A plausible answer is: at that point where the omission of the music would make the drama a fundamentally different work.[5] We are probably safe in assuming that a play with entire acts devoid of music may be omitted from consideration – even such works as Goethe's *Lila* or Johann Christian Bock's *Das Mädchen im Eichthale* which employ significant operatic or masque-like structures in their final acts. Here we are still in the realm of incidental music.

Where we are dealing with spoken dialogue in a fairly traditional eighteenth-century work, we naturally do not expect the composer to be charged with advancing the plot, and must not look to this feature in gauging music's involvement. But we do hope that the librettist will be sensitive to opportunities for the composer to sharpen a character's dramatic personality or emotional response, those time-honored prerogatives of the closed number in opera. The main characters ought to sing, and sing where it counts. And here we begin to find real diversity within a context we readily accept as operatic. For example, consider the following four attitudes toward musical numbers in a spoken "comedy with songs":

1. Heermann's translation of Favart's *Rosière de Salency*, *Das Rosenfest*, which achieved widespread popularity in Wolf's setting, includes no less than forty-seven musical numbers. Heermann indicates in the printed libretto[6] certain stanzas and even entire numbers which may be omitted (five of the forty-seven songs he felt could be left out completely). These are not dramaturgical exigencies of a specific performance, but a librettist's response to criticisms made of his music-dramatic planning.

2. In 1776 Caroline Luise von Klenke published *Der ehrliche Schweitzer*, "ein Schauspiel in zwey Handlungen," and included at the end of her play thirteen "Willkührliche Arien zum Ehrlichen Schweitzer," numbered and keyed to individual scenes. In several cases they clearly replace the spoken dialogue which they paraphrase, though their precise location is not indicated in the body of the play itself. As an opera the play was composed twice, by Johann Karl Mainberger for Nüremberg in 1790 and by Heinrich Christoph Hattasch for Hamburg in 1780.

3. Daniel Schiebeler's one-act comedy *Die Muse*, set by Hiller in 1767, has

---

[5] It is possible to omit the music of any opera and still have a reasonably coherent drama – as was done in the eighteenth century with Metastasio's works, for instance. Conversely, many people seem to find it rewarding to listen to the music of an opera without knowing anything about the text.

[6] *Das Rosenfest*, 3rd revised ed. (Weimar, 1774). Heermann notes in his preface that the publisher (Carl Ludolf Hoffmann) had decided upon this new edition, and so he wanted to take advantage of the criticisms made of his text, especially of the songs.

no musical numbers at all in its first six scenes, but then suddenly bursts into operatic flower in its last two scenes, which contain six musical numbers. The music is far from ornamental, for the heroine's conversion of Phaedria, who has determined to avoid the selfish and trifling fair sex for solitude and study, is brought off by her singing while disguised as the young poet's muse.

4. Baron Soden von Sassanfart's tasteless Gothic cliff-hanger *Mit dem Glockenschlag: zwölf!*, a South German libretto set by Nikolaus Mühle for Mitau in 1783, scatters its ten musical numbers haphazardly over two acts (the title page errs in promising an "ernsthafte Operette in drey Akten"). Neither act begins with music, and the first even ends with dialogue. Only three of the six principals sing, and the nuns are denied even a perfunctory chorus.

Obviously, alternating spoken dialogue and sung numbers created a different and more varied relationship from the Italian practice of alternating recitative and closed number. As in France, opinion was divided in Germany on the merits of combining speech and song, a controversy I have dealt with elsewhere.[7] For now, it is enough to observe that this mixture lay at the very heart of the diversity of North German opera. Especially in the 1760s and 1770s, there was never anything close to consensus on the integration of music into the individual scene, or even an entire act. As suggested above, it was by no means an inviolate rule that an act must either begin or end with a musical number (although this was more often than not the case). Scenes were seldom planned so as to culminate in a musical number, and frequently the turn to song (especially where no strong emotion was involved) was rationalized by a character's being asked to sing, or having a musical instrument handy, so that verisimilitude might lend a hand to reduce the abruptness of shifting from speech to song. Finales appear quite late in the era – they are not at all common before the final decade of the century.

The North German stage developed and perpetuated other kinds of musical theater which differ in essentials from our traditional conceptions of comic and serious opera. The *festa teatrale* had its more or less exact parallel in the musical "Vorspiel," a play usually in one act specially written and composed for the birthday of a sovereign, a wedding, coronation, or a similar event. Many of these are little more than miniature comic or pastoral operas. They tend to use plots drawn from classical antiquity and to work some manifestation of adulation for the personage honored by the occasion into their close. Recitative as a replacement for spoken dialogue made its first appearance in such pieces. While there are good reasons to consider the Vorspiel and similar occasional pieces as a separate, specific genre, several of them achieved some degree of general popularity when stripped of their topical trappings and presented as one-act operas. Schweitzer's *Elysium* (Hannover, 1770) is the best example of this.

---

[7] "Benda, the Germans, and Simple Recitative," *Journal of the American Musicological Society* 34 (1981): 119–31.

Another important genre, to which we shall turn in Chapter 4, is the melo-drama. There are compelling reasons for considering melodramas as quite separate from the rest of German opera, however obvious a country cousin they may be of the obbligato recitative in strictly musical terms. Melodramas were not written for operatic performers, but for tragedians, usually the best a troupe had to offer and almost always performers who otherwise did not participate at all in a company's musical offerings. Their tragic themes and dependence on an "argument" already familiar to the audience have no parallels in North German operatic practice.

Size, sources, and studies of the repertory

If we omit for the moment all incidental music, occasional pieces, and melo-dramas, we are left with a corpus of North German works of surprisingly small numbers. Table 1.2 presents the data. The statistics given here and

Table 1.2. *Operas composed and librettos written in North Germany,
1766–1799*

Music:		Text:[b]	
Operas composed[a]	277	Librettos written	266
Music survives			
(wholly or in part)	127	Librettos composed	221
Music survives		Text published	
(wholly – score or keyboard reduction)	106	(all or arias only)	136
		Text published	
		(arias and dialogue)	126

[a] Includes different settings of the same text.
[b] Includes South German, Rhenish, and Austrian texts set by North German composers.

through the following seven chapters derive from the catalogue of North German operas appended to this study. Part I of this catalogue presents by composer all 276 operas written for performance in North Germany from 1766 to 1799 with additional information on first performance, manuscript locations, and the printing history of the music. Part II lists the 264 texts emanating from Northern librettists or set by Northern composers. This list of titles includes cross-references to Part I, showing how many times each text was set and by whom, and it also indicates sources of the plot, publication history, and a bibliography of eighteenth-century references to each text and its settings. Part II also includes a separate listing of the 43 texts which were published in North Germany but apparently were never composed during the period. Finally, Part III presents the librettists with cross-indexing to Part II.

A strong caveat must be introduced at this point. The information con-tained in the catalogue and intabulated in the chapters of this study represent one student's efforts to attain as comprehensive a listing as possible of all North German operas meeting the formal definitions, geographic constraints, and temporal frame proposed in the present chapter. I dare say relatively few works have escaped notice, and hopefully no important ones, yet in an area so little studied before now no claim to completeness can be made. In particular, there are undoubtedly some sources – both musical and literary – which I have not discovered. Therefore, any claim about the survival of an opera's music or the publication history of a text must always carry the implicit qualification, "to the best of the author's knowledge." The composite figures derived from the catalogue, such as those presented here, are introduced only to support repertorial generalizations, for whose relative accuracy I believe a reasonable confidence level may be assumed.

This having been said, Table 1.2 does seem to imply that we have lost a significant proportion of the music to be discussed in this study – about 60 percent, in fact. Of the librettos actually composed, I have located the full texts of roughly half. On the whole, in a period of thirty-four years we are dealing with the production of, on the average, only eight new operas each year. Naturally, the more popular works survive in far greater numbers than the obscure ones, but we cannot always assume that the generalizations we may hazard based on the music and texts that come down to us extend to specific works for which we have only a title, perhaps a date of first performance, and in a few cases a contemporary evaluation or chance remark.

The graph in Figure 2 illustrates how the 277 operas are distributed over time. There are clearly two periods of peak activity in the production of new German operas, one from 1775 to 1782 and one from 1795 to 1799. Does this pattern concur with the way we apprehend the development of North German

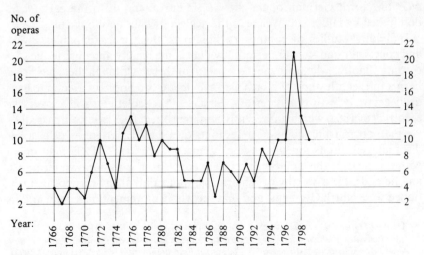

Figure 2   New operas produced in North Germany, 1766–1799. (16 unperformed operas not included)

opera today? It is appropriate to reflect for a moment on the present state of
our knowledge and some of the lacunae and misconceptions we shall be dealing with in the coming chapters. Let us begin with Alfred Loewenberg's *Annals
of Opera*.[8] Its selective policy yields a countercurve to Figure 2 by choosing
fewer and fewer North German works over time in its chronology of significant
European operas. Table 1.3 lists by five-year segments the number of North
German works included in the second edition of *Annals of Opera* along with
our total numbers for the same segments.

Table 1.3. *North German operas, 1766–1799, included in Alfred
Loewenberg's* Annals of Opera *(1954)*

Years	Loewenberg	Total composed	Percentage
1766-1770	6	17	35
1771-1775	8	38	21
1776-1780	8	53	15
1781-1785	2	33	6
1786-1790	1	28	4
1791-1795	1	38	3
1796-1799	3	54	6

There is nothing wrong, of course, with ignoring operas which are poor or
uninteresting. Loewenberg offers us an implicit judgment that North German
operas became steadily more so over time, and it shall be our task to determine whether this assessment is an accurate one. Nor is Loewenberg alone.
A glance at the contributions of Anna Amalie Abert to *MGG*, *NOHM*, and
NG[9] on North German opera show a similar attention to the early years
dominated by Hiller and Weisse to the neglect of later developments.

Individual studies of composers, librettists, theatrical companies, cities,
and courts abound for this period. It will become readily apparent in the succeeding chapters which are the more useful of these. Although there has never
been a full-length study of North German opera, two books can claim to have
dealt centrally with our repertory. First, H. M. Schletterer's *Das deutsche
Singspiel* of 1863, which has recently been reprinted, tries to encompass all of
German opera from medieval times to its own day. Schletterer ends a rather
disorganized discussion of the first "glänzende Periode" of German opera
with the close of the eighteenth century, concurring with our own terminus,
and he adds: "It is worthy of remark that almost all of the composers mentioned were North Germans, and that the whole movement in general and its

---

[8] *Annals of Opera, 1597–1940*, 2nd ed. (Geneva, [1954]).
[9] *Die Musik in Geschichte und Gegenwart*, s.v. "Oper," vol. 10 (1962), cols. 21–2, 30–2. *The
New Oxford History of Music*, vol. 7: *The Age of Enlightenment, 1745–1790* (London, 1973),
pp. 65–89. *The New Grove Dictionary of Music and Musicians*, s.v. "Opera," vol. 13 (London, 1980), pp. 585–6.

growth and diffusion was almost exclusively limited to North Germany."[10] As flattering as such a conclusion may be to our immediate purposes, it is not really valid. If we apply the same criteria to the Rhineland and South Germany that produced our total of 276 German operas in the North, we come up with nearly 250 operas in those regions. And the qualitative superiority of the Viennese operas of Mozart, Dittersdorf, and Wranitzky in the 1780s and 1790s for all German stages is beyond dispute.

A more recent study, *Das deutsche Singspiel* by Hans-Albrecht Koch (Stuttgart, 1974), approaches German opera of the seventeenth and especially eighteenth centuries from a literary perspective. The book's dual intent is to serve as a broad descriptive survey and as a guide to research. Unfortunately, in the restricted space he was allowed, Koch let many important operas pass unmentioned and scarcely touched on changes in musical style and their effect on libretto writing. Furthermore, unimportant works sometimes receive arbitrary emphasis,[11] and, although Koch's organization of his chapters is a vast improvement on Schletterer's, it ignores everything after 1778 in the North except settings of Goethe's texts.[12]

A preliminary summary

In the following seven chapters we have divided the history of North German opera from 1766 to 1799 into seven fairly distinctive phases. While such a division has been adopted principally for convenience of exposition, it does seek to mirror the most meaningful discontinuities in operatic developments in North Germany by reflecting the way in which various cities and courts moved in and out of prominence as troupes, talent, and taste shifted about. As a preliminary overview of our divisions, we shall conclude this introductory chapter with an abstract of the seven to follow:

CHAPTER 2: THE BIRTH OF SAXON OPERA (1766–70). After the sporadic and disorganized experiments with German opera between the demise of the Hamburg Opera in 1738 and the end of the Seven Years' War, the modern genre of German comic opera with spoken dialogue was created at Leipzig by Hiller and Weisse at the instigation of the principal Koch. The genre explored the farce at first, a legacy from the past and a style too popular to ignore, but particularly Weisse came to prefer strong links with the rustic, sentimental mode of early opéra-comique. Hiller, handcuffed by poor singers for the

---

[10] *Das deutsche Singspiel* (Augsburg, 1863), p. 142.
[11] The preface to J. W. A. Schöpfel's *Frühlingnacht*, which Sonneck had already printed, is run past us once more, although this as well as Schöpfel's other mediocre librettos was never set.
[12] Christoph Friedrich Bretzner, whose dozen librettos were set more times than the texts of any other German during the entire period, is mentioned only in the sections on South German and Viennese opera. The chapter on Goethe's librettos does not even come close to doing this celebrated topic justice and pads its bibliography with many irrelevant items.

most part, tried at first to move beyond Weisse's musically restrictive conception of the genre in his collaborations with Schiebeler. *Lisuart und Dariolette* introduced a more elevated vision of German opera, but Hiller quickly returned to the channels mapped out by Weisse. *Die Jagd* codified the ideals of early Saxon opera as the most enduring monument of the genre's infancy.

CHAPTER 3: THE DIFFUSION OF SAXON OPERA (1770–3). In the early 1770s North German opera explored possibilities still close to the lines Hiller and Weisse had drawn. The Weimar Kapellmeister Wolf developed a heavier dialect of Hiller's musical style, and his chief librettist Heermann, although he based two of his texts on local Saxon history, in fact simply grafted traditional rural plots onto this background. Among a younger generation of composers, Hiller's pupil Neefe showed brilliant farcic verve and originality in his first operas. The principal Koch, who had stood godfather to German opera at Leipzig, left for Berlin in 1772 and in so doing contributed materially both to the dissemination of the works of Hiller, Wolf, and Neefe, and to the decline of Leipzig after 1773 as a major operatic center.

CHAPTER 4: NEW DIRECTIONS: THE SEYLER COMPANY (1773–6). During the next few years, center stage shifted to the small Central German courts at Weimar and Gotha by virtue of the activities of the Seyler company at both centers. The troupe's music director, Anton Schweitzer, catapulted German opera into a new world with his setting of Wieland's serious opera *Alceste* in 1773. His importance suffered a sharp decline when a fire at Weimar forced the Seyler company to move to nearby Gotha, where Georg Benda was the court's Kapellmeister. Here Benda rather than Schweitzer followed through on the promise of *Alceste* with two impressive serious operas retaining spoken dialogue, *Walder* and *Romeo und Julie* (both 1776). A year earlier he had composed two of the earliest and greatest melodramas of the century. On the comic side, both Schweitzer and Benda moved well beyond the scope of Hiller's technique in response to witty librettos (both by Gotter) tailored to the taste of the court audiences for which they were intended.

CHAPTER 5: PRUSSIAN STIRRINGS AND GOETHE'S EARLY LIBRETTOS (1773–7). In the mid-1770s two natives of the Rhineland arrived in North Germany. Johann André dominated an otherwise lacklustre era at Berlin during his early years there as music director to Koch's successor, Döbbelin. André's popularity had been secured even before his arrival by his setting of Goethe's *Erwin und Elmire*. Goethe himself took up residence at Weimar in late 1775, and the next year his opera was given with Duchess Anna Amalia's music, setting the tone for Goethe's courtcentered dabbling in opera with other amateurs during the next decade. His first libretto achieved unprecedented favor among German composers during the latter 1770s, but his second, *Claudine von Villa Bella*, proved too bold for them, both in subject matter and structure (it hazards the first true finale in North German opera). Herder's verse tragedy *Brutus* similarly paid the price of its daring, disorderly unconventionality by remaining in obscurity.

CHAPTER 6: PRUSSIAN DOMINION AND THE END OF SAXON OPERA (1778–83). At least partly by default, Berlin emerged around 1780 as the operatic capital of North Germany. André continued to dominate the genre's development there. He and several other composers turned with enthusiasm at this time to the early librettos of Bretzner, which favored the lambent, witty spirit of Molière and the colorful, supernatural fables of Gozzi over the rustic sentimentality of earlier years. Technical improvements appeared only sporadically. André's *Belmont und Constanze* (1781), one of his last triumphs at Berlin, included a full-scale finale structure in the abduction scene. Goethe attempted an even grander finale in *Jery und Bätely*, but for this and for his most frankly Italianate libretto *Scherz, List und Rache* he could not find a worthy collaborator. Meanwhile, with the late 1770s came the cold chill of autumn for Saxon opera. The legacy of the Seyler company inspired several Dresden composers to the creation of a brief Indian summer. Both Joseph Schuster and Franz Seydelmann had inherited high standards of craftsmanship from their teacher Naumann, but both were committed primarily to Italian opera. They abandoned the German theater as soon as Italian opera was reinstituted at Dresden.

CHAPTER 7: LEAN YEARS (1784–91). The 1780s in North Germany were not a decade rich in new works, and what was produced tended to remain a local phenomenon. No more did North German operas march triumphantly from stage to stage, and the reason is not difficult to find: Austrian and Italian comic operas were sweeping into German repertories everywhere, an assault led by Dittersdorf, Mozart, Wranitzky, Salieri, and Piccinni. Symbolic indeed was the success on all German stages of Wranitzky's *Oberon*, based on a North German libretto, while an earlier setting by the Northerner Hanke died on the vine. During the drought, composers devoted more and more attention to serious opera. Some Northern librettists broached tragic themes during this vogue, but others, sensing the rising tide, tried to keep up with the new fashionable imports by beginning to retool for greater spectacle and musical control. Goethe's new recitative versions of his first two librettos ratified this major shift in thinking. Reichardt produced creditable settings of these refashioned librettos, but most composers struggled with only limited success to master the ascendant Italian-Viennese style. Wolf's several attempts at rejuvenating his operatic career under the new conditions failed completely.

CHAPTER 8: THE ASSIMILATION OF SOUTHERN STYLES (1792–9). The 1790s saw a cautious awakening from the doldrums of the preceding decade. At Brunswick, Leipzig, Oels, Breslau, Dresden, Königsberg, and even Hamburg German opera slowly returned to flower. North German composers began demonstrating that they had learned their lesson from the influx of Austrian and Italian opera. Librettists who had absorbed the same lesson – Bretzner, Herklots, Kotzebue, and Bürde – were preferred by these composers. Changing fashion left behind even Dittersdorf, whose late operas for the court at

Oels in Silesia never achieved the universal popularity of his best Viennese works. Although they do not betray declining powers, they cling to his popular style of the 1780s, now quite outmoded next to the latest Viennese magic operas securing triumphs on nearly every German stage. A final testament to the new state of affairs came in the last libretto of Benda's collaborator in the 1770s, Gotter. His *Die Geisterinsel*, an adaptation of Shakespeare's *The Tempest* written with Mozart in mind, sought to encompass both earlier Northern ideals and modern paradigms. In Reichardt's setting it eventually achieved an unqualified success at Berlin.

The relative longevity of Reichardt's score, which enjoyed a revival even after the musical "nova" *Der Freischütz* burst on Berlin and the North in 1821, suggests many continuities from German opera of the 1790s to the unabashed romanticism of Weber, Marschner, Spohr, and Hoffmann. Vital elements of the operatic style young Wagner was to inherit can be found as far back as Benda and André, as we shall discover. In tracing a theatrical and musical continuum, however, one can go back no further than the portentous years in which Viennese and Italian style transformed opera in every German-speaking region of Central Europe. Thereafter, the contributions of North German composers and librettists lost their distinctive voice and merged with a mainstream to which all German-speaking lands contributed in like measure.

2

The birth of Saxon opera

The first decade of sustained developments in German opera during the Enlightenment, extending from 1766 to 1775, is by far the best-known period in its history. The operas of Johann Adam Hiller and his immediate followers Ernst Wilhelm Wolf and Christian Gottlob Neefe define what we presently think of as North German comic opera; similarly, discussions of attempts at serious opera in the North limit themselves to the operas written by Anton Schweitzer for Weimar and Georg Benda for Gotha.

There are good reasons to regard these important years in the history of German opera in general as specifically North German. The works of Holzbauer, Danzi, Peter Winter, Cannabich, and others active in South Germany come slightly later, as does the establishing of the Mannheim National Theater in 1778. In Austria, too, the impulse to significant developments in German opera comes first with the founding of the National Singspiel by Emperor Joseph II in the same year. By that time, North German opera had already moved from the enforced simplicity of Hiller's early comic operas to the impressive, ambitious scores of Schweitzer and Benda. This initial decade of Northern activity, which took place almost entirely within Saxony and Thüringia, will occupy us in this and the following two chapters.

Before the beginning

The dawn of this era can be fixed precisely on 28 May 1766. On that day at Leipzig the theatrical company of Heinrich Gottfried Koch first presented Johann Adam Hiller's revision of the popular musical farce *Der Teufel ist los*, now rechristened *Die verwandelten Weiber*. This event ended nearly three decades of sporadic, disorganized operatic activities all across North Germany. At the same time, it rose from roots cast deep in the experiences of these decades. Therefore, before studying Hiller's first operas we must glance briefly at the German stage between German opera's last stand at Hamburg and the new beginnings made at Leipzig.

Upon the closing of the Hamburg Opera in 1738, the owner of the opera house at the Goose Market rented it to the traveling company of Caroline Neuber, an event symptomatic of things to come. The preceding October at Leipzig the Neuber troupe had carried out a celebrated mock *auto-da-fé* for

Harlequin, at the end of which the company had banished the poor fellow from their stage (or at least his licentiousness, costume, and extemporizing). The Hamburgers at the old opera house missed his antics, however, and even more so the pomp and splendor of opera. The most that the Neuber company could offer in recompense was the likes of *Das ruchlose Leben und erschreck-liche Ende des Welt bekannten Ertz-Zauberers D. Johann Fausts* (*The Infamous Life and Terrifying End of the World-Renowned Arch-Magician Dr. Johann Faust*), given on 7 July 1738 with two arias and a ballet of Furies included.[1]

Two years later Caroline Neuber and most of her company left for the court of Empress Anna at St. Petersburg, and her many opponents at Hamburg saw to the establishing of an Italian opera soon after. The Pietro Mingotti company appeared on this stage from time to time during the 1740s. Together with many other traveling bands of Italian buffists, they represented the standard musical fare of the day for civic and court theaters alike. German companies could not begin to rival their musical offerings and made no attempt to do so. At times, in fact, a German and Italian troupe would strike an agreement to share the same stage, performing German spoken dramas and Italian comic operas on alternate evenings.

The Neuber company's position of pre-eminence in Germany devolved on a new troupe founded by Johann Friedrich Schönemann. In 1743 he introduced into his repertory at Berlin a musical novelty, *Der Teufel ist los*, a translation of Charles Coffey's popular ballad opera *The Devil to Pay* (1728). The adaptation of the music for the original English version had been the work of a German at London, a certain Herr Sydow (or "Mr. Seedo"), and apparently through his connections with the Prussian court at Potsdam the work made its way to Germany.[2] The translator, an official in Frederick the Great's administration named Caspar Wilhelm von Borck, used a pseudonym so that his standing at court might not be disadvantaged by knowledge of his collaboration with vagrant actors.

Schönemann must have achieved a certain success with *Der Teufel ist los*, for he guarded the text jealously and would not allow it to be published, although his spoken repertory appeared in the series *Schönemannsche Schaubühne* (1748–55). A playbill for a performance at Hamburg by the Schönemann company on 29 June 1747 recommended the work on grounds certain to please a Hamburg audience: "This piece, which is filled throughout with satires, arias, pranks, and transformations of the theater, will hopefully kindle special delight as one of the first attempts at the practices of the English stage on our own."[3]

---

[1] The playbill for this performance has been reprinted by Friedrich Johann Freiherr von Reden-Esbeck, *Caroline Neuber und ihre Zeitgenossen* (Leipzig, 1881), pp. 233–4.

[2] The circumstances surrounding Sydow's version in Germany have been studied by Walter Rubsamen, "Mr. Seedo, Ballad Opera, and the Singspiel," *Miscellánea en homenaje a Mons. Higinio Anglés* (Barcelona, 1958–1961), pp. 775–809.

[3] This playbill, including the cast of twelve, is reprinted by Hans Devrient, *Johann Friedrich Schönemann und seine Schauspielergesellschaft*, Theatergeschichtliche Forschungen, vol. 11 (Hamburg and Leipzig, 1895), p. 77, n. 118.

Despite the popular appeal of *Der Teufel ist los* everywhere Schönemann presented it, he took no further comic operas into his repertory for the rest of his career, which ended in 1757. Further developments were to come through the efforts of Heinrich Gottfried Koch. Like Schönemann, he had learned his craft under Caroline Neuber, from 1728 to 1749. In 1750 he organized his own troupe at Leipzig. He cultivated among other things the Italian intermezzi, perhaps more than any other German principal, interspersing them between the acts of comedies and tragedies.

Then, in 1752 Koch had a respected German poet at Leipzig, Christian Felix Weisse, retranslate *The Devil to Pay* into German and had Johann Standfuss, a musician attached to his troupe, set this libretto to music. Gottsched, who saw here the seeds of a German comic opera, initiated a pamphlet war which did him little honor and only encouraged public interest.[4] The première of this new work, with Standfuss's music, was an extraordinary success on 6 October 1752, inclining Christian Heinrich Schmid to remark in 1775 that the origins of German comic opera were to be traced from that date.[5]

Koch's two leading singers for this production excelled as actor and actress, but lacked any substantial musical training. The Bohemian Johann Anton Bruck became especially famous for his pantomime skills as Jobsen Zeckel, the surly cobbler in *Der Teufel ist los*, and Caroline Elisabeth Steinbrecher, who took the part of his wife Lene, enchanted one and all. Only nineteen years old in 1752, she remained with Koch and lent her talents to Hiller's and Weisse's major comic operas produced at Leipzig, Weimar, and Berlin from 1766 to 1773. Weisse took unalloyed delight in her skills, dubbed her "our Favart," and created the female leads in these comic operas with her uppermost in mind.

A German troupe's ability to perform musical works depended on having not only adequate singers but also a decent orchestra, and this in turn usually depended on the degree to which a troupe cultivated the ballet. When Schönemann had presented the English version of *Der Teufel ist los* in 1743, few companies in Germany regularly gave ballets. Koch's cultivation of the intermezzi, on the other hand, provided him with both the instrumental and vocal resources necessary for his production of Standfuss's setting of *Der Teufel ist los* nine years later. The novelty for Koch's audiences lay not so much in a comic opera as such as it did in Standfuss's German music. Schmid summed up his strengths and weaknesses as a composer:

---

[4] The documents which constitute this impoverished attempt at an imitation of the Quérelle des Bouffons have been reprinted in an appendix to Jakob Minor's *Christian Felix Weisse und seine Beziehungen zur deutschen Literatur des achtzehnten Jahrhunderts* (Innsbruck, 1880). Among them is a translation by Gottsched's wife of Grimm's *Le Petit Prophète de Böhmischbroda*, which she was able to make appropriate to the situation at Leipzig simply by changing the names and references. As Minor notes, the entire campaign was against the principal Koch (Weisse is never mentioned in the documents), "whose performances of intermezzi and comic operas were viewed as a transplantation of Viennese local farces to Leipzig" (p. 155).

[5] *Chronologie des deutschen Theaters*, ed. Paul Legband, Schriften der Gesellschaft für Theatergeschichte, vol. 1 (Berlin, 1902), p. 102.

Herr Standfuss, rehearsal musician with the company, had much theatrical talent, especially for vocal composition for the theater, as his mostly appropriate comic expression indicates; only he lacked the deeper knowledge a true composer must have, and he died too early to acquire it [around 1759]. Thus occur the not infrequent errors against correct writing in his scores, the anxious modulations, the flat bass parts, and thus also to an extent the frequent similarity. Had he known how to make sufficient use of harmony, he would have been able to hide at least the last from his listeners' ears. He is more successful with droll and low comic arias than with more set and serious ones.[6]

We are unfortunately not in a position to judge Schmid's evaluation in all its details, since all of Standfuss's full scores are lost, and the numbers by him in the printed keyboard reductions of *Die verwandelten Weiber* and *Der lustige Schuster* have been edited by Hiller. Nonetheless, Standfuss's mastery of a cheerful, folk-like style is still abundantly apparent in these later sources, and so are inklings of what Schmid may have meant by "öftere Aehnlichkeit." Example 2.1 shows the composer's inclination to use the same thumping contredanse pattern in two songs for the cobbler Jobsen Zeckel in *Die verwandelten Weiber.*

Example 2.1   Standfuss: *Der Teufel ist los.* Vocal incipits of two songs for Jobsen.
    A: "Let the great, for all that, plague themselves with affairs of state."
    B: "A woman who is cheerful, young, and nimble is really quite a nice thing!"

The difficulties created at Leipzig by the initial hostilities of the Seven Years' War forced Koch to dissolve his troupe in 1756. But two years later he agreed to head the tattered remnants of Schönemann's old company in Lower Saxony. The new Koch troupe was brought up to full strength and enjoyed a profitable first year in the cities around Hamburg, safe from wartime perils.

[6] *Ibid.*

Koch did not forget about *Der Teufel ist los*, however, and also added at this time Weisse's translation of the sequel, *Der lustige Schuster (The Merry Cobler)*, set by Standfuss, who had rejoined Koch at Hamburg. In early 1759 it received its première at Lübeck, and in the same year Standfuss also completed another farcical opera, *Jochem Tröbs, oder der vergnügte Bauernstand*. The text came from a member of the troupe hired specifically as the company's theatrical poet, or Theaterdichter, Johann Christian Ast. Both text and music are lost, so we cannot know whether this may have been the first original German libretto of the new era.

Koch's decision to stay at Hamburg and Lübeck had been a wartime expediency. With the Peace of Hubertusburg in 1763 he hurried back to Leipzig to arrange for his company's return, and the following year the Koch troupe established itself permanently there. Hamburg, meanwhile, passed to Konrad Ackermann, a native of Königsberg driven from East Prussia by the Russian advance of 1756 and into years of unsteady wandering. Ackermann successfully petitioned the Hamburg Senate for citizenship and permission to build a new playhouse at the site of the old opera house on the Goose Market, inaugurated on 31 July 1765.

Under the pressure of public demand, opera was to play an increasingly important role in Ackermann's offerings at his new playhouse. Johann Friedrich Schütze, who chronicled Hamburg's theatrical life in 1794, looked back on these operas as a severe decline:

The principal was all too quickly led to a sin against taste. He summoned wretched intermezzists to his aid; he had *Eine wankende Schäferin* performed under the title "eine deutsche Oper"; he also mounted Italian intermezzi with awful singers, for example *La pace campestre*, in which Signore Ferini, supported by silent machines, performed every vocal prank alone on stage; yes, he even allowed, in a two-act pantomime-opera *Die ägiptische Piramide, oder Arlequin der verliebte Bauer*, a miscarriage from the Harlequin family in his very worst form to pull stunts.[7]

In 1766 things had come to such a pass that Ackermann tried reviving Reinhard Keiser's opera *Circe*, first performed in 1734 at Hamburg, and decked it out with "entertainment for the cruder mind of the herd. . . The rush of people was extraordinary – a quantity of theatrical decorations, transformations, and dances made the work so colorful and sensuous, that nothing can surpass it."[8] The text of this "Zauberstück mit Gesang und sechs Baletten" had been reworked by Ackermann's theatrical poet Ast, who had earlier provided Standfuss with *Jochem Tröbs*.

On the whole, during the thirty-year hiatus from 1738 to 1766 only Standfuss had aroused any interest as a composer of German opera in the North. There are traces of German operatic activities elsewhere – Gottfried Heinrich Stölzel at Gotha, for example, wrote several operas or possibly occasional pieces for the local court in the early 1740s, and a few stray librettos have

---

[7] *Hamburgische Theater-Geschichte* (Hamburg, 1794), pp. 327–8.   [8] *Ibid.*, p. 330.

come down to us suggestive of sporadic production here and there[9] – but, unlike the three operas set by Standfuss, these and other efforts excited little interest and did not survive in post-war repertories. Further, as already suggested in the case of Ackermann, most companies were still content to ply their audiences with translations of Italian intermezzi, sometimes using Italian singers as well.

The disruptive effects of the Seven Years' War had severely undercut what stability and continuity German troupes could muster. It had also wrought important changes in the life of Weisse, who fled to Paris with his patron when the forces of Frederick the Great pressed into Saxony in 1759 and began threatening Leipzig. Weisse found little to please him at Paris save the theater, which he attended almost every evening. In his autobiography he mentions seeing such works as Rousseau's *Le Devin du village* and Sedaine's *Blaise le savetier* (with music by Philidor). What Weisse says of the pieces he saw at Paris applies with little emendation to those he was to write himself in collaboration with Hiller:

They did not seek to arouse loud laughter with buffoonery and grotesque caricatures, as do most Italian ones, but put on stage a pretty fable and usually people living in the country, in whose mouths the melody of a little song was quite natural. These *chansons* had such apprehensible and singable melodies that they were very quickly learned by the public and repeated, and they enlivened social life . . . I saw clearly that the operettas were no works of dramatic art, and I did not hope to elevate the love of art in my nation with them.[10]

When Weisse returned to Leipzig he renewed his friendship with Koch, and it was not long before the principal was entreating him to revise first *Der Teufel ist los* and then *Der lustige Schuster* for his theater. Koch apparently considered the works out of date in their earlier form, for he also had prevailed upon his friend Johann Adam Hiller to revise Standfuss's music.

In so doing Koch had forged a makeshift triumvirate which was to rule virtually unchallenged over the creation and elaboration of a distinctive new genre of music drama in Germany, one we shall refer to as Saxon opera. But these first two revisions which inaugurated the new genre compromised themselves in many ways with the bygone decades which had welcomed their high spirits and unruliness. They derive their importance more from circumstance than from any pathbreaking stylistic novelty: they were the first operas to unite Weisse, Hiller, and Koch; the first to draw inspiration from opéra-comique, on which Saxon opera would continue to depend; the first to have both text and music published; and the first – so it came to pass – in an uninterrupted stream of North German operas extending to the end of the century and beyond. With them German opera became a consistent phenomenon in German cultural life.

[9] At the British Library, for example, one finds such evidence as a verse pastorale opera *Der Kuss, oder Das ganz neu musikalische Schäfer-Spiel* (Frankfurt and Leipzig, 1748) and *Der Soldat in den Winterquartieren* (Quirlequitsch [Berlin], 1759), also with verse dialogue.

[10] Christian Felix Weisse, *Selbstbiographie*, ed. Christian Ernst Weisse and Samuel Gottlob Frisch (Leipzig, 1806), p. 103.

Koch and Leipzig's theaters

Before examining these operas in more detail, however, we must consider the cultural climate and theatrical exigencies at Leipzig which brought them forth and shaped their character. Both versions of *Die verwandelten Weiber* – Standfuss's *Der Teufel ist los* of 1752 and Hiller's revision of 1766 – were given on the same stage at Leipzig, Quandt's Court on Nicolaistrasse. It had been built in the late 1740s and followed a suggestion of Gottsched that the amphitheater be arranged along antique classical lines in the shape of a semicircle.

Even as Koch began enriching his repertory with the new operas of Weisse and Hiller in 1766 at Quandt's Court, a new theater was under construction at the old "Bastey" ("bulwark") at the Rannstadt Gate. This new theater came to be called Koch's Theater, for his company performed there exclusively until 1771, when he began establishing a foothold at Berlin. Yet Koch's role in the planning and executing of the theater is unclear. In 1751 he had petitioned the Elector at Dresden for permission to build a new "regular opera- and comedy-house," since the theater at Quandt's Court "is all too small with respect to the stage for comedies, and is wholly unsuitable for operas."[11] In 1765, however, a local businessman captained the efforts to secure both Electoral permission for the Rannstadt Gate project and the financial means to carry it out.

The reviving of *Die verwandelten Weiber* that May was probably unconnected with the project, which was already under way. Had this been the case, Koch would presumably not have allowed the botching of the orchestra pit which resulted. As Schering describes it, the orchestra had its music stands nailed to the stage in a row, and so close together that a larger number of musicians would have been hampered in their movements. Only in 1773 did the impresario Bustelli correct matters.[12]

Koch opened the new Theater am Rannstädter Thore on 10 October 1766 with a German verse tragedy (*Hermann* by Johann Elias Schlegel), a ballet (*Die vergnügten Schäfer*), and a French afterpiece (Jean-François Regnard's one-act comedy *Le Retour imprévu* in an anonymous translation, *Die unvermuthete Wiederkunft*). Goethe remembered that the tragedy was a big bore. The disappointing turnout could be partly blamed on the diversion of public attention that same day to a spectacle elevated in quite a different way – the replacing of the weathervane on the Thomaskirche.[13]

---

[11] Quoted by Julius Vogel, *Goethes Leipziger Studentenjahre* (Leipzig, 1899), p. 12.
[12] Arnold Schering, *Johann Sebastian Bach und das Musikleben Leipzigs im 18. Jahrhundert* (Leipzig, 1941), p. 437.
[13] The diary of Johann Salomon Riemer records how on that day "the weathervane (Windstern) on the tower of the Thomaskirche was put back on the spire by the local slater Andreas Daniel Eydam with great solemnity, a very dangerous thing to behold which a prodigious number of spectators witnessed with astonishment." Gustav Wustmann, *Quellen zur Geschichte Leipzigs*, vol. 1 (Leipzig, 1889), p. 238.

As on many an opening night before and after, the spectators at the new theater were more interested in taking in the decorations and architecture of the new building than in the inaugural offerings. The curtain and its allegorical painting by Adam Friedrich Oeser was described and commented on by many, including Goethe.[14] Like the works selected for the inaugural evening, this curtain stressed the theater's role as a temple of spoken drama. The evening gave little hint of the role German comic opera had already begun to play in Koch's fortunes. For many years to come the genre, like Abel Magwitch, would bank-roll the well-being of others without sharing in the esteem they could command.

The new theater held nearly 1,200 spectators, a considerable number in a city of 25,000 inhabitants. Of course the three annual fairs for which Leipzig was famous swelled its population. Around them Koch planned his theatrical seasons. The New Year's Fair, the least important, ran from 2 January for about three weeks. The Easter Fair – the major one for the book trade – began the Tuesday after Easter Sunday and lasted five weeks. The Michaelmas Fair (named for the Feast of the Archangel Michael, 29 September) usually ran from mid-September to mid- or late October. Koch often obtained permission to perform for several weeks after each fair. Leipzig had already gained the upper hand on Frankfurt am Main as the center of Germany's book-publishing trade, and it dominated music publishing as well. Those who came to the fairs in connection with these trades supplemented an already considerable native coterie of sophisticated theater-lovers.

As a university town and intellectual center, Leipzig attracted a remarkable number of young men who contributed to the development of German opera as a literary genre in the next two decades – Goethe, Johann Benjamin Michaelis, Johann Jakob Engel, Daniel Schiebeler, and Johann Joachim Eschenburg to name the most prominent. Weisse was loved and esteemed by all of them and offered them models of gracious clarity in his French-inspired dramas and verse (Biedermann suggests that "the tendency to the natural and true" in Goethe's poetry of the period may have owed something to him[15]).

Die verwandelten Weiber

Neither Koch nor Weisse nor Hiller had approached the creation of Saxon opera with high artistic ambitions. Koch had been induced by concern for his dangerously depleted cash-box more than anything else to seek the aid of Weisse and Hiller in reviving Standfuss's two operas. The principal had

---

[14] *Dichtung und Wahrheit*, pt. 2, book 8. A more elaborate description by Franz Wilhelm Kreuchauf appeared in a Festschrift issued for the opening of the theater. See Gertrud Rudloff-Hille, "Das Leipziger Theater von 1766," *Maske und Kothurn* 14 (1968): 224–5. This description is also reprinted by Johann Friedrich Reichardt in his *Briefe eines aufmerksamen Reisenden die Musik betreffend*, vol. 2 (Frankfurt and Breslau, 1776), pp. 96–8.

[15] Woldemar Freiherr von Biedermann, *Goethe und Leipzig*, vol. 1 (Leipzig, 1865), p. 94.

begun to perceive that Leipzig was only marginally capable of supporting his company and its repertory as a year-round standing, unsubsidized theater. From 1766 until the arrival of the Wäser company from Dresden for the fairs of 1770, Koch had Leipzig virtually to himself, yet despite the crowds at fair time his repertory soon saturated his potential audience. Koch's instincts called Standfuss's comic operas to mind, and in their new versions they almost immediately righted his foundering fortunes.

Little in Hiller's career apart from his fortuitous presence at Leipzig and friendship with Koch suggested him for his role as the first great master of Saxon opera. His life-long ideals of musical taste in general and opera in particular were dominated overwhelmingly by the model of Hasse. Hiller had produced nothing for the theater apart from an unperformed one-act afterpiece by Gellert prior to his association with Koch. Further, during the entire span of his career as a composer of comic operas he devoted most of his energies to a host of other duties: conducting the Leipzig "grosse Konzerte" since 1763; giving lessons in singing and composition; and writing, editing, and translating. Certainly he approached *Die verwandelten Weiber* with limited ambitions. He agreed to compose only the new musical texts Weisse had added in revising his earlier version for Standfuss, and this as a favor for the struggling Koch. Georgy Calmus tells us that eventually Hiller was supposed to recompose the entire libretto,[16] but, although Hiller later replaced Standfuss's overture and four of his songs with new music "which has hitherto not been sung in any theater" in the published keyboard reduction of 1770, he otherwise left his predecessor's numbers stand, for "they had pleased the public." In this final version Hiller had composed or recomposed twenty-four items and had preserved fourteen by Standfuss. *Der lustige Schuster* he scarcely altered at all – just seven arias and the overture are his, the other thirty-three numbers are by Standfuss.

Weisse also maintained a circumspect attitude toward these two revisions, divorcing them rather sharply from his later librettos for Hiller. He was to give pride of place to *Lottchen am Hofe* and *Die Liebe auf dem Lande* in the first volume of the first edition of his *Komische Opern* (published anonymously at Leipzig in 1768); the *Teufel* texts were relegated to volume two, although they are earlier works chronologically. Further, Weisse's preface to the collection apologizes for the two farces: they are being published at all only because he has heard that some companies have got hold of Standfuss's music and have added the spoken dialogue after their own conception, passing this off under Weisse's name.[17]

In his spoken comedies of the 1750s and 1760s Weisse pursued two well-trodden paths, one the witty intrigue-laden comedy developing familiar character types, the other the sentimental comedy exploiting static tableaux

---

[16] *Die ersten deutschen Singspiele von Standfuss und Hiller* (Leipzig, 1908), p. 17. Calmus does not document this claim.
[17] *Komische Opern*, vol. 1 (Leipzig, 1768), p. vii.

and emphasizing the emotional analysis of serious, sympathetic characters. Neither was to be transferred without alteration into his comic operas, which Weisse could never bring himself to regard as in the same league with his spoken dramas, and least of all into his adaptations of Coffey. As a brief summary of the plot of *Die verwandelten Weiber* will indicate, Weisse turned here to the realm of farce, a genre he avoided completely in his spoken works. At the cobbler Jobsen Zeckel's house we learn of his wife Lene's unhappy lot as the object of his violent outbursts, and at the home of the landowner Herr von Liebreich we find an equally offensive specimen in the lady of the house, who curses and beats her servants incessantly. Doktor Mikroskop, a wandering magician, promises to improve Lene's situation drastically. After being thrown out of both houses he casts a spell which transforms Lene into Frau von Liebreich and the latter into Lene. In both households the husbands and servants discover with astonishment the sudden transformation in each wife's character. Eventually Mikroskop reappears, explains his charm, and stops its effects. Jobsen and Frau von Liebreich, chastened by the experience, promise to mend their ways.

Since Weisse's first translation of *The Devil to Pay* (the one set by Standfuss in 1752) does not survive, we can gain only an indirect understanding of the changes he made in this retranslation for Hiller. The new version follows Coffey's general plot fairly closely, but its borrowings from Sedaine's *Le Diable à quatre* (1756, based on the same source) and Weisse's own additions are significant in illuminating his objections to certain features of the ballad opera.

Coffey's *The Devil to Pay* consists of eight scenes not divided into acts and eighteen musical numbers. This modest frame had been expanded by Sedaine to the three-act format also found in Weisse. In many scenes the German text follows the disposition of prose and airs found in Coffey, with alterations involving mainly softening the language or removing topical and religious references. For example, Jobsen drives Mikroskop from his house with a commonplace threat of violence in Weisse: "Out of my house, thief, or I'll conduct you out with my strap!" The English cobbler had a far more dramatic measure in mind: "Out of my House, you Villain, or I'll run my Awl up to the Handle in your Buttocks."

In another scene Weisse omits altogether an anti-Catholic sentiment aired by the puritanical Lady Loverule upon catching her servants at dance and drink:

BUTLER: I thought, Madam, we might be merry once upon a Holiday.
LADY : Holiday, you popish Cur! is one Day more holy than another? and if it be, you'll be sure to get drunk upon it, you Rogue. [Beats him] You Minx, you impudent Flirt, are you jigging it after an abominable Fiddle? all Dancing is whorish, Hussy. [Lugs her by the Ears.]

Nonetheless, the violent shrew's flailings here inspired Geyser to the fron-

Plate 1 *Die verwandelten Weiber*, Frau von Liebreich upbraiding her servants, act 1, scene 7

tispiece he executed for Weisse's published libretto (Plate 1).[18] With it he meant to capture the essence of the opera's rowdy character: this was what German audiences went to see when *Die verwandelten Weiber* stood on the playbill.

Weisse borrows several significant touches from Sedaine, and in general intensifies the process already begun by his French model of smoothing the rough edges of Jobsen and Frau von Liebreich and of harping on the good nature of Herr von Liebreich and particularly Lene. Weisse's retreat from the farce's traditional attributes of violence, satire, brevity, bawdiness, and extremes of character delineation pointed to a bourgeois ethical and aesthetic conception of comic opera which he would further refine in his next librettos and which would dominate North German opera for decades to come.

An instructive parallel may be seen in an adaptation made around this time for the Hamburg stage of Gay's *The Beggar's Opera*, called *Die Strassenräuber*. In a review of the published libretto, Christoph Daniel Ebeling cited the anonymous translator's efforts to ennoble the character of Polly as praiseworthy in every way (she seeks to dissuade Macheath from his life of crime). He even suggests that the hero's character could benefit from revision, in order to make him more worthy of Polly's love. Ebeling assumes that the political–social satire and realistic views of whorehouses and dens of thieves would not interest German audiences, and that the love relationship would be paramount.[19]

From what Hiller tells us in the preface to his keyboard reduction of *Die verwandelten Weiber* as well as from other evidence, we know that the opera was done in many different versions, troupes outside of Leipzig often retaining much of Standfuss's older music. Even Koch's company did not follow the new version as published by Weisse and Hiller faithfully, but stuck to some earlier numbers which had been dropped by the poet. Such a situation is understandable, for the music's partnership with the text is a casual and at times careless one. This first German opera of the era begins not with a song but with dialogue, and act one ends with a whole scene of nothing but prose. Eleven pages of act three go by before anyone sings a note. The dramatic self-sufficiency of the spoken dialogue seen here remained characteristic of Saxon opera, and so did the ungainly distribution of airs among the principals in every act. Perhaps owing to Koch's limited vocal resources, Weisse gave the lion's share of musical numbers to Jobsen and Lene (fifteen and twelve respectively) and only two each for Herr and Frau von Liebreich. On three different occasions Jobsen sings three numbers running, and Hiller went to the trouble of adding a new number in his keyboard reduction of 1770 so that

---

[18] *Ibid.*, vol. 2 (Leipzig, 1768). The original drawing was by Carl Philipp Emanuel Bach's son Johann Sebastian.

[19] *Allgemeine deutsche Bibliothek* 14:1 (1771): 207–10. Ebeling also notes that "the intermixed arias are largely translated from the English, and often the English metric structure is actually preserved. Hopefully this was not done because of their abominable melodies!" (p. 209). There were also some new arias added by the anonymous translator.

Lene is similarly honored when she first sings in act one. That all three of her numbers here begin with Lombard rhythms ("Scottish snaps") scarcely makes the effect less tedious. In general, the music is worked in wherever possible with little or no attention to complementary interaction among adjacent numbers, not to speak of even broader groupings.

Simple songs predominate, and both composers reacted to Weisse's texts with a light responsive touch, seen especially in the nine airs in multiple tempos and meters. Hiller will of course always be remembered first and foremost for the engaging, folk-like melodies in his operas, several of which attained the status of true folk songs. Their absorption into German popular culture has been pointed to as evidence of the national character of the operas which brought them into being, but one can argue even more cogently that it attests to their inherent separability from their original dramatic context.

Hiller wrote two da capo arias of modest scale for Lene in *Die verwandelten Weiber* and none for anybody else. The first is the extra number he slipped in for Lene near the beginning of act one and has no special difficulties or adornments attached to it. In act two, however, when through the magician's arts Lene awakes to find herself in the bed of Liebreich's wife, Hiller gives her a second, more spacious da capo in E-flat major. Here he drew on as much of Hasse's high art as he dared in order to illuminate something in Lene's character that makes her new situation appropriate rather than incongruous. The melodic style with its triplet motion and discreet harmonic support (Example 2.2) derives from Hasse's galant manner. But he

Example 2.2 Hiller: *Die verwandelten Weiber.* Da capo aria of Lene, act 2.
"This is surely heaven! Where else would I find such lovely things?"

never had to struggle to ennoble thoughts expressed with such words as "kriegt" and "Sachen," nor would he have confined himself so drastically to Hiller's square phrasing, which brings this aria nearer to the simple Lieder in the opera. Lene's two cadenzas in the A parts are brief and of restricted compass, affective rather than virtuosic. The first eight bars of the B part are canonic, an idea that Hiller probably derived from studying Hasse's arias.

Several of the French-derived numbers in the score present types which became standard features of German comic opera. The work closes with a "Rundgesang" followed by a "Schluss-Chor." The former (which Hiller also calls a Divertissement) gives each of the principals a crack at its tune to a different stanza of text, with everyone joining in to echo the last line of each. The closing chorus alternates another group of solo stanzas with a choral refrain.

Another number, Standfuss's "Es war einmal ein junges Weib," is an early prototype of one of the most popular character pieces in any German comic opera, the Romanze. Several of this example's features link it with the explicitly labeled Romanzen in later German operas: it is strophic, it tells a story, and the story told is clearly a reflex of the opera's own plot. In this instance Jobsen sings to his suddenly imperious wife (Frau von Liebreich transformed into Lene) a tale which goes back to Chaucer's Wife of Bath: a husband refuses to let his wanton wife into heaven after she dies, but she blames Adam's transgression for the fall of women. The two characters on stage are precisely those in need of emendation. In all three versions of this number found in Coffey, Sedaine, and Weisse, dialogue interrupts the strophes, a technique the Romanze was to develop as a means of pointing up the song's role as a gloss on the drama under way.

Hiller's operatic experiments with Schiebeler

After his first two operas Hiller turned from Weisse to the young student Daniel Schiebeler for two of his next three operas. If the tone of the two Coffey adaptations was low, Hiller clearly set his sights too high with his first opera for Koch's new theater, *Lisuart und Dariolette*. Schiebeler's drama, based ultimately on Chaucer and filtered through Dryden and Voltaire, was written originally as a spoken afterpiece in 1764. Calmus surmises that the popularity of the *Teufel* twins prompted his turning it into an opera for Hiller,[20] and the success scored one year earlier at Paris by Duni's setting of Favart's four-act opéra-comique on the same subject, *La Fée Urgèle*, may also have had a hand in his decision.

In striking out from the low road of the *Teufel* revisions, both librettist and composer seized on Hiller's new periodical *Wöchentliche Nachrichten und Anmerkungen, die Musik betreffend* as a propaganda tool. Here they separate their endeavor from both the earlier operas of Hiller and Standfuss and from French opéra-comique, defend its use of da capo arias, and even hint at the possibility of turning the spoken dialogue into recitative. All this points to a predisposition toward imitating Italian opera. Hiller hoped the

---

[20] *Die ersten deutschen Singspiele*, p. 27.

work would prove to be "the herald of more serious taste on the lyric stage" in Germany and warned against slavish imitation of the French.[21] Young Johann Friedrich Reichardt, however, found little that was Hiller in the score and surmised "that Hiller was still too full of his Hasse" when he wrote it.[22] He also very properly reproved Hiller for his sloppy declamation – not something one worries over too much in comic operas, but as jarring as his hapless four-square phrasing in a more elevated style.

Hiller called *Lisuart und Dariolette* "eine romantisch–comische Oper" in the first edition of the keyboard reduction, unduly exciting those in search of the roots of German Romantic Opera. Schiebeler published a long essay on serious, comic, and romantic epic poetry in which he gingerly suggested that *Lisuart und Dariolette* might deserve the label Hiller was to give it in the 1768 print.[23] But all Schiebeler meant by the designation was a comic drama derived from the "romantic epic," an adventure poem dealing with the exploits of knights errant. Curiously, none of the extant editions of the libretto call it a "romantic–comic opera," and Hiller too dropped the label in the second edition of the keyboard reduction in 1769 and called it simply a "comische Oper."

Calmus and others have suggested Schiebeler's libretto as the possible source of some elements in Schikaneder's *Die Zauberflöte*: in the story the heroine Dariolette first appears as an old hag; Queen Ginevra is attended by three ladies; Lisuart is given a portrait of her daughter and bends all his efforts toward discovering the abducted beauty, who is to be married to a dwarfish dolt named Bubu. The first printed version of the libretto to come down to us is in fact Viennese,[24] but *La Fée Urgèle* was also produced at Vienna in 1780, and one is inclined to believe that this much finer telling of the story is the more logical and proximate source. Still, as we shall see later, it is sufficiently remarkable for a North German opera to be produced at all at Vienna for us to take note of *Lisuart und Dariolette*'s appearance there.

On 7 January 1767, by chance the day after the Viennese première of the original two-act version, *Lisuart und Dariolette* was given at Leipzig in a three-act expanded version. Why this was done is not clear, although it may have been simply an effort to invest the opera with dimensions equal to its ambitions. Apart from strengthening the new act ending introduced, Hiller and Schiebeler expand significantly the role of Dariolette: five of the nine new solo numbers are for her. The basso buffo Derwin, Lisuart's cowardly squire, picks up four new songs. Perhaps not by any coincidence, these represent the character types best suited to Hiller's talents. Far from redressing imbalances among the singers, the additions extend already prominent musical roles –

---

[21] *Wöchentliche Nachrichten und Anmerkungen, die Musik betreffend* 1 (1766/7): 219, 256.

[22] *Briefe eines aufmerksamen Reisenden*, vol. 2, p. 29.

[23] *Wöchentliche Nachrichten* 2 (1767/8): 135–9.

[24] Schatz 4726 (see Appendix). This libretto bears the date 1766, although the work was first given at Vienna on 6 January 1767.

ones no doubt created by the same singers in Koch's troupe who took the roles of Jobsen Zeckel and Lene in *Die verwandelten Weiber.*

None of the new numbers pursues the serious path Hiller and Schiebeler had earlier vaunted in their opera. Instead, they develop elements already present in the *Teufel* operas. Derwin's Romanze-like "Der Teufel kam vor vielen Jahren" is a case in point. In the two-act version Schiebeler and Hiller had already provided a number in the Romanze tradition, and one which mirrors the predicament of the drama's hero. This "Romanze" of the Three Ladies – about a beautiful young shepherdess, the sight of whom reforms a vice-prone and unruly prince – serves to introduce the subject of Lisuart in the opening scene of the opera. The second "Romanze" added to the three-act version, by contrast, tells the story of how the devil came to earth and took a wife named Honesta; she beshrewed him to such a degree that he fairly wished himself back in hell, so he left her and recovered his malicious good spirits by entering the soul of a poet; he amused himself with various antics in this guise until a doctor exorcised him by invoking the name of Honesta.

Friedrich Nicolai's *Allgemeine deutsche Bibliothek* carried a lengthy review of Hiller's keyboard reduction written by Johann Friedrich Agricola, Germany's foremost singing master, a staunch supporter of Italian opera, and the periodical's most active contributor of music reviews during the later 1760s. He praises the introduction of da capo arias for the serious parts and rather anxiously points out that even the French have begun making their comic operas "more properly musical" of late: "It could be that Philidor has perhaps even got a few da capos."[25] That having been said, however, Agricola proceeds to devote all his attention to the comic arias. He caps his review with a detailed discussion of Lisuart's embarrassed efforts to utter his response to the question he must correctly answer or lose his head: "What is most pleasing to women?" Agricola praises Hiller's musical stammering and the eventual whole-note answer, "Oberherrschaft" ("supremacy"). Hiller's efforts at musical substance and seriousness earned Agricola's respect, but his comic style won his enthusiasm, and in this the reviewer probably reflected the opinion of many.

Hiller and Schiebeler collaborated on one further work, a short afterpiece called *Die Muse*, first given on 3 October 1767. Its first six scenes are all in prose, and most of the singing in the last two is meant to be just that – Monime disguised as a poetic muse singing to Phaedria. Hiller moved further toward a refined, cantata-like musical assertiveness in these scenes, which include three arias, a duet, a simple Lied, and a recitative introducing a final chorus. Only the duet is in da capo form. In the first aria Hiller uses pizzicato strings effectively to imitate the lute to which the muse appears and he also includes an obbligato wind part for oboe or flute. The stylish Italianate vocal writing shows what Caroline Steinbrecher, still Koch's leading soprano, was capable of only seventeen months after she first appeared as Lene in *Die ver-*

wandelten Weiber. And Koch apparently had by now scraped together a tolerable orchestra, which in the closing chorus included trumpets and timpani.

Schiebeler's wandering off to classical antiquity had no effect on the story itself, about a young poet maniacally devoted to his art (and bearing some similarities to the hero of Lessing's comedy *Der junge Gelehrte*, first performed at Leipzig in 1748). *Die Muse* is one of the earliest German comic operas to use the technique of an elaborate pseudo-supernatural deception to bring an obsessed character to his senses. Here, the whole scheme of the epiphany of the muse is dreamt up by a conventional servant pair, and they are predictably rewarded with each other and a generous gift from the young poet's father at the end.

The breakthrough to French-derived "komische Oper"

Between Hiller's two operas written in collaboration with Schiebeler appeared his setting of Weisse's *Lottchen am Hofe* at Koch's theater on 24 April 1767. A year later followed their next joint effort, *Die Liebe auf dem Lande* on 18 May 1768. With these two works Weisse and Hiller established in paradigmatic form Saxon comic opera. They and their imitators were to follow the tone, setting, character types, and restricted role of music in these operas with little deviation up to 1773, when both Hiller and Weisse fell silent for half a decade. The high water mark of their collaboration came in early 1770 at Weimar, where Koch had found a warmer alternative to the New Year's Fair at Leipzig. Here his company produced at the court theater the most enduring and beloved achievement of Weisse and Hiller, *Die Jagd.*

Before discussing these works in detail, we must appreciate how overwhelmingly these men, and especially Hiller, dominated the North German operatic scene from *Die verwandelten Weiber* to *Die Jagd.* Table 2.1 lists all known German operas composed in the North during this period of nearly four years, with dates of first performance and publication histories of text and music. Of the sixteen works listed there, seven are by Hiller; of the eight keyboard reductions published, seven are again Hiller's, not to mention the multiple editions of four of his operas; and of the eleven texts that survive, seven were for his works. With the exception of a few stray arias and the lone keyboard reduction not by Hiller (Ernst Wilhelm Wolf's *Das Gärtnermädchen*), the only music to be preserved from these years is Hiller's. We can also glean from this table a distinction among Hiller's works listed there: the operas whose music was not published soon after the first production (the two *Teufel* operas and *Die Muse*) do not see further editions of their keyboard reductions. Nor were the librettists of these works in a hurry to bring out the texts.

None of the three new, seminal works of Weisse and Hiller uses an original plot. *Lottchen am Hofe* is a straightforward adaptation of Favart's *Le*

Table 2.1. *North German opera from* Die verwandelten Weiber *to* Die Jagd

Date of première	Title	Composer–Librettist	Date of publication Music	Text
28 May 1766	*Die verwandelten Weiber*	Hiller–Weisse	1770	1768
mid-1766	*Der lustige Schuster*	Hiller–Weisse	1771	1768
25 Nov 1766	*Lisuart und Dariolette*: two-act version	Hiller–Schiebeler	–	1766
1766	(*[Der lustige Schulmeister]*)	Krause–Nicolai	–	–
7 Jan 1767	*Lisuart und Dariolette*: three-act version	Hiller–Schiebeler	1768[a]	1769
24 Apr 1767	*Lottchen am Hofe*	Hiller–Weisse	1769[b]	1768
3 Oct 1767	*Die Muse*	Hiller–Schiebeler	1771	1770
18 May 1768	*Die Liebe auf dem Lande*	Hiller–Weisse	1769[c]	1768
1768	[*Lukas und Hannchen*]	Beckmann–Eschenburg	–	1768
1768	(*[Der Kapellmeister und die Schülerin]*)	Laube–Ast	–	–
1768	(*[Matz und Anna]*)	Laube–Ast	–	–
9 Jan 1769	(*[Fräulein von Ueberklug und Herr Gleichzu]*)	Frisch–unknown	–	–
1769	(*Das Erntefest]*)	Weisflog–Weisflog	–	–
1769	[*Das Monden-Reich*]	Frischmuth–unknown	–	n.d.
unperformed	[*Walmir und Gertraud*]	Schweitzer–Michaelis	–	1769
1769	*Das Gärtnermädchen*	Wolf–Musäus	1774	1771
29 Jan 1770	*Die Jagd*	Hiller–Weisse	1771[d]	1770

Key:
( ) – text does not survive.
[ ] – music does not survive.
— – unpublished.
[a] 2nd edition issued in 1769.
[b] 2nd edition issued in 1770 and 3rd edition in 1776.
[c] 2nd edition issued in 1770.
[d] 2nd edition issued in 1772 and 3rd edition in 1776.

Caprice amoureux, ou Ninette à la cour (itself based on Goldoni's *Bertoldo, Bertoldino e Cacassenno* of 1749, probably in the reduced two-act intermezzi version produced at Paris in 1753 and 1754). *Die Liebe auf dem Lande* cleverly intercalates Anseaume's one-act *La Clochette* of 1766 as an extended episode between the two outer acts based on Madame Favart's *Annette et Lubin* (1762) – a testimonial to the interchangeability of parts among opérascomiques which trade in rustic innocence. Finally *Die Jagd*, which we shall take up in the next section, draws on two French versions of Robert Dodsley's story "The King and the Miller of Mansfield" (1736): the first is Sedaine's important opéra-comique of 1762, *Le Roi et le fermier*, and the second is a "nationalized" spoken drama by Collé, *Le Partie de chasse de Henri IV.*

Die Jagd and *Die Liebe auf dem Lande*, as their titles imply, are set wholly in the country. *Lottchen am Hofe*, however, is two-thirds "am Hofe" and explores the familiar theme of plucky rustic innocence versus jaded courtly corruption far more thoroughly than the other two. The bluff good humor of the country folk can turn here to bitterest reproach. Lottchen, having been brought to court and decked out by Astolph for obvious purposes, is unexpectedly accosted near the end of act two by Astolph's fiancée, Emilie. She asks Lottchen rather haughtily how she likes the court, and Lottchen replies with a damning list of its hypocrisy:

LOTTCHEN: One is busy without having done anything: one eats without being hungry: one goes to bed without sleeping: people embrace each other in order to strangle each other, and they flatter each other in order to do each other harm. [To Emilie, who laughs:] One laughs with a victorious expression in order to hide one's secret vexation: cheerfulness is a mere grimace, and amusement is just a noisy din.

Touché, and Emilie must vexedly await the conclusion of Lottchen's aria following this sermon (which evokes the honest pleasures of country life) before she can pour her scornful, sarcastic contempt on the upstart peasant girl.

In act three Lottchen's betrothed, Gürge, shows up and has a falling out with her (he does not recognize her in court finery and she avails herself of the chance to test his fidelity, but he is bent on making Lottchen jealous and feigns infatuation). Lottchen runs off, and since misery loves company ends up conspiring with Emilie on a scheme for punishing both lovers, which has a number of similarities to the act-four finale of Da Ponte's *Le nozze di Figaro*. Astolph lavishes endearments on Lottchen in semi-darkness as Gürge overhears; Lottchen plays up to Astolph briefly, then substitutes Emilie for herself. After a quartet Astolph ends up on his knees in the awkward position of making love to his own fiancée.

Weisse made no attempt to nationalize Favart's drama, as he was to do with his subsequent adaptations – Astolph, for example, is still the Duke of Lombardy – possibly because he had retained so much of the spirit of Favart's social criticism and felt that a noble who had to be caught in the act in order to repent and promise to reform was better left on French soil. In *Die Liebe auf dem Lande*, Weisse returned to the rustic atmosphere he would maintain in all his subsequent operas. The intruders from court life, as always, complicate matters for a pair of country lovers, but Weisse now tempers their vicious inclinations. The Schösser (bailiff), who has buried three wives already, wishes to marry young and tries to separate the rustic arch-innocents Lieschen and Hänschen by poisoning Lieschen's simple mind with scruples about the sinfulness of her relationship with Hänschen (although Weisse does not go so far as to make the young lovers blood relatives, as Favart had done). The count who lords it over the village has the whole matter brought before him. Immediately infatuated with Lieschen, he decides that the law requires that she and Hänschen part, and he has her taken away to his court. Hänschen, armed with a stick and in high dudgeon, runs off and frees her. The count good-naturedly relents of his decision and allows the happy pair to marry. The Schösser is not so generous. In the Rundgesang he sticks to his guns as the feisty antagonist of Hänschen and Lieschen while everyone else rejoices in their felicity. In another German operatic version of *Annette et Lubin* by Eschenburg, *Lukas und Hannchen*, the bailiff relents and recognizes his self-deception at the same spot in the Divertissement. Weisse, however, would not play the sentimental blindling here. His notion of wholesome rusticity in no way precluded realistic touches of a coarse, earthy, or even violent nature.

Weisse and Eschenburg define with their interpretations of the bailiff two poles toward which other conceptions of the malefactor in North German opera will gravitate. Where we have no villain, but simply a venal vice in need of correction, or inept wickedness outwitted and made laughable, the Enlightenment stage is instructing us to optimism. But we shall also find unrepentant souls who refuse to drop character for the sake of a contrived spirit of universal love of virtue at the end. Eventually this type can develop into a dark being who must either be punished or purged – in other words, to the likes of Pizarro and Caspar in *Fidelio* and *Der Freischütz*.

As a literary type, the Schösser in *Die Liebe auf dem Lande* is the traditional old fool with a matrimonial eye on a young maiden. He comes away empty-handed, of course, but with little damage compared with other specimens of his type – just a tumble from the roof of a hut into a sheep-pen in act two. Musically, he also follows strong traditions of characterization as one of the most gruff and violent characters in all Hiller's scores. In his c-minor storm aria, "Wenn uns der Sturm die Felder verwüstet," he seeks to frighten Lieschen with visions of the evils which will surely be visited upon the whole village owing to her sinful relationship with Hänschen. Reichardt described it as "an example of raging fire," but added an interesting observation on a comic detail in Hiller's musical characterization of this blustering buffoon:

> For all the seriousness of this piece, I still find a very comic trait in it, which makes it fully commensurate with the character of the Bailiff. Of all the hideous consequences of guilty love, none moves him as much as the destruction of the wine crop. After he has repeated the whole line:
>
> Der Hagel den Wein in Gebirgen zerstört
>
> he says again:
>
> Den Wein, den Wein zerstört.
>
> That this does not happen just by chance, but may perhaps be the effect of a critical refinement, seems to prove itself quite clearly in the second part [of the aria] where Herr Hiller not only repeats again the words "den Wein zerstört" but also breaks off at the last repetition of the word "Wein" and inserts a pause; immediately thereafter he lets follow the dolorous contemplation of dying of thirst in the most dolorous tones.[26]

The passage from the second half of the aria which Reichardt is discussing is reproduced from Hiller's keyboard reduction of 1770 in Example 2.3.

[26] *Briefe eines aufmerksamen Reisenden*, vol. 2, p. 102–3.

Example 2.3 Hiller: *Die Liebe auf dem Lande.* Bailiff's aria, act 1.
"When lightning and thunder consume the harvest, when hail destroys the wine crop in the highlands, when we are dying of thirst and hunger, then you are to blame for the destruction."

Reichardt might also have mentioned how carefully Hiller prepared this detail. The extensive circle of fifths in bars 61 to 69 propels the Schösser downward on a linear descent from the C in bar 62 to, eventually, the C in bar 80 (with a nice reminder of the compass spanned in his outburst in bars 77 to 78). Lieschen presumably listens with waxing consternation to the ever darker consequences of her wickedness, and indeed at the end of his descent the Schösser lays the guilt directly at her and Hänschen's doorstep. The business on "Wein," however, interrupts the Schösser's admonition. He seems to lose the thread of his argument on the dominant, as if this one disaster were almost too much to bear. The comic bass singing the part is invited to dwell plangently on the last "den Wein" in bars 70 and 71, which so pleased Reichardt, before hastening back to his present purpose.

The lovers, most essential of comic characters, can occur in sets of one, two, or even three pairs in Weisse's operas. In *Lottchen am Hofe* the two pairs parallel the two interacting milieux. Weisse was no doubt attracted to this text in the first place by the situations Favart develops out of this interaction. The substitution trick in act three is one, and the denouement following on its heels is surely another. Here, after Gürge and Lottchen have mended fences, Astolph offers Emilie his heart and hand anew with a promise of a wedding that very night: "I would deserve an even greater humiliation were I not to follow their example."

This same promise prompted Weisse at this point to the most elaborate, most French Divertissement of his career, which casts a final high relief of the differences between the two couples. To begin with, the Divertissement requires a scene change to a sumptuous ballroom and a costume change for Gürge and Lottchen, who must appear in their country clothes once again. After several danced entrées come the stanzas of the Divertissement proper, four pairs of sextains sung by antithetical representatives of court and country:

> stanza 1 A proud courtier – Gürge
> stanza 2 A woman of fashion – Lottchen
> stanza 3 A philanderer[27] – Gürge
> stanza 4 A courtesan – Lottchen

Then begins a grand ballet, but it is soon interrupted by Gürge. In dialogue he tells Lottchen that he has had enough. They sing the Rundgesang and leave, after which the interrupted ballet is resumed to conclude the opera. Needless to say, this Divertissement has nothing to do with a comic finale (it echoes the work's social theme rather than concluding the dramatic action, and it incorporates spoken dialogue) and instead represents a genial expansion of the traditional Divertissement–Rundgesang conclusion to reflect the two inimical social spheres of the opera. Hiller, as ill disposed toward the ballet as he was toward French music in general, did not compose the ballet music required. The full score and the printed keyboard reduction include only the paired sextains outlined above (which he calls the Divertissement) and the Rundgesang.

The simple songs which pepper *Lottchen am Hofe* are sung mostly by the rustic lovers, which is precisely what Weisse expected of Hiller. In addition, Hiller took his serious protagonist Astolph down a peg from the level of his knightly predecessor Lisuart. Astolph interacts musically with Lottchen, but not with his fiancée Emilie. None of his more elaborate arias are either da capos or dal segnos. At the same time, Lottchen and Gürge gain ground musically. Astolph's d-minor self-examination in act one, "Stolz und Liebe quälen

---

[27] Weisse's word, "Hofnäscher," means literally a "court nibbler of sweets." These four courtiers are an expansion of Favart's "Courtisans, sous différens habits de caractère." The French Divertissement consists of several entrées, verses for Ninette only, and a concluding ballet général.

mich," is no more serious or profound than Gürge's b-minor "Ach, Lotte geht davon!" later in the same act. The innocent duet near the beginning of the opera, in which Lottchen and Gürge imitate the wedding bells that are to ring for them the next day, concludes with the two of them entwined in the traces of an extended imitative sequence – a nice presentiment of their nuptial prospects, but not precisely what one expects of two peasants (Example 2.4).

Example 2.4 Hiller: *Lottchen am Hofe*. Imitative section of duet, act 1.
> LOTTCHEN: "Then it goes 'bim, bim, bim,' and I think that tomorrow I shall be yours. Then my heart leaps and joins in the song."
> GÜRGE: "I imagine myself at your side, then my heart chimes."

Ex. 2.4 (*cont.*)

While in *Lottchen am Hofe* Astolph is clearly one of the principals
(secondo uomo of a sort with six arias and one duet to Gürge's seven arias
and five duets[28]), in *Die Liebe auf dem Lande* the same position devolves on
the Schösser (seven arias, three duets) vis-à-vis Hänschen (ten arias, five
duets) rather than on his liege. In fact the count sings only one aria, a cavatina
near the beginning of act one where his disposition to goodness is already
apparent, in sharp contrast with his irascible underling. Among the other
characters, a more serious style is brought in only for parodistic purposes:
Hänschen sings a song he picked up at court, "Der Schwelgereyen Ueberfluss,"
to show how ridiculous manners are there.

Die Jagd

Die Jagd is the culmination of the collaboration between Hiller and Weisse.
Standing at the midpoint of their works, it both epitomizes and perfects the
features common to all their comic operas. Weisse's text is based for the first
time principally on a spoken drama, Collé's *La Partie de chasse de Henri IV*

---

[28] Lottchen sings eleven arias and five duets. Emilie does not sing except in two quartets. Four
further numbers in Weisse's libretto of 1768 which exacerbated this imbalance (two arias for
Lottchen and a duet apiece with her for Gürge and Astolph) were not set by Hiller.

(1762), a three-act prose comedy. Although he also borrowed several features from Sedaine's opéra-comique *Le Roi et le fermier,* Weisse shied away from its tendency to turn the reins over to Monsigny at important dramatic moments.

Collé centers dramatic interest in his version on France's beloved Henry IV and strives for a realistic historical picture by careful stage directions, use of contemporaneous French, and a first act devoted almost entirely to the political atmosphere at Fontainebleau. Sedaine, on the other hand, sought to preserve the concision and English flavor of his model (Dodsley's "The King and the Miller of Mansfield"). The action takes place in England, and the forest in the opening scene is pointedly English rather than French, with "trees planted here and there on the stage, and without order." Even Dodsley's English names for the main characters are preserved. Weisse followed neither lead in relocating Dodsley's story. Instead he created a good-hearted German king, a generic royal figure devoid of all traces of historical color or politics.

Following Collé rather than Sedaine, Weisse introduced an unprecedented three rustic pairs into *Die Jagd*: the elderly couple Michel and Marthe, a comic pair of young lovers composed of their daughter Röschen and her Töffel, and a serious couple composed of their son Christel and his Hannchen. The only problem confronting Röschen and Töffel is her parents' decision to dispose of Christel before she can marry. Christel, however, has gone off to court to look into the disappearance of Hannchen with the evil Graf von Schmetterling. A great deal of time is spent in preparing for the arrival of the king and his hunting party, and in reconciling Christel, who returns empty-handed from court, and Hannchen, who escapes her abductor and must convince Christel of her being kidnapped and her unbroken faithfulness. A storm separates the king from his party after this, and he pretends to be a member of his own retinue in order to observe Michel's honest and happy household, to hear his own praises sung, to learn of Schmetterling's attempt on Hannchen, and to dispense punishment to vice and reward to virtue.

Compared with his French models, Weisse created a König who moralizes and reflects more than acts and is in general more completely absorbed into the rustic milieu. Although Weisse's König is not identified with any specific time or place, it would not have been difficult for his Saxon audiences at Weimar and Leipzig to think of their Elector at Dresden. In fact, at least one score and a very early print of the musical texts of the opera substitute the word "Churfürst" for "König" in the last stanza of the Divertissement when it is repeated by the whole chorus.[29] This refrain appropriately concludes a work in which a disguised king not only sups with a village judge and his

[29] D-B mus. ms. 10638, of which the score at US-Wc is an early twentieth-century copy. The print of the arias in question (*Arien und Gesänge zur komischen Oper, die Jagd, in dreyen Ackten* [n.p., 1770]) is the only print connected with Hiller's opera which deviates more than in details of wording and numbers of stanzas from Weisse's original text (it omits Röschen's aria "Die den Bruder Christel liebt" in act two).

family but even offers to stand godfather to his grandchildren. In the keyboard reduction Hiller directs that the lines be repeated by everyone, either as a chorus or as a four-voice canon, which is the way it is sung on stage (Example 2.5).

Example 2.5 Hiller: *Die Jagd*. Canonic section of Divertissement, act 3.
"Long live the Elector, my sweetheart, and I; the Elector for everyone, my sweetheart for me."

The König represents one of Weisse's and Hiller's happiest accomplishments, certainly in the eyes of their contemporaries. Dramatically, this ideal of an enlightened monarch in German *Kleinstaaterei* represents the utterly human friend and protector of the humblest hearth; musically, he not only joins in a duet with old Michel but also sings three arias without once resorting to da capo or dal segno structures. Reichardt, who published a number-by-number analysis of *Die Jagd* in 1774, could think of no better term than "stille Grösse" for the introductory aria of the König after the storm has separated him from his hunting party in act two (Example 2.6):

One hears a melody in which silent grandeur and true majesty reign. As gladly as I would otherwise grant the usual form of extensive grand arias as a mark of distinction for the persons of high rank, still the emphatic shortness of this aria of the König pleases me uncommonly; and I believe that this contributes the most to the majesty of its character.[30]

The aria does indeed seem to claim a dual pedigree. In figure, harmony, and scoring it aspires to the heroic style, but without heroics. The melody falls into unvarying four-bar phrases, which force line 1 and 3 of the text to scamper a little at their endings. Perhaps the melody is poised a little too securely on A toward the beginning, but its rise and fall in bars 21 to 32 achieve a measure of dignified spaciousness.

[30] Johann Friedrich Reichardt, *Ueber die deutsche comische Oper* (Hamburg, 1774), p. 79.

Example 2.6 Hiller: *Die Jagd*. King's aria, act 2.
"What fools people are! No one is free from weakness. No matter how high-born he may be, still he always remains a human being."

Ex. 2.6 (*cont.*)

Important changes in tone occur in Weisse's rustic lovers as well. In basic cast the types they present can be found not only in his models but in his earlier comic operas as well, but more and more Weisse exaggerates the features important to him. Reconciliation and reunion he seems to have especially prized. In act two, Christel and Hannchen settle their misunderstanding and return to each other's arms with unnecessary haste, whereas Collé more sensibly did not loosen this knot until the general denouement. Weisse laid such

Plate 2 *Die Jagd*, the reunion of Christel and Michel, act 3, scene 3

stress on the tearful reunion of Michel and his son Christel in act three that this scene was chosen for the frontispiece of the third volume of his *Komische Opern* (Leipzig, 1771), seen here in Plate 2. Michel has been introducing the disguised König to his family when Marthe (far right) directs his attention to "perhaps an even better guest." Michel fairly knocks the König over (states Weisse's stage direction) in order to embrace his son. This scene may be compared with the one from *Die verwandelten Weiber* chosen for illustration by the same artists (Plate 1). The contrast in subject, scene, and dress bespeak the differences between the early, farcical *Teufel* operas and the rural sentimental ones that became characteristic of Weisse and Hiller.

Not only did Hiller echo Weisse's emphasis on the humanitarian side of the König, he also carried to its logical musical conclusion the distinction Weisse made between his comic and serious lovers. For the more earthy comic pair, simple songs in 2/4, 3/8, and 6/8 predominate. Hannchen and Christel prefer common time for their solos, as well as for their d-minor duet preceding the storm in act two, or a moderato 3/4. Hiller's numbers in 3/4 are never trivial or light-hearted in character; the "Alla Polacca" aria of the König, for example, is also in 3/4. Hiller chose the same meter for the aria with which Hannchen first appears on stage. It invests her with the same seriousness and nobility of character that Hiller sought to create for Lene in *Die verwandelten Weiber* when she awoke as Frau von Liebreich (see Example 2.2). Both arias are in E-flat, but Hannchen's 3/4 cavatina, marked "Con tenerezza," obviously strives for a more natural seriousness of character than Lene's 3/8 da capo aria had. Reichardt expressed boundless enthusiasm for Hannchen's cavatina: it is the high point of the Singspiel, he claims, its opening melody filled with "the sweetest contentment"[31] (Example 2.7). He especially admired Hiller's expressive setting of "wohl, wohl mir!" which is brought about by a diminished octave between the voice and bass, a device of which Hasse was fond in similar instances.

Ensembles are not plentiful in *Die Jagd* – only two duets, two trios, and three quartets out of forty-one numbers. None of the ensembles, even the quartets, required more than one staff for the vocal parts in Hiller's keyboard reduction. The most memorable is the duet of Christel and Hannchen preceding the storm in act two. Reichardt was the first of many commentators to notice the motivic connection between Hiller's duet and storm. Monsigny's *orage*, which Hiller must have known, had also retrojected the approach of the storm into the duet, but the effect is quite different in each case. Monsigny is much more vivid in his tone painting, and he fashioned the duet itself as a combination of lyric exchanges and short bursts of recitative, all intermingled with the approaching storm. Hiller's motives, on the other hand, fall far behind Monsigny's in harmonic daring and graphic potential. He attempts nothing so dramatic as Monsigny's fluid discourse, and actually integrates his storm motive into Hannchen's melodic line – only possible because of its

[31] *Ibid.*, p. 49.

Example 2.7 Hiller: *Die Jagd*. Hannchen's first aria, act 1.
"Sweet home of quiet joys, little village, happy am I!"

conventional make-up, in contrast to Monsigny's amelodic and virtually arhythmic swells of harmonic turbulence.

Hiller's friend Johann Jakob Engel addressed himself to the question of storm symphonies in his essay "On Musical Painting" of 1780. He asserts there that "it is always better in a storm symphony (and these occur in various operas) to paint the inner movements of the soul during a storm rather than the storm itself which occasions these movements."[32] His opinion, typical of

[32] *J. J. Engel's Schriften* (Berlin, 1844), vol. 4, p. 146. Not surprisingly, Engel prefers Hiller's storm symphony to Monsigny's (actually, Engel identifies the composer of *Le Roi et le fermier* as Philidor in this passage).

Northern critical and theoretical thought of the day, went hand in hand with the view that music could portray only general concepts or states of mind.

Die Jagd illustrates in its attitude toward the picturesque the modest confines in which Hiller chose to work for his entire career. One sees further evidence of this in the role of Graf von Schmetterling. He is one of Weisse's most callous malefactors, yet he scarcely appears on stage at all until the very end, when the König metes out his punishment. Weisse leaves him in the lurch musically as well by reducing him to a spoken part. Sedaine, in contrast, kept Dodsley's Lurewell in the thick of things both musically and dramatically.

By restricting the role played by the Graf, Weisse insured that Hiller need never depart from the cheerful, tender, or noble sentiments with which he otherwise deals in *Die Jagd*. Hiller's own activities which competed with and complemented his musical association with Weisse and Koch suggest that he was entirely capable of far more than he hazarded in his comic operas. Nonetheless, he happily acceded to Weisse's resolute refusal to let musical considerations limit his own prerogatives. Weisse was later to confess to a wholly ulterior purpose in writing his comic operas in the first place: "The special aim that I set myself with them was to introduce the little social song among us."[33] It cheered and enlivened everyone when conversation flagged, and the comic opera seemed the most potent means of making songs generally known. Hiller, he added, understood his purposes. Indeed, it is true that Hiller's dramatic gift, neither sophisticated nor fruitful, led him to accept Weisse's texts with little or no alteration. The four arias he left unset in *Lottchen am Hofe* were about as far as he was willing to go in rethinking what Weisse gave him. Not surprisingly, it took little effort on a certain Heufeld's part to turn *Lottchen am Hofe* into a spoken comedy at Vienna, in which form it was presented at the Kärntnerthor Theater in 1769.

Weisse's philistine attitude was uttered in 1778 and seems to reflect his dismay over the turn comic opera had taken in North Germany during the 1770s, a turn away from his literary conception of the genre to a more equitable partnership between poet and composer. Yet Weisse's conception did not die, as we shall see, nor did his operas disappear from repertories when both he and Hiller gave up the lyric stage for didactic and pedagogic matters. Even late in the century there were those who thought back nostalgically to these early comic operas.[34]

---

[33] *Komische Opern*, vol. 1 (Carlsruhe, 1778), p. ii.
[34] The lament of Johann Friedrich Schink in 1789, occasioned by a performance of *Die Jagd* at Hamburg, is representative: "Our musical taste has become proper. Opera will have nothing to do anymore with such a common thing as healthy human understanding. The light simplicity of Hiller's melody bores us, we want bass viol runs and leaps of a tightrope dancer . . . Things have gone so far with us that we are ashamed of a taste for simple and artless melody . . . But to feel shame, in the true sense of the term, is in general not the custom of our decade." *Dramaturgische Monate* 3 (1789): 654–9. Schink concludes that there will always be a place for Hiller's compositions. "They will always retain their worth, and everyone who has a true conception of Nature and of the goals of melody will continue to render them his applause, without thereby having to be any less fit to be a connoisseur" (p. 662).

Just as Weisse and Hiller were not the sole architects of early Saxon opera, so were they not solely responsible for its limitations. Koch's poor singers and the principal himself (who performed only in spoken dramas) kept Hiller from pursuing the direction he and Schiebeler had struck out in with *Lisuart und Dariolette*, as Hiller himself explained in his autobiography:

The theater had no actual singers [at the time Koch had approached Hiller with the idea of reviving Standfuss's operas], but anyone whom Nature had granted a tolerable voice and a little sense of meter undertook to sing in the operettas, and with so much success that I could easily take it into my head little by little to demand more from these singers, in order to bring them by degrees closer to true singing. To this end I composed the operetta *Lisuart und Dariolette*, written by Schiebeler. Unfortunately Koch was not of the same opinion; he maintained that everything should be song-like, simple, and in such a manner that every spectator would be able to sing along if he wished.[35]

When Charles Burney visited Leipzig in September of 1770 Hiller took him to a rehearsal of one of his comic operas. "I found this music very natural and pleasing," Burney noted, "and deserving of much better performers than the present Leipsic company can boast; for, to say the truth, the singing here is as vulgar and ordinary as our common singing in England, among those who have neither had the advantage of being taught, nor of hearing good singing."[36]

Other stirrings

Friedrich Nicolai declared in a review of the first two volumes of Weisse's *Komische Opern* that when comic operas are valuable as plain comedies, "then both parties, the friends of good comedy and the friends of pleasing music, will be satisfied." Decisive in his view for achieving this goal was adherence to French models:

If even more comic operas are brought onto our stage, it would certainly be quite desirable that the authors do not depict the mores of the lowest riff-raff, as Coffey does in the *Devil to Pay*, or indeed wish to imitate the Italians, who in their comic operas support the most tasteless and ill-bred chatter with a loutish caricature, and by this spectacle corrupt good morals, good taste, and beautiful music to the same degree. Here one should imitate the French, who in their best comic operas seek to unite a refined drollery with naïve and sentimental scenes.[37]

Even as Nicolai wrote, Weisse and Hiller were confirming his position with *Die Jagd* at Weimar. However, theirs was not the only show on the road. Before turning to the repercussions of Weisse's and Hiller's achievement, we

---

[35] Johann Adam Hiller, *Lebensbeschreibungen berühmter Musikgelehrten und Tonkünstler neuerer Zeit* (Leipzig, 1784), pp. 311–12.
[36] *An Eighteenth-Century Musical Tour in Central Europe and the Netherlands*, ed. Percy Scholes (London and New York, 1959), p. 154.
[37] *Allgemeine deutsche Bibliothek* 11:2 (1770): 2.

should pause to consider the handful of other works in Table 2.1 from these years.

Except for *Das Gärtnermädchen*, which we shall consider in Chapter 3, only three texts and two arias have been preserved from these works. Eschenburg's *Lukas und Hannchen*, we have mentioned, is another translation of *Annette et Lubin*. Instead of dialogue, however, it follows Madame Favart's original in being entirely in verse. So, too, is *Das Monden-Reich*, in which a young woman and her lover play upon the moon-mania of her guardian in order to secure his permission to marry. After drugging him they pretend that he has been transported to the moon and commence to plague him in various guises – Mercury, a French dancing master, a hairdresser, a *miles gloriosus*, a Prague student, a doctor, a dialect-speaking Croatian, a chimneysweep, and finally an astrologer. Such foolery had no place in Weisse's art, but it did not disappear from German stages.

The two lost works in Table 2.1 set by Anton Laube reappear on the Berlin stage in 1777, and the playbills connected with these performances indicate that they were intermezzi-like works for only two singers. *Matz und Anna* is described as a musical farce in the Italian manner with recitatives, and was in two acts.[38]

A playbill for a performance of *Fräulein von Ueberklug und Herr Gleichzu* at Brunswick on 9 January 1769 reports that a ballet was performed between its two acts.[39] These and other examples of the drastic low-comic style continued to delight audiences and outrage critics everywhere in Germany both in translations of Italian works and German imitations such as these.[40]

Johann Benjamin Michaelis's *Walmir und Gertraud*, dating from 1766, is a sentimental, almost serious drama, or as he himself put it: "an attempt to transfer the sentimental comedy to the lyric stage."[41] Set on a desert island, it involves a test of loyalty of Gertraud, who a year prior found her husband transformed into lifeless stone. She remains faithful to the statue despite the energetic suit pressed on her by the knight Marbott. Eventually his patience wears thin – she must marry him or die. "Sey mir, süsser Tod, willkommen," she sings, but (in a scene that was perhaps not lost on Wieland), when the sacrificial altar is ignited, a transformation to a temple reveals Marbott as

---

[38] Herbert Graf, *Das Repertoire der öffentlichen Opern- und Singspielbühnen in Berlin seit dem Jahre 1771* (Berlin, 1934), p. 24.

[39] Adolf Glaser, *Geschichte des Theaters zu Braunschweig* (Brunswick, 1861), p. 62.

[40] The company of G. F. W. Grossmann gave a popular sibling of these works, *Pierre und Narcisse*, at Göttingen in 1784 and a reviewer in Johann Christian Friedrich Dietz's *Beiträge zum Theater, zur Musik und der unterhaltenden Lektüre überhaupt* summarized the plot of this lost work. A runaway French hairdresser and an out-of-work chambermaid try to outfox one another by assuming a variety of disguises until a dealer in second-hand clothes puts an end to their antics by demanding that his costumes be returned. Pierre and Narcisse marry each other "and hit upon the sound idea that each of them should seek his pleasures out of the company of the other," 1 (1785): 263.

[41] *Walmir und Gertraud, oder Man kann es ja probiren* (n.p., n.d.), p. [3]. One of Michaelis's aims was to remove gods and mythological characters from regular plays and put them in a work "in which one seeks to unite all the fine arts in the most probable manner."

Oberon and a reanimated Walmir is restored to his faithful wife. The same
wager between Oberon and Titania which Wieland borrowed from Chaucer
in *Oberon* in 1780 explains the motivation of her trial – that true love even
unto death was nowhere to be found on earth.

Michaelis later brought his fondness for the supernatural to the level of
farce in a three-act comedy appropriately titled *Je unnatürlicher, je besser*,
published in 1769. A magician charged with the care of young Irene has conceived a passion for her although she is intended for Philint, son of the goddess Armide and a cold, moralizing, passionless lover to boot. As a punishment for the magician, Armide has placed Irene under a spell which can only
be broken by finding the most unnatural thing on earth. Assorted spirits
which the magician summons up produce several human specimens – a verse-
spouting shepherd, a hyper-romantic knight, and a Robinson Crusoe. But the
charm is unwittingly broken by Philint, whose exaggerated moralizing and
want of passion are judged far more unnatural than the deranged antics of
the other three.

Mildly reminiscent of *Lisuart und Dariolette*, Michaelis's broader comic
canvas did not attract a composer, although Christian Gottlob Neefe set two
arias from it. *Walmir und Gertraud* had been set earlier by Anton Schweitzer,
but proved too difficult for the North German troupe with which he was
associated to perform. In general during the 1760s and 1770s such instances
of farce and the supernatural or mythological remained clearly subordinated
to an elaboration of North German comic opera as Weisse and Hiller had
defined it.

3

The diffusion of Saxon opera

During the first years of the 1770s new North German operas came almost exclusively from Hiller and his immediate followers, notably the Weimar Kapellmeister Ernst Wilhelm Wolf and Hiller's young pupils Christian Gottlob Neefe and Johann Friedrich Reichardt. With few exceptions, librettists also pursued the paths marked out by Weisse, not just in theme but in characterization and technical construction as well. Similarly, despite the proliferation of operatic production as troupes all over North Germany took up these new works, Koch's company retained its position of pre-eminence in bringing forth new comic operas.

In Table 3.1 we continue the chronology of new operas produced in North Germany begun in the preceding chapter. The bounds of the present table are *Die Jagd*, which occupied us at the end of Chapter 2, and *Alceste*, the astonishing phenomenon which will demand our attention in Chapter 4. Three theatrical centers account for eleven of the twenty works listed in Table 3.1 – Leipzig, Berlin, and Weimar – and the four composers who form the main constellation of this chapter – Hiller, Wolf, Neefe, and Reichardt – account for twelve of them.

The German theater and the rise of Saxon opera

Around North Germany, the decade after the Seven Years' War saw the important traveling companies attempt more than ever before to establish themselves in one or two locations, to become incorporated into court or civic life if even at an indifferent social level, and to put together repertories which would make both of these possible. For some principals, gaining a foothold meant building a theater. By no means all of these construction projects resulted from the initiative of wealthy theater-lovers as had Koch's new Theater am Rannstädter Thore at Leipzig. Konrad Ackermann, as we saw, had built his own theater at Hamburg in 1765 (and he had done the same at Königsberg before the war). The same year saw the completion of a new theater at Berlin, the Theater in der Behrenstrasse, built by the principal Franz Schuch the Younger with his father's fortune.

Telling changes toward higher ideals took place in many repertories during these years as well. The lofty aspirations of the Hamburg National Theater (1767 to 1769), to which we shall turn later, represent the most extreme case of

Table 3.1. *North German opera between* Die Jagd *and* Alceste

Date of première	Title	Composer–Librettist	Place of première
21 May 1770	[*Der lustige Schuster*]	Schweitzer–Weisse	Celle
4 Sep 1770	*Das Rosenfest*	Wolf–Heermann	Weimar
early 1771	*Der Aerndtekranz*	Hiller–Weisse	Leipzig
18 Apr 1771	*Der Dorfbalbier*ᵃ	Hiller/Neefe–Weisse	Leipzig
10 Oct 1771	*Clarisse*	Röllig–Bock	Hamburg
13 Dec 1771	*Die Apotheke*	Neefe–Engel	Berlin
1771	*Clarisse*	Uber–Bock	Breslau
1771	*Das Orakel*	Fleischer–Gellert	*
10 Feb 1772	*Die Dorfdeputirten*	Wolf–Heermann	Weimar
10 May 1772	*Amors Guckkasten*	Neefe–Michaelis	Leipzig
18 May 1772	*Die Dorfgala*ᵇ	Schweitzer–Gotter	Weimar
14 Jul 1772	*Die treuen Köhler*	Wolf–Heermann	Weimar
17 Aug 1772	*Der Krieg*	Hiller–Weisse/Ramler	Berlin
late 1772	*Der Einspruch*ᶜ	Neefe–Michaelis	Leipzig
1772	*Hänschen und Gretchen*	Reichardt–Bock	*
1772	*Amors Guckkasten*	Reichardt–Michaelis	*
1772	[*Der Deserteur*]	Helmig–unknown	Breslau
1772	[*Das Milchmädchen*]	Helmig–unknown	Breslau
1772	[*Das Frühstück auf der Jagd*]	Weisflog–Weisflog	Sagan
5 Apr 1773	*Die Jubelhochzeit*	Hiller–Weisse	Berlin

Notes:
[ ] – music does not survive.
ᵃ Two-act version first performed at Leipzig on 1 August 1771.
ᵇ Two-act version first performed at Hamburg on 21 January 1779.
ᶜ Two-act version, retitled *Die Einsprüche*, first performed at Berlin on 16 October 1773.
* – no performance recorded.

the struggle to elevate taste in the German theater. On a more modest scale, Franz Schuch, who had built his reputation on Harlequin pieces and other forms of improvised low comedy, gave these up soon after opening his new stage at Berlin. The newly formed company of Theophil Döbbelin began championing the best original German dramas in the late 1760s; in 1767 his troupe gave the première of Lessing's *Minna von Barnhelm* at Berlin, and it took the audiences by storm.

Critical writings on the theater also came into their own around this time. French classical tragedy, Shakespeare, sentimental comedy, Marivaux, Goldoni, the *drames* of Diderot and others, domestic tragedy, farce, *commedia dell'arte* elements, and opera all found adherents and opponents. Lessing's *Hamburgische Dramaturgie*, admired today as one of the greatest monuments of theatrical criticism from any age, can scarcely be too highly rated as a shaping force on opinion in its own day. The repertory Lessing was evaluating – that of the Hamburg National Theater in its first year – included no musical works, however,[1] and the debate over the nascent German comic

[1] Both opera and ballet were originally excluded as inimical to the goals of literary purity and moral decency. Public pressure soon forced the reinstatement of ballet, but musical theater remained out in the cold save for incidental music.

opera (Should it exist at all? What ought its character to be?) never achieved the focus of that dealing with spoken repertories. Voices were raised, nonetheless, signaling opera's participation in the German theatrical renaissance.

By the mid-1770s, not only major contributions to dramatic criticism but also regular theatrical journals were appearing nearly everywhere in Germany – at Berlin largely through the efforts of Christian August von Bertram, at Hamburg with the *Unterhaltungen*, and most importantly at Gotha with the institution of Heinrich August Ottokar Reichard's *Theater-Kalender* (1775–1880) and *Theater-Journal* (1777–84), periodicals which achieved pan-Germanic influence on a plane with the literary prestige of Wieland's *Teutscher Merkur* and Nicolai's *Allgemeine deutsche Bibliothek* during the same era. As a vital cultural institution, the German stage had come into its own.

These literary and theatrical trends strongly influenced opera's development in the North. German opera's distinctive "bi-focal" character, which we have discussed at length in Chapter 1, is readily apparent in the unique physiognomy of its publication format. In the 1750s, texts and music had seldom if ever been published. Their literary and musical qualifications remained dubious beyond their value to the individual company as a jealously guarded repertory novelty. With the comic operas of Weisse and Hiller, the genre gained an aura of musical and literary respectability. Librettos, to begin with, were published as literary works in their own right, in prints unconnected with a specific production of the opera, and usually with no mention of the composer. For a specific performance only the texts of the musical numbers were printed, usually as cheaply as possible, often without place or date, and nearly always with the composer specified.

Full scores of German operas were a losing proposition for publishers throughout the century and scarcely ever appeared. Usually the score was available in manuscript either from the composer himself, as many notices inserted in periodicals and at the end of keyboard reductions tell us, or from a commercial house such as Breitkopf at Leipzig.[2] The musical public at large normally purchased an opera only in a printed keyboard reduction. At first these were somewhat paltry, with the keyboardist's right hand and the vocal part sharing the same staff. Inner voices were omitted, if there to begin with, and the figuration was sometimes changed to make it more idiomatic to the keyboard. Later these reductions became fuller, often approaching the faithfulness of a short score, but almost never did they include the spoken dialogue.

One is tempted to see in these printing norms further evidence of the loose partnership which made up North German opera in its early days, the text going one way and the music another. The tailoring of a text to a particular composer's needs or the music to a particular singer's demands was scarcely

[2] See *The Breitkopf Thematic Catalogue*, ed. Barry S. Brook (New York, 1966).

known during Hiller's ascendancy. When composers did think of their singers, it was more often of their weaknesses than of their strengths. Though the most notable collaborations during these years involved a librettist and composer at the same court or city, it was not unusual in other cases for them to be far removed from one another in time and space. Would-be librettists even published opera texts which never received a single setting, a phenomenon we shall deal with in Chapter 5.

At the same time, it must be observed that reviewers of keyboard reductions tend to dwell at length on dramatic considerations such as musical characterization, obviously assuming not only that these are the principal measure of the music's success, but also that the purchaser will be familiar with the dramatic context which the reduction itself fails to supply. The essential problem German opera faced was not one of its credentials as dramatic music, but of how it reconciled itself to the competing demands of its theatrical heritage in spoken drama and musical proclivities potentially incompatible with this heritage.

Leipzig and Berlin

Already in the early 1770s the significance of Leipzig for the new operatic tradition to which it had given birth began to decline. The comic operas of Weisse and Hiller depended for their production and dissemination on Koch and his company rather than on the new theater at Leipzig and its audiences, and Koch's commitment to Leipzig was far from wholehearted. As early as 1767 he had applied to the Prussian court for permission to perform at Berlin, but was turned down. The attraction of a metropolis with five times the population of Leipzig remained, however. The year 1770 brought increased pressure on Koch at Leipzig from other troupes coming for the fairs and from restrictions on theatrical presentations sought by worried professors at the university.

Koch began spending some of his time at the Weimar court, where his comic operas made him especially welcome. While he was there in January 1770, the troupe of Johann Christian Wäser gave performances at Leipzig in what was described as "a large shed built at Grossbosen's Garden before the Grimm Gate."[3] When Koch returned for the Easter Fair in April and May, Wäser also came back. By the next year his improved theater was called the "Wäserisches Comödienhaus," and Leipzig had the makings of a true theatrical rivalry. For the Easter Fair of 1771 the new stage was leased to the formidable Döbbelin company from Berlin, but Koch was by then in a position to avoid potentially ruinous competition at Leipzig. Early in 1771 the principal Franz Schuch the Younger had died and Koch had purchased from his widow not only Schuch's privilege to perform in Prussia, but also his

---

[3] Wustmann, *Quellen zur Geschichte Leipzigs*, vol. 1, pp. 489–90.

theater at Berlin in the Behrenstrasse. Over the next two years occurred a slow transition of the Koch company from Leipzig to Berlin, completed by early 1773. They remained at Berlin as the chief German troupe in Prussia until Koch's death in early 1775.

Koch's repertory during his first visit to Berlin in 1771 was documented in Christian August von Bertram's anonymous pamphlet *Ueber die Kochische Schauspielergesellschaft*.[4] In his first seventy-two evenings Koch gave:

> 7 performance of tragedies
> 45 performances of comedies
> 19 performances of afterpieces
> 24 performances of comic operas

As these figures indicate, Koch overwhelmingly favored comic genres – spoken comedies, afterpieces, and comic operas. Döbbelin's company, in contrast, devoted considerable attention to serious genres such as the tragedy and *drame*. Bertram compared the offerings of both companies in these various genres, always to the disadvantage of Koch. In their operatic productions he judged Caroline Steinbrecher inferior as an actress to Döbbelin's wife Katharina in *Lottchen am Hofe* and *Die Jagd*. Koch's leading soprano had the better voice, Bertram conceded, but "was far from equal to the engaging Lottchen of [Madame] Döbbelin in innocence, naïveté, and rustic manner."[5]

As a non-musician, Bertram evaluated only the acting of both troupes, but this at least affords us some insight into mimetic practices then current for operatic productions. From his remarks we learn that the Koch company's greatest strength lay not in the rural sentimentality of Weisse's most popular operas but in a heartier comic style derived from the farce. For example, Bertram took uncommon pleasure in the singer Johann Carl Löwe's rendering of the comic antics of the matrimonially minded old Martin in Wolf's *Das Gärtnermädchen*. In one scene Simon, a chamberlain, is having fun at Martin's expense by professing love not just for the country girl Hannchen but also for the gardener's maid Julie, on whom Martin has set his sights. Simon pursues an outrageous comparison to a ship at sea in describing his being tossed between his two loves. Wolf pursued the possibilities for extravagant tone painting to the fullest, as seen in Example 3.1. What caught Bertram's attention, however, was not Simon's parody of serious opera but the pantomimetic excesses of old Martin. The actor Löwe "bent forward and kept peering, as if to see if he could not spot the ship, which Simon painted for him so nicely with voice and hands." In general, Bertram adds, Löwe "knew how to insert inarticulate sounds of joy, displeasure, astonishment, and so forth, always in an excellent fashion."[6] All this was part of the company's characteristic *vis comica*.

---

[4] (Berlin and Leipzig, 1771). The review of this print by Christian Heinrich Schmid in his *Theater-Chronick* (Giessen, 1771) gives the imprint place as "Halle bey Curt" (p. 59).
[5] *Ibid.*, pp. 24–5.
[6] *Ibid.*, pp. 92–3.

Example 3.1 Wolf: *Das Gärtnermädchen*. Simon's comparison aria, act 1.
"Soon it sinks deep down into the abyss."

In his spoken repertory Koch's ambitions were clearly not as high as those of his predecessor at Berlin, even allowing for Bertram's partisanship for Döbbelin. Particularly in his latter days Koch tended to emphasize variety, urging his performers to learn new roles as fast as possible, luring them to the operatic repertory with bonuses, and not setting much store by careful rehearsals. Despite these tendencies, his contribution to the goals of stability, respect, and artistic improvement on the German stage was far from insignificant. On 24 September 1771 Crown Prince Friedrich Wilhelm honored Koch's little theater at Berlin with his presence at a performance of Wolf's *Das Rosenfest*,[7] and even Frederick the Great conceded in a memorandum concerning Koch that "his stage deserves to be distinguished from other common comedians"[8] – this from a sovereign who in 1746 had scornfully written that "the German stage is given up to smutty clowns or wretched purveyors of farce who present works without genius, which revolt good sense, and make modesty blush."[9]

The new operas of Hiller and Weisse

The four operas composed by Hiller after *Die Jagd*, all for Koch's company and all on librettos by Weisse, constitute a second and concluding phase of this triumvirate's elaboration of Saxon opera as they conceived it. After 1773, both Hiller and Weisse avoided the genre they had created for the next five years – years that reshaped German opera along lines that neither had dared explore nor probably would have condoned. The four works they produced in the early 1770s divide into two shorter derivative works with roots in the 1760s – *Der Dorfbalbier* and *Der Krieg* – and two lengthy comic operas treading the

[7] For this occasion a new aria was composed to replace the "Arie ans Parterre" at the end of the opera. It borrows imagery from the play to point up the benefits of Friedrich Wilhelm's protection.

[8] A[dalbert] E[mil] Brachvogel, *Geschichte des königlichen Theaters zu Berlin*, (Berlin, 1877), vol. 1, p. 241.

[9] Quoted in Heinz Kindermann, *Theatergeschichte Europas*, vol. 4: *Von der Aufklärung zur Romantik (Part 1)* (Salzburg, 1961), p. 504.

path of their previous triumphs, both of them for the first time on original subjects – *Der Aerndtekranz* and *Die Jubelhochzeit*.

Weisse acknowledged *Der Dorfbalbier* to have been one of his earliest efforts at comic opera and claimed that only pressure from Koch for something new had induced him to blow from its pages the dust "in which it had lain for many years and should have remained lying." In the second edition of his *Komische Opern* he put it in volume two along with its fellow farces *Die verwandelten Weiber* and *Der lustige Schuster*. Further, he pleaded the same motive in publishing it at all as he had used for its brethren – lest other theaters "add dialogue to the music which [the author] would wish to see reckoned to his account even less than that given here."[10] The cast consists of sixteen roles, but except for the closing chorus only four of these sing in the opera (a duet involving a fifth character was left uncomposed). In the story, based very closely on Sedaine's one-act *Blaise le savetier* of 1759, a barber and his wife, finding themselves pressed for funds, compromise another couple entertaining extramarital designs on each of them. Weisse's translation (or "imitation," as he called it) was originally performed in one act, but he expanded it to two the same year.[11] It is not surprising in light of its one-act origins that Weisse's *Der Dorfbalbier* contains only twenty-four numbers, the least of any of Hiller's multi-act operas. Even at that, Hiller farmed out the composing of ten of the numbers to young Neefe, then a law student at Leipzig, and left unset the duet mentioned above.

The colorful "Soldatenstück" *Der Krieg* also dates back to the mid-1760s in conception. At Koch's prompting the Berlin poet Karl Wilhelm Ramler had revised the translation by a certain Saal of Goldoni's prose comedy *La guerra*, but the play was not very successful. The big cast and half-dozen sets had cost Koch a considerable amount, however, and in order to salvage his investment he persuaded Weisse to convert the drama into a comic opera. Weisse did so by slipping in some fifteen numbers wherever Goldoni's fast-running plot allowed, and by adding several episodes, only marginally relevant, centering on a pair of country lovers.

The cast runs to nineteen (not including supernumeraries), of which eleven sing in the scant twenty-seven musical numbers. The characters who figure in the seige and treaty – the two generals and Graf Claudio – do not sing, nor does the serious female lead, Fräulein Florida. Among the military subalterns only Cirillo, a lame lieutenant, figures at all musically, and this principally in one of Weisse's interpolated episodes. On the whole, the drama resembles a Restoration semi-opera, with its musical numbers allotted only to secondary characters.

[10] 2nd expanded ed., vol. 2 (Leipzig, 1772), p. [3]. The libretto was also published separately by Dyck the same year.

[11] Two years later Neefe also changed *Der Einspruch* from one to two acts, claiming "that without this alteration the piece would not have been played at the theater here [in Leipzig]" and pointing to both *Der Dorfbalbier* and his own setting of *Die Apotheke* as other instances of expansions for the Leipzig stage. *Die Einsprüche* (Leipzig, 1773), p. [iii].

The play's martial theme prompted Weisse's rustic lovers in one of his added scenes to articulate anti-war sentiments, which move beyond the cautious social complaints of the peasantry in his earlier operas against the destructive hunting methods of the nobility, and which could scarcely have passed lightly over the ears of North German audiences with unhappy memories of the desolation wrought by the Seven Years' War. Peter and Lisette long for the end of the conflict because, for one thing, they cannot marry until the war is over. Hiller sets their duet elaborating this theme in a stern d minor and further strengthens its seriousness in adopting a through-composed plan with a modulation past the relative major to a minor:

R_1	A		B			R_2	C		R_3
i	i	→ ♭III	→iv	→v			→ i		
	Peter		Lisette				both		
	(1st quintain)		(2nd quintain)				(3rd quintain)		

In the C section, Weisse's eloquent plea for a return of peace elicited from Hiller an imitative elaboration over a dominant pedal (Example 3.2) preparing the musical oxymoron in which "let . . . the shepherds be happy" is set to a deceptive and closed cadence in d minor. (This passage may be compared with the similar but much lighter touch of imitation between Lottchen and Gürge in Example 2.4.)

At the same time, one senses even here (in bars 74 to 77) something mechanical and old-fashioned in Hiller's melodic style and declamatory skills. Other passages in *Der Krieg* reinforce this impression, for instance the two given in Example 3.3. The first is from the beginning of a duet for the venal commissary Polidor and his kindred spirit Orsoline. The second is the opening of a wrathful da capo aria for Orsoline after Polidor tries to cast her off upon learning that her faro tables have gone bankrupt.

In the two other operas of the early 1770s, Hiller and Weisse returned wholeheartedly to the pattern established in their French-derived rustic operas. Both *Der Aerndtekranz* and *Die Jubelhochzeit* take place entirely in the country (Weisse goes so far as to set the former precisely, outside Dresden), both also add an elderly married couple to the younger lovers, and both turn on rivalry over the rustic heroine. Weisse's methods remain those of spoken comedy, and a great deal of the music he calls for does little more than interfere with the inertial force of the drama. This force was not much to speak of in *Die Jubelhochzeit* with its three generations of peasant couples preparing for the golden anniversary of the eldest. As in the earlier operas, scenes are not constructed around the musical numbers they contain, which are worked in wherever moments of repose or reflection are to be found. Both operas include no less than three Romanzen, always set as strophic Lieder with unvaried repeats, and act one of *Die Jubelhochzeit* concludes with a song comprising fourteen quatrains in the original libretto (of which Hiller

Example 3.2 Hiller: *Der Krieg*. Plea for peace in duet, act 2.
"Gracious peace, return again! Lodge with the shepherds! Hear their pious songs, let all princes be brothers, all the shepherds be happy."

included only five in his keyboard reduction).[12] In these as in other instances, sheer repetition stands in place of any serious effort at generating new, larger musical structures.

Der Aerndtekranz was the more highly regarded of the two and remained in repertories throughout the eighteenth century. It harks back somewhat to *Lottchen am Hofe* in developing a plot in which a husband unwittingly woos his own wife. The affections of Amalia's husband, Herr von Lindford, have been transferred to the country girl Lieschen, whom he wishes to establish in town. Amalia comes to the country, disguises herself as Lieschen's cousin,

---

[12] In the third edition of his *Komische Opern* (Carlsruhe, 1778), Weisse remarked that in his simple songs he had often written more strophes than need be sung in the theater: "Here one is often enough, and the directors do well to arrange things to fit the circumstances in this regard" (vol. 1, p. iii).

Example 3.3 Hiller: *Der Krieg*. Two incipits from acts 1 and 3.
  A: "Let money be joined with money, that's the marriage I like."
  B: "Tremble before a woman's revenge, which glows like her love."

and avails herself of the opera's first Romanze to disabuse her of her naïve views on Lindford's generosity. Amalia tells her the story of how a noble seduced a simple maid by means of a sham wedding ceremony; after this everyone spurned the unfortunate girl, and before too long she was dead. Later, in order to reconcile Lieschen to her erstwhile country swain, Peter Pumpernickel, Amalia infatuates him with herself, which has the desired effect of nurturing jealousy and remorse in Lieschen.

Christian Heinrich Schmid sensed something new in Weisse's libretto when it first appeared and labeled it a "musikalisches Intriguenstück" in which the country interest is secondary to that for Amalia.[13] Ebeling, too, found the characters well drawn, striking, and important to the course of the plot, but

---

[13] *Theater-Chronick*, pp. 115–16. Schmid argues here that the comic opera must be as similar as practicable to spoken comedy if it is not to be a mere "Rhapsodie von Vaudevillen." He then explains how Weisse's comic operas parallel the various categories of comedy.

he also thought that Weisse had peppered the libretto with far too many songs "which are insignificant, in which neither serious nor comic feeling rules, whereby the composer falls into a musical tittle-tattle – that is, he must write melody without expression."[14]

Ebeling's charge that the opera's music is dramatically irrelevant rings true for many numbers in *Der Aerndtekranz*, but occasionally Hiller reveals his ability to point up a situation succinctly and effectively with the modest means he was allowed. In act three, when Lieschen is alone with Lindford, his advances begin to kindle her fears of a fate similar to that of the girl in Amalia's Romanze. To express these misgivings she sings to Lindford an admonitory song that her father had sung to her the day before (Example 3.4). Hiller tells us that Lieschen has taken the song's message to heart, using such simple elements as a genial opening IV–V–I cadence for the orchestra, a

Example 3.4 Hiller: *Der Aerndtekranz*. Song of Lieschen, act 3.
"My daughter, do not trust him! What a Junker promises you are only pretty, golden lies. You are whistled to [sung to] with flattery, your willing ear is opened, then your heart can [soon] be deceived."

[14] *Allgemeine deutsche Bibliothek* 19:1 (1773): 430. Ebeling is speaking of both *Der Aerndtekranz* and *Die Jagd*, which form the third volume of Weisse's *Komische Opern*. *Der Aerndtekranz* contains 38 numbers, *Die Jagd* 40, and *Die Jubelhochzeit* 42.

Ex. 3.4 (*cont.*)

whole-measure pause placed strategically at the words "fine golden lies," and the return of the opening cadence at the end. The effectiveness of these means depends on Hiller's penchant for eight-bar phrases. Here he sets Weisse's *aabccb* sextain in two complementary six-bar phrases: the first dramatizes the empty measure 9 (we expect another two bars here to complete an eight-bar phrase), and the second demands the two-bar cadence as a necessary conclusion. As a result, the empty bar 9 wittily portrays the emptiness of the Junker's promises, and the closing cadence harks back to the opening with an emphatic orchestral Q.E.D., driving home the moral of the story.

Alas, the infelicities of text declamation which plague Hiller's vocal writing in general are not absent here. In bars 10, 11, and 14 a later hand saw fit to change Weisse's text in the Berlin manuscript score of the opera so it would fit better under Hiller's stiff rendering of the last half of the first sextain. (The emendations are indicated in square brackets in Example 3.4.) On balance, nonetheless, the virtues of Hiller's interpretation of the song in its dramatic context outweigh such defects.[15]

---

[15] These virtues seem not to have counted for much with the unknown adapter responsible for the manuscript copy of the score now at Vienna. After discarding the viola he proceeded to fill out all Hiller's rests with ceaseless activity in the two violin parts, not even sparing the eloquent emptiness of bar 9. The fine opening unison on E-flat is also harmonized on the downbeat, and Hiller's figuration for the second violins is throughout altered beyond recognition.

The early operas of Reichardt and Neefe

Hiller's interest in the stage was never a whole-hearted one. After 1773 he directed his energies away from the production of further comic operas to editing, conducting, and teaching. The training of German singers to a competence equaling that of the best Italian singers, achieved with the sopranos Gertrud Elisabeth Schmeling and Corona Schröter, now became his chief concern, one complemented by his didactic publications on singing, which began to appear in 1773.

These were not Hiller's sole teaching roles, however. In the early 1770s two students, Reichardt and Neefe, studied vocal composition with him, apparently on an informal basis. All the operas of these young composers from these years were originally in one act, and with the possible exception of Reichardt's *Hänschen und Gretchen* (a translation of Sedaine's *Rose et Colas*) they also tend toward the low comic. It may well be that Hiller deemed such a humble dramatic milieu proper to the first efforts of young composers. Both Neefe and Reichardt set Johann Benjamin Michaelis's *Amors Guckkasten* at about the same time – a farcical pastoral comedy with several mythological characters, far removed from the rustic goodness Hiller and Weisse celebrate in their most popular works. Whether Hiller put the two of them up to it must remain speculation, as must the very thin case Irmgard Leux makes for a rivalry or falling out between the two young composers in the 1770s based in part on these settings.[16]

Not much is known of Reichardt's early comic operas except that he had precious little success with them. That a performance of any of them ever took place is at least doubtful. He had a keyboard reduction of his first two efforts, *Amors Guckkasten* and *Hänschen und Gretchen*, brought out back in his native East Prussia, at Riga in 1773. Rolf Pröpper evaluates them accurately as well within "the bounds of the typical operas of those years."[17]

Neefe, on much more intimate terms with Hiller,[18] achieved far greater success in the 1770s with his comic operas. He found immediate critical favor, for one thing, and his name came to be linked with Hiller's as his closest pupil and follower. According to Neefe's autobiography, Hiller promoted his career not only by having him collaborate in composing *Der Dorfbalbier* and in editing the *Wöchentliche Nachrichten*, but also by using his influence to get Neefe's early works published at Leipzig (by Junius and Schwickert).[19]

[16] *Christian Gottlob Neefe (1748-1798)* (Leipzig, 1925), pp. 22-3.
[17] *Die Bühnenwerke Johann Friedrich Reichardts (1752-1814)*, vol. 1 (Bonn, 1965), p. 65. Pröpper errs, however, in adding that such works were announced "by the dozens" in the Gotha *Theater-Kalender*. Quite apart from the fact that Reichardt's two operas appeared in print two years before the *Theater-Kalender* was first issued, only thirty-five new German operas were produced in the North from 1766 to 1773, an average of five per year.
[18] Neefe's keyboard reduction of *Die Apotheke* (Leipzig, 1772) is dedicated to Hiller with the hope that the student may prove worthy of the master.
[19] Neefe's autobiography first appeared in Friedrich Rochlitz's *Allgemeine musikalische Zeitung* in 1798 and 1799. It was reprinted by Leux, *Christian Gottlob Neefe*, with the passages omitted by Rochlitz restored (pp. 188-98).

The two keyboard reductions by Neefe and Reichardt of *Amors Guck-kasten* afford us the opportunity of comparing the two young composers. Though each sailed close to Hiller's flagship, Neefe achieved more varied and felicitous results. At this early stage in both men's careers, he is clearly the better melodist and the more artful in choice of tempo, meter, and figure. Example 3.5 presents both settings of a relatively simple song (with ritor-

Example 3.5 A. Reichardt: *Amors Guckkasten*. Song of Comus. B. Neefe: *Amors Guckkasten*. Song of Comus.
   "They wanted to see and wanted to see, and had they done so, although they didn't, they would have looked and looked for as long as there was anything in there to see."

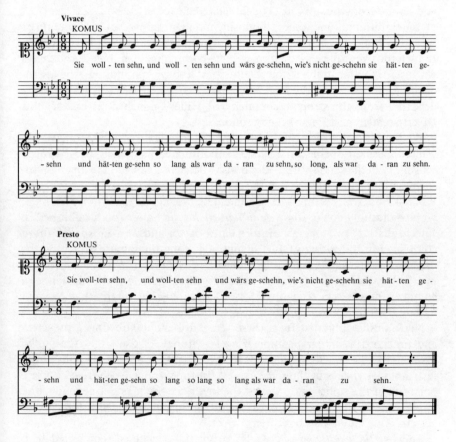

nellos omitted), a strophic Lied of two septains for the rascally bass Komus. He has stolen a shadow-box ("Guckkasten") from the sleeping Cupid (Amor) so that the nymphs Arkadia and Hermione may look in it and satisfy their ardent curiosity. Komus, however, demands a kiss of each as his compensation, and as votaries of Diana the two refuse. Along come two shepherds to defend the nymphs as a shouting match develops, and Komus explains to them in this song the nymphs' desire to peep into the purloined box.

Both composers chose a fast 6/8, but Neefe's g minor is more appropriate to the disgruntled old thief's mocking the curiosity of the two nymphs. Neefe's declamation is also much more careful, and the high squawk on E-natural (on "nicht" and, happily, "guckt" in the second stanza) offers an inventive comic touch which makes Reichardt's one effort in the same direction, a three-fold repetition of "so lang," seem pedestrian.

Michaelis concluded his delightful libretto with a Divertissement which marks a considerable advance on the formulaic Rundgesang. Amor cranks the shadow-box as his Psyche looks in. Arkadia and Hermione both want a turn, and Komus cranks for them. Each of the three women sees her own folly and reward from the story just concluded re-enacted in the box – a clever twist on the traditional function of the closing number as purveyor of the moral of the story. But then each wants another turn and forces her way back to look. In turn they describe a swan aproaching a bathing maiden, but before things get carried too far in the in the shadow-box "the curtain falls and the instruments alone play out the last lines pizzicato." Both Reichardt and Neefe departed from the strophic simplicity of Hiller's conclusions and set this Divertissement as a free-wheeling rondo.

We have already seen that such aesthetic arbiters as Nicolai and Weisse wanted German opera's farcical side subordinated to French-derived rustic sensibility in the service of good morals. Michaelis came to take up an opposite position. As we observed as the end of the preceding chapter, he followed his first libretto, the three-act sentimental romance *Walmir und Gertraud*, with the frankly comic romp *Je unnatürlicher, je besser* (both published in 1769). His last two operas, *Amors Guckkasten* and *Der Einspruch* (both completed in the spring of 1772), continue along the same path within the dimensions of a single act. In the preface to *Der Einspruch* Michaelis recommends this format for German opera in general: as a one-act afterpiece, a comic opera would be recognized for what it should be, "a farce that may find its buyer without harming the more respectable pieces."

Neefe's other librettist from these years, Johann Jakob Engel, preached and practiced a similar position. Engel ventured to assert that the public really liked low comedy while pretending to despise it, and he saw substantial instructional virtues in the farce as well. In functioning as "a true, accurate portrait" of the follies and vices of the lower classes, it better acquaints the upper classes with the lower ones, including their judgments of their social betters, which are harsh but often correct.[20]

Engel's *Die Apotheke* is not, as is sometimes claimed, connected with Goldoni's *Lo speziale* of 1754. Engel states in his preface to the printed libretto that a composer friend had asked him for an opera "in which there reigned not the naïve mode but instead the truly comic." He seized the first idea that occurred to him and set to work. His friend became ill, but passed

---

[20] *Die Apotheke* (Leipzig, 1772), pp. viii-ix. The print carries no author designation on the title page, and the preface, dated Leipzig, 10 November 1771, is signed only "-l".

the first arias along to a young composer of promise, and Engel completed the libretto for his sake. It is all but certain that the unnamed principals in this incident were the hypochondriac Hiller and his protégé Neefe. If so, this suggests that Hiller himself was not wholly content with Weisse's naïve rustic manner, which Neefe avoided in his first operas. Koch, too, who had pressed a reluctant Weisse for both *Der Dorfbalbier* and *Der Krieg*, may have had some role in the creation of *Die Apotheke* by Engel and Neefe: Engel frequented his performances, and Neefe mentions in his keyboard reduction that several of the arias were written with Koch's theater in mind.

One episode of *Die Apotheke* will serve to communicate its character. The old apothecary Enoch, awaiting his prospective son-in-law and his father, decides he must be clean-shaven for the occasion and so has the barber Trist sent in. Trist (like Hiller, Neefe, and Michaelis) is a hypochondriac. As he sets to work he complains to Enoch of his malaise and blames it on Latin. "But Latin is practically child's-play compared with Greek," he adds with waxing discomfort. "Whoever feels that pulsing in his limbs is lost forever." Enoch, all soaped up, refuses to let this melancholic near him with a razor and fends Trist off with a shaving-towel. At length Trist gathers up his things and runs off, and a little later Enoch receives his guests, unaware that his face is still covered with lather.

Neefe set about satirizing the barber's allergy to Classical languages with relish, putting Trist's complaints into a mock-heroic Lamentoso section of dotted accents in d minor (Example 3.6) followed by a feverish run-through in F major. The plan is a succinct ABA' with the reprise beginning in the subdominant:

	R_1	A		R_2	B		R_3	A'		R_4
	i	$\rightarrow$	v		bIII			iv	$\rightarrow$ i	
Lamentoso					Tumultuoso			Lamentoso		
		1st tercet			2nd tercet			3rd tercet		

Young Neefe's gift for musical characterization grew even stronger in his third opera, Michaelis's *Der Einspruch* (or *Die Einsprüche*, as Neefe called it after having expanded it to two acts). Again, Neefe seems to have come to his text through Hiller. When Michaelis had begun work on the libretto he apparently got Hiller to undertake its composition,[21] but the collaboration was broken off when Michaelis moved to Hamburg in April of 1770. Neefe completed his setting of the opera after the text was published in mid-1772.

The cast of *Der Einspruch* is compact and to the point, in contrast with the low comic operas of Hiller and Weisse. A married couple have hatched conflicting matrimonial schemes for their daughter: Märten has settled on a Latin-spewing idiot of a schoolmaster for his Hannchen, his wife Anne on the girl's present young lover Barthel. The schoolmaster accuses his rival of

---

[21] Ernst Reclam, *Johann Benjamin Michaelis* (Leipzig, 1904), p. 28.

Example 3.6 Neefe: *Die Apotheke*. Aria of the barber Trist, act 2.
"Poor Trist is nearly suffocated, his diaphragm is sorely pressed, in his stomach he has cramps."

trucking with the devil, which turns Anne against her first choice but suggests to Märten a silver lining in the spells Barthel might be able to cast. A series of magic tricks, including kneading the schoolmaster's wig like dough so that it expands to comic dimensions, convinces Märten and outrages the God-fearing Anne. Finally, Hannchen appears as the schoolmaster's departed wife and frightens a promise from him to relinquish his claim.

In his long and interesting preface to the keyboard reduction, Neefe apologizes for the uniformity of his music to this story but points out that the librettist had written it completely in the low comic mode. In *Die Apotheke* Neefe had departed from this style into more elevated numbers (two da capos and a ternary), but none occurs here. He especially stresses the dependence of the musical numbers in *Die Einsprüche* on a knowledge of the plot: "In order to understand the songs and to perform them appropriately at the keyboard, one must be acquainted beforehand with the complete contents of the work, since the arias and songs are mostly very closely related to the dialogue."[22]

The opening duet for the parents at matrimonial loggerheads makes this immediately apparent. Example 3.7 presents the opening and closing vocal sections of Neefe's skillful setting of this duet. Boldly he leaps without a close from the C-major overture into e minor and immediately sets Märten and

---

[22] *Die Einsprüche*, p. [iii]. Neefe adds that most of the numbers are short, "for I believe that the prolix and expansive are incompatible with the truly comic."

Example 3.7 Neefe: *Die Einsprüche*. Two sections of the opening duet.

A. MÄRTEN: "Protest here and protest there!"
   ANNE: "Resisting here and resisting there!"
   MÄRTEN: "Barthel will never get her!"
   ANNE: "Barthel will never leave her!"

B. MÄRTEN: "I don't want to hear any more about him."
   ANNE: "Just wait, soon you'll have to!"
   MÄRTEN: "I'll take that chance!"
   ANNE: "Well, they are going to ask you."
   MÄRTEN: "Asking here and asking there!"
   ANNE: "Chancing here and chancing there!"
   MÄRTEN: "Barthel will never get her."
   ANNE: "Barthel will never leave her."

Ex. 3.7 (*cont.*)

Nur Ge - dult, du wirst schon müs - sen; nur Ge-

Ich will nichts von ihm mehr wis - sen ich will nichts von ihm mehr

dult, du wirst schon müs - sen! Ey, sie wer - den dich auch fra - gen, ey, sie

wis - sen. Dar - auf will ichs wa - gen! Dar - auf will ichs

wer - den dich auch fra - gen! Wa - gen hin, und Wa - gen

wa - gen! Fra - gen hin, und Fra - gen her!

Ex. 3.7 (*cont.*)

Anne upon each other with close-quarter responses, as if we had just dropped
in near the end of a long quarrel. Neefe also tells us right away who has the
upper hand in these vociferations. A deceptive cadence undercuts Märten's
words of opposition to Barthel in bars 16 and 17, whereupon Anne sets him
straight with a vigorous perfect cadence in bare octaves. In the retransition to
e minor (bars 61 to 72) Anne's victory is even more telling. After a bit of contrapuntal squabbling, Märten turns things toward the subdominant (a
minor), in which he begins recapitulating the main idea (bars 69 to 71). The
i–v harmonic motion of the first two bars plays right into Anne's hands,
however. What was e minor/b minor in bars 12 and 13 now returns as a
minor/e minor. Anne seizes on this e minor and reasserts it as the real tonic,
after which Märten must give up his thoughts of a minor and meekly repeat
his "nimmermehr" to a second deceptive cadence in e minor, with Anne's
same perfect rejoinder an inevitable sequel.

Like his mentor Hiller and all the others who followed Hiller's lead in the
early 1770s, Neefe pursued Saxon opera's chief goal of characterization
within the dimensions of poetic structures lacking all but trace elements of
dramatic development. By this time not only Italian opera buffa but French
opéra-comique as well had moved far beyond this conservative text–music
relationship. North German librettists were not providing their composers
the same amount of room to maneuver, nor, it seems, were composers dun-
ning them for it. Neefe made the best of the situation owing to the skill of
Michaelis in weaving his poetic texts into the processes of character delineation. He did so as well without resorting to Weisse's Romanzen, songs accompanying work, and other instances of internally generated singing meant to
rationalize the incursions of song into spoken dialogue. While there was as
yet no such thing as a true dramatic ensemble in North German opera, the
duet just discussed illustrates the importance music could achieve as an

amplifier and clarifier of dramatic situations. We should stress again that – at their best – German composers were not writing collections of songs and arias but dramatic music.

Wolf's comic operas for Weimar

At Weimar we encounter circumstances significantly different from those at either Leipzig or Berlin. Virtually every aspect of the lives of Weimar's 6,000 inhabitants revolved around the court and, until the maturity of Prince Karl August, everything at the court revolved around Duchess Anna Amalia. As at most small German courts, significant achievement in any area of the arts or sciences reflected the interests and taste of the sovereign, and the flourishing of musical and theatrical life in the 1760s and 1770s at Weimar was no exception. As a young princess at the Brunswick court she had been trained to a taste for Italian opera and became a creditable keyboardist and amateur composer as well. After the death of her twenty-one-year-old husband in 1758, she began early in her regency to build a solid musical establishment at Weimar. In 1761 she invited Ernst Wilhelm Wolf, a young traveling keyboard virtuoso, to stay on at court. By 1768 he was Kapellmeister of a much improved orchestra, which boasted several first-rate soloists, and remained securely under Anna Amalia's wing, despite Goethe's pointed dislike for him and a strong streak of selfish vanity in Wolf's personality.

Wolf's activities as a composer of opera commenced with the first visit of Koch's company in September 1768. Koch faced a wholly different situation at Weimar from any at the public stages he had hitherto known. His troupe performed in the small theater located in a wing of the palace itself, an intimate hall which held only about one hundred persons, all admitted free and only by invitation of the court.

Koch's company divided its time between Weimar and the major fairs at Leipzig from September 1768 until April 1771. They were succeeded at Weimar that autumn by the Seyler company, and as it turned out, they relinquished not only Weimar to the new troupe but also their pre-eminence as the North's leading purveyor of new operas. In the next chapter we shall study the crucial role played by Seyler, his troupe, and their musical repertory in North German opera's coming of age.

Wolf, although he wrote several operas for the Seyler company, was not really a part of their new directions. Instead he embraced Saxon opera in its early guise and clung to its canons until he too, like Hiller, fell silent in 1774 for half a decade. His librettists at Weimar, while no slavish imitators of Weisse, made no real technical or conceptual changes in adapting his models for a court audience. Johann Carl August Musäus, supervisor of the court pages and professor at the Weimar Gymnasium, provided Wolf with his first text in 1768, *Das Gärtnermädchen*. Koch gave its première during his first visit to Weimar and kept it in his repertory into his Berlin years, but Seyler never took it up at all, even during his troupe's stay at Weimar.

Schmid censured the opera on several occasions for its departures from Weisse's rustic manner, but Musäus would not limit his conception of German comic opera to the touching and sentimental: "Must the operetta always be tender only, is it founded solely on this affect?" His own aim was rather "to hold a middle course between the grotesque of opera buffa and the vacuity of the French operetta, which seems a course tailored to German taste."[23]

Das Gärtnermädchen follows the course Musäus charted. It is based on a French novel but seems to owe something to Goldoni's *La buona figliuola* as well. In the scope and function of his musical numbers Musäus follows Weisse, but he makes significant departures from Weisse's methods in his treatment of the noble protagonist. The count in question had at one time made indelicate attempts to conquer the gardener's daughter, Julchen. Her unshakeable virtuousness in the face of these assaults raised her in his eyes as much as it lowered himself, inspiring him to take on the humble disguise of a gardener's helper to win her heart in earnest. The play nowhere sanctions the idea that he might simply marry her outright once her affections were his, however. Well before the end we learn that Julchen's mother is actually a lady of rank who fled to America after marrying against her parents' wishes, leaving Julchen with the gardener. The solution by discovered patent of high birth is a familiar one in seventeenth- and eighteenth-century comedy,[24] but was not one in Weisse's repertory.

For the highborn characters and court officials (four of the five principals, as it turns out) Wolf included several dal segno arias. In a style more elaborate than Hiller's or Neefe's, they no doubt contributed to the early perception of Wolf's manner as more ponderous than it should be.[25] As the following diagram of the heroine's one dal segno aria illustrates, Wolf characteristically preferred to begin his A_2 section away from the tonic and to borrow the opening of A_1 for this spot upon repetition:

R_1	A_1	A^2		R_2	B		R_3	$A_2{}'$	
		on					on		
i		→v iv→V →♭II i		♭III→♭VI		→V	i		D.S.
Non troppo lento				Allegretto			Tempo primo		

---

[23] *Das Gärtnermädchen* (Weimar, 1771), p. [viii]. Musäus published the libretto anonymously after a member of the Koch company had brought out a corrupt (and hitherto untraced) version at Berlin. He remarks that Schmid is wrong to censure his short arias apart from their context in the dialogue.

[24] Venetian law forbade a noble's marrying a woman from the lower class on pain of forfeiting his title and its emoluments.

[25] [Bertram,] *Über die Kochische Schauspielergesellschaft*: "Although he has composed this comic opera splendidly, one must still admit that he seems to have taken no account of German actors in doing so; he has taken much too high a flight in his arias, which our singers cannot reach" (p. 89). Schmid, *Das Parterr* 1 (1771): 259: "Herr Wolf is a perfectly fine composer, but writing for the theater is not his business. He is too affected and doesn't understand the art of writing for the throats of his singers."

The portion of A_1 which also appears at the end of the diagram as A_2' is shown in Example 3.8. Its Mozartean accompaniment figure anticipates the accentuated setting of "zitternd" in bar 10. In general Wolf's partiality to such tone painting was the most outspoken of any practitioner of Saxon opera. It betokened no allegiance to French style, however: in Example 3.8,

Example 3.8 Wolf: *Das Gärtnermädchen*. Dal segno aria of Julchen, act 2.
"In feeling tender joys golden days have fled from me. Trembling. . ."

for instance, the imitative sequence inserted into the initial proceedings as a vehicle for sliding around a circle of fifths from tonic to dominant is a badge of conservative North German style. The cadential triplets which Wolf favors everywhere had also seen better days.

Gottlob Ephraim Heermann, Wolf's second and principal librettist, turned to writing operas only because Anna Amalia urged him to do so. He began cautiously in choosing to translate Favart's *La Rosière de Salencie* as *Das Rosenfest*, a long opera with a substantial cast and forty-seven musical numbers, more than Weisse himself had ever included in a single opera. The plot itself is none too compact and full of familiar elements. A nobleman, having decided that purity and innocence would be more assiduously cultivated in his domain if there were some tangible reward for them, has instituted an annual competition to determine the most chaste girl in the village.[26] The inevitable rivalry between the young ladies involves not only their mothers and country-bumpkin admirers but also the official from the city who has come to judge the competition and becomes infatuated with the heroine.

Wolf's keyboard reduction, which appeared in 1771, is dedicated to his patroness Anna Amalia. He had it brought out by Winter at Berlin, where

---

[26] This strange conception is based on true circumstances, as Favart's libretto relates in the author's preface. The contest was begun in the time of Clovis by the Bishop of Noyone and the Sieur de Salencie. The first winner, unanimously chosen, was one of his sisters.

Koch had introduced the opera that July as one of his first productions.[27] The Sinfonia is anomalous in German opera: its three traditional movements are in three different keys which ascend through a circle of fifths to the opera's first number (F–C–G–D). Wolf had several of the opera's numbers printed on three staves in order to do justice to his heavier accompaniment style. One of these numbers, "Was der Hagel in Feldern," displeased an anonymous reviewer who objected to Wolf's chronic tone painting in a passage "where hail, thunder, and mildew follow one another, and where, as far as we can rightly tell, the mildew in its turn seems to thunder and hail more than the thunder and hail themselves."[28]

Heermann did not work a Romanze into his story. Instead he put it after the Rundgesang, where its glossing of the opera's plot leads naturally into a closing septain of advice to young girls on the advantages of being virtuous. The story of this "Romanze zum Ballet die Zauberrose am Ringe genannt" is presumably to be danced. A North German opera was characteristically followed by a ballet on the programs of nearly all troupes at this time, and the subjects of opera and ballet were often related. *Die verwandelten Weiber*, for instance, was normally followed by a "cobbler ballet." Several of Weisse's librettos specify that a country dance is to close the piece, and Friedrich Ludwig Schröder followed his productions of *Die Jagd* at Hamburg with the ballet "Töffels Hochzeit." Heermann and Wolf were building on this tradition.

For his second libretto Heermann turned to Goldoni's spoken comedy *Il feudatorio*, and, after more far-reaching alterations than he had applied to Favart, produced *Die Dorfdeputirten*. Had Goldoni himself constructed a comic opera out of his play, he would have divided the cast into *parte serie* and *parte buffe*. On the serious side, a baroness sets about reforming her skirt-chasing son by promoting a marriage between him and the virtuous Louise, an orphan but the true heiress of the property the baron now occupies. The comic doings center on the three silly village deputies and also their wives, each of whom the baron tries to seduce.

Heermann removed as un-Saxon the *commedia dell'arte* roles in Goldoni's play by eliminating Harlequin altogether and transforming Pantalone into an unnamed overseer of the baron's property. He also localized the small-town administrative business of the deputies, which they carry on with ridiculous accesses of strained protocol and swaggering self-importance. A Hamburg reporter in 1788 remarked that "one is too little acquainted here with the

[27] Over the next three and a half years Koch gave *Das Rosenfest* forty more times at Berlin, a number matched by only one other opera in his repertory, *Der Aerndtekranz*. The choice of a Berlin publisher was possibly influenced by the opera's popularity there.

[28] The passage is quoted by Wolf himself in the preface to the first edition of his keyboard reduction (Berlin, 1771), p. [iv]. Wolf writes in his own defense that nature painting had not been his aim, "but rather I have directed my attention to the anger and indignation which have been aroused here in the Amtmann [Magistrate], and in which state of mind he sings the aria" (p. [v]).

Upper Saxon peasant ceremonies for them to be effective on our stage,"[29] but the local color helped promote the work's popularity in Saxony.

It also indicated the direction in which Heermann's interests as a librettist were heading. He based his third opera for Wolf, *Die treuen Köhler*, on an incident from local Saxon history, the kidnapping of the two sons of Elector Friedrich II at Altenburg in 1455 and their rescue by a brave collier named Triller. Heermann observed in his preface to the libretto that "the happy recovery from smallpox of the illustrious princes of Saxe-Weimar gave the occasion for this piece, to which among several other allusions the words 'Wir haben unsre Prinzen wieder' also refer." It may come as a disappointment, but certainly as no surprise, that Heermann did not capitalize on the dramatic potential of the kidnapping and rescue. Eschenburg's incisive critique of the libretto explains what he chose to do instead:

> The author has not, indeed – as would have been more advantageous in our judgment – made the saving of the princes itself the subject of this piece, but only the conse-quence of this: the rewarding of the collier, his being summoned to court, and his departure. On the side of theatrical art, very little is contributed by this – almost no complications, nothing that can arouse the spectator's expectations for very long, only purely small occurrences.[30]

Yet Heermann's blend of history and "small occurrences" brought his works favor among composers and audiences, and not just in Saxony. Both *Die treuen Köhler* and *Die Dorfdeputirten* were set by South German and Viennese composers, the first by Knecht (Biberach, 1786) and Schubaur (Munich, 1786), and the second by Schubaur (Munich, 1783), Teyber (Vienna, 1785), and Dieter (Stuttgart, 1786). Lukas Schubaur, a talented musical amateur and doctor of medicine by trade, wrote in the printed libretto connected with his setting of *Die treuen Köhler* that he had chosen this opera for his leisure hours "especially because it is by the author of *Die Dorfdeputirten*. The gift of expressing naïve feeling well, or presenting in fluent verse small portraits of objects which to all common appearance are far from easy to portray, he possesses to the highest degree."[31]

Heermann and Wolf were inspired to a sequel, *Der Abend im Walde*, which Seyler produced on 10 December 1773, a year and a half after the première of *Die treuen Köhler*. Heermann had perhaps deliberately left the door open for such a possibility by ending the earlier opera with Triller's

---

[29] *Annalen des Theaters* 2 (1788): 95. The opera had been given at Hamburg on 28 April in Schubaur's setting and had been "hissed off the stage." The correspondent judged the music fine in and of itself, but less appropriate to the characters than Wolf's.

[30] *Allgemeine deutsche Bibliothek* 21 (1774): 190. The Swabian Christian Friedrich Daniel Schubart was even less kind to Heermann. He lumped this text with Bertuch's *Das grosse Loos*, also set by Wolf, and calls them "childish things. . . Senile amusement, tasteless ideas, and the most insupportable pertness of peasant girls are encountered everywhere." *Deutsche Chronik* 1:3 (1774): 478–9.

[31] *Die treuen Köhler* (Munich, [1786]), pp. 8–9. Schubaur also found it necessary to recount the story of the abduction of the Saxon princes so that the opera would be more interesting and the references in it better understood by his Bavarian audience.

poignant farewell to his friends and children. Like Weisse's *Die Jubelhoch-zeit*, first presented earlier the same year, *Der Abend im Walde* is almost totally inert dramatically. Everything works toward a concluding celebration, as in Weisse's libretto; in this case a nocturnal feast dripping with local atmosphere honors Triller's return to the country after eight years at court. Even from otherwise sympathetic critics it received a round censure.

In the keyboard reduction of *Der Abend im Walde* Wolf included a concert aria for Triller's son-in-law, the collier Brix, printed in twenty pages of full score – an indication of directions others would pursue after *Alceste*, which Seyler had produced seven months earlier. The aria appears in act two of the libretto with the remark: "This scene is retained here owing to the composition. It can be omitted along with the following one. . ."[32]

Again Heermann had gone to the chronicles for much of his material (anecdotes about court life), and he even specified local Altenburg dress for the colliers. The opera's Romanze, about Landgrave Ludwig, is also based appropriately in Saxon history. A mild ruler with evil and power-hungry courtiers once went hunting and stopped incognito at a blacksmith's for the night. The smith, talking to his guest as he worked, wished the Landgrave firmer with every hammerstroke. Ludwig took the unsolicited advice to heart, returned to court, and did battle with the usurpers of his power. Wolf set this text in the primitive format of one eight-bar melody for all six stanzas (Example 3.9) and introduced strong modal flavoring by means of prominent

Example 3.9 Wolf: *Der Abend im Walde*. Romanze, act 1.
"In the time of Landgrave Ludwig it was like blind man's buff, with the goings-on among all the knights."

---

[32] The next scene is one of the sillier episodes which pad out the story: Koriander, a basso buffo cook, climbs up into a tree to catch a raven for dinner and has the ladder snatched away by two girls, who proceed to taunt him.

secondary dominants. Such "antique" touches were entirely in the spirit of
the Romance as practiced and preached by Rousseau.[33]

Wolf uses these secondary dominants with unexpected frequency in *Der
Abend im Walde*, especially V of vi. The overture's one movement prefigures
both the descending repeated-eighth bass line and the initial harmonic
progression (I–V/vi–vi) of the opera's first number (the parallel passages are
shown in Example 3.10). Possibly Wolf was seeking to unify the score by such

Example 3.10 Wolf: *Der Abend im Walde*. A: Incipit of sinfonia. B: Incipit of the opening trio.
"When working long nights, I commend a little rest to myself."

devices. There are other instances of his thinking along these lines in his
operas of the 1770s, but none of them has much to do with sound dramatic
planning: they are disembodied musical niceties at best and inappropriate
artifice at worst. A clear instance of his powers of miscalculation may be seen
here in Example 3.10, where Wolf uses the dignified Alla Polacca manner in a
trio for two colliers and a woodland blacksmith. Lack of good instincts lay at
the heart of nearly all Wolf's difficulties and limitations as a dramatic com-

---

[33] In his *Dictionnaire de musique* Rousseau defines the Romance as an "Air sur lequel on chante
un petit Poëme du même nom, divisé par couplets, duquel le sujet est pour l'ordinaire quelque
histoire amoureuse & souvent tragique. Comme la *romance* doit être écrite d'un style simple,
touchant, & d'un goût un peu antique, l'Air doit répondre au caractère des paroles" (Paris,
1768), p. 420. One of the earliest and most perfect realizations of these instructions to the
musician occurs in the celebrated Romance in Rousseau's own intermède *Le Devin du village*,
"Dans mon cabane obscure."

poser. Perhaps he simply reflects a cultural inclination pushed too far in what Schmid complained of as "much unwieldiness and anxiety" in his style.[34] It should not surprise us, at any rate, when we later witness Wolf's utter failure to re-establish his operatic career in the 1780s under new and more demanding conditions which made of Saxon opera a thing of the past.

In the provinces: Breslau, Hamburg, and Brunswick

No other theatrical centers pursued the cultivation of German opera with half the vigor we find at Leipzig, Berlin, and Weimar. The reason does not lie in the absence of creative talent, but of the likes of Koch and Anna Amalia. Berlin owed its initial rise to significance, for example, not to its local poets or composers but to Koch's purchasing of the Prussian privilege and to his continued commitment to the new genre.

Breslau in Silesia offered German companies an attractive alternative to Leipzig or Berlin. Like them, it could support a company from autumn through spring, but the privilege to play there had to be secured from the Prussian court. The company of Schuch the Younger performed there, from 1766 until his death in 1771, in the theater his father had built in 1755, which carried the charming name Theater on the Cold Ashes. Schuch brought the first Hiller operas to Breslau in 1770, and his successor Johann Christian Wäser introduced many more.

In addition, Breslau saw the premières of three new operas of its own in 1771 and 1772. The two by the utterly obscure Helmig, a rector at Breslau, were written for the Wäser company. Possibly his *Das Milchmädchen* and *Der Deserteur* were only adaptations: their titles suggest connections with Anseaume's *Les Deux Chasseurs et la laitière* (1763, set by Duni) and Sedaine's *Le Déserteur* (1769, Monsigny), and it is difficult to understand why Wäser would have bothered with Helmig's music when the scores of Duni and Monsigny were proving their great value to other German principals (Koch took both French operas into his repertory in 1772).

Christian Benjamin Uber called his *Clarisse*, the one other Breslau opera of these years, "the modest first fruits of my perhaps not wholly misspent leisure hours," and he added that, as a musical amateur, he knew it could not be judged as one did the products of "natural talents" such as [František] Brixi, [Anton] Laube, Hiller, and Wolf. The four composers Uber chooses to mention here – two from Saxony and two from Prague – illuminate the nature

---

[34] *Theater-Chronick*, p. 94. Schmid had set himself the task, in analyzing *Das Rosenfest*, not only of proving Wolf inferior to Hiller, but also of showing "why one judges differently in Leipzig than in Berlin" (p. 93). Schmid had earlier noted the cool reception Koch had been given when he mounted the opera at Leipzig during the Michaelmas Fair in 1770. When he repeated it nine days later "with very many abridgements," it still failed to please (*Das Parterr*, p. 267). As mentioned earlier (Note 27), *Das Rosenfest* was very successful at Berlin in Koch's production.

of the musical horizons of a Silesian civil servant in 1772. Though a part of Prussia since 1742, Silesia still had strong memories of its former Hapsburg days, and these are reflected in Uber's musical consciousness as well. In musical style, nonetheless, he follows Hiller closely. Only on one occasion does he write a lengthy bravura aria (and at a highly inappropriate moment). The overall character of the score may be gleaned from Uber's overwhelming preference for 3/8 and 2/4 meter: of the work's fifty-one movements, numbers, and sections of numbers in a single meter, thirty are in 2/4 and ten in 3/8. Prior to the denouement in act three, Uber sets five consecutive numbers in 2/4 meter and in the minor mode.

The librettist of *Clarisse*, Johann Christian Bock, declared himself openly to be a disciple of Weisse's art. Indeed, although the story Bock adapted differs in several fundamental respects from Weisse's norms, still in tone, versification, and musical structuring he remains close to his model. Two unhappy city dwellers have come to the country. Clarisse's husband had committed suicide after deserting the army to stay with her, and she has buried him under an oak tree near the home of the elderly rustic couple she now serves. Fritzgen, meanwhile, has run away from home to search for Clarisse, whom he saw by chance and with whom he fell in love. He exchanges clothing with a peasant, buys his hut, and in this guise becomes a rival with another peasant, Gürge, for Clarisse's affections. Bock included two sets of parents in his story, the elderly village couple Clarisse serves and Fritzgen's parents, who come to the country in search of their son, and he also throws in a delightful specimen of the idiot-savant village schoolmaster, Donatius, who is fond of quoting Latin proverbs and then mistranslating them with totally unrelated German ones.

In a scene in which Gürge and his cronies burn down Fritzgen's hut, Bock explicitly calls the composer to his aid with stage directions demanding "music appropriate to the situation." But in Uber's keyboard reduction the composer provided only the aria occurring in this scene, and later composers of the libretto such as Johann Christian Frischmuth followed suit. One sees here that it was not wholly the librettists' doing that North German composers failed to expand their musical control to larger, more challenging canvases.

The distance between librettist and composer in this case was physical as well as artistic. Bock, born in Dresden, was working at Leipzig as a teacher[35] when he wrote *Clarisse* in 1770 and almost certainly had no contact with the two composers, both non-Saxons, who set his libretto in 1771. Besides Uber, Karl Leopold Röllig also set *Clarisse*, produced with success at Hamburg in October 1771 by the Ackermann troupe. The next Easter this company engaged Bock as its Theaterdichter.

Bock and Röllig, the music director of the Ackermann troupe, did not fol-

---

[35] A Viennese edition of Bock's comedy *Der Bettler* (1773) calls him "Magister Bock." This casts a special light on his portrayal of the schoolmaster Donatius in *Clarisse*.

low up on the popularity of *Clarisse* with more German comic operas, however. The reasons for this lay in theatrical realities at Hamburg. After the collapse of the Hamburg National Theater in 1769, three important troupes vied for popular approval there. Most welcome among them was the French troupe of Hamon, which played at the Dragonerstall theater and made a specialty of opéras-comiques.[36] The two German companies visiting Hamburg, those of Seyler and Ackermann, adopted French operas in translation to the extent they were able, but Seyler left Hamburg and Lower Saxony in 1771, and after Ackermann's death late in the same year his successor Schröder began reining in comic opera in favor of serious spoken dramas. Bock resigned himself to translating French and Italian operas, seeing that there was little room left for original German operas. After Röllig's *Clarisse* of 1771, Hamburg did not see the première of a new German opera until Carl David Stegmann's setting of the same libretto was produced in 1778.

Elsewhere in the region, the Brunswick court finally opened the door to German opera when it disbanded its extravagantly expensive Italian opera under Nicolini around 1770. Two years later the court named Döbbelin "Hofschauspieler," and during his visits to Brunswick he may possibly have taken into his repertory the sole German comic opera written at Brunswick in the 1770s, a setting of Gellert's *Das Orakel* by Anna Amalia's former keyboard instructor, Friedrich Gottlob Fleischer. However, no performance of the work is documented, and it may well have existed solely as a keyboard reduction.

Gellert wrote the libretto in 1747, translating Saint-Foix's prose afterpiece *L'Oracle* into rhymed verse. Its two acts contain twelve consecutive arias – each of five to nine lines and with a da capo explicitly indicated – and two duets and a trio to conclude the work. The plot turns on an incredible, elaborate test of Lucinde, whom a sorceress had abducted at birth by command of an oracle and has brought up served only by machines. Lucinde is destined for Alcindor, the sorceress's son, but in this controlled existence she must try to love him in spite of believing him a puppet like the other machines – supposedly unfit to speak or think, to feel joy or pain. Alcindor, who has been wondering why he must play deaf and dumb before Lucinde, is brought to grasp the genius of the plan: "Reason is easily deceived, but not the heart." Such a frankly artificial story functions principally as a vehicle for exploring philosophical and moral issues.

Fleischer left Gellert's verse dialogue to sort out such matters without his assistance and set only the arias and ensembles. For eight of the twelve arias he honored the poet's instructions with da capo or dal segno structures, which Reichardt found old-fashioned: "There are a number of the most

---

[36] Schütze, in his *Hamburgische Theater-Geschichte*, exaggerated only a little in recalling that during the early 1770s "the ascendant theatrical taste in Hamburg, and more or less in all Germany, turned at that time to the operetta (and almost exclusively French music)" (pp. 380–1).

familiar thoughts in [the opera], and they are often repeated. . . the arias all resemble each other too much."[37]

By far the best number in the opera is the first duet. The sorceress has explained to Lucinde that Alcindor is not wholly mute: he can sing, but only like a parrot who doesn't know the meaning of what he says. Gellert's duet, in which Alcindor is supposed to imitate his mother, was set by Fleischer as a two-part canon at the octave. The composer thought highly enough of this duet to include an extra staff for the violins in the keyboard reduction; it is given in full except for the opening and closing ritornellos in Example 3.11. Here, as in the famous act-one quartet in *Fidelio*, the technique of canon symbolizes unwilling submission to necessity. Beethoven's canonic inter-

Example 3.11 Fleischer: *Das Orakel*. Canonic duet.
ZAUBERINN: "He who loves must be able to dissemble if he wishes to be loved."
ALCINDOR: "He who loves must be able to make himself known if he will have his happiness."
ZAUBERINN: "Let his heart burn as intensely as it may, still he will keep silent out of wisdom."
ALCINDOR: "Once his heart really begins to burn, his mouth will surely not remain silent. And ten oracles will not prevent love from speaking out of him."

Ex. 3.11 (*cont.*)

Ex. 3.11 (*cont.*)

zehn O - ra - ckel hin - dern nicht, und zehn O - ra - ckel hin - dern nicht, dass

nicht aus ihm die Lie - be spricht.

weaving of four disparate views of a dramatic situation occurs in the opera's exposition, however, whereas the one in *Das Orakel* is part of the denoue-ment. Though Alcindor's parroting of his mother is exact musically, he twists each of her verses to his own ends, communicating his true feelings to Lucinde. His flagrant contradiction of her last line breaks the canon's hold on him – as well as the oracle's – and he sings the coda of the duet alone.

Fleischer dedicated his keyboard reduction to Catherine the Great (who for the first fifteen years of her life had been a German princess at Stettin). His motives in doing so are unknown, beyond the obvious one of a pecuniary expression of gratitude. At all events, this dedication removes his work one step more from Brunswick and from the operas we have been studying. Its old-fashioned text with its rhymed verse dialogue, da capo arias, lessons in moral education, and artificiality of plot and character also set *Das Orakel* apart as an anomaly of German opera's early years. It is somewhat surprising to learn, in consequence, that Hiller had taken the libretto in hand in the spring of 1754:

I once hid myself for three weeks from the noise of the [Easter] Fair and composed Gellert's *Orakel*; now, however [1784], I look upon the work as nothing but the raw material for a good setting of this piece, which I would have undertaken had not Fleischer in Brunswick made this effort superfluous.[38]

One cannot imagine an Italian composer entertaining such an attitude toward a libretto. It is a measure of the strength of Saxon opera's roots in spoken drama that one setting was deemed sufficient, a second "superfluous."

Saxon opera: a summary

Just as the operatic innovations of Hiller's and Weisse's heyday all owe important debts to Koch and his company, so are the much more far-reaching changes in German opera from 1773 to 1776 nearly all beholden to the Seyler company, to whom we shall turn in Chapter 4. At this juncture, let us summarize the essential theatrical, literary, and musical characteristics of North German opera during its first seven years.

At Koch's instigation North German opera had been coaxed onto the stage, and at his prodding, suggesting, and soliciting new works continued to arise. In turn, he and his troupe depended on the newcomer, who had saved him from financial ruin and was to do so for other principals as well later on. Actors turned singers performed these works, and playwrights turned librettists wrote them. At the outset, therefore, Saxon opera was fundamentally conditioned by the German stage, and more specifically by the demands and limitations of a company trading chiefly in spoken comedy.

By good fortune, North German opera arose coevally with the great awakening of German drama after the Seven Years' War. At first the effects of this propitious conjuncture were indirect. The quest for permanence and higher social status elevated the profession, fostered patronage, attracted the best artistic talent, and generated more sophisticated and discriminating audiences. North German opera, which had been born at the Leipzig Fairs, was to be brought up at the courts and cities which cultivated the most serious aspirations of the German stage. Saxon opera would not long remain unchanged in this stabler, more discerning and demanding environment. The modest number of works, largely of more or less one stamp, and produced by a handful of men connected to a single stage, would soon yield to greater, more diffuse, and more diverse activity.

As a literary genre, Saxon opera involved a complex of writers nearly all connected with Leipzig. Weisse's initial translations and adaptations in the 1760s adumbrated the two basic alternatives these men would explore – the low comic ethos of the farce and the rustic sentimentality Weisse himself came to prefer. Other librettists, notably Michaelis and Engel, were not so quick to sell the low comic short, while other important dramatists such as Heermann and Bock followed Weisse's lead with minor variations. All depended to an extent on foreign models, but never directly on opera buffa

[38] *Lebensbeschreibungen*, p. 309.

(Goldoni, for instance, only as a writer of prose comedies). Large casts, extensive dialogue, and only the most faint-hearted efforts at allowing for musical flourishes attest to the influence of spoken comedy on the fledgling genre. Works based on opéra-comique tended to select models from early in the genre's history, texts which could easily accommodate themselves to Saxon opera's basic conception of music's role – as a delineator of character within set dramatic situations prescribed by the spoken dialogue.

Experiments, though seldom successful, must not be given short shrift. The ambitions to seriousness of *Lisuart und Dariolette* were not to be forgotten, nor its medieval setting. The local color of Heermann's librettos inspired by events in Saxon history also held unrealized potential. Tendencies to the antique and supernatural in Schiebeler's *Die Muse* and more especially Michaelis's *Walmir und Gertraud* are of immediate importance to Wieland's *Alceste* and reflect the importance of the celebratory Vorspiel as a source of inspiration for a dangerously uniform German opera in 1773.

On the whole, however, the alternatives to Weisse's models of German operatic librettos were limited. Similarly, Hiller's blend of songful simplicity and discreet Hasse-inspired elegance imperfectly realized dominated most composers' apprehension of the genre. Neefe was only beginning to demonstrate his superior dramatic instincts, and Wolf lay bogged down at the opposite end of the spectrum. Without exception, all of these composers of Saxon opera had docilely accepted the artistic constraints their librettists had laid on them, working out the potential of simple song, aria, and character piece within strictly defined limits to the degree that their varying dramatic instincts allowed. In short, the alternatives to Hiller's definition of opera seemed as limited as the literary alternatives to Weisse's.

Incipient dramatic experiments with music's role, found in ensemble numbers and Divertissements, only hinted at new possibilities. Models were not difficult to find. They were all around, in the newest Italian and French operas which were already infiltrating the repertories of German companies as they became capable of performing them, and which were also being given all across Germany by traveling Italian and French troupes. To absorb their lessons, however, German opera required a new complex of librettists and composers – men with first-hand knowledge of the foreign achievements from which North German opera had so much to learn.

4

New directions: the Seyler company

The period of North German opera's development we have just observed was in many ways an infancy. And like those of opera buffa before mid-century or opéra-comique prior to 1762, it was an infancy sternly governed by the traditions which had fathered the new genre. From 1773 to 1776, however, new phenomena arose in astonishing succession, phenomena which made of the mid-1770s the most distinctive and significant era in the history of North German opera, especially serious opera, from the collapse of the Hamburg opera in 1738 to the Napoleonic age. All of the important innovations in these four years – the through-composed Vorspiel, the melodrama, and serious opera both with and without recitative – broke ranks with the modest comic dimensions of Saxon opera. Furthermore, they all arose under the aegis of a single theatrical company, the Seyler troupe, and were nurtured by the small-court system of Germany rather than by its civic stages.[1]

In light of this, the present chapter will be devoted to the Seyler company and its musical repertory. We must trace the growth of this extraordinary troupe from its rise from the ashes of the Hamburg National Theater through unsteady days in Hannoverian lands to its idyllic and fruitful years at the courts of Weimar and Gotha. We must also pursue the aftermath of these vital years – the formation of the Gotha Court Theater in 1775 and Seyler's fortunes at Dresden and Leipzig before his removal to the Rhineland in 1777. Along the way, we shall have an opportunity to acquaint ourselves with some of the typical problems a German theatrical company had to contend with and to observe how certain personalities could work profound changes on a musical repertory not yet rigid with tradition.

Table 4.1 sets out in chronological order the musical works of the Seyler company and Gotha Court Theater during these years. It includes not only their German operas but also French and Italian works as well as occasional pieces and melodramas. By good fortune, a precise account of the day-by-day offerings of the Seyler company and the Gotha Court Theater was kept by the leading actor of both enterprises, Konrad Ekhof. From this and other

---

[1] Most of the present chapter is based on my unpublished doctoral dissertation, "Music and Drama in Germany: A Traveling Company and Its Repertory, 1767–1781" (University of California at Berkeley, 1977).

92

Table 4.1. *Musical repertories of the Seyler company and the Gotha Court Theater, 1769–1779*

Times Performed

No.	Title (Original title)	Librettist–Composer	Lower Saxony 9/69–9/71	Weimar–Gotha 10/71–8/75	Gotha Ct. Th. 9/75–9/79	Dresden 10/75–2/77	Leipzig 1776–1777
1	*Die verwandelten Weiber*	Weisse–Standfuss/Hiller	24	6	4		
2	*Elysium*	Jacobi–Schweitzer	15	2	3		
3	*Die Liebe auf dem Lande*	Weisse–Hiller	18	13	9		
4	*Lottchen am Hofe*	Weisse–Hiller	15	7	8		
5	*Der lustige Schuster*	Weisse–Schweitzer	9	4		x	
6	*Apollo unter den Hirten*	Jacobi–Schweitzer	2	3			
7	*Lisuart und Dariolette*	Schiebeler–Hiller	1	5	6		
8	*Herkules auf dem Oeta*	Michaelis–unknown	2				
9	*Der stolze Bauer Jochem Tröbs*	Ast–Standfuss	2				
10	*Die Stufen des menschlichen Alters*	Musäus–Schweitzer			2		
11	*Milchmädchen und Jäger (Les Deux Chasseurs et la laitière)*	Anseaume–Duni		18	8	x	
12	*Die Schnitter (Les Moissoneurs)*	Favart–Duni			2		
13	*Die Dorfdeputirten*	Heermann–Wolf			5		
14	*Der Fassbinder (Le Tonnelier)*	Audinot–Gossec et al		15	7	x	
15	*Pygmalion*	Rousseau–Schweitzer		8	1		
16	*Die Dorfgala*	Gotter–Schweitzer		8			
17	*Die treuen Köhler*	Heermann–Wolf		16		x	
18	*Aurora*	Wieland–Schweitzer		4			
19	*Das Rosenfest*	Heermann–Wolf		7			
20	*Alceste*	Wieland–Schweitzer		25	4	x	
21	*Die Jagd*	Weisse–Hiller		16	15	x	
22	*Die Wahl des Herkules*	Wieland–Schweitzer		4			
23	*Ceres*	Einsiedel–Wolf		3			
24	*Der Abend im Walde*	Heermann–Wolf		3			
25	*Der Töpfer*	André–André		4			
26	*Das grosse Loos*	Bertuch–Wolf		3			
27	*Das redende Gemälde (Le Tableau parlant)*	Anseaume–Grétry		3	6		
28	*Ariadne auf Naxos*	Brandes–Benda		10	7	x	x
29	*Der Jahrmarkt*	Gotter–Benda		13	11	x	x
30	*Der Aerndtekranz*	Weisse–Hiller			4	x	x
31	*Polyxena*	Bertuch–Schweitzer			1		
32	*Medea*	Gotter–Benda		8	3	x	x
33	*Der Deserteur (Le Déserteur)*	Sedaine–Monsigny		1	15	x	
34	*Das Fest der Thalia*	Reichard–Schweitzer			1		

Table 4.1 (*cont.*)

No. Title (Original title)	Librettist–Composer	Times Performed				
		Lower Saxony 9/69–9/71	Weimar–Gotha 10/71–8/75	Gotha Ct. Th. 9/75–9/79	Dresden 10/75–2/77	Leipzig 1776–1777
35 *Der Freundschaft auf der Probe* (*L'Amité à l'épreuve*)	Voisinon/Favart – Grétry			8		
36 *Zemire und Azor* (*Zémire et Azor*)	Marmontel–Grétry			19		
37 *Walder*	Gotter–Benda			8	x	x
38 *Rose und Colas* (*Rose et Colas*)	Sedaine–Monsigny			5		
39 *Der zaubernde Soldat* (*Le Soldat magicien*)	Anseaume–Philidor			8		
40 *Heinrich und Lyda*	d'Arien–Neefe			5		
41 *Die zwei Geizigen* (*Les Deux Avares*)	Falbaire–Grétry			11		
42 *Romeo und Julie*	Gotter–Benda			9	x	
43 *Der Hufschmidt* (*Le Maréchal ferrant*)	Quétant–Philidor			6		
44 *Der Kaufmann von Smyrna*	Schwan–Stegmann			6		
45 *Heyrath aus Liebe*	Schack–Hönicke			1		
46 *Der Freund vom Hause* (*L'Ami de la maison*)	Marmontel–Grétry			8		
47 *Der Holzhauer*	Gotter–Benda			3		
48 *Lucilie* (*Lucile*)	Marmontel–Grétry			1		
49 *Das gute Mädchen* (*La buona figliuola*)	Goldoni–Piccinni			1		
50 *Pygmalion*	Rousseau–Benda			1		
51 *Robert und Kalliste* (*La sposa fedele*)	Chiari–Guglielmi				x	x
52 *Der Zauberer* (*Le Sorcier*)	Poinsinet–Philidor				x	
53 *Der Barbier von Sevilla* (*Le Barbier de Séville*)	Beaumarchais– F. L. Benda				x	x
54 *Sophonisbe*	Meissner–Neefe					x
55 *Pyramus und Thisbe* (*Piramo e Tisbe*)	Coltellini–Hasse				x	x

Key:
x – number of performances not documented.

sources[2] the performance figures in Table 4.1 are derived, showing us the popularity as well as longevity of each musical work in the repertory.

Seyler before Weimar

Abel Seyler was a Hamburg businessman whose fascination with the tragic actress Sophie Hensel as much as with the stage itself prompted him to participate in supporting the idealistic Hamburg National Theater in 1767. After its demise scarcely two years later, the bankrupted Seyler took to the road with Sophie and a creditable gleaning of the failed enterprise's best talent. His chief rival in Lower Saxony was Ackermann, who had secured a position at the Brunswick court. Seyler settled for the smaller Hannoverian court, which offered such limited possibilities that much of his time had to be spent wandering from one small city to another in the realm.

Seyler began performing in September of 1769 and by early December was already giving comic operas, henceforth to be one of the mainstays of his repertory. The Hamburg National Theater had shunned musical works, and so Seyler had to build a musical wing of his troupe from the ground up in order to perform them. First he hired as the troupe's music director a young chamber composer from the recently dissolved Kapelle at Hildburghausen, Anton Schweitzer. Trained at his duke's expense at Bayreuth and in Italy, Schweitzer was immediately dissatisfied with the musical dimensions of North German opera as he found them in 1769. He had brought with him his setting of Michaelis's comic opera *Walmir und Gertraud*, but Seyler's poor singers could not master it. Schweitzer was not ready to pull in his horns and abandon the operatic styles and ideals he had absorbed in Italy, however. Rather than accepting the limitations he found, he traveled around looking for new musical talent and pursued vigorously his duties as singing instructor until he had brought Seyler's singers to a pitch of competence which would make the composer's *Alceste* possible less than four years later.

Seyler's musical repertory in Lower Saxony – the first ten items in Table 4.1 – is exclusively German. Apart from the occasional pieces written for the Hannoverian court, it contains nothing but comic operas of Hiller, Stand-

[2] Ekhof's notebooks were summarized in a series of tables drawn up by Rudolf Schlösser, *Vom Hamburger Nationaltheater zur Gothaer Hofbühne, 1767–1779*, Theatergeschichtliche Forschungen, vol. 13 (Hamburg and Leipzig, 1895). Most of the first half-year at Weimar, missing from Ekhof's notebooks, is supplied from an article attributed to Gustav Friedrich Wilhelm Grossmann in J. J. A. von Hagen's *Magazin zur Geschichte des Deutschen Theaters* (Halle, 1773). Repertory lists, but not performance figures, for Seyler's years at Dresden and Leipzig are drawn from Arnold Schering, *Johann Sebastian Bach und das Musikleben Leipzigs im 18. Jahrhundert* (Leipzig, 1941) and Moritz Fürstenau, "Die Theater in Dresden: 1763 bis 1777," *Mittheilungen des Königlich Sächsischen Alterthumsvereins* 25 (1873): 44–78.

fuss, and Schweitzer.[3] Hiller's more ambitious *Lisuart und Dariolette* failed to please (though it regained ground before court audiences at Weimar and Gotha) whereas *Die verwandelten Weiber* proved the runaway favorite of all the works in Seyler's repertory, spoken or sung.

Prior to the troupe's arrival at Weimar, Schweitzer's musical development unfolded largely within the confines of the occasional piece. It is easy to understand why. Such works, written to celebrate the birthdays of the King and Queen of England, were performed at Hannover where one found both competent musicians and a cultivated audience. The other places in which Seyler performed – Lüneburg, Stade, Celle, Hildesheim, Osnabrück, and even Hamburg and Lübeck – offered no such advantages. At Hamburg, as we mentioned earlier, the Seyler company had to compete with the French troupe of Hamon and with Ackermann. The latter had quickly embraced the opéras-comiques of Philidor and Monsigny, a delicacy especially pleasing to the Hamburg palate, but which Seyler avoided completely. Seyler played little over a month there in the summer of 1770 and never returned.

The Vorspiel, or celebratory dramatic piece, had its own tradition in the German theater both as a spoken work (usually in verse) and as a musical equivalent of the *festa teatrale*. Schweitzer's first two occasional works for Hannover, however, retain spoken dialogue. *Apollo unter den Hirten* and *Elysium*, apart from their mythological trappings, thus suggest a structural kinship with German comic opera. No doubt this state of affairs was a child of necessity, a result of the constraints the musical skills of the troupe's singers imposed on Schweitzer. At Hildburghausen he had been able to give his ambitious pen full reign, composing in 1769 among other things an Italian secular cantata ("Furibondi tempesti, irati venti") on a text by his patron. But in *Elysium*, where all of the dialogue is in prose, the librettist afforded him no opportunity for anything but closed numbers. The opening monologue of *Apollo unter den Hirten* is cast in free verse – fairly demanding that it be set as a recitative preparing for Apollo's ensuing aria – but Schweitzer left it uncomposed.

These celebratory pieces were not intended to be staple items in the company's offerings. All the more surprising, therefore, are the fifteen performances achieved by *Elysium*, making it one of the most popular works in the entire repertory. The librettist, Johann Georg Jacobi, was no servile Hannoverian courtier, but a canon and poet at Halberstadt with relatives at the court of Hannover. By 1770 he had already made a name for himself in Germany as a sentimental-rococo poet, and the court turned to him during one

---

[3] Schweitzer's lost setting of *Der lustige Schuster* may possibly be a revision retaining some of Standfuss's and Hiller's music. Schmid claims that Schweitzer composed it for the troupe "in Piccinni's manner" but that it is not indicative, as are his later works, of Schweitzer's independence from Hiller's style. *Chronologie*, p. 182. A report in the Hamburg journal *Unterhaltungen* describes Schweitzer's setting as "completely in Piccinni's taste, but more correct in its composition, only it is two steps too high for the spirit of the piece" 10 (1770): 259.

of his visits to Hannover for this text. Only the prefatory verses make specific reference to the Queen's birthday, and in general a reading of Jacobi's *Elysium* calls to mind not so much a band of fawning courtiers lavishing praise on a sovereign as it does the sort of sentimental audience which the author envisaged for his works as a whole and which were flocking to hear Hiller's comic operas.

In his score to *Elysium*, Schweitzer ventures beyond the bounds Hiller had set only in the numbers for Franziska Koch, the troupe's newly acquired leading soprano who was to be the first Alceste at Weimar three years later. Schweitzer's two arias for her are the most memorable numbers in *Elysium*. In one, the nightingale aria "So leise schlug mit ihrem Flügel die Nachtigall," he includes an obbligato flute part against which the singer must pit her budding virtuosic talents. At Hannover Schweitzer had the court orchestra at his disposal, but one wonders whether he was always able to scrape together instrumentalists equal to the score's demands in the towns away from Hannover where the company gave *Elysium* as an afterpiece. (The first twelve measures of the opening ritornello are shown in Example 4.1.) Not the instrumentation itself, but the way Schweitzer uses his band distinguishes him from Hiller. The features that became watchwords of his style – depth, complexity, elaborateness, heaviness – became more pronounced as Schweitzer's compositional ambitions soared at Weimar. *Elysium* stands at the beginning of his dealings with texts based on subjects from antiquity, which proceeded hand in hand with the intensification of these basic features of his style.

Example 4.1 Schweitzer: *Elysium*. Ritornello of nightingale aria.

Ex. 4.1 (*cont.*)

For the entire time he was in Lower Saxony, Seyler experienced financial difficulties, stemming in large part from the need to travel constantly, and exacerbated by the embezzling of underlings. In the summer of 1771, now under Ekhof, the troupe gave up on Hannover and environs. They tried their luck at Wetzler and Darmstadt, recuperating some of their losses. Then came the irresistibly attractive offer from Weimar: a generous stipend made it unnecessary to supplement earnings with trips to Leipzig for the fairs (as Koch had done); properties, costumes, music, and all other production requisites were provided by the court; and the company had only to perform three times a week (five or six was the norm for most troupes). In short, the Seyler company had been offered a theatrical utopia.

Weimar: Schweitzer's operatic apprenticeship

During the nearly three years the troupe spent at Weimar, a pervasive spirit of amity reigned. From the beginning the court showed great respect for the Seyler company, whose fame in Germany was by now considerable. All the theatrical personnel were regarded as well-bred and often visited the best homes in town. Court members with literary inclinations readily contributed to the troupe's repertory with comic operas, occasional pieces, and ballets. Troupe members were enthusiastically welcomed into the court's intellectual life, and a circle of theater-lovers met "almost every evening" at Seyler's home.[4]

The theater became a center of more than local attention during the Seyler troupe's years at Weimar. Visitors came regularly from Gotha, Erfurt, and Jena to performances, supplementing an already educated, critical, and refined audience. Much about a performance was subsumed under the stylization of manners typical of court life, as one courtier recalled: "The loges and parterre were always filled, and those in attendance showed their respect

[4] So reminisced Wieland to Karl August Böttiger, who recorded such matters in his *Literarische Zustände und Zeitgenossen*, published by his son in two volumes at Leipzig in 1838. See vol. 1, p. 276.

when the ducal party entered. . . Only the ducal loge applauded particular successful scenes, and was answered by the actors involved with bashfully lowered eyes and an imperceptible bow."[5]

New personalities were taken on at Weimar, and many of these recruits were to play central roles in the troupe's activities. Two of the most important – probably discovered by Schweitzer on his journeys in search of talent undertaken early in 1771 – were Josepha and Friedrich Hellmuth. Josepha had been a member of the Marchand company in the Rhineland, where she gained experience in performing German translations of opéras-comiques. Her voice was extremely broad in range and considered more astonishing than touching in character. Her husband possessed a fine, full baritone voice.

Schweitzer's occupation with the Vorspiel continued unbroken at Weimar. Each year the birthdays of Duchess Anna Amalia (24 October), Crown Prince Karl August (4 September), and Prince Konstantin (9 September) had to be seen to with special musical, dramatic, and balletic works. Musäus, who had supplied Wolf with *Das Gärtnermädchen* in 1769, ungraciously taxed the company's musical resources to their limits at the very beginning of their stay with his Vorspiel *Die Stufen des menschlichen Alters*, which calls for eight singing parts – a man and a woman for each stage of life, each pair complaining about its lot.

This first celebratory piece for the Weimar court closed with a ballet – not a hold-over from the troupe's Hannoverian days but a new work conceived as a concluding part of the Vorspiel itself. The troupe's balletmaster, Franziska Koch's husband Friedrich, was its inventor. The company, in fact, had seen at once that the ballet was taken seriously at Weimar, far more so than had been the case in the North. To create and participate in such spectacles, therefore, the balletmaster of Heinrich Gottfried Koch's troupe at Berlin, Karl Schulz, was enticed back to Weimar so that the company could now claim the unusual distinction of having two balletmasters.

Among the new dramatic ballets taken up at Weimar were Wieland's chivalric *Idris und Zenide* (set by Schweitzer in 1772), Koch's *Inkle und Yariko*, and Karl Schulz's *Orpheus und Eurydice*, which ends with a band of raving bacchantes beating Orpheus to death. Possibly these new ballets owe something to Viennese example. Taken together, they satisfy Noverre's definition of the ballet as "a vivid portrait of the passions, manners, customs, ceremonies, and costume of all the people of the earth."[6] His other tenets – avoidance of symmetry, the pursuit of naturalness, the ethical need to punish vice and reward virtue, and the presence of a clear and central plot – are also observed in these dramatic ballets.

[5] Karl Freiherr von Lyncker, *Am Weimarischen Hofe unter Amalien und Karl August*, ed. Marcè Scheller (Berlin, 1912), p. 18.
[6] Quoted in Hermann Abert's "J. G. Noverre und sein Einfluss auf die dramatische Ballet-komposition," *Gesammelte Schriften und Vorträge*, ed. Friedrich Blume (Halle, 1929), p. 268. Noverre's *Lettres sur le danse* had been translated and published at Hamburg and Bremen in 1769.

In contrast to the hapless years in Lower Saxony, those at Weimar saw only one new comic opera by Hiller, *Die Jagd*, among the ten new ones in Seyler's repertory. The remaining nine comprise four by Wolf, three opéras-comiques, a lone late Rhenish afterpiece, and Schweitzer's first surviving comic opera, *Die Dorfgala*. Its librettist, who in this chapter must occupy center stage in that capacity, was Johann Friedrich Wilhelm Gotter, a legation secretary of the Gotha court. He had first met the Seyler company at Wetzlar and sent the text along with them when they departed for Weimar in September of 1771.

Gotter modestly admits in a dedicatory poem prefixed to the printed libretto that his effort belongs in the "valley of the farce," and indeed he follows Michaelis and Engel far more than Weisse in tone, characterization, and story. Gotter builds his main plot around a scheming Frenchwoman past her prime (Antoinette) who enlists the aid of a meddlesome schoolmaster's wife (Liese) to win the tutor Treumund away from Klärchen, an innkeeper's daughter. The schoolmaster during all of this busies himself with rehearsing a fustian musical play he has composed for the birthday celebration of the local noblewoman. Liese presses a match between her buffoon of a son Christlieb and Treumund's Klärchen, but to no avail. A judicial scene defuses Antoinette's manufactured claim that Treumund had promised to marry her, and happily an itinerant puppeteer turns out to be Antoinette's first love from long ago.

Gotter's colorful and varied dialogue helps sharpen the contrasts among his characters. Antoinette is always speaking (and singing) half French and half German, and the pompous and officious investigator in the courtroom scene lards his official jargon with legal Latin such as Gotter no doubt remembered from his school days at Göttingen. The schoolmaster sings a Latin cantata – really an eight-line poem – which Schweitzer sets as a ponderous slow introduction and "fugato" which deliberately runs its subject into the ground. At the other extreme, Liese's method of congratulating Treumund and Klärchen in song on their prospective marriage reveals her colorful commonness at its most unadorned:

> Ein junges Paar
> Bringt man mit wahrer Lust zu Bette.
> Ihr braucht kein Jahr,
> Neun Monden nur, dann wird, ich wette,
> Mein Glückwunsch wahr.
> Ein junger Sohn!
> Ich seh' ihn schon –
> Ich hör' ihn schon –
> Papa! Mama!
> Haha! Haha!
>
> (She runs off laughing.)

[One brings a young couple to bed with true delight. You don't need a year, just nine moons, then I'll bet my good wishes will come true. A young son! I see him already – hear him already – "Papa! Mama!" Ha ha! Ha ha!]

Both rustic directness and poetic fulsomeness are raised to the level of parody in the scene from Samson and Delilah which the schoolmaster chose for his theatricals in honor of the local patroness. Gotter laid out this rehearsal scene as follows:

(1) a slumber duet (with dialogue of the schoolmaster and innkeeper);
(2) Delilah's [Klärchen's] sarcastic recitative addressed to the sleeping hero [Christlieb], during which she cuts his hair (interrupted by Samson's awaking ahead of cue);
(3) a jubilant chorus of the Philistines with the triumphant Delilah and befuddled Samson.

At the beginning the schoolmaster shouts for just what Schweitzer provides: "Wahre *Opera*-Musik, wahren italienischen *Gosto!*" The music, which Julius Maurer has reprinted in full score,[7] serves up all the characteristic elements of Schweitzer's style. His vocal lines are as much triadic as conjunct, with wide leaps especially between phrases. His accompaniments are sometimes heavy, never thin, and always persistent. In Delilah's recitative (section 2 above) his figures are happily chosen, in particular the depiction of her busy shears by means of pizzicato strings.

Schweitzer betrays in *Die Dorfgala*, as in all his scores, a fondness for the minor mode. Later he would explore the impassioned side of the minor rather than its more folk-like uses, but here the latter govern his choice of the mode, for example in Liese's a-minor song vaunting her abilities as a marriage counselor in act two. Gotter's text (Example 4.2, which includes all three

Example 4.2 Schweitzer: *Die Dorfgala*. Song of Liese.
"1. Yes, come to me, for I understand every doubt in marriage. No injured maiden has ever asked my advice in vain.
"2. To rekindle love, to make men faithful and tame, as tame and faithful as my own is, that only my cunning can do.
"3. But if I don't succeed in bringing a man back, I am ready to suggest a means by which a woman can be comforted."

[7] *Anton Schweitzer als dramatischer Komponist*, Publikationen der IMG, Beihefte, n.s. vol. 11 (Leipzig, 1912), Musikbeispiele, pp. 1–19.

Ex. 4.2 (*cont.*)

mir denn ich ver - ste - he je - den Zwei - fel in der E - he kein ge - kränk - tes Mäd - chen

bat mich ver - ge - bens noch am Rat mich ver - ge - bens noch am

Rat. Lie - be

quatrains in translation) amounts to a brilliant portrayal of this sardonic matchmaker, with its subtle indications of Liese's exasperation at seeing the hopes of a match between Klärchen and Christlieb shattered. The sarcastic innuendo in the last quatrain reveals the sophisticated, amused detachment Gotter brought to his portrayal of a low character such as Liese. Schweitzer's music captures something of Gotter's intent. He introduces d minor rather than the relative major in measure 10, and reinjects it in measure 12 to bring out the rhyme of the final couplet.

Five days before the première of *Die Dorfgala* at Weimar, yet another novelty from Schweitzer's busy pen saw the light of day – a setting of a German translation of Rousseau's melodrama *Pygmalion*. It was not very successful, however, and three years later this first attempt at transferring Rousseau's idea of musically accompanied spoken dialogue was eclipsed by the great tragic melodramas of Benda, also written for the Seyler company. Schweitzer's *Pygmalion* is lost, but Gustav Friedrich Wilhelm Grossmann admired its "transitions from the violent to the tender"[8] in a review of the première – suggesting that Schweitzer was already drawing from the stylistic well of obbligato recitative. We should note, too, in anticipation of Benda's masterworks, that the first Pygmalion, Johann Michael Böck, was not a singer but a "fiery and visceral" actor with exceptional pantomimetic skills.[9]

Alceste

By the time Wieland moved to Weimar from Erfurt in September of 1772, he had already collaborated with Schweitzer that summer on the allegorical ballet *Idris und Zenide*, and the two were also charged with producing a Vorspiel for the duchess's birthday on 24 October. In contrast to the celebratory piece Musäus had provided a year earlier, which had called for eight singers, Wieland included only three in his *Aurora*: Diana (Franziska Koch), Aurora (Josepha Hellmuth), and Amor (Friedrich Hellmuth), the three best-trained vocalists at the company's disposal. With these resources, Schweitzer carried his musical ambitions one step further by using recitative rather than spoken dialogue in his score. While *Aurora* thus served as a proving ground for *Alceste* seven months later, Wieland nonetheless followed the accepted pattern for a celebratory work in minimizing dramatic tension, maximizing flattery, and even including a ballet.

Wieland approached all his operatic activities with a long-standing respect and admiration for Metastasio's art, his shining ideal in the field. In 1771 he wrote to a friend, "I wish it were possible to learn from my favorite, my Metastasio, the art of the aria; I feel and recognize the difficulties our language creates against this only too well; but they are not totally insurmountable."[10] For a long time he had been toying with the idea of a full-length serious opera in German, but never found the right composer until he met Schweitzer. Immediately after he had seen what Schweitzer could do with *Aurora*, Wieland set to work on the libretto of *Alceste*, completed by the end

---

[8] In his contribution to Hagen's *Magazin* already cited, p. 64.

[9] *Gallerie von Teutschen Schauspielern und Schauspielerinnen*, ed. Richard Maria Werner, Schriften der Gesellschaft für Theatergeschichte, vol. 13 (Berlin, 1910), p. 13.

[10] J. G. Gruber, *Wielands Leben*, vol. 52 of *C. M. Wielands sämmtliche Werke* (Leipzig, 1827–8), p. 33.

of 1772. Wieland intended the opera for Schweitzer, upon whose virtues he insisted even when Anna Amalia suggested her favorite Wolf as a composer. In all his writings about *Alceste* Wieland emphasizes the complete artistic sympathy in which the two worked, a prerequisite for a successful opera in his mind, and as soon as he was able to hear Schweitzer's music for the opera the panegyrics began. Here was a composer Germany could hold up against the best Italy had to offer, declared Wieland:

This opera is in its way an unusual phenomenon in Germany. But it is perhaps even more unusual that we have here in our troupe an Amphion, or more correctly a Galuppi, a Sacchini, and perhaps even more than this – in short, we have a man who has so excellently composed this *Alceste*, with all its recitatives and arias, that the poet himself, even though he demands much of his composer, could wish for nothing more.[11]

From the very beginning, Wieland viewed his *Alceste* as a production of national significance, yet as one of Germany's most cosmopolitan Aufklärer, he did not seek to make it in any way nationalistic. Externally he turned to the shapes and techniques of Italian opera seria, simplifying Euripides in ways that even Metastasio would not have dared. Following norms for spoken tragedy, he cast his libretto in five spare acts:

ACT I (Alceste's room.) Alceste awaits anxiously the decision of the Delphic oracle which will determine ailing Admet's fate. Parthenia, her sister and confidante, arrives with the bad news: he will die unless someone offers himself in Admet's place. His father, she reports, cannot bring himself to this noble act. Alceste decides to offer herself. Parthenia cannot dissuade her, and rushes off to seek help.

ACT II (A front hall with pillars.) Admet wonders about his sudden return to health. Parthenia comes in great agitation. (Alceste's room is opened to view.) Admet senses immediately what has happened. He cannot turn Alceste from her purpose, however. She calls for her children, takes leave of everyone, and expires. Admet is carried off in a stupor. Parthenia sings her grief to the gods.

ACT III (A front court, the royal palace in the background.) Herkules arrives, tired, at his friend's court. He sings to Virtue, "whose name I carry on my brow." He senses foreboding, justified when Parthenia explains the sad events. Herkules is so moved that he decides to fetch Alceste back from Orcus itself, or to die himself in the attempt. (A palace hall.) Herkules tells Admet of his plan.

ACT IV (A front hall.) Parthenia describes in a monologue the great despair that has overcome Admet. (Admet's room.) He himself recalls his golden days of joy, and imagines Alceste in the Underworld at the River Lethe. Parthenia seeks to console him. They go to prepare a funeral offering to Apollo, scheduled for that midnight.

[11] *Wielands gesammelte Schriften*, ed. Wilhelm Kurrelmeyer, pt. 1, vol. 11, p. 65.

ACT V (A small temple in the palace.) Offertory duet and chorus. Herkules returns with, he says, a beautiful woman to comfort Admet and make him forget his misery. He refuses, upbraids Herkules, and leaves in a rage. Parthenia also chides Herkules, who produces Alceste. Parthenia goes to get Admet. Herkules tells Alceste to draw back into the shadows. She reflects on the strangeness of her feelings back on earth. Parthenia returns with Admet, Herkules asks forgiveness, then produces Alceste. Herkules refuses to explain how he did it. Final quartet.

Wieland's basic constructive tenet in *Alceste*, thoroughgoing simplicity, was a virtue the poet thought he was reviving from Greek tragedy. But in essence the opera reflects the values that animated and colored the modern genres of the domestic tragedy, the sentimental comedy, and the *drame*: a unified plot, static tableaux, feminine virtues, and the family as the center of dramatic interest.

Wieland reduced Euripides' cast to only four, prompted by the small number of competent singers in the Seyler company. He turned each of these four into a familiar eighteenth-century dramatic type, a process which demanded profound changes in Herkules especially. "Ill-bred Herkules!" Wieland lamented of Euripides' character. His own virtuous demigod must have no drunken clownishness about him: the retrieval of Alceste, for example, must not be an act of expiation but "the meritorious deed of a free decision, worthy of a man who *does everything, dares everything for Virtue*."[12] Wieland thought for a while of enlivening things with a love-intrigue between Herkules and the seconda donna Parthenia but quickly scrapped the idea. It would have made of the former "an ordinary opera hero" and of Parthenia something less than a sister distracted by grief.

In his merciless send-up of the libretto, *Götter, Helden und Wieland*, Goethe imagines Wieland suddenly whisked off in his nightcap to the Underworld, where Mercury, a man of letters, Euripides, and the original Admet, Alkestis, and Hercules all ridicule the unfortunate poet. Euripides complains that he was so bored by Wieland's *Alceste* that it nearly put him to sleep. The characters, he snorts, are like so many eggs "stirred together into this meaningless pap":

There is a wife who wishes to die for her husband, a husband who wishes to die for his wife, a hero who wishes to die for them both, so that nothing remains but the boring object Parthenia, who is gladly fastened by the horns like a ram in the bush in order to make an end of this wretchedness.[13]

Goethe was outraged not that Wieland had written a poor opera, but that he had prostituted the characters and spirit of Greek drama. Wieland took this mauling in good grace, knowing that his libretto spoke to the sensibilities of his own age, and even complimented Goethe publicly by comparing his

---

[12] *Der deutsche Merkur* 1:1 (January, 1773): 48. The italics are Wieland's.
[13] See *Der junge Goethe*, ed. Max Morris, 2nd. ed., 6 vols. (Leipzig, 1910), vol. 3, p. 337.

gift for caricature to that of Aristophanes. He also argued his own defense in two essays which he published in his *Teutscher Merkur*,[14] and in them he makes no bones about having consciously fashioned all of his characters into eighteenth-century personages. He also defends simplicity of plot and the use of German in opera, and disagrees with Algarotti's arguments for spectacle and extremes of passions. He justifies all these restrictions by proposing a narrow role for music as an expressive medium: for its sake everything must be "warm feeling or glowing affect."

A large number of intellectuals, literati, nobles, and friends of art flocked to Weimar for the première of *Alceste* on 29 May 1773 and united in declaring the opera a grand success opening a bold new horizon to German theatrical aspirations. Schweitzer's singers distinguished themselves famously in practically everyone's judgment. Not surprisingly, historical costuming was not used. An oil painting of Franziska Koch made by G. M. Kraus (who also drew up the sets for the production) shows her not in a flowing robe but a typical eighteenth-century hooped dress (Plate 3). The setting here is the only attempt at breathing something of antiquity into the painting – but this background corresponds to no scene in the opera itself, where Alceste appears only inside Admet's palace.

Schweitzer's fame has always rested on *Alceste*. "Many and diverse things," wrote Gerber in 1792, "have the critics found to fault in it, and indeed not without cause. In spite of this, it has now held up on our German stage for sixteen years, always with the same enthusiastic praise and applause."[15] It is manifestly unfair to single out Schweitzer's opera for comparison with Gluck's *Alceste* of 1767 purely on the basis of the subject employed. The reforms embodied in Gluck's opera were literary, musical, and dramatic all at once. Wieland's on the other hand were almost entirely literary, touching on the musical shape of the opera only in its inner content rather than its outer complexion, which duplicates Italian opera seria as Schweitzer had experienced it in the early 1760s. Schweitzer himself was wholly unsympathetic to Gluck's reforms.[16]

Emotionally, the opera sits on a single plane, and as if in response to this Schweitzer turned at the very beginning to the homogeneous contrapuntal busywork of a French overture, as he was to do again in his next serious opera, *Rosamunde*, and as several other North German composers of serious opera were to do after him. Once beyond the overture, Schweitzer was at Wieland's mercy, so to speak, since the libretto had already been published

---

[14] "Briefe an einen Freund [Friedrich Heinrich Jacobi] über das deutsche Singspiel Alceste," 1:1 (January, 1773): 34–72, 1:3 (March, 1773): 223–43. "Versuch über das Teutsche Singspiel, und einige dahin einschlagende Gegenstände," 1775:3 (July–September): 63–87; 1775:4 (October–December): 156–73.

[15] Ernst Ludwig Gerber, *Historisch-Biographisches Lexikon der Tonkünstler*, vol. 2 (Leipzig, 1792), col. 484.

[16] See the letter to the Mannheim theatrical intendant Dalberg, written on 24 June 1778, which is reprinted by Maurer, *Anton Schweitzer*, p. 80.

Plate 3　*Alceste*, Franziska Koch in the title role

when he began composing it. The absence of Alceste from the stage for a full half of the opera (for Wieland does not permit us a visit to the Underworld) forced the poet to concentrate full attention on her in the first two acts: she sings all three of the arias which comprise act one (where one feels the absence of Calzabigi's chorus with special keenness). One can understand how the first two of them – in f minor and g minor and right on the heels of Schweitzer's dour g-minor overture and anxious opening recitative – would have led Mozart to complain at Mannheim of "die traurige Alceste."

Wieland crowed loudly about the second aria for Alceste in act one, especially his own text: "Metastasio himself has few arias that could have a stronger effect."[17] In his setting of it Schweitzer sought to embody the firmness of Alceste's resolve to die in Admet's stead, but he characteristically overshot the mark. "Yes, unlucky the singer," wrote Mozart to his father, "who falls into Schweitzer's hands; for all his life long he will never learn how to write singably."[18] Wieland, however, was especially impressed with Schweitzer's music for the aria's B part (Example 4.3), whose verses the poet had modeled closely on Euripides' language. The music here, Wieland declared, sent cold shudders racing through his veins.

Characteristic in this excerpt are the busy bass line (in the viola), the suspensions, and the elaborate harmonic route from c minor to g minor (i–iv_7–v [without root so as to avoid parallel fifths]–$^\flat VI$ [without fifth] –i_4^6–vii_7^0/v–V_7/v etc.). Perhaps all of this, combined with the narrow ambitus of the vocal part's opening phrase and the fussy ado over the dominant of g minor made by the strings was all intended to set off Alceste's sudden leap to a high g on "Mein Gemahl" – the object of her suffering as it is the linear and harmonic goal of Schweitzer's phrase.

For one critic at the première, the most impressive aria in *Alceste* was Parthenia's beautiful, irrelevant "O! der ist nicht vom Schicksal ganz verlassen," capping her obbligato recitative in act four. Here Schweitzer reckoned not only on the dazzling virtuosity of Josepha Hellmuth but also on the brilliant concertmaster of the Weimar Kapelle, Karl Göpfert, for the demanding obbligato accompaniment for solo violin.[19] Throughout this act, in which Wieland's tenuous plot has ground to a complete halt, Schweitzer is in top form. The *ne plus ultra* of his obbligato talents occurs here in a long recitative for Admet, "O Jugendzeit," which aroused universal admiration. Maurer has reproduced both the recitative and ensuing aria in full score.[20]

All through *Alceste* it is clear that the obbligato recitative afforded Schweitzer a format far more congenial to his stylistic proclivities than did the aria.

---

[17] *Der deutsche Merkur* 1:1 (January, 1773): 45.

[18] *Briefe und Aufzeichnungen*, 7 vols. (Salzburg, 1962–75), vol. 2, p. 477.

[19] E. W. Wolf, while traveling through Halle, heard Parthenia's aria in a concert performance in which the vocal and violin parts were sung by two boys. *Auch eine Reise aber nur eine kleine musikalische in den Monaten Junius, Julius und August 1782* (Weimar, 1784), p. 9.

[20] *Anton Schweitzer*, Musikbeispiele, pp. 53–115.

Example 4.3 Schweitzer: *Alceste*. B-part of Alceste's second aria, act 1.
"Ah, the greatness of your pain is the measure of my sorrow. My spouse!"

By tradition such recitatives were saved for moments of great emotional turmoil or confusion. After act one there are only a few such opportunities in *Alceste*, but an important one occurs in act five when Herkules produces the heroine, who even after a scene with Parthenia has not yet got her terrestrial bearings back. The passage, Wieland later recalled, cost Schweitzer a great deal of trouble. He knew it demanded a "powerful transition" but could not find the right notes. Wieland encouraged him, and eight days later Schweitzer returned "with sunshine in his eyes." The librettist considered the solution that Schweitzer at last hit upon to be one of the most sublime moments in the score.[21]

[21] Böttiger, *Literarische Zustände*, vol. 1, p. 228.

Few would disagree. Perhaps more than any other passage from the opera, this spot sums up the composer's virtues (Example 4.4). Schweitzer's delicate motives in the strings and winds, gently punctuated by the horns, rustle here above measured harmonic motion tipped downward toward the sub-dominant, A-flat, and then momentarily toward its subdominant, D-flat, for two plagal cadences in bars 55 and 56. Here inspiration dictated to Schweitzer an ethereal harmonic transfiguration of "Unvergänglichkeit" ("immortality," $^{\flat}$VI $_{\sharp 6}$ of E-flat reinterpreted as V$_7$ of E major as Alceste relives for a moment her brief sojourn in the Elysian Fields). This stroke is linked to what preceded it through its own descent by fifths to A major and by the whole passage's long-range bass ascent (G–A$^{\flat}$–A).

In an obvious external sense, *Alceste* marks an extreme swing of the pendulum away from the early comic operas North Germany had known prior to its sudden manifestation at Weimar. Given the opera's technical difficulties, its rapid spread across Germany is surprising. *Alceste* remained popular with both court and civic audiences throughout the rest of the century. Immedi-

Example 4.4 Schweitzer: *Alceste*. Obbligato recitative of Alceste, act 5.
"From eternally blooming fields there yet breathes toward me the spirit of immortality."

Ex. 4.4 (*cont.*)

ately it became the most performed item in Seyler's repertory – and not just at Weimar and Gotha but at the Leipzig fairs as well. Marchand's company at Frankfurt, hitherto almost exclusively devoted to opéra-comique in translation, became the first to follow Seyler's with a new production of *Alceste* less than a year later, again for a fair-time audience. Many subsequent performances, we should note, were concert presentations, usually because the singers skilled enough for Schweitzer's ambitious score had to be recruited from a Kapelle rather than a theatrical company. The concert format was used not only for other serious North German operas written in imitation of *Alceste*, but also for foreign operas in the same league – including Gluck's Italian and French works of the 1760s and 1770s.

Whatever the merits of *Alceste* when considered *sub specie aeternitatis*, it considerably widened the range of possibilities later North German librettists and composers could consider feasible, and its influence on opera with spoken dialogue during the following years is unmistakable.

The transition to Gotha

A year after the première of *Alceste* a fire broke out above the kitchens at the Weimar court and destroyed the entire wing of the Wilhelmsburg, including the playhouse and all its properties. Anna Amalia was forced to dismiss the Seyler company with a quarter year's wages and a letter of recommendation to Duke Ernst II at nearby Gotha. He agreed to engage the company for a trial period of three months.

Ernst II was a serious, enlightened monarch who equaled Anna Amalia in love of propriety, concern for his subjects, and commitment to the arts and learning. Gotha, both as a court and city, was larger than Weimar and also boasted a court Kapellmeister, Georg Benda, whose contributions to the theater under Seyler and later the Gotha Court Theater were to outshine even those of Schweitzer in past years. Benda had been at Gotha since 1750, when he replaced the worthy Gottfried Heinrich Stölzel. Benda's operatic manner and taste had been formed at the court of Frederick the Great. At Gotha he had produced an Italian opera seria in 1765, and shortly thereafter had gone to Italy for six months to polish his style and bring it up to date.

The arrival of the Seyler company at Gotha kindled great interest and enthusiasm in both the court and city. During the trial period the troupe made itself so popular that Ernst II readily agreed to renew Seyler's contract for a full year in September 1774. His terms were less liberal than Anna Amalia's (and he also charged spectators admission fees), but socially and professionally the company was as well off as before. The duke took great interest in their performances and personally approved each evening's program.

Though Seyler received only 6,500 Thaler a year at Gotha, he was allowed to play at the lucrative Michaelmas and Easter Fairs at Leipzig. Döbbelin was still plying these fairs in 1774, but when Seyler appeared at Wäser's theater at the Grimm Gate that autumn Döbbelin was forced to surrender the field and the Theater am Rannstädter Thore to his formidable rival after only three weeks. The next Easter Döbbelin did not return (he was by then in a debtor's prison). In his place came Wäser and company from Breslau, but they fared no better against Seyler.

The money to be made in Saxony at fair-time obviously attracted Seyler, and even before his year's contract with Gotha expired he secured Döbbelin's troubled Saxon privilege from the Dresden court. Many of his players, however, unwilling to leave such an amiable home as Gotha, agreed to stay on there as the nucleus of an unprecedented undertaking proposed by the court in order to keep the troupe at Gotha – a theater directly under the control and supervision of the court itself, the first "Hoftheater" or Court Theater in the history of the German stage.

During Seyler's year and a half at Gotha and Leipzig, from June 1774 until September 1775, little change took place in his spoken repertory or the ballets. But the Gotha court's love of everything French and the presence of Benda generated several major additions among the eight new musical works introduced (items 26 to 33 in Table 4.1).

The new opéras-comiques to appear differ from the harmless, timid kind brought into the repertory at Weimar. With *Le Tableau parlant* Grétry – already all the rage in South Germany, the Rhineland, and Lower Saxony – finally broke into Seyler's repertory.[22] On the eve of the inauguration of the Court Theater, Seyler added Monsigny's *Le Déserteur* (1769) to his repertory, an extravagant and sentimental story (which Sedaine went so far as to label a *drame*) significant for its novel blending of tender pathos and arch comedy.

Next to *Alceste*, the most popular work at Gotha and Leipzig was Benda's first comic opera, *Der Jahrmarkt*, an opera whose genesis is almost as colorful as the village fair it brings to life on stage. Like Schweitzer's *Die Dorfgala*, its libretto is by Gotter and is pure farce. Gotter originally intended to adapt a popular afterpiece in the company's repertory, Engel's *Der dankbare Sohn*, but when Ekhof heard that one of his favorite roles was to become part of a comic opera, he flew into a rage, and the duke ordered the project halted. Benda, however, was already well advanced on the composition and so both Gotter and Engel himself (who had come to Gotha in 1774) decided to use the recruiting episode as the basis of a new text. As a one-act work *Der Jahrmarkt* received its première on 10 February 1775 at Gotha. Then, at Leipzig, a new two-act version was presented by Seyler on 26 April, with additions not just by Gotter and Benda but by Engel and Hiller as well. (We have already

---

[22] The duke's sister had requested that H. A. O. Reichard, the court librarian, translate Anseaume's text. In so doing he added two new arias, which Schweitzer set to music.

seen Leipzig's strong preference for two-act rather than one-act musical works.)[23]

As in his earlier libretto, Gotter built his plot around a simple and familiar central strand. Bärbchen has a falling out with her fiancé Lukas when he detects a lieutenant flirting with her; the lieutenant has his recruiting sergeant, Fickfack, get Lukas drunk and enlist him; Bärbchen arrives too late to undo the damage Lukas's despair over her has wrought, so she runs off and fetches the benevolent colonel who straightens everything out. Most of the characters are tried-and-true types already developed by other German librettists, and so are the constructive techniques involved. The musical numbers are sprinkled around here and there, with greatest emphasis on the heroine and the comic bass Fickfack. The lubricious, scheming lieutenant does not sing at all (like Graf Schmetterling in *Die Jagd*) although Gotter makes his presence felt throughout and develops his character very deftly in the spoken sections.

Conceptually, we are dealing with a work squarely in the camp of Saxon opera's farcical tradition, but the changes Schweitzer had worked in Seyler's singers prompted Benda to adopt a more elaborate musical style, one which comes fully into the open in the closing number, a virtuosic concert aria written especially for Josepha Hellmuth. And – let it not be overlooked – Hiller too rises above the technical level of his own comic operas in his contributions to the two-act version, now that he had better singers to write for.

Even in his orchestral style Benda made advances, for example in the opera's Romanze, "In unserm ganzen Dorf." Although he employs the same lovely f-minor tune for all four of its stanzas, Benda varies the accompaniment in the second and third as the small tragedy Bärbchen relates (about two lovers who fall into a lime-pit) unfolds. The second, the beginning of which is shown in Example 4.5, provides deft coloring with the bassoons doubling the soprano and the strings working exotic chromatic inflections into their figuration.

As with the collaborations we have already studied in earlier chapters, Benda and Gotter still coordinate rather than combine their efforts. The central characters Fickfack and Lukas, whose recruiting scene begat the opera and forms the high point of both versions, receive less careful, detailed musical delineation than Bärbchen, who does not rise much above a stock character in Gotter's hands. The ensembles, too, build on personality rather than dramatic interaction.[24]

---

[23] The full score has been published in a modern edition – at present the only North German opera of the period so honored – including the different versions of both the music and the text. *Denkmäler deutscher Tonkunst*, vol. 64 (Leipzig, 1930; 2nd ed., 1955).

[24] "Characteristic" was the word Reichardt chose to describe Benda's duets in reviewing the published keyboard reduction for the *Allgemeine deutsche Bibliothek* 34 (1778): 222. Good examples are the duet in which Lukas and Bärbchen have their falling out and the trio in which Fickfack and the Tyrolian Lehnchen try to convince the befuddled Lukas that duty and honor await him as a soldier.

Example 4.5 Benda: *Der Jahrmarkt*. Romanze, act 1.

"The banns had already been published, indeed for the second time, and tomorrow was to be the wedding, the bed and feast were prepared."

Benda's two great melodramas, written like *Der Jahrmarkt* in early 1775, have received much attention,[25] and, although they are not strictly speaking operatic works, it is both useful and appropriate to raise several points concerning them at this time. Most important, they were not written for members of Seyler's musical ménage but for the finest tragic actresses in the troupe – *Ariadne auf Naxos* for the touching pathos of Charlotte Brandes (on a text by her husband), and *Medea* for the overpowering, bone-chilling art of Sophie Seyler (amply provided for by Gotter's text). One must therefore trace two hereditary lines of descent in accounting for the genre's pedigree – (1) the development of the monologue from French classical tragedy through the English-inspired reforms which commence after mid-century with Lessing, Weisse, Gerstenberg, and others; and (2) the acclimatization of Italian techniques of obbligato recitative, especially as refined after mid-century by the generation of Jommelli and Traetta, among German composers connected with court-based theaters inclined to welcome such ambitions. Though the rise of the German melodrama was coeval with the appearance of *Alceste*, which owes much to this same musical heritage, Schweitzer's opera and Benda's melodramas are distinctive developments. True, the melodrama preferred subjects from classical antiquity (at least in the North), but it lived on vibrant tragic realism, and no such claim can be made for *Alceste*. It is worth noting in this connection that *Ariadne auf Naxos*, at Duke Ernst II's personal stipulation, used a natural, flowing Greek robe for its heroine, lending persuasive visual realism to its violent emotions, just as historically accurate costuming did at the same time for Goethe's *Götz von Berlichingen* at Berlin and Hamburg. Opera, on the other hand, still clung to eighteenth-century dress, and not just in the North but all across Europe.

While there was no necessity that a composer think any further than the immediate line of text or gesture each musical interpolation accompanies in a melodrama (and this is the case with the *Pygmalion* of Rousseau and Coignet), Benda's triumph and claim to the international recognition which his melodramas earned him lay in shaping both scores into unified large-scale canvases. "How everything is so new and still so true!" exclaimed Neefe of the two works, "so varied and still so coherent!"[26] Mozart, it is well known, carried them around with him constantly in the later 1770s and entertained high hopes of integrating the technique into opera, a step that was soon to be taken in the North.

The overnight success of Benda's melodramas instantly earned him flattering national and international attention. Schweitzer was eclipsed, and remained in Benda's shadow. his melodrama *Polyxena* cut a poor figure

[25] The principal studies are Edgar Istel's *Die Entstehung des deutschen Melodramas* (Berlin and Leipzig, 1906) and Jan van der Veen's *Le Mélodrame musical de Rousseau au romantisme* (The Hague, [1955]). Only in connection with Goethe has the genre received serious attention as a literary phenomenon in Germany.
[26] *Theater-Journal für Deutschland* 1777:1, p. 75.

indeed against his rival's scores, and never achieved more than a single performance. When the Gotha Court Theater was formed in 1775, Schweitzer did not leave with Seyler but remained at Gotha as the music director of the new enterprise. He contributed nothing at all of significance to the Court Theater. Most of his creative activities came in collaboration with the Weimar court, most notably a commission that Wieland and he provide a new serious opera along the lines of *Alceste* for the court at Mannheim, from which resulted their ill-starred *Rosamunde*.

Benda, on the other hand, determined to avail himself of the Court Theater to capitalize on his new-won fame. He and Gotter (with whom he continued to collaborate exclusively) faced changed circumstances under the court-sponsored undertaking. Both tragediennes for whom Benda had written his two melodramas had left with Seyler. So had the Hellmuths, and Franziska Koch remained only until mid-1777.

Taste in music at Gotha, as in everything, continued to run heavily toward anything French. Of the seventeen new musical works the Court Theater introduced (items 34 to 50 in Table 4.1), eight are opéras-comiques, and a rank ordering is even more telling: of the seven works performed eight or more times, five are French. Grétry's opéra-ballet *Zémire et Azor* swamped everything else in the repertory as the most popular work, spoken or sung – an honor previously held by *Alceste*.

Possibly these realities helped dissuade Gotter and Benda from any thought of pursuing German serious opera as Wieland and Schweitzer had defined it. Instead, they took stock of the new company and struck out upon an important new path that effected a new amalgamation of the melodrama's heritage of serious opera and serious spoken drama. They began cautiously with *Walder* (first performed on 23 February 1776), which transforms Marmontel's one-act opéra-comique *Silvain* into a musical equivalent of the *drame*. Their second, more ambitious and uncompromising effort, *Romeo und Julie*, transforms prose tragedy into unremitting serious opera.

Walder

Silvain was already popular all across Germany in Grétry's setting, and in an adaptation by Weisse as a spoken afterpiece as well. The story, familiar to German readers in Salomon Gessner's prose idyll *Erast*, must have exerted considerable fascination for Gotter to dare yet another version.[27] The

---

[27] The story had already served as the source of Graf von Spaur's one-act libretto *Milton und Elmire*, set by Josef Michl (Frankfurt, 1773) which was revised and presented in a two-act version at Meiningen in 1776. Shortly after the appearance of Benda's *Walder*, it also found employment in Johann Friedrich Schink's libretto *Rosalia*, published at Gotha in 1777 and set that year by Josef Schubert for Berlin. Finally, Christian Jacob Wagenseil began his one-act libretto *Ehrlichkeit und Liebe*, as an adaptation of Gessner's *Erast*, but the close similarities with *Walder* forced him to change the plot. The text was set by Wolf and published at Weimar in 1776.

significance of Gotter's *Walder*, however, lay not in the sentimental story but in his sensitivity to the musical possibilities to be developed for Benda. *Walder*, in contrast with Gotter's first two librettos, is a true collaboration of poet and musician, another step away from the primitive division of labor which characterized early Saxon opera. Johann Nikolaus Forkel, who fairly scorned most German opera of his day, devoted a long and enthusiastic review to *Walder* in his *Musikalisch-Kritische Bibliothek* in 1778. He heaps praise on Gotter's libretto not only because it is filled with "purely noble, touching, and interesting situations," but more especially because "the music is given an opportunity to work at its most powerful and to appear with a dignity that must in no case be denied it if one wants it to display the useful influence that one is justified in expecting of it."[28]

The plot of Gotter's version is simple and dignified, and a far cry from the color and excitement of *Der Jahrmarkt* of a year earlier. Walder had forsaken the advantages of good birth in order to marry Sophie. His father (Dolmon Vater) had envisaged a wife in better circumstances, and in anger disinherited Walder, who moved to a small village to support his wife and children. Now the old landowner of this village has been superseded by none other than Walder's father, together with his younger brother (Dolmon Sohn). The opera begins with Walder telling Sophie that they must leave their beloved village. He goes off to hunt, but returns unexpectedly, holding off several armed guards carrying out a new suspension of the peasants' hunting rights. Walder's brother is behind this. When he appears only Walder recognizes him, and answers the high-handed insolence of Dolmon Sohn with boldness and spite. The latter tells him that Dolmon Vater is coming and will punish him. In the greatest agitation, Walder leaves Sophie and his children to soften his father's heart before he himself dares confront him. Dolmon Vater needs converse only a little with Sophie (whom he has never seen) to perceive that she was not born to her present lowly condition. She turns his anger to curiosity, then enchantment, and the two daughters win him over completely. Dolmon Vater recognizes Walder at once when he finally appears, and forgives him everything over the objections of the nasty Dolmon Sohn.

Gotter deviates only occasionally from Marmontel's text. He lengthens the concluding scene of reconciliation considerably, not just to exploit this highly prized theatrical commodity, but to bring Dolmon Sohn back into the picture for a final confrontation of the two brothers. The unpleasant sibling serves as the keystone of the great quartet with which Benda caps the drama, a scene strengthened by Gotter's decision to have Dolmon Vater reject the intractable Dolmon Sohn at the end.

[28] 2 (1778): 233. For Forkel, *Walder* turned decisively from the path German opera had been treading, and he hoped the example would not be lost on other composers and librettists: "May it frighten away all the unruly bunglings around it, which seem to have amused a part of our musical public for many years, and may it arouse in their place a lively feeling for the worth, so misunderstood, and true employment of art! Nothing can more easily give a new advantageous turn to a widespread false taste than a work of art which is a masterpiece in the contrary taste." *Ibid.*, p. 230.

Walder, in sum, confronts serious problems of reconciliation among antagonistic familial elements rather than dealing in the comic stock-in-trade of courtship and marriage braving all obstacles. A comedy, Byron has observed, always ends with a marriage. By this facetious definition, *Walder* is no comedy; in fact, with its decided subordination of the young lovers (Walder's daughter Hannchen and her fiancé Christel) to the trials of Walder and Sophie, it approaches the realm of the *drame.*

Grétry's *Silvain,* produced in 1770, offered a potential model of musical interpretation along current opéra-comique lines, but it was apparently ignored by Benda and Gotter. The librettist had his own ideas about how music ought to be integrated into the story. He eliminated several numbers in order to remove two singing parts from the drama and turned into prose the septet which Marmontel used to highlight the confrontation of Silvain and the guards.[29]

Benda broke with tradition both in issuing his score under the new rubric "eine ernsthafte Operette" and in adopting the format of a short score "to please those amateurs of music who are not satisfied with a bare keyboard reduction of a Singspiel, but wish to see or hear something more complete."[30] Above the two-stave keyboard reduction and vocal part or parts appear the violins and whatever obbligato woodwinds are employed in each number. Occasionally even the viola appears. But Benda did not bother putting the overture (labeled "Eingang") into anything more than a two-stave keyboard format, even though the score includes a concertante part for solo violin and runs into the first number.

In adopting the adjective "ernsthaft," Benda published his intention of conquering an international style which remained the supreme touchstone of operatic excellence. Though nearly all foreign critics in this period voice displeasure at German composers' "laboured contrivances" and lack of mastery over Italian "cantabile" style,[31] this was no insuperable cultural blight. Eximeno y Pujades made exception to such strictures for composers, like Hasse and Johann Christian Bach, who had studied in Italy for a long time. Benda and others in the North did not enjoy the educational advantages of these two composers, but nonetheless sought to improve their native musical language by attending to Italian example.

Let us consider three of Benda's fourteen numbers in *Walder* to illustrate

---

[29] Action numbers such as this septet of Grétry's are rare in German opera of the 1770s. The Germans also looked upon dramatically developing arias in opéra-comique as something unusual. A reviewer of Weisse's spoken afterpiece – also entitled *Walder* – based on *Silvain* remarked in Schmid's *Das Parterr* that Weisse had been forced to turn many of Marmontel's arias into prose rather than simply to omit them "since the French often advance the plot in their arias" (Erfurt, 1771), p. 18.

[30] See the preface to Benda's published short score (Gotha, 1777), p. [iii], which is signed by the publisher, Carl Wilhelm Ettinger.

[31] See for the former charge Burney, *The Present State of Music in Germany, passim,* and for the latter D. Antonio Eximeno [y Pujades], *Dell'origine e delle regole della musica colla storia del suo progresso, decadenza, e rinnovazione* (Rome, 1774), p. 450.

the opera's special character. First, the composer gave his heroine Sophie an especially beautiful obbligato recitative and aria at the very mid-point of the drama, where she is left alone on stage to prepare herself for the arrival of Dolmon Vater. Marmontel had constructed this scene as a "Récitatif obligé" followed by an "Air vif." Gotter changed each of these elements into a recitative-arioso pair, and Benda's setting of this scene is even more fluid than this textual disposition would suggest. The composer moves smoothly into and out of the two ariosos and also brings back the first to round the whole:

Recitative	Arioso I	Recitative	Arioso II	Arioso I (Varied)
Eb (c f)	Eb Bb	g	c (Eb) c	Eb

Benda's interpretation of the heroine's scena lacks Grétry's color and sweep, which may in general be taken as typical of the divergent national styles. However, Benda's overall sense of dramatic form is stronger. He shades deftly from the first recitative into the following arioso (Example 4.6)

Example 4.6 Benda: *Walder*. Sophie's scena.
"He is coming, he is coming! I hear already the voice of offended Nature. That is she, take your revenge, that is she who made off with your son, who transformed the finest youth into a rebel. She is the enemy, the enemy of your peace, the source of your grief.
"Yes, my father; yes, my judge: I am to be punished — take your revenge."

Ex. 4.6 (*cont.*)

with a plaintive Adagio open cadence in bars 35 to 36, softening the rather routine orchestral bluster preceding it. In the arioso, warm lyricism brings out the more passive dignity Gotter had breathed into Sophie's part and which answered perfectly to the dramatic and musical abilities of the first Sophie, Franziska Koch. In bars 39 to 41 in particular, the falling sixth of "räche dich" and the beloved and poignant melodic seventh outlined against a ii§ harmony on "ich bin strafbar" ensure that no one will seriously believe that Dolmon Vater would ever seek revenge as a father or hold her guilty as a judge in the face of such sweet innocence. Later on the second arioso section in c minor – too long and imposing to be labeled a B part, despite its contrasting tonality – brings forth the noble side of Sophie's character.

The second of our examples from *Walder* is Sophie's A-major rondo in which she imparts advice on marriage to her daughter Hannchen, soon to be wed to Christel. It is the first example of the rondo in North German opera. As with nearly all subsequent rondos, "Selbst die glücklichste der Ehen" follows the seven-part pattern ABACADA with all statements of A setting the same text to the same refrain in the same key. The shorter form ABACA (familiar from Gluck's "Che farò senza Euridice" in *Orfeo ed Euridice*, 1762) occurs less often. The rondo enjoyed two periods of sustained cultivation in the North, first from 1776 to 1783 and later from 1791 to the end of the century. It was apparently abandoned completely in operas produced during the lean years between these periods.

The early vogue of the rondo in the North was initiated by Benda's aria for Sophie, and subsequent examples during the rondo's first efflorescence are almost without exception also assigned to the prima donna of the cast. Musically, these rondos are akin to the Romanze, whose relentless repetitive strophic character they lighten with episodes, but whose simple, memorable melodic stamp they try to duplicate.[32]

The introduction of a simple rondo into an "ernsthafte Operette" seems somewhat surprising. Forkel speculated that Benda included it to lure listeners to the opera's more substantial musical essays, and it is also possible that composer and librettist conceived it as a substitute for the inevitable Romanze (which does not appear in *Walder*). At any rate, the little rondo for Sophie was to be heard all over town on the lips of the young ladies of Gotha, and it quickly became the equal of Hiller's best-loved songs in German society. The opening of its refrain is given in Example 4.7.

The third number we shall consider, the quartet which closes the drama, Forkel rightly singled out as the crowning eminence in Benda's score. In general, as we have seen, German librettists and composers practiced in ensembles what their theorists preached concerning music's incapacity to advance the plot. In so doing they set themselves clearly apart from both the finale, which opéra-comique was already beginning to absorb, and also dramatic ensembles. Furthermore, even the emotional relationships between the participants seldom change in the course of a North German operatic ensemble.

---

[32] There are precedents for the German rondo in both French and Italian comic opera of the 1760s and early 1770s. The genre has, however, received little study. Malcolm Cole, who wrote the entry "Rondo" for *The New Grove Dictionary of Music and Musicians* (London, 1980), vol. 16, pp. 172–7, musters scant interest for the rondo as a vocal phenomenon.

Example 4.7 Benda: *Walder*. Refrain of the rondo.
"Even the happiest of marriages, my child, has its trouble. Even the best men often follow their whims."

In the quartet in *Walder*, however, Gotter provided Benda with the opportunity to deal musically with a knot left tied to that point, Dolmon Sohn's disturbing recalcitrance. Perhaps inspired by the theme of fraternal discord,[33] Gotter lades the part of Dolmon Sohn with a wholesale condemnation of the "Empfindsamkeit" of the other three, who harp on being touched, the sweetness of forgiving, and the power of love and happiness. Dolmon Sohn seems actually to borrow a rhythmic figure of an important earlier aria sung by his father, a lament on the sorrows of parenthood, for his opening salvo directed at his father, whom he finds reconciled with Walder and Sophie (Example 4.8). Benda follows every nuance of the attempts to soften Dolmon Sohn with upward inflections of supplication and ever more unremitting downward responses, culminating in plunging octaves on Dolmon Sohn's words "hasst mich immer" – a magnificent final gesture which will brook no further attempts at reconciliation. The stubborn spoilsport departs.

[33] An early example of the theme in German sentimental literature of the eighteenth century occurs in another idyll by Gessner, *Der Tod Abels*. It contrasts Cain's manliness with Abel's "womanish weakness," and this contrast is to an extent explored musically by Johann Heinrich Rolle in his sacred music drama of the same name (Magdeburg, 1769) based on Gessner's idyll. It is of interest that the role of Adam in seeking to reconcile Gessner's brothers parallels that of Dolmon Vater in the quartet here. The words of Dolmon Sohn include Cain's "weibisch" as well as scornful reference to reconciliation and tears. The importance of the topic of fraternal strife throughout German literature is explored by Michael Mann, "Die feindlichen Brüder," in *Germanisch-Romanische Monatsschrift*, n.s. vol. 18 (1968): 225–47.

Example 4.8 Benda: *Walder*. A: Aria of Dolmon Vater. B: Incipit of quartet.
  A: "I have children, but in vain."
  B: "Does your heart break at false tears?"

As theatrically effective as this close may be, Gotter and Benda were not content to end the opera here. Dialogue follows, and then the three characters remaining on stage repeat the quartet's final section with Dolmon Sohn's bass part omitted. Very possibly the original version of the opera ended here, but Benda's keyboard reduction, issued in 1778, includes one further number, a mammoth dal segno comparison aria for Sophie ("He who was almost shipwrecked wavers still on dry land. . . thus the danger that threatened us, barely escaped, still pales my cheeks with fear"). Gotter's original libretto, also not published until 1778, included this aria in an "Appendix for the Use of Some Theaters," preceding it with a brief dialogue serving to empty the stage of everyone but the heroine. Probably Benda did not compose this aria for Franziska Koch, who had been the original Sophie, but for her successor in the role, his star pupil Sophia Elisabetha Preysing. The number is far better suited to what we are told of her sparkling vocal skills than to what we know of Franziska Koch's.

With or without this accretion, *Walder* remains exactly what Forkel called it, a major departure from German comic opera even as it had been practiced by the same poet and composer only a year before. This first step toward greater "seriousness" in opera with spoken dialogue was apparently not out of step with German theatrical sensibilities and realities, for it was successful not only at Gotha but nearly everywhere in Germany. Seyler took it up at Dresden almost at once, and others followed suit. Schröder at Hamburg had to compromise with local prejudice, which ran heavily in favor of Grétry's *Silvain*, already an old favorite there. His solution was to amalgamate the two works by adopting six of Grétry's numbers and five of Benda's.[34]

Romeo und Julie

No such contamination with another opera could be imagined for the next collaboration of Gotter and Benda, *Romeo und Julie*, a three-act serious opera with spoken dialogue. In many ways it is their answer to Schweitzer's *Alceste*, sharing with it a total commitment to seria style, and it also parallels the earlier opera in adopting a simple plot and a small cast. As we saw earlier, the Court Theater was deprived of two of Seyler's best singers when the Hellmuths left with him, and it continued to have difficulty in finding and keeping good singers. Gotter reduced a potentially populous cast to just four singing roles through the first two acts and two very minor additional ones in act three. Further, he concentrated musical attention heavily on Julie, sung by the seventeen-year-old Sophia Preysing, and secondarily on her confidante Laura, in which role Benda's own daughter Justina ("Justel") made her debut.

Gotter's cast had already been whittled down from Shakespeare's in his immediate source, Weisse's prose tragedy of 1767. Gotter also followed Weisse in preserving the unities and avoiding what Weisse had censured in Shakespeare as "many trivial, superfluous things not necessary to the plot."[35] Gotter's most controversial change had no precedent, however – the substitution of a happy ending. "Partly the musical economy seemed to me not to allow the retention of the all-too-tragic catastrophe," he observed in the preface to the printed libretto, "partly the consideration of the capabilities of

---

[34] All five of the numbers preserved from Benda's setting are for Sophie, whereas other impressive numbers such as the quartet just discussed were not included. The fact that Benda's daughter Justel sang the part of Sophie in the Hamburg production must surely have played a part in Schröder's decision to use precisely these numbers from Benda's setting.

[35] Weisse's tragedy and its preface are reprinted by Fritz Brüggemann in *Die Aufnahme Shakespeares auf der Bühne der Aufklärung in den sechziger und siebziger Jahren* (Leipzig, 1937), the quotation here occurring on page 236. The relationship of Gotter's text to other German versions of Shakespeare's play is discussed in my article, "Opera *versus* Drama: *Romeo and Juliet* in Eighteenth-Century Germany," *Eighteenth-Century Studies* 11 (1977/8): 186–203.

the singers impelled me to this."[36] The price of serious opera, he seems to be saying, is serious acting.

Thus, just as Wieland had adjusted his basic conception of plot, emotional content, and language in *Alceste* to the needs and limitations of music as he conceived them, so did Gotter in a work whose spoken dialogue brought it much closer to non-musical traditions. Benda, on the other hand, was more than ready to yield to the claims of the story's affiliation with domestic tragedy. In an essay "On Simple Recitative," which he published in Cramer's *Magazin der Musik* in 1783, he thanks Gotter publicly for putting the dialogue of his serious opera into prose "and thereby sparing me the pain of weakening the plot of this touching work with common operatic language." And later, echoing Gluck's famous dedicatory preface to *Alceste*, Benda philosophizes: "Music itself suffers when one sacrifices everything for its sake."[37]

This is consideration with a vengeance – a librettist short-circuiting the tragic close of his drama to suit a composer, and a composer deferring to the dramatist's expressive needs. Many critics felt that it was Gotter who had gone too far in yielding to convention – and it was not reverence for Shakespeare but admiration for Benda's powerful score which animated them. Reichardt in 1780 called the setting "a magnificent, ravishing work that penetrates the heart!" But he added in irritation, "If only the poet had not cut up his material so irresponsibly into well-behaved, everyday opera garb!"[38]

Yet we should not take Gotter too severely to task. His text is fully as dignified as that of Weisse's tragedy, and he drew a far stronger heroine than had Weisse. Especially where Gotter calls on the composer's obbligato skills, his Julie gathers strength, for example in her final monologue before taking Friar Laurence's potion, a musical complex capped by an f-minor aria whose last line came straight from Shakespeare: "Romeo, diess trink ich dir zu!" ("Romeo, I come! this do I drink to thee"). Weisse had avoided such a flourish by letting his heroine drink the potion well before the end of her monologue, where she falls on her bed trembling with terror. Gotter considerably toned down both Romeo and Capulet as personalities, although they receive adequate attention musically. In so doing he aligned Julie with the tragic heroines of Benda's melodramas, who stand in splendid isolation from the males (Theseus and Jason) who generate the situations which make their dramatic monologues possible.

---

[36] *Romeo und Julie* (Leipzig, 1779), p. [8]. Gotter wrote this preface in October 1778, two years after the première of the opera. In the meantime, Heinrich Leopold Wagner had viciously attacked his libretto for replacing Shakespeare's tragedy "with 19⁄20 water." *Briefe, die Seylerische Schauspieler-Gesellschaft und ihre Vorstellungen zu Frankfurt a. M. betreffend* (Frankfurt am Main, 1777). Gotter addressed this critique directly, and it appears that at least part of his motivation for publishing his libretto was to counter these criticisms.

[37] *Magazin der Musik* 1 (Hamburg, 1783): 755. I have published a translation of this essay in the appendix to my article, "Benda, the Germans, and Simple Recitative," *JAMS* 34 (1981): 119–31.

[38] *Allgemeine deutsche Bibliothek* 40 (1780): 129.

The best number in the opera, the justly famous chorus at the beginning of act three, seems to draw inspiration from Gluck. At first it stood alone in the score, followed by a duet for Capulet and Laura, but when Gotter's friend Schröder mounted the opera at Hamburg, he recommended changes in this scene. Gotter incorporated these in the printed text of 1779 and Benda provided additional music. Musically a second duet was added and the chorus was repeated so as to lend the scene more architectural strength and solemnity after Capulet leaves in despair. The stage action was also enhanced: Laura, accompanied by maidens with burning candles, sings the added duet with one of them, then places a wreath on Julie's coffin and leaves; during the final chorus the coffin is closed and the crypt darkened and shut, and in the end an empty stage awaits the entrance of Romeo and his servant. More and more, German librettists and composers were to learn how to think in terms of such visual-architectural planning.

The dignified and measured last exequies for Julie must have been of powerful theatrical effect when accompanied by Benda's chorus (Example 4.9). The pitiless unison descent of the tonic triad bristles with Gluckian

Example 4.9 Benda: *Romeo und Julie*. Funeral chorus, act 3.
"In the grave dwells the oblivion of cares."

power. The unaccompanied, contrapuntal surge that follows, however, is purely North German. In many ways the chorus suggests a Lutheran motet, a genre which after Bach had turned to discreet polyphony and free combinations of voices within a homophonic context (and a motet was a frequent adjunct to a funeral service as well).

Elsewhere in the opera, Benda stints nothing in writing for Julie and Laura, and even in the less demanding numbers for Romeo and Capulet he nowhere touches on the easy apprehensibility which he occasionally had invoked in *Walder*. The high expressive profile in all of Julie's recitatives and arias at times recalls the daring sallies in Benda's melodramas. To take but one example, consider the jolting half-step relation seen in Example 4.10

Example 4.10 Benda: *Romeo und Julie*. Obbligato recitative of Julie, act 1. "No, he still delays."

from Julie's opening recitative. She anxiously awaits Romeo's arrival, jumping at every imagined footfall. Benda aptly portrays her unrest over each false alarm with a jarring harmonic shift from the dominant of b minor to F major, a tritone away from the expected chord of resolution.

Julie's most celebrated number was "Ihn wieder zu seh'n," an aria intermixed with recitative elements sung in response to Friar Laurence's suggestion that he may have a way to reunite her with Romeo. Reichardt praised it lavishly as "the highest expression of rapture that art is capable of reaching,"[39] and as late as 1797 Goethe's friend Karl Friedrich Zelter published an analysis of this scene. He also discusses Julie's equally impressive recitative and aria, already mentioned, culminating in her taking the potion at the end

[39] *Ibid.*, p. 130.

of act two. Zelter follows this latter scene from its quiet beginning as Friar Laurence leaves through all Julie's doubts and fears to her final determination, and he concludes that "taken all together, it seems a single, capital outpouring of a great tragic poetic fantasy, which will be passed on to posterity as surely as there were poets and artists in the days of Pericles."[40]

As with Schweitzer's *Alceste*, the seriousness of Benda's and Gotter's opera in no way jeopardized its popularity in Germany. The Court Theater revived *Romeo und Julie* at Gotha in 1778, and chose it for the benefit performance for the players given when the enterprise closed in September 1779. Practically every important theatrical company in Germany had taken it up by that time, and it continued to enjoy popular approval throughout the following decades.

The final operatic collaboration of Benda and Gotter for the Court Theater, the one-act "comische Operette" *Der Holzhauer*, represents a wholesale retreat from *Walder* and *Romeo und Julie*. Based on an outmoded one-act opéra-comique, *Le Bûcheron* (1763), it attained popularity nowhere. At Hamburg, *Der Holzhauer* had to compete with a French version with Philidor's music. It was indifferently received, and Schröder wrote to Gotter in exasperation: "Why do you and Benda busy yourselves with such thankless tasks? with operas that already exist? that have prejudices in their favor? I could mention and give you twenty pieces by Holberg, Goldoni, and the old French theater that are more grateful to the poet, composer, public, and director."[41]

The two did not follow this advice, but instead abandoned operatic collaboration. Benda decided to end his nearly thirty years as the court Kapellmeister at Gotha in order to travel. Besides the prospect of lucrative performances of his works under his own direction, he was interested in furthering the careers of Justel, whom Schröder wanted to engage, and his son Christian Hermann. After spending the summer and autumn of 1778 settling Justel at Hamburg, father and son visited briefly at Mannheim, then traveled to Vienna. Benda's *Medea* had already aroused admiration there, and arrangements were made for him to conduct several of his stage works at the Burgtheater, at which Joseph II had established a German National-Singspiel in early 1778. Benda disappointed expectations by offering *Der Jahrmarkt*, chosen perhaps because of its vogue in the North, perhaps because it allowed his son to shine as Lukas. He made no attempt to mount the serious operas he had earlier presented with success and profit at Hamburg. *Der Jahrmarkt* was given only three times in 1779 and once more in 1780, whereas *Medea* and *Ariadne auf Naxos* remained in Viennese repertories until 1795 and 1798 respectively. On the whole, in fact, North German operas fared poorly indeed at Vienna, although Austrian composers and audiences welcomed Northern

---

[40] "Ausstellung einer Szene aus dem musikalischen Drama *Romeo und Julie*, von Georg Benda," *Lyceum der schönen Künste* 1:1 (Berlin, 1797): 141.

[41] The letter is reprinted by Berthold Litzmann, *Schröder und Gotter* (Hamburg and Leipzig, 1887), p. 124.

librettos. From 1778 to 1784 at the Burgtheater, *Der Jahrmarkt* was the sole North German opera to appear in the repertory of the National-Singspiel.

Seyler in Saxony

In September 1775, Seyler and those loyal to him had left Thuringia for Leipzig, where the Michaelmas Fair was just beginning, and later for Dresden, where they enjoyed a successful winter. Seyler returned to Leipzig for the Easter Fair of 1776; he made money and received a year's extension on his contract with the city fathers to play there. His company was now back to full strength, numbering forty-two persons. As they had done elsewhere, the members of his company established close ties with artists, musicians, and nobles at Dresden. Bustelli, who headed the opera buffa establishment there, began intriguing at court against his new rival, but the Seyler company's offerings, and especially the musical ones, met with great enthusiasm.

In September of 1776 Seyler hired the fiery young dramatist Friedrich Maximilian Klinger as his theatrical poet, and at the Easter Fair the next spring gave the première of his new drama *Sturm und Drang*. That winter Seyler had received an invitation from the Palatine court at Mannheim to accept an engagement there. While the position eventually went to the Marchand troupe, the opportunity of leaving Saxony for the Rhineland apparently appealed to Seyler. He demanded better terms for the renewal of his contract with the Dresden court. These were rejected, and so Seyler decided to depart for Mannheim after the Easter Fair of 1777.

Although this final Saxon episode in Seyler's career was brief and not without difficulties, his troupe remained one of the most respected and admired in Germany. He had scored something of a coup when, Schweitzer having elected to remain at Gotha, he secured Hiller as the troupe's new music director. Exactly how much this entailed for Hiller is not known, but he apparently soon discovered that the duties of music director involved more time and energy than he was willing to devote. After a falling out with Seyler, at any rate, he prevailed on Neefe to take over.

Despite the young composer's presence, Neefe's comic operas were not taken into Seyler's repertory, nor was his one-act opera *Heinrich und Lyda* of 1776, a serious work along the lines of *Walder*. Seyler did give the première of Neefe's most important score from this period, however, the melodrama *Sophonisbe*. Sophie Seyler took the title role, created specifically for her at Seyler's request.

There were other additions to Seyler's musical repertory at Dresden. In November 1776 the troupe attempted to mount Hasse's intermezzo *Piramo e Tisbe* in German – a serious work with a tragic ending whose production epitomized the repertory's drift toward seriousness and Italian style. Seyler may have been seeking to flatter the Dresden court, to whom the memory of "il caro Sassone" was still dear, but he kept the work in his offerings at Leipzig and later Frankfurt. Possibly it was Neefe who suggested that the intermezzo be taken up: he cited several examples from Hasse's works, including *Piramo e Tisbe*, in an essay "On Musical Repetition" which he published in the *Deutsches Museum* in 1776.

Apart from Neefe's melodrama, Seyler introduced only one new German opera in Saxony, a version of Beaumarchais's *Barbier de Séville* with musical numbers by his new first violinist, Friedrich Ludwig Benda – another son of the Gotha Kapellmeister. The music consists of only thirteen numbers spread over four acts. Far from reaching out for any Spanish character, young Benda's music preserves many of the features his father had been developing earlier in 1776 with *Walder* (including a rondo). In contrast to the music Beaumarchais himself had published for his comedy, Benda's numbers are mostly quite long. About half parallel vocal numbers in the original version, but with heavy alterations. The count's simple, strophic *romance* with which he introduces himself to Rosine as Lindor in act one is changed by Benda into a species of da capo aria, with the second and third couplets of Beaumarchais's text serving as A_2 and B sections. When Almaviva at last wins Rosine, he breaks into a D-major bravura aria with a traditional triadic main melody and a long cadenza on "wieder*hall*en." Even Rosine's Spanish air in young Benda's hands becomes a long, virtuosic aria with a big opening ritornello. No doubt he had Josepha and Friedrich Hellmuth in mind when composing both Rosine's and the count's arias and duets.

The departure of the Seyler company left a void in Saxony, doubly felt inasmuch as North Germany's most vital operatic composers of the 1770s, Schweitzer and Benda, were approaching the ends of their careers. As we have seen, after 1777 both sought opportunity and fame elsewhere. Central Germany by that time had little else to fall back on, with Hiller and Wolf grown silent, Reichardt at Berlin as Frederick the Great's Kapellmeister, and Neefe gone to the Rhineland with Seyler.

The operatic legacy of Seyler's years in Saxony and Thuringia was a considerable one. The principal himself neither acted nor wrote nor composed anything in his repertory, yet he had an uncanny gift for finding opportunities and the artists to exploit them. His troupe also contributed to the bridging of the gap between the two theatrical worlds of court and city in Germany during the 1770s. Most importantly, in elevating the social and intellectual status of both these worlds, they fostered an aesthetic and critical environment in which Schweitzer's and Benda's experiments in ever more serious and elevated musical form and expression could flourish. Once created in the happy conjunction of persons and events at Hannover, Weimar, Leipzig, and Gotha, the new Vorspiele, operas, and melodramas these men produced attained widespread and lasting popularity throughout Germany and in so doing set new standards for German theatrical repertories and the composers supplying to them.

In addition, new German operas felt increasing pressure from the strong competition offered by new French and Italian works which now came under the competence of the steadily improving operatists in German companies. We have already mentioned the works of Grétry and Monsigny introduced by Seyler at Gotha. The assiduous cultivation of French opera had continued under the Court Theater, bringing its offerings into line with those at Berlin, Hamburg, Frankfurt, and elsewhere in Germany. In addition, German audiences began showing an increasing fondness for opera buffa in translation, especially less farcical, more sentimental ones. Piccinni's *La buona figliuola* (1760) and Guglielmi's *La sposa fedele* (1767), both of which appear in Table 4.1, were the most popular and stand in the vanguard of an invasion which was eventually to force German librettists and composers to rethink the terms in which they defined their own operatic traditions.

Schweitzer and Benda had created lasting models of what could be done with serious opera, and the years to come were to be devoted largely to the much more difficult task of asserting a new identity for German comic opera. The proving ground for this endeavor would not be in Saxony, however, which lost with Seyler its last claim to leadership in the cultivation of North German opera, but at Berlin.

5

Prussian stirrings and Goethe's early librettos

In the preceding chapter we devoted exclusive attention to the contributions of the Seyler company and Gotha Court Theater to North German opera, which involved us with not only some of the most experimental works of the decade but also some of the most serious. We should now survey the more varied, if generally less distinguished activities going on elsewhere in the North during the halcyon days of Seyler and the Gotha Court Theater. Table 5.1 lists the North German operas written from *Alceste* to the end of 1777 exclusive of those composed for Seyler and the Gotha enterprise. In this entabulation the domination of Berlin and its Prussian provinces is overwhelming. The six most active centers are:

Berlin	15	Weimar	2
Breslau	6	Leipzig	2
Königsberg	4	Bückeburg	2

Yet while these raw figures reflect Berlin's growing prominence in North Germany, the troops she commands are by and large a scruffy, sorry lot, as witness the wholesale disappearance of the scores and librettos of many of them. For twenty-four of these thirty-nine works we have no surviving music, and not even the texts for seventeen of them. By contrast, the music survives for seven of the eight new German operas produced by Seyler and the Gotha Court Theater – in both printed and manuscript copies in most cases – and all of the texts come down to us.

The Berlin stage, 1773–1777

As we saw earlier, Koch ruled the roost at the Theater in the Behrenstrasse until his death in early 1775. His widow made an effort to carry on (by no means an uncommon occurrence in the traveling companies of eighteenth-century Germany, built more out of families than individual performers). However, Christiane Koch soon gave up, and Döbbelin, who in 1773 had been forced into a period of unsteady wandering around Prussia and Saxony, seized the moment. By skillful maneuvering he obtained not only Koch's Prussian privilege but also his theater, appurtenances, and many of his players as well.

Koch's partiality for comic opera, as we saw, had been an outspoken one,

Table 5.1. *New German operas not written for the repertories of the Seyler company or the Gotha Court Theater, 1773–1777*

REGION: Date Title	Librettist–Composer	Place of première
BERLIN:		
1773 [(*Die kranke Frau*)]	unknown–Frischmuth	Berlin
Der Kaufmann von Smyrna	Schwan–Holly	Berlin
1774 *Der Bassa von Tunis*	Henisch–Holly	Berlin
[*Der Holzhauer*]	Eschenburg–Koch	Berlin
1775 *Clarisse*	Bock–Frischmuth	Berlin
Erwin und Elmire	Goethe–André	Berlin
[*Der alte Freyer*]	André–André	Berlin
1776 *Heinrich und Lyda*	d'Arien–Neefe	Berlin
1777 [*Rosalia*]	Schink–Schubert	Berlin
[(*Pierre und Narciss*)]	unknown–Laube	Berlin
[(*Braut, Friseur, Hexe und* *Advocat in einer Person*)]	unknown–Fleischer	Berlin
[(*Deukalion und Pyrrha*)]	unknown–Laube	Berlin
[(*Der studierte Jäger*)]	unknown–Laube	Berlin
[(*Der italienische Garkoch zu Genua*)]	unknown–Schubert	Berlin
Die Bezauberten	André–André	Berlin
PRUSSIAN PROVINCES:		
1773 *Der Kaufmann von Smyrna*	Schwan–Stegmann	Königsberg
1775 (*Das redende Gemälde*)	unknown–Stegmann	Königsberg
Die Recrouten auf dem Lande	unknown–Stegmann	Königsberg
[*Das Gärtnermädchen*]	Musäus–Holly	Breslau
[(*Gelegenheit macht Diebe*)]	Henisch–Holly	Breslau
[(*Der Frühling*)]	Kellner–Feige	Breslau
[(*Die Kirmess*)]	Kellner–Feige	Breslau
1776 *Zemire und Azor*	Schubert–Baumgarten	Breslau
Erwin und Elmire	Goethe–Stegmann	Königsberg
Das Grab des Mufti	Meissner–Baumgarten	Breslau
[(*Die Erbschaft*)]	unknown–Weisflog	Sagan
SAXONY AND THURINGIA:		
1773 [(*Der bestrafte Hochmuth*)]	unknown–Fischer	Leipzig
1776 [*Zemire und Azor*]	Thümmel–Neefe	Leipzig
Erwin und Elmire	Goethe–Anna Amalia	Weimar
Ehrlichkeit und Liebe	Wagenseil–Wolf	Weimar
Die Schadenfreude	Weisse–Weimar	Erfurt
1777 [(*Der blaue Montag*)]	Berger–Rust	Dessau
LOWER SAXONY AND THE NORTH:		
1774 [*Brutus*]	Herder–J. C. F. Bach	Bückeburg
1775 [*Philoktetes*]	Herder–J. C. F. Bach	Bückeburg
1776 [(*Crispin und Eliante*)]	unknown–Krebs	Rostock
1777 [(*Der Kobold*)]	Thomas–Escherich	Stralsund
UNPERFORMED:		
1775 [*Erwin und Elmire*]	Goethe–Schweitzer	
[(*Der Holzhauer*)]	unknown–Reichardt	
1777 [(*Der Kobold*)]	Thomas–Frischmuth	

Notes to Table 5.1 (*cont.*)

NOTES:
[] – music does not survive.
() – complete German text does not survive.
[For published librettos from this preiod not set to music, see Table 5.3.]

along with a predilection for lighter comedies in his spoken repertory. In 1774 he had begun inclining more toward serious spoken drama at Berlin with the likes of Goethe's *Götz von Berlichingen* and *Clavigo*, but the same could not be said for his repertory of comic operas. As one contemporary saw it, his musical offerings actually took a turn for the worse in response to popular demand: by 1774 the Berliners' taste "had turned without any discrimination so decisively toward Singspiele, that finally not only *Jochem Tröbs* but also *Megära* and *Der hinkende Teufel*, which Henisch had brought to Koch from Prague, could be given very often and with large crowds – by which, naturally, taste suffered no small detriment."[1]

Carl Franz Henisch, a born Viennese, came to Berlin with his wife (Franziska Koch's sister) in 1773 and won "extraordinary applause"[2] in his low comic roles. Henisch had established an intimate artistic relationship at Prague with the Kapellmeister of the Brunian troupe there, Andreas Franz Holly. Three of the four librettos Holly had set at Prague were by Henisch (including a fresh translation of *The Merry Cobler*), the other being Holly's composition of Weisse's *Die Jagd*. We have already mentioned the ambivalent position of the Prussian province of Silesia as a center of German opera, poised between Saxon and Viennese example. Holly and Henisch exemplify the similar position of the German stage at Prague, largely ignored by the Hapsburg-linked patriciate and therefore inclined to look northward.

Holly followed Henisch to Berlin and became Koch's Kapellmeister sometime in 1773. He added several works of his own, mostly on his friend Henisch's texts, to the company's repertory in 1773 and 1774. When Koch died in early 1775, however, Döbbelin chose to do without the services of the Henisches or Holly, and they left Berlin for the Wäser troupe in Silesia.

Among the original North German works in Table 5.1 only Henisch's libretto *Der Bassa von Tunis* deals with an exotic or supernatural subject, although these dominate the French and South German librettos set by Northern composers during these years. As was customary, the principals of Henisch's story are Europeans. Julie, in fact, is an Italian born in Germany. She appears improbably disguised as the Bassa of Tunis, a position she uses as a vantage point from which to test the fidelity of her lover Alzindor (she has written to him, pretending to be a slave at Tunis, and hopes he will try to rescue her). Henisch introduces into this fabric several elements which will inform later North German librettos on exotic subjects. One is the overt con-

---

[1] C. M. Plümicke, *Entwurf einer Theatergeschichte von Berlin* (Berlin and Stettin, 1781), p. 275.
[2] *Gallerie von Teutschen Schauspielern*, ed. Werner, p. 64.

trasting of Western and Eastern morality. Principally this is the business of the black slave Omar, by birth an American, sold to a European, and much traveled in the world. Another element appears in the opera's opening scene, where Omar and Hassan, the overseer of the slaves, are drinking. Northern librettists never tired of portraying weak-willed Moslems infringing Mohammed's ban on wine. Bretzner's *Belmont und Constanze*, which we will study in the following chapter, is the best-known example of later elaborations on these themes.

Koch gave *Der Bassa von Tunis* nineteen times during the sixteen months it was in his repertory, making it something of a popular success. Further, it was apparently revived at some later date in an expanded three-act version. Yet in 1775 it left with Holly and Henisch when they departed Berlin, and in this respect it was not alone but part of a large-scale retrenchment by Döbbelin, Koch's successor. To illustrate musical developments at Berlin under these two principals Table 5.2 presents the musical works introduced by each from Koch's advent in 1771 until the end of 1777.[3]

Prior to the arrival of Henisch and Holly, Koch had departed from the Saxon operas of Hiller, Wolf, and Neefe only with the opéras-comiques of Monsigny, Duni, Grétry, and Philidor. The new personnel from Prague, however, brought with them not only their own wares but also works Brunian had absorbed from Viennese repertories, and in his final year Koch also turned for the first time to opera buffa.

The musical works Döbbelin retained from Koch's repertory (see the right-hand column in Part I of Table 5.2) reveal interesting patterns. The earlier Saxon operas were already in his offerings, at least the more popular among them,[4] and he added many more when he took over Koch's theater at Berlin. Döbbelin also took up nearly all the French works Koch had adopted (although he was to add no new ones until late 1778), but he dropped all of the Prague and Viennese works, even though they had been popular items. Döbbelin had apparently decided he could do without this Southern farcical tradition as well as Henisch and Holly. (As mentioned, he declined to take them on when he picked over Koch's disbanded players in 1775.) Neither Italianate style nor the farce *per se* displeased him in their works, however, since he kept both of Koch's opere buffe and also Johann André's popular one-act farce *Der Töpfer*.

Döbbelin's failure to adopt new French works during his first three years at Berlin may owe something to external circumstances. In 1774 Frederick the Great had decided to build a new playhouse at Berlin for his French company,

---

[3] Our table is derived with only a few emendations from the repertory study of Herbert Graf, *Das Repertoire der öffentlichen Opern- und Singspielbühnen in Berlin*, based largely on a collection of playbills of Koch's and Döbbelin's offerings. We have omitted occasional pieces, melodramas, and plays with incidental music.

[4] Döbbelin's repertory prior to his succeeding Koch at Berlin in 1775 has not been reconstructed. We know from Günter Meyer, *Hallisches Theater im 18. Jahrhundert* (Emsdetten, 1950) that Döbbelin performed *Lisuart und Dariolette*, *Lottchen am Hofe*, *Die Liebe auf dem Lande*, and *Die Jagd* while at Halle in May and June of 1771.

Table 5.2. *Musical works in the repertories of Koch and Döbbelin at Berlin, 1771–1777*

PART I: KOCH'S MUSICAL REPERTORY, 12 JUNE 1771–15 APRIL 1775

Berlin

Première	Title	Librettist–Composer	Place of origin	Taken up by Döbbelin
12 Jun 1771	Lottchen, das Bauermädchen am Hofe	Weisse–Hiller	Leipzig	x
18 Jun 1771	Die Jagd	Weisse–Hiller	Weimar	x
2 Jul 1771	Das Rosenfest	Heermann–Wolf	Weimar	x
13 Jul 1771	Die verwandelten Weiber	Weisse–Standfuss/ Hiller	Leipzig	x
20 Jul 1771	Der lustige Schuster	Weisse–Standfuss/ Hiller	Leipzig	x
26 Jul 1771	Lisuart und Dariolette	Schiebeler–Hiller	Leipzig	
1 Aug 1771	Der Dorfbalbier	Weisse–Hiller/ Neefe	Leipzig	x
13 Aug 1771	Die Liebe auf dem Lande	Weisse–Hiller	Leipzig	x
5 Sep 1771	Das Gärtnermädchen	Musäus–Wolf	Weimar	
14 Oct 1771	Der stolze Bauer Jochem Tröbs	Ast–Standfuss	Hamburg	
25 Nov 1771	Die Muse	Schiebeler–Hiller	Leipzig	
13 Dec 1771	Die Apotheke	Engel–Neefe	BERLIN	
17 Feb 1772	Der Aerndtekranz	Weisse–Hiller	Leipzig	x
12 May 1772	Der Deserteur ·	Sedaine–Monsigny	Paris	x
15 Jun 1772	Die Dorfdeputierten	Heermann–Wolf	Weimar	x
5 Aug 1772	Das Milchmädchen	Anseaume–Duni	Paris	x
17 Aug 1772	Der Krieg	Ramler/Weisse– Hiller	BERLIN	
5 Apr 1773	Die Jubelhochzeit	Weisse–Hiller	BERLIN	
26 May 1773	Erast und Lucinde	Marmontel–Grétry	Paris	x
2 Jul 1773	Sancho Panssa	Poinsinet–Philidor	Paris	
7 Jul 1773	Die kranke Frau	after Gellert– Frischmuth	BERLIN	
16 Oct 1773	Die Einsprüche	Michaelis–Neefe	BERLIN	
22 Oct 1773	Bastien und Bastienne	Favart–parody	Paris	x
13 Nov 1773	Der Kaufmann von Smyrna	Schwan–Holly	BERLIN	x
20 Nov 1773	Der Zauberer	Henisch–Holly	Prague	
6 Jan 1774	Der Bassa von Tunis	Henisch–Holly	BERLIN	
15 Feb 1774	Der hinkende Teufel	Kurz–Haydn	Vienna	
20 Feb 1774	Der Holzhauer	Eschenburg–Koch	BERLIN	
30 Mar 1774	Der kluge Mann	after the French–?	?	
31 May 1774	Das redende Gemälde	Anseaume–Grétry	Paris	x
18 Jun 1774	Das Schnupftuch	Henisch–Büchel	Prague	
25 Jul 1774	Mägera, die fürchterliche Hexe	Haffner–Böhm	Brno (?)	
13 Oct 1774	Das Gespenst	Henisch–Holly	Prague	
10 Nov 1774	Die Nacht	Goldoni–Piccinni	Lisbon	x
19 Dec 1774	Das grosse Loos	Bertuch–Wolf	Gotha	
14 Feb 1775	Der Töpfer	André–André	Hanau	x
8 Apr 1775	Robert und Kalliste	Chiari–Guglielmi	Venice	x

Table 5.2 (*cont.*)

PART II: DÖBBELIN'S MUSICAL REPERTORY, 17 APRIL 1775–2 DECEMBER 1777

Berlin

Première	Title	Librettist–Composer	Place of origin
4 May 1775	Die Herrschaftsküche auf dem Lande	?–Jommelli	?
26 May 1775	Clarisse	Bock–Frischmuth	BERLIN
29 May 1775	Der bestrafte Hochmuth	?–K. L. Fischer	Leipzig
17 Jul 1775	Erwin und Elmire	Goethe–André	BERLIN[a]
17 Aug 1775	Elysium	Jacobi–Schweitzer	Hannover
2 Oct 1775	Der alte Freyer	André–André	BERLIN
26 Mar 1776	Heinrich und Lyda	d'Arien–Neefe	BERLIN
8 Mar 1777	Rosalia	Schink–Schubert	BERLIN
10 Apr 1777	Pierre und Narcisse	?–Laube	BERLIN
17 Apr 1777	Matz und Anne	?–Laube	BERLIN
21 Apr 1777	Braut, Friseur, Hexe und Advocat in einer Person	?–Fleischer	BERLIN
28 Apr 1777	Il marito giocatore[b]	Salvi(?)–Pergolesi	?
5 May 1777	Der Kapellmeister und die Schülerin	?–Laube	BERLIN
12 May 1777	Deukalion und Pyrrha	after St. Foix–Laube	BERLIN
26 May 1777	Der adelige Braut und der bürgerliche Bräutigam	?–?	?
11 Jun 1777	Der studierte Jäger	?–Laube	BERLIN
1 Jul 1777	Philemon und Baucis	?–?	?
12 Jul 1777	Der italienische Garkoch zu Genua	?–Schubert/ Laube	BERLIN
8 Sep 1777	Das gute Mädchen	Goldoni–Piccinni	Rome
18 Oct 1777	Die Bezauberten	André–André	BERLIN

[a] Privately performed at Frankfurt in May 1775, possibly without music.
[b] German recitative and Italian arias.

and the new (and rather ineptly designed) structure at the Gendarmenplatz was completed and inaugurated on 22 April 1776. But the French troupe which performed there was dismissed at Frederick's order in 1778, after which Döbbelin began introducing new opéras-comiques once again, beginning with Grétry's universally popular *Zémire et Azor*.

As Döbbelin expanded his spoken and musical offerings his company grew apace. It counted thirty-nine persons in April 1775, to which twelve were added from the old Koch troupe, and seven more in 1776, bringing his ranks to fifty-eight (or sixteen more than Seyler had at that time). Not only had Döbbelin hired many new singers, he also sought to improve his orchestra. In July of 1777 Johann André took over leadership of Döbbelin's twenty-man orchestra. Three of his comic operas were already in the troupe's repertory, and his setting of Goethe's *Erwin und Elmire* especially, given fifteen times in its first year at Berlin, had prompted Döbbelin to lure André there from Offenbach. (We shall take up *Erwin und Elmire* later in this chapter.)

Once secure in his eventual position as principal music director, André dominated the German operatic scene at Berlin for the next seven years. In 1777 he began cautiously, however, adding to the three operas by him Döbbelin had already adopted (plus two plays with incidental music) only a Vorspiel for the birthday of Prince Friedrich Wilhelm and a cheerful two-act comic opera, *Die Bezauberten*. André, who had translated countless comedies and opéras-comiques for Marchand in the Rhineland, provided himself here with his own close translation of Madame Favart's *Jeannot et Jeanette, ou Les Ensorcelés*, a harmless story of a naïve young pair of country lovers whom a blacksmith *cum* horse doctor and a local noblewoman seek to separate by convincing them that they are bewitched rather than in love. The process whereby the lovers "cure" themselves loses nothing of its benign humor and delicate eroticism in André's translation. And music is allowed to play an integral role. Peter and Hannchen first think of following the example of the frolicking sheep and warbling birds by singing together a Romanze-like story: a maiden chased a butterfly and fell into a brook, a lad sprang out and saved her, she took him home and now she no longer chases butterflies. These measures do not help their mutual yearning so they try sleeping on a grassy knoll. In an action duet they begin to inch closer together, then hold hands, and finally, when Peter kisses Hannchen's hands, their pain begins to abate.

Apart from André's opera, Döbbelin's early Berlin repertory introduced only a handful of new works by German composers. Earlier, we had briefly mentioned Johann Christian Frischmuth's *Das Mondenreich*, which Döbbelin produced at Berlin in 1769. Frischmuth's second opera *Die kranke Frau*, also in one act, saw its first production there as well (in 1773 by Koch), and so did his setting of Bock's *Clarisse*. Though dated 1771 in the manuscript keyboard reduction at Berlin, it does not seem to have been produced before Döbbelin mounted it in 1775. Its style differs little from that of the amateur Uber's setting of 1771. The reduction is so spare, however, as to indicate little beyond Frischmuth's melodic style, as shown in Example 5.1. The presence of dialogue cues and tie-overs suggests that this manuscript was used in connection with a performance of *Clarisse*, but Frischmuth's whereabouts in 1771, the date carried by the manuscript reduction, are not known. He seems to have had no direct contact with the Berlin stage until 1782, when he joined Döbbelin's company. In 1784 he succeeded André as the troupe's music director.

Joseph Schubert, born on the Saxon–Bohemian border and trained at Prague as well as Berlin, collaborated when only twenty with Johann Friedrich Schink on *Rosalia*, an adaptation of Marmontel's *Silvain*. A correspondent for the Gotha *Theater-Journal* found Schubert's setting derivative, to put it mildly:

Schink's *Rosalia* has found a young composer at Berlin who in his entrance into the musical world, like the crow in the fable, has decked himself with all the foreign feathers possible; for there is probably not an operetta from which one could not find

Example 5.1 Frischmuth: *Clarisse*. Song of Fritzgen, act 3.
"Let this stranger sit by your side, to reconcile your hard fate and his adverse fortune through tears and laments."

entire passages in *Rosalia*. This operetta was given by the Döbbelin company on March 8th in this setting with little applause.[5]

Schink also contributed to Döbbelin's stage in 1777 a new melodrama on the beloved subject *Inkle und Yariko*, set by Friedrich Wilhelm Rust. It is one of the genre's first departures from subjects drawn from classical antiquity and includes several songs as well as accompanied dialogue. Schink also wrote the text of the celebratory Vorspiel composed by André for Friedrich Wilhelm's birthday that September.

Finally, we must direct attention to a shabby little barrage of intermezzi introduced at Berlin in April, May, and June of 1777. As their titles indicate, these eight works are for two persons (see Table 5.2). Some have recitative throughout instead of spoken dialogue and one even has Italian arias with German recitative. For none of them is the librettist identified. A reporter on the Berlin stage explained how these works came to be given at Döbbelin's theater:

[Anton Berger] came to Berlin in April of 1777 with Madame [Maria Josepha] Vink and made an agreement with Herr Döbbelin to perform twice a week in his theater and in return to give him a quarter of the receipts each time. The pieces which both persons gave for roughly two months are what the Italians call musical Intermezzi.

[5] *Theater-Journal für Deutschland* 1 (1777): 88.

They consist of recitatives and arias. After this period both were engaged by Herr Döbbelin so they are now on the payroll just like the other members.[6]

Both singers left, however, in January 1778.

None of these works seems to have survived, and there is a strong possibility that they had earlier been given elsewhere by Berger and Vink. The composers are apparently unconnected with Berlin and Döbbelin. His music director prior to André's arrival in mid-1777 was an obscure Herr Schindler, who was not a composer (one source designates him the troupe's "singing master").

Other Prussian and Saxon developments

Apart from those for Berlin, the German operas in Table 5.1 stem largely from the Prussian-controlled provinces of Silesia and East Prussia. The Wäser company continued to perform at Breslau, where their privilege gave them the exclusive right to theatrical representations, but they left each summer to supplement their modest receipts. In 1775 they toured with good success at Leipzig, Magdeburg, and Potsdam, where Crown Prince Friedrich Wilhelm attended every evening. A venture to the Kärntnerthor Theater at Vienna the following summer, however, proved a disaster. While at Berlin in 1775 Wäser had welcomed both Henisch and Holly when Döbbelin elected not to engage them. The same year he also took on the bass Johann Gottlieb Feige and his wife, and that year Holly and Feige each provided him with two new comic operas, of which not a note remains.

Wäser also produced two operas published by a Prussian lieutenant resident in Silesia, Gotthilf von Baumgarten, both of them based on French librettos. The German version of Marmontel's opéra–ballet *Zémire et Azor* which he set, by Karl Emil Schubert, follows its model scrupulously, honoring all of Marmontel's musical items without addition or subtraction. The work is dubbed a "Romantisch-komische Oper" in both the published keyboard reduction and the libretto, apparently an allusion to the integral role the marvelous plays – this is, at any rate, the common ground it shares with its sole German predecessor bearing the designation "romantisch," *Lisuart und Dariolette*.

Baumgarten's Sinfonia follows the common opéra-comique model of outer exposition and recapitulation sections (Allegro) flanking an Andante middle section in the subdominant (in other words, a ternary aria structure).

---

[6] *Ibid.* 4 (1777): 143. Schütze, *Hamburgische Theater-Geschichte*, states that Berger and Vink gave intermezzi at Hamburg with the help of the tenor Liebich and music director Frischmuth in 1767 (p. 346), but Madame Vink was said not to have made her stage debut before 1770 (*Gallerie von Teutschen Schauspielern*, ed. Werner, pp. 158, 377). Schütze describes *Matz und Anne* as a hen-pecking piece, adapted from the Italian, in which a man and wife insult and beat one another.

The vocal numbers differ very little from Hiller's except in externals: for example, most of them carry German rather than Italian tempo markings, and the rather exceptional key of b-flat minor appears in Ali's aria "Noch beb ich vor Zittern und Zagen" at the beginning of act four. In the same act, expanding on Marmontel's lead, Schubert created a broad accompagnato-aria-accompagnato complex for the suicidal Azor which links directly to Zemire's ensuing aria:

Recit. (Mässig)		Aria (Azor: Klagend)		Recit. (_____)		Aria (Zemire)
a	c	F	V/B♭	g	c	F

Such a dramatic musical canvas, never found in Weisse, suggests French influence and distinguishes Schubert's libretto from earlier German practice, even if the same cannot be said for Baumgarten's music here. The composer does follow Grétry in linking act one (at Azor's palace) with act two (at Sander's country house) with an entr'acte depicting the flight of Sander and Ali on a magic cloud. Not only does this entr'acte smooth over the disrupted unity of place for squeamish neo-Aristotelians, as Marmontel perhaps intended, it recalls in Baumgarten's hands the key and motives of the ritornello of the first aria in act one (where, as in Marmontel, the music is specifically requested to contradict Ali's wishful statement that the storm is over).

Baumgarten's second opera, *Das Grab des Mufti*, also competed with a popular Grétry original, in this case Falbaire's *Les Deux Avares* (1770). Baumgarten sets a translation published in 1776 by the Saxon August Gottlieb Meissner, which had carried in its preface a note on Hiller's intention of setting it.[7] In his keyboard reduction Baumgarten explains that his knowledge of this had at first dissuaded him from publishing his own setting, but an over-zealous friend had announced it in print, and delays in the appearance of Hiller's setting seemed to confirm reports "that Herr Hiller, after his total falling out with Seyler, would leave his scarcely begun work uncompleted."

Like *Zémire et Azor*, Falbaire's two-act libretto *Les Deux Avares* adopts an exotic setting (a street scene in Smyrna with a pyramidic grave of a Mufti in the center), but here magic plays no role. Instead we have a comedy of character: two old misers make plans to plunder the treasure buried with the Mufti while the niece of one connives to run off with her lover Jérôme, the cousin of the other. The lovers, both wards of the misers, are aided by the servant-confidante Madelon. All five of these principals are French. The second act brings in the only Turks in the opera, a drunken band of Janissaries, to introduce a string of comic complications.

---

[7] *Das Grab des Mufti; oder: die zwey Geizigen* (Leipzig, 1776). The preface is dated Leipzig, 8 March 1776. In his letter of dedication to Engel (by then a professor of philosophy at the Joachimsthal in Berlin) Meissner explains that he is offering him "the first fruits of the field," not necessarily the best.

The story as Falbaire constructed it would not do in the eyes of Meissner. His own version, Meissner observes, while unable to redress all the flaws in Falbaire's well-known piece, seeks to improve it with "wholly new songs, a third new scenes, more dialogue instead of the almost continuous singing, and a total reworking of the character of Karl and Wilhelmine." A literal translation had already been made by André for the Marchand company, retaining Grétry's music, but Meissner was more interested in serving Hiller, "who saw this work in manuscript and promised immediately to give it through his composition advantages which it does not now have." Whatever these may have been, they could not be as material as the ones Falbaire allowed Grétry. Especially Meissner's point about less "continuous singing" and more dialogue harks back to the restrictive policies of Weisse.

Baumgarten's setting again approximates Hiller's style – indeed, this was precisely the reason he so feared comparison with a setting by the grand master of Saxon opera of the same text. There are several changes from Baumgarten's earlier opera, in line with the arch comedy of this second libretto. The da capo arias he had included in *Zemire und Azor*, for instance, are missing entirely, and in general everything is more succinct. The comic business awaiting the audience is prefigured in the three-movement overture, in particular the final Allegro, marked "droll, in the character of Madelon" (whose first aria is also marked "droll").

Wilhelmine's e-minor Romanze in act two (an ariette in Falbaire) begins with a tune appropriate to the genre which exploits the modal interplay of tonic minor and relative major (Example 5.2). Baumgarten uses the same binary tune for the Romanze's first three stanzas but introduces variations in the last three. Perhaps these changes reveal mild discontent with the primitive strophic Romanze as Hiller had practiced it; at any rate, they offer musical

Example 5.2 Baumgarten: *Das Grab des Mufti*. Romanze, act 2.
"More tenderly than Tell and Lyda two souls never loved one another; he was her only hope and she his whole happiness."

reactions to the little tale Wilhelmine sings to Karl: Tell and Lyda, who passionately loved one another, finally gained their parents' consent to marry, but at their wedding feast a storm arose, lightning struck Lyda dead, and Tell, taking her in his arms, died too.

That Karl wipes a tear from his eye after the last stanza strikes one as odd: such mortal forebodings are out of place in Falbaire's witty comedy; but a German opera without a Romanze was unthinkable, and Meissner probably introduced it in order to ply this deep main channel of Saxon opera. He reveals his distance from modern French tendencies even more strikingly in the ensuing trio. Falbaire gave Grétry a delightful action ensemble here in which Jérôme is lowered into the well, and Grétry artfully describes this descent with the violins. Meissner gave his composer instead a static moment of anxious foreboding, enlarging on what he had already done in the preceding Romanze.

Both of these two French-derived operas by Baumgarten made no changes in the spirit of Saxon opera, and in East Prussia a similar conservative situation obtained. Here the principal troupe was that of Franz Schuch the Younger, whose death at age thirty in 1771 had left the company in the hands of his widow Karoline and the troupe's operatic talent, the tenor-composer Carl David Stegmann. A native Saxon who had broken into acting with Wäser in Silesia, Stegmann produced a series of four early operas in the East Prussian cities the Schuch company toured, where they met with great favor. Three of them appeared in published keyboard reductions.

In the late 1760s Schuch had done without a musical repertory at Danzig, Königsberg, and Mitau. But once introduced there, German comic opera made many fast friends – including Immanuel Kant, who took such pleasure in *Der lustige Schuster* that he seldom missed a performance.[8] A Danzig critic named Gomperz, writing in 1773, felt his bile rise when even thinking about this new theatrical phenomenon, but especially full-length operas with pretensions to the heroic. What irked him most was that these works seemed insusceptible of the critic's art: "They say: it's only an operetta! Fine! Farewell, dear theatrical rules! Go back to your teachers Diderot, Lessing, Sonnenfels and other artistic judges! Tell them that we don't need rules any more, for we have operettas!" Thereupon he pointed out indignantly that at Königsberg in 1773 *Der Aerndtekranz* was given three times running, followed by *Matz und Anna* and *Amors Guckkasten*. Would this ever happen with the best comedies or tragedies? "What do all these operettas teach us? What virtues do they stress?"[9]

The structure of Stegmann's early operas, both musical and literary, is the familiar pattern of Weisse and Hiller. *Die Recrouten auf dem Lande*, for example, is peppered with little songs (thirty-two of them) set quite apart from the ongoing intrigue. On the other hand, in addition to the pair of

---

[8] E[rnst] A[ugust] Hagen, *Geschichte des Theaters in Preussen* (Königsberg, 1854), p. 313.

[9] Quoted in *ibid.*, pp. 311–12.

country lovers and benevolent protector of the wronged, the plot also breathes the more farcical spirit of Engel, Michaelis, and Gotter (a foolish schoolmaster seeks to get his heart-throb's lover recruited).

Like Baumgarten, Stegmann also recomposed a translation of one of Grétry's most successful opéras-comiques (*Das redende Gemälde*, a German version of *Le Tableau parlant*). In this case as with Meissner's reworking of *Les Deux Avares*, the original was expanded considerably, from Anseaume's one-act *parade* into a two-act opera with seven new vocal numbers and an entr'acte. Stegmann does not fare so badly in comparison with his worthy Belgian predecessor in the opera's grandest number, Frontin's storm aria, which modulates wildly in response to the vivid and extended poetic text (Stegmann also had the number printed in three staves rather than two in order to do his hyperactive accompaniment justice).

The cast of five sorts out into the conventional pairs of serious and light lovers and the old guardian Cassandre, but in the French opera the leading tenor has no solo numbers at all and just one duet with the heroine. French opéra-comique in general observes few hierarchical niceties with respect to distribution of arias. German opera tended to trade in more numbers with fewer ensembles among them. All six of the numbers added in Stegmann's version are solo pieces (and Colombine's interjections are eliminated from Frontin's storm aria to boot). That three of the six new arias went to the tenor Frontin strongly suggests that Stegmann may have composed the role for himself.

Stegmann's other two operas from this period, and the *Clarisse* he wrote for Hamburg in 1778 as well, set texts already composed by other North Germans. He and Holly took up Christian Friedrich Schwan's *Der Kaufmann von Smyrna* at nearly the same time, in 1773, and both published keyboard reductions of their scores. Reichardt reviewed Holly's, which appeared in 1775, two years after Stegmann's, and declared that the existence of the latter made the issuing of Holly's "wretched thing" so much worse. Reichardt surmised that Holly had written down here the Italian comic operas he had heard at Prague as a young man.[10] The opera in this first version (which Schwan later lengthened to three acts) is brief – nine musical numbers in Stegmann's setting, ten in Holly's – and no doubt owed much of its popularity to its voguish plot concerning a noble Turk whose generosity frees a Frenchman and his bride from a merciless slave-dealer. Finally, Stegmann also published his setting of Goethe's *Erwin und Elmire*, which took its place alongside those of André, Schweitzer, Anna Amalia, and Carl Christian Agthe. We shall return to his music in considering Goethe's first libretto later in this chapter.

Next to nothing is known about the comic operas produced in the Lower Saxon towns of Rostock and Stralsund, and also those at smaller central German cities such as Dessau and Sagan. Rudolf Czach discusses Friedrich

[10] *Allgemeine deutsche Bibliothek* 33:1 (1778):173.

Wilhelm Rust's *Der blaue Montag* (Dessau, 1777) on the basis of both a libretto and score of the work, both of which seem to have disappeared. It was clearly a low comic work in which a husband and wife berate each other for their vices.[11] Rust, apart from his duties as director of the ducal Kapelle at Dessau, was an indispensable participant in an amateur theater there, first formed in 1774. A report to the *Theater-Journal* noted with approval "how far this amateur society has already advanced, especially in operettas, in which it surpasses the best theaters, although performing only seldom."[12] Later we shall discuss a similar enterprise begun in 1776 at the Weimar court.

Apart from Seyler's visits, Leipzig saw little new musical activity in its theaters. For the two new works produced there that are listed in Table 5.1 we do not have music, and indeed nothing at all is known about *Der bestrafte Hochmuth*. It was composed and perhaps written by the theatrical principal Karl Ludwig Fischer, who visited Leipzig with his small troupe during the winter of 1773 and 1774 for about a month and played at Wäser's comedy house at the Grimm Gate. This opera, whose cast consists of a father, his daughter, her lover, and a scissors-grinder, was perhaps not far different from Fischer's standard fare – "now extemporized, now written pieces, one as absurd as the next."[13]

The other Leipzig opera was a different matter. The company of Simon Koberwein, otherwise active in Bohemia and Austria, came to Leipzig in 1775 and gave a new work by Neefe, *Zemire und Azor*, Marmontel's text now freshly translated by the Leipziger August Moritz von Thümmel. Why Koberwein ventured northward to Leipzig is not clear, but the Saxon privilege may have had a hand in his appearance. Even as he gave Neefe's new opera on 5 March 1775, Seyler was negotiating for this privilege at the Dresden court, and the date of Koberwein's performance was the name day of the Elector of Saxony. Seyler of course won the privilege, and Koberwein never returned to Saxony.

Unset librettos and the issues they raise

The picture we see emerging from our study of the ranks assembled in Table 5.1 contrasts sharply with the high tide of innovation we witnessed in the preceding chapter. The terrain is not utterly bleak, nonetheless, and at the

---

[11] *Friedrich Wilhelm Rust* (Essen, [1927]). Italian provenance of this sort of farce is likely (cf. Note 6 above), but Czach also mentions a Romanze about a shrewish wife who after her death must go around as a poltergeist, which appears to be firmly in the German traditions of the genre.

[12] *Theater-Journal für Deutschland* 4 (1777): 148. The group had already performed *Die Muse*, *Der Töpfer*, and *Der Kaufmann von Smyrna* in a little theater erected for them; then at a bigger one opened on 10 August 1776 they produced *Der Aerndtekranz*, *Die Dorfgala*, and *Ariadne auf Naxos* (to which Rust composed a prologue).

[13] *Gallerie von Teutschen Schauspielern*, ed. Werner, pp. 49, 290.

end of this chapter we shall consider two bright spots in the persons of two of Germany's greatest literary eminences of the age, Herder and Goethe. First, however, in order to offer the widest possible view of the literary background against which their activities as librettists may be viewed, we should pause here to consider briefly a group of librettos which we have ignored until now – published texts which were never set to music. This phenomenon, which seems to have been far more extensive in Germany than in the rest of Europe, invites speculation on the directions explored by would-be librettists but not seconded by North German composers. Table 5.3 lists the nine works in this category to appear during the period we are considering:[14]

Table 5.3   *Uncomposed published North Geran librettos, 1773–1777*

Date of publication	Title	Librettist	Place of publication
1773	*Die Frühlingsnacht*	J. W. A. Schöpfel	Frankfurt and Leipzig
1773	*Das vornehme Suschen*	G***	Chemnitz
1773	*Das Testament*	G***	Chemnitz
1774	*Palaemon*	J. W. A. Schöpfel	Frankfurt and Leipzig
1775	*Das Urtheil des Midas*	C. M. Wieland	Weimar[a]
1775	*Die Dorfkirmse*	unknown	unknown
1775	*Jeder Topf find't seinen Deckel*	unknown	Magdeburg
1777	*Achills zürnender Schatten*	T. B. Berger	Leipzig
1777	*So prelt man alte Füchse*	Mylius and d'Arien	Halle

[a]Published in Wieland's periodical *Der Teutsche Merkur* 1775:1 (January), pp. 1–19.

Die Frühlingsnacht, the earliest of these, is often mentioned owing to its preface, where the new-won pre-eminence of comic opera over spoken tragedy and comedy in Germany is attributed to "the tender feeling" ("das weichliche Gefühl") which the genre arouses. Schöpfel, a Leipziger, fairly scorns opera buffa in exalting the works of Hiller and Weisse, and he openly confesses his desire to imitate the latter in this "the first-born of my muse." The one long act of *Die Frühlingsnacht* distributes its eighteen numbers among only three characters – Dorchen, a farmer's daughter who must stay up all night to keep the animals out of the family's grain field; Heinrich, her lover, whom she must meet secretly, since her father opposes their marriage on the grounds that Heinrich is poor; and the father Andreas, who is brought to see reason in the end when his own son runs off to join the army and he is left without a strong back to turn his soil. The only ensemble is the closing Rundgesang – there is not even a single duet. The arias favor the heroine (nine

---

[14] Omitted are works never seriously intended for stage production, notably satires or polemic pieces masquerading as music dramas such as *Wieland und seine Abonnenten* (Weimar, 1775). Johann Georg Jacobi's attack on his critics, *Die Dichter, eine Oper gespielt in der Unterwelt* (Halberstadt, 1772) is actually a poem.

for Dorchen, including the Romanze, five for Andreas, three for Heinrich), and are wholly peripheral to Schöpfel's overlong story. The libretto's sole strong point is its evocative nocturnal setting.

Das vornehme Suschen and *Das Testament*, published together, are country cousins to Schöpfel's initial effort. Their preface, replete with abject begging for criticism of "these flawed trifles," confesses that the author is young and inexperienced. Both again adhere to Weisse's conception of North German opera as spoken comedy seasoned with songs, but in a more farcical spirit. Although the contrasting of corrupt city morals and sound rustic ones is still the relentless burden of *Das vornehme Suschen*, the author intensifies this contrast by exaggerating his characters beyond anything Weisse had thought proper. The title role, a widow whose head has been turned by visits to Leipzig, eventually makes a total fool of herself in aping urban morals, manners, and fashions – crowned by the revelation that the Frenchified Monsieur Flink whom she intends as her daughter Dorchen's spouse is an impostor, a former servant of the local prince who had run off with his master's silver service.

Suschen's foolishness is eclipsed by that of the schoolmaster Bakel, a character already developed by those of Weisse's contemporaries who had opted for the more farcical touch Weisse had abandoned in the 1760s. Flink teases Bakel in one scene about a scathing review of his learned tract *Gemeinnützige Käseform* (*A Cheese-Mould of Public Utility*). Later at Suschen's garden coffee hour the others play catch with the schoolmaster's collected works, *Bakeliana*; his wife cuffs him on the ear when he tries to order her around; and he is made out to be an arch-coward in a duel with Flink's companion, Herr Badin.

Had a composer tried to set *Das vornehme Suschen*, he would have faced the task of writing a record-breaking fifty-four musical numbers for an opera already bloated with dialogue. Many of the song texts are of the short, aphoristic sort which Weisse had already popularized; others relate all sorts of anecdotes, including two sung by Dorchen to her young beau Christel about babies born out of wedlock to various country girls.

Das Testament explores the same tendency to farce in a rather more mechanistic plot. Lieschen, the daughter of a rich farmer, confronts a series of wooers – a touchy, aging captain; a poor young poet, timid and unassuming; a laconic bailiff; a blustering Junker (whose first act on stage is an improper attempt on Lieschen's bosom); and her true sweetheart Fridel. After each has vaunted his merits as a potential husband, Lieschen's father Peter has his will drawn up before them, leaving everything but a small yearly stipend to a neighbor whose house had burnt down. Only Fridel will have Lieschen on these terms, whereupon Peter blesses their union and tears up the will. Again the humor tends to the low comic (one critic described it as "a farce like those which used to be extemporized"[15]), reflected as well in the

---

[15] *Allgemeine deutsche Bibliothek* 24:1 (1775): 100. The reviewer is Johann Carl Musäus.

descriptive surnames for the parade of suitors: Hauptmann Hohlmilch, Junker Pflugschaar, Schösser Sportel, and the poet Seltenreich.

All of the three works just discussed are long texts by inexperienced young men with no known theatrical connections. Schöpfel's Arcadian drama *Palaemon* may also be included among them, for even though he set it in misty antiquity and invoked the supernatural to restore his hero's sight, Schöpfel (inspired by Gessner and his own "enchantment with nature and innocence") leads his flock of indistinguishable shepherds and shepherdesses to a point which makes an obscenity of virtue. If the neglect of all these texts proves a point, it is possibly that the old order had already saturated its market among Northern composers and audiences, both with rural romances and farcical comedies.

The other farce in Table 5.3, *So prelt man alte Füchse*, stands apart from these works in spirit, if not in technical construction, by drawing for the first time on a major source of inspiration for the years to come – Molière. Into Wilhelm Christhelf Siegmund Mylius's close translation of the timelessly popular *Les Fourberies de Scapin* the young dramatist Bernhard Christoph d'Arien wove twenty-five musical numbers, all of them brief. A ballet concludes each of the opera's three acts. Mylius restored to the *commedia dell'arte* masks lurking behind Molière's cast their original Italian names, including Harlequin, Brighella, Dottore Balanzoni, and Pantalone de Bisognosi.

As mentioned in Chapter 2, in 1737 the Neuber troupe had staged at Leipzig a formal banning of Harlequin from their theater, but it was more the irregularities and vulgarities of improvised comedy than the masks themselves whose day was passing, and later theatrical critics were not slow to defend Harlequin and his lot as worthy purveyors of a hearty if uninstructive brand of humor. Heinrich Justus Möser earned Lessing's praise with just such an effort in *Harlekin, oder Vertheidigung des Groteske-Komischen* of 1761, which saw a second edition in 1777, the same year Mylius's libretto appeared. Möser also argues in defense of opera, stressing the decisive role of music in creating the reality in which the characters live. Yet, although *So prelt man alte Füchse* is both libretto and harlequinade, it attracted no composer, and doubtless for good reason; there is nothing in it for the music to do – no situations to develop, only the most fleeting emotions which vanish quickly into the tightly torqued dialogue. The "decisive role" of which Möser wrote required a differently fashioned libretto, to begin with, and then techniques German composers had not yet tried to master. In a nutshell, these were to be the genre's problems for the next two decades.

Möser came to join other North Germans who firmly opposed the combining of spoken dialogue and song, and in addition he favored mythological or otherwise remote topics as the most fitting for opera. Both of these desiderata are fulfilled in the two remaining operas in our Table 5.3. The first, Wieland's *Das Urtheil des Midas*, is little more than a farce decked out in the garb of verse dialogue and a collection of gods, muses, fauns, and citizens of ancient Phrygia in order to send up artistic delusions of grandeur and aesthetic incompetence. Long-eared Pan has challenged Apollo to a singing contest and has stacked the deck by naming as judge his waddling, prattling friend King Midas. Pan more or less Beckmessers his way through his prize song "with much gesticulation," interrupted by Midas's cries of bravo. Apollo realizes the score but good-naturedly sings his elegant recitative and aria anyway, after which Midas gives the crown to Pan. Apollo, observing that their judge must not go unrewarded, causes a pair of ass's ears to appear on Midas's head. Even Pan thinks them rather smart and everyone forms a circle around the enraged Midas as the fauns offer to take him into their order.

One is tempted to assume that autobiographical considerations lay behind Wieland's adaptation of Lafont's *Le Jugement d'Apollon et de Pan par Midas* (1721). His *Abderiten* of 1778 represents an outstanding example of this penchant in his writings, and even in *Alceste* there are parallels with his own family.[16] Goethe is only one of a younger generation of detractors upon whom Wieland may have wished the ass's ears which crown Midas.[17] Whatever his design, the connection of art and personal experience at play here is far more pervasive and inescapable in Goethe's own writings, and, as we shall see shortly, did not leave his early operas untouched.

Finally, we find in Traugott Benjamin Berger's *Achills zürnender Schatten* of 1777 the first attempt by a North German librettist to follow the lead of *Alceste* in exploring full-length verse opera set in antiquity. Though contemporary reviewers took scant note of it, the twenty-three-year-old Berger's libretto (dedicated "to all musical actors") is a daring experiment in transferring five-act verse tragedy to the German operatic stage. Musical inspiration could have come only from Gluck's operas – for example, in the participation of the chorus in thirteen of the text's thirty-four numbers (which are not distinguished in the print) including the concluding number of each of the opera's five acts. In good operatic tradition there are just five principals – Agamemnon, Ulysses, Pyrrhus, Hecuba, and Andromache. As in *Alceste*,

[16] Late in life Wieland reminisced to Böttiger, "My wife had been dangerously ill and had, as it were, returned from the Underworld. So I suddenly hit upon Alceste, whom my Euripides had made so agreeable to me . . . I was especially pleased with the idea of giving Alceste two children, since I myself had only two at that time." *Literarische Zustände*, vol. 1, p. 227.

[17] Just after the appearance of *Das Urtheil des Midas*, under date 27 January 1775, Friedrich Heinrich Jacobi wrote to Wieland from Frankfurt, where he was staying with Goethe, and energetically denied that "the extraordinary praise Goethe gave your cantata of Apollo in *Midas* is persiflage. O, a thousand times could I place my hand over my heart on this point and swear that this approval was as entire and deep as it can be." *Friedrich Heinrich Jacobi's auserlesener Briefwechsel* (Leipzig, 1825–7), vol. 1, p. 199. Wieland had perhaps not entirely forgiven Goethe his satire on *Alceste*, and in general he opposed all the young Turks who adopted "the tone of Herder in our prose," which he described to Jacobi as "the affectation, pursued everywhere it is possible, of giving dignity, grandeur, beauty, and even *grace* to the condition of savagery and barbarity" (*ibid.*, letter of 9 December 1774, p. 196).

the two children do not have speaking roles, but no longer are they present merely to lend familial poignancy to a tearful tableau. Polyxena, the daughter of Hecuba, must be run through by Ulysses's sword to placate the shade of Achilles, and Astyanax, the son of Hector and Andromache, is cast from a cliff so that the Greeks may obtain favorable winds to return home. Throughout Berger's stern drama all the principals and even the chorus give vent to extreme emotions of a kind Wieland had unequivocally ruled out of opera's sphere.[18] Yet there was as yet nowhere in Germany for such a work to strike root; in the next two decades, however, we shall encounter classical musical tragedies in the North prefigured by this impressive and daring, if unpolished, work. In spirit, the only Northern predecessors of *Achills zürnender Schatten* were two works Berger could scarcely have known anything about, the two operatic librettos completed in 1774 by Johann Gottfried Herder.

Herder and German opera

In a much quoted dithyramb from his *Journal meiner Reise im Jahr 1769* Herder exclaims: "O, a German opera to be created anew! on a human foundation and basis; with human music and declamation and embellishment, but with feeling, feeling; o grand purpose! grand task!"[19] However, he was talking about something that the German stage had not shown the slightest inclination to pursue, and his comments were an exasperated reaction to the very genre from which German opera chiefly drew inspiration – French comic opera. This he dismissed acerbicly as a genre for deaf people who see, and Italian opera as fare for blind people who hear.

Herder could have been speaking to no one but himself (he had no intention of publishing his journal, which did not appear in print until 1846). And three years later he in fact set about this "grand task." In nearly every respect, his methods and ideals ran counter to North German norms in 1772. To begin with, he chose an utterly noble, tragic figure from Roman history – Brutus. Nor was it the historian in Herder who prompted this choice, but the Shakespearean. "Brutus!" he wrote to his fiancée Karoline Flachsland in 1771 of *Julius Caesar*, "noble in everything – more I will not say, but his portrait lies very deep in my heart!"[20] Second, he cast his drama in verse, but such inflamed verses as neither Metastasio nor Wieland would ever have dreamt of writing. They answer perfectly, however, to Herder's designation of one draft of the opera: "words strewn about, for music." Third, he put much of the responsibility for the drama's effectiveness on the composer's shoulders. The

---

[18] In the "Briefe an einen Freund über das deutsche Singspiel *Alceste*," Wieland writes concerning music, "All subjects that allow for no broken colors, all wild and stormy passions that are not moderated by hope, fear, or tenderness lie outside of its sphere."

[19] *Herders Sämmtliche Werke*, ed. Bernhard Suphan, vol. 23.

[20] Johann Gottfried Herder Briefe; *Gesamtausgabe, 1763–1803* (Weimar, 1977–82), vol. 2, p. 71.

earliest manuscript of the libretto carries many marginalia instructing, urging, or cautioning the composer, and, when he sent this draft to his fiancée, Herder warned: "Without music it is only a framework and netting: on top of that, the best traits aren't mine. History and Shakespeare. Actually, I only wrote it for myself, in order to pour out my favorite situations."[21] Fourth, as the last sentence intimates, the drama is a compact digest of the most compelling and emotionally charged moments in a history the librettist more than half assumes his audience already knows. Finally, Herder observes none of the unities in selecting from Shakespeare such disparate situations as Cassius's storm scene, Caesar before the Capitol, the funerary orations of Brutus and Antony, and finally Brutus's death at Philippi.

In May of 1772 Herder disclosed that his drama was being set to music. Though he does not mention the composer, it must have been the court concert master Johann Christoph Friedrich Bach, whom Herder had quickly befriended upon coming to Bückeburg in 1771. However, nothing came of it at the time, and by the end of 1772 Herder had begun revising his text, a process which lasted a year and included such changes as shortening many lines from the prevailing iambic pentameter, rewriting several scenes completely, and adding Brutus's wife Portia to the cast, under the inspiration of Plutarch's moving portrayal of her farewell scene with Brutus. Of the original eleven arias and ensembles, only two were left relatively intact.

Bach finished setting this second version by January 1774, whereupon Herder submitted his text to Duke Wilhelm as a birthday present. The duke immediately began translating *Brutus* into French. In addition he personally supervised the printing of the German text in preparation for the work's première, which took place on 27 February at the court theater. Unlike *Alceste*, the work was apparently not a success and attracted no attention, and Herder's libretto remained virtually unknown to anyone beyond his immediate circle.

Herder appears to have been dissatisfied with Bach's setting (which is lost). In November 1774 he sent *Brutus* to Gluck in hopes of kindling the interest of the dramatic composer he – along with Goethe, Wieland, and many other German literati – admired most. The accompanying letter compares his text to the inscription on a painting or statue, "an *explanation*, a *guide* for the stream of music, by means of words scattered between."[22] Gluck did not take up the project, no more than those from Wieland and Goethe which came his way in the 1770s.

In 1777 Herder's friend and teacher Hamann urged him to consider having their fellow East Prussian Reichardt tackle *Brutus*: "It pleased him a great deal and he believed that in many places the structure of this music drama

---

[21] *Ibid.*, p. 173.
[22] *Ibid.*, vol. 3, p. 125. My translation differs from that offered by H. and H. E. Müller von Asow in *The Collected Correspondence and Papers of Christoph Willibald Gluck* (London, 1962), p. 50.

came very close to his ideal of the duties of the poet toward the virtuosos or the composer, duties until now unrecognized."[23] But two years later the collaboration had got nowhere and nothing further was ever heard of it.

Herder had completed another music drama in 1774, the "Scenen mit Gesang" *Philoktetes*, begun in 1772 along with *Brutus* and also set to music by J. C. F. Bach, sometime before late 1775. Herder's source was the *Philoctetes* of Sophocles, with the character of Odysseus omitted and the confrontation of Neoptolemus and Philoctetes reduced to a bare abstract of the Greek drama. Internal evidence suggests that the work may have been intended as a dramatic cantata (there are no scenic divisions or stage descriptions, and all the stage activity is described in the recitatives). Again, the dramatic action is elliptical and obscure unless one knows the story it reenacts. The versification is beautifully wrought, and an especially happy inspiration is the substitution of a beguiling chorus of a band of island nymphs, "Schlummre sanft zum letztenmale," for Sophocles's chorus of sailors. Bach's music, alluded to in a letter from the Riga publisher Hartknoch to Herder, does not survive, and no performance is recorded.

Herder contributed nothing further to German opera until the early years of the next century. By that time both German opera itself and Herder's ideas about the genre had changed radically. His efforts in the 1770s fell victim in part to circumstance – the provincial court where he worked, perhaps even the merits of Bach as a dramatic composer – and in part to the lack of contact between his originality and the more restricted norms still controlling the genre. In turning now to Goethe's first two librettos, we shall discover that their fortunes were similarly linked to the extent to which they adhered to these norms.

Erwin und Elmire

If we look over the works in Table 5.1 once again, we find several librettos drawn from the Rhineland, a source previously ignored by North German opera. Such works represent no very wide departure from earlier paths, however, insofar as the Rhenish region was wholly dominated by the example of opéra-comique. André, while still at Offenbach, and the Mainz professor J. H. Faber translated assiduously from the French for the major theatrical company in the Rhineland, that of Theobald Marchand. Similarly, Goethe's early taste in comic opera was formed almost exclusively by opéras-comiques given at Frankfurt.

As we have seen, Goethe had been present at Leipzig during the years in which Weisse and Hiller codified early Saxon opera. "Weisse's operas,"

---

[23] Quoted by Walter Salmen, "Herder und Reichardt," in *Herder-Studien*, ed. Walter Wiora (Würzburg, 1960), p. 108. Reichardt was exceptional among his German contemporaries in opposing Metastasio's art on the grounds that it allowed "no room for the free flight of genius" (*ibid.*, p. 107).

Goethe later recalled in *Dichtung und Wahrheit*, "enlivened in a light manner by Hiller, gave us much pleasure," but the genre elicited no immediate creative reaction in him. The earliest we can securely date such efforts is late 1773, and at that time the direct stimulus was Goethe's budding friendship in the Rhineland with Johann André, whose house at Offenbach he frequently visited. The opera they eventually completed, *Erwin und Elmire*, like the poet and composer themselves, was Rhenish by birth and only became a part of North German traditions by adoption.

Very little is known of the genesis of the libretto, or the exact nature of relations between Goethe and André when preliminary work began in late 1773. In mid-1774 Goethe read from his "Operette" to Lavater in Switzerland, and in early 1775 he was hard at work on the libretto under the watchful eye of his new-found friend, the philosopher Friedrich Heinrich Jacobi. In March Jacobi's brother, Johann Georg (the librettist of Schweitzer's *Elysium*) brought out *Erwin und Elmire* in his *Iris*, a journal directed principally at female readers. Included as well were André's settings of two songs from the opera, but neither he nor Goethe is mentioned anywhere as composer and author.

Goethe based *Erwin und Elmire* on the ballad "Angelica and Edwin" in Goldsmith's *The Vicar of Wakefield*, a novel which Herder had read to him in early 1771 and which Goethe continued to re-read with pleasure and unstinted admiration to the end of his life. The ballad develops a single, vivid scene in which Angelica, disguised as a young man, meets a hermit in the wilds. After revealing her true sex, she confesses to having driven her lover Edwin to despair by feigning indifference to his attentions. Thereupon the hermit reveals himself as Edwin and the lovers reunite.

Goethe's libretto differs in several important ways from this pattern, not all of which may be attributed to the change from a narrative to a dramatic genre. An initial act (though not so labeled) prefaces the confrontation of the lovers with details of the unhappy course of their relationship and the introduction of two new characters. In the opening scene Olimpia, Elmire's mother, indulges in a long digression on the inferiority of new-fangled manners of social deportment in the young to the free-and-easy ways of her own youth. In the second half of the act Bernardo, Elmire's French instructor and fatherly friend, hears her self-reproaches and persuades her to meet an old hermit in a secluded valley, who may bring her comfort. The reuniting of the lovers, the subject of the second act, comes as no surprise, for immediately Erwin is introduced in his own right to us. Bernardo, who engineers the entire anagnorisis, provides him with the hermit's costume in which he hears Elmire's confession.

Behind the libretto's familiar theme of reconciliation in healthy rustic directness of emotion, clearly opposed to the pretense and artificiality of urban manners, lie several important new features.

Firstly, the rural setting is sought out as a temporary stage on which to set things to rights between two lovers otherwise unconnected with this rustic world.

Secondly, Elmire's mother (who figures only in the opening scene) is not a typical parent of the operatic ilk. Far from being a bar to her daughter's happiness, she approves of Erwin and in consequence seems to have been produced only for the sake of her philosophical ramble. Several writers have suggested that she is a thinly veiled Frau Rat Goethe. While her connection with the drama may be a slender one, the subject on which she spoke was a welcome one in Jacobi's journal, which carried such contributions as "World History for Women," "Ossian for Women," and "The Raising of Daughters."[24]

Thirdly, the libretto places in the background a benevolent rather than a corruption-ridden court which has nothing to do with Elmire's insincere flatterers or the artificial mode of behavior she adopts. Bernardo arranges for a position there for Erwin, in fact.

Fourthly, as the manipulator of events Bernardo is without strong precedent. Both lovers mistrust his apparent lack of warm sympathy, yet he shows strong emotional attachments to both of them: he is at once friend, mentor, confidant, and apothecary to disjointed souls. Superficially, he recalls the title role of Rousseau's *Le Devin du village*, but his function as a bastion of reason over passion suggests rather a kinship with Albert in *Die Leiden des jungen Werthers*.

Finally, Goethe chose for his drama the designation "Schauspiel mit Gesang," one apparently never used before in Germany, and we are perhaps not too far off the mark in translating "Schauspiel" here with the French term *drame*. External events count for little in this libretto (seen most strikingly in Goethe's rejection of the element of surprise as found in Goldsmith's ballad); rather it is built around careful analysis of a central emotional problem – the deleterious effects of the social circle Elmire has been moving in on the deep and unadorned affection which Erwin offers and which she would reciprocate.

This may or may not have been Goethe's original intention, but it is abundantly clear that in its published form the libretto mirrors the turmoils of his passionate attachment to Lili Schönemann which took fire in the three months preceding the publication of *Erwin und Elmire*. Her upbringing, her parents, and the circle around her kindled misgivings in Goethe that are clearly reflected in his portrait of the social ambiance surrounding Elmire. Possibly there is some connection between Bernardo and an uncle of Lili's at Offenbach named Bernard. A quatrain Goethe placed as an epigraph on the

---

[24] The first of these was contributed by Goethe's brother-in-law, Johann Georg Schlosser, the second by Jakob Michael Reinhold Lenz. In January 1775 Goethe and Friedrich Heinrich Jacobi wrote a joint letter to Johann Georg Jacobi in which Fritz Jacobi remarked about *Erwin und Elmire*, "The strange thing is that the whole work fits so splendidly into *Iris*; I could almost say it was expressly composed for it." Johann Wolfgang Goethe, *Gedenkausgabe der Werke, Briefe und Gespräche*, vol. 18 (Zurich, 1951), p. 255.

drama's title page speaks of "the small bouquet" he has gathered from his heart for "Belinde" (his literary sobriquet for Lili). In May of 1775, when Goethe was at Mannheim and an amateur performance was being planned back at Frankfurt, he wrote anxiously to his aunt for a report on the performance, and specifically whether Lili was present.

Goethe's contemporaries needed no details concerning the deep stratum of autobiography in the libretto to recognize the attraction Goethe's "small bouquet" held for the German opera stage. In the next three years it was set more times than any German libretto before it. André was of course the first to do so. Nothing is known for certain of the projected performance at Frankfurt in May 1775, but it may have been with his music. In June he announced his intention of publishing by subscription both a keyboard reduction and full orchestral parts. One month later Döbbelin mounted his setting at Berlin, where its popularity was immediate and pervasive. In August the Berlin poetess Anna Luise Karsch sent a letter to Jacobi describing how at her request Daniel Chodowiecki had made a drawing of "the loving maiden, who comes flying down the hill, and seeks her beloved, and sings: 'Er ist nicht weit' ['He is not far']."[25] Soon after Daniel Berger made an engraving of it for the second volume of Himburg's (unauthorized) edition of Goethe's works, brought out at Berlin in 1776, and in this form it comes down to us (see Plate 4). As the enthusiastic poetess describes it:

A lovely girl in an ethereal-colored, billowing dress; everything is grace, from her flowing hair down to her winged foot; one could consume her with one's eye; one finds her more beautiful, the longer the eye is fixed on her. The warmest feeling of sweet anticipation, the whole rapture, which Elmire is promised in the coming moment; everything, everything is expressed. Her arms spread, her eyes lifted upward, everything speaks delight.

Possibly something in the acting of Sophie Huber in the part of Elmire made its way into Chodowiecki's conception of the moment (she had become the darling of the Berliners in this role, and Chodowiecki had just moved to within a few doors of the Theater in der Behrenstrasse) – but in general we must not regard such engravings as accurate representations of prevailing styles of acting, staging, or costume.

Berlin was not the only place to welcome *Erwin und Elmire*. Christian Friedrich Daniel Schubart declared in his *Deutsche Chronik* that "*Erwin und Elmire* is in the feeling of all good readers the best German Singspiel,"[26] and he goes on to mention performances with André's music at Frankfurt, Cologne, and Amsterdam.

In November of 1775 occurred the most decisive event in Goethe's long life, his removal to Weimar. After the destruction of the court theater in the fire of 1774, there was little or no theatrical activity there until the founding of an

---

[25] The letter was first published in *Iris* 4:1 (1775): 58–9, and was reprinted in the *Berlinisches Litterarisches Wochenblatt* 1 (1776): 54–5.
[26] Issue of 25 September 1775.

Plate 4   *Erwin und Elmire*, Sophie Huber as Elmire, scene 2

amateur theater shortly after his arrival, in January 1776. The court and city were well stocked with enthusiasts for both music and the theater, and none more so than Anna Amalia, who in September 1775 had ended her regency when Karl August reached his majority. Before this she had brought to Weimar several courtiers and musicians who were to play a central role in theatrical affairs over the next decades. Especially significant among them was Siegmund von Seckendorff, a much-traveled former Austrian officer, master of six modern languages, and an amateur composer. Wolf remained under the duchess's protection, but Goethe took a deep dislike to him and he played no role in the new theatrical undertaking.

From Goethe's arrival to the end of 1776, Weimar's new duke presided over a disorderly court, a period of "Genie-Treiben" in which Goethe took a prominent part. But by the end of the year young Stürmer like Lenz, Klinger, and Christoph Kaufmann had departed, and gentler winds prevailed. During 1776, the fledgling amateur theater mounted a variety of works, some in French, some in German, and only occasionally did the stormy side of the new court find its way into the theater. The few comic operas were largely French. An exception was Anna Amalia's own setting of *Erwin und Elmire*, first performed on 24 May 1776.

For this new setting, whose production Goethe himself supervised, the poet provided several new arias in the first act for Elmire, Bernardo, and Olimpia. In addition, Olimpia is integrated into the closing ensemble. Dialogue cues in the manuscript score indicate that Goethe made changes in the spoken portions as well, but the revised text does not survive.

The duchess's music was universally admired. Lenz published a poem on her score in Wieland's *Teutscher Merkur* which concludes:

> Und kann der Dichter uns in sel'ger Raserei
> Bis an des Todes Schwelle führen:
> So fürst Du uns von da noch seliger und lieber
> Bis nach Elysium hinüber.

(And if the poet can lead us in blissful madness to the threshold of death: then do you lead us from there yet more blissfully and agreeably across to Elysium.)[27]

Lenz was far too inept socially to have been flattering insincerely, and anyone studying the modern edition of Anna Amalia's setting must agree that it merits his high praise. Comparison with the other surviving versions from the 1770s, those of André and Stegmann, instructs us in the nuances distinguishing the different dialects of German opera. All three composers, to begin with, set Goethe's libretto in a style commensurate with its serious tone. André, not surprisingly, tends to follow the models of French opera, especially Grétry. Stegmann, on the other hand, speaks with severely Northern accents derived from examples such as Schweitzer's *Alceste*. Duchess Anna Amalia tends almost everywhere toward the rich, more cheerful lyricism of

---

[27] *Der Teutsche Merkur* 1776:2 (May): 197–8. Lenz himself went off in a rather Erwin-like fashion later that year and lived as a hermit in Berka.

the Italianate style she had grown up with at Brunswick and to which she remained devoted throughout her life.

Only two of the libretto's sixteen numbers proved susceptible of a simple, Lied-like setting – Elmire's laying bare of her soul to a disguised Erwin in act two ("Sieh mich, Heiliger, wie ich bin: / Eine arme Sünderin"), and the celebrated "Das Veilchen." Goethe had written the latter exquisite lyric more than a year before the completion of the libretto – in January 1774 it was in Lotte Jacobi's hands as part of "several Romanzen."[28] Psychologically, however, it could not be more appropriately placed in the opera. Elmire sings it when Bernardo mentions to her the "little song" Erwin had written after one of her acts of feigned coldness. In a simple, poignant setting, its words not only bring Erwin's voice to life in the first half of the drama but also complete Goethe's portrait of Elmire's remorse.

André's setting (Example 5.3) builds with two-bar phrases perfectly attuned to the poetic structure (no other number in his score avoids textual repetition as this one does). The second half of the melody is agreeably varied: the early arrival of "Mit leichtem Schritt und munterm Sinn" in the two-bar scheme of things is not only "light" and "cheerful" (and perhaps a little heedless of the order of things, like the young shepherdess), but moves the tonic

Example 5.3 André: *Erwin und Elmire*. Romanze.
  "A violet stood in the meadow, bent down and unnoticed. It was a charming violet. Then along came a young shepherdess, with light step and cheerful mien, into the meadow and sang."

[28] See Hanna Fischer-Lamberg, *Der junge Goethe*, 2nd ed., 5 vols. (Berlin and New York, 1963–73), vol. 4, p. 337.

Ex. 5.3 (*cont.*)

accent onto "Schritt", where it belongs, rather than on "leichtem". The final phrase expands to four bars in order to give the wistful "daher! daher!" its expressive due as the culmination of a long series of Grétry-like descending seconds, which are the principal ingredient of André's tune.

Anna Amalia, though also adopting G major (as Mozart did nine years later), varies the accompaniment in each strophe, enriching it with beautiful obbligato woodwind parts for the virtuosi in the Weimar Kapelle. We have already seen in the preceding chapter the principle of orchestral strophic variation used by Benda for the Romanze in *Der Jahrmarkt*. The decision to follow this lead here is a happy one, for it allows a combination of the duchess's elaboratedly wrought style and a fairly simple melody generated from the lilting 6/8 meter, the wistfulness of the dramatic situation caught by the expressive E^b–D inflections against a tonic pedal (Example 5.4).

Example 5.4 Anna Amalia: *Erwin und Elmire*. Romanze, act 1.

Ex. 5.4 (*cont.*)

Stegmann combined Anna Amalia's 6/8 meter and André's simple strophic style in his version of "Das Veilchen," which he labeled a canzonetta, but he chose the key of E-flat major for this song, a key associated with Elmire throughout his score (which is one of the most carefully planned in its choice of tonalities in all of eighteenth-century German opera). He also used this setting of "Das Veilchen" as the slow movement of his overture, which begins with a c-minor Adagio in sharp contrast with the bright Allegros André and Anna Amalia wrote. The whole overture is planned as a ternary structure:

	Adagio	Un poco vivace ("Das Veilchen")	Adagio	
	c	E♭	E♭	f	c

Example 5.5 presents the opening Adagio and the beginning of the Un poco vivace. Stegmann reflects the conservatism of Northern symphonic style in the Adagio with its square, sealed-off c-minor opening and his mixture of repeated phrases and old-fashioned sequence-writing. The novelty of such an

Example 5.5 Stegmann: *Erwin und Elmire*, Overture.

Ex. 5.5 (*cont.*)

overture for North German opera lay in choosing such serious ruminations to begin the work and in the thought devoted to the overall plan.

Elmire's first aria, a restless dal segno soliloquy, echoes the overture's interest in c minor and E-flat major, although here Stegmann tacks toward e-flat minor until the very end of the A₁ section, shown in Example 5.6. The pervasive spirit of the minor mode infects even the ritornello in bars 40 to 44, which returns to the tonic minor rather than confirming the arrival of the relative major. Throughout the emphasis is on intensity, but the histrionic opening and the bristling chromatic activity disguise the moderate demands Stegmann felt he could make on his heroine's range and agility when writing for the Schuch company.

Stegmann published his *Erwin und Elmire* in the spring of 1776 and soon thereafter he and his wife left East Prussia for the Gotha Court Theater and later Hamburg. Wolf at Weimar registered surprise at Stegmann's publishing

Example 5.6 Stegmann: *Erwin und Elmire*. First aria of Elmire.
"Erwin! Oh, see, you are avenged. No god hears my distress, no god! My pride broke his heart, oh Love! give me death!"

his opera at his own cost,[29] but the composer mentioned in his preface to the keyboard reduction his intention of seeking fame in the great world of German theater beyond Königsberg, and his ambitious, earnest setting was no doubt a part of his plans to recommend himself to Northern stages.

[29] On 30 May 1776 Wolf wrote to Breitkopf, "Herr Stegmann must have more money than I do, else he might have lost the courage to have Goethe's *Erwin und Elmire* as well as *Apollo unter den Hirten* [a Vorspiel by Johann Georg Jacobi] printed at his own expense." Wilhelm Hitzig, "Beiträge zum Weimarer Konzert, 1773–1786," *Der Bär: Jahrbuch von Breitkopf & Härtel*

All three of the composers of *Erwin und Elmire* we have been discussing treat the first act as a preamble to the second, and Goethe's planning made it inevitable that musical emphasis in each case would fall on the scene of reunion, the core of the drama and the section most directly derived from Goldsmith's ballad. The musical high point is not the same in all three cases, however. André and Stegmann stress the entrance of the heroine. Goethe had intended this event to assume some musical importance. Elmire is heard singing from afar just after Bernardo has told Erwin that she loves him. His transports at hearing her voice are brief, however, for Bernardo immediately whisks him into the hut to assume his disguise. Elmire enters, with the stage to herself, and sings tandem arias connected by eight lines of recitative, the second a storm aria fairly inviting the extensive treatment both Stegmann and André gave it.

Stegmann's keyboard reduction contains no special music for Elmire's singing off stage, but André set this moment as a short melodrama, uniting the lovers in our ears even before they are both on stage. The music used, shown in Example 5.7, consists of the first fifteen bars of Elmire's aria reduced to only a flute and bassoon placed behind the scenes.

Though Anna Amalia does not short-change her heroine at her entrance in act two, the high point of her setting of their encounter comes later. It corresponds to the moment around which Goldsmith built his ballad, and the one Chodowiecki drew for Anna Luise Karsch. Elmire has been handed a mes-

Example 5.7 André: *Erwin und Elmire*. Offstage singing of Elmire.

ELMIRE: "With deep breaths . . ."
BERNARDO (spoken): "Listen!"
ELMIRE: " . . . I draw from you, Nature, a painful pleasure."
ERWIN (spoken): "I am lost!"
ELMIRE: "How my heart lives and throbs and aspires!"
ERWIN (spoken): "That is her voice! How its tone runs through all my senses!'"
ELMIRE: "How my heart beats!"

auf das Jahr 1925 (Leipzig, 1925), pp. 89–90. Earlier in the month he mentioned talk at Weimar of printing Anna Amalia's music to *Erwin und Elmire* at the time of its première. Wolf, however, had misgivings about publishing an opera "under the name of a sovereign" (p. 89). The same year, in fact, he published the cantata *Polyxena* with Breitkopf under his name only, although the arias are by Anna Amalia. As a result, even today she is never credited with their composition.

Ex. 5.7 (*cont.*)

sage by a mute Erwin in his hermit garb, and he motions that she go off in the distance to read it. Erwin and Bernardo hide in the shrubs as she flies back to the hut, singing a dizain which commences with the words Erwin has written for her: "Er ist nicht weit!" and culminating in an ecstatic "Erwin! Erwin!" At that moment he springs forth:

ERWIN: Elmire! (Er springt hervor)
ELMIRE: Weh mir!
ERWIN (Zu ihren Füssen.): Ich bin's.
ELMIRE (An seinem Halse.): Du bist's.
(Die Musik wage es, die Gefühle dieser Pausen auszudrücken.)

This last rubric, "Let the music dare to express the feelings of these pauses," aroused the wrath of one critic, who re-worded this thought as: "Let the music dare to wish to move as I can," and sneered: "More shameless pride we would never have thought to discover in anyone."[30] Goethe's challenge, at all events, was lost on André, who preferred to filch from Grétry at this juncture (Zémire's "Azor! Azor!" in act four of *Zémire et Azor*). At Erwin's appearance he contents himself with a Lombardic figure and a fermata when the lovers embrace, after which he rushes headlong into the trio initiated by Bernardo (Example 5.8). Stegmann, too, made only a tentative effort toward

Example 5.8 André: *Erwin und Elmire*. Reunion scene.
ELMIRE: "Erwin! Erwin! Erwin!"
ERWIN: "Elmire!"
ELMIRE: "Woe is me!"
ERWIN: "It is I!"
ELMIRE: "It is you!"
BERNARDO: "O look down, ye gods, on this happiness!"

30 *Beytrag zum Reichs-Postreuter*, 22 May 1775, reprinted in *Goethe im Urtheile seiner Zeit-genossen*, ed. Julius W. Braun (Berlin, 1883), vol. 1, p. 109. The writer, who signs his name "Clwd.", was reviewing a copy of the libretto which did not name Goethe as the author.

amplifying the moment of reunion musically with a sequential Adagio figure (Example 5.9). Elmire's preceding Presto rounds out in its tonic E-flat even before she calls Erwin's name, and Bernardo continues in the same tonality, creating a static effect apart from the changes of tempo.

Example 5.9 Stegmann: *Erwin und Elmire*. Reunion scene.

Anna Amalia, on the other hand, while setting the interchange of the lovers as simple recitative, responds to the spirit of Goethe's rubric with a dignified Adagio ritornello mediating between the embrace of the lovers and Bernardo's entrance at the commencement of the trio, "O schauet hernieder" (Example 5.10). There is a tonal point as well: while Stegmann sticks doggedly to Elmire's E-flat throughout and André fastens aria, reunion, and trio to an overriding E–B–E canopy, in Anna Amalia's rendering we hear F major (in which Elmire also sang upon arriving earlier in the act) transformed into E-flat major as a reflex of the drama's progression to the awaited reconciliation. The composer, poised on the threshold of opera seria, moves fully into its accents with the spaciousness created by the ritornello establishing E-flat. The reconciliation *à trois* only implicit in Goethe's libretto (that Bernardo too has made his peace with the lovers, who so mistrusted his putting sense before sensibility) is made musically explicit by the composer as the three are bound together in the closing Allegro molto section of the trio (Example 5.11).

Example 5.10 Anna Amalia: *Erwin und Elmire*. Reunion scene, act 2.

Example 5.11 Anna Amalia: *Erwin und Elmire*. Stretto of trio, act 2.
   ELMIRE: "I have you again. . ."
   ERWIN: "I have you again, here I am. . ."
   BERNARDO: "O look down, ye gods. . ."

The amateur theater at Weimar mounted Anna Amalia's setting five times in 1776, then twice in each of the next two years. The part of Olimpia went to Kapellmeister Wolf's wife Karoline, daughter of the Berlin violinist Franz Benda, and Elmire was sung by Friederike Steinhard, a soprano who had come to Weimar with her husband Johann Friedrich Steinhard, a virtuoso flautist from the Stuttgart Hofkapelle. On 1 March 1777, however, her role passed to Corona Schröter. Goethe, who had heard this beautiful and somewhat retiring soprano at Leipzig while he was a student there, heard her again in 1776. She was even more stunning than before. For some time, however, she had stood in the shadow of Gertrud Schmeling (La Mara), a fellow pupil of Hiller, at least in part because Corona's modesty kept her from pursuing a career on the public stage. Nonetheless, she readily agreed to an offer from Weimar to become a court singer and became yet another vital addition to its musical and theatrical resources in November 1776.

Claudine von Villa Bella

Less than a month after *Erwin und Elmire* had been published in Jacobi's *Iris*, Goethe wrote to Johanna Fahlmer: "I have exhumed *Claudine*." This first explicit reference in his writings to his next libretto suggests that it had been begun and then set aside earlier. No later than May 1776 the libretto was published by August Mylius at Berlin. Unlike its predecessor, *Claudine von Villa Bella* appeared as a separate publication and with Goethe's name on the title page. Equally as characteristic of the work itself are its connections with Weimar: Goethe sent the drama to Carl Ludwig von Knebel there in June 1775 with instructions to show it to Karl August, and after Goethe himself arrived that autumn he spoke of himself and his fellow hell-raisers as Crugantino and Basko, the two vagabonds in the story. Though also called a "Schauspiel mit Gesang," Goethe's second libretto differs from his first in many ways: it is a full-length, technically unruly, dramaturgically demanding, and emotionally charged work – every inch a Storm and Stress libretto, the first in the history of German opera:

(Garden scene at Villa Bella.) A procession celebrates the eighteenth birthday of Donna Claudine, only child of Don Gonzalo. A conversation between him and Don Sebastian praises her modesty and perfection and notes the awkward love of young Don Pedro for her. He and Sebastian have come seeking Pedro's older brother, who has fallen in with a band of vagabonds. Two nieces of Don Gonzalo, jealous of Claudine, believe she is secretly meeting a lover at night and plot to expose her.

(Room in a low village inn.) Amid gaming and boasting about their exploits, the vagabonds try to guess the girl their leader Crugantino is occupied with now. He tells his comrade Basko that he is determined to approach Claudine on one of her evening strolls.

(Moonlight. A terrace at Villa Bella.) While Basko sits guard in a chestnut tree, a masked Crugantino makes advances on Claudine which send her running off in terror. Pedro comes seeking her, Crugantino smells a rival, duels, and wounds him. Basko carries Pedro off to the inn. Gonzalo, alerted by the jealous nieces, finds not Pedro but Crugantino, who feigns the innocent bystander and is invited in for a glass of wine.

(A room in Villa Bella.) Crugantino amid refreshments tries to talk with Claudine. With his zither he sings to the group a Romanze, interrupted by a cry from Claudine, who faints upon being told that Pedro is wounded. Sebastian enters with soldiers, but Crugantino escapes. Claudine recovers and determines to disguise herself and find Pedro.

(Toward morning, before the inn.) Crugantino meets Claudine and quickly recognizes her beneath her disguise. Words again do not work, so he tries force, but a barely recovered Pedro stops him from carrying her off. Guards come and arrest everyone.

(A narrow prison cell.) Sebastian learns of these activities, exposes Crugantino, and reveals to him who Pedro is. Crugantino shows no contrition, though sorry for the harm done Pedro and Claudine. There is no place for him, he insists, in Sebastian's bourgeois world. Don Gonzalo comes, Claudine faints once more and they all fear her dead. But she recovers and, at Sebastian's urging, Gonzalo takes pity on her and promises her to Pedro.

As early as 1777 Eschenburg speculated on the basis of the strong element of adventure in this plot that it may have been derived from a Spanish novella,[31] but a principal literary source for the drama has yet to be found. Some have suggested the Don Juan legend, and indeed *Claudine von Villa Bella* does share elements with versions of this legend by Tirso di Molina, Molière, and Goldoni. There are many contradictions as well, however.

---

[31] *Allgemeine deutsche Bibliothek* 31:2 (1777): 494. "The material is indeed somewhat adventurous, and very similar to a Spanish novella, from which it is perhaps drawn; but the execution breathes pure life and warmth, and betrays a poet of no common genius."

Most scholars have stressed autobiographical connections with Lili Schönemann and her circle. To do so in this case, they have been compelled to split Goethe's personality into two aspects – the rebellious-poetic (Crugantino) and the bourgeois-social (Pedro). But Claudine's lack of any reciprocation for Crugantino's advances, among many other incongruities, makes this hypothesis difficult to uphold.[32]

Whatever one chooses to believe about the opera's sources, Goethe was surely correct in regarding *Claudine von Villa Bella* as something new to German opera. Common ground with anything in Weisse is out of the question.[33] Among other North German operatic predecessors, only one has a Spanish setting – Grossmann's adaptation of Beaumarchais's *Le Barbier de Séville* – and it differs in every other respect from Goethe's libretto. The theme of inimical brothers had similarly been explored in Gotter's adaptation of Marmontel's *Silvain*, but it virtually eliminates the component of rivalry and breathes a wholly different, rustic spirit.

We might well ask, all the same, whether there is any indication of indebtedness to German practice in the musical disposition of the text. With *Erwin und Elmire* this was at least plausible, especially in the first act with its long passages of dialogue. In the second act, however, after the appearance of Elmire, Goethe had placed the musical numbers ever closer together and, as we just saw, had called on the composer at important dramatic junctures, much as the writers of opéras-comiques were wont to do. Even the closing trio departs sharply from the Rundgesang tradition and invites a true ensemble setting.

[32] Indeed, Goethe seems to reject it himself, while just as vigorously affirming the connection of *Erwin und Elmire* with Lili, in a preliminary draft for *Dichtung und Wahrheit*: "In company [Lili] keeps on playing the role of attracting and repulsing and still cannot refrain from comforting, sometimes fleetingly, the faithful lover whom she sees suffering ceaselessly . . . Were all the poems of that epoch gathered together, they would portray the situation better than can be done here; for there was no peak of happiness, no abyss of pain to which an accent was not dedicated; from social party-songs to the smallest note accompanying a present, everything was living. Erwin's song 'Ihr verblühet süsse Rosen' belongs here, like *Erwin und Elmire* in general in its first version. On the bittersweetness of *Stella* this situation exerted not a little influence. *Claudine von Villa Bella* was completed earlier, when I aspired to work with romantic subjects as opposed to operas about tradesmen and contemplated uniting noble sentiments with vagabond activities as an auspicious motive for the stage, which indeed is not uncommon in Spanish poems, but at that time was new to us." *Werke*, ed. in commission from Sophie von Sachsen [=Weimarer-Ausgabe], vol. 29, p. 216. Willy Krogmann proposes that Goethe did not recall the order of events improperly here, that *Claudine von Villa Bella* at least in substance antedates *Erwin und Elmire*, and that it owes its life to the same unhappy triangle of 1772 – Goethe, Charlotte Buff, and her fiancé J. C. Kestner – which also inspired *Die Leiden des jungen Werthers* in 1774. "Die persönlichen Beziehungen in Goethes Schauspiel mit Gesang, *Claudine von Villa Bella*," *Germanisch-Romanische Monatsschrift* 19 (1931): 348–61. Among many problems left unsolved by this interpretation is Goethe's decision to make Crugantino and Pedro brothers as well as rivals. And why would he pass over in silence its autobiographical source when he so explicitly asserted one for *Erwin und Elmire*?

[33] We may dismiss at once Woldemar Martinsen's attempts at establishing character pairings between *Claudine von Villa Bella* and Weisse's librettos in his *Goethes Singspiele im Verhältnis zu den Weissischen Operetten* (Dresden, 1887).

Claudine von Villa Bella tends even more strongly away from German practice. In the elaborate introductory complex, the birthday celebration, the relationship of Pedro and Claudine already begins to develop (she later sings to the bouquet he gives her in this scene). The duets between them occurring later are nothing unusual, but Crugantino in both his confrontations with Claudine carries on his amorous attempts in action duets, as befits his character. The second of these, in front of the inn, initiates what we should not hesitate to proclaim the first North German operatic finale:

(1) (à 2, lines 1–19) Crugantino asks if he can hope that his love may be returned. Claudine is insulted and pushes him away.

(2) (à 3, lines 20–60) Pedro, at the inn's window, hears her voice as Crugantino's entreaties grow warmer and her repulses sterner. When Crugantino assails her she draws a knife, but he easily wrests it from her. In vain she struggles to escape his grasp. Pedro has left the window and appears at the door, dagger in hand. Crugantino draws his own and holds it to Claudine's breast.

(3) (à 4, lines 61–73) At this moment of impasse Basko is heard offstage, responding to the disturbance. Crugantino calls him and he knocks the dagger from Pedro's hand. As Crugantino carries Claudine off she cries for help.

(4) (tutti, lines 74–89) The guards come to see about the tumult. Crugantino releases Claudine and he and Basko fight with the guards, some of whom detain Claudine and Pedro when they try to flee. The vagabonds are overpowered and all four principals are led off in various states of distress and disgrace.

Only from Italian practice could Goethe have gleaned the brilliant inspiration of setting the first notes of this finale at the moment Crugantino recognizes Claudine beneath her male clothing, and in the finale itself the mounting dramatic tension through the four sections duplicates in this deadly serious context the acceleration to imbroglio of an internal opera buffa finale.

As had also been the case with *Erwin und Elmire*, Goethe indicated no act divisions in *Claudine von Villa Bella*, but the present finale strongly resembles an act-two finale in Italian practice, where confusion and dramatic tension soar to their highest pitch. On this assumption, the opera is an implicit three-act drama. However, a hypothetical conclusion to act one would have to come at the musically undistinguished close of the exposition – the vagabond scene – with the first act's musical demands overflowing German operatic banks only in the introductory procession. On the other hand, this three-act conceptualization helps explain why Goethe's last scene has struck many critics as a relatively weak conclusion. It may be viewed as a case of the hereditary disease of operatic third acts, compelled to mop up after the confusion wrought in the act-two finale.

North German composers had never seen the likes of Goethe's operatic tour de force, and they greeted it diffidently. André's setting was never performed, and he published only the two songs which appeared in Reichard's *Theater-Kalender* in 1778. A production was planned by the Weimar amateur theater for Ettersburg in 1779, but Goethe's departure for Switzerland forestalled it. Whose music was to be used is not known, though Seckendorff is sometimes mentioned. Significantly, the first known production of *Claudine von Villa Bella* came at the Burgtheater in 1780 with music by Ignaz von Beecke.

Critical reaction in the North is also illuminating. The *Berlinisches Litterarisches Wochenblatt* presented the party line which treated German librettos as essentially literary products: "The plot is without anything episodic; very simple, but too precipitous and abrupt; and because of this it seems to us that the good situations are not exploited in the way the author of *Götz von Berlichingen* and *Die Leiden des jungen Werthers* could have."[34] One Altona journal greeted the libretto with untempered sarcastic irony. Another could not believe it to be Goethe's work save that his name stood on the title page; the reviewer decided that it must be a satire on operettas, for "there are things sung that can scarcely be tolerated when spoken in the theater, for example duels, fighting with the watch, and so forth." But he liked the Romanze.[35] A critical journal from Lemgo (near Hannover) found the whole thing too "novelesque, unnatural and therefore uninteresting" and also concluded that "in general it seems that Nature has not fashioned Herr G[oethe] to be a musical poet."[36]

Only Eschenburg brought sympathetic insight to the libretto. He found it incomparably better than *Erwin und Elmire*, its songs light and musical and demanding "a lively, indeed succinct composition, especially those which are constructed in the manner of the finales in Italian operettas and are united with lively action."[37] Unlike many of his fellow German critics, Eschenburg had first-hand experience with the genre he mentions, having prepared German translations for Guglielmi's *La sposa fedele* and Piccinni's *La notte critica*. Nonetheless, the majority opinion among critics, coupled with the feeble response of North German composers, reduced Goethe's far-sighted endeavor to a local aberration in German operatic developments.

In the spring of 1776, when *Claudine von Villa Bella* appeared and Anna Amalia's *Erwin und Elmire* was in production, Weimar was as rich in theatrical talent as any other center in Germany and could easily have assumed a role of leadership in the fostering of German opera. That it did not was no fault of Goethe's, as the next two chapters will show, but of larger, seemingly inevitable trends. One of Weimar's difficulties lay in the function an amateur court theater served – the occasional and exclusive entertaining of a small, non-paying audience. Not just talent and inclination, but the enterprise to employ and develop them was a necessary ingredient.

Although there were lean years ahead, North German opera experienced an Indian summer for five or six years after 1777, in part owing to the bright

---

[34] Reprinted in Braun, *Goethe im Urtheile seiner Zeitgenossen*, vol. 1, p. 281.
[35] Both Altona reviews are in *ibid.*: that of the *Beytrag zum Reichs-Postreuter* on pp. 285–7, that of the *Neuer gelehrter Mercurius* on p. 288.
[36] *Ibid.*, pp. 310–14, reprinted from *Auserlesene Bibliothek der neuesten deutschen Litteratur* 10 (1776): 490–8.
[37] *Allgemeine deutsche Bibliothek* 31:2 (1777): 495.

spot of André's presence at Berlin, where Döbbelin's fortunes were beginning a long, inexorable decline, and in part owing to an efflorescence of interest in German opera in Dresden's impressive musical establishment. Goethe, meanwhile, moved more and more wholeheartedly into the spirit of Italian opera, and in so doing blazed the trail his countrymen would later follow.

6

Prussian dominion and the end of Saxon opera

The years 1778 to 1783 were decisive ones for the German operatic manner established in Saxony a decade earlier. Many of its practitioners stubbornly refused to abandon ship and continued to uphold the dramatic subordination of music as a predicate of their conception of German opera's answerability to the canons of spoken drama. More and more, however, other composers and librettists turned their backs on the founders of North German opera as pressure toward change and models to follow arose both internally and externally. We have already detected realignments in subject matter and in musical technique, and more importantly a growing awareness among some librettists that composers were their colleagues in the enterprise of operatic creation, not sub-contractors. An even more persuasive kind of pressure was felt when German audiences began responding to the latest and best comic operas from France, Italy, and Vienna.

Although some of the most significant composers and librettists in this period were attached to courts, public stages under the private management of a principal brought forth the great majority of new German operas from 1778 to 1783, as seen in Table 6.1. Patterns of popularity and the survival of sources (the music for thirty and the texts for forty-four of the sixty-one works listed) direct our attention toward but a few centers: Berlin, Breslau, Dresden, and Leipzig are the only cities for which we have more than a single score to evaluate. Berlin once again outstrips other centers, even when lumped together, in the production of new German operas. Nor is this simply a quantitative advantage as it had been during the preceding half decade. Both in music and text Berlin was beginning to find its own voice, and its echoes were already resounding throughout Prussia and North Germany.

Berlin: Döbbelin's theater

The War of the Bavarian Succession, initiated in 1778 and over by May of the following year, was of no great moment to Prussian security. Its only effect on theatrical affairs there came when Frederick the Great ordered the dissolution of the French comic troupe at the Gendarmenmarkt and thereby enriched Döbbelin's orchestra with new players.

The signal acquisition Döbbelin made in 1778, however, was the engaging

174

Table 6.1. *New North German operas, 1778–1783*
(listed alphabetically by composer)

COMPOSER		Première	
Title	Librettist	Date	Place
JOHANN ANDRÉ			
Der Alchymist	Meissner	11 Apr 1778	Berlin
[*Azakia*]	Schwan	26 Nov 1778	Berlin
(*Der Barbier von Bagdad*)	André	19 Feb 1783	Berlin
Belmont und Constanze	Bretzner	25 May 1781	Berlin
[*Claudine von Villa Bella*]	Goethe	unperformed	
(*Eins wird doch helfen*)	unknown	24 Aug 1782	Berlin
Elmine	von Drais	14 Feb 1782	Berlin
(*Kurze Thorheit ist die beste*)	F. L. W. Meyer	18 Jul 1780	Berlin
Laura Rosetti	d'Arien	23 May 1778	Berlin
(*Der Liebhaber als Automat*)	André	11 Sep 1782	Berlin
Die Schadenfreude	Weisse	1778	Berlin
Das tartarische Gesetz	Gotter	31 May 1779	Berlin
Das wütende Heer	Bretzner	22 Nov 1780	Berlin
ANNA AMALIA			
Das Jahrmarktsfest zu Plundersweilern	Goethe	20 Oct 1778	Weimar
GEORG BENDA			
Der Holzhauer	Gotter	2 Jan 1778	Gotha
DAVANDER			
[*Julie*]	Nesselrode	1781	Dresden
EHRENBERG			
([*Die Alpenhütte*])	unknown	unperformed	
FRIEDRICH CHRISTOPH GESTEWITZ			
(*Die Liebe ist sinnreich*)	unknown	27 Nov 1781	Dresden
([*Der Meyerhof*])	unknown	20 Sep 1780	Leipzig
JOHANN AUGUST HALBE			
Die Liebe auf der Probe	d'Arien–Halbe	1781	Mitau
HEINRICH CHRISTOPH HATTASCH			
([*Der Barbier von Bagdad*])	unknown	after 1780	Hamburg
[*Der ehrliche Schweitzer*]	Klenke	1780	Hamburg
JOHANN ADAM HILLER			
[*Das Denkmal in Arkadien*]	Weisse	unperformed	
Das Grab des Mufti	Meissner	17 Jan 1779	Leipzig
Die kleine Ährenleserinn	Weisse	unperformed	
Poltis	Brunner	unperformed	
FRANZ ANDREAS HOLLY			
Der Irrwisch	Bretzner	1779	Breslau
JOHANN CHRISTOPH KAFFKA			
[*Der Äpfeldieb*]	Bretzner	26 Jun 1780	Berlin
[*Der Guckkasten*]	Kaffka	1782	Breslau
[*So prellt man alte Fuchse*]	Meyer–Kaffka	1782	Breslau
Das wütende Heer	Bretzner	Jan 1782	Breslau
JOHANN MATTHEUS KÖNIG			
(*Lilla*)	unknown	unperformed	
OTTO CARL ERDMANN FREIHERR VON KOSPOTH			
Adrast und Isidore	Bretzner	16 Oct 1779	Berlin

Table 6.1 (*cont.*)

| COMPOSER | | Première | |
Title	Librettist	Date	Place
Der Irrwisch	Bretzner	2 Oct 1780	Berlin
[*Karoline*]	Seidel	unperformed	
NIKOLAUS MÜHLE			
[*Der Äpfeldieb*]	Bretzner	1781	Danzig
[*Fremore und Melime*]	Spaur	1778	Königsberg
[*Mit dem Glockenschlag: zwölf!*]	Soden	1783	Mitau
[*Der Schiffbruch*]	Spaur	1778	Königsberg
JOHANN CHRISTIAN OHLHORST			
([*Adelstan und Röschen*])	Schink	1782	Neustrelitz
([*Das Jahresfest*])	Neumann	1783	Neustrelitz
FRIEDRICH PREU			
Adrast und Isidore	Bretzner	22 Feb 1779	Dresden
[*Der Irrwisch*]	Bretzner	1779	Leipzig
JOHANN FRIEDRICH REICHARDT			
Liebe nur beglückt	Reichardt	autumn 1781	Dessau
JOHANN HEINRICH ROLLE			
([*Der Sturm*])	Patzke	28 Mar 1782	Berlin
KARL SIEGMUND SCHÖNBECK			
([*Der Küster im Stroh*])	unknown	1778	Königsberg
CORONA ELISABETH WILHELMINE SCHRÖTER			
Die Fischerinn	Goethe	22 Jul 1782	Tiefurth
JOSEPH SCHUBERT			
([*Das blaue Ungeheuer*])	unknown	1781	Schwedt
([*Die Entzauberung*])	unknown	1781	Schwedt
JOHANN ABRAHAM PETER SCHULZ			
[*Clarisse*]	Bock	unperformed	
JOSEPH SCHUSTER			
Der Alchymist	Meissner	Mar 1778	Dresden
Die wüste Insel	Meissner	30 Sep 1779	Leipzig
ANTON SCHWEITZER			
[*Das wütende Heer*]	Bretzner	unperformed	
KARL SIEGMUND FREIHERR VON SECKENDORFF			
[*Jery und Bätely*]	Goethe	12 Jul 1780	Weimar
FRANZ SEYDELMANN			
Arsene	Meissner	3 Mar 1779	Dresden
[*Der Kaufmann von Smyrna*]	Schwan	1778	Dresden
Der lahme Husar	Koch	17 Jul 1780	Leipzig
([*Der Soldat*])	unknown	1783	Gotha
CARL DAVID STEGMANN			
[*Clarisse*]	Bock	Nov 1778	Hamburg
[*Das Mündel*]	Korb	1783	Altona
CHRISTIAN GOTTHILF WEISFLOG			
([*Das glückliche Unglück*])	unknown	ca. 1780	Sagan
([*Der Schatz*])	Weisflog	12 Jan 1781	Sagan

Key:
[ ] – complete music does not survive.
( ) – complete text does not survive.

of the South German soprano Marie Sophie Niklas, the undisputed empress of opera at Berlin throughout this period. The tender as well as astonishing qualities universally prized in her voice and acting were described in detail by a Berliner in 1780:

> Her voice is not strong, but full and so meltingly sweet as is not easy to find. Her range is from G to f″ and thus encompasses nearly three octaves. However, the middle range is the most excellent. She has great perfection to her voice and sings especially descending *passaggi* with the greatest precision from a full chest, yet her Adagio is still to be preferred to her Allegro, since she has complete command over her *portamento* with her magical tone. Her triumph is the rondo. She sings staccato and trill impeccably. As an actress everything strong, ponderous, or overwrought lies outside her sphere. She makes great efforts to bring it off, but is not convincing. Her fire is but a higher grade of warmth, her pride but cold reserve with a small addition of scorn. On the other hand in every tender, innocent, merry, and good-hearted role she plays with great naturalness.[1]

These abilities, so perfectly attuned to the character of German opera of the 1770s, were all the more welcome at Berlin in that Sophie Huber, having felt herself undervalued by Döbbelin, had left a worshipping public for Bondini's company at Dresden and Leipzig. Marie Niklas took over all of Sophie Huber's roles, although the latter's most celebrated piece, *Erwin und Elmire*, was not revived until 1782. Döbbelin was careful to keep his new diva satisfied with her lot at Berlin. One journalist complained in 1782 that he allowed her to sing in public concerts whenever she pleased, even though as "the crown of our operetta" she received nearly 1,500 Thaler a year. He implicitly stressed Berlin's pre-eminence as a center of operatic cultivation in adding: "Also I would remind this excellent young lady that in other places the heavens are not hung full with violins: few leave the Berlin theater without soon regretting it."[2]

By 1781 Döbbelin had the largest theatrical company in Germany with a staggering seventy-eight members. Brachvogel has published a complete list with each person's specialty,[3] allowing us to break down the Berlin company in terms of their involvement with the musical repertory:

Male	42	Female	36
Actors only	18	Actresses only	21
Singers only	2	Singers only	2
Actor-singers	11	Actress-singers	7
Actor-singer-dancers	2	Actress-singer-dancers	1
Others	9	Others	5

The actor-singer, rather than the virtuoso specializing in opera, still

---

[1] *Abbildungen berühmter Gelehrten und Künstler Deutschlands, nebst kurzen Nachrichten ihrer Leben und Werke* (Berlin, 1780), pp. 73–8, quoted in *Gallerie von Teutschen Schauspielern*, ed. Werner, pp. 105–6.

[2] [Christian Friedrich] von B[oni]n, *Berliner Theater-Journal für das Jahr 1782* (Berlin, 1783), p. 534.

[3] *Geschichte des königlichen Theaters zu Berlin*, vol. 1, pp. 302–5.

dominates in the company's musical ranks. While more and more troupes sought out a few singers equal to the challenge of the most ambitious operas and audiences kept up pressure for vocal pyrotechnics, the versatile performer remained characteristic in the German troupe system.

In 1778 an anonymous traveler wrote an informative report on Döbbelin's stage. The troupe, he noted, played in its very small and narrow theater every day but Friday, when the weekly grand concert took place at the innkeeper Corsica's hall. Sundays there was no performance during the summer, and in the winter the theater was usually quite empty that day, since most of Berlin was out in the Tiergarten. The traveler registered more than a little surprise at the independence of the audiences at the Behrenstrasse – no one stood up or took special notice when the princes entered their loge – and at their exemplary deportment: "Other theaters are manned with guards in order to avoid disorders; nothing is known of that here, and a guard is nowhere to be seen."[4]

Many of the actors in the large company the writer judged as terrible, and Döbbelin himself clung to the old style of overacting in pathetic roles, but the comic operas kept the public indulgent toward such exaggeration, our observer notes, and he adds that these works were responsible for keeping Döbbelin in business. Indeed, the company's commitment to opera grew stronger with each passing year, and the trend crested in 1783 with 151 performances of operas (up from 117 two years earlier). The forty-six new operas introduced at Berlin from 1778 to 1783 were still dominated by North German works (twenty-one, mostly by André and Benda) and French ones (eleven, nearly all by Grétry), but slowly fourteen new operas imported from the Rhineland, Italy, and Vienna made their way onto Döbbelin's stage.

During 1779 and 1780 important operas from central Germany, in particular the serious works of Benda and Schweitzer, entered the Berlin repertory, but not a one from that region appeared in the succeeding three years. French operas continued to do well, but André's new works pleased less and less with each passing year. Döbbelin's receipts in the early 1780s dwindled despite his increasing commitment to the comic operas his audiences craved. Christian Friedrich von Bonin issued a day-by-day account of his offerings for 1782 and summarized the problem Döbbelin faced in that crucial year:

It must be remarked that the taste for operettas seems to be abating here – although on the whole they are really always very well cast. A mediocre comedy has for some time been as effective as a good operetta. One finally becomes tired of the eternal plinking and planking, for which probably the uniformity of the compositions is partly to blame; we hear almost nothing here but Italian, French, and – André – from the last we enjoy always at least *three* operas before we are served up one by another composer.[5]

The vigor he detected in Döbbelin's spoken offerings was something new,

4 *Deutsches Museum* 1779:2, p. 271. The traveler signed his contributions on several German cities "Wz." Presumably he is Johann Carl Wezel, a major contributor to this journal.
5 Bonin, *Berliner Theater-Journal*, 534.

and lay with the likes of Schiller and Shakespeare: "High tragedy and comedy that approaches farce are now most effective here," Bonin continued. "Our public no longer desires weak fare; one wants either to be shaken or to laugh from the belly – everything that is simply *sentimental* won't do."[6] As if to prove his point, the next year Döbbelin took up Schiller's *Die Räuber* and it swept everything else in the repertory before it.

André produced only one opera of his own in 1783, *Der Barbier von Bagdad*, and it failed. Thereafter the company's musical repertory swerved suddenly toward an important new source – Vienna. All six of the other operas introduced in 1783 came from the Burgtheater, and not just the latest products of the National Singspiel there but Italian, German, and French works spanning two decades:

> *I filosofi immaginari* (Paisiello, in Stephanie the Younger's translation of 1781)
> *L'amore artigiano* (Gassmann, 1767, in Neefe's translation)
> *Der Rauchfangkehrer* (Salieri, 1781)
> *Diesmal hat der Mann den Willen!* (Ordoñez, 1778)
> *La Rencontre imprévue* (Gluck, 1764, in an unknown translation)
> *Le Cadi dupé* (Gluck, 1761, translated by André)

As the succeeding two chapters will show, these six works were but the vanguard of a Viennese invasion which eventually transformed virtually all of North German opera in the later 1780s and 1790s.

The literary background: Bretzner's early librettos

If we extract from Table 6.1 the most popular librettists in North Germany from 1778 to 1783 and compare these with the most frequently set librettists from the preceding six years, one name fairly leaps out at us:

1778–1783		1772–1777	
Bretzner	11	Goethe	5
Meissner	5	Gotter	5
Goethe	4	Heermann	4

Christoph Friedrich Bretzner, born at Leipzig in 1748 and a businessman there all his life, began writing plays in 1771. In 1779 he issued a collection of four comic operas which immediately struck a responsive chord. All four of them were set more than once by North German composers, *Der Irrwisch* and *Das wütende Heer* three times, *Adrast und Isidore* and *Der Äpfeldieb* twice. An auspicious beginning, and one on which Bretzner followed up: by the end of the century, his librettos accounted for more German operas than those of any other writer.

Bretzner's first four operas may be divided into two pairs. The more tradi-

---

6 *Ibid.*, pp. 536–7. The term used by Bonin for "sentimental" is not the common "empfindsam" (which Bode had used, for example, in translating Sterne's *Sentimental Journey*) but the more pejorative "sentimentalisch."

tional pair comprises *Adrast und Isidore, oder Die Serenate*, a skillful reworking of Molière's *Le Sicilien* into a two-act comic opera, and *Der Äpfeldieb, oder Der Schatzgräber*, originally a one-act spoken comedy published by Bretzner in 1771. Both these farces display Bretzner's keen relish for comic complications. In *Der Äpfeldieb* a gardener's assistant named Martin has taken to stealing apples from his employer by night. One evening he is interrupted by an assortment of lovers and forced to hide in an apple-tree, from which vantage point he overhears their dealings. The landowner's daughter Juliane and her lady-in-waiting tryst with a young nobleman and his servant. Juliane's mother sends these four into hiding when she appears in order to meet her own lover. We learn that she has been systematically making life as sour as possible for her husband in order to hasten his end. Her assignation is also interrupted, this time by her husband and a confidence man named Fuchs, who has convinced the credulous old man that a treasure lies buried in his orchard. Fuchs has nearly swindled him of his valuables when a scene of mass confusion develops as the various hiders are discovered, capped by Martin's falling out of the tree with his basket of apples. He need fear nothing from this disclosure of his activities, however, since he has compromising information on just about everybody. At a sign from the wayward wife he refrains from divulging her affair, and he also lets Juliane's maid make off with her master's valuables on being given to know that he will share in the booty.

The size of the cast, the conduct of the intrigue, and the personalities of several of these characters betray strong French and Italian comic influence. The professional bilker Fuchs was something new to German opera, and so was the thieving gardener's assistant. Needless to say, an adulterous wife hastening a foolish husband's end had hitherto been utterly unthinkable.[7] There is not even a token effort at promoting virtue, and, though vice is ridiculed, none of the evildoers is punished.

The musical complexion of Bretzner's libretto is not striking. The imbroglio scene he left entirely in dialogue, a feature which most prominently marks this as an early libretto, for he would not miss the chance of developing an extended musical ensemble out of such a scene later on. The set numbers are oddly distributed. The young lovers are allowed two duets, but otherwise just a single aria for Juliane. Her maid is given both the Romanze and the rondo. Martin, though in hiding for most of the drama, receives the greatest musical attention with four arias and a duet.

Bretzner placed at the front of his collection the more adventuresome pair of librettos, *Der Irrwisch, oder Endlich fand er sie* and *Das wütende Heer, oder Das Mädchen im Thurme*. In his preface he called them "Märchen"

---

[7] It was certainly not to be tolerated in a Viennese setting by Friedrich Jast "performed at the imperial royal court Nationaltheater by young people studying dramatic art" (so reads the title page of the printed libretto of 1781). In this version both Frau von Althayn and her lover are eliminated entirely from the cast. The version adds a fair-sized ensemble when the two pairs of young lovers first meet, including asides from Martin in the apple-tree.

("fairy tales") and acknowledged Gozzi as his general model. He embraced the medieval in *Das wütende Heer*, as Schiebeler had done with *Lisuart und Dariolette*, but rejected its Anglo-Frankish flavor in earlier works in favor of the Teutonic, initiating a vogue that was to find its way across the next forty-two years to *Der Freischütz* in 1821. In *Der Irrwisch* Bretzner was more cautious, duplicating the familiar fairy-tale milieu of an enchanted island, which Michaelis had already explored in *Walmir und Gertraud* and for which Kotzebue was to have such a decided taste in his librettos.

Der Irrwisch follows the fortunes of Alwin, Prince of the Green Island, under a fairy's curse brought on by careless gallantries with the ladies at his court. He must wander through the swamps each night as a will-o'-the-wisp, appearing to various maidens as a humble shepherd until he finds a pure innocent who will love him for himself. He finds her in Blanka, adoptive daughter of a foolish fisherman and his unprincipled, scheming wife. This step-mother substitutes herself for Blanka but fails the ceremonial test, held in "a temple in old Gothic style" and conducted by priests and white-clad virgins. Blanka, who passes the test by firmly rejecting the prince until he dons his shepherd's disguise, is discovered to be of noble birth as tradition sanctioned in such instances.

Das wütende Heer moves much more assertively into the castled, spectred world of "Schauerromantik," which was soon to invade English and German drawing rooms through collections of folk tales and the Gothic novel. Laura, while out hunting one midsummer's day with her father, Graf Conrad, had become lost in a primeval forest where the "wütendes Heer" (a supernatural army of wild huntsmen) haunts the environs of an ancient castle tower. More than twenty young knights, inspired by Laura's portrait, have lost their lives trying to free her from this haunted tower. Now young Albert sets out to try his luck. As he and his faint-hearted squire Robert near the tower, a mist envelops it, a storm with thunder and lightning arises, and an eerie chorus sings offstage: "Heraus, o wütendes Heer zur Jagd!" Robert is petrified with fear but Albert is undaunted. A female voice tells him to catch a white dove at midnight, two feathers of which will open the tower. The dove duly appears and Laura is rescued, but act three is barely off the ground, so the moment her father kisses her she turns to a marble statue. Robert decides that the dove is to blame and stabs the bird, whereupon a blue flame appears behind Laura and she comes to life.

Bretzner's plot is an arbitrary, disorderly riot of romantic folk-legend motives planned around the midnight tower scene. As in the other early librettos of this set, the musical disposition is conservative. Squire Robert's endless string of songs dominates act one, and the second act droops after the wild hunt sings offstage (and the act actually ends with dialogue). Music is also kept out of the supernatural goings on involving Laura's petrifation, the dove, and the flame in act three. A reviewer of Bretzner's first four operas suggested a cure: "If he were to study the finale of the Italians and the dialogue duets, trios, quartets, etc. of the French, he will soon excel them. As heterodox as it may seem to many German art critics, yet it is true that entire scenes set to music make the most splendid effect on stage, but the subject must be well chosen."[8]

The sort of larger musical canvas suggested here the librettist allowed for only once in these four works, and not in either of the supernatural extravaganzas but in his adaptation of Molière, *Adrast und Isidore*. A young French nobleman and his Turkish slave attempt to free a beautiful Greek girl jealously guarded by her Sicilian master. The young Adrast arranges musicians and lanterns for an extended evening serenade. This long musical number is nothing more than a small cantata of three arias separated by recitative, however, and only when it concludes does the plot regain its momentum. As we shall see, Bretzner moved decisively in the direction of the Italian finale in his one other libretto from this period, *Belmont und Constanze*, completed in 1780.

The attraction of these early librettos for musicians lay not in their inviting musical structure but in their colorful and lively plots. Here Bretzner was not alone, however. His interest in Molière echoes in an adaptation of *Le Mariage forcé* by Friedrich Ludwig Wilhelm Meyer, *Kurze Thorheit ist die beste*, a revision for Berlin of his *Alter schützt für Thorheit nicht*, first performed at Mannheim with André's music in 1779. A writer present at the Berlin première in 1780 could not praise the text enough: in the comic additions the poet approached Molière himself, "who is almost inimitable here," and he excelled him on the side of sentiment. The song texts were very skillfully woven in, "and in them the action continues, which undoubtedly provides greater liveliness than the usual method, and is more advantageous for the composer, but demands sharper attention on the part of the auditor."[9]

The farcical element which figures strongly in these operas derived from Molière seems also to have informed the librettos which André wrote for himself. Although only the arias survive, they are both works adapted from the French. In 1782 von Bonin noted with approval the broad comic character of one of these, *Der Liebhaber als Automat* – "for the public is justly tired of the tearful or insipidly naïve Singspiel."[10]

Bretzner's fascination with the marvelous reverberates in one other new opera produced at Berlin during this period, an adaptation of Shakespeare's *Tempest* by the Magdeburg minister Johann Samuel Patzke, set to music by the same city's music director, Johann Heinrich Rolle. However, the lost text had reduced Shakespeare's romance to a single act and was apparently intended as an occasional piece.

Finally, the trend toward an operatic equivalent to the *drame* took a turn toward the hyper-emotional at Berlin with young Bernhard Christoph

[8] *Litteratur- und Theater-Zeitung* 2 (1779): 695.   [9] *Ibid.* 3 (1780): 765–6.
[10] *Berliner Theater-Journal*, p. 411.

d'Arien's music drama *Laura Rosetti*. Published at Leipzig in 1777, it was set by André and enthusiastically received at Berlin in 1778. Schink, who had befriended d'Arien, did not hesitate to class this libretto with Gotter's *Romeo und Julie* as an example of "dramas that demand something more than a voice, that also demand a head."[11]

Franzesko is to marry Donna Rosa Sensali, but has fallen in love with her lady-in-waiting, Laura Rosetti. His friend, the cavalry captain Cesar Rinaldi, warns him not to deal lightly with Donna Rosa, but Franzesko is determined to break with her. Sensing this, she throws herself into a jealous frenzy, and when she finds Laura with Franzesko's portrait her worst fears are confirmed. She confronts the lovers and, after an inept attempt at poisoning them with chocolate, has Laura locked away. She offers Franzesko a dagger, dares him to kill her, faints, and awakens with her wits disjointed. Rinaldi, the cold realist, suggests that Franzesko take them both, one for money and the other for love, which earns an icy rebuff. Rinaldi then tells Laura that Franzesko has gone back to Donna Rosa, throws himself at her feet, and proposes to save her from the waiting convent if only she will return his affection. This elaborate test convinces Rinaldi of her steadfastness and worth. Meanwhile, Donna Rosa regains her senses, forgives Franzesko with a warning ("you were born to nobler purposes than languishing, sighing, and tender raptures"), and leaves a paper giving half her estate to Laura.

One thinks often of Goethe in studying d'Arien's libretto. The connection is further cemented by d'Arien's adoption of the designation Goethe had chosen for his first two librettos, "Schauspiel mit Gesang," and by explicit reference to the notorious denouement of *Stella*, made by Franzesko when Rinaldi proposes a triangular accommodation with both Laura and Donna Rosa. D'Arien's concern for strongly drawn characters had many precedents in Storm and Stress drama and few or none in German opera. Donna Rosa is of course an arch-operatic species, the spurned aristocrat whose obsession with revenge drives her insane.[12]

The defects in d'Arien's hero, who borrows heavily from the indecisive Fernando in *Stella*, translate into a defective, forced plot. Nor could the author seek refuge in claims of operatic immunity, for he had not given his composer much room in which to manoeuvre. The drama freezes for every one of his twenty-eight numbers. Twenty-two of these are arias, and four of the five for Donna Rosa are raging exit arias of more or less the same character. André remained the only composer in North Germany to set *Laura Rosetti*, but elsewhere its high emotional charge complemented the sort of librettos current in South Germany and the Rhineland, and settings appeared

---

[11] *Dramaturgische Fragmente* (Graz, 1781–2), vol. 2, p. 460.
[12] Somewhat surprisingly, Wieland went against all his own laws of operatic moderation in hazarding a similar character at nearly the same time with Queen Elinor in *Rosamunde*, written with Schweitzer for Mannheim in 1777. The triangular predicament here is also similar to d'Arien's.

over the next decade and a half at Mannheim (Danzi, 1781), Pressburg (Teyber, 1784), Stuttgart (Dieter, 1787), and Münster (Bruckhausen, 1791).

André's operas for Berlin

André dominated the operatic scene at Berlin with twelve of the sixteen new German operas produced there. His control was even more pervasive than these figures suggest, for he also composed most of the celebratory Vorspiele and pantomime ballets mounted by Döbbelin and, beyond that, he composed incidental music (including numbers for Shakespeare's *Macbeth*) and translated texts of both French and Italian operas for the Berlin stage.

Yet by 1782, the date of Bonin's complaint about too many performances of André's operas, his fortunes were on the decline. *Das wütende Heer* played to an empty house by its fifth performance in 1781, and *Der Barbier von Bagdad* was booed off the stage after only a few evenings in early 1783. André produced nothing more for Berlin thereafter, and in April of 1784 retired from his position at Berlin and returned to his languishing printing business back at Offenbach.

Not all of André's misfortunes were of his own making. The failure of his *Elmine* in 1782, in which he returned to the serious style which had made a great success of *Laura Rosetti* in 1778, has been justly charged by critics to the account of the librettist, a Nüremberger named von Drais. Elmine and Philidor have received the permission of her father Ebhardo to marry, but must first gain that of Philidor's father. Just then Vanderhök, an unattractive and mercenary old friend of Ebhardo, turns up to help his friend out of some sudden pecuniary straits, in return for which he demands Elmine's hand in marriage. Ebhardo reluctantly lays the choice of duty or inclination before his daughter. Elmine repairs to her mother's graveside, her favorite spot for meditating, where she determines to adhere to her mother's dying adjuration to obey Ebhardo in all things. Her obedience is celebrated and rewarded by the revelation that Vanderhök was a disguise under which Philidor's father had sought to sound out her character, for he could learn nothing from his son's "shallow, new-fangled gibberish."

André's over-elaborate musical means are wholly inappropriate to the maudlin dramatic ends of *Elmine*, except perhaps when he deals with Ebhardo, the one bearable character in the story. No sooner is the curtain up than Philidor adopts the unnatural attire of an obbligato recitative to tell Elmine that her father has agreed to their marriage. By the time the fourth number rolls around, André reminds us of what precious little headway either plot or characterization has made by recalling a large section of the opening duet. Worse is still to come, and wastes no time in doing so. Elmine's silly little sister Lore, who suffers from adolescent obsession with romance, catches her sister and Philidor exchanging endearments – and all this André sets as a melodrama! But such a melodrama as Germany had never seen, a galant G-major Andante grazioso issuing in Lore's imbecilic 6/8 aria, "Ha, ha, ha, ha! Ich sah euch winken."

Thereafter André recoups somewhat. Ebhardo's Pantalone-like goodness of heart as a father devoted to his child's happiness permeates the music, if not the words, of the aria in which he enjoins Elmine to choose between Vanderhök and Philidor. "Consider, struggle, and choose!" hardly deserves the rich harmonic depth of attachment lent Ebhardo in one of the composer's favorite keys, B-flat (Example 6.1). The poignant solo oboe yields after the

Example 6.1 André: *Elmine*. Aria of Ebhardo, act 1.
"Consider, struggle, and choose. . ."

ritornello to high flutes rather than the composer's usual string accompaniment, and his chronic fascination with secondary dominants is enriched by reliance on accented diminished-seventh chords, a musical equivalent all in all of Goldoni's sweet Venetian dialect in conveying more than a well-meaning father can say with his honest words alone. Through such numbers, André helps to draw attention away from any suspicion that the whole dilemma facing Elmine is an artifice to which Ebhardo was privy from the start.

André resorted to the melodrama twice more in the opera after his first mis-
fortune with it, both times much more appropriately, and as usual he
provided Marie Niklas with a recitative and aria tailored to her considerable
talents. The spot chosen for this is a favorite one with North German librett-
tists and composers – right after the release of dramatic tension, where a
poetic simile on the remembrance of dangers past or the happy prospect of
coming felicity animates the heroine to ariatic heights.

All in all, André showed himself not a little anxiously ambitious in *Elmine*.
Such is not the case in his more popular scores. Witty apprehensibility marks
his fine setting of Meissner's *Der Alchymist*, a text we will consider in more
detail when examining Joseph Schuster's exquisite setting. The lovely four-bar
theme of an aria for the *soubrette* Christine, shown in Example 6.2, almost

Example 6.2 André: *Der Alchymist*. Aria of Christine.
"If a kiss could move you, willingly I'd give it to you."

brings to mind "Il mio tesoro" or Beethoven's C-major Rondo for piano.
But its gaiety is calculated. Christine is playing up to Magister Kybbutz, a
meddlesome pedant who is threatening to expose the escape plan of
Christine's mistress and her lover. So in setting "Could a kiss move you,
willingly I'd give it to you," André inserts a coquettish pause (inviting
appropriate stage gesture) which delays "willig" a half bar. In the middle part
of the aria Christine moves off to the relative minor and an undulating 6/8
Allegretto which graphically depicts her seductions as she winds toil after
amorous toil around her quarry (Example 6.3). The implication of a sultry
siciliana is enhanced by the augmented second in the vocal line (filled in by
the hypnotic echoes of the flute), and by the four-fold textual repetition over
a G pedal. Now the poet Meissner swings into action along with André.
Together they press anatomical allurements onto the victim as the two-bar
phrases urge the relentless motive upward. For a moment Christine keeps
Kybbutz dangling in mildly erotic syntactic uncertainty over whether "soft
and round and white" refers to her heaving breast just described. But no, it is
her "little arm," and both poet and composer can congratulate themselves at

Example 6.3 André: *Der Alchymist*. Aria of Christine.
"See how my little mouth glows, and my breast swells for you alone, soft and round and white is this little arm, and it binds you."

Ex. 6.3 (*cont.*)

the end that the final line of text, "and may it bind you," is a wish already half realized.

André shows in this and similar instances a mastery of comic effects closely linked to text and suggestive of gesture at every turn. It lay at the heart of his popularity at Berlin along with his pleasing melodic style. Something of another order altogether was demanded for the eerie chorus of the wild hunt in *Das wütende Heer*, however. To set it André departed sharply from the conservative stamp of earlier storm numbers in North German opera (which followed the example Hiller had set in *Die Jagd*) and helped himself liberally to a wide range of stock components from French opera: string tremolos, piccolos, sudden dynamic shifts, harmonic irregularities, diminished sevenths, syncopation, monophonic choral declamation on reciting tones, and even the key of c minor. André anticipates something of Weber's structural fascination with the diminished seventh chord with the chorus's bold opening statement on E-flat (bars 19 to 44 in Example 6.4) under which the outlined diminished seventh resolutely refuses to resolve its low F♯ to the dominant and instead creeps up against the chorus's relentless whole notes to the dominant of e-flat minor. André sidesteps this anticipated resolution as well and instead winds his way back to c minor.[13]

---

[13] André's chorus seems not to have been well performed at Berlin. One reviewer complained: "On this occasion we remember having noted that several men, whom we could name, must consider it a mere bagatelle to sing in the chorus, since – seemingly either to make a joke or to highlight their voices – they often scream and explode so as to make things most unpleasant for the audience. And thus the best and most splendid music is not infrequently unrecognized, music which cost its worthy composer many a difficult hour." *Litteratur- und Theater-Zeitung* 4 (1781): 112. Nonetheless, as shown in Example 6.4, André specifically instructs his chorus to sing "in a fearsome, strong, cavernous voice."

Example 6.4 André: *Das wütende Heer*. Chorus of the Wild Hunt, act 2.
"Come out! oh wild hunt to the chase, out to the chase. The midnight hour sounds. . ."

Ex. 6.4 (*cont.*)

Ex. 6.4 (*cont.*)

Belmont und Constanze and Mozart's *Die Entführung aus dem Serail*

With the founding of the National Singspiel at Vienna in early 1778 German opera became an accredited part of the city's cultural life, and the possibility arose for fruitful exchange with South and North Germany. Yet, as we saw earlier, North German composers fared quite poorly in the new repertory, and South Germany had as yet generated only a handful of German operas.

Nonetheless, the widespread admiration for North German literary achievement in all fields at Vienna made itself felt in the National Singspiel. In addition to Stephanie the Younger's well-known adaptation of *Belmont und Constanze* for Mozart, all four of the librettos published by Bretzner in 1779 saw productions at Vienna in settings by local composers, and three of them just prior to Mozart's *Entführung aus dem Serail* of 1782:[14]

Der Äpfeldieb (Jast, 1781)
Adrast und Isidore (as *Die Nachtmusik*, Miča, 1781 – an earlier version by Bretzner which won a prize at Vienna)
Der Irrwisch (Umlauf, 1782, adapted by Stephanie at the same time he was working on Mozart's libretto)
Das wütende Heer (Ruprecht, 1787, in an anonymous adaptation)

[14] The only North German libretto to precede Bretzner's in the repertory of the National Singspiel was Engel's *Die Apotheke*, set by Umlauf and first produced in 1778. Other early North German librettists, such as Weisse, Heermann, and Gotter, found new composers in South Germany, but not at Vienna's new enterprise.

This Viennese vogue of Bretzner's librettos strikingly parallels his domination of the Berlin stage during the same period. An astonishing five of the six premières at Berlin from 1779 to 1781 were settings of his first five librettos. Mozart's *Die Entführung aus dem Serail*, then, is simply the best known opera from a broad cultivation encompassing all of Bretzner's librettos, first at Berlin, and then at Vienna.

An immediate model for Bretzner's story has yet to be identified. The exotic setting of a seraglio formed the basis of the strenuous search undertaken by Walter Preibisch.[15] All the connections he draws with opera buffa are unimpressive, save those to Martinelli's *La schiava liberata*,[16] and there are no strong links with the English sources Dent mentions.[17] Freiherr von Knigge dismissed Bretzner's text as "derived from a few opéras-comiques," but to date a clear source in French literature – the most likely place – has not emerged.[18]

Among German operas there are a few common motives with *Der Bassa von Tunis* by Henisch, as we noted earlier, but a great many more with a contemporary Rhenish opera, *Adelheit von Veltheim*, written for Neefe by Grossmann in 1780. The situation here between Adelheit and the Bassa Achmet is substantially that between Constanze and Bassa Selim. Mehmet, the overseer of the seraglio, is an explicit eunuch and thus cannot function as a comic parallel to his master, as Osmin does in Bretzner's libretto. Karl von Bingen, the Bassa's gardener and Adelheit's fiancé, combines Belmonte and Pedrillo. Grossmann adds many secondary characters (a haremful of Europeans to play up national differences, Adelheit's father, and a band of German knights) and adopts a much lower tone which is variously crude, jingoistic, and sarcastic, already hinting at the mental breakdown which ended Grossmann's career.

Bretzner claimed to have completed his own libretto of *Belmont und Constanze* before he read Grossmann's,[19] but, while he presents a very convincing

---

[15] "Quellenstudien zu Mozart's "Entführung aus dem Serail," *SIMG* 10 (1908/9): 430–76.

[16] The father–son relationship dominating this libretto – a sultan wishes his son Selim to marry the Turkish beauty Elmire, but Selim stubbornly pursues the captive Spanish woman Dorimene – minimizes anything more than incidental motivic borrowing by Bretzner. On the other hand, he is likely to have known this source, since not only was it performed at nearby Dresden in 1777 with Schuster's music, but also the libretto saw publication there in a bilingual edition (Schatz 9754).

[17] Dent, who never refers to Preibisch's study, claims that Bretzner's play "was imitated from an English comic opera, *The Captive*, performed in 1769 with music by Dibdin and others" (*Mozart's Operas*, 2nd ed. (London, Oxford, and New York 1947), p. 71).

[18] Knigge's remarks occur in his review of the printed libretto in the *Allgemeine deutsche Bibliothek* 49:1 (1782): 127–8. He was no doubt thinking of Favart's *Solimann II* (1761), popular all over Europe. Rudolf Angermüller's efforts to connect Bretzner's libretto with the spoken drama *Les Époux esclaves*, in the *Mozart-Jahrbuch 1978/9* (pp. 70–88), are less than convincing inasmuch as this work is known to exist only in manuscript at Paris.

[19] A prefatory letter to Grossmann's printed libretto is dated 10 September 1780. Less than a month later, under date 4 October, Bretzner sent an open letter to André, printed in the *Litteratur- und Theater-Zeitung*: having just read *Adelheit von Veltheim*, he notes, he was amazed "that we both, without knowing the slightest of each other, have by chance pursued

case in support of his claim that he had had no contact with *Adelheit von Veltheim*, Grossmann may well have inspired Stephanie the Younger to his modification of Bretzner's denouement, in which the Bassa turns out to be Belmonte's father. Grossmann's Bassa Achmet frees Karl and Adelheit even though they had exposed him to the torment of a fruitless passion and had betrayed his friendship. In so doing he enjoins them to reflect "that you have found in so-called barbarous lands a human and a friend, . . . that I surely did not learn to act thus from the history of your conquest of foreign parts of the earth."[20] Stephanie, too, concludes with the Bassa's magnanimity as a lesson in humanity, in this case for the son of his arch-enemy.

Speculation on sources is less important for our present purposes than gaining an appreciation of how Bretzner's fifth libretto differs from the four he had published in 1779, and what these differences meant to André. While much of this libretto still adheres to traditional North German practice, several of its features clearly suggest the inspiration of foreign models, and particularly opera buffa. The characters, independent of what the musician does with them, already have shifted toward types who receive their stamp not from moral sentence and episodes pursued at length in the spoken dialogue, but from confrontation with one another inviting musical participation. The pairings of Constanze and the Bassa, Pedrillo and Osmin, and Osmin and Blonde offer familiar examples, though at this stage Bretzner does not exploit all of these musically. In fact, a clear musical reflex of these interactions does not come until the end of act one, in the trio of Osmin, Belmonte, and Pedrillo ("Marsch! Marsch! Marsch! trollt euch fort!") which Stephanie passed on to Mozart without alteration. The second appears with the drinking duet "Vivat Bachus!" of Osmin and Pedrillo in act two, which became something of a folk song around Berlin in André's setting (Example 6.5).

Example 6.5 André: *Belmont und Constanze*. Drinking duet, act 2.
"Long live Bacchus, long live Bacchus, Bacchus is a fine fellow."

almost the identical path" 3 (1780): 672. To avoid the reproach of imitation he added that the text of *Belmont und Constanze* had been sent to André in July, and a reviewer writing on the première of André's opera for the same journal's issue of 7 July 1781 recalled having seen the text at André's "schon vor Jahr und Tag."

[20] *Adelheit von Veltheim, ein Schauspiel mit Gesang in vier Akten* (Leipzig, 1781), p. 127.

Bretzner's *tour de force* in this regard, wholly unprecedented in his earlier librettos, occurs near the beginning of act three, a huge and impressive finale structure encompassing the entire elopement scene. Most North German composers had little or no practice in dealing with the compositional problems Bretzner posed here. Guidance was needed, from Italian models in particular. A few such works André already knew quite well from preparing them for performance in German versions at Berlin – Piccinni's *La buona figliuola* in 1777, Sacchini's *L'isola d'amore* (for which André wrote the German translation) in 1779, and Anfossi's *Il geloso in cimento* less than three months before the première of *Belmont und Constanze* in 1781. André, it may be remembered, was the only North German composer to hazard a setting of Goethe's *Claudine von Villa Bella*, the only earlier North German libretto with anything remotely approximating Bretzner's abduction scene; it may be remembered as well that Goethe's grand ensemble in that libretto involved an attempted abduction foiled by the arrival of the town watch.

Not surprisingly, however, the dimensions in which André cast his setting of the abduction scene in *Belmont und Constanze* still resemble those of Galuppi and Piccinni in the 1750s and early 1760s, that is to say, the early stage of the development of the opera buffa finale.[21] Table 6.2 lays out the musical and dramatic structure of Bretzner's ensemble in André's setting. The action develops slowly, lingering at the start in order to create an element of anxious anticipation, introduced as a prime emotional color of Section 1 – a ternary aria for Belmonte – and Section 2, in which Pedrillo seeks to restrain his nervous master. André's light touch – ever at his behest in 6/8 sections such as this and the one from *Der Alchymist* discussed earlier – proves especially effective here, as seen in Example 6.6. André chooses economical and apt figures to bring the situation to musical life: the lulling motion in the violins floats over an undercurrent of unrest in the basses and violas, touching off the anxious spasm of a diminished octave in bar 92, a heartbeat figure at "still," and a slightly skitterish mention of "die Wach" as Pedrillo vaults suddenly toward the dominant. Belmonte's reply is more frankly disconcerted, nice use being made of an augmented second in his rising line and the traditional feint toward the dominant minor before settling into the major. At this point, the tense palpitations of Belmonte's heart are now explicit.

Dent has dismissed André's music in Section 3, Pedrillo's Romanze, as "trivial."[22] In André's defense, one should point out that in the original libretto, which Dent never looked at, Bretzner had already extended the

---

[21] André's setting of the elopement scene tends more to the technical procedures of Galuppi than to those of Piccinni. The distinctions to be made between them and the historiographic fortunes of their finales are discussed by Daniel Heartz, "The Creation of the Buffo Finale in Italian Opera," *PRMA* 114 (1977/8): 67–78.

[22] *Mozart's Operas*, p. 80. This one word sums up Dent's attitude toward North German vocal music in general, but in confronting his attitude one must bear in mind his ardent championship of Italian vocal style – so important to the formation of our present stylistic understanding of the eighteenth century – and the unhappy state of Anglo-German relations at the time he wrote (1913).

Table 6.2. *Music-dramatic structure of André's "Welch ängstliches beben," Belmont und Constanze*

Section	Characters	Tempo	Key	Meter	Measures	Text incipit	Action
1	B	Andante–Allegro–Andante	F–f–F	2/4	1–85	Welch ängstliches beben	B, alone, sings while playing the mandolin, caught between fear and hope.
2	B,P	Allegretto	F	6/8	86–207	Alles ruhig, alles still	B wants to rush into action, P reins him in, B stands guard as P prepares to give the signal.
3	B,P	ROMANZE: Andante	Bb	2/4	208–240	Im Mohrenland gefangen war	P, playing the mandolin, sings four stanzas as B urges him to hurry; finally he coughs as a signal and C opens her window.
4	B,P,C,	Allegro	V/D D	C	241–322	Sie öfnet, sie öfnet!	P sets up the ladder, B climbs in, he and C come out the door, P sends them off to the shore, sets the ladder at Bl's window and climbs in. O comes out with a mute servant, who finds the ladder and gesticulates.
5	O,M,P, Bl	Più allegro	d–C–d	C	323–380	Gift und Dolch!	O thinks thieves and murderers are in the house and sends the mute for the Watch. As P descends Bl sees O; P scampers back in as O climbs up after; P and Bl then slip out the door.
6	O,W,P, Bl,M,	Allegro assai	F	2/4	381–490	Zu Hülfe!	O cries out on seeing them, the Watch detains O until the mute convinces them of their error; others return with P and Bl. O longs to hack off their heads.
	B,C				491–603	Schändliche lasst mich	The rest of the Watch come with B and C; they try to bribe O, but he and the Watch are unmovable: it's off to the Bassa over all protests and pleas.

Key:
B – Belmonte   C – Constanze   P – Pedrillo   Bl – Blonde   O – Osmin   M – mute   W – Watch

Example 6.6 André: *Belmont und Constanze*. Abduction scene, act 3.

PEDRILLO: "All is peaceful, all is still. Everyone is asleep, and the watch has already retired."
BELMONTE: "Oh, then come to rescue her, for anxious as if in chains my suffering heart beats for her."

Ex. 6.6 (*cont.*)

ensemble's static beginning with an ariatic section for Belmonte (Section 1), and here Pedrillo must provide only a short bit of stage music (although it is not short enough for Belmonte) as a foil for the cough in the night air signaling to Constanze and Blonde that the elopement is under way. It is a small fish in a big sea, unlike the separate number surrounded by dialogue which it became in Stephanie's adaptation.

Coordinated with Pedrillo's cough and Constanze's opening of her window is the one major tonal shift in André's finale, up a major third from B-flat to D major at the beginning of Section 4. The slower tempos similarly give way to an accelerating series of Allegros as the stage action shifts into high gear. The business with ladders, windows, and doors demands skillful coordination. The pantomimetic contributions by Osmin's Moorish mute are another essential ingredient. André could have done much more here: he was an old hand at writing for the pantomime ballet, an important part of nearly all North German repertories. But the most telling betrayal of his lack of practice in dealing with the compositional problems posed by a finale structure occurs in Section 6, where he scurries back to the tonic and asserts the final tempo well before the conclusion of the dramatic action – a tonal event that a more practiced hand would have held in reserve until bar 491 (indicated separately within Section 6 in Table 6.2).

Mozart, who owned a copy of Bretzner's printed text and referred to this ensemble in act three as a "charming quintet or rather finale," began composing Bretzner's original abduction scene in 1781, but broke off his preliminary draft just prior to Pedrillo's Romanze. In Mozart's version the scene was to serve as the finale of act two, but this left virtually nothing for the third act, and so Stephanie provided Mozart with a new intrigue with which to end act two and broke up the abduction scene at the beginning of act three into dialogue and three set pieces: a new aria for Belmonte to replace Section 1, Pedrillo's Romanze intact, and a new aria for Osmin ("O! wie will ich triumphiren!") expanding on a single line in Section 6.[23]

---

[23] His sketch has been printed in the appendix to *Die Entführung aus dem Serail*, edited by Gerhard Croll, in the *Neue Mozart-Ausgabe*, series 2, work-group 5, vol. 12, pp. 436–41. Croll's introduction, especially his remarks on the genesis of the opera's libretto and music,

There are other important deviations from Bretzner's plan in *Die Entführung aus dem Serail*. Eight of Bretzner's fifteen numbers survived more or
less unaltered, five were replaced with new texts, four new ones were added
where dialogue had stood, and only one was eliminated entirely. Thus, unlike
the Viennese adaptations of Bretzner's other librettos, this one grafted more
than it pruned. Most of the substitutions involve arias Mozart wanted to
tailor to his singers at Vienna, particularly the great comic bass Ludwig
Fischer, who took the part of Osmin. Others, however, involve the altering of
specifically Northern features, and so does the only excision made in Bretzner's plan, the omission of a concert aria for Constanze in the denouement,
just before the closing chorus in act three. As we have seen both in Benda's
Walder and André's earlier operas, such a spot had become traditional for the
exercise of the leading lady's virtuosity. With the plot safely conducted to its
conclusion, Northern dramatic sensibilities argued, one could indulge the
prima donna without harming the drama. The counterpart in *Die Entführung aus dem Serail*, Constanze's "Martern aller Arten," has dismayed most
critics by doing precisely the opposite, but it is an undeniable corollary of
Mozart's view of the relative roles of text and music that it is better for the
musician to risk interrupting a strong dramatic situation than to make much
ado about a weak one.

"Martern aller Arten" and Blonde's delightful "Welche Wonne, welche
Lust" highlight a new scene Stephanie had substituted in act two, and in this
context they replace another Northern specialty, the rondo, which Bretzner
had included in the omitted scene for both singers. As mentioned earlier, the
rondo was the strong suit of Marie Niklas, the original Constanze at Berlin.
In Bretzner's original scene Blonde, seeking to cheer up her unhappy mistress, explicitly commends the form to her: "Let's at least keep up hope!" she
chirps. "But, dear miss, the rondo! Certainly you know with what magic
music affects the heart; and it is your favorite piece, you know, so melting, so
tender!" To accommodate both characters Bretzner wrote a rondo-duet in the
shorter ABACA form, both women joining in the refrain and each singing a
quatrain in the two episodes. The rondo was soon to slip from favor in the
North, and Bretzner's adaptation to limit its repetitive structure is already
suggestive in this instance. Still, it adds nothing to a slack, inert moment in
the drama, and its defects are the more deeply felt today in that we have two
brilliant character pieces by Stephanie and Mozart to show what could
replace the lacklustre moralizing a rondo inevitably brought with it.

---

are warmly to be recommended. The ensemble's aspirations to the status of finale apparently
became a reality at Berlin. The manuscript of André's score there carries in a later hand at the
end of this number: "Here the third act may be concluded." Though a logical division in light
of the ensemble's character and also because a transformation to the inside of Bassa Selim's
palace follows, this makes explicit the musical and dramatic weakness of the concluding
scene.

Other Prussian personalities

André was not the only composer at Berlin, although the degree to which he dominated new operatic production there is equalled only by Hiller's reign at Leipzig from 1766 to 1773. Reichardt, as we saw, had come to Potsdam as Frederick the Great's Kapellmeister in late 1775, a prestigious position which bound him to commit most of his time and energy to Italian opera at the court. He seems to have had little to do with Döbbelin's stage beyond his fine melodrama on a text by the eminent Berlin poet Ramler, *Cephalus und Prokris*. His lone German opera from this period, *Liebe nur beglückt* (1781), saw its première not at Berlin but at Dessau.

In his preface to the libretto of this opera, which he had written himself, Reichardt offered his ideas on the position music ought to occupy in German opera – advice the genre was in no mood to take seriously, at least at Berlin, where André and Bretzner were beginning to move in the very directions it proscribed. Reichardt will allow singing only where high passion moves the listener to sighs and tears, and only for the main characters, not for the likes of confidantes, servants, and parents. The libretto itself offers nothing new. Wilhelmine, a count's daughter, is to marry a well-connected Baron, though she loves Hermann. The depth of this love quickly brings her father and the Baron around to supporting the match, and the class differences impeding it are taken care of when Hermann is made a major in the army. Reichardt experimented with several modern techniques of musical organization to bolster the drama: he introduced melodramas for the most important monologues and also made thematic connections between the overture and entr'actes on the one hand and his arias and melodramas on the other.[24]

Baron Otto Carl Erdmann von Kospoth, since 1776 *maître des plaisirs* at Potsdam, enjoyed some success with his settings of Bretzner for Döbbelin. His version of *Der Irrwisch* was given five times in a row after its première in 1780. "All his works have very lovely melodies," wrote von Bonin, "and will therefore always please on stage, for here the connoisseurs of music stand in at most a one-to-one-hundred ratio with plain dilettantes."[25] Kospoth published twelve favorite songs from his two Bretzner settings, showing the full gamut from simple Lieder (his tune to the rondo in *Adrast und Isidore* was sung all over Berlin) to bravura arias. The last item in this set is a song the factotum Hali sings near the beginning of *Adrast und Isidore* in praise of the keys of B-flat major and b-flat minor. The two excerpts given in Example 6.7 offer a fair representation of Kospoth's general comic style, with their wooden prosody and the mock-pathetic Neapolitans in bars 46 and 48 of the second.

East Prussia continued under the domination of Karoline Schuch's company. Her troupe played winters at Königsberg, summers at Mitau, and

---

[24] The opera is discussed in greater detail by Pröpper, *Die Bühnenwerke Johann Friedrich Reichardts*, vol. 1, pp. 70–3.
[25] *Berliner Theater-Journal*, p. 338.

Example 6.7 Kospoth: *Adrast und Isidore*. Serenade, act 1.
  A: "Believe me, no oath is needed, as a connoisseur I esteem only B-flat major."
  B: "But if one wishes to whimper and lament, cry, sigh, tremble, and quake, if it is to sound really pitiful, then it has to be in b-flat minor."

autumns at Danzig. They gave "tragedies seldom, comedies frequently, and operettas as often as the strength of the singers allows,"[26] strengthening a trend begun under her husband. The company had only six singers and drew its orchestra from an infantry regiment. At Königsberg they played at a private house, at Mitau in a specially built theater, and at Danzig in a "comfortable and roomy booth."

[26] Mohr, *Königsbergisches Theaterjournal*, preface.

Nearly all the new German operas, as well as several celebratory Vorspiele, which were produced by Madam Schuch from 1778 to 1783 came from two members of her troupe – the actor Johann August Halbe and the troupe music director Nikolaus Mühle. Halbe took d'Arien's sentimental one-act opera *Heinrich und Lyda*, already set by Neefe, expanded it to three acts, and renamed it *Die Liebe auf der Probe*. He retained all of Neefe's nine musical numbers and composed the eleven additional ones himself.

None of Mühle's music survives, but he was single-minded enough in his choice of texts to tell us something of his operatic taste. In addition to Bretzner's *Der Äpfeldieb*, he set three Rhenish librettos while in East Prussia with the Schuch company, and while at St. Petersburg he had already composed Bretzner's *Der Irrwisch* and two other texts from the Rhineland. The emotions in all these Rhenish texts are less carefully governed than was the norm in North Germany. *Fremore und Melime*, for instance, trades in a pair of young English lovers already secretly married and blessed with issue, who are discovered to be brother and sister and go through an entire act of torment until papers prove Fremore to be the changeling son of another man. *Mit dem Glockenschlag: zwölf!* goes just as far: in a moment of ecstasy Eugenius had robbed Laura of her innocence; as a result he was sent on travels to England and she was put in a convent. A happy ending is pulled out of the fire at the last second, just before Laura takes final orders.

Mühle also ventured into the exotic-romantic, not only with *Der Irrwisch* but also with Graf von Spaur's "Märchen" in four acts, *Der Schiffbruch*. The libretto borrows heavily from Shakespeare's *Tempest*. In the opening scene, for example, a magician whose brother has banished him from his native land (Egypt) commands his familiar spirit to bring about a shipwreck, but to save all on board and to bring him the young lady and the love-sick slave pursuing her.

In Silesia Holly produced one last German opera for Wäser, right in step with the trend elsewhere in Prussia, a setting of Bretzner's *Der Irrwisch*. A new figure arose in his stead to dominate the company's musical offerings, the actor-composer Johann Christoph Kaffka. The *Gallerie von Teutschen Schauspielern und Schauspielerinnen* of 1783 paints a detailed and none too flattering portrait of him. The writer begrudged Kaffka modest ability as a composer, dismissed his singing voice as raw, denied his acting any soul or insight, and closed with the remark, "With the publication of several wretched plays he has prostituted himself as a poet."[27]

Kaffka's gigolo qualities seem to have commanded the writer's special attention. The actor's "extremely advantageous figure" especially disturbed him: "Among the female part of the public this advantage is never obscured; in their eyes Kaffka is the greatest actor in Germany. 'Today the beautiful Kaffka is performing, we must go to the theater,' thus say mothers and daughters." Born at Regensburg, he studied to be a Jesuit, then a Cistercian (when

[27] *Gallerie von Teutschen Schauspielern*, p. 76.

the Jesuits were suppressed), but left for Prague and became Brunian's music director in 1775. There he also changed his name from Engelmann to Kaffka. He acted with a long string of German troupes at Nürnberg, Frankfurt (Marchand), Leipzig (Bondini), Regensburg, Stuttgart (Schikaneder), Berlin (Döbbelin, from 1779 to 1781), Brno, and finally Breslau, where he remained until 1789.

With Döbbelin at Berlin Kaffka had written incidental music, a ballet, and a melodrama (*Antonius und Cleopatra*) in 1779, and composed Bretzner's *Der Äpfeldieb* in 1780. When he joined the Wäser company in 1781 the principal had just died. The troupe thrived through the 1780s at Breslau under Wäser's very capable widow, Maria Barbara, who improved the company measurably and in May 1782 had their old playhouse at Breslau torn down and replaced with a much finer new one.

Kaffka's compositions for the Wäser company include the same ingredients already popular at Berlin – the melodrama, Bretzner, and Molière. He also explored the possibilities of both dramatic ensembles and finales, especially in the operas for which he acted as both librettist and composer. The former function, it is true, must be broadly construed in Kaffka's case. His *So prellt man alte Füchse*, for example, is not so much "after the French of Molière" as it is after an earlier German adaptation, Meyer's *Alter schützt für Thorheit nicht* mentioned earlier. Except for some adjustments in the gypsy scene, Kaffka uses all of Meyer's song texts verbatim.

He published this libretto at Breslau in 1784 along with two other comic operas he had translated. The first was *Die befreyte Sklavin*, a German version of Martinelli's *La schiava liberata* to be used with Schuster's music. The second, *Der Guckkasten, oder: Das Beste komt zulezt,* "after an Italian text," was set to music by Kaffka himself. His music is lost, but the libretto shows that he confronted true finales at the end of both acts. This, along with the small cast and frequent use of exit arias (seven of twelve), suggests that Kaffka had translated an opera buffa rather than an Italian spoken comedy, the more common source for German opera up to that time.

Kaffka proved very energetic during his first years at Breslau. He edited a collection of German operatic arias, including two of his own, in 1783 and a year later issued his setting of Bretzner's melodrama *Rosamunde*.[28] On 24 January 1783 he marked the birthday of Frederick the Great with a new "ernsthaftes Singspiel," actually an allegorical one-act Vorspiel using recitative throughout, *Bitten und Erhörung*, on the subject of the new theater at Breslau. Kaffka published his music in short score and immediately a reviewer in Cramer's *Magazin der Musik* cried plagiary: "Herr Kaffka has *composed* this work in the literal sense, that is, he has *copied out* and *put together* the

---

[28] In the preface Kaffka remarked that *Rosamunde* had been performed twenty times within three months at Breslau. Johann Abraham Peter Schulz, however, believed that the applause Kaffka earned was really for Benda, whose melodramas he had plundered without mercy. What was not stolen Schulz judged "insufferably vapid and paltry." *Allgemeine deutsche Bibliothek* 72:1 (1787): 163–4.

whole score from Naumann, Benda, Gluck, Schuster, and beyond that from the works of all musical Christendom on earth."[29] We shall later discover Kaffka appropriating the efforts of others as a librettist in the 1790s.

Finally, the Mark Brandenburg north of Berlin, under the control of several royal relatives, and Pomerania further northward produced only a few new German operas, only the names of which survive. Margrave Friedrich Heinrich of Schwedt had set up a private theater in the mid-1770s, dedicated mostly to comic opera and put together at first from members of his own Kapelle and local talent. Soon he enriched his troupe with professional singers drawn from Leipzig and Berlin, and in 1780 he secured the playwright Heinrich Ferdinand Möller as director, who continued to improve the excellent company. Later on, after André left Berlin in 1784 the Margrave named him Kapellmeister in return for his providing the theater with several of his operas. At the same time Marie Niklas left the Berlin stage to join his theater. A private opera stage was a common ornament to the court of a noble closely connected to the Prussian throne, but one devoted to German opera was an anomaly in Brandenburg. The tone for such theaters was set by Prince Heinrich at Rheinsberg: he kept a full-time French troupe, concocted performances mostly for birthday celebrations and visiting nobles, and provided a great many French texts for these revels himself.

Theatrical decline at Hamburg, Gotha, and Weimar

After a half decade of silence, Hamburg and Altona saw the production of five new German operas from 1778 to 1783. Not a note of the music comes down to us, and the few texts that survive suggest that creative production there was not keeping pace with developments elsewhere, but continued along earlier paths. The Schröder–Ackermann company welcomed new works from elsewhere in Germany, especially Berlin and Gotha. At Hamburg, however, Stegmann was still composing the likes of Bock's *Clarisse*, which dates from 1770. *Das Mündel*, also set by Stegmann, spreads only eight arias, one duet, and a closing Rundgesang over two acts of conventional plot: a runaway ward finds protection from her greedy and violent guardian, who wishes to marry her for her fortune.

Caroline von Klenke's *Der ehrliche Schweitzer*, published in 1776, declares its kinship with Weisse's literary conception of German opera in printing its thirteen "optional arias" at the end of the play without even indicating their precise location in the dialogue. The story itself draws a piously inept

---

[29] *Magazin der Musik* 2 (1784): 876. The reviewer adds that he has spoken with his friend Naumann, who agrees with him. "I have the commission from Herr Kapellmeister Naumann of informing Herr K. that the former is very irritated by the way his works are corrupted by such copying and augmenting, and that in the future he would have such plagiaries forbidden. For new editions of his works, should they be necessary, he would rather provide himself" (p. 878).

portrait of a young soldier of the Swiss Guard put in a Parisian prison for a crime he did not commit. He forgives the man whose false testimony put him there, and he refuses to escape when the opportunity presents itself, lest it bring discredit on his well-meaning prison master. He even exposes as inauthentic a marriage certificate which his beloved has coaxed from a soft-hearted priest in order to join him in slavery.

As at Berlin, opera in general figured more and more prominently on the Hamburg stage during these years, especially the perennial local favorite Grétry. Schütze saw this trend as a clear countercurve to theatrical health: "Much as we value a good operetta, still we believe that it is always an indication of the decline of a stage and of theatrical taste when the Singspiel gets the better of true comedy."[30] To keep up with operatic expansion strides were made in improving the musical resources of the company even as the best actors in the spoken repertory departed (Brockmann, Schröder, and his wife all went to Vienna between 1778 and 1781). The orchestra was improved, several fine singers were engaged, and the company tried out several music directors. The last of these, Johann Friedrich Hönicke, had come from Gotha as had many of the best musicians and singers at Hamburg. Like his predecessors he composed nothing of importance for the stage there, but "almost everything was done for the music drama, and Hönicke conducted the orchestra and trained the singers eager for instruction with incessant zeal."[31]

At Gotha, as we saw in Chapter 4, the Court Theater came to an abrupt end by order of Duke Ernst II in 1779. The musical repertory had declined along with theatrical standards in general. After the première of Benda's *Romeo und Julie* in September 1776, the Court Theater introduced only two new German operas in its last three years of existence, and neither is a distinguished contribution. The theater's Kapellmeister, Schweitzer, went totally to seed and produced nothing for the enterprise but an inaugural Vorspiel. If he indeed composed Bretzner's *Das wütende Heer*, as the title page of the published libretto of 1779 states, his music seems never to have been performed and has disappeared altogether.

Benda too lapsed into old-guard ineffectuality. His last attempts at German operas – *Der Holzhauer* (Gotha, 1778) and *Das tartarische Gesetz* (Mannheim, 1787) – were disappointments, the latter in fact a miserable failure, although Gotter had presented him with an up-to-date and popular exotic piece. André had set it almost as soon as it had seen print in 1779 and three South German settings quickly followed. Based on an episode from Gozzi's play *I pitocchi fortunati*, Gotter's libretto trades in whimsy, fine character drawing, and efforts to capitalize on the story's local color. In the opening duet – it comprises all of the first scene – the rich Samarkand businessman Tauhari divorces his wife Zenide, though secretly still in love

---

[30] *Hamburgische Theater-Geschichte*, p. 649.   [31] *Ibid.*, 507.

with her. Almost at once he repents of this impulsive deed, but the "law of the Tartar" states that he can remarry her only if a beggar marries and divorces her on the same day. Tauhari hires one to do just that. Unluckily, he chooses her lost lover Saed. When Saed discovers that he has married Zenide he refuses to divorce her and a public lashing is ordered. In a remarkably fast-paced conclusion (in which Gotter departs from Gozzi's plan) the Cadi orders Saed released; Tauhari feigns reconciliation, but pulls a dagger when about to embrace Zenide; Saed saves her and the Cadi condemns Tauhari to death, but then acquiesces to Zenide's pleas for leniency and gives Tauhari's fortune to her.

In this conclusion – a nearly ideal spot for an action ensemble – Gotter contented himself with dialogue and a traditional closing chorus.[32] Elsewhere, however, he cast his ensembles as brilliant interactions – especially the opening divorce scene and a duet in which Tauhari explains Saed's unusual task with a mixture of anxiety, fear, and jealousy, continually calling him back for further instructions and advice.

Nine years elapsed between Gotter's completion of his libretto and the production of Benda's setting, and this event took place not at Gotha but at Mannheim. From 1779 until 1806 Gotha received only a few visits from troupes and actors on tour. Gotter organized an amateur theater, but his attention was more earnestly directed toward Mannheim, where his advice was eagerly sought after by Baron von Dalberg, intendant of the National Theater there. Gotter provided him with several adaptations of spoken dramas and he also planned a new opera for Mannheim, to be based on Gozzi's *Il corvo*, but Benda's indifference ended the project. After the Bellomo troupe gave Franz Seydelmann's *Der Soldat* at Gotha in 1783, not a single new German opera was to see its première there for the rest of the century.

At Weimar four personalities – Goethe, Seckendorff, Corona Schröter, and Anna Amalia – accounted for nearly all the operatic activities of the amateur theater. And two main principles – brevity and adaptability to local limitations – governed their musical productions. Goethe's two true operas from this period, *Jery und Bätely* and *Die Fischerinn*, are both in one act. His occasional pieces, comprising a wide variety of works honoring the birthdays of the new duchess Luise (30 January) and Anna Amalia (20 October), are also brief. For Luise these include the likes of *Lila* (in its original more festive version, now lost, 1777) and *Der Triumph der Empfindsamkeit* (1778), both set by Seckendorff. The latter included, quite incongruously, Goethe's melodrama *Proserpina*, written for Corona Schröter.[33]

[32] André added an aria in the concluding scene for Zenide (in his usual manner of providing for the prima donna) so as to expand this brief choral conclusion. He also split the second act in two, transforming the whole work into a three-act opera.

[33] Seckendorff used all the latest techniques of the genre which Benda's successors (Neefe, Rust, Reichardt) had developed: music underneath speech, notation of relative pitch and duration of declaimed syllables, incorporation of song for the heroine, and the addition of a four-part chorus.

A work *sui generis* among German operas, the "Schönbartspiel" *Der Jahrmarktsfest zu Plundersweilern* marked Anna Amalia's birthday in 1778 (along with Einsiedel's new translation of Molière's *Le Médicin malgré lui*). Goethe had completed the first version, only 350 verses long, in early 1773. Using principally "Knittelvers" (irregular four-foot verses in couplets, common in Hans Sachs), it presents humorous vignettes of a traveling troupe at a fair, including two snippets of a tragedy on the story of Esther. At Weimar Goethe nearly doubled the drama's length. Anna Amalia herself set all the strophic parts to music (seven songs) and also treated three other sections musically – a duet, a trio, and a melodrama (for the Schattenspielmann). Seckendorff orchestrated all these numbers and presumably added instrumental numbers of his own.[34]

The production of Goethe's farce typifies the atmosphere of aristocratic self-indulgence surrounding much of the theatrical activity of the amateur stage at Weimar. It was given not at Hauptmann's small hall in the city, where anyone decently dressed was admitted, but at the ducal hunting palace, Schloss Ettersburg, where admission was by invitation only. The play required much expense and three weeks of feverish preparation. After the final rehearsal in town six coaches bore the cast of twenty-four to Ettersburg with an escort of torch-bearing hussars. A banquet followed the theatricals, and after the guests left a ball was given for the players, which lasted until dawn.

Seckendorff added a few arias to another early work of Goethe's, the Alexandrine pastorale *Die Laune des Verliebten*, and it too was mounted at Ettersburg, on 20 May 1779. That same year the court rejoiced in a merciless parody of Wieland's *Alceste* (called *Orpheus und Euridice*, its music arranged by Seckendorff), performed on the duke's birthday and in Wieland's presence, with Anna Amalia herself among the performers. When Alceste's dying aria "Weine nicht, du meines Herzens Abgott" paraded forth with obbligato posthorn, Wieland jumped up screaming and stomped out of the hall.

Shortly thereafter Goethe and Karl August left for Switzerland, the inspiration and the setting for *Jery und Bätely*, completed there in late 1779. The drama turns on reforming a common operatic type of the day, "die Spröde," a stand-offish heroine who rejects all suitors. Bätely primly refuses to accept her devoted lover, the cheese-maker Jery. His friend Thomas, a recently discharged soldier, invents a scheme to correct matters: he raises holy terror with Bätely and with her father's property, culminating in a set-to with Jery, who appears to champion Bätely's cause. Moved by his heroics (suggested to Goethe by contests between young Swiss men which he saw on his journey), Bätely relents and offers Jery her hand.

Goethe wrote this libretto for his childhood friend Philipp Christoph Kayser, then at Zurich, on whom the poet came to pin nearly all his hopes for

---

[34] Wilhelm Bode, *Der weimarische Musenhof 1756–1781* (Berlin, 1920), p. 309.

settings of his librettos during the next decade. Goethe sent him *Jery und Bätely* on 29 December 1779 from Frankfurt in company with a famous and much-quoted letter describing the three kinds of music it required – Lieder, arias, and "rhythmic dialogue." The last was no doubt to come into its own in the conclusion, which Goethe himself described in a later letter to Kayser: "From the moment that Thomas begins to sing the Quodlibet, the music continues unbroken to the end and becomes, if one wished to stamp it with a technical term, a monstrously long finale."[35] With its 338 verses and many sections this long finale moves far beyond the one Goethe essayed in *Claudine von Villa Bella*. It encompasses more than half of the entire drama and, despite its loose structure, exemplifies Goethe's further progress in the emancipation of the German composer from subordination to literary goals. "It consists of the very simplest outlines," Goethe wrote to Kayser of his libretto, "which you must then throw into relief with light, shade, and colors, if they are to strike and to please."

Kayser, as was to be his wont, dragged his feet in setting this challenging libretto, and Goethe, anxious for a performance at Weimar "while the interest in Swiss stories has not yet evaporated," turned to Seckendorff. He set it quickly and, in Goethe's opinion, very poorly. Its dramatic consistency was leaden, to judge from a remark Goethe wrote to Charlotte von Stein on 30 June 1780, just before the opera's première: "*Jery und Bätely* still won't float."

Local conditions could scarcely play a more vital role than they did in shaping Goethe's next libretto, *Die Fischerinn* (1782). Dortchen, vexed at the lateness of her father and her fiancé Niklas in returning from fishing on the river, arranges appearances so that upon getting back they think she has fallen into the river and perhaps drowned. They frantically call out a search party, and after she believes they have come to feel her own anxieties in their absence, Dortchen comes out of hiding. Goethe wrote the title role for Corona Schröter, who also composed the ten musical numbers, but the drama itself owed its conception principally to the natural theater at Tiefurth on the banks of the Ilm where it was first performed. Goethe planned the story around the scene in which the roused neighbors search for Dortchen:

The audience sat, unsuspecting, so that they had the whole winding river before them. At the moment in question, torches were seen moving close by. After several cries, they also appeared in the distance; then fire leapt up from the headlands jutting out, and with their light and reflection they gave nearby objects the greatest clarity while the surrounding region further off lay in deep night. Seldom has a more beautiful effect been seen.[36]

Perhaps with Corona's compositional abilities in mind, Goethe drew back

[35] Goethe, *Briefe der Jahre 1764–1786*), p. 481 (letter of 20 January 1780 from Weimar).
[36] This notice appeared as a footnote in the original printed edition (*Litteratur- und Theater-Zeitung* 5 [1782]), referring specifically to the chorus's lines: "Und brennet Fackeln / Und Feuer an!"

from his earlier finale experiments in *Die Fischerinn*. The scene described above represents his only attempt at a large musical complex in the opera. It extends from the father's first cries for help through the illumination, Dortchen's aside on the success of her plan, further searching, and her appearance before her father and Niklas.

The opera commences with Dortchen's singing "Der Erlkönig," clearly in the Romanze tradition but on a dramatic theme unconnected with the opera's. Goethe had written the famous ballad four years earlier in 1778, working from a Danish folk poem published by Herder. Goethe took other poems from Herder's collection of folk songs as well,[37] and the pervasive note of pessimism surrounding Dortchen combines with the dark, ancient hue of these lyrics to set *Die Fischerinn* sharply apart from the healthy moralizing of Weisse's rustic portraits.

Time, place, and personnel limited operatic horizons at Weimar, and Goethe's progressive conception of opera – drifting with each passing year more and more toward Italian models – set these limitations in high relief. The absence of a composer with skill and sympathy enough to do his ideas justice remained Goethe's lot until his return from Italy in 1788. Meanwhile, theatrical matters showed some improvement at Weimar. The duke and his theater-loving mother built a new playhouse opposite her palace in town, inaugurated in early 1780. Several principals sought permission to play there, and finally in late 1783 the company of Joseph Bellomo was invited to Weimar from Dresden.

Leipzig: the last works of Weisse and Hiller

Though it had slipped considerably from its position as the undisputed capital of German opera during the triumviral years dominated by Weisse, Hiller, and Koch, Leipzig remained one of the two poles around which opera gravitated in Saxony. But its role was limited now largely to its librettists, such as Bretzner, and its publishing houses; theatrically it fell wholly under the shadow of Dresden. The court there had established a new German company after Seyler's departure in 1777, put under the direction of the former head of the court's Italian opera, Pasquale Bondini. The troupe divided its year between winters at Dresden and summers at Leipzig.

The overall tone at Leipzig was a conservative one. The city fathers still claimed the right to control theatrical performances in order to protect the social, economic, and moral standards of the city and the university – Goethe's *Stella* and Schiller's *Die Räuber*, for example, were banned during this period as morally offensive. Bretzner's librettos, which had taken all Prussia by storm, saw life in his native Saxony only in the two operas of the obscure Friedrich Preu. André's operas also held little interest for Saxony. At

[37] Several of these are listed by Hans-Albrecht Koch, "Die Singspiele," in *Goethes Dramen: Neue Interpretationen*, ed. Walter Hinderer (Stuttgart, 1980), p. 55.

Koch's old theater at the Rannstadt Gate nothing had changed from the early 1770s – not even the sets.

Hiller's position as the dean of Leipzig's musicians remained a solid one throughout the 1770s. The duties connected with several new appointments from 1778 to 1783 and his editorial and pedagogic activities demanded most of his energies. After his falling out with Seyler in 1776 his direct contact with the German stage withered. Operatic projects ceased to interest him. His setting of *Das Grab des Mufti*, promised by Meissner in early 1776, did not see its première until three years later. Gottfried Samuel Brunner had similarly appended a note to his 1773 libretto *Poltis*, stating that Hiller was to set it, but the keyboard reduction did not appear until 1782.[38]

Hiller believed that the improvement of German opera depended on what became his own pedagogic hobby-horse in the 1770s – raising the standards of singing among Germans. He communicated his impressions in the preface to the third of six collections of "the best yet unpublished arias and duets of the German theater" which appeared from 1777 to 1780. Hiller notes that the first step toward the improvement of German singing had been taken in his own and similar comic operas: "I see this as the first level of singing among Germans. To remain for a long time at this level would have been a harmful stagnation for the growth of art." But then Wieland and Schweitzer gave us *Alceste*, "a work that requires toil in performance, but also richly rewards this toil."[39] The level of skill Hiller thought German singers now ought to aim at and its Italianate character are reflected in the best represented composers in his six collections – Guglielmi (10), Hiller (9), Schuster (7), and Hasse (6).

Weisse, meanwhile, had entered a species of operatic second childhood. In 1777 Dyck had issued the last Leipzig edition of his collected operas, and the Carlsruhe publisher Schmieder followed a year later with the last edition anywhere that the century was to see. By this time these librettos and similar texts by Heermann and others had taken on the character of a conservative rallying point for those opposing the drift toward Italian practice and greater musical control.[40]

After *Die Jubelhochzeit* (1773), Weisse wrote no more full-length operas. He limited his production as playwright and librettist to a periodical for children which he wrote almost single-handedly from 1776 to 1782, *Der Kinderfreund*. The journal enjoyed great popularity (it went through many editions up to 1818 and was twice translated into French) and saw a sequel in Weisse's *Briefwechsel der Familie des Kinderfreundes* in the 1780s.

[38] Johann Gottfried Dyck announced in his libretto *Der neue Guthsherr* (Leipzig, 1781) that Hiller was setting it, but the promised score never materialized.

[39] *Dritte Sammlung der vorzüglichsten, noch ungedruckten Arien und Duetten des deutschen Theaters, von verschiedenen Componisten* (Leipzig, 1778), p. iii.

[40] In 1783, for instance, Wolf's *Das Rosenfest* saw revivals at both Berlin and Danzig to the joy of reviewers and audiences at both cities. "The full playhouse," reported a writer at Danzig, "was a strong proof of how greatly our public loves this and similar pieces, and it is a shame both for us as well as for Madame Schuch herself that this operetta is a dish only served up to us at most once a year." *Litteratur- und Theater-Zeitung* 7 (1784): 117–18.

Der Kinderfreund brings to life German Enlightenment ideals concerning the education of children through the ongoing fortunes of the fictitious family of Mentor (Weisse himself), his wife, four evenly spaced children from 11 to 5, and four family friends who pop in from time to time and discuss a variety of topics. Weisse also employs moral stories and plays to this didactic end in both *Der Kinderfreund* and the *Briefwechsel*. All of the plays are in one act and could be put on by children; four of them are "Kinderoperetten."

The title of the earliest of these four, *Die Schadenfreude*, presents a concept for which we have no simple term in English, the malicious pleasure taken in the misfortunes of others. While Frau Gärtner is away, little Fritz finds his sister Julchen nibbling in the pantry and locks her in. She begs and bribes him in vain; he goes so far as to call in four of his schoolmates to laugh at her distress. Herr Gärtner's arrival cuts this short, however. Julchen confesses her guilt; he releases her and makes Fritz take her place in the pantry until bed-time for his "Schadenfreude." Julchen pleads his case, but to no avail, and as Fritz creeps weeping into the pantry his friends romp around singing, "Du kleiner Schadenfroh!" For Weisse this represents stern chastisement indeed. In her social study of *Der Kinderfreund*, Bettina Hurrelmann observes: "Very seldom is someone punished in Mentor's family; misbehavior in the children is in the rule clarified through conversation."[41]

In the later librettos Weisse departs from the obvious didacticism of this first effort and constructs plots closer to the norms of his full-length sentimental operas. *Die kleine Ährenleserinn* (1777), an especially tearful specimen, prints its musical texts as footnotes keyed to the dialogue and thus, like *Der ehrliche Schweitzer*, invites performance with or without music.[42] Hiller's keyboard reduction of the opera appeared four months later. The publisher of *Der Kinderfreund*, Siegfried Lebrecht Crusius, had requested him to set it despite, Hiller noted, the "little desire" he now had of working for the theater, and also his being greatly "hindered by other duties."

Hiller had begun writing his music specifically for children and a small family theater, with scoring for only two violins and keyboard. In this form Crusius published it, and for the first time included the spoken dialogue along with the musical numbers. Hiller the singing master, meanwhile, got the better of Hiller the Kinderfreund. He decided that the opera might also do well in a large theater and completed a second version in full score, which changes the male lead to a baritone and includes coloratura for the parts to be

---

[41] *Jugendliteratur und Bürgerlichkeit: Soziale Erziehung in der Jugendliteratur der Aufklärung am Beispiel von Christian Felix Weisses "Kinderfreund" 1776–1782* (Paderborn, 1974), p. 210.

[42] An explanation appeared in the same installment of *Der Kinderfreund* (8 [1777]: 132). When Herr Spirit brought the play to the children, Lottchen asked for little songs to be added. He complied, "since he is too galant to refuse anything to a lady, be she great or small." Weisse explains that he has included them here in his text "in case some of you, my dear readers, wanted to perform it as an operetta." He adds that he had already heard that "one of our good composers" is busy setting it to music. This was Hiller.

taken by adults. Apparently the opera was never publicly performed in either version.

Hiller also set Weisse's next opera for children, *Das Denkmal in Arkadien* (1781) – the only one of his works not to come down to us in any form. The story, set in ancient Greece, gives great sentimental play to the reuniting of a young Arcadian girl, carried off as a child by Spartans, with her repining father Palämon. Everything is cleared up with five of the opera's twenty numbers still to come, indicative of the static monument-wreathing, moralizing, and praising of the virtues and joys of Arcadia which dominate the work from beginning to end.

Weisse's last libretto is possibly the worst he ever wrote, *Unverhoft kömt oft, oder: Das Findelkind* (1786), a long and boring tale of a rustic foundling reunited with his mother, a well-to-do officer's wife. It is the most prolix of his children's operas. Though in only one act, it includes twenty-six numbers, every one of them set in Georg Benda's keyboard reduction of 1787. By this late date both men, like Hiller, had lost all contact with developments in German opera.

The German operatic efflorescence at Dresden

With more civic pride than objectivity, the Leipzig publisher Dyck declared in the late 1770s: "There is no Dresden Court Theatrical Company, which travels to Leipzig for the fairs, but the Leipzig Privileged German Theatrical Company goes in the winter to Dresden."[43] Yet Bondini's company seldom did new pieces there, and played to many empty loges.[44] When they left each autumn after the Michaelmas Fair, the theater remained closed for the winter. In 1779 Bondini split his quarreling players into two troupes and let one perform through that winter at Leipzig, but went back to a single company the next spring when receipts there proved poor.

Especially in the production of German opera, Leipzig had become little more than a commercial entity for Bondini. The important new operas in his repertory all came from Dresden. Beginning in 1778, a group of important composers there turned their attention to German opera. One was the music director of the new enterprise, Friedrich Christoph Gestewitz. But the chief musical architects were two students of Kapellmeister Johann Gottlieb Naumann, both of whom had accompanied their teacher to Italy in 1765 and had hitherto devoted themselves exclusively to Italian opera – Joseph Schuster and Franz Seydelmann.

In its first year, which began as soon as Seyler had left in May of 1777, Bondini's German company almost totally avoided opera of any kind. In 1778,

[43] Quoted by Friedrich Schulze, *Hundert Jahre Leipziger Stadttheater* (Leipzig, 1917), p. 3.
[44] So remarked the same traveler who commented on Döbbelin's stage at Berlin (see Note 4 above). He had also stopped at Leipzig in 1778 and in general found the theater there boring. *Deutsches Museum* 1778:2, pp. 465–74.

however, the War of the Bavarian Succession caused the Saxon court to dismiss the Italian opera buffa as an economizing measure. One correspondent explained what this meant for the Bondini company: "Just as everything in the world seems black on one side and white on the other, thus precisely this wicked war perhaps holds something good for Germany's Singspiel. Since the Italian opera is wholly dismissed, now the composers here work only for our theater."[45]

Schuster produced the first in this series of Dresden operas, *Der Alchymist* – one of the finest and most popular German operas of the decade. The librettist was Meissner, who was to be the mainstay of Dresden's German operatic interlude. He based his libretto only very loosely on a spoken comedy by Legrand. A silly old man named Tarnow, addicted to alchemy, has vowed not to let his daughter Louise marry until he has discovered the philosopher's stone. He has locked her up in her room, prompting her lover Bellniz to busy himself with constructing an apparatus in the apartment below with which to effect their elopement. The plan is nearly foiled by Kybbutz, tutor to Louise's little brother, and by the sudden appearance of Tarnow himself. The lovers and Bellniz's resourceful servant play on the old man's superstitions with a mock visitation by the devil in order to gain his consent, and after Tarnow is disabused of his mania he reluctantly renews this promise in good faith.

Musically, the possibilities Schuster faced came nowhere near those in *La schiava liberata* – no finale, no dramatic ensembles, no moments of emotional extremes. On the other hand, Meissner had made the most of his alterations in Legrand's play precisely because "scenes with song necessarily have a wholly different structure from those which are merely spoken." Hence, as with the best works of Gotter, *Der Alchymist* lives on what a composer can do with strategically placed opportunities for musical characterization. We have already seen how André brought one such moment to life, Christine's coquetry directed at Kybbutz (Examples 6.2 and 6.3). Characteristically, Schuster proceeds less drastically in this same aria. He also chose B-flat and duple time, and even delayed "willig" as André did, but in general he used deft orchestral accents to paint in most of the colors, as seen in Example 6.8.

Schuster's powers of characterization never saw happier use than in his arias for Gustel, the heroine's ten-year-old brother, and his tutor, Magister Kybbutz. Gustel (a trouser role) struggles for uncertain command over the exaggerated heroic accents in his two arias – especially the first, in which he proclaims his intention of running off and joining the army, "Wie lang, so wächst der Bart mir schon!" (reminiscent of Flute the bellows-mender's "I have a beard coming"). Schuster lavishes his strongest comic effects on the pedant Kybbutz, a typical North German object of ridicule. At his first appearance he discovers the lovers together in Louise's room. Finding that he is not to be bribed to silence, they appeal to his sensibilities – they love each other. For that, remarks Kybbutz archly, an improper education is to blame,

---

[45] *Ibid.*, p. 382.

Example 6.8 Schuster: *Der Alchymist*. Aria of Christine.
"If a kiss could move you, willingly I'd give it to you."

and he proceeds to lecture them on this point in his first aria. His interlarding of Latin and German finds a delightful parallel as Schuster's violins interweave above a bustling bassoon, aided by violas (Example 6.9). Schuster's economy of means makes itself especially evident in the second half of this excerpt (bars 12 to 30), the fruits of his years in Italy. As a contributor to Baron von Knigge's *Dramaturgische Blätter* put it, "We find here neither an overburdening with winds nor a shoring up with harmonies and vacuous artifices, which we Germans still often prefer to sweet and simple Nature."[46]

[46] 26 (18 April 1789): 410.

Example 6.9 Schuster: *Der Alchymist*. Aria of Magister Kybbutz.

"Idleness is vice,' says the proverb. Sloth is the name of the black seat of repose. One's energy for better activities is diminished, then one thinks of stratagems and with delight lets lust ensnare one, until in the end one presents oneself at the grave limping on a staff."

Ex. 6.9 (*cont.*)

Franz Seydelmann, who shared many duties at court with Schuster, also explored German comic opera along the lines his friend followed. Closest in spirit to *Der Alchymist* is *Der lahme Husar*. The stiff libretto by Friedrich Carl Koch, a seasoned veteran of many stages now with Bondini, is poetically and technically inferior to Meissner's. The farce deals with deceiving a blustering old farmer, Hanns Struff, into giving his daughter to her lover Fritz. The lame hussar Brause arrives on the scene in time to engineer the deception: Fritz must appear to have stabbed himself in the heart with a bread-knife in despair, and Brause convinces Hanns to pity the wretch and assent to Fritz's marrying his daughter before he expires. Again musical patterning follows earlier German preference for the closed number, although Fritz sings a pathetic recitative with the bread-knife sticking out of his chest. Like Meissner, Koch provided a rondo for the heroine, and also made room for a Romanze, set by Seydelmann in a traditional style closely resembling Benda's.[47]

These two comic operas occupy one extreme of German operatic production at Dresden. At the other lay serious opera. Seydelmann's lost setting of Schwan's popular *Der Kaufmann von Smyrna* already points in this direction. The only music to survive, a recitative and aria added to Schwan's text and published in keyboard reduction by Hiller, indicates Seydelmann's deepest stylistic proclivities, toward substantial Italianate arias. This tendency came into its own in *Arsene*, translated by Meissner from a fairy piece by Favart already popular all across Germany in Monsigny's setting of 1773.[48]

Seydelmann runs the gamut here from a song-like cavatina and rondo to sprawling arias, two with preceding recitatives. Rudolf Cahn-Speyer has reprinted one of these, though he omits the obbligato recitative.[49] Prince Alcindor has fallen in love with Princess Arsene, but his knightly exertions in her name only increase her unbearable pride and cold disdain for all her suitors. Arsene's foster mother, the fairy Aline, decides to help Alcindor with Arsene's cure, counseling him to fight coldness with coldness. Like most operatic knights, Alcindor is not cut out for such stratagems, and in this aria at the beginning of act two he beseeches Nature to soften Arsene before his powers fail. The two quintains clearly invite a recursive (da capo or dal segno) rendering, even though by the end of the first Meissner has scarcely got Nature's attention. Seydelmann opts for an $A_1A_2A_3BA_2'A_3$ dal segno-like plan, which provides more textual repetition than other North German composers cared to use in similar arias. The A_2 section, shown in Example 6.10, maintains an active harmonic profile, as befits Seydelmann's slightly old-fashioned structural planning, which still depends on ritornellos for tonal affirmation. His tendency to think in two-bar phrases, only occasionally relieved with distension to three, limits the breadth of his cantabile. Schuster, with his thoroughgoing absorption of Italian example, surpasses his colleague in this respect.

Meissner translated *Arsene* for Bondini and Seydelmann under some duress. Originally he had intended only to rewrite the arias of Johann Heinrich Faber's Rhenish translation for Seydelmann, but he found the entire text so wretched and "stiff beyond all measure" that he started from scratch. After explaining these circumstances in his preface he added: "Anyway, this is the last Singspiel that I will adapt from the French; I give my word on it." With his next libretto Meissner kept his word – he translated Metastasio's

---

[47] This number has been reprinted in full by Rudolf Cahn-Speyer, *Franz Seydelmann als dramatischer Komponist* (Leipzig, 1909), pp. 159–65.

[48] Döbbelin took it up five months after the première of Seydelmann's version at Dresden, and during the next year Monsigny's opera was the most performed work in his repertory.

[49] *Franz Seydelmann*, pp. 132–8. The keyboard reduction shown here in Example 6.10 is that of Cahn-Speyer, not Seydelmann (his *Arsene* was the only Dresden opera of the group we are studying to appear in a keyboard reduction [Leipzig, 1779]).

Example 6.10 Seydelmann: *Arsense*. Aria of Alcindor, act 2.
"You who pour the fire of love into my veins, you who infuse tender agitation through every one of my nerves, hear me, Nature!"

L'isola disabitata for Schuster. By preserving the Imperial Poet's recitatives Meissner made of *Die wüste Insel* the first through-composed North German opera since *Brutus* and *Alceste*. He left the order of scenes intact and translated all the recitatives literally, but some of Metastasio's arias displeased him, especially those with elaborately wrought similes or precious conceits. Still, though he made of his source a more Germanic "ernsthaft empfindsam" music drama, as one critic labeled it,[50] Meissner did nothing to change its simple, static musical plan of six arias (five of them exit arias) plus a concluding coro. Indeed, there was hardly need to, for Metastasio's scene planning was little different from the aria-centered ideal he had been striving for in his other librettos for Schuster and Seydelmann.

Warmed to their task with *Die wüste Insel*, Schuster and Meissner set about producing a full-length through-composed German opera. Forgetting his public promise for a moment, Meissner chose Marmontel's *Les Incas, ou la destruction de l'empire de Pérou* as his model. When Schuster left for Italy in 1778 once again, he had the first act of Meissner's *Cora* in hand. From Venice he wrote to the librettist that he had set everything he had taken with him, "and I am now waiting impatiently for more."[51] But the project withered as Schuster's rising star in Italy prolonged his stay there. A more compelling reason may have dissuaded Meissner from pursuing the project. Naumann had just set a Swedish text, *Cora och Alonzo*, based on the same source, for the Swedish court. It saw a German keyboard reduction and partial performance at Dresden in 1780, two years before its Swedish première at Stockholm in 1782. Naumann's opera found admirers all over Germany. A concert performance at Halle in 1781 set one Carl Wilhelm Bumbrey in raptures:

No masterpiece of such a nature yet exists. . . I would assure you, that the splendid compositions produced by German heads, which we Germans have received in recent times, have been clearly left behind by *Cora*, a work which must be well-nigh the highest peak of human perfection. . . All the treasures of musical art lie united here in a single piece. . . [52]

Nonetheless, Naumann produced nothing for the German stage. Instead, he continued to write Swedish operas for Stockholm and Italian ones for Dresden and Berlin. In 1780 the Dresden court had reinstituted its beloved Italian opera, and two years later Bondini, never enthusiastic about German opera, abandoned the genre altogether. The lone comic opera Seydelmann wrote after 1780, *Der Soldat* (1783), sought its fortune with the Bellomo troupe, then playing the small theaters around Dresden and soon to be off to Weimar.

The German interlude at Dresden was over. Having summed up many German operatic tendencies of the 1770s in terms of the local Italianate dialect, her composers returned to the fold of court patronage and to Italian opera. In the coming years, as we shall see next, German opera fell on hard times everywhere. At Dresden it vanished completely.

[50] *Allgemeine deutsche Bibliothek* 42:1 (1780): 87.
[51] *Deutsches Museum* 1779:1, p. 187.
[52] *Briefe über Musikwesen, besonders Cora in Halle* (Quedlinburg, 1781), p. 33.

7

Lean years: 1784–1791

After André's return to Offenbach in the spring of 1784, Döbbelin's company struggled to retain its position of leadership in North German operatic affairs. It succeeded, but only by default as production nearly everywhere slackened. Only forty-six new operas emerged in the North from 1784 to 1791 (see Table 7.1), less than six works per year on the average, whereas the six years just discussed averaged eleven. Furthermore, posterity exercised little care in its stewardship over this meager patrimony – the music of only eleven operas comes down to us, and only twenty-five full texts (seven of them from earlier days).

The Weimar court kept pace with the Prussian capital's *faute-de-mieux* pre-eminence owing almost entirely to the late works of Ernst Wilhelm Wolf, a problematic resurgence of a figure bred to the norms of Saxon opera. Apart from these cities, however, little of interest can be said about local manifestations. Instead, several major realignments of taste command attention in these years – a flowering of serious opera, flickers of interest in Gluck's masterpieces, and a more widespread cultivation of the Italian and German operas of a small group of Viennese and Italian composers. These are the important issues for the present chapter and for what follows.

Except for a setting of one of Weisse's children's operas, the names Leipzig and Dresden do not appear in Table 7.1. Elsewhere, the procedures of early Saxon opera emit a crepuscular glow here and there, but by and large librettists had begun to understand how to plan for music as an integral factor rather than an ornament. Still, this earlier restrictive legacy, born of close practical and literary ties with the spoken theater, had been slow to disappear. The following discourse by a Berlin reviewer would have sounded silly from a French critic, and preposterously irrelevant from an Italian, but still needed saying in Germany in 1783:

A Singspiel must be seen and heard, not read: if it reads excellently, then it is surely a tragedy or comedy embroidered with songs, and no true Singspiel, and for that reason creates a bad or at least musically untoward effect. Song will interrupt the discourse inappropriately, and, to the extent that the dialogue or music is better, so will one wish that the other would go to the devil. Usually the music is the best; then one ends up not paying any attention to what is spoken, but only to the arias: the opera becomes a concert. The Singspiel in all its perfection is more than a concert, and something other than a tragedy, drama, and comedy: it seeks to excite the feelings and thus move the

Table 7.1. *New North German operas, 1784–1791*

COMPOSER		Première	
Title	Librettist	Date	Place
AUMANN, DIEDRICH CHRISTIAN			
([*Das neue Rosenmädchen*])	unknown	1789	Hamburg
BENDA, FRIEDRICH LUDWIG			
(*Louise*)	Fr. Ernst Jester	16 Jan 1791	Königsberg
(*Mariechen*)	Fr. Ernst Jester	1791	Königsberg
([*Die Verlobung*])	Fr. Ernst Jester	1789	Königsberg
BENDA, FRIEDRICH WILHELM HEINRICH			
[*Alceste*]	Wieland	15 Jan 1786	Berlin
Orpheus	Lindemann	16 Jan 1785	Berlin
BENDA, GEORG			
Das Findelkind	Weisse	unperformed	
BIRNBACH, CARL JOSEPH			
([*Die Fischerweiber in Paris*)]	unknown	1790	Breslau
([*Saphire*])	unknown	1788	Breslau
BURGMÜLLER, AUGUST FRIEDRICH			
([*Das hätt' ich nicht gedacht!*])	C.A. Vulpius	1788	Weimar
DROBISCH, J. F.			
[*Der blinde Ehemann*]	J. Fr. Jünger	Oct 1791	Lübeck
EHRENBERG			
[*Azakia*]	C. Fr. Schwan	1790	Dessau
FLORSCHÜTZ, EUCHARIUS			
([*Richter und Gärtnerin*])	unknown	1790	Rostock
HANKE, KARL			
([*Doktor Fausts Leibgürtel*])	B. C. d'Arien	1786	Hamburg
[*Hüon und Amande*]	Fr. Sophie Seyler	1789	Schleswig
([*Xaphire*])	B. C. d'Arien	1786	Hamburg
HANSEL, JOHANN DANIEL			
Cyrus und Kassandane	C. W. Ramler	1786	Halle
HUNT, KARL			
[*Das Denkmal in Arkadien*]	Weisse	1791	Dresden
HURKA, FRIEDRICH FRANZ			
[*Das wütende Heer*]	Bretzner	1788	Schwedt
KAFFKA, JOHANN CHRISTOPH			
[*Der blinde Ehemann*]	J. Fr. Jünger	1788	Breslau
(*Der Talisman*)	Bretzner	1789	Breslau
KALKBRENNER, CHRISTIAN			
Demokrit	C. Fr. Schröter	1791	Rheinsberg
KÖNIG, JOHANN MATTHEUS			
([*Die Execution*])	unknown	1784	Ellrich
KOSPOTH, OTTO CARL ERDMANN FREIHERR VON			
[*Bella und Fernando*]	C. A. Vulpius	1790	Berlin
[*Karoline*]	C. A. G. Seidel	unperformed	
Der kluge Jakob	J. C. Wezel	26 Feb 1788	Berlin
KRAUS, BENEDIKT			
([*Amors Zufälle*])	Jos. Bellomo	1785	Weimar

Table 7 (*cont.*)

COMPOSER		Première	
Title	Librettist	Date	Place

MÜHLE, NIKOLAUS			
[*Der Eremit auf Formentera*]	Kotzebue	1790	Königsberg
OHLHORST, JOHANN CHRISTIAN			
([*Meister Johannes*])	Ch. G. Korb	1791	Neustrelitz
PHANTY, OTTO CHRISTIAN FRIEDRICH			
[*Doktor Fausts Zaubergürtel*]	Mylius and Schink	1784	Lübeck
REICHARDT, JOHANN FRIEDRICH			
Claudine von Villa Bella	Goethe	29 Jul 1789	Charlottenburg
RELLISTAB, JOHANN CARL FRIEDRICH			
[*Die Apotheke*]	J. J. Engel	May 1788	Berlin
ROLLE, JOHANN HEINRICH			
(*Melida*)	Sucro	early 1784	Magdeburg
SCHWANENBERG, JOHANN GOTTFRIED			
([*Der Deserteur*])	unknown	1784	Brunswick
SECKENDORFF, KARL SIEGMUND FREIHERR VON			
([*Der Blumenraub*])	Seckendorff	1784	Weimar
WEBER, EDMUND KASPAR JOHANN JOSEF MARIA FREIHERR VON			
([*Der Transport im Koffer*])	unknown	30 May 1791	Hamburg
WESSELY, CARL BERNHARD			
[*Psyche*]	C. Fr. Müchler	18 Nov 1789	Berlin
WITTROCK, G. H. L.			
[*Die kleine Ährenleserinn*]	Weisse	1787	Lübeck
WOLF, ERNST WILHELM			
Alceste	Wieland	1786	Weimar
([*Angelica*])	Wieland	1788	Berlin
[*Der Eremit auf Formentera*]	Kotzebue	1786	Weimar
[*Erwin und Elmire*]	Goethe	1785	Weimar
[*Der Schleyer*]	C. A. Vulpius	1786	Weimar
[*Superba*]	Seckendorff	30 Jan 1785	Weimar
([*Die Zauberirrungen*])	Einsiedel	24 Oct 1785	Weimar
ZELLER, GEORG BERNHARD LEOPOLD			
[*Der ehrliche Räuber*]	Ch. G. Korb	2 Jul 1787	Neubrandenburg

Key:
[ ] – music does not survive.
( ) – complete text does not survive.

will through the heart; the other genres of drama seek to excite ideas, and speak to the heart through the reason. A Singspiel which can still be performed with the songs omitted, as a well-known German writer of operettas demands [Weisse], would surely be a most wretched Singspiel, to which Figaro's definition of the operetta would apply (in *Le Barbier de Séville*): an opera is a play in which one allows to be sung what is not worth speaking; whereas on the contrary in the true Singspiel the song is the most essential, and one speaks what is not worth singing. Therefore, we cannot concur with the wish of a German philosopher [J. J. Engel] to transform farces into comic operas; for the plan of a Singspiel must be wholly different from that of a play. All comedies which have hitherto been transformed into operettas confirm our opinion; they are all disastrous miscarriages which can only delight those who will put up with anything![1]

More unset librettos

One way to illustrate how unwilling North German composers and audiences were to put up with just anything is to examine those published librettos from this and the preceding period which were never set to music. As Table 7.2 shows, the population of such literary spinsters rose sharply from 1778 to 1780. Many richly deserve their fate. Both *Der Einsiedler* and *Erano* deal with a father cast from a position of power and living out his days in the wilderness; in addition, both seek to escape the familiar rusticity of earlier comic operas: the former is set in Commonwealth England, the latter in Palestine during the Crusades. In *Der Einsiedler* the reunion of the embittered and world-weary hermit Grimaldo and his son Helley works along predictable lines and at least limits its fulsome moralizing to one act. *Erano*, on the other hand, aspires to new heights of excruciating homiletics, compound improbability, dramaturgic incompetence, and romantic hyperinflation of setting, mood, and language. Except for three guardian spirits who materialize to sing its closing number, act one includes only Erano himself. We learn very little from all his ramblings as he sits by moonlit fallen walls, a sinking triumphal arch, and broken columns: long ago he left his wife and son, fell from power, and escaped from those who desecrate God's temples and pollute His rites. He falls asleep. Act two: the guardian spirits have transported him to another region, just in time to meet up with an impossibly virtuous German knight, Sigmund, off to save the maid Leda from the Saracen. Once this is done, we are confronted with a battlefieldful of corpses and a task as daunting as Sigmund's own – sorting out that Zatera, in male clothing and on the point of expiring next to the body of one Bassa Selim, is Leda's sister; that the Bassa's slave Sarri is their brother Anton; and that Sigmund's companion Kronberg is also their brother and had sold them into slavery. Furthermore, Sigmund himself is Leda's fiancé, and Erano's son. Erano begins a sermon on

---

[1] *Litteratur -und Theater-Zeitung* 6 (1783): 349–50. The anonymous critic is reviewing the first installment of Neefe's keyboard reduction *Gesänge aus dem Neuen Guthsherrn* (Leipzig, [1783]).

Table 7.2. *Unset published North German librettos, 1778—1791*

Date	Title	Librettist	Place of Publication
1778	(*Die beschleunigte Hochzeit*)	Berger	Leipzig
	Komala	Bouterwek	Dresden
	(*Lykon und Agle*)	unknown	Leipzig
	Der Sklav	Seidel	Berlin
	(*Wilhelm und Hannchen*)	Titzenhofer	Breslau
1779	Erano	Batsch	unknown
	Hannchen Robert	Matthesius	Gotha
	Pandora	Wieland	Weimar
1780	Agaton und Psiche	Schlenkert	Leipzig
	(*Die Arzeney der Liebe*)	unknown	Hamburg
	Der Barbier von Badgad	Mylius & Schink	Gotha
	(*Die dankbare Tochter*)	Hartmann	Budissin
	Der Einsiedler	L.	Leipzig
	Peter der Grosse, Kayser von Russland	Hempel	Leipzig
	(*Wunna*)	Kosegarten	unknown
1783	Das Hallorenfest	Schlicht	Magdeburg
	(*Der Rekrut*)	Hagemann	Hamburg
	(*Selinde*)	Weismann	Rudolstadt
1784	(*Der Rangstreit*)	Matthesius	Chemnitz
	Die Wassergeister	Einsiedel	Dessau
1786	(*Das Familiengelübde*)	unknown	Hildburghausen
1787	Der Lindwurm	Weber	Berlin
1788	(*Selim und Zelinde*)	unknown	Breslau
1789	Rudolph von Mohelli	unknown	Breslau
1791	(*Eimsbüttel*)	Schütze	Hamburg
	Theseus auf Kreta	Rambach	Leipzig

Key:
( ) – libretto has not been traced.

all their trials after a round of forgiving and embracing. Luckily he dies before he can finish, but the others take up the theme.

The burgeoning vogue of the historical and topical seen in this Crusade piece fascinated other librettists at this time. Like the exotic and the supernatural (also present here), such subjects offered a quick avenue of escape from a genre overpopulated with Töffels and Hannchens. Christian Gottlob Hempel's turgid five-act "musikalisches Drama" *Peter der Grosse, Kayser von Russland* celebrates an episode out of modern history, Peter's outwitting of the Turks at the River Prut in 1711. Hempel crowns his fawning adulation of the emperor with the unmotivated appearance of a Greek monk. A sudden prophetic raptus seizes the monk, and he describes a long line of heroes and heroines ruling Russia for many generations to come. Thereupon the Genius of Russia sings an aria and calls forth the shades of emperors and empresses from Catherine I to Peter III and his wife Catherine the Great, with the monk driveling on in praise of each.

Hempel obviously knew nothing about writing a libretto. He deliberately included long passages of dialogue: "Since in general the dignity of a tragedy demands lengthier rather than shorter declamation, the period-rich speech of the English, which I have striven to imitate from their best dramatic works, must needs be the most decorous for my tragic interlocutors as persons of the highest rank." Needless to say, Hempel did not miss the opportunity of dedicating his work to Catherine the Great and her son, Grand Duke Paul Petrovich.

Friedrich Gustav Schlicht exploited a colorful local tradition of Halle in *Das Hallorenfest* – the Whitsuntide celebration of the Halloren, an ethnic group largely employed in the extracting of salt from four springs near the town. In his long preface Schlicht explains their special dress, institutions, dialect, and customs. The drama develops the amorous rivalry between one of these young men, Franz, and a student at the university, Baron von Klehr, which comes to a head in the rowdy young baron's room with a struggle over a pistol. The baron faints when the weapon fires and Franz is arrested for murder in order to sustain dramatic interest until the sobered student can repent of his ways and clear the air for the festival.

All of these dramas offer the composer little chance to do more than pick up on emotions or aphorisms already present in the dialogue. One must include here as well *Hannchen Robert*, also a drama of rivalry (between a young scholar and a crude young boor of a country nobleman), which maintains an old-fashioned complexion of thirty-four short numbers distributed over its three acts, two of which end in prose.

The two librettos set in ancient Greece differ markedly in this respect. Friedrich Christian Schlenkert's *Agaton und Psiche* relates the trials of its titular lovers with frightful poetic mediocrity. In blissful innocence these two love each other, but Psiche's mistress Pitia, priestess of Apollo, has conceived "an ignoble, animal passion" for Agaton. The author's purpose was apparently to celebrate sexual self-control (Pitia overcomes her desire and renounces claim to Agaton) and non-sexual love (Psiche turns out to be Agaton's sister). The bland moral rectitude of these three contrasts sharply with the turpitude of the hypocritical high priest Teogiton, who not only exploits his position for financial gain but also has taken to seducing the temple's flock of virgins. He decamps when his game becomes known, dismissed from the drama with the remark, "Thus does vice punish itself."

With his musical planning Schlenkert makes some tentative efforts in directions important for the future. The chorus (or choruses) appears in seven of the opera's seventeen numbers, including a substantial complex around an oracular prophecy. Usually it introduces a change of scenery – an ever more important visual component of opera amply provided for here. An ingenious musical innovation forms the center-piece of Pitia's major assault on Agaton's virtue in act two. Reclining "in a seductive negligée," she asks him to read to her, choosing a passage from Homer in which Zeus becomes inflamed at the sight of Hera and makes love to her in a golden cloud. Agaton is instructed to read "mit Accompagnement." Pitia's stratagem nearly works, forestalled only by the untimely appearance of a messenger.

The best of the unset librettos in Table 7.2, also on a classical theme, is Wieland's last libretto *Pandora*. Its opening scene (Prometheus falls in love with Pandora but refuses to accept the gods' box) forms a verse prologue to the prose drama with arias which analyzes the evil workings of the opened box on an utterly harmonious pastoral community. Wieland was never more in his element, and this libretto, like all his writings, bears the stamp of the Enlightenment's joy in instruction pleasingly imparted. Mercury (Harlequin in Lesage's *Boëte de Pandore*, Wieland's model) explains to Pandora the nature of the box's contents: it holds the passions, and "with the passions it is entirely a matter of measure and purpose, time and place. They can be good or evil, depending on how they are handled." Wieland plans her opening of the box as an extended pantomime: tiny winged monsters climb out to thunder, lightning, and a thick mist; Prometheus arrives, Pandora drops the box and runs off; he cries out after her and leaves.

Wieland returned to verse for the drama's conclusion. The happy, bucolic world of Prometheus's creatures has fallen apart and wavers on the brink of insurrection. Prometheus again appears, heaping scorn and reproach on Jupiter and Mercury for ruining his creatures. Mercury replies:

> Cousin Prometheus, if the foul mood
> That makes you speak in iambs
> Otherwise leaves you at liberty to hear reason,
> Then listen. . .

Eternal sameness is not life, Mercury observes, and Pandora has hastened what would have happened anyway. Prometheus, the plastic artist, loves *pure forms*, however: this mixture of light and dark, sweet and bitter, gives him no joy. Tender music announces Pandora's arrival. She obtains forgiveness, and Mercury foretells that she will bear Prometheus a daughter – Hope – who will live forever among men, and the opera concludes with a musical tableau honoring Irene, the goddess of peace.

Pandora differs from Wieland's earlier operas – *Alceste* and *Rosamunde* – and from the dramatic Vorspiele he wrote for various occasions at Weimar in its variety of character and in the degree of musical participation it invites. With Addison's Sir Trusty in *Rosamunde*, it is true, Wieland had made a timid attempt at mixing high and low, but he also badly botched the opera's dramatic construction, whereas *Pandora* is beautifully proportioned. Its theme is perhaps several rungs too high on the philosophical ladder for opera of its day (which perhaps accounts for its neglect), but the drama embodied a realization Wieland had come to, and which others could mull over with profit: the variety opera craves will assert itself one way or another; its dynamic will eventually supersede the "immer Einerley" of pure forms.

Table 7.2 reflects a fairly substantial falling off in the number of unset librettos for the eight years under study in this chapter, compared with the six preceding years. And in the last eight years of our study, to be considered in the next chapter, the unset libretto virtually disappeared as a phenomenon of North German operatic life. Only six examples will confront us there. Among those from the period 1784 to 1791, the two worthy of serious consideration – *Rudolph von Mohelli* and *Theseus auf Kreta* – are both tragedies. With the latter in particular one can see how far serious opera had traveled in North Germany after *Alceste*. We shall take it up, as well as the important essays published with it, when we consider German serious opera as a special topic later in this chapter.

Döbbelin's end and the Berlin National Theater

At his narrow little theater in the Behrenstrasse, Döbbelin saw his entrepreneurial fortunes decline steadily in the 1780s. By 1784, the year both André and Marie Niklas left, receipts were running at about two-thirds of what they had been five years earlier. A traveler in 1785 reported that his theater "is not so well attended as it is thought elsewhere. The playhouse is only a small booth for such a city, and still with its small dimensions it is very seldom full."[2]

On 17 August 1786 Frederick the Great died, and all theaters were ordered closed until October. For Döbbelin this spelled ruin, or so he claimed in a private audience with the new sovereign, Friedrich Wilhelm II. Happily, the king's long-established sympathies for the German stage proved anything but empty – Friedrich Wilhelm granted Döbbelin outright the old French playhouse at the Gendarmenplatz, together with its decorations, and a royal subvention of 6,000 Thaler per year, creating thereby the Berlin National Theater out of Döbbelin's company.

Despite these happy events, Döbbelin's days were numbered. He was growing old, discipline had become lax in his troupe, his casting left much to be desired, he still gambled, and not least important he was wholly unpracticed in the art of court intrigue. Brachvogel attributes his fall to one man, Johann Jakob Engel, now a professor of fine arts at the Joachimsthal and a favorite of the king's, a man animated by selfish ambitions and open disdain for Döbbelin.[3] Between Döbbelin and the king's supervisors (his financial advisor Johann August von Beyer and the esteemed poet and professor Carl Wilhelm Ramler) Engel carved out for himself a position of great practical

---

[2] *Der Teutsche Merkur* 1785:2 (May): 136. The correspondent later notes a local complaint about inflation at Berlin, including theater tickets: "Everything here rises and rises in price, and many of the inhabitants must do without many pleasures, since they do not have enough money to take part in them in the proper style" (p. 137). The writer's barber, for example, considered it beneath his station to sit in the gallery at Döbbelin's theater, although that was the only place he could afford.

[3] *Geschichte des Königlichen Theaters zu Berlin*, vol. 2, pp. 15–16. Throughout his discussion Brachvogel backs up this assertion with strong documentary evidence.

power as artistic director of the theater. This was made official on 31 July 1787, demoting Döbbelin in effect to a mere stage manager. Two years later the court pensioned off old Döbbelin.

Despite the dark picture drawn of him, Engel made vital contributions to the enterprise, including the rebuilding of its sluggish, indolent musical wing into an excellent cadre capable of mounting the most challenging new works with brilliance and polish. The composer Johann Christian Frischmuth, who had replaced André, proved a lackadaisical sort with a tendency to dawdle in preparing new operas. To help him out, and more specifically to improve a small and sloppy orchestra, Engel hired Carl Bernhard Wessely as second music director. Under him the orchestra expanded from around eighteen players to nearly forty.[4]

Engel also acquired important new singers, whose styles and strengths we can illustrate, along with those of the singers inherited from Döbbelin, by listing the distribution of roles at the Berlin premières of the three Mozart operas taken up by the new enterprise:

Name (Year joined National Theater)	Die Entführung aus dem Serail (16 Oct 88)	Le nozze di Figaro (14 Sep 90)	Don Giovanni (20 Dec 90)
Friedrich Carl Lippert (1788)	Belmonte	Almaviva	Don Giovanni
Carl Wilhelm Unzelmann (1788)		Figaro	Leporello
Christian Hermann Benda (1786)	Osmin		
Ferdinand Ernst Greibe (1786)	Pedrillo	Basilio	
Friderieke Unzelmann (1788)	Constanze	Contessa	Donna Anna
Henriette Baranius (1786)	Blonde	Susanna	Zerlina
Mariane Hellmuth (1789)		Cherubino	Donna Elvira

The Unzelmanns, though excellent singers, were engaged to perform in both spoken and sung works. He had served under Döbbelin earlier. Among the singers on hand at the inception of the National Theater in 1786, only Henriette Baranius proved important, and she too performed in spoken dramas. Friedrich Lippert was another matter altogether: he came from Vienna in early 1788 and demanded a salary nearly equalling that of the company's premier tragic actor, Johann Friedrich Ferdinand Fleck. The supervisor Beyer, on hearing and seeing him in Dittersdorf's *Doktor und Apotheker*, was inclined to take him on his terms. He wrote to Engel: "A good tenor who at the same time is a good actor is by common consent considered the rarest theatrical specimen. Therefore Herr Lippert should be worth

---

[4] In 1786 the National Theater began life with 7 violins, 2 violas, 1 cello, 1 bass, 2 oboes (one doubled on the flute), and 2 horns. See Gerhard Born, *Die Gründung des Berliner National-theaters und die Geschichte seines Personals, seines Spielplans und seiner Verwaltung bis zu Döbbelins Abgang (1786–1789)*, Ph. D. Diss., Erlangen (Borna-Leipzig, 1934). Brachvogel reports (vol. 2, p. 150) that in 1788 Wessely brought the orchestra to 14 violins, 3 violas, 4 cellos, 4 basses, and 4 each of all the winds.

twenty-four Thaler a week. . . . A better tenor and actor is probably not to be had just now."[5] Engel agreed to pay him twenty-three Thaler if he would also coach the other singers at rehearsals. This in effect put the control of Berlin's singers in the hands of a Viennese. With the arrival of the bass Frankenberg the same year and of Mariane Hellmuth[6] in 1789 all the leading singers of the company were of first rank.

The king's interest in the National Theater waxed with its burgeoning musical establishment. At first his influence extended little beyond the scheduling of premières on Tuesdays, the day the king regularly attended the theater. In 1788 he began requesting specific works for the evenings he attended; that year fifty-three requests came from the court (and the public also submitted signed "demonstrations" asking for a certain work). Later that year the king for the first time called members of the company to Potsdam for command performances. In 1789 he began lending some of his own best singers to the enterprise. He offered them the illustrious bass Ludwig Fischer, for example, in 1791 to sing the title part of Salieri's *Axur* (*Tarare*) at Potsdam and then made a present to the National Theater of the sets created for this production by his stage designer Verona.

What were the new musical works taken up by the ever-improving musical establishment of the National Theater? Döbbelin had produced only a few new operas before 1788, when fresh musical talent arrived. Thereafter, the National Theater offered its patrons a banquet of foreign operas. By original language the thirty-eight works break down into fifteen French, twelve German, and eleven Italian, but the truly successful works come from only two places – Paris and Vienna. Grétry's *Richard Coeur-de-Lion* became a special favorite of the king's (no surprise, considering its theme), and Dalayrac's *Nina* delighted the sentimental set. The major innovation in the repertory, however, came from Vienna – twelve works in all, seven German and five Italian. Dittersdorf and Mozart led the pack: *Der Apotheker und der Doktor* created such a sensation in 1787 that it was given six times in a twelve-day period following its première. *Die Liebe im Narrenhaus* carried the day in 1791. When *Don Giovanni* saw its première in December 1790, Berliners could revel fully in the topical allusions in the act two finale – all three operas quoted there had entered the National Theater repertory since 1788.

Against this grand parade new North German operas cut a figure we can only call pathetic. During these eight years Berlin witnessed only three local operatic premières by the National Theater, and all three works met with little or no approval. Baron von Kospoth tried his luck first. He had felt himself slighted by Döbbelin and sought immediately to ingratiate himself with

[5] Brachvogel, *Geschichte des Königlichen Theaters zu Berlin*, vol. 2, p. 131.
[6] She came with her mother Franziska Hellmuth from Schwedt on the dissolution of the court theater there. She led an exemplary life and married very high up in the king's administration. At the same time Marie Niklas returned to Berlin from Schwedt, but took a position as a chamber singer at Potsdam.

Engel in 1787.[7] Engel granted his request for a free pass to performances and also listed the baron's new opera *Der kluge Jakob* for production.

Johann Carl Wezel had brought out this libretto earlier that year at Leipzig. It is a veritable ward for flawed personages, including a king who lacks resolution, a cowardly and philandering young nobleman, a gullible and fortune-hungry soldier, a hopelessly romantic mayor's daughter, and lastly the farmer Jakob himself – incapable of making proper use of opportunity, oversusceptible to delusions of grandeur, and given to sloth – together with his wife Lise, a penurious, small-minded shrew. The various classes mix with remarkable freedom, a modern development, but Wezel offered Kospoth little room for the kinds of comic musical techniques to which Berlin audiences were fast becoming addicted. The opera's thirty-one musical numbers are mostly short and aphoristic, for instance Jakob's opening Lied, "Wer kein Geld im Beutel hat, / Kann kein Geld daraus verlieren."[8] The National Theater produced Kospoth's opera on 26 February 1788, and, as Gerhard Born reports, it did not please and in fact "was booed off the stage three times running."[9]

Carl Bernhard Wessely, second music director to the company and sole music director after Frischmuth's death on 31 July 1790, tried his hand at an opera with *Psyche* in 1789. He had gained much esteem in Berlin with his funeral music for his fellow Jew Moses Mendelssohn in 1786, but his first and only German opera fell from the repertory after only three performances. One journal blamed this on its mythological subject, now passé at Berlin.[10]

Musically and poetically, *Psyche* is worlds removed from *Der kluge Jakob*. In the opening introduzzione (not so labeled) the people assembled in the temple of Apollo ask the god for a prophecy. King Nicetas, Psyche's father, enters with a heavy heart: he has come to learn why no one has asked for the hand of his third and dearest daughter. The oracle speaks: her husband is to be no mortal, but a false monster whom even Jupiter avoids. She must leave her father and sisters. All present lament her fate, but Psyche refuses to

---

[7] He wrote to Engel in July: "Herr Döbbelin, for whose theater I have already written three operas, with which he has certainly earned a lot, was never so good as to offer the smallest thanks to me, rather he always inclined to suppress my work, which naturally rather angered me, and I therefore determined never to set foot in his theater again, which I have not done to this day." Brachvogel, *Geschichte des Königlichen Theaters zu Berlin*, vol. 2, pp. 67–8.

[8] The score of *Der kluge Jakob* in West Berlin (D-B mus. ms. 11880, apparently autograph) gives us an idea of how quickly Kospoth worked on the opera. After the Overture the beginning of the first act bears the inscription "Berlin den 27^t October 1787" and the act concludes with the note "geendet den 16 November 1787 Baron v. Kospoth." The title page of the entire score carries one further date: "Der kluge Jacob Eine komische Oper in drey Ackten für Das Berliner National Theater in Music gesetzt von Kammerherrn Freyherrn von Kospoth Berlin in December 1787." It took him about two months, therefore, to compose the entire opera.

[9] *Die Gründung des Berliner Nationaltheaters*, p. 72. The German term is "ausgepocht": at the theater disapproval was expressed by beating the floor with a stick or one's foot.

[10] "*Psyche* was the effort of two young authors, but, since subjects based on mythology no longer tend to succeed on our German stages, thus even Psyche did not quite suit the Berliners." *Journal des Luxus und der Moden* 5 (1790): 115.

shrink from it. She gives a farewell kiss to her father and to her two sisters (who are delighted to be rid of the object of their envy). As the music dies out Psyche falls asleep, alone in the temple, and Amor descends in a cloud to sing his first aria, about the grand deception he has just perpetrated.

Wessely's setting of this opening tableau illustrates the shortcomings of his score, only half of which is preserved. The choral writing is fine, but functions marginally rather than structurally. Internally, each episode moves to a new key, meter, and tempo with little effort directed toward overall effect. In one striking passage, the oracle speaks in melodrama over chromatically ascending whole notes in the bass (prefiguring Caspar's "Kugelsegen" in Weber's Wolf's Glen Scene). Wessely does not even observe the unity of key in this opening complex. It begins in D major, the key of the overture, and ends in C major, the key of Amor's ensuing aria. Thereby Wessely underscores the expository nature of Müchler's opening scene without much effort toward establishing its own musical integrity.

Shortly before the production of *Psyche*, one other new German opera saw its première under the National Theater on 29 July 1789 at Charlottenburg – Reichardt's setting of Goethe's *Claudine von Villa Bella*. The court audience received the new work coldly, a reaction duplicated when the National Theater repeated it at the Theater am Gendarmenplatz. We shall have more to say about this opera in considering Goethe once again later in this chapter. For now it is sufficient to remark that it did nothing to alter the wholesale insignificance of North German opera for the Berlin National Theater during these eight years.

Serious opera and Gluck's reception in North Germany

Although the center-piece of theatrical activity at Berlin, the National Theater was not the only show in town. The concert-hall, especially that run by the hotel-keeper Johann Friedrich Corsica, provided another forum for opera, and indeed the preferred forum for serious opera in German. We have already seen that *Alceste*, the bold undertaking of Schweitzer and Wieland at Weimar in 1773, did not exactly open the flood-gates to similar new works. Despite the triumphs scored all over Germany by this seminal work, later serious North German operas looked to spoken dialogue and less remote subjects; Benda's *Romeo und Julie* was the bellwether of this trend. In the mid-1780s, however, there emerged no less than five through-composed serious operas in North Germany, four of them set in antiquity and two of them new compositions of Wieland's *Alceste*. All were given in concert performances:

> Johann Heinrich Rolle: *Melida* (Magdeburg, 1784)
> Friedrich Wilhelm Heinrich Benda: *Orpheus* (Berlin, 1785)
>   *Alceste* (Berlin, 1786)
> Ernst Wilhelm Wolf: *Alceste* (Weimar, 1786)
> Johann Daniel Hensel: *Cyrus und Kassandane* (Halle, 1786)

The two re-settings of Wieland remained obscurities – partly perhaps owing to the formidable competition Schweitzer had already fielded, but perhaps owing as well to the conservative character of Wieland's libretto. The other operas fared better: all three were issued in keyboard reductions and drew critical attention.

Although the last of these works, *Cyrus und Kassandane*, differs from the others in some respects – it is in only one act and was composed by an amateur – in other ways it typifies this brief classicizing vogue. Both music and text, for example, are connected by their creators to royalty. Hensel, a pedagogue at Halle, dedicated his keyboard reduction to Prince Heinrich of Prussia. Ramler wrote his text (prior to his involvement with the Berlin National Theater) for Duke Peter of Curland. The duke himself had selected the opera's subject; he hoped to mount it at Mitau in order to fête the Russian Grand Duke Paul, but a death in the family brought the project to nought. The visit was to have occurred in the autumn, Ramler explains in his preface, and so the story is set in that season. He added other topical references: the rising sun is the future regent, a reference to religious devotions without images alludes to the banning of all statues by the Russian Orthodox Church, Cyrus's taking an assumed name in the opera reflects the Grand Duke's traveling incognito, and so forth. Ramler also included some flattering verses in the text describing the mother of Cyrus as lawgiver, patroness of the arts, and victorious heroine in obvious reference to Paul's mother, the Empress Catherine.

As one would expect, these flattering emblems accompany a story which holds fast to the techniques, personages, and sensibilities of opera seria. The Erfurt music director Georg Peter Weimar took Ramler rather severely to task for his failings as a musical poet in *Cyrus und Kassandane* and was lukewarm about Hensel's music as well: "Original features, thoughts startling in their novelty, bold turns of phrase, artful modulations, and passages by which the singing personages can be distinguished in character from one another one seeks in vain here."[11]

The earliest of the works listed above, Rolle's *Melida*, invited no such censure. To begin with, the young poet Christoph Joseph Sucro chose a subject anything but traditional: he wrote, in fact, a "cloister drama" and the first unequivocal tragedy in the history of North German opera. Before the opening curtain, the heroine has been forced to change religions on the death of her parents and to enter a cloister, where she was pursued by the lustful Franciscan monk Bernhardo. Her husband Julius has freed her and taken her to

---

[11] *Musikalische Real-Zeitung* 3 (1790): 188. The review is signed "Wr." Weimar's other frequent contributions to this journal make it very likely that he also wrote this review. Ramler indulged in the pedantic habit of printing the classical meters he employed at the beginning of his librettos, including *Cyrus und Kassandane* and his melodrama for Reichardt *Cephalus und Prokris*. Weimar found his verses unmusical, however: "Hard, intractable verses, which must be veritable thumb-screws for the composer to provide with music, are to be found not only in the recitatives, where they just might be forgiven, but also in the arias and duets" (col. 187). He cites the verse "Dis war mein Wunsch, dis bleibt mein Stolz" as an unhappy concatenation of monosyllables.

his country estate, but his friend Gustio Ojeda, a religious fanatic, has filled Melida with scruples and has informed the cloister of her whereabouts. The drama itself takes place entirely on Julius's estate and trades mostly in intensive emotional analysis of the principals along with nocturnal nature-painting. Then a contingent of monks and nuns arrives. Melida, filled with contrition, resolves to leave with them, but she recognizes her would-be seducer Bernhardo and confronts him with his vice. She hears Julius's voice and rushes toward him; Bernhardo interposes and stabs her to death.

The mixture of sentiment and wild dramatic vigor in Sucro's text was nothing new to Rolle. He had been dealing with precisely these ingredients all along in his religious dramas for Magdeburg such as *Der Tod Abels* (1769), *Abraham auf Moria* (1777), and *Thirza und ihre Söhne* (1779), as well as in his secular oratorios. While others had followed the introspective, meditative lead of Karl Heinrich Graun and Ramler in *Der Tod Jesu* (1755), Rolle sought to combine his penchant for musical Pietism with the ideals of Handel's dramatic oratorios. Chronologically he was of Gluck's generation (he completed *Melida*, his only full-length opera, when sixty-eight years old), and occasionally his sense of scale and dramatic flexibility incline one to think of Gluck. Act one begins with one of Rolle's most expressive obbligato recitatives, incorporating a d-minor arioso and arching to Melida's vision of Retribution crying "Forsworn!" ("Meineyd!"). As she sinks exhausted to the ground, a second arioso in b minor intensifies the effects of the pale moonlight in Julius's garden on her soul (Example 7.1). The second half of this arioso, fol-

Example 7.1 Rolle: *Melida*. Arioso of Melida, act 1.
"Do not look down with such paleness, oh moon, and with such gloom upon me! He who created you, star of the night!, gave love to this heart!"

Ex. 7.1 (*cont.*)

lowing a few bars of recitative, turns to new material in a new tempo (Vivace moderato) in keeping with the sudden change of mood in Sucro's text ("Gott! wie kämpft in mir Pflicht um Pflicht!"). In the present example as well, one sees that Sucro has skillfully provided for the composer's modulation to the relative major with a change of mood in the second couplet (bars 97 to 105).

As one can already infer from this example, Rolle's most profound stylistic affinities lie not with Gluck but with another of his generation's greatest masters, Carl Philipp Emanuel Bach – not surprising, since they had worked together at the court of Frederick the Great in the 1740s. A host of examples could be drawn from *Melida* or any of Rolle's dramatic oratorios and keyboard works to instance the common language they spoke, an especially idiomatic northern strain of the so-called "empfindsamer Stil," which young North German composers had all but abandoned by the mid-1780s. A brief aria-like section sung by Ojeda in act one provides most of the requisites. He is anxious to carry out his high deed (returning Melida to the Mother Church), but thoughts of the despair this would visit upon his friend Julius nag at Ojeda's human side. Without missing a stride, Ojeda moves from recitative to arioso (Example 7.2). Especially characteristic – beyond tempo,

Example 7.2 Rolle: *Melida.* Recitative and arioso of Ojeda, act 1.
   "You, however, you! My poor friend, my Julius! Feel now for the last time joys that your good fortune gave you."

Ex. 7.2 (*cont.*)

key, and meter themselves – are the bass pattern, cadence on "-male", appoggiaturas, and drooping figures on the downbeat beginning in bar 32. Rolle sets the text once through without repeating the first quatrain and devises a fluid tonal plan carefully tailored to the affective content of Sucro's poetry:

key:	G		g	B♭	d	G
bars:	28–46		47–59		60–75	76–82	83–97
lines:	1–2		3–4		5–7	5–7	8

1 Fühle nun zum lezten male
2 Freuden, die dein Glück dir gab!
3 Ach! der Leiden volle Schaale
4 sinkt an deines Lebens Wage, sinkt herab!
5 und die Stunden
6 sind verschwunden,
7 da ein Traum dir ew'ge Lust verhiess.
8 Ruhe denn zum letzten male sanft und süss.

(Feel now for the last time joys that your good fortune gave you. Ah! the cup filled with sorrows sinks on the scale of your life, sinks down! and the hours have vanished when a dream promised you eternal pleasure. Rest, then, for the last time, gently and sweetly.)

Rolle was at his best in planning such solo scenes. His ensembles represent little more than a traditional extension of ariatic patterns to two or three voices. On the other hand, he was justly famous all over Germany for his choruses, which always appeared in his keyboard reductions with each voice printed on a separate staff. Sucro offered him only two opportunities in *Melida*, a chorus of monks and nuns at the beginning of act two and a choral lament of onlookers at the end of the opera. The first of these Rolle set as an imposing, militantly square e-minor unison prayer, with protean open intervals at its start and a splendid low A on the word "Nacht" (Example 7.3). The

Example 7.3 Rolle: *Melida*. Chorus of monks and nuns, act 2.
"In the depth of this night, inasmuch as we make our pilgrimage for Your glory, Mother of God, sublime and majestic, be full of grace, and full of might with all of us pilgrims!"

Ex. 7.3 (*cont.*)

effect is as dramatically stark as Gluck himself could have wanted, but Lutheran choral traditions more than anything else lie behind Rolle's art in such instances.

Considering how skillfully recitative, arioso, and aria intergrade in Rolle's hands, his decision to set *Melida* as a through-composed opera is not surprising. Like other North Germans, he set all his oratorios this way, and *Melida* shared their method of performance, the public concerts at Magdeburg which Rolle himself supervised. Through-composition was apparently the norm for concert performances of any opera with pretensions to grandeur. A libretto for an unspecified revival of Seydelmann's *Arsene* reduced Meissner's prose dialogue to recitative "in order to make this Singspiel all the more serviceable for the concert."[12] The opposite could also happen when a concert opera migrated to the stage. A certain J. C. Fischer of Güstrow took it upon himself in 1787 to dress *Melida* "in the garb of a tragedy with arias (like

---

[12] *Arsene, Ein Singspiel in drey Akten nach Favart, von A. G. Meissner. In Musik gesetzt von Franz Seydelmann, Churfürstl. Sächsischen Kapellmeister* (n.p., n.d.). As the full imprint just given indicates, the opera was also reduced from four acts to three, accomplished by omitting three of the six numbers in Meissner's act one.

Benda's *Romeo und Julie*)" by writing extensive prose dialogue to replace its recitatives. In this form he had it mounted at Strelitz, "and the repeatedly ordered performances of the same convinced me anew that Rolle's arias produce the most splendid effect even on the stage."[13]

In discussing Rolle's operas we have alluded to Gluckian features here and there, but in no case does a resemblance overwhelm one. Composer and librettist have moved forward from the likes of *Alceste* in matters of color and characterization, but only the catastrophe shows signs of dramatic life, and the chorus is ignored as a vehicle for expanding the music-dramatic architecture. A more thorough-going reorientation of serious opera does occur in the Dresdener Lindemann's *Orpheus*, set by Friedrich Wilhelm Heinrich Benda, son of Franz Benda and a lifelong chamber musician at the Prussian court.

It seems that Lindemann originally intended his libretto for Naumann,[14] and part of it, along with translations from Calzabigi, made its way into the Danish opera Naumann eventually completed, *Orpheus og Eurydike* (Copenhagen, 1786). In the form in which Friedrich Benda set it, *Orpheus* differs from Calzabigi's libretto principally in retaining from the legend Eurydice's rival Hersilia. She tries to gain Orpheus's affections in act one even as he grieves for his lost wife. Spurned and beside herself with fury, she rather than Apollo appears after Orpheus loses his beloved for a second time in act three. Hersilia and her band of female Bacchantes find Orpheus insane with grief and she orders him clubbed to death. But Olympus is revealed in all its glory with Eurydice among the gods, and they restore Orpheus to her.

Orpheus demands no less than six different choral groups (no practical difficulty, of course, for a concert performance), which participate in nine of the opera's twenty vocal numbers. The first chorus to be heard – an a capella Largo for double chorus in c minor – is repeated in part after Orpheus's first aria, and the chorus of shades in the Elysian Fields scene beginning act three sees similar re-use.

In sharp contrast to previous North German practice in serious operas, Benda's score contains not a single da capo or dal segno aria. Instead, in nearly all cases young Benda turns to the cavatina in the form A_1A_2 (that is, just the first part of the old da capo form). As with Rolle, several numbers reveal a refreshing flexibility of formal and dramatic planning. Time and again, when presented with two quatrains by his librettist, Benda chooses to set the first in cavatina form and the B part as a transition, usually to an ensuing chorus. Each ensemble is composed in a different formal pattern. Even the final aria for Eurydice – after the dramatic tension has been resolved and one expects something along the lines of a concert aria   leads into a closing choral couplet rather than into a repeat of the A part of her aria. Preceding

[13] *Ephemeriden der Litteratur und des Theaters* 6 (1787): 404.
[14] A certain F. D. at Dresden reported in a letter of 9 September 1778: "Naumann. . . is said to be busy with an opera, *Orpheus*, by Hofr. Lindemann; its musical merit is extolled to me by various persons." *Deutsches Museum* 1778:2 (October): 382–3.

the wild chorus of the Bacchantes, Orpheus sings a dramatic aria whose key plan faithfully reflects his state of mind as he works himself into "Oresteian madness."

Allegro					Andante
A_1	A_2		B	Acc. recit.	
c–Eb–eb	B–c	G→c	Db–Eb–f		→ ab

Modulating to E-flat major, then switching to the parallel minor of that key to conclude the first quatrain reverses a common pattern, but is not unprecedented (Mozart ends the first half of the great E-flat major quartet in *Idomeneo* this way). But after a belated return to the tonic at the end of A_2, what seems like a B part (the second quatrain of text) moves to the Neapolitan, then the relative major, then the subdominant, and finally dissolves into an accompanied recitative as Orpheus takes final leave of his senses. Eventually he exhausts himself in a-flat minor, far from his opening tonic, c minor.

Orpheus also has its share of conservative features. Nearly half the arias are introduced by substantial ritornellos. Although there is some attempt at tonal unity in having the overture begin in B-flat, a key important to Orpheus and the one in which the opera ends, the overture itself is motivically and spiritually unconnected with the opera. In fact, Benda adopts Schweitzer's practice in *Alceste* and *Rosamunde* of writing a French overture. The fugue subject of the Allegro is fully worked out in four voices with a rather self-conscious augmentation near the end (Example 7.4). Whether the opera used simple or orchestrally accompanied recitative is difficult to judge today from the only surviving source, the published keyboard reduction.

Benda's letter of dedication in this print, to the Prussian Princess Friderike Charlotte Ulrike Catherine, refers to his "bold undertaking" in "treating musically for the first time in the German style and art a subject which has already been treated by the ablest foreign masters." He does not go into details concerning what "the German style and art" consists in, but the Berliners had no trouble distinguishing it from Italian fare. In 1788, when the king's Italian opera company substituted Bertoni's *Orfeo ed Euridice* (Calzabigi's text) for a *Medea* commissioned of Naumann but not yet completed, Benda sought to get his *Orpheus* performed again at Berlin, this time in the amateur "Stadt Paris" concerts, as pointed opposition to Bertoni's opera. The king, however, forbade any such performance until after Carnival season. Benda's *Orpheus* was indeed revived that March and, notes Brachvogel, "The composition harvested great applause, especially among the *opponents* of Italian music and everyone *with a taste for demonstrations*."[15]

A month earlier, a concert performance in French of *Iphigénie en Tauride* had brought a serious opera by Gluck to the Berliners' ears for the first time. As the following list culled from Loewenberg indicates, this was one of only

[15] *Geschichte des Königlichen Theaters zu Berlin*, vol. 2, p. 113. See also L[ouis] Schneider, *Geschichte der Oper und des Königlichen Opernhauses in Berlin* (Berlin, 1852), p. 220.

Example 7.4 F. W. H. Benda: *Orpheus*. Overture.

eight performances of Gluck's serious operas in North Germany in the thirty years from 1762 to 1791:

1770	Breslau	*Orfeo ed Euridice*	German (concert)
1775	Hamburg	*Orfeo ed Euridice*	unknown (concert)
1782	Hannover	*Armide*	Italian
1783	Rheinsberg	*Iphigénie en Tauride*	French (private)
1783	Hannover	*Orfeo ed Euridice*	Italian
1783	Hannover	*Alceste*	Italian
1788	Berlin	*Iphigénie en Tauride*	French (concert)
1790	Magdeburg	*Iphigénie en Aulide*	German (concert)

This record accurately reflects Gluck's overall fortunes in the North. While *literati* there, as we have seen, ranked him as the foremost German operatic master, North German composers were slow to accept the reforms associated with his name. In 1771 Frederick the Great's Kapellmeister Johann Friedrich Agricola greeted the printed score of *Alceste* with an extensive and searching review filled with misgivings over the new manner it represented.[16] After preliminaries, he spends fourteen pages in point-by-point objections to the famous dedicatory preface and then only nine pages on the music itself. To

---

[16] *Allgemeine deutsche Bibliothek* 14:1 (1771): 3–27.

his credit, Agricola does not attack the ideas to which Gluck set his name by denigrating his music to *Alceste*, but by repeated recourse to the argument that it is the excesses of opera seria rather than the genre's sound rules that are under the preface's critical gun. In the notorious "servant squabble" Agricola sides with Mozart and the Italians: "It surely does not follow that music, for the poetry's sake, must be robbed of half its charms and appear only as a servant: but rather that in a true Singspiel it has dominion and makes use of the aid of poetry to render what it is to express that much more distinct and clear."[17] He even defends coloratura as essential to the proper spaciousness of an aria.

On the whole, his evaluation of *Alceste* itself is a laudatory one. Yet – typically Northern and anti-Viennese – the slightest offense against the dignity of serious opera's musical demeanor meets with swift and stern reproof. The conclusion of the chorus "Che annunzio funesto" offers an instance (Example 7.5). "We understand that the composer wished to express

Example 7.5 Gluck: *Alceste*. Chorus, act 1.
"Let us flee, let us flee this place of horror."

Ex. 7.5 (*cont.*)

- giam   fug - giam   fug - giam

a dark murmuring of the people. But this expression, in this manner, is beneath the dignity of music. It is quite as low as it is also unnatural."[18] Nearly every passage Agricola censures, in fact, fails on grounds of low pedigree.

Agricola's review set the tone for the stand-offish attitude of many North German professional musicians toward Gluck into the 1780s. When all the ratiocination is stripped away, the bare truth emerges that embracing Gluck meant abandoning Hasse and Graun, and even Germans such as Hiller who were unconnected with Frederick the Great's musical establishment were unprepared for such a step. Hiller, writing in 1781, repeated most of Agricola's objections and hinted as well at the close connection of serious opera and concert performances in the North: Gluck's operas pursue the French ideal of a balance between the contributing arts, Hiller notes,

. . . but whether thereby these works have become *monumenta aere perenniora*, time must tell; it does not appear so, since far from all connoisseurs have wished to take his side, and even among those who did so in the heat of the moment, several have already thought better of it. It seems to me that a composer using this plan always has *one* disadvantage. If he fears that every lengthy ritornello, every melismatic dilation, or emphatic repetition of the words will interrupt the action or bring it to a halt, then all the pieces will become so short, so meager and undeveloped, that – however effective with respect to the whole they may be – they will still cut no figure at all when they are sung outside of this context in concert and at the music stand. . .[19]

Amateurs, on the other hand, took up the cudgel on Gluck's behalf. Wieland published notices of the fortunes of Gluck's operas at Paris in his *Teutscher Merkur* during the 1770s, and even printed Philipp Christoph Kayser's rhapsodic jumble, "Empfindungen eines Jüngers in der Kunst von

[18] *Ibid.*, p. 22.
[19] *Ueber die Musik und deren Wirkungen*, edited and annotated by Johann Adam Hiller (Leipzig, 1781; photo-reprint: Leipzig, 1974), p. 190, n. 22. This work is a translation of Michel-Paul-Guy de Chabanon's *Observations sur la musique et principalement sur la métaphysique de l'art* (Paris, 1779).

Ritter Glucks Bildnisse,"[20] although Wieland himself wrote to Kayser about the essay: "I have observed with amazement that you seem to be still unacquainted with the *Orfeo ed Euridice* of your holy man. In my feeling there is nothing greater, more lovely, or more melting for the soul than the aria, 'Che farò senza Euridice' in this Singspiel."[21] In the early 1780s, Carl Friedrich Cramer showed himself an especially ardent partisan of Gluck's music in his *Magazin der Musik* (Hamburg, 1783–4), openly ridiculing Agricola's animadversions (which Forkel had reprinted in 1778[22]) and championing recent works of Salieri, Naumann, and Johann Abraham Peter Schulz which breathed the spirit of Gluck's ideals.[23] Reichardt raised his voice around this time as well.[24]

The few classicizing concert operas just discussed provided the clearest opportunity for creative absorption of Gluck's legacy into German opera. And, as we have seen, Friedrich Benda alone made a serious effort in this direction. Neither he nor his reviewer ever mentions so obvious a predecessor, but in touting the forthcoming keyboard reduction of *Orpheus*, the publisher Rellstab could almost have been writing of Gluck rather than Benda:

> Through a continual alternation of choruses, arias, accompagnati, and dances, attention is sustained in a pleasing and moving manner, so that the boredom vanishes which one so often encounters with Italian operas. We are convinced that these pieces together do not determine the worth of an opera by a long stretch: yet Herr Benda has forged these individual parts together with such art and made them into a *whole*, that the principal feeling everywhere maintains the upper hand and, independent and recognizable, strides through the mélange as his hero does through Tartarus.[25]

After the two settings of Wieland's *Alceste* by Benda and Wolf in 1786, no new serious operas of any sort saw production in the North. Librettists, however, had not given up interest in the genre. In 1788 Friedrich Bouterwek published an impressive musical tragedy, *Menöceus*, eventually set by Bernhard Anselm Weber in 1792. On the other hand, Friedrich Rambach's "lyrisches Drama" *Theseus auf Kreta*, in spirit starkly Greek and in construction starkly Gluckian, offered North German composers a challenge which was doomed to go unanswered. Like Benda's *Orpheus* it mixes recitative, aria, chorus, and dance, but now the text moves so fluidly in

[20] *Der Teutsche Merkur* 1776:2 (September): 233–47.
[21] Quoted by C. A. H. Burkhardt, *Goethe und der Komponist Ph. Chr. Kayser* (Leipzig, 1879), pp. 8–9. Kayser sent his essay to Wieland through Goethe.
[22] *Musikalisch-Kritische Bibliothek* 1 (1778): 176–99.
[23] Cramer used his musical series *Polyhymnia* to disseminate Gluckian opera in German: the most prominent examples were Salieri's *Armida* (1783, translated by Cramer himself) and Naumann's *Orpheus und Euridice* (1787, translated from the Swedish by Eschenburg).
[24] He reprinted "No, crudel, non posso vivere" from *Alceste* together with the equivalent aria from Lully's *Alceste* (1674) and observed: "No very exhaustive analysis is needed to indicate how infinitely more truly and beautifully [the scene] is treated in Gluck. . ." *Musikalisches Kunstmagazin* 1 (1782): 91. Nine years later he remarked about the same opera, "The passionate expression of lament in Gluck's aria 'Misero e che farò?' is perhaps the highest that any composer has ever reached." *Ibid.*, 2 (1791): 66.
[25] *Der Teutsche Merkur* 1785:2 (September): cxlvii–viii.

continual unrhymed verse that it is virtually impossible to compart it into the traditional categories of recitative and aria. In an eighty-page historical essay appended to the drama, Rambach sounds the burden of recurrent operatic decadence and the necessity of reform. Germany must return to the example of ancient drama, the model for the present effort. His libretto follows only the laws of "Dramatik und Lyrik," knowing that its sister art will follow step by step.

Rambach adopted Herderesque ideas in defending his use of German in *Theseus auf Kreta*: ". . . this language is our possession, the echo of our character and heart. The grandeur, strength, and fullness of feeling and deed, which moves the German most, lies in it, and its words will also bend themselves to tender sentiment and tone in a skilled poetic hand."[26] He made ample provision in his drama for all these properties, and also for modern operatic sensibilities with frequent scene changes, offstage choruses, and a spacious introduction for the minotaur's appointed victims. The gods move freely in and out of the action. The last act begins with a pantomime ballet which Rambach integrates fully into his libretto: not only does it sketch out an important sub-plot necessary to the denouement, but it also connects seamlessly by means of an entr'acte with the end of the preceding act, the love scene of Theseus and Ariadne.

The eminent Johann Joachim Eschenburg lent his prestige to young Rambach's "first fruits" with his prefatory remarks to the reader. In them he speaks in pessimistic terms of the present state of serious opera in Germany. No one, be he patrician or commoner, goes to a serious lyric drama today expecting noble entertainment or strong, spirit-lifting feelings, or sentiments arousing lively interest. No one thinks of the total impression of an opera. Our connoisseurs confess that they would rather read the libretto for this – the performance serves better for enjoying details. The connoisseurs had their way with *Theseus auf Kreta*, at least. Although both Eschenburg and Rambach mention that "the young, talented music director Schwenke in Hamburg" was laboring on its composition, neither this nor any other setting ever materialized.

Silesia and East Prussia

All of the serious operas just discussed arose in a relatively small area of Prussia with its center at Berlin, prefiguring the more intensely "classical" persona the city's cultural institutions were to assume in coming decades. One thinks first of the Weimar court in seeking kindred attitudes elsewhere, of course, but here only Wolf's setting of Wieland's *Alceste* gives any evidence of classicizing trends in German opera. While the rest of North Germany all

---

[26] "Ueber das dramatisch–lyrische Gedicht," appendix to *Theseus auf Kreta* (Leipzig, 1791), pp. 209–10.

but ignored this part of Berlin's musical personality, it echoed other developments in the Prussian capital's cultivation of German opera. At Breslau, Dittersdorf's comic operas made their earliest conquests, beginning with a successful production of *Der betrogene Bräutigam* (*Lo sposo burlato*) in 1783. In March of 1790 Dittersdorf himself attended the Wäser company's performances of *Hieronymus Knicker*, one of which was a benefit for the composer. That May he also received as an honorarium the receipts from the Breslau première of *Das rothe Käppchen*, soon to be a favorite everywhere in Germany. His pupil Carl Joseph Birnbach also provided the Wäser company with two comic operas during this period.

Kaffka got into the act as well. He offered to other German theaters in April 1789 copies of "a newly completed comic operetta, *Hieronimus Knicker*" by Dittersdorf, who needed no further recommendation than that of "the author of *Doktor und Apotheker*,"[27] an opera the Wäser company had already given countless times. Kaffka also offered his own recent creative efforts, *Der blinde Ehemann* and *Der Talisman*, both of which had fared well at Breslau. The text of the latter, Bretzner's one libretto from these years, does not survive. The former, adapted from a fine comedy by J. C. Krüger of 1744, offers a study in infidelities past and present, real and imagined. A serious triangle involves the virtuous Laura, her blind husband Alfonso, and the prince of the island, Astolfo, bent on seducing his friend Alfonso's wife. A comic triangle develops parallel entanglements: Florine, of light virtue and exasperated by the continual drunkenness of her husband Krispin, has taken Astolfo's chamberlain Marottin as her lover. Alfonso and the prince turn out to be half brothers by means of yet another triangle, for the old prince had sired Alfonso, and, just to complicate matters, he had thereby angered another of his lovers, the fairy Oglyvia, who took revenge on him by blinding Alfonso. With these ingredients Krüger's adapter Johann Friedrich Jünger found rich opportunities for characterization and interaction. Especially in his musical structures he took advantage of these situations, not only in the finales concluding both acts, but in several extensive ensembles involving the comic trio. Marottin's feigned muteness for most of the opera opens the door to much pantomimetic participation, which Jünger carefully prescribes.

Madame Wäser provided new costumes and splendid decorations for her production of Kaffka's opera. A local critic lauded her care and expense for this and each new production. "We do not know a time when the public has visited the theater in such numbers as the current autumn and winter,"[28] he remarked in early 1789.

In East Prussia theatrical matters changed little despite the death of Karoline Schuch in 1787. Her children and the tenor Ackermann took over, and Mühle continued as music director. The troupe's operatic repertory derived largely from Berlin's. A survey of new works and their reception at

---

[27] *Neues Theaterjournal für Deutschland* 2 (1789): 112.   [28] *Ibid.*, p. 44.

Königsberg, which appeared in 1789, illustrates how closely public taste in opera there approximated that of audiences at Berlin and Breslau:[29]

Doktor und Apotheker (Dittersdorf): the favorite piece of the public
Der Hypochondrist (Naumann): moderate applause
Der Automat (André): little applause
Die Entführung aus dem Serail (Mozart): pleased greatly
Der Alchymist (André): pleased more because of the piece than because of the music
Die drey Pächter (Dezède): pleased greatly
Die Reue vor der Hochzeit (André): did not please
Das Narrenhospital (Salieri): pleased greatly
Walder (Benda): pleased greatly
Die Wäschermädchen (Zanetti): pleased

Four new German operas sprang up between 1789 and 1791 at Königsberg, three of them by Georg Benda's son Friedrich Ludwig. In the early 1780s he and his wife Felicitas had been with Döbbelin at Berlin, then the Hamburg Theater, and finally Duke Friedrich's court in Mecklenburg-Schwerin. Most of their time was taken up with giving concerts, including a successful trip to Vienna in 1782–3. A second major tour brought them to Königsberg in 1788, where Benda was offered the position of director of the amateur concerts. Felicitas had no interest in the town, nor in Friedrich Ludwig. She left him and filed for divorce "on grounds of drunkenness, fornication, or rather frequent adultery, and malicious abandonment, also prodigality."[30]

Benda lived at Königsberg in the house of Friedrich Ernst Jester, the librettist of his three last comic operas, and died there in early 1792, not yet forty, of an apoplectic stroke. In his last operas he kept faith with the Saxon traditions to which he had been bred without totally losing sight of modern trends in German opera. His first effort with Jester, *Die Verlobung*, failed – in the opinion of one correspondent because the music "perhaps approaches the chamber style too much" and the libretto had none of the caricature of opera buffa.[31] But then in early 1791 their *Louise* appeared and all Königsberg talked of little else. Its songs were sung everywhere, pirated editions of some of them cropped up, and so Benda quickly got out a keyboard reduction. An unprecedented three hundred copies were subscribed to in Königsberg alone, sixty-eight more outside of town, although the opera was apparently never performed elsewhere.

The same year Benda and Jester worked up a sequel, *Mariechen*, "since continuations are beginning to be fashionable," quipped one writer, "even where there is nothing to continue. . . The poet had observed that in *Louise* the action is often held up too long by the arias, so he sought to weave the fast-paced action more into the singing." The effects on *Mariechen* were such

[29] "Gegenwärtiger Zustand der ehemaligen Schuchischen Bühne in Preussen," in *ibid.*, pp. 78–83.
[30] Hugo Hagendorff, "Friedrich Ludwig Benda," in Franz Lorenz, *Die Musikerfamilie Benda: Georg Anton Benda* (Berlin and New York, 1971), p. 126.
[31] *Musikalisches Monatsschrift* 1 (7192): 51.

that "one does not find in it so many popular, easily repeated songs as in *Louise.*"[32]

Both operas conclude their inner acts with finales, perhaps better classified as dramatic ensembles, each with four or five key and tempo changes but not much dramatic momentum. The operas owed their success, as had Hiller's twenty years before, to their short, memorable melodies. Everyone in Königsberg knew the opening number of *Louise*, "Heitre Sinn und froher Muth" (which returns in the act one finale). Benda and Jester went so far in this direction as to include a Romanze in each of the opera's three acts, and even one of Benda's introductory recitatives leads not into a substantial aria but into a tender cavatina (Example 7.6), showing to advantage his mastery of Lied style.

Example 7.6 F. L. Benda: *Louise*. Recitative and Cavatina of Louise, act 2.
"The determination that heartened me is gone, I submit. Ah, have mercy, have pity on the grief that eats into me, and forgive the poor one when she wavers and trembles disconsolately."

Further up the Baltic coast at Reval, an amateur theater had opened its doors in 1784. One of its mainstays in the 1780s, August von Kotzebue, began producing his first significant dramatic works for this stage and for private entertainments at the home of Baron Friedrich Rosen. One of these pieces, the opera *Der Eremit auf Formentera*, was to be set ten times by German composers before the century was out. It neatly epitomizes the literary character of North German opera during these years with its exotic theme, varied characters, liberal moral tone, and unabashed joy in strong situations deftly directed toward a happy ending. Only its fairly cautious disposition of musical materials sets it apart from later more Italianate texts, including Kotzebue's own librettos of the 1790s.

The overture, so Kotzebue instructs, describes the end of a storm and daybreak on the desert island of Formentera off the Spanish coast, where a hermit and his old servant Fernando live. They find and revive Selima, a young Turkish maid washed up on shore. Later, Don Pedro, the young Spanish captive with whom she was fleeing, lands with his servant Pedrillo. Then Turkish music announces the arrival of the proud Algerian pirate Hassan Machmut, Selima's father come in pursuit of her. Kotzebue establishes some secondary connections – we learn that Hassan was impressed by Don Pedro's valor in their sea battle, and that he makes yearly visits to the hermit – but in line with modern tendencies the dialogue is kept short. Act two spins off a volley of multiple confrontations and revelations. The hyper-emotional Hassan believes his daughter drowned, the hermit promises to restore her to him if he will forgive her, and at first Hassan agrees to this, but then refuses to do so when the hermit produces her. With Don Pedro he also swings from one extreme to another: he rejoices to learn that he is the hermit's long-lost son, but draws his dagger in fury when Don Pedro also confesses to being his daughter's abductor. Magnanimity, of course, prevails in the end. Kotzebue's strength here, as in his spoken dramas, lies in careful dramatic pacing of strongly charged emotional situations, which at times borders on the exploitative.

Kotzebue wrote his first libretto in 1785 and tailored the role of Selima to the abilities of Baron von Rosen's daughter Maria. The first edition of the libretto (Reval, 1787) already mentions Ernst Wilhelm Wolf's setting, the first North German one (followed by Mühle's for the Schuch troupe in 1790). This edition contains several interesting textual variants from later editions, indicative of Kotzebue's combative moral and religious ideas. One aria, for example, originally began:

> Einst sagt' ein Capuziner mir,
> ein Heyde, Freund! ist nur ein Thier!
> Und Thiere darf man schlachten.

(A Capuchin monk once told me, "A heathen, friend, is nothing more than an animal, and one may slaughter animals.")

A later print changed "Capuziner" to "Hochstudierter," and most others omitted the aria altogether.[33]

In 1789 Friedrich Wilhelm sent Kotzebue's libretto to Engel along with the music of the Mannheimer Peter Ritter. Engel, who knew the text already, wrote back to the king:

> ... it bears unmistakable traits of the genius of its author, although it is in fact one of his earlier and thus less mature works. The principal fault would concern the fact that the excellent opinions on tolerance are at times so incautiously expressed as to suggest that indifference to all revelation is being preached, which could scarcely be the intention of the noble-minded author. The direction of the Mannheim theater has, however, already happily remedied this flaw through the omissions and changes it has made.[34]

Engel may well have had in mind the original closing refrain of the final chorus, the most stridently counterdenominational passage in the opera:

> Ja gewiss! wir sind einander
> Alle, alle gleich!
> Juden, Türken, Christen, Hayden,
> Wandeln ohne sich zu neiden!
> Hand in Hand ins Himmelreich!
> Drum so ziehet hin in Frieden
> Unser aller Gott mit euch!
> Unser Glaube ist verschieden
> Unsre Herzen sind sich gleich.

(Yes, surely! we are everyone of us the same! Jews, Turks, Christians, heathens walk hand in hand without envying one another into the heavenly kingdom. So go thus in peace, the God of us all with you! Our faith is different, our hearts are the same.)

The lesson Kotzebue has borrowed here from Lessing's *Nathan der Weise* was lost on weak-minded Friedrich Wilhelm. In 1791, less than two years after the opera's première, he permitted the cornerstone of Wöllner's notorious Religionsedikt to be laid, initiating an era of official intolerance wholly unprecedented under his uncle's enlightened reign.

Hamburg and the North: Viennese and Italian opera in full flood

Nowhere in Germany did Italian and Viennese opera triumph more decisively than at Hamburg. Production of new German opera had never amounted to much there, but French comic opera had become something of an institution by the early 1780s. A turning point came in 1784, however, when Italian buffists joined the Hamburg company, now under the indefatigable Seyler.

---

[33] "Capuziner" occurs in Lo 3984 as well, "Hochstudierter" in Schatz 11081 (apparently "Capuziner" was too much for Catholic Regensburg – and this print changes another aria's mention of "Franz von Assissi" to "heil'ger Holofern"). The aria does not occur in the *Deutsche Schaubühne* edition (Augsburg), nor in Schatz 8822a. See Part II, Section A of the Catalogue.

[34] Brachvogel, *Geschichte des Königlichen Theaters zu Berlin*, vol. 2, p. 223.

When he left that year the new directors retained the Italians and even suffered them to sing their roles in Italian while the rest of the cast sang in German. The next year brought another administration which went so far as to rent the theater to an Italian troupe for a month. It also brought Schröder back from his travels. He organized a new company at Altona and after Easter in 1786 began his second directorship at Hamburg.

Always a strong partisan of a strong spoken repertory, Schröder at first banned both opera and ballet from his offerings. This, it turned out, would not do. Public demand and poor receipts forced him to reinstate the opera after six months. Thereafter, two principles dominate his expanding operatic repertory at Hamburg – buffa and spectacle. Neefe's *Adelheit von Veltheim* was the first new opera taken up. As Schütze puts it, "Mindboggling decorations (some with illumination), richness of costume, nocturnal adventure, cheerful music and scenery charmed the masses continuously with this operatic farce. It became fashionable not to miss *Adelheit*, and he who did not go from a taste for opera went with the crowd for the society."[35] Other special favorites with the Hamburgers over the next three years include Dittersdorf's *Doktor und Apotheker* and Mozart's *Entführung aus dem Serail* and *Don Giovanni*.

Hönicke remained music director through the various theatrical regimes which struggled to keep the Hamburg stage afloat in the 1780s. Karl Hanke came as co-director in 1784, and his wife also joined the troupe. She began studying with Sophie Seyler, and, after the renowned actress left to join her husband's company, the Hankes also left Schröder. Eventually they rejoined the Seylers at Schleswig, where the Landgrave Carl had established a court theater in early 1787 with Seyler in charge and Hanke as music director. Here Sophie Seyler wrote and Hanke set to music *Hüon und Amande*. Her libretto, completed in July 1788 and dedicated to Schröder, is a creditable adaptation of Wieland's immortal epic *Oberon* (bits of which had been pilfered here and there in North German fairy operas throughout the 1780s), but along fairly conservative lines. Hanke's music, now lost, remained a local phenomenon. Later in 1789, Wranitzky's setting of Karl Giesecke's adaptation, *Oberon, oder König der Elfen*, began its triumphal sweep from Vienna to every corner of the German-speaking world and beyond.

Apart from the significance of *Oberon* for German opera in general and for Mozart's *Die Zauberflöte* in particular, it provides a unique opportunity to study how much distance still separated Northern and Southern conceptions of libretto construction. It is especially instructive to compare the musical numbers in the original *Hüon und Amande* with the version of Wranitzky's *Oberon* performed at Frankfurt (1790) and Hamburg (1791) which had several added arias written by Heinrich Gottlieb Schmieder and composed by Stegmann, who was now attached to the court theater at Mainz.

The new version omits thirteen of Sophie's thirty-one numbers altogether,

[35] *Hamburgische Theater-Geschichte*, p. 599.

revises six others, and substitutes new texts (including two finales) for another five. By the time he finished, Giesecke had left only seven of Sophie's original numbers in unaltered state. Six of his new numbers replace dialogue in the original version, and the two finales also incorporate much of the action preceding the act-ending choruses they engulf. Besides reducing the drama to three acts, Giesecke also cut back on the number of arias for the principals and redistributed the duets in favor of the comic pair Scherasmin and Fatime (Sophie had lavished four duets on Hüon and Amande):

	Seyler (1788)		Giesecke–Schmieder (1790)	
	arias	duets	arias	duets
Hüon	6	5	2	5
Amande	4	4	1	2
Scherasmin	5	1	3	3
Fatime	1	0	1	1
Almansaris	0	0	2	1

Sophie conceived Almansaris, the jealous wife of the Bassa von Tunis, as a spoken role – very possibly for herself – and provided a pathos-laden melodrama for her at the end of act four. Schmieder made all his changes in Giesecke's adaptation around this role, providing her with a dramatically charged duet with Hüon and two arias, one of them a rondo which blossoms out of her melodrama. Stegmann composed these additions for Margarethe Schick, prima donna of the Mainz National Theater.

Wranitzky's *Oberon* with Stegmann's additional music received its Hamburg première on 17 October 1791. Schröder gave it eleven times before the year's end and sixteen times the next year. It enriched his box office as had no previous work. "There has never been a greater and more lasting approbation than that for *Oberon* for as long as the Hamburgers love, see, praise, and admire operas. The public has hastened to no operatic pomp more constantly, indeed more insatiably than to this *King of the Elves*."[36] *Oberon* set the seal on Viennese–Italian dominion over North German operatic stages, and ironically, it did so by suborning a libretto of one of the greatest practitioners of Northern spoken drama to the task.

Elsewhere in the northerly districts of Germany the Viennese–Italian fashion made itself felt even in the wholly Frenchified theater of the Prussian Prince Heinrich at Rheinsberg. In 1790 Christian Kalkbrenner had taken over as music director, and a year later he produced his new German opera *Demokrit* – very closely based, it is true, on Regnard's popular comedy *Démocrite* (1700), but brought up to modern operatic standards by the Viennese writer C. F. Schröter. He reduced the original five acts to three and ended each with an extensive finale. This required some rearranging, since

---

[36] *Ibid.*, pp. 646–7.

Regnard followed the French practice of closing each act with an empty stage. In general the long speeches Regnard favored become shortened or turned into arias – a delightful dialogue in the original between the comic lovers in which they discover they are man and wife, separated for twenty years, thereupon putting an immediate stop to amatory preambles, is transformed with very few changes into a lively duet.

One would be hard pressed to find a stronger contrast with this cheerful, musically alive French-derived comedy than a strange drama published at nearby Neubrandenburg in 1785, *Der ehrliche Räuber.* C. G. Korb based it on events which occurred in Saxony during a severe famine in 1772. Kühn, a laid-off miner with six children, is driven to distraction by the sight of his family nearing death from starvation. He tries to hold up a peddler to get money, but breaks down in the middle of the enterprise. The peddler hears his story, goes with him to see his starving brood, and gives them his purse. The eight musical numbers are little more than byways. As Korb explains in his preface, "This subject is of such a serious nature that it permits no weaving in of humorous and least of all comic episodes, and I have therefore sought to uplift the piece by adding several other situations and by mixing in arias. . . " With its sober subject, marginal employment of music, rustic setting, and forceful moral assault on the audience's sympathies, *Der ehrliche Räuber* may have been typical of North German opera of the past, but it stood wholly counter to everything German audiences now wanted in an opera.

Weimar, Wolf, and Goethe's conversion to Italian opera

The troupe of Joseph Bellomo performed under contract with the Weimar court at the new ducal theater from 1784 to 1791. During this period Bellomo played at Weimar three times a week from September or October until Easter, then traveled to two or three other towns during the summer months. His troupe suffered from a continual coming and going of players, and neither their spoken nor their operatic offerings achieved great distinction. The music directorship changed hands several times; two of its short-lived occupants, Kraus and Burgmüller, contributed insignificant comic operas to the Bellomo repertory.

Goethe took no great interest in the company, which he considered "mediocre" at best. Several other members of the court, however, did provide the company with new operas, most of them set to music by Wolf. Only one of these, *Der Schleyer,* by Goethe's brother-in-law Christian August Vulpius, traveled beyond the confines of the Weimar theater for a second production elsewhere, in this case Hamburg. The text suffers more than most other German fairy operas from riotous over-indulgence in the knightly, exotic, and supernatural motifs employed with such point and elegance by Wieland in *Oberon.* A description of the principal characters illustrates this:

Prince Markomir, a knight from Gaul in search of his Ideal, carries with him a veil which will reveal her to him.

Soldan Issuff, King of Egypt, has had a crown affixed permanently to his brow by a jealous fairy. If any but the truest knight tries to remove it, the king gets a three-day headache.

Mandane, his wife, is carrying on with one of the king's knights ("I have drawn you to a pillow where only kings have lain," she tells him), but she also tries to coax the veil from Markomir, hearing that it preserves a woman's beauty forever.

Bellamira, the king's sister and Markomir's Ideal, has already dreamt of him. Protected by a magic talisman, she fends off the unwelcome suit of:

Mervillo, Prince of Loango and a magician. He uses all his powers to win her and to overcome Markomir; when defeated by the Fairy Marzinde, he throws himself into a flaming crevice in the earth.

Hamburg did not think much of the opera in 1788, allowing it only two performances even though it contained the spectacle, finales, and diverse characters audiences there craved. One reviewer remarked that it borrowed far too freely from Wieland, and that "the drinking scene between the dwarf and Arzanto [Markomir's squire] resembles that in Bretzner's *Entführung aus dem Serail* as one egg does another." He added: "The music is insignificant and especially the finales are insupportably boring and without any action."[37]

All of the poets with whom Wolf worked in the 1780s lived at Weimar (excepting Kotzebue, who nevertheless was a native of the city). His old collaborator Heermann, however, was not among them. Furthermore, although Wolf had published every one of his seven operas written before 1780 in keyboard reductions, he made no such effort for any of the seven written after that date. As a result, only his atavistic setting of *Alceste* survives. Textually, all of these late operas differ markedly from his earlier Saxon ones, *Der Schleyer* being the most extreme example. The lost *Angelica* (originally titled *Medor und Angelica* and probably based on Metastasio) dates from 1774; Wolf and Wieland had completed one act when the destruction of the court theater halted the project. They no doubt had conceived *Angelica* as an attempt to capitalize on the success of *Alceste*, and it finally saw completion as a pendant to Wolf's late setting of Wieland's famous libretto.[38]

Bellomo gave Wolf's *Die Zauberirrungen*, a "Schauspiel mit Gesang" based on Shakespeare's *Midsummer Night's Dream*, on 24 October 1785, the birthday of Anna Amalia – ever a staunch supporter of the composer. The

---

[37] *Annalen des Theaters* 2 (1788): 101.
[38] Possibly a remark Goethe made to Karl August in a letter dated 8 April 1786 refers to *Angelica*: "Wieland. . . wants with all his might to write another opera; I believe he has already begun." *Gedenkausgabe*, vol. 18, p. 919. The opera was not produced until two years later, apparently in a concert performance, at Berlin.

company repeated the opera a month later "by great demand" and revived it for a third performance in March of 1787. All that survived the fire of 1825 at the Weimar theater is a playbill,[39] which at least yields an inkling of how closely Einsiedel followed his model. He preserved with only slight reductions the major character-groups (nobles and lovers, fairies, and rude mechanicals), but nationalized the drama, as a comparison of his cast of characters with that of Shakespeare illustrates:

Einsiedel	*Shakespeare*
Prinz	Theseus, Duke of Athens
Prinzessin	Hippolyta, Queen of the Amazons
Hugo, ein Ritter am Hofe des Prinzen	Egeus, father to Hermia
Ottilia, dessen Tochter	Hermia, daughter to Egeus, in love with Lysander
Adelbert, für Ottilia bestimmt	Demetrius, suitor to Hermia, approved by Egeus
Cordula, liebt Adelbert	Helena, in love with Demetrius
Amandus, von Ottilia geliebt	Lysander, beloved of Hermia
Oberon	Oberon, King of the Fairies
Titania	Titania, Queen of the Fairies
Piuck	Puck, or Robin Goodfellow
Eine Fee	[Peaseblossom, Cobweb, Moth, Mustardseed]
Peter Squenz, Prologus und Souffleur, ein Maurermeister	Peter Quince, a carpenter; Prologue in the interlude
Klaus Zettel, ein Leinweber	Nick Bottom, a weaver; Pyramus in the same
Schnock, ein Schneider	[Tom Snout, a tinker; Wall in the same, Robert Starveling, a tailor; Moonshine in the same]
Schlucker, ein Hufschmidt [Tischler in the second performance]	Snug, a joiner; Lion in the same

Einsiedel more or less transliterated the names of the tradesmen except for the great bully Bottom: he received a surname appropriate to his craft ("Zettel", meaning "warp" in weaving).

If Bellomo's troupe at Weimar did not earn Goethe's admiration, at least they offered him the sort of operatic fare he longed for. The poet's letters of the 1780s are replete with admiring comments on opera buffa and with a special delight in Paisiello (the first opera buffa he heard was Paisiello's *Infanta di Zamora*, during his Swiss journey in 1779). In a letter to Kayser dated 28 June 1784 he declared his partisanship openly ("Ich bin immer für die Opera buffa der Italiäner"), and he wrote *Scherz, List und Rache* that year in this spirit. Goethe also mentions in the same letter that he had heard "a dozen" opere buffe at Weimar performed since winter by the Bellomo company. German opera, on the other hand, brought him no pleasure. In December 1785 he saw the Bellomo company's production of Mozart's

[39] Reprinted by Karl Elze in *Jahrbuch der Deutschen Shakespeare-Gesellschaft* [*Shakespeare-Jahrbuch*] 5 (1870): 364.

Entführung aus dem Serail and wrote to Kayser in no very flattering terms about it, to the dismay of those historians who seek a just concord among the immortals:

Everyone was in favor of the music. The first time it was performed indifferently; the text itself is very poor and even the music I could not swallow. The second time it was performed very poorly and I actually walked out. Still the work held its own and everyone praised the music. When they gave it for a fifth time I went once again. They acted and sang better than before, I put the text out of mind, and now I understand the difference between my judgment and the impression of the public, and I know how things stand with me (weiss woran ich bin).[40]

Goethe was not one to ignore a defective text – or a poor performance – for the sake of the music. His stern evaluation in this instance may have been influenced by his outspoken admiration for the Italian librettos he studied during these years and for the musical style that beseemed them. A passage from the letter to Kayser already quoted summarizes his views: "Life, movement spiced with feeling, all kinds of passions find their arena there. I am especially delighted by the delicacy and grace with which the composer fairly hovers as a heavenly being over the earthly nature of the poet." If *Die Entführung aus dem Serail* failed to satisfy Goethe in this way, one must not overlook the fact that its most Italianate feature, as we saw in the last chapter, disappeared from its musical fabric in Stephanie the Younger's revision – the abduction scene itself. Later on, Kayser complained to Goethe that *Scherz, List und Rache* was "zu angezogen, zu angestrengt" ("too tight, too strained") for a music drama. Goethe admitted that in retrospect it did seem "überdrängt" ("overdriven"), but nevertheless stood by his belief that "my highest conception of drama is restless action."[41]

The first flush of aesthetic commitment to opera buffa led Goethe to extremes. This apostleship was but one element in his deep disaffection for his cultural surroundings, a mood he tended to generalize: the boring insignificance of Weimar's court life he projected onto Germany *partout*, and the spiritless torpor of the Bellomo company's performances he projected (not wholly without justice) onto all of the German theater. Even Mozart's *Entführung aus dem Serail*, it seems, fell victim to this wholesale disgust. At Gotha, only a month after writing to Kayser about Mozart's opera, Goethe leafed through Reichard's *Theater-Kalender auf das Jahr 1786*:

. . . it brought me near to despair; I have never purposefully gone through it as I do now, and never has it and its subject matter appeared so empty, insipid, tasteless, and loathsome to me.

One cannot perceive how bad a business is until one performs a thorough audit and casts up its accounts in detail. A state of affairs is displayed here with the most desolate coldness and honesty, from which one can see clearly that everywhere – especially in the field that interests me at present – everywhere there is nothing and can be nothing. I pity the poor operetta I have started [*Die ungleichen Hausgenossen*] as one can pity

[40] *Gedenkausgabe*, vol. 18, p. 894.   [41] *Ibid.*, p. 902.

a child that is to be born to a black woman in slavery. . . Had I only known twenty years ago what I know now! I would at least have acquired a command of Italian so that I could work for the lyric theater, and I would have mastered it. I only pity dear Kayser that he is throwing his music away on this barbaric tongue.[42]

Goethe never completed the "poor operetta" he was writing. He also found himself alone in his admiration for what Kayser had sent him of *Scherz, List und Rache*. His commitment to his new operatic aesthetic remained firm, however, and in 1786 he even began turning his thoughts to the possibility of revising his earlier operas along the lines of the new ideals he had embraced. Then, on 3 September 1786, he departed secretly for Italy, and there he refashioned *Erwin und Elmire* and *Claudine von Villa Bella* in accordance with these new ideals.

Elmar Bötcher has summarized most of the significant differences between the earlier and later versions of both operas:[43] in general descriptions and long narratives are omitted or shortened (details of Crugantino's youth, Gonzalo's speech in praise of Claudine); sentimental, satiric, and moralizing scenes are similarly cut back or omitted (lovers' meetings, the recognition scene of Crugantino and Pedro, Erwin's speech on woman's fickle nature, Pedro's sermon on his brother's misdeeds). In both new versions Goethe created a secondary pair of lovers. For *Erwin und Elmire* this meant doing away with two very un-Italian creatures, the mother Olimpia and the tutor-confidant Bernardo. Their replacements, Rosa and Valerio, initiate the drama with professions of renewed love after a falling out occasioned by Rosa's jealousy; she returns abruptly to her old ways when she discovers Valerio tenderly comforting Elmire. The reunion of Erwin and Elmire reveals to Rosa Valerio's good intentions and thus brings about their own reconciliation. In *Claudine von Villa Bella* Goethe conflated the two envious nieces into one (he had also eliminated the old moralizer Don Sebastian) and made her rather than Claudine the object of Crugantino's attention. The young Stürmer storms much less in the new version, even though Goethe added a falling out with Basco which splits the vagabonds into two factions and prompts Basco to declare himself Crugantino's rival in love as well as leadership. Goethe went so far in his toning down of Crugantino as to rename him Rugantino after the young castrato Rugantino Caparolini (a favorite of Goethe and other German artists who assiduously attended Rome's small stage for opera buffa, the Teatro della Valle) – scarcely a model of Storm and Stress virility.

Clearly the source of all these changes lies in the dramatic principles of opera buffa. Even more clearly did they dictate the technical changes wrought. Goethe rewrote all the dialogue of both operas as recitative – with considerable shortening, of course – and incorporated more of the action into the ensembles. The implicit act divisions of both plots became explicit,

[42] *Ibid.*, pp. 906–7. (Letter of 26 January 1786 to Charlotte von Stein.)
[43] *Goethes Singspiele "Erwin und Elmire" und "Claudine von Villa Bella" und die "opera buffa"*, Ph.D. Diss., Univ. of Marburg (Marburg, 1911).

and every act ends with a finale structure. *Erwin und Elmire* remained idyllic enough so that Goethe could retain five of its sixteen original numbers intact and five more with minor modifications, including the reunion of the lovers. The changes in character and action had been too drastic in *Claudine von Villa Bella*, however, to permit the salvaging of more than three numbers without alteration. Goethe even scrapped the ambitious finale-like ensemble of Crugantino, Claudine, Pedro, and the Watch. As we noted earlier, this structure makes an anemic third act all but inevitable, and no doubt Goethe amalgamated what he could save of the old scene in his new act-three finale so as to avoid a local climax detrimental to the whole. A remark to Kayser in a letter of 5 May 1786 had touched on this issue:

The Italians have produced the greatest effects with individual situations which hang by bare necessity on to the general thread of the plan. One does not want to move ahead because the whole is not interesting, because in each particular spot one is at ease. Yet that too has its inconveniences; among others, the total discredit of the third act is the fault of this manner.[44]

From Rome Goethe dispatched both revised operas via Herder to his publisher Göschen at Leipzig, who included them rather than the original versions in his authorized complete edition of Goethe's works in 1788. Reichardt, having heard of the new versions beforehand, was already pestering Herder for copies. He set to work with gusto and in April 1789 showed up at Weimar with his setting of the new *Claudine von Villa Bella* under his arm. He remained eleven days, living at Goethe's home and going through the score with him. Herder's wife Karoline heard his music and could discover only a few good things in it, "but Goethe finds everything charming."[45]

Reichardt's opera was performed only six times at Berlin and Charlottenburg between 1789 and the end of the century. Goethe staged its only other production, at the Weimar Court Theater, in 1795. It generated enthusiasm nowhere. The première production at Berlin left Goethe's blank verse unset, the Weimar version had it set as recitative, and a 1799 revival at Berlin actually turned Goethe's verses back into prose – all to no avail.

Once *Claudine von Villa Bella* was out of the way, Reichardt set to work on *Erwin und Elmire*. Although his setting was not performed until 1793, we should consider it here because of its connections not only with Goethe but also with several of the issues we have been discussing in this chapter. To begin with, Reichardt set the entire text to music: "The work is wholly through-composed," he wrote in a 1791 advertisement, "and can be used in concert performances as well as in the theater."[46] The former, in fact, were to be the opera's lot – no full stage production of *Erwin und Elmire* ever occurred. Reichardt used accompanied recitative throughout – the first time a German opera had followed Gluck's lead in this respect.

[44] *Gedenkausgabe*, vol. 18, p. 926.
[45] Quoted by Rolf Pröpper, *Die Bühnenwerke Johann Friedrich Reichardts*, vol. 1, p. 83, n. 18.
[46] *Musikalisches Kunstmagazin* 2 (1791): 125.

The keyboard reduction of the opera, issued in 1791, saw a second edition in 1793 – something of a rarity for a German opera by this decade. *Claudine von Villa Bella*, which Reichardt never published, may have suffered under the pressure of his preparing what became the masterpiece of his Italian operas, *Brenno*, for the king's birthday on 16 October 1789. *Erwin und Elmire*, written in 1790 when Reichardt produced nothing at all for the king's Italian opera, shows greater care in every number. Wessely found the declamation flawless, and Naumann wrote an open letter in praise of the music.[47] Goethe was also delighted with the music and requested a full score from Reichardt.

"Since I now know the needs of the lyric theater more exactly," Goethe wrote in February 1788, "I have sought to work for the composer and actor by means of many sacrifices."[48] His sacrifices demanded that the composer take up the slack. Goethe's ensembles in particular no longer occupy points of dramatic rest, and occasionally he even breaks up arias (including "Das Veilchen") among several voices to create at least a semblance of interaction. He moved some numbers in *Erwin und Elmire* to new locations, out of the path of developing dramatic momentum. For example, the scene in act one between Bernardo and Elmire originally concluded with a short duet after Bernardo's lengthy description of the hermit, the romantic region he inhabits, and the comfort he could offer Elmire. Once she has left, Bernardo treats himself to a monologue of self-congratulation and a bravura aria to conclude the act. In the second version Goethe moved his closing aria all the way back to the opening scene and let Rosa join in at the end of it. He also injected her into Elmire's and Valerio's static duet: Rosa enters in the middle of it to discover Elmire and the consolatory Valerio hand in hand and reacts in a heart-broken aside. Reichardt, of course, was expected to respond musically to bring her access of jealous pain immediately to life (Example 7.7). He did so with the kind of economy Goethe longed for in his composers – a single, telling harmonic stroke (V-$^\flat$VI$_{\sharp 6}$ in bars 23–4) and a familiar rhythmic figure to suggest Rosa's palpitating heart (bars 24–6).

The act-two finale commences with Elmire's flying in on wings of Erwin's message: "Er ist nicht weit!" and proceeds to their reunion, but no longer does Goethe bid the composer pause to savor the moment as he had in 1775. Instead, Valerio steps in immediately for his quatrain before rushing off to fetch Rosa. Reichardt achieved the musical continuity Goethe wanted and did so again with grace and understatement (Example 7.8). He times the first step away from the dominant's orbit to coincide with Erwin's appearance, and thereafter maximizes the effectiveness of the simple, time-tested musical resources which return us to the tonic.

Reichardt was the only German composer of his day to set Goethe's revised

---

[47] Both are to be found in *Berlinische Musikalische Zeitung historischen und kritischen Inhalts* 32 (14 Sep 1793): 125, and 45 (23 Nov 1793): 177.

[48] Pröpper, *Die Bühnenwerke Johann Friedrich Reichardts*, vol. 1, p. 80.

Example 7.7 Reichardt: *Erwin und Elmire*. Trio, act 1.

ELMIRE: "The comfort from your mouth is nourishment for my pain."
VALERIO: "It heals your wounds and enlivens your heart."
ROSA: "Oh, what a deep wound! My heart is breaking!"

Example 7.8 Reichardt: *Erwin und Elmire*. Reunion scene, act 2.

ELMIRE: "Hear me, ye gods, oh give him back! Erwin! Erwin!"
ERWIN (stepping forth): "Elmire!"
ELMIRE: "Woe is me!"
ERWIN (at her feet): "It is I!"
ELMIRE (on his neck): "It is you!"
ERWIN: "It is I!"
VALERIO: "Oh look down, ye gods, on this happiness!"

Ex. 7.8 (cont.)

librettos to music. Although Reichardt's own restrictive dicta on German opera, dating from 1781 and 1782,[49] contradict in many essentials the character of Goethe's revisions, Pröpper dismisses the possibility that his sole aim had been "to link his own name even more closely with that of Goethe."[50] It is true that Reichardt was entirely capable of changing with the times from his youthful idealization of Hiller's *Die Jagd* to a sympathetic understanding of the new realities facing German opera by the end of the 1780s. Nonetheless, his devotion to everything lyric–dramatic from Goethe's pen until the rupture

[49] The preface to his libretto *Liebe nur beglückt* (Berlin, 1781) and the essay "Ueber das deutsche Singeschauspiel" in *Musikalisches Kunstmagazin* 1 (1782): 161–4.

[50] *Die Bühnenwerke Johann Friedrich Reichardts*, vol. 1, p. 82.

in their relationship and even beyond runs very deep and sets him clearly apart from all his contemporaries. In addition to the revised librettos we have been discussing, Reichardt also set *Jery und Bätely* in 1790 and *Lilla* in 1791, and planned several further operatic projects with Goethe (including *Der Gross-Cophta*). In 1791 Reichardt made so bold as to announce a projected six-volume series of *Musik zu Göthes Werken*, to comprise Lieder, operas, and incidental music to the plays.[51]

More deeply and accurately than other German texts of their day, Goethe's new versions of *Erwin und Elmire* and *Claudine von Villa Bella* together with *Scherz, List und Rache* had rendered practical testimony to the exemplary stageworthiness of opera buffa in German and had also implicitly put to discredit German operatic practices of the past. Yet in so doing Goethe had turned his back on several features of the German lyric stage which were proving their worth in the 1780s despite years of poor harvests – the marriage of German and Italian ideals in the Viennese operas of Dittersdorf and Mozart, the mounting tide of spectacle and the supernatural, exotic settings and stronger character types (often with political undertones), and continuing developments along closely related lines in French opera, particularly after the Revolution created entirely new institutional arrangements at Paris. Goethe would make good this temporary neglect in the 1790s as director of the Weimar Court Theater and as the author of a sequel to the coming decade's greatest and best-loved opera, *Die Zauberflöte*.

[51] Only three volumes actually appeared: *Erwin und Elmire* (1793), *Goethes lyrische Gedichte* (1794), and *Jery und Bätely* (1794).

8

The assimilation of Southern styles

In the last decade of the eighteenth century, the sway foreign operas held over nearly all German stages grew even stronger. Concomitantly, and in contrast to the preceding decade, a large segment of North German librettists and composers rethought the dramaturgic and aesthetic bases of their own operatic traditions, drinking deep draughts of the foreign operatic elixir around them, and began trying to produce new German operas more in step with popular taste.

Our examination of the operas produced in the North from 1792 to 1799 must begin with a brief look at the prominence given foreign works in operatic repertories there. The changing patterns of new North German operas may then be judged against this background. The keen competition offered by Italian, French, and especially Viennese operas added an economic dimension to the difficulties which faced struggling Northern composers: the preparation and expense demanded by these new operas, with their more complicated musical complexion and penchant for spectacle, restricted the number of new works a theater could consider mounting; success elsewhere became an important recommendation, since long runs were needed to recover initial costs.

Three representative stages: Weimar, Berlin, and Hamburg

With minor variations, a remarkably uniform foreign domination marked the operatic repertories of German court theaters, national theaters, ambulatory stages, and standing civic theaters. The most successful operas in all these theaters tended to come from the same small group of Viennese, Italian, and French operas, with each center adopting and adapting according to local taste and resources. To illustrate these points we shall consider briefly the operatic activities of the Weimar Court Theater under Goethe, the Berlin National Theater, and the German theater at Hamburg.

The court-sponsored enterprise which replaced Bellomo's company at Weimar did its best to assemble resources – especially singers – for perpetuating the Italianate operatic fare to which Weimar audiences had grown accustomed. Karl August, however, was not so open-handed as to indulge in the level of subsidies required for rivaling the operatic pomp of the largest court theaters, and the actor-singer rather than the virtuoso remained the company's characteristically German basic ingredient. The new troupe played at Weimar from autumn to spring, then spent the summer touring various towns for the purpose of reducing the considerable deficit incurred at Weimar each year. New works were very seldom introduced on these summer excursions.

Goethe pushed the operatic offerings even more decisively in the direction of Viennese and Italian opera than had been the case under Bellomo. Although more given to opera buffa than other principals of the 1780s, Bellomo had still introduced a respectable cross-section of North German operas (works by André, Schweitzer, Benda, Schuster, Wolf, Kospoth, Hiller, and Seydelmann), though none was especially popular.[1] Goethe, on the other hand, turned his back on North German opera. From 1791 to 1799 the Weimar Court Theater produced – apart from Benda's three major melodramas – only two North German operas, Schuster's *Der Alchymist* and Reichardt's *Claudine von Villa Bella*, both of them revivals. Not a single new North German opera saw its première at Weimar during these years.

Table 8.1 lists the most-performed operas in the Weimar Court Theater's repertory.[2] Just three cities account for the fourteen operas listed there: ten came from Vienna and two each from Prague and Naples. Altogether only four French works appeared in the Weimar repertory from 1791 to 1799; the most popular among them, Grétry's *Richard Coeur-de-Lion*, saw ten performances during these years.

The overwhelming triumph of *Die Zauberflöte*, duplicated on nearly every other North German stage, lay at the center of the enthusiastic favor with which every one of Mozart's major operas from *Die Entführung aus dem Serail* on was greeted. Dittersdorf's collaborations with Stephanie the Younger shared in Weimar's devotion to Viennese style. After 1793, however, no new operas by Dittersdorf were introduced, neither his earlier works nor those he wrote for Oels from 1794 to 1797. Instead Weimar turned to other German composers active at Vienna – Wenzel Müller, Süssmayr, Wranitzky, Weigl, and Peter Winter.

Die Zauberflöte, like nearly all its Viennese sisters, saw production at Weimar with its text severely altered by Goethe's brother-in-law Christian August Vulpius. It has remained an unexplored minor mystery why Goethe

---

[1] The *Annalen des Theaters* published a chronology of the Weimar theater covering the years 1784 to 1794. None of the eighteen German operas listed was performed more than five times. 20 (1797): 43–56.

[2] These figures, taken from Alfred Orel, *Goethe als Operndirektor* (Bregenz, 1949), pp. 115–85, cover the full span of the court theater's life in addition to the period relevant for this chapter so as to present a fairer picture of works introduced in the last years of the 1790s. The principal study of the musical and non-musical works of the court theater is C. A. H. Burkhardt's *Das Repertoire des Weimarischen Theaters unter Goethes Leitung, 1791–1817* (Hamburg and Leipzig, 1891).

Table 8.1. *Most popular operas in the repertory of the Weimar Court Theater*

Title (Original Title)	City, Year of première	Composer–Librettist	Introduced at Weimar	Weimar Performances 1791–1817	1791–1799
Die Zauberflöte	Vienna, 1791	Mozart–Schikaneder	16 Jan 1794	82	53
Don Juan (Don Giovanni)	Prague, 1787	Mozart–Da Ponte	30 Jan 1792	68	36
Die Entführung aus dem Serail	Vienna, 1782	Mozart–Bretzner/ Stephanie	13 Oct 1791	49	29
Das rothe Käppchen	Vienna, 1788	Dittersdorf–Stephanie	7 Jun 1791	39	30
Lilla (Una cosa rara)	Vienna, 1786	Martin y Soler– Da Ponte	19 May 1791	35	22
Hieronymus Knicker	Vienna, 1787	Dittersdorf–Stephanie	24 Nov 1791	34	26
Doktor und Apotheker	Vienna, 1786	Dittersdorf–Stephanie	17 Jul 1791	33	21
So sind sie alle (Così fan tutte)	Vienna, 1790	Mozart–Da Ponte	10 Jan 1797	33	14
Die Müllerin (La molinara)	Naples, 1788	Paisiello–Palomba	11 Nov 1797	28	5
Titus (La clemenza di Tito)	Prague, 1791	Mozart–Metastasio/ Mazzolà	12 Dec 1799	28	3
Oberon, König der Elfen	Vienna, 1789	Wranitzky–Seyler/ Giesecke	28 May 1796	27	11
Die theatralische Abentheuer (L'impresario in angustie)	Naples, 1786	Cimarosa–Diodati	24 Oct 1791	23	19
Das unterbrochene Opferfest	Vienna, 1796	Winter–Huber	10 Jun 1797	23	1
Die Hochzeit des Figaro(Le nozze di Figaro)	Vienna, 1786	Mozart–Da Ponte	24 Oct 1793	20	8

suffered the ineptitudes perpetrated by Vulpius in revising Mozart's opera, whose libretto Goethe admired, to creep onto the court theater's stage.[3]

Despite this mutilation, *Die Zauberflöte* became a household phenomenon at Weimar, and within a year of the first performance there Goethe had begun work on a sequel. Though Mozart's music undoubtedly lay close to Goethe's heart in the 1790s, he also admired the libretto as an effective piece of

[3] Schikaneder himself took umbrage at the changes Vulpius wrought on several of his librettos. Peter Branscombe has discussed the Weimar versions of Schikaneder's texts in his article, *"Die Zauberflöte*: A Lofty Sequel and Some Lowly Parodies," *Publications of the English Goethe Society* n.s. 48 (1977/8): 1–21. "Not the least edifying aspect of the Weimar adaptations of Schikaneder's works," Branscombe remarks, "is the petty skirmishing in which he and Vulpius indulged in the prefaces they attached to their libretti – for instance, in a ten-page-long 'Pro memoria!' that introduces *Der Königssohn aus Ithaka* (Vienna, 1797), Schikaneder takes Vulpius to task for maltreating *Der Spiegel von Arkadien*" (p. 5). Vulpius, it may be added, responded to this by visiting the same treatment on the libretto in which Schikaneder's "Pro memoria!" appeared.

stagecraft.[4] In fashioning his own sequel Goethe kept practical considerations uppermost in mind. The cast in *Die Zauberflöte, zweiter Theil* was to remain unchanged, for "the persons are all known, the actors are practiced in these characters, and one can, without exaggerating, intensify the situations and relationships, since one already has the first work before one, and give such a piece much life and interest."[5] Even the costumes and decorations of the original libretto were to be retained so that directors could mount the sequel that much more economically if they wished.

In 1796 Goethe offered terms of collaboration to Paul Wranitzky, who had written to him to ask for a libretto. But Wranitzky feared that the project as Goethe outlined it would bring him in uncomfortably direct competition with Mozart. Furthermore, the management of the Burgtheater balked at the idea of mounting a sequel to an opera whose first part they had not given. Here the matter rested, a tantalizing possibility that would have given concrete expression to the strong operatic bias of Weimar toward Vienna. As it happened, Weimar remained exclusively a consumer in the musical market of the 1790s. In a letter to Karl Friedrich Zelter of 29 May 1801 Goethe summed up the court theater's one-sided balance of trade during the preceding decade: "On the whole I do not live in a musical sphere; we reproduce now this, now that music all year long, but where there is no productivity an art cannot be sensed as a living thing."[6]

At Berlin the National Theater also occupied itself in the early 1790s almost exclusively with Viennese and Neapolitan operas. Thereafter Parisian opera asserted itself, but with an emphasis on non-French composers (Kreutzer, Gluck, Bruni, Sacchini, Piccinni, Cherubini) as much as on Grétry, Dezède, and Gaveaux. In the period 1792 to 1799 four cities provided all but seven of the forty nine new operas produced by the National Theater: Vienna (17), Paris (14), Naples (5), and Berlin itself (6).

Glowing reports of *Die Zauberflöte* at Vienna and Prague prompted Friedrich Wilhelm to ask Engel to explore the possibilities of a Berlin production as early as March 1792. But the aging director protested that the stage at the Gendarmenplatz was too small, that the libretto's only virtue lay in the extravagant visual effects it demanded, and finally that "the public, unacquainted with certain mysteries and unable to peer through the heavy, dark veil of allegory, cannot possibly take any interest in it."[7] The king relented, but scarcely three months later ordered the opera to be made ready for

---

[4] Frédéric-Jacob Soret related a conversation he had in 1823 with Goethe about Schikaneder's libretto: "He finds the first part full of improbabilities and silly things but rich in contrast, and attributes to its author a great understanding of the art of producing theatrical effects." Quoted in Hans-Albrecht Koch, "Die Singspiele," *Goethes Dramen*, p. 58.

[5] *Ibid.*, p. 59. These lines come from a *pro memoria* Goethe enclosed with his letter to Wranitzky of 24 January 1796.

[6] *Gedenkausgabe* vol. 19, pp. 408–9.

[7] Letter of 8 March 1792, quoted in Brachvogel, *Geschichte des Königlichen Theaters zu Berlin*, vol. 2, p. 302. Engel adds: "I regret in this case that the great composer Mozart was forced to waste his talent on such a thankless, mystic, and untheatrical subject" (pp. 302–3).

production. Engel squawked louder: mounting the work would be hideously expensive (over 2,000 Thaler), even with using some of the costumes already made for *Oberon*, and the Glockenspiel essential to the plot was unknown in Prussia. Again, the king relented.

For two years the project languished, then in an unaccountable move Engel brought *Die Zauberflöte* on to the boards in May 1794, while the king was away with his troops in the Rhineland. Angered, the king forced Engel's resignation, an action to which other factors also contributed. Engel had remained a firm supporter of the theater's music director Wessely despite lies, arrogance, and dereliction of duty,[8] whereas Friedrich Wilhelm favored the promising young co-director Bernhard Anselm Weber, hired in 1792. Engel had also run a rather uneconomical show at the National Theater and had introduced many failures in the early 1790s, which hurt attendance. His forced retirement indicates the sway royal prerogative exercised over the German theater at Berlin.

The presence of Weber revivified the National Theater's operatic establishment in the 1790s. His production of Gluck's *Iphigénie en Tauride* in 1794 scored a brilliant success, to the consternation of the moribund Italian establishment at Potsdam. The Francophile Prince Heinrich attended a performance with the express intent of laughing it off the stage (he had never previously set foot in the German theater), but the production left him astonished – especially since the young music director had never been to Paris.

During the directoral interregnum following Engel's retirement, the rivalry between Wessely and Weber polarized nearly everyone. Soon, however, Wessely was off to Rheinsberg where he succeeded Kalkbrenner as Kapellmeister to Prince Heinrich, and Weber's dominion over operatic affairs at the National Theater for years to come was assured. The directorship, too, stabilized when in December 1796 Friedrich Wilhelm succeeded in appointing August Wilhelm Iffland as sole director, a man the king had been seeking to lure to Berlin since 1790. His arrival marked a watershed for the spoken repertory, but the operatic offerings continued under Weber along paths already marked out. Earlier triumphs, namely Mozart's operas and Gluck's *Iphigénie en Tauride*, continued to fill the house. New operas met with little success by and large, with the exceptions *Das unterbrochene Opferfest* of Peter Winter and *Palmyra, Regina di Persia* of Salieri, both Viennese works, and Reichardt's finest German opera, *Die Geisterinsel*, to which we shall return at the end of this chapter.

In late 1797 Friedrich Wilhelm II died, and the colorless son who succeeded him as Friedrich Wilhelm III allowed affairs at the National Theater

---

[8] In his annual report to his co-director Ramler, Engel remarked concerning the necessity of hiring Weber: "We have lost so much under present circumstances, and principally through the neglect and lies of Wessely, that in order to cover our debts and to guard against perhaps even greater ones in the future we probably will have to suffer this new expense." *Ibid.*, pp. 312–13.

to continue unchanged in the early years of his reign. The American diplomat John Quincy Adams drew a neat summary of an operatic performance by the National Theater on 18 May 1798 which suggests how dominant Southern ingredients, namely spectacle and music, had become there:

At the play in the evening – *Palmira, Princess of Persia* [by Salieri], a German translation of an Italian opera. The scenery was magnificent, the music pretty good, the performers tolerable, the house small and very badly lighted. The royal box in front of the stage was as full as it could hold. The King, Queen, and all the younger part of the royal family were there. Upon the Queen's entrance the company in the boxes rose, and she bowed complaisantly all round. No sort of notice was taken of the King when he came in, and he kept altogether at the hindmost part of the box. Play over before nine.[9]

At Hamburg, Schröder's company, despite differing circumstances and pressures, evolved an operatic repertory not far different from that at Berlin. The raw statistics of forty-five new operas introduced, seventeen of them Viennese, ten French, and five Italian, differ little from those of the National Theater. Similarly, the Hamburg stage gave premières of only four new German operas from 1792 to 1799, not one of them of any particulr significance.

A major shift in the Hamburg offerings coincided with Schröder's retirement at the end of 1797. For the preceding six years only one new French opera per year had been taken up, whereas four new ones appeared in 1798. In late 1794 a certain Bursai, with members of the disbanded Brussels Court Theater, had received permission to perform plays and operas in French at Hamburg – offerings aimed in part at the considerable population of post-Revolutionary French immigrants around the city, but also at the many Francophiles among the natives. A writer reported in May of 1797 on the competition they offered:

The French theater is winning more and more of the public's favor – and not undeservedly – to the cost of the German theater; the public finds its orchestra, decorations, costumes, and so forth, without considering acting, better than those of Schröder. . . That the influence of the French actresses extends even to the area of fashion is proved by a female hat called *à la caravane*, which an actress in *La Caravane du Caire* [Grétry] first wore, and now is worn in imitation by a great part of Hamburg's beauties.[10]

As we have seen, opera formed no part of Schröder's higher artistic goals as a theatrical director. Where it could not feasibly be banished, it was to function as an economic tool. The Viennese operas which predominated after the dazzling triumph of *Oberon* in 1791, including *Die Zauberflöte*,[11] served

---

[9] *Memoirs of John Quincy Adams: Comprising Portions of His Diary from 1795 to 1848* (Philadelphia, 1874), vol. 1, p. 216.

[10] *Der Teutsche Merkur* 1797: 2, p. 189.

[11] Schröder's was the first North German stage to produce *Die Zauberflöte*, an event eagerly awaited by Hamburg's theater-goers. Schütze devotes more pages to this opera than to any other in his *Hamburgische Theater-Geschichte* (pp. 684–90), but, as with other Viennese

this end. So did the concert series Schröder instituted in May 1792, by means of which both Gluck's *Iphigénie en Tauride* and Mozart's *La clemenza di Tito* made their way to Hamburg.

Apart from Viennese operas, the backbone of his musical repertory, Schröder also took up several Rhenish operas, notably the works of Ignaz Walter. In late 1792 Stegmann had returned to Hamburg from the combined Mainz and Frankfurt stage. He became one of the co-directors who assumed control of the Hamburg theater after Schröder's retirement, and may well have been responsible for the French turn the repertory took in 1798. By that time, however, the operatic establishment had fallen on evil days, mostly through the loss of its best singers. In mid-1799 a correspondent complained that if operas such as *Die Zauberflöte* could not be given any better than it was at Hamburg, then they ought not to be given at all![12]

Here and there across Germany, desultory efforts were made to reanimate German opera in its earlier guise. In his dotage, Ramler tried in the mid-1790s to revive some older operas at Berlin, including works of Hiller and André, but, except for Benda's *Romeo und Julie* (which saw new productions at Berlin in 1793 and 1796), none of these revivals kindled much enthusiasm.

New operas, new librettists

After eight years of slow and sporadic production, North Germany brought forth in the period from 1792 to 1799 an ever-increasing stream of new operas. The eighty-four works are grouped according to five regions in Table 8.2. Except for the prolific Gottlob Benedict Bierey, music director of the undistinguished Seconda troupe, and for Dittersdorf, no composer is represented by more than two or three works. Bierey's many operas for his company's sojourns at Leipzig and Dresden have not been traced and remained of local importance. Dittersdorf's activities at Oels represent a special byway, albeit a symbolic one, of German opera toward the end of the eighteenth century. All in all, no composer during these years can claim anything close to the exalted exemplary roles played in earlier decades by Hiller, Schweitzer, Benda, and André.

Most of the scores to the operas represented in Table 8.2 have been lost to time and neglect. The disappearance of sixty-four of these eighty-four operas leaves a small and perhaps not wholly representative sample for evaluation, especially inasmuch as seven of the twenty survivors are works of Dittersdorf. This sharp drop in transmitted scores does not proceed wholly from the mediocrity or lack of success of most of these works, for, as North German opera moved further and further from the character of Hiller's operas toward

operas, his remarks deal mostly with decortions and costumes. Like many North Germans, he felt that Mozart had thrown his music away on an unworthy text.
[12] *Allgemeine musikalische Zeitung* 1 (1798/9): 714.

Italianate ideals, keyboard reductions for amateurs became less and less practicable. Several of the works in Table 8.2 (marked with an asterisk) saw partial publication in the "favourite songs" format Italian opera had experienced much earlier in England.

Although it is difficult to identify a leading group of composers or stages, four librettists form a band of influential and popular purveyors of texts. Two of them, Kotzebue and Bretzner, we have discussed earlier. Two others, Carl Alexander Herklots and Samuel Gottlieb Bürde, hailed from the Prussian provinces and began writing for the theater in the 1790s as an avocation. Together they account for a considerable proportion of the German operas of this period:

> Herklots's 6 texts account for 9 settings,
> Kotzebue's 3 texts account for 8 settings,
> Bretzner's 5 texts account for 7 settings,
> and Bürde's 2 texts account for 6 settings.

These four writers constitute the progressive wing of North German libretto production during the 1790s, and in this regard provided a vital service to the composers their librettos attracted. Paradoxically, North German opera's deepening estrangement from the traditions and procedures of spoken drama to which it had hitherto been intimately linked was spearheaded by librettists rather than composers. In fact, however, these writers came from the lower echelons of Germany's literary world, as they themselves admitted. Their models and often their direct sources tend to be the works of their confrères in Austria and Italy, whereas earlier writers had preferred spoken dramas and opéras-comiques.

In assessing the attempts of these four men to bring North German opera up to date, we would do well to shift to an important model at Vienna, Gottlieb Stephanie the Younger, the architect of Dittersdorf's most successful German operas there. In the rambling preface to his *Sämmtliche Singspiele* of 1792 Stephanie devotes a long and fascinating passage to the librettist's art on the modern German stage and goes so far as to lay down putative rules governing the proper construction of a German opera:

Neither too few nor too many musical numbers must occur; one can accept twenty-four in an entire Singspiel as the maximum and eighteen as the minimum; these must be properly divided into arias and concerted pieces and then again divided up proportionally so that especially the chief voices are not overtaxed and even more are not neglected. The Singspiel must begin with a concerted piece and each act must conclude with an action finale in which the main characters appear. More than two arias must seldom follow one another and must not be sung by one person; a duet, trio, or quartet must then create a sort of segment. Each of the principal voices must have at least three arias and a duet or trio, and appear especially in the finales. Furthermore, the composer must be given opportunity to vary the style of the music. One must also take care not to let the musical pieces follow one another too closely, nor to strand them too far apart; what is unavoidably necessary to know of the plot is not to be accompanied by music, since it can then easily become lost, and thereby the spectator

Table 8.2. *New North German operas, 1792–1799*

REGION: Composer	Title	Librettist	Year	Place
SAXONY-THÜRINGIA				
Bergt	*List gegen List*	Bretzner	1797	Leipzig
Bierey	[*Der Äpfeldieb*]	Bretzner	1793	Leipzig
	[*Die Ehestandskandidaten*]	Kaffka	1796	Leipzig
	[*Jery und Bätely*]	Goethe	1795	Leipzig
	([*Die Liebe im Lager*])	unknown	1792	Leipzig
	([*Liebesabentheuer*])	Grossmann	1794	Dresden
	[*Der Mädchenmarkt*]	Herklots	1794	Leipzig
	([*Die offene Fehde*])	unknown	1794	Leipzig
	[*Phaedon und Naide*]	Jacobi	1793	Leipzig
	([*Der Schlaftrunk*])*	Bretzner	1797	Leipzig
	([*Der Zauberhain*])	Berling	1799	Dresden
Dunkel	[*Lieb' um Liebe*]	Zschiedrich	1796	Dresden
Eberwein	([*Szenen der Vorwelt*])	unknown	1799	Rudolstadt
Kopprasch	([*Einer jagt den Andern*])	unknown	1795	Dessau
Lichtenstein	([*Bathmendi*: 1st version])	Behrisch	1798	Dessau
	Bathmendi: 2nd version	Lichtenstein	1799	Dessau
	([*Die steinerne Braut*])	Lichtenstein	1799	Dessau
Schmiedt	([*Melida*])*	unknown	1797	Leipzig
Volanek	([*Die Ueberraschung*])	Barchielli	1797	Leipzig
PRUSSIA				
Agthe	[*Der Spiegelritter*]	Kotzebue	1795	Ballenstädt
Bianchi	(*Der Insel der Alcina*)	Herklots	1794	Berlin
Bierey	[*Die böse Frau*]	Herklots	1792	Stettin
Cartellieri	(*Die Geisterbeschwörung*)	Herklots	1793	Berlin
Ebell	([*Der Schutzgeist*])	unknown	1798	Berlin
	([*Seliko und Berissa*])	Kinderling	1799	Berlin
Essiger	([*Barbier und Schornsteinfeger*])	Authenrieth	1798	Lübben
	[*Sultan Wampum*]	Kotzebue	1797	Lübben
Fliess	*Die Regata zu Venedig*	Bürde	1798	Berlin
Gürrlich	[*Das Inkognito*]	Herklots	1797	Berlin
Haack	[*Die Geisterinsel*]	Gotter	1798	Stettin
Kallenbach	([*Ehestandsszenen*])	unknown	1795	Magdeburg
	[*Die Opera buffa*]	Bretzner	1798	Magdeburg
	[*Das Schattenspiel an der Wand*]	Bretzner	1797	Magdeburg
Müller	[*Don Sylvio von Rosalva*]**	Bürde	1799	Berlin
Reichardt	*Die Geisterinsel*	Gotter	1798	Berlin
Reymann	([*Der Derwisch*])	Rathje	1797	Neustrelitz
Schubert	([*Die nächtliche Erscheinung*])	unknown	1798	Stettin
Weber	[*Der Theater-Prinzipal*])	Herklots	1796	Berlin
EAST PRUSSIA				
Halter	[*Die Kantons-Revision*]	Baczko	1792	Königsberg
Mühle	([*Die schöne Fürstin*])	Langbein	1799	Königsberg
	[*Die Singschule*]	Baczko	1794	Königsberg
Schmidt	[*Der Schlaftrunk*]	Bretzner	1797	Königsberg
Schönbeck	([*Esther*])	Jester	1793	Königsberg
	(*Der Wunderigel*)	Jester	1793	Königsberg

Table 8.2 (*cont.*)

REGION: Composer	Title	Librettist	Year	Place
SILESIA				
Dittersdorf	Don Quixotte der Zweyte	Dittersdorf	1795	Oels
	Das Gespenst mit der Trommel	Dittersdorf	1794	Oels
	Gott Mars	Dittersdorf	1795	Oels
	Die lustigen Weiber	Römer	1796	Oels
	Der Mädchenmarkt	Herklots	1797	Oels
	(Der Schah von Schiras)	Kotzebue	1795	Oels
	(Ugolino)	unknown	1796	Oels
Grüger	Hass und Aussöhnung	Rordorf	1797	Breslau
Hensel	[Daphne]	Hensel	1799	Hirschberg
	[Die Geisterbeschwörung]	Hensel	1799	Hirschberg
	[Die Geisterinsel]	Hensel	1799	Hirschberg
Hinze	[Der Eremit auf Formentera]	Kotzebue	1797	Waldenburg
	[Der Spiegelritter]	Kotzebue	1797	Waldenburg
Sander	[Don Sylvio von Rosalva]	Bürde	1797	Oels
	[Die Regata zu Venedig]	Bürde	1796	Oels
Schaum	[Jery und Bätely]	Goethe	1795	Oels
Spindler	([Achmet und Zenaide])	unknown	1796	Breslau
	([Don Quixotte])	unknown	1797	Breslau
BRUNSWICK, HAMBURG, AND THE NORTH				
Bachmann	Don Sylvio von Rosalva	Bürde	1797	Brunswick
	[Phaedon und Naide]	Jacobi	1795	Brunswick
	[Der Tod des Orpheus]**	Jacobi	1798	Brunswick
Bornhardt	Der Eremit auf Formentera	Kotzebue	1797	Brunswick
	[Sultan Wampum]**	Kotzebue	1796	Brunswick
Ebers	([Die Blumeninsel])*	unknown	1797	Brunswick
	[Der Eremit auf Formentera]	Kotzebue	1793	Schwerin
	([Der Liebeskompass])	unknown	1797	Brunswick
Eule	([Der verliebte Werber])	unknown	1799	Hamburg
Hattasch	([Helva und Zeline])*	unknown	1795	Hamburg
Hausing	([Der Eichenstamm])	unknown	1798	Stade
Hiller	([Adelstan und Röschen])	Schink	1792	Güstrow
Kallenbach	([Der Schlaftrunk])	Bretzner	1799	Altona
Kospoth	[Der Mädchenmarkt]*	Herklots	1793	Hamburg
Lichtenstein	([Glück und Zufall])	Lichtenstein	1793	Hannover
Löwe	[Rinaldo und Alcina]*	Baczko	1797	Brunswick
Neumann	([Das Mädchen nicht ohne den Ring])	unknown	1798	Altona
Phanty	[Don Sylvio von Rosalva]	Bürde	1796	Schleswig
Stegmann	(Der Triumf der Liebe)	Jester	1796	Hamburg
Stengel	([Amadis, der fahrende Ritter in Gallien])	Giesecke	1798	Hamburg
Walter	Die böse Frau	Herklots	1794	Hannover
	(Doktor Faust)	Schmieder	1797	Bremen
Weber	[Menöceus]	Bouterwek	1792	Hannover

Key:
[ ] – music does not survive.
( ) – full text does not survive.
  * – selected numbers published in keyboard reduction.
** – no copies of keyboard reduction survive.

remains in uncertainty. The fewer the persons a Singspiel is limited to, the better it will turn out, since the third and fourth roles are mostly weak vocally and musically, and not uncommonly disturb the good humor of the spectator. One should be especially wary of choruses, as much as possible, for not only do they occasion great expense, but also not infrequently spoil the whole with their stiffness and, like the supernumeraries in tragedies, ever remain but a poor aid to the poet in lending his matter lustre.[13]

Stephanie presents a remarkably explicit description of the rhythm of a comic opera as audiences expected it at the time of the greatest contributions to the genre by Mozart and Dittersdorf at Vienna and, with little emendation, the contemporaneous Italian comic operas of Paisiello, Cimarosa, and Salieri. It also provides us with a useful framework against which to measure the major North German librettos of the 1790s, particularly since in the preceding chapters we have seen frequent infractions of nearly every rule Stephanie lays down.

Carl Alexander Herklots, easily the most prolific Northern librettist of the decade, came to Berlin from Königsberg in 1790 as a young lawyer in the Prussian high court. During his long relationship with the Berlin stage he translated nearly seventy operas, both French and Italian. Engel wrote to his colleague Ramler in December 1792 about Herklots's skills in this field:

After he had plagued himself with the unspeakably wretched verses in the most recent opera of Mozart, *Eine machts wie die Andere* [*Così fan tutte*], and at least made them bearable, he totally reworked all the verses from beginning to end in the opera of Salieri, *Die Chiffer* [*La cifra*], now at the copyist's, and adapted them excellently to the music.[14]

Herklots also began producing his own librettos, most of them intended for local composers (Bianchi, Cartellieri, Gürrlich, Kospoth, and Weber). He published four of his new operas in 1793, which brought them to the attention of other composers including Dittersdorf and Ignaz Walter. Only one of the four, *Die böse Frau*, is an original work; the other three Herklots adapted from Saint-Foix.[15] In all of them he strove to blend his North German heritage with modern fashions. *Die böse Frau*, set in the familiar rustic milieu of

---

[13] [Johann Gottlieb] Stephanie der Jüngere: "Vorrede." *Sämmtliche Singspiele* (Liegnitz, 1792), pp. ix-xi. This introduction is reprinted in *Das deutsche Singspiel im 18. Jahrhundert*, ed. Renate Schusky (Bonn, 1980), pp. 93-4. Stephanie does not include in this collection any of his earlier adaptations of Bretzner's comic operas for Viennese composers, works which to some degree depart from the rules he draws up here. Stephanie declares in his preface that his activities as a translator of librettos, his association with composers for whom he wrote, and his six years as the operatic director of the Viennese Court Theater are the practical experiences on which this codification is based.

[14] Brachvogel, *Geschichte des Königlichen Theaters zu Berlin*, vol. 2, p. 313. At this time Herklots was not paid for his services, but Ramler and Engel agreed to make him a gift of 100 Thaler.

[15] *Die böse Frau* appears also to be an earlier work than the other three. Bierey's setting for Stettin in 1792 antedates all versions of the other three texts, and in the 1793 published version *Die böse Frau* carries the date 1791 on its own title page, although it was placed fourth in the collection.

Weisse's librettos, does not dally over an extended scene of rural cheer or idyllic bliss, but jumps right to the heart of the matter with its opening Lied. The fifty-year-old Niklas laments his marital miscalculations: his first wife was a dragon, this second one is a very devil, though only twenty-three. The prince and his friend the count, both incognito, overhear Niklas's complaint and, after being treated to a scene of his wife Hanne's snarling shrewishness, determine to free this henpecked disgrace of a man from his self-made martyrdom. The other characters enriching this procedure are all familiar German comic types: Niklas's daughter and her headstrong lover, the schoolmaster (whom Hanne wants as her step-daughter's husband), a swindler masquerading as a recruiting sergeant, and the self-important town mayor.

Herklots's borrowings from North German traditions do not extend to the musical structure of his libretto. The total of twenty-five numbers is only a shade over Stephanie's limit, and nearly half of these are ensembles and choruses. Both acts end with extensive, active finales composed of clearly marked episodes. The chorus sings only in the finales and in two numbers in act two, including an evocative opening hunting chorus to establish the scene at the count's hunting lodge. In general, Northern specialties such as rondo, Romanze, and aphoristic Lied rub shoulders with more active numbers which advance the plot or pursue extremes of character delineation.

The three dramas by Saint-Foix which Herklots adapted also allowed him to pursue the development of themes and characters firmly embedded in German opera. Saint-Foix had been an early purveyor of motifs we have come to associate with Rousseau – unspoilt Nature, the noble savage, rural virtues, cultural degeneration, and an interest in the exotic. *Das Inkognito*, in one act, cultivates the most familiar and traditional of these ideas. A prince has been wooing Juliane, the daughter of a grumpy old count withdrawn from city and court to the peace and quiet of his country estate. The prince has given himself out to be a young count in his own entourage and now must test Juliane's loyalty by setting his true princely self up as rival to the young count he has been feigning.

Herklots's other two adaptations of Saint-Foix explore more problematic moral issues in much more exotic settings. *Schwarz und weiss*, the more radical of the two, studies the interactions of various shipwrecked Spaniards on an island in the East Indies inhabited by a tribe of white-hating blacks. The noble savage among them, the old man Omar, protects the haughty Olivie and her twin daughters and tries to restrain his violent and overbearing son Kuxko. In one scene Olivie instructs her daughters in the evil effects of passion after Kuxko has attempted to drag both girls off as his brides: if they fall in love, they will turn black like him, and therefore his whole race should be a perpetual reminder of the hateful effects of passion. The value of Olivie's advice becomes a source of great puzzlement to her two daughters when the young Spaniard Pedro washes up on shore and they fall in love without the promised epidermal reaction.

Schwarz und weiss was Herklots's only published libretto never set to music, owing perhaps in part to the ticklish issues it broaches. His opera *Der Mädchenmarkt*, in contrast, was set five times in North and South Germany. Love and money are the amusing and slightly cynical drama's main ingredients. The colonists of an island in the South Seas, after having landed twenty years ago, produced in rapid succession a considerable progeny, now all of maritable age. The governor, inspired by the female market formerly at Nineveh, has set up a plan for compulsory universal marriage. Each young woman is rated for relative beauty or ugliness. The men then choose among them, but must pay a tax for a beautiful wife, the proceeds of which will be used to subsidize the ugly ones, whose husbands receive a rebate. Young Belcourt, fearing that he will be unable to pay the high tax his beloved Karoline is certain to carry, browbeats his servant Paul into dressing up as a woman and entering the derby; as the incontestably ugliest creature in the running he will surely fetch the largest subsidy, which will return to Belcourt through another of his servants who is to choose Paul. But Holbeck, a money-hungry old widower from the country, complicates matters by taking an instant fancy to Paul's subsidy.

Here as in his other librettos Herklots amalgamates Southern and Northern features. Up to date are the skillfully contrived introduzzione, Holbeck's rooster aria (complete with barnyard noises), the finales capping the first two acts, the liberal use of choruses, and the strategic placing of ensembles along the lines advocated by Stephanie. Yet Herklots also runs the number of musical pieces in the opera far beyond what Stephanie had thought proper, to thirty-three in all. And as in the other librettos of the 1793 print, the secondary characters enjoy as much musical attention as the prima donna and primo uomo.

Herklots placed a long preface at the head of his *Operetten*, pursuing *ad infinitum* the conceit of the genius of German drama fallen ill from a poor diet of modern comic operas. He summarizes the development of North German opera up to his own day in terms of this metaphor:

In the beginning it was very forgivable that, lulled to sleep like other children with good-humored folk songs to the tinkling of lovely silver tones, he allowed beguiling little bundles of sweets to be put in his mouth rather than solid fare; for originally these were intended more for his amusement than his nourishment, and indeed were also for the most part imbued with such genial essences that the most tasteful epicure could allow himself to be turned into a steer with pleasure in order to be able to partake of such morsels.

But the days are gone when men like Engel [to whom Herklots dedicated his collection], Weisse, Gotter, Michaelis, and later on Goethe let themselves be charged with the care of the poor child and provided it from time to time with a few surplus scraps. Its ingratitude has almost completely forfeited their favor.

A musical genius blown here from Italy by a hot scirocco set himself up despotically as the tutor of his German brother, filled his little bundle with strongly spiced macaronis and dried preserves, insinuated himself into his ear with the magic power of lovely melodies, a tendency to adventuresome romances and prankish fairy tales, and in a short time so completely ruined the physical and moral taste of his pupil that the latter wantonly scorned all native dishes in order to fall that much more insatiably upon the insipid fruits from abroad which had wholly lost in transit the small degree of potency they originally had.[16]

Two years after this collection appeared, another new librettist, Samuel Gottlieb Bürde, brought out two texts. The weaker of the two, *Die Regata zu Venedig*, found two composers, and *Don Sylvio von Rosalva* was set no less than six times, twice by composers at Berlin in the early nineteenth century. Günther Bobrik is perhaps overharsh in castigating the latter as a text "that unites in itself virtually all the flaws a librettos can have,"[17] yet it cannot be denied that, like its predecessor *Oberon*, Bürde's work owed a great deal of its popularity not to its own merits but to its model, Wieland's *Der Sieg der Natur über die Schwärmerei* (Ulm, 1764). In this delightful novel Wieland sets about curing the enthusiastic knight-errant Don Sylvio of a host of delusions, not the least of which is his belief that his lady love has been changed into a blue butterfly.

Bürde falls far short of Herklots as a poet and librettist. His most serious error in constructing *Don Sylvio von Rosalva* lay in basing it too closely on his well-known model. Not only did this render his work too episodic, it also led him into serious inconsistencies in the plot. Similar problems recur in his other libretto, *Die Regata zu Venedig*, a three-act drama based on an actual event at the Venetian regata of 1784. The three finales are short and only minimally dramatic. Again no use is made of the introduzzione technique, which Stephanie had warmly recommended. The undue emphasis on the culminating regata race (which not surprisingly occurs offstage and is reported by onlookers) forced Bürde into fashioning an exposition and central episodes more dilatory than generative of suspense. Furthermore, the tomfoolery adored by opera lovers everywhere in the 1790s and present in good measure in *Don Sylvio von Rosalva* nowhere appears here; in its stead the tiresome virtue-vaunting and sermonizing long familiar in the North hold forth.

Bretzner and Kotzebue

Unlike Bürde, the two seasoned librettists among the four most popular ones of the decade – Bretzner and Kotzebue – found little trouble in making the transition to the omnipotent buffa style. In 1796 Bretzner, still at Leipzig, issued a sequel to his enormously popular collection of librettos which had appeared in 1779. He admits frankly in his preface to these three new two-act

---

[16] *Operetten von Karl Herklots* (Berlin, 1793), pp. [iii]-iv.
[17] Günther E. G. Bobrik, *Wielands Don Sylvio und Oberon auf der deutschen Singspielbühne*, Ph.D. Diss., Ludwig-Maximilian University, Munich (Königsberg, 1909), p. 21.

comic operas that he had modeled them in the Italian form: "It is the currently beloved fashionable form, without which a product of this sort can seldom be promised success."[18] Bretzner echoes Herklots's dismay that at a time when love of opera has reached its highest pitch in Germany "nearly all of Germany's good poets seem to have conspired to remain silent or at least not to wish to provide anything in the comic genre (for wholly serious operas seldom meet with success) which would be *usable* for the theater."[19]

These three librettos, along with the intermezzo *List gegen List* of a year later, represent the most whole-hearted Northern rapprochement with the buffa manner of the Italians. Intrigue, buffoonery, a variety of disguises and deceptions, and emphasis on the theme of jealousy mark every one of them. Both *Der Schlaftrunk* and *Schattenspiel an der Wand* include a contrived incantation of spirits near the end of act two, and both the latter and *Opera buffa* employ a play within a play to lay bare the unfoundedness of the jealous hero's suspicions. Bretzner went over to the Italian camp completely in putting the entire text of *List gegen List* into verse.

Though he was not reticent about vaunting his connections with Mozart through *Die Entführung aus dem Serail*, Bretzner nonetheless avoided the elements which distinguished Viennese opera in German from Italian comic opera of the later eighteenth century. A writer who saw the Seconda troupe's production of *Der Schlaftrunk* at Ballenstädt, with music by the company's music director Bierey, hailed the text as "a new opera, yet not one of the so beloved spectacle and magic operas, but a wholly simple, domestic, and quite agreeable piece."[20]

In sheer technical terms, Bretzner advanced from his librettos of André's era to as complete a mastery of buffa libretto construction as any North German writer achieved. His finales show a recurring fondness for garden scenes such as that in the act-four finale of Da Ponte's *Le nozze di Figaro*. In both *Opera buffa* and *Schattenspiel an der Wand* the internal finale at the end of act one whisks various lovers in and out of hiding places from which they can fuel their suspicions and fears in order to bring the imbroglio to its zenith. Bretzner had exploited this milieu and technique as early as 1771 in the prose comedy on which his libretto *Der Äpfeldieb* had been based. He uses the introduzzione brilliantly in *Opera buffa*: the entire opening scene encompasses one broad musical number of four distinct sections. Again Bretzner exploits a situation already worked out less fully in one of his earlier librettos, in this case the serenade scene in *Adrast und Isidore*.

Often Bretzner's fondness for things Italian comes out into the open. In

---

[18] *Singspiele von C. F. Bretzner* (Leipzig, 1796), p. iv.
[19] *Ibid.*, p. [iii].
[20] *Journal des Luxus und der Moden* 13 (1798): 44. For a reviewer writing in the *Hamburgisch- und Altonaische Theater- und Litteratur-Zeitung* the libretto was if anything too flat: "It does not even contain the otherwise common overdrawn operatic nonsense, but rather absolutely nothing that could pique the curiosity of the spectator. He who possesses even a little delicacy is not vouchsafed even a single laugh" 1 (1799): 422–3.

Schattenspiel an der Wand he introduces as one of his comic lovers the
Kapellmeister Signor Campanello, who sings among other things a ridiculous
bravura aria (after offering ample proof of his cowardice) full of musical
imagery and terminology and with a middle section mostly in Italian. The
small entertainment *Der beschämte Eifersüchtige*, put on in *Opera buffa* in
order to hold up to the baron a mirror reflecting his foolish suspicions, is
announced by the baroness's lady-in-waiting Laurette with an aria sung
entirely in Italian. Prior to this aria, however, she presents "a poor devil cast
into misery innocently and most cruelly by the famous Signora Neuber," and
so saying she whips off her mantle to reveal herself attired as Arlecchino, her
part in the play about to be presented.[21] The baron adduces all the traditional
objections to Harlequin, each of which Laurette parries, even to the point of
addressing the audience. The spectators play an important role in her ensuing
aria as well. Bretzner provided it with two endings, the first to be sung if the
audience applauds or at least does not stomp in disapproval, the second
"should the parterre not find the personage of Harlequin to its taste and
express displeasure. . . She thereupon puts on a top-coat and plays her role
without mask." With or without his lozenges showing, Harlequin dominates
the intermezzo that follows. As Bretzner remarked at the end of his preface,
"In *Opera buffa* I need hardly remind the composer that I imagined the composition of the little opera in the burlesque Italian style."[22]

Kotzebue moved less quickly and less decisively toward the new realities of
German libretto-writing in the 1790s. His first libretto, *Der Eremit auf Formentera*, the closest of all his operas to the spirit of his spoken plays,
remained popular, finding three new composers between 1793 and 1797.[23] In
1790 Kotzebue left Reval on a journey which would eventually take him to
Paris, and on his way he stopped in the Rhineland and provided two of its
composers with new librettos. The first, *Sultan Wampum*, differs little from
the musical makeup of his *Der Eremit auf Formentera*. The title role,
significantly, does not sing. Stegmann set the opera for the Mainz National
Theater in 1791, then carried it with him to Hamburg where Schröder himself
took the role of the corpulent and impossibly tyrannical Shah Wampum.[24]

---

[21] "Harlequin's costume," remarks Bretzner in a footnote at this point in the libretto, "must be
that of the Italian Arlecchino, and not that of the German Hanswurst."

[22] *Singspiele von C. F. Bretzner*, p. vi.

[23] Kotzebue reflected this libretto's relatively conservative musical character by adopting the
designation Goethe had introduced to German opera with his early librettos, "Schauspiel mit
Gesang." In 1790 the Grossmann company actually gave *Der Eremit auf Formentera* as a
spoken play at Hannover. Bernhard Anselm Weber, then music director of the company,
provided a symphony and a Turkish song for the performance. See *Journal des Luxus und der
Moden* 5 (1790): 142.

[24] Schink notes in his *Hamburgische Theaterzeitung* 2 (1792): 766 that Stegmann's setting was
given at Hamburg "in a considerably altered form" on 8 December 1792, although the book
of arias printed for this production (Schatz 10043) does not differ from the published full text.
Schink alludes to "the two finales" which he found "truly dramatic," but nothing of the sort
appears in this book of arias nor in any other published version of Kotzebue's text. Nor does
Stegmann's music itself come down to us. We do know that he revised the most popular of his

Kotzebue veered suddenly toward current fashions with *Der Spiegelritter*, set by Ignaz Walter and first presented at Frankfurt in September 1791. The librettist looked upon his venture into heroic–comic opera with amusement: "I have often been requested to write for once an opera in today's style, and now I have finally made one. Hopefully the reader will find that it is just as foolish and adventuresome and silly as its older siblings on the German stage. Among all *operibus* of a writer such an opera is the simplest *opus*."[25] With more fancy and good humor than care and thought, Kotzebue threw together a ragout of motives, situations, characters, and techniques of Viennese magic opera. Prince Almador of Dunnistan, brought up sheltered and pampered at court, must set out with his squire Schmurzo to prove his manhood. A magic shield with a mirror, given to him by the magician Burrudusussusu, will protect him against all dangers. By luck a storm makes his first port of call the Black Island, where the beautiful Milmi lies under a spell which has made her a cannibal of male flesh. Almador's trials include slaying both a dragon and the giant sentry Kroxbox, refusing the food and wine offered by Milmi's virgins and dwarf, and resisting the rather overt erotic overtures of several young ladies. The shield's mirror eventually breaks Milmi's spell after she fails in an attempt to cut out Almador's heart, and she settles for marrying him instead.

Kotzebue provides generously for all the musical trappings the subject could possibly endure – characteristic arias and ensembles, choruses (including one to a storm and shipwreck), a melodrama, and three lengthy finales – the last one aspiring to Da Ponte's ideal of a self-contained drama within the drama.

The moral tone of the play sets it clearly apart from Kotzebue's other librettos and from Northern norms in general. Seducing or consuming male flesh obsesses nearly all the female characters, and Kotzebue does not strive very energetically to veil bawdy allusions, as in the exchange between Schmurzo and several ladies of the court who have been flirting with the prince:

FIRST LADY: You will long often enough for our flesh pots.
SCHMURZO: For your flesh pots? (He measures them contemptuously with his eyes.) The fat has already been ladled off.
SECOND LADY: But still much too good for you, fatso.
SCHMURZO: I don't like to gnaw on bones the prince has thrown under the table. (They begin to beat him.)

The deficiencies of Kotzebue's text compared with its exact contemporary,

early operas, *Der Kaufmann von Smyrna*, at this same time, and that his major alteration to bring it up to date was the addition of a substantial finale (the musical numbers of this new version are preserved in Schatz 10040).

25 Schatz 10865a (n.p., n.d.), p. [323]. Kotzebue's Viennese orientation is made clear in the rest of his preface: "May heaven make me as fortunate as it has made the Messrs. Eberl & *Consorts*; that is: may it grant my Knight of the Mirror music like that of Dittersdorf, Mozart, Martin, or Reichardt, then the fellow may well make his way in the world."

Schikaneder's *Die Zauberflöte*, are obvious and may be traced to the librettist's low opinion of the specific genre, his unconcern for deeper human values, and not least of all the speed with which he manufactured *Der Spiegelritter*. A reporter at the first Mannheim performance remarked, "Herr von Kotzebue wanted to have some fun and said during his stay at Mainz: an opera may be written in a couple of days; in that manner he wrote this one, and – it looks like it, too."[26]

North German composers and the major librettists

Nine of the twenty surviving operas in Table 8.2 involve texts by the four librettists just discussed, but none of these nine is among the significant or successful operas produced in North Germany from 1792 to 1799. Apart from the relevant operas by Ignaz Walter and Dittersdorf, these works by and large show a battery of obscure Northerners struggling with an idiom to which they had not been born or bred. Stiff competition from foreign masterworks consigned many North German operas to early oblivion when they failed to secure footholds in local repertories.

Casimir Antonio Cartellieri produced his first and only opera, Herklots's *Die Geisterbeschwörung*, at Berlin in 1793. Originally a one-act opera on the scale of the same librettist's *Das Inkognito*, it was produced by the National Theater as a two-act opera with an extra aria added. The critic Carl Spazier liked some things in it, but thought the young composer had tried too hard to imitate Dittersdorf.[27] Cartellieri shows a fondness for the clarinets, used in eight of the opera's sixteen numbers, and with Herklots's help the multi-sectional finale provides a series of carefully contrasted sections and an appropriate tonal plan.

Cartellieri, son of an Italian tenor and a German actress, had been born to a theatrical life which kept him abreast of operatic developments. Yet even amateurs in Germany tried to affect an appearance of modernity. The obscure J. B. Fliess, known only for his setting of Bürde's *Die Regata zu Venedig* for Berlin, offers a case in point. For this production an unknown reviser considerably altered Bürde's weak plan: he reduced it from three acts to two, retained only four of the original two dozen numbers intact, combined two others into a true finale structure (all three of Bürde's are mere ensembles), reworked another, and wrote thirteen other entirely new numbers. A Berlin journal, it is true, still considered the opera in this new version "mediocre music to a less than mediocre operetta,"[28] but while the score never sparkles, Fliess nonetheless strives to invest it with an *au courant* appearance by using a medley of ideas and techniques picked up here and there. The overture seems modeled on Mozart's to *Die Entführung aus dem Serail*:

[26] *Zeitung für Theater und andere schöne Künste* 7 (1793): 129–30.
[27] *Berlinische Musikalische Zeitung historischen und kritischen Inhalts* 16 (25 May 1793): 61–2.
[28] *Berlinisches Archiv der Zeit und ihres Geschmacks* (1798): vol. 2, p. 308.

Allegro	Andante	Tempo primo
C → G	c	C
	(=melody of the	
	Romanze, #5)	

Much use is made of the winds, notably in the instrumental numbers for this section of the orchestra played behind the scene as the festivities get under way in act two. A four-part ensemble in the opera's second finale (Nane Deo has won the race and his Bettina as well), accompanied by woodwinds alone, sets an almost motet-like aphoristic seal on the hero's good fortune (Example 8.1). Fliess adds several harmonic touches in the second phrase (augmented and diminished chords) to enliven the cadence and avoid a perfectly square consequent.

Example 8.1 Fliess: *Die Regata zu Venedig*. Finale, act 2.
"May friendship, love, and fidelity tie this knot for eternity, and may our entire life be one of walking hand in hand."

Ex. 8.1 (*cont.*)

In an "alla Polacca" aria for the chatty gondolier's wife Justine, we see how far the polonaise has moved in German opera from its regal restraint in Hiller's *Die Jagd* to a text on gossiping, set off by all the nuances familiar to us in the polonaises of Carl Maria von Weber and his generation (Example 8.2).

Baron von Kospoth, whose dealings with the Berlin theater we have already touched on, apparently found himself constrained to turn to Hamburg for a production of his score to Herklots's *Der Mädchenmarkt*. Schütze reports that it did not please much: "Opera subjects betraying a French sense and

Example 8.2 Fliess: *Die Regata zu Venedig*. Song of Justine, act 2.
"Call me a chatterbox in spite of everything. Gossiping is no sin. I enjoy it!"

Ex. 8.2 (*cont.*)

plan with German music run counter to the local taste of today."[29] Yet in fact the baron ought to have taken pride in his "German music" in light of the improvements he had made over his trivial tunes in his first Berlin operas of 1779 and 1780. He included at the head of a published collection of selections from *Der Mädchenmarkt* an especially impressive c-minor aria. In it the hero Belcourt vents his despair over the governor's plan for mass nuptials which is certain to deprive him of his Karoline. The harmonic plan of this impassioned ternary aria exploits a clever relationship:

[29] *Hamburgische Theater-Geschichte*, p. 679. Heinrich Gottlieb Schmieder, in making free use of these comments a year later, twisted their meaning in a way typical of the French-dominated post-Revolutionary Rhineland: "[it] did not please greatly, – it was French human feeling and a good plan with *German* music!" *Taschenbuch fürs Theater* 1 (Mannheim, 1795): 104.

tempo:	Allegro						Più lento	
section:	A						B	
key:	i			$\flat$III			$\flat$VI	$\flat$iii
cadences:	dec	op ($\flat$VI$_{\#6}$-V)			cl	cl	op	
line:	1 1	2	3		4-5	4-5	6-7	8-

tempo:		Tempo primo			
section:		A'			
key:		i	$\flat$ii-V/vi I		i
cadences:	op (#IV$_7$-V$_7$)			cl	cl
line:	9	1 1-2 -3 -3		4-5	4 - 5

A portion of the aria from the middle of the B section to the arrival on tonic major in the A′ section appears in Example 8.3. Earlier, after a deceptive cadence, Kospoth had availed himself of a typical feint in minor-mode tonal planning – a jump from the dominant of i directly to the relative major ($\flat$VI $_{\#6}$-V- $\flat$III in the diagram above). In the reprise, when he reaches the same deceptive cadence on A-flat major, Kospoth prolongs it (bars 86-8) even to the point of exponentiation by giving it a deceptive cadence of its own. But

Example 8.3 Kospoth: *Der Mädchenmarkt*. Aria of Belcourt, act 1.
"In so doing you dishonor the pain of hopeless love! Despair rages in my soul! The deep grief this heart suffered knows only the feeling of thwarted love. Why, oh Lina. . ."

Ex. 8.3 (*cont.*)

See - le; Ver - zweif - lung tobt in mei-ner See - le! den tie - fen

Gram, den die - ses Herz er - fuhr, kennt das Ge -

-fühl ge - trenn - ter Lie - be nur, kennt das Ge -

-fühl ge - trenn - ter Lie - be nur.

Wa - rum, o! Li - na,

he is far from finished with his gambit: to our puzzlement Kospoth ups the ante again with a deflection to iv of A-flat, then an enharmonic twist to $^\flat$VI $_{\#6}$ of A-flat. That too resolves deceptively for prolongation and eventually the announcement that a-minor – of all things – is upon us. The arrival of C major at this point (bar 98) realizes a precise equivalent of the $^\flat$VI$_{\#6}$–V–$^\flat$III relationship in the first A part, making retrospective sense out of the surrogate tonic a minor which was needed if such a progression was to land us in the true tonic major for the complementary material first heard in $^\flat$III.

German this intensively wrought harmonic footwork certainly is, but, more importantly, it presents a thoughtfully conceived musical interpretation of Belcourt's despair. We already know at this point to what desperate lengths the governor's plan can drive him, for in the introduzzione his servant Philipp had created a public riot by appearing as a mountebank and singing a song which attacked the governor. In the present aria Kospoth paints a telling tonal portrait of Belcourt's shaky control over his despair (and perhaps even hints at the Byzantine scheme the hero is about to hatch).

A German composer could feel right at home in grappling with an aria such as this. A light touch – apart from the folk-like, at least – came much less readily to many, though all around them they could see that it was securing the popularity of many a Viennese and Italian opera. It stood high among compositional priorities for Bretzner's Italianate librettos. André had excelled in this respect earlier, but his day had passed. A delightful successor to his manner appeared in 1797 with the Seconda troupe's production of the intermezzo à 4, *List gegen List*, by Christian Gottlob August Bergt. With deft understatement he follows every comic nuance in Bretzner's text, moving freely from aria to recitative to arioso. The opening partenza of the jealous Erich and his Röschen communicates at once the spirit of the piece. After a first tender goodbye he reminds her to set the dog Sultan on guard; after another he goes off but returns at once to remind her to lock the door; after yet another he returns to admonish her to be on her guard against soldiers, who will surely try to seduce her. Erich returns later, disguised as a soldier, to test her loyalty to him. With most unsoldierlike fainthearted anxiety he makes sure that all is perfectly quiet (Example 8.4). Bergt captures with his

Example 8.4 Bergt: *List gegen List*. Arioso of Erich.
"Silent, silent, softly, softly. Everything's peaceful, everything's still. Ha! who goes there? It was a fancy. Still! Who sighs? What's up? I'll bet it's. . . only Sultan on his chain. Everyone's asleep; now I'll see, my little one: I am tricking you in order to see proofs of your constancy."

Ex. 8.4 (*cont.*)

Ex. 8.4 (*cont.*)

dei - ner Treu   zu sehn.

spindly accompaniment and carefully placed pauses Bretzner's implicit equating of jealousy and timorousness in Erich's personality. A long preparation for d minor, for instance, dissolves back into F major after he satisfies himself that the noise which had startled him was nothing more than the watch-dog Sultan.

Other librettists and their composers

The few surviving texts apart from those of the four major librettists discussed earlier allow us only a partial glimpse of how closely their example was followed by others. For sixteen works in Table 8.2, all of them lost, we do not even know who the librettists were. Eleven other authors contributed a single lost opera, and, in the case of Friedrich Ernst Jester, all three of his late librettos seem to have disappeared. The arias preserved from his *Der Triumf der Liebe* demonstrate that he had swung away from the old-fashioned rustic plays with songs he had written for Friedrich Ludwig Benda to a wholehearted acceptance of the trappings of Viennese magic opera. The cast includes fairies, princes, pages, nymphs, sylphs, knights, a monster, monks, shield-bearers, heralds, furies, and graces.

Jester divided *Der Triumf der Liebe* into four acts, an unusual configuration in the North, and included a finale of goodly size at the end of each. The opera has only ten arias (two with chorus, one with trio) plus six duets, two trios, a chorus, and a melodrama. Stegmann's score struck one auditor as "in the Mozartean taste and not unsuccessfully so,"[30] but it did not fare well at Hamburg. Jester's plan allowed Stegmann to exert himself in a variety of styles (another of Stephanie's desiderata), and the composer rounded his work very happily with a recall of the opening chorus's "Tempo di Contredance" at the end of the opera. The idea of accompanying the Silphengesang in act four with a "Harmonica hinter dem Theater" no doubt came from Schink, Schröder's theatrical poet for most of the 1790s. In his *Hambur-*

---

[30] *Annalen des Theaters* 18 (1796): 44.

gische Theaterzeitung he had published an article, "Noch etwas über die Harmonika," suggesting its use in opera "where situation and character demand an expression raised above the limits of contemporary life, such as oracular pronouncements and the proclamations and visitations of spirits."[31] He had especially in mind the scene of Ferdinand alone on the beach in Shakespeare's *Tempest*, which Schink had heard his "excellent friend" Gotter was adapting for the operatic stage.

Jester's fellow-Königsberger, the blind historian Ludwig von Baczko, published three librettos in 1794. As with Jester's, his more rustic and earthy ones had already found local composers – *Die Kantons-Revision* (Halter, 1792) and *Die Singschule* (Mühle, 1794) – whereas his first venture into a magical fairy spectacle, *Rinaldo und Alcina*, had to seek elsewhere. Baczko had completed his libretto several years before its appearance in 1794, and had at first sent it to the blind Viennese composer-pianist Maria Theresia von Paradies. Her lost setting was produced at Prague in 1797, and the same year Friedrich August Leopold Löwe's music to *Rinaldo und Alcina* was performed at Brunswick.

Baczko's two operas set in small country villages trade in familiar German characters and problems and also maintain the older North German relationship of dialogue and musical numbers. The so-called finales in each are again merely concluding ensembles. In 1796 Kaffka revised *Die Singschule* for Bierey as *Die Ehestandskandidaten*. "It is absolutely necessary," he declared in his preface, "to retain the finales and other forms of the Italians in our German Singspiele if any product of this sort is to succeed on our stages."[32] In this spirit he restructured Baczko's story into an up-to-date comic opera, further complicating the intrigue, reducing the original thirty-three numbers to twenty-one and conflating the original three acts into two with true finales and several new concerted numbers.

Baczko's magic opera *Rinaldo und Alcina* could have benefited from similar pruning. He put the story's plot together with all sorts of motives from Ariosto's *Orlando furioso* and from several fashionable fairy operas – the young knight Rinaldo tempted by the fairy Alcina on the Island of Joy, a magician who protects Rinaldo's beloved Brandamanta and gives him a magic ring in his hour of need, a cowardly squire, a familiar spirit named Ariel, and assorted choruses, visible and invisible, of genies, sailors, and misshapen servants. There is even an admonitory chorus sung by those who have crossed Alcina in the past and as a result were turned into rocks, trees, and plants. The magic ring allows Rinaldo to see Alcina, the embodiment of

[31] 2 (1792): 667–72.

[32] *Die Ehestandskandidaten, oder Die Parodie aus dem Stegreife* (Riga and Leipzig, 1805), p. [iii]. Kaffka adds, "I rejoice that even one of our best operatic poets, Herr Bretzner, agrees with this opinion," and he cites the preface to Bretzner's 1796 collection of comic operas. Kaffka, always happiest when making use of other people's artistic property, did not abandon his ways here. The text of the polonaise cited earlier in this chapter (Example 8.2) from Bürde's *Die Regata zu Venedig* (1795) crops up verbatim in Kaffka's libretto.

carnal temptation, for the hideous creature she really is. Here, as throughout the opera, the moral trowel-work runs to the thick side.

Rinaldo und Alcina strikes an uneasy formal and spiritual compromise between North German and Viennese manners, eased to an extent by Baczko's choice of a supernatural fairy tale in which anything goes. The possibilities for strong contrasts between comic and serious, quite at home in such operas, he pursued vigorously. The first act finale is a comic romp: Alcina's nymphs have bewitched Rinaldo's squire Scudero; he must choose one but cannot, so they blindfold him, clap and chase around with him, and then produce the unfortunate old hag Malfatta, whom Scudero seizes and must then take as his own. The finale of the second act, in contrast, focuses on a deadly earnest struggle between Alcina and Brandamanta for Rinaldo's heart.

Critics of the period invoke a strong sense of character again and again as a meritorious ingredient of any opera score, and the composer Löwe took full advantage of the opportunities for clear delineation of comic and serious provided here by Baczko. The two realms he will straddle Löwe announces in his overture, a brief Allegro scherzando in 6/8 which yields to a weightier Allegro assai. Scudero's numbers are generously represented in Löwe's "Favoritgesänge," and in all of them the composer demonstrates a decided knack for imitating the comic manner of Dittersdorf, Paisiello, and their like (Example 8.5). Northern comic patter, we see here, has progressed from

Example 8.5 Löwe: *Rinaldo und Alcina*. Comic patter of Scudero, act 1.
 "Ah, by my poor soul, that's fine old wine! Now I'm at your service and shall make merry with you; if there is something to eat and drink, if I see full glasses sparkling, oh then joy has come to stay!"

Ex. 8.5 (*cont.*)

Hiller's succinct folkish instances through the crucible of Southern styles to broader and more directed harmonic motion, more emphatic repeated-note patterns, and a joy in motivic repetition which expands and enlivens the simplest triadic material. Hiller's practice narrowed itself to a more short-breathed syntax and a preference for several alternations of brief sections in the two contrasting tempos.

Scudero maintains his musical persona even when singing with his high-minded master. In their first duet Scudero's poetic burden is identical to that of the example just discussed – eating and drinking – whereas Rinaldo's thoughts fly to his beloved (Example 8.6). The clear stylistic distinctions

Example 8.6 Löwe: *Rinaldo und Alcina*. Duet, act 1.
RINALDO: "Were Brandamanta but here! She is happiness and joy to me."
SCUDERO: "Were there but something to eat here! I need something to drink as well."

between them can be traced in conception back to ensembles by Philidor and Monsigny dating from the 1760s, though more immediately it lay at the heart of ensemble practice in modern Italian comic operas and especially Mozart's masterpieces in that genre.

Adherence to Southern styles brought with it a falling away from several literary tendencies of earlier decades in the North. Fascination with magic, spectacle, and farce crowded out more characteristically Northern concerns with moral edification, sentimental tableaux, and classical subjects. The high-affect disorderliness of Storm and Stress drama was also a thing of the past. It made a lone appearance during the 1790s with the Breslau publisher Rordorf's *Hass und Aussöhnung*, an undisciplined tale of a sour, vindictive businessman whose hatred of his son's beloved prompts him to jail her father and to attempt poisoning her at her own birthday party. A scant eleven musical numbers slip into the histrionic and improbable goings on as best they can. Only the last act does not end with prose.

Five music dramas on classical subjects appeared in North Germany during these years, each quite different from the others. Friedrich Karl von Strombeck intended his two-act *Diana und Endymion*, a verse adaptation of Metastasio's early *Endimione* (1721), as an epithalamium for his sister. It was never set. Johann Daniel Hensel, whom we saw treading classical paths earlier in composing Ramler's *Cyrus und Kassandane*, expanded the plot of Weisse's one-act children's opera *Das Denkmal in Arkadien* into *Daphne*, a three-act verse drama unrhymed throughout. Hensel includes a generous measure of chorus and ballet – the chorus sings in seven of the nineteen vocal numbers and concludes each act – bringing his opera in line with the Gluckian proclivities of North German classicizing opera.

The other three classical operas were all conceived during the heyday of the genre in the 1780s. Friedrich Bouterwek's brilliant verse tragedy *Menöceus* refashions an episode from Euripides' *Phoenicians* from a larger portrait of intrafamilial rivalry and blood-guilt to a modern drama of self-sacrifice for moral principles. An old prophet declares that Thebes will fall in the struggle between its king Eteokles and his brother unless young Menöceus kills himself in the temple of Mars. At first the valiant youth agrees, but when his resolution falters his beloved Antigone sets the example by stabbing herself on their nuptial altar. Bouterwek published his libretto in 1788 and announced "that the choruses and musical scenes of this play have been fortunate enough to find a composer in Herr [Bernhard Anselm] Weber, director of the orchestra with the Grossmann company,"[33] but Weber's setting was apparently not produced for four years.

Johann Georg Jacobi, who had not written a libretto since his Vorspiel

---

[33] *Menöceus, oder Die Rettung von Thebe* (Hannover, 1788), p. 6. It is to be inferred from Bouterwek's comments that Weber did not set the verse dialogue (a tradition in tragedy which did not automatically demand treatment as recitative), and as much is implied by the libretto's label, "ein Trauerspiel mit Gesang."

Elysium had achieved the status of a widely popular one-act opera in the early 1770s, returned to the genre with two more texts during the vogue of classical operas in the 1780s. In 1784 Jacobi had received a call to the University of Freiburg (becoming the first Protestant ever appointed there). Within a year he was at work on an opera on the Orpheus legend. At Mannheim the intendant of the National Theater there, Freiherr von Dalberg, heard about it and asked for the manuscript, having Georg Benda in mind as its composer. The collaboration never materialized. Jacobi eventually published *Der Tod des Orpheus* in 1790, but it did not find a composer until Gottlob Bachmann set it in 1798.

Jacobi's verse tragedy (labeled "Singspiel" and thus probably conceived by the poet as a recitative opera) begins after Orpheus's return from Hades. The first act, a sort of prologue, recounts this familiar part of the legend briefly, then provides a dream-like doublet: in deep night, amid bare jutting cliffs, a "wild symphony, full of terror, fear, and despair" introduces an off-stage chorus of spirits; they storm out on to the scene with torches and in glowing chains; Orpheus's lyre and the wild symphony wrestle with each other until the latter is subdued; after a lament by Orpheus, spirits of Elysium bring in Euridice; she is to follow him silently during the night and at daybreak will be his provided he does not look back; Orpheus imagines he sees the light of day too soon and once again loses Euridice. Jacobi no doubt felt that this varied re-enactment of the legend was required to prepare dramatically for Orpheus's ensuing destruction by the Thracian women.

In spirit and musical–technical requirements *Der Tod des Orpheus* yields nothing to the most demanding operas of its day. Such is not the case, however, with Jacobi's other libretto, *Phaedon und Naide*, published in 1788, which returns to the circumscribed manner of *Elysium*. Only four characters appear, unity of action is scrupulously preserved in both acts, and only thirteen musical numbers interrupt the prose dialogue. Phaedon, an elderly judge, has left Thessaly and intends to marry the young shepherdess Naide. Eurydamos, a young epicure from Crete, chances into their valley and tries to take liberties with Naide. Phaedon stops him, and in revenge Eurydamos poses as the oracle of Apollo, said to speak prophecies from an enchanted tree, and when the betrothed couple visits the shrine he augurs ill for their marriage. The noble sorrow of the lovers draws a confession from the youth as well as a revelation from Apollo's priestess that the oracular tree is a sham.

Phaedon und Naide explores sympathetically a theme usually reserved for ridicule or farce. Even more directly than had Goethe, Jacobi drew on his own life for this unusual story. He had fallen in love with his housemaid, a young and beautiful woman though neither rich nor highly placed socially. Jacobi undertook her aesthetic and religious education and set down the problems he faced in this task in his libretto.[34]

---

[34] When Jacobi's former fiancée read *Phaedon und Naide* she wrote to him at once: "I would think that without a living Naide no such beautiful portrait could have been formed, and

Not surprisingly, the element of instruction figures prominently in this conservative libretto, but Naide and Eurydamos are not its sole recipients. Apart from an implicit exorcizing of fears concerning a young wife's fidelity to a husband twice her age, the opera corrects the gullibility of Phaedon himself with respect to the oracle – perhaps a reminiscence of Jacobi's earlier devotion to the sentimental, covertly homoerotic cult of friendship into which Gleim had drawn him. Eurydamos admonishes Phaedon near the end of the opera, "Are you perhaps angry, good Phaedon, that I have cured you of your enthusiasm (Schwärmerey)? One breathes far more freely when one keeps to earth where one is at home and does not seek to ascend to the Immortals, or to coax them into a miserable little valley."

Baron von Knigge's *Dramaturgische Blätter* praised Jacobi's libretto warmly when it appeared. He found the allegory "almost too delicate for our frivolous theatrical taste. . . but so much the worse for our taste and so much the better for the head and heart of the author, who would give the Singspiel such dignity."[35] Knigge made his own aesthetic preferences known in the next installment by printing a long and damning essay on comic opera, against which it championed the serious operas of Handel, Gluck, and Hasse.

One cannot dispute the assertion that dignity had become a commodity in very short supply on the operatic stage. One cannot doubt either that any of the few operas remaining for brief consideration in this section would have pleased the baron. First, in the same collection with his Arcadian sentimental verse drama *Daphne*, Hensel also published *Die Geisterbeschwörung*, a reflex to the mania for séances in Germany which had also contributed to Goethe's *Der Gross-Cophta* (originally planned as an opera). Hensel roasts once again the old chestnut about a young couple's disabusing an old man of his passion for spiritualism and at the same time exposing the confidence man who has been reaping profits from the gullible fool's obsession.

The minor Dresden official K. A. Zschiedrich also availed himself of familiar themes with *Lieb' um Liebe*, but unlike Hensel pushed them all to extremes. The two acts of this "Romantisch–komische Oper" make mincemeat of the unities. Act one, set in Valencia, brings the tensions between the governor, who has a senator picked out as his prospective son-in-law, and his daughter Isabella, whose heart belongs to Don Rodrigo, to such a pitch that the poor girl throws herself into the Guadalaviar at the commencement of the finale. Act two finds Isabella in a harem in Asia Minor. Even more ineptly than in the first act characters are batted about as Don Rodrigo lands, passes the usual test for fidelity fabricated by a veiled Isabella, and prepares to battle her master Almanzor, Khan of the Tartars. The latter adamantly refuses to

since Phaedon resembles strikingly the Professor himself, I cannot but imagine that he has actually found such a maiden – of a higher sort, it is understood, and her language betrays this – and that he has introjected his own fate into the libretto for his own pleasure. . . and at the same time to give the shallow-minded a good lesson." *Ungedruckte Briefe von und an Johann Georg Jacobi*, ed. Ernst Martin (Strassburg and London, 1874), p. 40, n. 69.

[35] 14 (17 Jan 1789): 223–4.

part with her, but a band of priests fresh from the temple foretell a rout if he does not, and so Almanzor quickly assents.

Finally, at the Dessau court the noble amateur Baron Karl August von Lichtenstein brought his multi-faceted talents to the new court theater there, opened on 26 December 1798 ("on one of the coldest days of this century"[36]) with his opera *Bathmendi*. Lichtenstein's original score has not been traced (nor has the libretto), but a Berliner in attendance who amused himself with the score gave it high marks, even though one had to allow that in the choruses "study of Mozart's manner shows through quite clearly, although it is almost impossible to write in this area without encountering him in style and manner at times."[37]

Scarcely five months later Lichtenstein produced another new opera on a magic theme, *Die steinerne Braut*. Not only did he write both text and music, he acquitted himself famously as primo uomo with his wife as prima donna. Three months later, in August of 1799, Lichtenstein completely rewrote the text of *Bathmendi*, substituting an entirely new plot and cast. A critic praised the new text for its manifold surprises which elevated the beauties of the score, previously lost in the uniformity of action in Ernst Wolfgang Behrisch's original libretto.[38] Possibly in this same form *Bathmendi* was produced at Vienna in 1801, a rare honor for any North German opera. The *Allgemeine musikalische Zeitung* printed a lovely duet from the original version which bears witness to Lichtenstein's melodic gift and mastery of instrumental dialogue.[39] The Berlin critic Carl Spazier praised Lichtenstein for the very virtues that had brought Viennese and Italian operas to the boards of the Berlin National Theater in droves.[40]

---

[36] *Journal des Luxus und der Moden* 14 (1799): 82.

[37] *Ibid.*, p. 86.

[38] *Ibid.*, p. 401.

[39] *Allgemeine musikalische Zeitung* 1 (1798/99): Supplement No. 10.

[40] "One receives the liveliest conviction that Herr von L. is wholly suited to be a theatrical composer; that he knows how to conceive a whole with poetic and philosophical insight and to order and elaborate the individual parts according to their aesthetic importance and their striving together toward the total effect; that he knows how to guard against *monotony of manner*, to adjust the theatrical action precisely with the musical expression, to apportion skillfully interest everywhere between the fantasy and the heart, and in so doing to utilize the orchestra to the fullest extent and in general to present a work that interests the masses through many apprehensible and memorable melodies and at the same time allows the connoisseur to perceive many true perfections, conjured up from the innermost sanctuary of art, which afford him pleasure and amuse him for a long time.

"It is possible that the composer provides somewhat too amply for instrumental music after the currently ruling fashion, that his decided partiality for the wind instruments, which indeed often occasions the happiest thoughts for embellishing an effect, sometimes misleads him to poor control in the conduct of the harmony, and that the text occasionally permits of a more critical and careful revision. Yet all this is outweighed by so many beauties that, though there remains the wish for this kind of perfection, it would be at the very least unjust and ungrateful not to apply to such works by him the same forbearance that one is used to granting to even the most famous works." *Ibid.*, pp. 513–14.

Walter and Dittersdorf in the North

The popular musical style and large-scale control which composers like Lichtenstein were seeking to absorb and master entered Northern repertories not just through such imitations and through the importation of the most successful operas abroad, but also through the appearance of Ignaz Walter and Carl Dittersdorf as direct contributors of new works to Northern stages.

Walter, a Bohemian trained at Vienna, had made a creditable name for himself as a tenor at Augsburg, Prague, Riga, and Mainz before becoming the Grossmann company's music director in 1792. Sometime prior to this appointment Walter began collaborating with the Mainz National Theater's theatrical poet Heinrich Gottlieb Schmieder on a Faust opera. The subject had been treated before in two adaptations of Rousseau's *Le Ceinture magique*, but Schmieder became the first to use the German dramatic versions of the legend. Indeed, he helped himself without scruple to the works of Goethe, Maler Müller, Klinger, and Lessing. Philipp Spitta devoted a lengthy study to the sources of the musical numbers in Schmieder's *Doktor Faust*, which is all that survives of the libretto. One expects a certain freedom in borrowing, Spitta observes, "but among the hundreds of operatic texts I know from the eighteenth century, there is not a one in which the freebooting has been carried so far."[41] Two of Goethe's best-known lyrics from the Faust fragment published in 1790 appear virtually unchanged – the Romanze "Es war ein König in Thule," and Gretchen's spinning song, "Meine Ruh' ist hin." The extensive finales, too, are deeply in Goethe's debt.

Spitta grants qualified approval to Walter's score for lightness of touch and inventiveness. Walter, he remarks, "belongs to the very few German operatic composers who stood wholly within Mozart's sphere of influence," a comment which does not do justice to the strong impression Mozart's style made all across Germany. Also, Spitta dates the opera too early, 1792 or before, on the basis of Walter's "Churfürstlich Maynzischer Hofsänger" on the score; such embellishments actors, singers, and composers often retained after leaving court service, and one journal's report that Walter was "nearing completion" of his *Doktor Faust* in 1797 should probably be accepted as accurate.[42]

Walter had also completed a setting of Herklots's *Die böse Frau* for the Grossmann company. He set it straight through without alteration and the troupe gave its première at Hannover in 1794. All the traits Spitta noted in *Doktor Faust* appear in the music to this small-town farce as well. Less folklike than Dittersdorf, Walter nonetheless shares his simplicity of material and instinct for the appropriate gesture. In act one, for example, his first ensemble generates its substantial length from only a few ideas which serve to bind the characters together as the opera's main predicament is broached: old Niklas has offered the disguised prince and count a glass of milk, but his wife refuses

[41] "Die älteste Faust-Oper und Goethe's Stellung zur Musik," in his collection of essays *Zur Musik* (Berlin, 1892), p. 209.

[42] *Journal für Theater und andere schöne Künste* 1799: 263. Quoted in *ibid.*, p. 201.

to give it to them and beshrews her husband for extending generosity to un-invited guests. In Example 8.7 the two nobles remark ironically that in place of the milk peace and quiet will do, since Niklas seems to have promised more than he can deliver; Hanne rejoices over the discomfort she has inflicted on her husband; and Niklas resolutely refuses to go back on his word. Walter unites all four voices in an imitative passage (bars 157–69) but sets Hanne off clearly from the other three with her repeated eighth notes – an apt portrayal with the high woodwinds chirping along, as is Niklas's thankless plodding as harmonic beast of burden to the others in the cadence section which follows. The text lies very well under the notes, and the pointed "rasch" of the prince and count receives an appropriate dynamic poke in the ribs.

In much of Walter's score he indulges a love of the woodwinds, using them soloistically, as a choir, and in dialogue with the strings. The young hero Peter's first aria offers a characteristic example in its opening ritornello and first phrases (Example 8.8). The kind of "zerbrochener Stil" seen here springs less from an abhorrence of a vacuum than from a joy in a rich orchestral palette. Walter's orchestral style probably derives from his years of study at Vienna, and certainly the opening eight-note motive in the winds is an unmistakable borrowing from Viennese comic opera. Walter uses the clari-nets frequently, often with a Mozartean chromatic tinge. Like most German composers of this era, Walter distinguishes the orchestral and vocal versions of his principal melody, seeking to make each as idiomatic as possible.

Walter composed Herklots's two long finales with finesse. In the first espe-cially he employs frequent choral interjections and textual repetition to extend and alter the finale's proportions as sketched out by Herklots. As a result, careful musical preparation enhances the theatrical effectiveness of the two foci of the finale – Peter's drawing of a lot in the recruiting episode and the news that Niklas has apparently beaten his wife to death. In general Walter uses key in ways similar to Mozart's tonal architecture in his mature operas: the home key, marked off by the overture and last-act finale, returns for several important numbers; opposing it, a rival non-dominant tonal center asserts itself in other major arias and in the inner finale as a tonal emblem of the high point of dramatic tension; other keys function along traditional affective lines sanctioned by use throughout the century.

Dittersdorf's connections with Germany – apart from his role as a univer-sally beloved comic master and as a model – consists in a journey to Berlin in 1789, several visits to Breslau, and his association with the ducal theater at Oels from 1794 to 1797. Dittersdorf describes this period in his *Lebens-beschreibung* only sketchily. He spent the last decade of his life, years of declining health and popularity, mostly on his estate in Bohemia. He traveled to Oels several times in 1795 and 1796 to rehearse and conduct the premières of his new operas *Der Schach von Schiras*, *Ugolino*, and *Die lustigen Weiber von Windsor* but otherwise never spent any time at the small Silesian princi-pality.

Example 8.7 Walter: *Die böse Frau*. Quartet, act 1.

HANNE: "Good advice is dear. Oh how I rejoice in silence; let the fool fulfill what he has promised."

FÜRST AND GRAF: "A little quiet would suffice for us; one can't always fulfill what one has promised in haste."

NIKLAS: "Just leave me in peace, for one must keep one's word when one has promised something."

Ex. 8.7 (*cont.*)

Example 8.8 Walter: *Die böse Frau*. First aria of Peter, act 1.
"Everything around me here weighs heavily on my heart."

Duke Friedrich August, a member of the house of Brunswick, had acquired Oels through marriage in 1792. He established his court theater in
1793 and for the first winter season contracted with Madam Wäser's company at nearby Breslau for a series of Saturday performances. As we saw
earlier, her repertory was already replete with operas by Dittersdorf, and at
least six of them figured in her offerings at Oels from November 1793 to
March 1794. After this initial season Friedrich August decided to establish
his own standing company and lured several important singers away from
Madam Wäser to head his new troupe. The bass Joseph Franz Alexi became

director and brought with him from Breslau the rest of his theatrical family, most prominent among them his daughter Caroline. The duke also acquired the Wäser company's first tenor Rösner. Obviously all of these singers had distinguished themselves in the Wäser performances at Oels of Dittersdorf's operas, and it was only natural that the duke would seek more operas from the composer.

A letter from Dittersdorf to Friedrich August, reprinted by Lothar Riedinger,[43] tells us at least a little about the composer's relationship with patron and performers. We can deduce that the duke personally approved the librettos Dittersdorf intended to set and also determined the distribution of roles, that when his health permitted Dittersdorf came to Oels to supervise rehearsals with both the singers and the orchestra, and – not surprisingly – that he knew his singers' abilities, both musical and dramatic, quite well. An illustration of these points occurs near the end of his letter. Dittersdorf has asked if he might suggest a distribution of the three principal parts of his serious opera *Ugolino* – Alexi as Ugolino, Rösner as Fernando, and Caroline Alexi (rather than the prima donna Wotruba) as Laura:

> The fiction one must accept with other subjects on the stage of father–daughter–lover becomes Nature [i.e. literally true], since in the first two cases it is perfect reality and in the last is a very great probability. Herr Rösner would have to have no feeling were he not to find Caroline lovable. Still! – if I have spoken too much on this last point, at least I have said it only to Your Highness (not as the ruler of your court but as a connoisseur and friend of man).[44]

Dittersdorf produced seven new German operas at the ducal theater at Oels. The librettos show varied provenance. Three of them the composer himself wrote: one – *Gott Mars* – is apparently original, whereas the other two are translations from the Italian. Dittersdorf may also have prepared the text of his serious two-act opera *Ugolino*, taken not directly from Gerstenberg's tragedy but from "a French manuscript."[45] In 1795 Dittersdorf set Kotzebue's *Sultan Wampum*, but its simple musical format would not do: the plot was changed and alterations made to give the musician greater scope. Dittersdorf himself, who may have been responsible for the new version, retitled *Der Schach von Schiras*, described it as "after Aug. v. Kotzebue's play with songs, refashioned into a regular comic opera."[46]

The other librettos Dittersdorf set, both by South and North German writers, required no such alterations to accommodate the composer's conception of "eine förmliche komische Oper." One of these texts, Georg Römer's *Die lustigen Weiber*, had already been composed for the Mannheim National Theater by Peter Ritter. The other was Herklots's *Der Mädchenmarkt*.

---

[43] "Karl von Dittersdorf als Opernkomponist: Eine stilkritische Untersuchung," *Studien zur Musikwissenschaft* 2 (1914): 311–12.

[44] *Ibid.*, p. 312. Riedinger's dating of the letter (December, 1795) is to be accepted on strong internal evidence.

[45] *Ibid.*, p. 230.

[46] *Intelligenz-Blatt zur Allgemeine musikalische Zeitung* 1 (1798/9): 19.

(Dittersdorf also set a Bretzner libretto in 1798, *Die Opera buffa,* but by then the Oels court theater had closed on the death of Friedrich August, and the première of this opera apparently took place at Vienna.)

None of these later works came anywhere near the popularity of his German operas for Vienna of the 1780s based on texts by Stephanie the Younger. Dittersdorf wrote bitterly about their neglect in his autobiography, but to little avail. Only one of his operas, *Das Gespenst mit der Trommel,* saw a production outside of Oels, this at the Berlin National Theater in 1795. In editing the posthumous edition of the composer's *Lebensbeschreibung,* Carl Spazier tinged his introductory remarks with nostalgia for other masters of a disappearing era:

> With respect to the operetta [Dittersdorf] is for us in a certain sense what Grétry is for France. His dramatic works have for the most part natural life, cheer, character, and truth, and especially a certain affability and popularity that addresses an emotion directly, as formerly in a smaller genre the unforgettable operettas of Hiller had done.[47]

When Dittersdorf began composing for the operatic establishment at Oels he no doubt faced certain constraints – Northern singers rather than Viennese-trained ones, for instance, and a small orchestra (without clarinets) – but so immensely pleasing was his music to all German-speaking lands in the early 1790s, he could have felt no need to rethink his operatic *modus operandi,* and indeed the Oels scores bear this out. Let us consider as an example his music for Herklots's *Der Mädchenmarkt,* a work of which Dittersdorf thought well enough to turn it into an Italian opera buffa in 1798 (*Il mercato delle ragazze,* never performed). A gleaning of its melodies demonstrates that the composer continued to pursue the "certain affability and popularity" Spazier had praised in his operettas (Example 8.9).

Similarly, Dittersdorf had changed little in his deft portrayal of situation and character in ensembles. Herklots's libretto had provided wide scope for such exercises. The second-act finale begins with a scene between Paul, disguised as a brutally ugly lady, and the money-hungry old Holbeck. Paul pleads in vain for Holbeck to put off his suit but the latter will brook no delay nor hear any more excuses. Dittersdorf's technique in this section is his typical one (Example 8.10). He chooses a simple but effective accompaniment motive with which the strings can snigger in amused detachment at the foolish couple. He permits it to run on at great length without variation or substitution, keeping the harmonic underpinnings militantly simple. Thereby he drenches the section in a single prime color and also helps along Herklots's linking of the dialogue with similar syllables sung by Paul and Holbeck – "ach," "bit-," "ge[h]" – in addition to the unification provided by the rhymes. The declamation of each participant is also carefully moulded to the situation. Indeed, Dittersdorf changed Herklots's opening line, "Herr Holbeck!

[47] (Leipzig, 1801). A modern edition with Spazier's introduction is that edited by Norbert Miller (Munich, 1967). This quotation appears there on page 11.

Example 8.9 Dittersdorf: *Der Mädchenmarkt*. Four excerpts in popular style.
A: "Joy empties the tankards and gives them to us for filling."
B: "Then you should know that twenty years ago today. . ."
C: "Is there one among the male sex whom none of the patterns fit. . ."
D: "Still I don't know why, if you're able to put up with hearing that. . ."

ach! ich bitte sehr," by slapping an additional "ach" at the beginning. He sensed, no doubt, the need for a plangent accent to set the finale's tone stronger than "Herr" could provide. Dittersdorf's desire to create some sort of unity in the finale – by the later 1780s typically a sprawling affair – led him to repeat the opening Vivace section in the act-one finale as a Presto at the end. A ballet and chorus function in a somewhat analogous way in the masque which serves as the finale of act three.

Example 8.10 Dittersdorf: *Der Mädchenmarkt*. Finale, act 2.
PAUL: "Ah, Herr Holbek, ah I beg of you. . ."
HOLBEK: "I'll not hear another plea."
PAUL: "Just a moment of your time, then the quarrel can be smoothed out."
HOLBEK: "No, no, I'm going to the governor to tell him everything."

Ex. 8.10 (*cont.*)

Das Gespenst mit der Trommel traces its direct literary lineage through Goldoni's opera buffa *Il Conte Caramella* to Addison's *The Drummer*. The latter had created a thoroughly English version of a familiar dramatic pattern: a young nobleman, thought killed in battle, returns to his estate to find his wife besieged by suitors for her considerable jointure; one, Fantome, has taken to haunting the manor as a nocturnal regimental drummer; another, Tom Tinsel, is a shallow fop of a free-thinker from the city; disguised as a conjurer, the husband unmasks the ghostly drummer (whose apparition has already frightened Tinsel off) and reclaims his faithful wife.

Goldoni presents only a single suitor, the Marchese, who has hired a drummer to play the supposedly dead conte's spirit – a standard operatic simplification which Dittersdorf also follows. But Goldoni is closer to Addison in developing the secondary love interest between the comic couple Ghitta and Cecco. Dittersdorf, working in the modern two-act frame, could spare no room for them and, after following Goldoni's exposition scrupulously up to its finale, departs sharply from then on.

All in all *Das Gespenst mit der Trommel* is an excellent piece of work, perhaps the best of all the later operas. The characters are sharply etched and neatly interlaced in the unified plot. The planning for musical numbers is impeccable. Several features seem tuned precisely to Dittersdorf's style. The Graf, for example, first appears not in his steward's chamber (as in Addison) or in a courtyard (as in Goldoni) but in a village scene with a dairy farm and his own castle on either side. Further, he sings an aria extolling the verdant beauty of his lands, "Holde Haine, holde Fluren!" in place of the monologue Goldoni had provided him. For good measure, Dittersdorf grants him a second nature aria at the beginning of act two. Both numbers allow the Graf to assert his healthy, warm character, otherwise hidden beneath his pilgrim's disguise.

The German libretto's most brilliant innovation consists in a sextet in which the Graf conjures up himself as a soldier. Not only does this bring vividly to life another side of his personality, it deals a mortal blow to the baron's scheme of passing off his drummer as the Graf's spirit, which will not be laid to rest until the Gräfinn marries the baron. In D major the principals await with sharpened curiosity the promised spectacle ("Ich bin begierig bald zu sehn / Was uns der Mann versprochen hat"). After suitable preparations a mirror falls away and a March in E-flat commences, played by a wind band behind the scene. The Graf appears and runs through some military exercises to the accompaniment of the wind band. Dittersdorf set this as a melodrama – one of the most unusual in eighteenth-century German opera – and the technique could hardly have been bettered (Example 8.11). The march rounds out the vignette as the Graf marches off and the mirror returns to its normal position. As if to demonstrate how deep an impression this apparition has made on those watching it on stage, Dittersdorf has them repeat the opening Andante of the sextet with a modified text ("Ich muss wahrhaftig eingestehn / ich hab so etwas nie gesehn") and with a modified key (the E-flat major of the march instead of D major). This relationship of a suspended half-step will never lack for employment during all of the next century as a tonal analogue

Example 8.11 Dittersdorf: *Das Gespenst mit der Trommel*. Melodrama and sextet, act 2.
    GRAF: "Attention! The whole company load! Get ready! One, two, three. Up, take aim! One. Down! One. Half company take aim. One. Fire! Look to the battery. One. Shoulder arms. One, two, three. Attention! March right by rows. Right face in rows. March!"
(*Note*: The preceding march is played again without repeats.) There follows immediately:
    GRÄFINN, MARTHA, KAROLINE, BARON, KONRAD: "I must truly confess that I've never seen such a thing."

Ex. 8.11 (cont.)

of divine, supernatural, or otherwise unearthly visitations.[48] The melodrama
technique and off-stage winds were already stock items in the operatic composer's arsenal for similar situations. The novelty here lies not in Dittersdorf's willingness to end an operatic number in a key remote from the one in

[48] Such half-step relations between repeated sections were not the exclusive property of the later
eighteenth and nineteenth centuries. J.S. Bach uses a crucial one in the *St. Matthew Passion*
in flanking Peter's vehement denial that he will disown his discipleship three times before
the cock crows with the "O Haupt voll Blut und Wunden" chorale, first in E major and
then in E-flat major. While the half-step depression creates an undeniable darkening effect, its
use was no doubt also symbolic – the chorus sees the same notes written on the staff, but the
key signature has changed their meaning.

which it began, but his making compelling dramatic capital of this skewed relationship by harking back to the music whose key is transmuted in the sextet.

Both finales include a healthy amount of action. In the act-one finale, for instance, the Graf as pilgrim is brought before his wife, prophesies, and comes to blows with the baron (who thinks him an interfering fraud); the drumming commences suddenly, the baron's henchman Wirbel appears and announces that his spirit will not lie in peace until the Gräfinn marries the baron. The Graf counters with a promise to restore her husband and exorcise this ghost within twenty-four hours.

Dittersdorf fills his score with short, contrasting sections, contributing greatly to the finale's compact energy. In Example 8.12 the Graf is in the midst

Example 8.12   Dittersdorf: *Das Gespenst mit der Trommel*. Finale, act 1.
GRAF: "Oh, keep still or I'll tell the Gräfinn right now what passed between you and the messenger who, when the Graf received his bride's consent, was not exactly singing psalms with you."
MARTHA: "I beg you, keep silent!"
(Drumming is heard.)
GRÄFINN, MARTHA, FRIEDERIKA, BARON, KONRAD: "Oh, alas! I'm done for! Here comes the ghost. God help us!"
GRAF: "Fear not, for I shall drive it away. . ."

Ex. 8.12 (*cont.*)

of threatening Martha with some revelations about her earlier conduct through his necromantic powers when Wirbel's drumming breaks in on them. An obligatory chromatic outburst of terror follows: the Graf, of course, is silent, and Martha and the baron only feign fear – indeed, he seems almost to lead the congregation in their supplications with his high E's reinforced by the horns. Dittersdorf permits them to quake no longer than ten measures before interposing the Graf. He takes command of the situation with a Tempo di minuetto, an emblem of his true station and character. In the short space of this excerpt the composer has traversed three tempos, meters, and keys (G–C–a/A). Though he has avoided the dimensions and looseness of modern Viennese finales, with their distinct episodes and transformations, Dittersdorf has preserved the dramatic *raison d'être* of the form.

On the whole the adjustments Dittersdorf made in his style for the Oels operas do not amount to much more than minor deviations from his earlier manner. His light, apprehensible melodic style still couples with a simple, by now conservative harmonic vocabulary. He sought variety rather than unity in his tonal planning. *Das Gespenst mit der Trommel* begins in D major, ends its first act in C major, and concludes in A major. Not a single one of its twenty-two numbers is in the minor mode save the last finale, which begins in a minor. Dittersdorf does use different styles effectively to establish and contrast characters, but never does he hazard the extremes of Mozart's stylistic spectrum in *Don Giovanni* and *Die Zauberflöte*. The Gräfinn he treats as a true prima donna with an impressive aria with concertante flute in act one and a modish two-tempo Rondeau in E-flat just prior to the last finale, precisely where Vitellia sings hers in *La clemenza di Tito*. But for the ignoble young baron (direct dramatic descendant of Addison's Tom Tinsel) he could think of nothing better than recourse to his popular style for the poetic coarseness of the baron's first aria (Example 8.13). In the autograph score, Dittersdorf at first wrote C#'s for the two B's marked with asterisks in Example 8.13 but then changed them to the Baron's triadic thumping seen here; he also adhered to the same square, open–closed, repetitive phrasing seen earlier in *Der Mädchenmarkt* (Example 8.9).

In his last operas Dittersdorf chose subjects which had nothing to do with the spectacle and magic so pervasive in popular Viennese and Italian librettos. Equally foreign to him was any tincture of the political mongering of post-Revolutionary French opera. Instead, and perhaps with his courtly audience at Oels uppermost in mind, he confined himself to texts of good sense which celebrate the kind of virtues to which no enlightened thinker could object. *Gott Mars*, his one original text for Oels, offers an illustration. It revolves around a retired Captain Bärenzahn, his daughter Emilie who has chosen a fiancé her father cannot abide, and two servants who have been embezzling the captain's household accounts. Emilie resists the temptation to elope throughout the drama, hoping for a change of heart in her father. In good time he does not fail her, even though his assent is forced – "I suppose I

Example 8.13 Dittersdorf: *Das Gespenst mit der Trommel*. First aria of the baron, act 1.
"To fall in love without hope is peculiar only to fools. The strong urges of my heart would never think of such a thing."

must, if the Singspiel is going to end. . ." – and he even forgives the larcenous servants.

Dittersdorf concluded his autobiography in 1799 with the remark that he had not lost his powers over the past five years and had completed "a considerable collection of wholly new works such as operas, symphonies, and a great number of pieces for the fortepiano." No one seemed interested, however. "I revere my dear, good German nation, but when it comes to support – there, alas, we are not at home."[49] In part Dittersdorf had fallen victim to circumstance by seeking to maintain his position as a favorite composer of comic operas from a provincial court theater rather than from the Viennese stage. More importantly, his musical style and the character of his librettos lacked novelty – an important asset in the 1790s. His old, familiar works would do just as well.

Die Geisterinsel: between two worlds

The 1790s in Germany, as Dittersdorf and others learned, were years of pervasive changes in operatic taste and aesthetics as much as they were years of

---

[49] *Lebensbeschreibung*, ed. Miller, p. 276.

political upheaval. The decade spelled the end of the cultural and intellectual pre-eminence in Germany of the system of values and habits of mind we call the Enlightenment, and it also spelled the end of North German opera as a distinctive entity in European music. In both musical and literary terms, as we have seen in this chapter, the cultural area we have defined in this study as North Germany had altered or abandoned its own operatic traditions under unprecedentedly strong pressure from foreign operas, and in so doing became swept up in counter-Enlightenment sensibilities.

Several librettos we have discussed effected a compromise between the old and new, and we must now turn for a concluding exhibit to the North's most important monument to this spirit of compromise, *Die Geisterinsel*. The idea and first plan of this operatic adaptation of Shakespeare's *Tempest* originated with the Weimar courtier Einsiedel, who had dug out a youthful effort in this direction in 1790 and sent it to his friend Gotter at Gotha. Over the next four or five years a new opera derived from Einsiedel's took shape. It was largely Gotter's work, and after his death in 1797 Schiller published the text in *Die Horen* with the inscription "aus Gotter's Nachlass" and no mention of Einsiedel.

The genesis of the text and its search for an adequate composer has been documented by Werner Deetjen and in the published correspondence of Caroline Schlegel.[50] Unfortunately, the libretto's connections with Mozart have led others to less helpful or reliable studies, including Einstein's short essay, translated with amusing incompetence into English as "Mozart and Shakespeare's *The Tempest*."[51] Einstein relies on the critical judgment of Gotter's biographer Rudolf Schlösser, who dismissed it on literary grounds as "an unpoetic fairy story of everyday ilk,"[52] and even refused to see any merit in Goethe's reported opinion of the text as a "masterpiece of poetry and speech: one cannot imagine anything more musical."[53]

Goethe had put his finger on qualities close to Gotter's heart, qualities which linked him with his beloved Metastasio. Early on in his labors, in February 1791, Gotter had written to Einsiedel: "I have sung every line to myself with my owlish voice in order to infuse as much euphony as can be attained in our raw language."[54] Gotter wrote all the musical numbers first, then went back and filled in the prose dialogue. He echoes Wieland's operatic ideals in his quest for mellifluous verse and also in his concern for seriousness, simplicity, and humanistic values. He stressed in a letter to Einsiedel that "the serious is the predominant tone" in the libretto: "The most difficult task is probably dispelling the darkness of the introduction and simplifying

[50] "Der 'Sturm' als Operntext bearbeitet von Einsiedel und Gotter," *Shakespeare-Jahrbuch* 64 (1928): 77–89. *Caroline: Briefe aus der Frühromantik*, ed. Erich Schmidt, 2 vols. (Leipzig, 1913).
[51] *Essays on Music* (New York, 1956), pp. 197–205.
[52] *Friedrich Wilhelm Gotter*, p. 298.
[53] Schmidt, *Caroline*, vol. 1, p. 399. Letter of 3 October 1796 to Gotter's wife Luise.
[54] Deetjen, "Der 'Sturm' als Operntext," p. 77.

the marvelous in the fable as much as possible. The more human, the more attractive."[55]

In upholding these virtues Gotter inevitably ran foul of critics attuned to other standards. Schiller, no great judge of the librettist's art, viewed the text from a purely dramatic standpoint as "kraftlos" and "eine dünne Speise," but printed it anyway for political reasons.[56] The *Berlinisches Archiv der Zeit und ihres Geschmacks*, like other journals, brought up Schikaneder's *Die Zauberflöte* and Gozzi as points of comparison. Gotter, the reviewer observed, fails with the masses as well as the strict judge of art principally because he neglects all of "the most advantageous opportunities to set the imagination of the spectator in motion through magic, song, and machinery." Gotter explains at length what Shakespeare left to the imagination.[57]

Johann Daniel Hensel repeated these criticisms almost verbatim in the preface to his own *Die Geisterinsel*, "a Singspiel in four acts, revised after Shakespeare, Gotter, and J. W. D.,"[58] brought out at Hirschberg in 1799. "We are now too *spoiled* with contrasts in the operetta," wrote Hensel in his long preface, "to be satisfied with a work that should be *spectacular* in the manner of *Die Zauberflöte* unless it also has very many contrasts, changes, surprises, etc. – in a word, unless it makes a *spectacle*." Hensel adds other objections, the most serious that Gotter excelled only at drawing soft characters – Fernando is too weak, Prospero not spirited enough, and Caliban far from evil enough. By 1799 villains blacker than death were waiting in the wings for German librettists to call them out, and once the French operas of Cherubini, Méhul, and Lesueur had asserted themselves sufficiently the Pizarros and Caspars took shape. Hensel also derides Gotter's versification on similar grounds: "Everything is soft, nothing wholly comic, nothing wholly cheerful or sad, nothing really sublime. This is very bad for the music."

Friedrich von Schlichtegroll, on the other hand, staunchly defended *Die Geisterinsel* when he reprinted it three years after Hensel's version had appeared. He praised it as "wholly calculated for musical effect. . . It seizes

---

[55] *Ibid.*, p. 78.

[56] In less than dignified tones Schiller wrote to Goethe in August 1797: "I have read the first act [of *Die Geisterinsel*], but it is quite without power and meagre fare. Nonetheless, I thank heaven that I have a few sheets to fill out *Die Horen* and indeed by means of such a classical writer, who had so bitterly complained about the *genie* and *Xenien* character before his death [18 March 1797]. – And so we are forcing Gotter (who would have nothing to do with *Die Horen* while living) to speak in it while dead." Quoted in Schmidt, *Caroline*, vol. 1, p. 718, n. 181.

[57] 1798:2, p. 298.

[58] Hensel knew no more than these initials of Johann Wilhelm Döring, author of *Der Sturm, oder Die bezauberte Insel* (Cassel, 1798), a two-act version based on Shakespeare. Hensel decided to make use of it owing to its strongly drawn characters and some fine verses, and also because he felt it most unlikely that it would be set now that *Die Geisterinsel* had been composed by the likes of Reichardt and Zelter. Nevertheless, Peter or Heinrich Ritter did set Döring's text in 1799; it was performed at Aurich, Emden, and Altona that year, then disappeared. Döring retains Prospero's brother Antonio (reported to have been assassinated in Gotter's version), but represents the clowns in Fernando's entourage with just Trinkulo and limits the characters from the spirit world to Ariel alone.

me anew every time I enjoy again even just reading this harmonious poetic creation, which through the music of speech, which the critical and careful author has put into it, is at the same time the finest monument he could make to what is most excellent in his abilities."[59]

Whether one ultimately sides with this retrospective point of view or with the progressive evaluations of others, it is clear that neither Gotter himself nor his posthumous critics deemed it proper to judge his libretto apart from its musical effectiveness. Indeed, so essential a part of a librettist's task had this finally become in the North that the writing of a serious text with literary aspirations by one of the old guard proceeded hand in hand with the search for a suitable composer. Gotter, no expert in such matters, sought advice elsewhere – from two of his friends who were professional actors, Schröder and Heinrich Beck, and most of all from Einsiedel, himself a gifted musician. Names taken under consideration included Dittersdorf, Mozart, Christian Friedrich Gottlieb Schwenke of Hamburg (suggested by Schröder), Grétry (suggested through Einsiedel by Karl August), Reichardt, Wranitzky, Haydn, Schulz, Friedrich Fleischmann of Meiningen, and the young Italian-trained Berliner Friedrich Heinrich Himmel.

Gotter and Einsiedel wanted Mozart first and foremost, won over by his music despite Schröder's caution that he had worked too much in the opera buffa, but Mozart died before a correspondence on the possibility had got off the ground. Most curious are the writers' dealings with Dittersdorf. A draft of the libretto had been sent to him in late 1792. His suggestions for revisions heartily displeased Gotter: "The suggestion of Herr von Dittersdorf for shortening the opera betrays too clearly the children of what kind of spirit are the insipid poetic products that for some time now he has thought good to compose and to send into the world to the exasperation of good taste."[60] Only two years later did Gotter recover the manuscript from Dittersdorf. Reichardt, a logical choice, was apparently passed over owing to his inflammatory political views, which had also cost him his position at Berlin and his friendship with Goethe. Finally, seeing that a major composer of repute was not to be had, Gotter and Einsiedel settled on Fleischmann and granted him an exclusive right to set the libretto.

No abstract ideal of an apposite musical adornment for their text spurred Gotter and Einsiedel in their search for a composer, but rather a strongly charged sense of the libretto's specific musical needs, made explicit here as Gotter had never done in his earlier music dramas, even in the melodrama *Medea*. Gotter's letters to Einsiedel on various numbers then in the casting mould mention again and again the advantages and burdens which will befall the composer. Gotter also acknowledged receiving several valuable hints from Reichardt, who would eventually set *Die Geisterinsel* after Gotter's

---

[59] [Johann] Friedrich Wilhelm Gotter, *Literarischer Nachlass* (Gotha, 1802), p. ix.
[60] Deetjen, "Der 'Sturm' als Operntext," p. 86. Gotter's letter is dated 2 March 1793, so he is of course referring to Dittersdorf's Viennese operas rather than those he was to write for Oels.

death, on musical matters in the libretto. Within the text Gotter labeled various sections of its numbers with musical designations such as "arioso," "recitativo," and "cavatina." Here and there he dropped even more direct hints for his composer. For instance, after Fernando's recitative which opens act two "the music repeats single ideas from the closing chorus of the first act;" an especially ethereal chorus of spirits in act three is to be set "without accompaniment of the orchestra and most preferably totally unaccompanied;" and a duet for Ariel and Caliban carries the rubric "with the accompaniment of a single guitar."

Gotter and Einsiedel also made careful provision for the singers and actors, with the special conditions of the German stage in mind. One reason Gotter shied away from verse dialogue was "the general inability of today's singers to recite verses without stiffness."[61] On Einsiedel's advice Gotter made both Ariel and the youth Fabio trouser roles, thereby redistributing the eight singing parts from seven male and one female to five male and three female, the norm for German opera. Similar considerations of a typical troupe's personnel prompted Gotter to write one of the libretto's major scenes – the return of Caliban's mother Sycorax after Prospero's powers over her have ended – as an extended pantomime. With the stage empty, the ground opens to lightning and thunder and Sycorax appears. A monument to Maja, a benign spirit native to the island, bursts and falls. As Sycorax makes for the cell to which Miranda has retired Maja appears and bars her way. Sycorax drops her staff, falls into a flaming crevice, and Maja returns to her gravesite, where a palm tree has replaced the monument. Gotter directed that the role of Maja be played by "the first tragic actress" and that of Sycorax by "the first tragic actor" of the troupe, players who would be skilled in the art of pantomime and melodrama; otherwise the roles would have fallen to the company's fourth and fifth female singers, a very weak alternative in every respect.

Fleischmann's setting of *Die Geisterinsel*, first performed at Regensburg in 1796, did not impress anyone. It failed at Weimar in 1798 when Goethe mounted it there, and a production planned for Frankfurt apparently never took place. Schröder did not like the music, and Iffland too decided that it was not worth much after having it sent to him at Berlin, and he turned instead to Reichardt for a new setting.[62] At nearly the same time Rudolf Zumsteeg composed the libretto for Stuttgart, a fine setting discussed at length in the *Allgemeine musikalische Zeitung*.[63] Both scores appeared in 1799 in handsomely printed keyboard reductions. Fleischmann had announced subscriptions for his own setting in September 1798, but two months later he died suddenly and with that all interest in his version evaporated. Finally, Friedrich Wilhelm Haack at Stettin became the fourth composer to set *Die Geisterinsel* in 1799. It was reported that "the richness, fullness, and elabora-

---

[61] *Ibid.*, p. 80.   [62] Schmidt, *Caroline*, vol. 1, pp. 450–1.
[63] 1 (1798/9): 657–76, 691–711, 785–813.

tion of the harmony, especially in solemn and sublime passages, are supposed to distinguish this composition greatly."[64]

At Berlin Reichardt's *Die Geisterinsel* received a less than enthusiastic reception at its première on 6 July 1798. But Friedrich Schlegel, who attended a rehearsal at Berlin, praised the music warmly as "very sparkling and romantic,"[65] and within a year reports from Berlin spoke with one voice of it as "one of the most pleasing and successful works of this famous master, which creates a growing sensation there with each new performance."[66] *Die Geisterinsel* saw revivals at Berlin in 1806 and 1825, by which date it had rung up a creditable fifty-five performances. Reichardt's score represents the only thorough-going triumph of all the eighty-four operas listed in Table 8.2. It is the last great North German monument to the spirit of the Enlightenment, and one already tinted here and there with the hues of a new era.

After his fall from royal favor in the early 1790s, Reichardt had retired to his estate at Giebichenstein near Halle. But the death of Friedrich Wilhelm II in November 1797 opened Berlin to him once again, and he lost no time in currying favor as a persecuted artist with the new sovereign, Friedrich Wilhelm III. In January of 1798 Reichardt's Italian opera *Brenno* was given in a concert performance at the royal opera house in a German translation, the first time an opera had been given by the king's operatic establishment in German.[67] The première of *Die Geisterinsel* came on "Huldigungstag," a day of official celebration of allegiance to Prussia's new king, to whom Reichardt dedicated his published keyboard reduction. Musically, the composer's stock had clearly suffered no decline at Berlin: Iffland paid him the unprecedented sum of 500 Thaler for the score to *Die Geisterinsel*, whereas he had paid only 70 for Fleischmann's.[68]

In composing Gotter's libretto Reichardt made very few changes and for the most part adhered to its musical instructions. The norms for a comic opera, even one with a generous helping of *parti serie*, would not do here, where what levity and imbroglio there is has assumed the role of a secondary episode. Rather Gotter had invited his composer to attend first to Miranda, Fernando, and Prospero, and then to choral and instrumental numbers; only in act two, overextended and by far the weakest of the three, do the comic figures move into prominence.

[64] *Ibid.* 2 (1799/1800): 135.
[65] Schmidt, *Caroline*, vol. 1, p. 452. Schlegel's opinion was reported by his wife to Gotter's widow.
[66] *Journal des Luxus und der Moden* 14 (1799). 355.
[67] So states L[ouis] Schneider, *Geschichte der Oper und des königlichen Opernhauses in Berlin*, pp. 276–7. Donald Jay Grout distorts this into the misstatement that this performance "was the first occasion on which opera was sung at Berlin with German words." *A Short History of Opera*, 2nd ed. (New York and London, 1965), p. 267.
[68] These figures are drawn from Appendix three in *Johann Valentin Teichmanns weiland königl. Preussischen Hofrathes ec. Literarischer Nachlass* (Stuttgart, 1863), which lists manuscripts and music bought for the National Theater from 1790 to 1810.

The storm which heads Shakespeare's play and gave it its title Gotter delays until the finale of act one, a good piece of operatic strategy by the standards of his day. Reichardt anticipates the storm capping this finale in his overture – and quite a good storm it is by eighteenth-century standards. Further, he seems to underscore its unruliness in the finale by ending not in its initial key of E-flat but in the D major of the overture. A neat symmetry results: the overture had modulated from D major to Miranda's opening Larghetto in E-flat; now her languishing E-flat Adagio at the beginning of the finale eventually loses itself in the return of the storm music in D major. Reichardt's overture anticipates the nineteenth-century German norm, seen clearly in Weber's brilliant operatic overtures, of building an independent instrumental argument of the drama about to unfold out of themes drawn from the music of the opera proper.[69]

Although Reichardt was on the threshold of developing the Liederspiel which dominates his operatic activities in the first decade of the nineteenth century, he keeps the folk-like simplicity of Hiller and Dittersdorf at arm's length. The closest he comes is in act two, where Gotter had specifically requested that the first two quatrains of the trio "Mögen unsre Weiber doch" be set "nach einer Volksmelodie" (Example 8.14). The characters who sing here

Example 8.14 Reichardt: *Die Geisterinsel*. Trio, act 2.
"Let our wives dwell there however they please, if we feast here in peace, free from the marital yoke. But we would rather that we were feasting there in peace, and instead of us our wives were dwelling here."

[69] A six-bar Largo leads to an Andante quotation in D major of the Geisterchor "Wolken verschweben," all this by way of slow introduction to the storm sonata-allegro (from the act one finale). Thereafter an Allegretto quotes two 6/8 numbers of Ariel (his first aria and his interpolation in the storm scene).

Ex. 8.14 (*cont.*)

are strictly second-class ones in the drama's musical pecking order. Neither Oronzio (Fernando's cook) nor Stefano (his wine steward) has a solo aria anywhere in the opera, and here they seem to duplicate the sounds of the male choral societies already springing up around Germany, rather than Hiller's folk style.

At the beginning of the opera Reichardt seems to strive for a leitmotivic sense of musical unity as Gotter establishes the dramatic situation which unites Prospero, Miranda, Ariel, and the spirit of Maja. A falling dotted figure, at any rate, recurs in each of the opera's first three numbers (Example 8.15). Possibly we are meant to associate this emblem with Miranda, who

Example 8.15 Reichardt: *Die Geisterinsel*. Dotted motive in first three numbers, act 1.
A: "Die upon the grave of my Maja! Maja. . ."
B: "The clouds float away."

dominates the opening scene. What Gotter did not take over directly from Shakespeare in her character he developed out of the long tradition of earnestly naïve heroines in North German opera and drama. He had complained that Einsiedel, in his original conception of Miranda, had transformed her from "an unrestrained daughter of Nature into a cultivated European. . . Let me make an effort to restore to her the Tahitian innocence and naïveté through which she is made so interesting in Master William!"[70] Gotter was equally displeased with Dittersdorf's suggestion that Miranda be given a bravura aria.

Reichardt sought a compromise between these two poles. His Miranda at Berlin was Margarethe Schick, the brilliant soprano for whom Stegmann had composed additional arias to enrich the character of Almansaris in Wranitzky's *Oberon*. When she arrived at the Berlin National Theater from Mainz in 1794 she instantly became the darling of the public, and she also sang in the king's opera, which now boasted of a considerable number of German singers.

To render her justice Reichardt made his only significant departure from Gotter by inserting a recitative and aria between Fernando's simple Romanze and the finale of act two. Instead of a straight bravura aria, however, he chose the more appropriate two-tempo rondeau. This was also the one number from the opera chosen for publication in the *Allgemeine musikalische Zeitung*.[71] Reichardt does not attempt to link the rondeau theme of the Un poco Adagio first half with that of the Allegro second half, a feature commonly encountered in the two-tempo rondeaux of Mozart and the Italians. He seems rather to have concerned himself with setting off two quite diverse sides of Margarethe Schick's voice in a way the four-part scena would soon be doing for nineteenth-century heroines. The results are closely akin to Agathe's first scena in *Der Freischütz*.

This rondeau shows with special clarity the goal-oriented character that this and other forms could assume by the later 1790s as a new era began to rethink the shapes which best expressed its self-image. The text specifically invites such directed momentum: contrary to both Gotter's poetic canons and his vision of Miranda, the anonymous supplier (possibly Reichardt himself) caps the closing quintain of the Allegro with Miranda's embracing Fernando and crying, "Hier ist dein Vaterland!" Reichardt sets this second quintain twice and thereby produces within the Allegro an ABB form, one which will be a hallmark of Italian opera and especially Bellini later on. It inevitably called for a kind of cadential one-upmanship in the second B part, but Reichardt does not enrich this spot as later composers would routinely do, making room only for greater vocal brilliance from the soprano.

Reichardt's finales, particularly the storm scene concluding act one, show

[70] Deetjen, "Der 'Sturm' als Operntext," p. 80.   [71] 1 (1798/9): Supplement No. 8.

his mastery of another modern accretion to North German operatic style, and several of Gotter's extensive ensembles also provided him a wide field in which to maneuver. These include not only the comic scenes for Caliban, Oronzio, Stefano, Fabio, and Ariel in act two, but even the lovers' duet of Fernando and Miranda which opens the third act, a potentially conventional spot which Gotter chose to expand into something approaching an introduzzione. At the end of the act-two finale Prospero had given each of them a sack of corals with instructions to separate and stay awake all through the night by counting the corals. At the beginning of their two-tempo duet, Fernando and Miranda set about this unhappy task, but by the end of the number Nature has overruled their enforced separation and Fernando throws himself at Miranda's feet. A clap of thunder sends them running. Reichardt moves immediately into the pantomime confrontation of Sycorax and Maja and the chorus of spirits which concludes it; nor does he stop here, but rather modulates into a large-scale duet of Ariel and Prospero to conclude the scene.

Rather than unifying this musical complex tonally, Reichardt intensifies the strong key associations he has already established in the first two acts for Miranda (E-flat major) and Prospero (C major). The simple Un poco Adagio melody with which Miranda submits to her father's demands at the start of her duet with Fernando presents Reichardt's loveliest musical portrait of his heroine, a truly Mozartean cantilena (Example 8.16). The accompaniment

Example 8.16 Reichardt: *Die Geisterinsel*. Duet, act 3.
   "Unhappy corals, I am to count you! Yet who counts the tears that, mingled with you, fall upon my lap?"

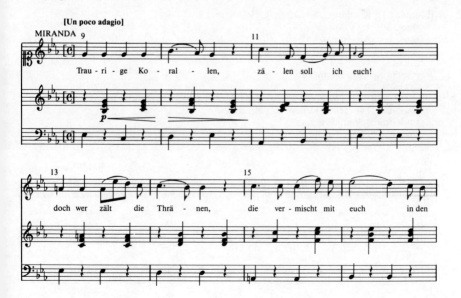

Ex. 8.16 (*cont.*)

figure begun in bars 23 and 24 anticipates the following section, in which she begins counting the corals, and foreshadows as well Reichardt's concern to link the sections of his larger structure in order to create a directed, chain-like dramatic continuity. Later in this duet, for example, he highlights the lovers' struggle to keep to Prospero's adjurations with several strongly marked deceptive resolutions (Example 8.17). The first cadence, V–ᵇVI in F major

Example 8.17 Reichardt: *Die Geisterinsel.* Duet, act 3.
 FERNANDO: "Ah, Miranda!"
 MIRANDA: "Ah, Fernando!"
 FERNANDO: "You complain as well?"
 MIRANDA: "I do."
 FERNANDO: "You call me?"
 MIRANDA: "Ah, no!"
 FERNANDO: "The complaint sounds sweeter when another heart joins in."
 MIRANDA: "Let each of us bear his pain alone."
 FERNANDO: "Solitude is pain!"
 MIRANDA: "I must remain alone!"

Ex. 8.17 (*cont.*)

Ex. 8.17 (*cont.*)

(bars 84–5), sets up a ten-measure parenthetical comment in D-flat; after it the delayed F major comes as a warm surprise (V_7–♮III in bars 94–5) and initiates a modulatory transition to yet another unexpected event (V–♭III in c minor) and the introduction of the duet's second tempo.

Elsewhere Reichardt is not so forward-looking. The pantomime music to which Maja overcomes Sycorax does not depart from the restrained practice of the century, and similarly the two supernatural choruses do not go in search of novel effects. Each, however, connects to the aria preceding or following it in order to enhance their psychological relevance to the human characters of the drama. At a later date these characters would be overwhelmed by the forces of destiny, irrational nature, and the supernatural, but not here. The softness and moderation critics began to disdain in Gotter's Miranda, Fernando, Prospero, and Caliban even before the century was out offer a last glow of the optimism, taste, good sense, and restraint already beginning to crumble under the transformation of Europe as it entered the age of Napoleon.

Catalogue of North German operas
1766–1799

Introduction

As a supplement to the foregoing study and as a general resource, there follows a comprehensive catalogue of all known German operas written and produced in North Germany from the initial triumphs of Hiller and Weisse at Leipzig in 1766 to the end of the 1700s. The geographical delimitation of the term "North Germany" has been set forth in Chapter 1. Excluded from the present catalogue are melodramas, occasional pieces (Vorspiele), and incidental music. Again, as explained in Chapter 1, definitions for the last two categories must necessarily involve a certain degree of arbitrariness. The catalogue is divided into three parts:

Part I offers an alphabetical listing by composer of all German-language operas first performed in the North and, in addition, unperformed settings written in North Germany. Entries follow this format:

COMPOSER

Title [*Alternate title(s)*]
Librettist (Genre [source of designation] – number of acts)
City of première (Date of première) Theater or troupe
Publication history of music and manuscript locations
    Notes

Where more than one title occurs in eighteenth-century sources for a work, preference is given to the most frequently used. Where differing genre designations occur in these sources, all variants are shown and the source of each is indicated in brackets as the libretto [L] or musical source [M].

The publication history of the music lists not only keyboard reductions – by far the most common format throughout the period, for which we use the widely adopted German abbreviation for Klavierauszug, KLA – but also printed excerpts in various collections and journals. Bracketed numbers after such printed items are those given in *RISM: Einzeldrücke vor 1800*, to which the user is referred for complete imprint information and locations of surviving copies. Manuscript locations are indicated with the library sigla of *RISM* as adapted in *The New Grove Dictionary of Music and Musicians*.

Finally, the Notes at the foot of each item present specific information on such matters as conflicting attributions; varying dates, act numbers, and so forth in standard secondary sources; and other pertinent information.

Part II is divided into two sections. Section A lists by title all texts set by composers for performance in North Germany during the years under discussion. Section B lists texts which were published but apparently never set to music. The format adopted is as follows:

TITLE
Librettist (source)
Composer(s) (city, date of première [except in Section B])
Publication history:
1. Title, if different from above (genre label, acts) [composer, if mentioned on title page]
   City: publisher, date OR collection or periodical [library and catalogue references]
BIBL.: mention of work in eighteenth-century periodical literature
   Notes

Several of these items require further explanation. Settings by composer are listed in chronological order and are meant to facilitate crossreferencing to Part I of the catalogue. Printed librettos appear chronologically in the publication history with undated works last. An "A" appended to a number in this list (for "arias") means that the print contains only the musical numbers and not the spoken dialogue. The genre label is taken from the title page of each print. If the number of acts does not appear there, it is supplied in brackets.

Library and catalogue references are of two kinds, supplied for two reasons. Three important catalogues of librettos – Sonneck's of the Schatz Collection and other librettos at the Library of Congress in Washington, Richard Schaal's of the libretto collection at the Clara-Ziegler-Theater-Museum at Munich, and the catalogue of the librettos at the Herzog-August-Bibliothek at Wolfenbüttel – are given so that more precise details concerning each print could be omitted here. Specific library references, using *RISM* sigla, are also given for those prints not found in any of these catalogues.

In Section B it was thought prudent to include works for which no surviving copy has been located, but which were nonetheless published in the eighteenth century and mentioned or reviewed in a contemporary periodical.

Part III lists in alphabetical order all the known librettists of the operas mentioned in the first two parts of the catalogue. Both title and composer or composers are given for each work so that this part may serve as an author index to both Part I and Part II. A publication date rather than composer is supplied for each item from Section B (unset librettos) of Part II. Collaborations appear under the writer thought to be the principal contributor, with cross-indexing.

Frequently cited sources in the first two parts of this catalogue are abbreviated as shown in the following key. Other short-title references in the catalogue are cited in full in the Bibliography.

Key to abbreviations
(Complete citations in Bibliography)

ABSS	*Allgemeine Bibliothek für Schauspieler und Schauspielliebhaber*
AdB	*Allgemeine deutsche Bibliothek*
AdM	*Almanach der deutschen Musen*
AdT	*Annalen des Theaters*
ALZ	*Allgemeine Literatur-Zeitung*
AMZ	*Allgemeine Musikalische Zeitung*
ATL	Ernst Ludwig Gerber: *Historisch-biographisches Lexikon der Tonkünstler*
BAZG	*Berlinisches Archiv der Zeit und ihres Geschmacks*
BLT	Bernhard Christoph d'Arien: *Beyträge zur Litteratur- und Theaterkunde*
BmZ	*Berlinische musikalische Zeitung historischen und kritischen Inhalts*
BTC	*The Breitkopf Thematic Catalogues*, ed. Barry S. Brook
BTJ	Christian Friedrich von Bonin: *Berliner Theater-Journal für das Jahr 1782*
BTML	*Beiträge zum Theater, zur Musik und der unterhaltenden Lektüre überhaupt*
DB	Adolf Freiherr von Knigge: *Dramaturgische Blätter*
DBW	Christian Adolph Klotz: *Deutsche Bibliothek der schönen Wissenschaften*
DM	*Deutsches Museum*
DOAM	*Deutsche Operetten im Auszuge mit Musik der besten deutschen Componisten*
ELT	*Ephemeriden der Litteratur und des Theaters*
GGO	*German Opera, 1770–1800* (facsimile series)
Graf	Herbert Graf: *Das Repertoire der öffentlichen Opern- und Singspielbühnen in Berlin seit dem Jahre 1771*
Hagen	Ernst August Hagen: *Geschichte des Theaters in Preussen*
HATLZ	*Hamburgisch- und Altonaische Theater- und Litteratur-Zeitung*
Hiller *L*	Johann Adam Hiller: *Lebensbeschreibungen berühmter Musikgelehrten und Tonkünstler neuerer Zeit*
HT	Johann Friedrich Schink: *Hamburgische Theaterzeitung*
JLM	*Journal des Luxus und der Moden*
Kade	Otto Kade: *Die Musikalien-Sammlung des Mecklenburg-Schweriner Fürstenhauses*

KT	Friedrich Samuel Mohr: *Königsbergisches Theaterjournal fürs Jahr 1782*
LAD	*Lieder, Arien und Duette beym Klavier*, ed. Johann André
LTZ	*Litteratur- und Theater-Zeitung*
Maurer	Julius Maurer: *Anton Schweitzer als dramatischer Komponist*
MdM	*Magazin der Musik*, ed. Carl Friedrich Cramer
MGG	*Die Musik in Geschichte und Gegenwart*
MKB	Johann Nikolaus Forkel: *Musikalisch-Kritische Bibliothek*
MM	*Musikalisches Monathsschrift*
MRZ	*Musikalische Real-Zeitung für das Jahr. . .*
MW	*Musikalisches Wochenblatt*
NG	*The New Grove Dictionary of Music and Musicians*
NOHM	*The New Oxford History of Music*
NTD	*Neues Theaterjournal für Deutschland*
NTL	Ernst Ludwig Gerber: *Neues historisch-biographisches Lexikon der Tonkünstler*
Pazdírek	Bohumil Pazdírek: *Universal-Handbuch der Musikliteratur*
Plümicke	C. M. Plümicke: *Entwurf einer Theatergeschichte von Berlin*
Pröpper	Rolf Pröpper: *Die Bühnenwerke Johann Friedrich Reichardts*
QL	Robert Eitner: *Quellen-Lexikon*
Reichardt BaRM	Johann Friedrich Reichardt: *Briefe eines aufmerksamen Reisenden, die Musik betreffend*
Riedinger	L. Riedinger: *Karl von Dittersdorf als Opernkomponist*
Riemann OH	Hugo Riemann: *Opern-Handbuch*
RISM	*Répertoire international des Sources Musicales: Einzeldrücke vor 1800*
SADdT	*Erste [–Sechste] Sammlung der vorzüglichsten, noch ungedruckten Arien und Duetten des deutschen Theaters*, ed. Johann Adam Hiller
Schaal	Richard Schaal: *Die vor 1801 gedruckten Libretti des Theatermuseums München*
Schink DF	Johann Friedrich Schink: *Dramaturgische Fragmente*
Schink DM	Johann Friedrich Schink: *Dramaturgische Monate*
Schmid C	Christian Heinrich Schmid: *Chronologie des deutschen Theaters*
Schmid DP	Christian Heinrich Schmid: *Das Parterr*
Schmid T	Christian Heinrich Schmid: *Theater-Chronick*

Schubart *DC*	*Deutsche Chronik*, ed. Christian Friedrich Daniel Schubart
Schütze	Johann Friedrich Schütze: *Hamburgische Theater-Geschichte*
Sonneck	Oscar G. T. Sonneck: *Catalogue of Opera Librettos Printed Before 1800*
Stauder	Wilhelm Stauder: *Johann André: Ein Beitrag zur Geschichte des deutschen Singspiels*
Stieger	Franz Stieger: *Opern-Lexikon*
STM	*Studien für Tonkünstler und Musikfreunde*
Teichmann	Franz Dingelstedt: *Johann Valentin Teichmanns literarischer Nachlass*
TfT	*Taschenbuch fürs Theater*
TJ	*Theater-Journal für Deutschland*
TK	*Theater-Kalender*
TM	*Der Teutsche Merkur*
TSS	*Taschenbuch für Schauspieler und Schauspielliebhaber*
TW	*Theatralisches Wochenblatt*
TZD	*Theater-Zeitung für Deutschland*
UeKS	Christian August von Bertram: *Ueber die Kochische Schauspielergesellschaft*
WNA	*Wöchentliche Nachrichten und Anmerkungen, die Musik betreffend*, ed. Johann Adam Hiller
Wolf.	E. Thiel and G. Rohr: *Kataloge der Herzog-August-Bibliothek Wolfenbüttel*, vol. 14: *Libretti*
ZTK	*Zeitung für Theater und andere schöne Künste*

Library sigla

AUSTRIA

| A-Wgm | Vienna, Gesellschaft der Musikfreunde |
| A-Wn | Vienna, Österreichische Nationalbibliothek: Musiksammlung |

BELGIUM

| B-Bc | Brussels, Conservatoire Royale de Musique |
| B-Br | Brussels, Bibliothèque Royale Albert Ier |

SWITZERLAND

CH-Bmi	Basel, Musikwissenschaftliches Institut der Universität
CH-Bu	Basel, Öffentliche Bibliothek der Universität: Musiksammlung
CH-Zz	Zurich, Zentralbibliothek

GERMANY

D-B	Berlin (West), Staatsbibliothek Preussischer Kulturbesitz
D-Bds	Berlin (East), Deutsche Staatsbibliothek
D-Bhbk	Berlin (West), Staatliche Hochschule für Bildende Kunst
D-Bhm	Berlin (West), Staatliche Hochschule für Musik und Darstellende Kunst
D-BNms	Bonn, Musikwissenschaftliches Seminar der Universität
D-Dl	Dresden, Bibliothek und Museum Löbau
D-Dlb	Dresden, Sächsische Landesbibliothek
D-DS	Darmstadt, Hessische Landes- und Hochschulbibliothek
D-F	Frankfurt, Stadt- und Universitätsbibliothek
D-Fmi	Frankfurt, Musikwissenschaftliches Institut der Johann Wolfgang von Goethe-Universität
D-GOl	Gotha, Forschungsbibliothek [Landesbibliothek]
D-HAh	Halle, Händel-Haus
D-HR	Harburg, Fürstlich Oettingen-Wallerstein'sche Bibliothek
D-KNmi	Cologne, Musikwissenschaftliches Institut der Universität
D-LEm	Leipzig, Musikbibliothek der Stadt
D-Lr	Lüneburg, Ratsbücherei
D-Mbs	Munich, Bayerische Staatsbibliothek
D-Rp	Regensburg, Bischöfliche Zentralbibliothek
D-Rtt	Regensburg, Fürstlich Thurn und Taxis'sche Hofbibliothek
D-SWl	Schwerin, Wissenschaftliche Allgemeinbibliothek [Landesbibliotek]
D-W	Wolfenbüttel, Herzog August Bibliothek
D-WRdn	Weimar, Deutsches Nationaltheater
D-WRtl	Weimar, Thüringische Landesbibliothek: Musiksammlung

FRANCE

F-Pc	Paris, Conservatoire National de Musique

GREAT BRITAIN

GB-Lbm	London, British Library: Reference Division [British Museum]

UNITED STATES OF AMERICA

US-BE	Berkeley, University of California: Music Library
US-Bp	Boston, Public Library: Music Department
US-NH	New Haven, Yale University: School of Music Library

US-NYp   New York, Public Library at Lincoln Center: Library and
                Museum of the Performing Arts
US-PHu   Philadelphia, University of Pennsylvania: Otto E. Al-
                brecht Music Library
US-U   Urbana, University of Illinois Music Library
US-Wc   Washington DC, Library of Congress: Music Division

UNION OF SOVIET SOCIALIST REPUBLICS
USSR-KAu   Kaliningrad [Königsberg], Universitetskaya Biblioteka

Part I

Settings of North German operas, 1766–1799: by composer

AGTHE, CARL CHRISTIAN (1762–97)

Der Spiegelritter
August von Kotzebue (Singspiel [L] – 3)
Ballenstädt (1795)

ANDRÉ, JOHANN (1741–99)

Der Alchymist [*Der Liebesteufel*]
August Gottlieb Meissner (Operette [L] – 1)
Berlin (11 Apr 1778) Döbbelins Theater
Excerpt: "Getrocknet die Zähren" *LAD* 2:1 (1781)
Ms.: D-B mus. ms. 603

Der alte Freyer
Johann André (Komische Oper [L] – 1)
Berlin (2 Oct 1775) Döbbelins Theater
[KLA and parts: Offenbach: André, [1776] – no copies survive]
    Stauder gives the date 2 Oct 1776; Sonneck, *Teichmann*, and Graf the one
    shown here. *QL* describes the lost KLA as a "Singspiel in 2 A." and Graf also
    gives the number of acts as 2.

Azakia
Christian Friedrich Schwan (Singspiel [L] – 3)
Berlin (26 Nov 1778) Döbbelins Theater
    Stieger dates the première 26 Oct 1778; Stauder and Graf give the date shown
    above.

Der Barbier von Bagdad [*Der Balbier von Bagdad*]
Johann André (Oper [M] – 2)
Berlin (19 Feb 1783) Döbbelins Theater
Ms.: D-B mus. ms. 610. US-Wc M 1500 A745B3 [copy of preceding]
    QL gives the date as 9 Feb 1783 and the designation as "Singspiel." Graf gives as
    first performance Mainz, 1778.

Belmont und Constanze [*Die Entführung aus dem Serail*]
Christoph Friedrich Bretzner (Operette [L, M] – 3)
Berlin (25 May 1781) Döbbelins Theater
Excerpts: All in *LAD*: "Wer ein Liebchan hat gefunden" 2:2 (1781), Romanze: "Im
    Mohrenland gefangen war" 2:2 (1781), "Ah! mit freudigem Entzücken" 2:2
    (1781), "Durch Zärtlichkeit und Schmeicheln" 2:3 (1782), Duet: "Vivat
    Bachus! Bachus lebe!" 2:3 (1782), Duet: "Hoffnung, Trösterinn im Leiden" 2:3
    (1782), Arie: "O wie ängstlich, o wie feurig" 2:4 (1782), Chor: "Oft wölkt
    stürmisch sich der Himmel" 2:4 (1782), Rondeau: "Traurigkeit ward mir zum
    Loose" 2:4 (1782)

Ms.: D-B mus. ms. 608. US-Wc M 1500 A745E4 [copy of preceding]
A later hand divides the Berlin ms. into four rather than three acts. Stauder and
QL give the première date 26 May 1781. The date given here is that of *Teich-
mann*, Sonneck, and Graf. Facsimile edition of the Berlin ms.: *GGO*, vol. 6

Die Bezauberten [*Peter und Hannchen*]
Johann André (Komische Oper [L] – 1)
Berlin (18 Oct 1777) Döbbelins Theater
Excerpt: "In einem Thal, bey einem Bach" (Romanze) in *LAD* 1:1 (1780) and in Voss's
Musen Almanach für 1778, pp. 68–71.
Ms.: D-B mus. ms. 602 [incomplete]
Ms. excerpt: "In einem Thal, bey einem Bach," D-Mbs autogr. mus. ms. 2774, vol. 2,
f. 14
   The Berlin ms. contains only numbers 1 to 9 and the first page of number 10
   (out of a total of 19 numbers).

Claudine von Villa Bella
Johann Wolfgang von Goethe (Schauspiel mit Gesang [L] – [3])
unperformed (composed 1778)
Excerpts: "Alle Freuden, alle Gaben" [A 1043] and "Es war ein Bube frech genug"
(Romanze) [A 1044] in *TK* 1778
   Nothing beyond these two songs is known of André's dealings with Goethe's
   libretto. *TK* 1777 reported that André was working on the opera.

Eins wird doch helfen [*Die Werbung aus Liebe*]
Johann Daniel Sander (Komische Oper [L] – 2)
Berlin (24 Aug 1782) Döbbelins Theater
Ms.: D-DS mus. ms. 28

Elmine
Freiherr Carl Wilhelm von Drais (Singspiel [M–KLA] Schauspiel mit Gesang
[L, M–Ms] – 3)
Berlin (14 Feb 1782) Döbbelins Theater
KLA: Berlin: Maurer, 1782 [A 1045]
Excerpt: Aria "Athme lieb und ruh" and Overture in Jakob Martius: *Sammlung ver-
mischter Clavierstücke . . . auf das Jahr 1783*, pt. 1 (Nüremberg, [1784]) [GB-Lbm]
Ms: US-Wc M 1500 A745E35

Erwin und Elmire
Johann Wolfgang von Goethe (Schauspiel mit Gesang [L] – [2])
Berlin (17 July 1775) Döbbelins Theater
KLA and Parts: Offenbach: André, [1776] [A 1046]
Excerpts: "Das Veilchen" (Romanze) and "Ein Schauspiel für Götter" in *Iris* 2:3
(March 1775): between pp. 182–3 and 190–1
Ms: D-B mus. ms. 600. US-Wc M 1500 A745E6 [copy of preceding]. D-Rtt (parts). A-
Wn s.m. 1041.
   The KLA and parts are announced in *BTC*: 588 and in *Iris* 3:3 (June, 1775):
   238–9. See also *BTC*: 758. It is possible that André's music was used for an
   amateur performance at Frankfurt am Main in May 1775.

Kurze Thorheit ist die beste [*Alter schützt für Thorheit nicht*]
Friedrich Ludwig Wilhelm Meyer (Operette – 1)
Berlin (18 Jul 1780) Döbbelins Theater
Excerpts: Rondo: "Es erwacht an jedem Morgen die Natur zu neuer Lust" in *LAD* 1:2
(1780), "Ich will sie nehmen, sie ist schon mein" 1:3 (1781)

Ms.: D-B mus. ms. 606. D-Rtt.
Riemann *OH* incorrectly identifies *Der alte Freyer* as an alternate title of this work. An earlier version was first performed under the title *Alter schützt für Thorheit nicht* at Mannheim on 20 Jun 1779.

Laura Rosetti
Bernhard Christoph d'Arien (Schauspiel mit Gesang [L] – 3)
Berlin (23 May 1778) Döbbelins Theater
KLA: Offenbach: André, [1778] [A 1047]
Excerpt: Romanze: "Bey kriegerischer Trompetenklang" in *TK* 1774 [A 1048]
Ms.: D-B mus. ms. 604
Stieger gives as date of first performance 21 May 1778.

Der Liebhaber als Automat [*Der Automat, Das Automat, Die redende Maschine, Der Antiquitätenhändler, Der Antiquitätensammler*]
Johann André (Operette [L –1738 – 1784] Singspiel [L–1787] – 1)
Berlin (11 Sep 1782) Döbbelins Theater
Ms.: D-B mus. ms. 609. D-Bhbk. D-DS mus. ms. 29
QL attributes this opera incorrectly to Johann Anton André.

Die Schadenfreude
Christian Felix Weisse (Kleines Lustspiel für Kinder mit Liederchen [L] – 1)
Berlin (1778)
Ms.: D-B mus. ms. 611
The above date is Stauder's. Stieger gives a 1780 private performance as the première.

Das tartarische Gesetz
Johann Friedrich Wilhelm Gotter (Schauspiel mit Gesang [L] – 3)
Berlin (31 May 1779) Döbbelins Theater
Excerpts: In *LAD*: "Noch weiss ich nicht wie mir geschah!" (recitative and aria) 1:1 (1780), Duet: "In deinem Arme leben" 2:2 (1781)
Ms.: D-B mus. ms. 605. B-Bc ms. 2376. D-Rtt.
See *BTC*: 758. The Brussel ms. is an "opéra en deux actes," and the ms. formerly at Mannheim was also described by Walter as a two-act opera.

Das wütende Heer [*Das Mädchen im Thurme*]
Christoph Friedrich Bretzner (Operette [L] – 3)
Berlin (22 Nov 1780) Döbbelins Theater
Excerpts: In *LAD*: Duet: "Unsre Freundschaft zu erneuen" 1:3 (1781), Ariette: "Schönheit, Jugend, Anmuth, Tugend" 1:3 (1781), Romanze: "Graf Siegfried einst in Welschland kam" 1:3 (1781), Lied: "Dieser sanfte, gute Junge" 1:4 (1781), "Holder Schlaf, du Freund der Matten" 1:4 (1781), Chor: "Nach überstandnen Schmerz und Leiden" 2:1 (1781)
Ms.: D-B mus. ms. 607
Ms. excerpts: "Unsre Freundschaft zu erneuern" (duet) and "Wie dank ich dem Glücke" in D-Lr (KLA)
QL incorrectly states that this opera has only two acts. The score it lists as being in D-Mbs is no longer there.

ANNA AMALIA, DUCHESS OF SACHSEN-WEIMAR (1739–1807)

Erwin und Elmire
Johann Wolfgang von Goethe (Schauspiel mit Gesang [L] – 2)
Weimar (24 May 1776)

Ms: D-WRtl sig. nr. 5. A-Wn ms. 16740
Stieger gives the date of first performance as 1 Mar 1777. A revised version,
with Corona Schröter as the heroine, was first given on that date. A modern,
not entirely reliable KLA, edited by Max Friedländer, appeared at Leipzig in
1921.

Das Jahrmarktsfest zu Plundersweilern
Johann Wolfgang von Goethe (Schönbartsspiel [L] – 2)
Weimar (20 Oct 1778) Liebhaber-Theater at Schloss Ettersburg
Ms.: D-WRtl sig. nr. 29
The première date is Anna Amalia's birthday. The score was orchestrated by
Karl von Seckendorff.

AUMANN, DIEDERICH CHRISTIAN (dates unknown)

Das neue Rosenmädchen
unknown (2 acts)
Hamburg (1789)

BACH, JOHANN CHRISTOPH FRIEDRICH (1732–95)

Brutus
Johann Gottfried von Herder (Drama zur Musik [L] – [3])
Bückeburg (27 Feb 1774) Court Theater

Philoktetes
Johann Gottfried von Herder (Scenen mit Gesang [L] – 1)
Bückeburg (1775)

BACHMANN, GOTTLOB (1763–1840)

Don Sylvio von Rosalva [*Der Sieg der Natur über die Schwärmerey*]
Samuel Gottlieb Bürde (Komische Oper [M] – 2)
Brunswick (1797)
KLA: Brunswick: Verlag des Musicalischen Magazins auf der Höhe, [1797]
    The KLA is not listed in *RISM*. *MGG* gives its date as [1796]. There is a copy at
    GB-Lbm.

Phaedon und Naide [*Der redende Baum*]
Johann Georg Jacobi (Singspiel [L] – 2)
Brunswick (1795)

Der Tod des Orpheus [*Orpheus und Euridice*]
Johann Georg Jacobi (Singspiel [L] – 3)
Brunswick (1798)
[KLA: Halle and Leipzig: Selbstverlag, 1795. Brunswick: Verlage des Musicalischen
Magazins auf der Höhe, n.d.]
    The Halle–Leipzig KLA is mentioned in *MGG*, the Brunswick KLA in *QL*.
    Neither is listed in *RISM*.

BAUMGARTEN, GOTTHILF VON (1741–1813)

Das Grab des Mufti [*Die beyden Geizigen*]
August Gottlieb Meissner (Komische Oper [M] – 2)
Breslau (1776) Wäser Company
KLA: Breslau: J. E. Meyer, 1778 [B 1374]

Zemire und Azor
Karl Emil Schubert (Romantisch–komische Oper [M] – 4)
Breslau (18 May 1776) Wäser Company
KLA: Breslau, J. F. Korn der Ältere, 1775 [B 1375]. 2nd ed. [B 1376]
    Stieger apparently dates the première from the KLA (1775); that given above is
    from Sonneck. The KLA was edited by "W.", that is, Ernst Wilhelm Wolf.

BECKMANN, JOHANN FRIEDRICH GOTTLIEB (1737–92)

Lukas und Hannchen
Johann Joachim Eschenburg (Operette [L] – 1)
Brunswick (1768) Fürstliches Kleines Theater

BENDA, FRIEDRICH LUDWIG (1752–92)

Der Barbier von Seville [*Die vergebliche Vorsicht, Die unnöthige Vorsicht*]
Gustav Friedrich Wilhelm Grossmann (Komische Oper [M] Lustspiel . . . mit unter-
mischten Gesängen [L] – 4)
Leipzig (7 May 1776)
KLA: Leipzig: Schwickert, 1779 [B 1847]
Ms.: D-B mus. ms. 1321
Ms. excerpt: "Dir unbekannt und ohne sich" (accomp. violin and bass) USSR-KAu
    See *BTC*: 700. Stieger gives the première place and date as Dresden 8 Jun 1776,
    Neues Theater vor dem schwarzen Tor. That given above is from *NG*. The over-
    ture has been recently issued in full score, edited by Edvard Fendler (London:
    Boosey & Hawkes, 1967).

Louise
Friedrich Ernst Jester (Komische Operette [M] Oper [L] – 3)
Königsberg (16 Jan 1791) Ackermanns Theater
KLA: Königsberg: F. Nicolovius, [1791] [B 1848]
    Hagen gives the place and date of the première as Danzig 1789. *QL* dates the
    KLA as [1790]. The date given here is from *NG*, Hagen, GB-Lbm and US-Wc.

Mariechen
Friedrich Ernst Jester (Komische Operette [M] – 3)
Königsberg (1791)
KLA: Königsberg: Hartung, [1792] [B 1849]
    This opera is a continuation of the same collaborators' *Louise*. *NG* gives the
    date as 1792, possibly from the date of publication. The KLA was prepared by
    Johann Wilhelm Schultz, apparently after Benda's death.

Die Verlobung
Friedrich Ernst Jester (Singspiel)
Königsberg (1789)
    NG gives the première date as 1790.

BENDA, FRIEDRICH WILHELM HEINRICH (1745–1814)

Alceste
Christoph Martin Wieland (Singspiel [L] – 3)
Berlin (15 Jan 1786) Corsika'scher Saal (concert performance)
    The above number of acts is from Stieger. *NG* lists 2. Wieland's original
    libretto was in 5 acts.

Orpheus
Gottfried Ferdinand von Lindemann (Singspiel [M] – 3)
Berlin (16 Jan 1785) Corsika'scher Saal (concert performance)
KLA: Berlin: Selbstverlage [Rellstabs Druckerey], 1787 [B 1852]
> The KLA is marked "No. IX," i.e., opus 9 (of the printing house, not the composer). The set of parts once in D-DS, listed in *QL*, was destroyed in World War II.

BENDA, GEORG ANTON [JIŘÍ ANTONÍN] (1722–95)

Das Findelkind [*Unverhofft kömt oft*]
Christian Felix Weisse (Operette [M] – 1)
unperformed
KLA: Leipzig: Schwickert, [1787] [B 1875]

Der Holzhauer [*Die drey Wünsche*]
Johann Friedrich Wilhelm Gotter and Wulff (Comische Operette [M] – 1)
Gotha (2 Jan 1778) Court Theater
Short score: Leipzig: Schwickert, 1777 [B 1876]
Ms.: D-B mus. ms. 135b. D-Dlb. US-Bp M.320,6
> See *BTC*: 668, 700, 881–2. *Teichmann's* date for the première, 20 Feb 1774, is in fact that of Johann August Christoph Koch's setting. Gotter's text uses the musical numbers of a 1772 Berlin libretto with slight modifications and omissions. Schlösser, *Friedrich Wilhelm Gotter*, ascribes this earlier version to a certain Wulff.

Der Jahrmarkt [*Der Dorfjahrmarkt, Lukas und Bärbchen*]
Johann Friedrich Wilhelm Gotter [2-act version adapted by Johann Jakob Engel] (Komische Oper [M] – 1 [later 2])
1-act version: Gotha (10 Feb 1775) Seyler Company
2-act version: Leipzig (26 Apr 1775) Seyler Company
KLA [*Der Dorfjahrmarkt*]: Leipzig: Dyk, 1776 (2 acts) [B 1873]
[*Lukas und Bärbchen*]: Leipzig: Schwickert, [1786] (1 act) [B 1874]
Ms.: D-B mus. ms. 1355. Us-Wc M 1500 B46D5 (copy of preceding). D-SWl
(2 scores and parts). (2 acts)
D-B mus. ms. 1358. A-Wn ms. 18635. (1 act)
> The later two-act version incorporates musical additions by Johann Adam Hiller. The alternate title *Der Dorfjahrmarkt* was proposed at that time in order to distinguish the two versions. A modern edition of the full score incorporating everything from the work's different versions was edited by Theodor W. Werner and appeared in *Denkmäler deutscher Tonkunst*, series 1, vol. 64. The Schwickert KLA includes an accompanying violin part. See also *BTC*: 588, 622–3, 700.

Romeo und Julie [*Julie und Romeo*]
Johann Friedrich Wilhelm Gotter (Oper [M-KLA] Ernsthafte Oper [M-MS] Schauspiel mit Gesang [L] – 3)
Gotha (25 Sep 1776) Court Theater
KLA: Leipzig: Dyk, 1778 [B 1883]. 2nd ed. Leipzig: Dyk, 1784 [B 1884]
Ms.: D-B mus. mss. 1354 and 1354/1. D-Dlb. D-DS mus. ms. 94. A-Wn ms. 18690. US-Wc M 1500 B46R5. D-Mbs St. th. 135b. D-Rtt (score and parts)
Ms. excerpts: D-G01 mus. 4°44b/12. US-NYp Drexel 5046
> See *BTC*: 668, 700, 883. Pazdírek lists an undated Haslinger print of the recita-

tive and aria "Ihn wieder zu seh'n." The ms. at Munich is a copy in German, although its title page reads "Atto 1mo 2do et 3^{tio} Romeo et julia. . ." and falsely ascribes the opera to Zingarelli. The set of parts and score in Regensburg are described on the title page as "orchestrated ("in stimen gesetzt") from Benda's keyboard reduction by Th[eodor]B. von Schacht, Regensburg 1779." Facsimile edition of the Berlin ms. 1354: *GGO*, vol. 5.

Walder
Johann Friedrich Wilhelm Gotter (Ernsthafte Operette [M] Operette [L–1776] Ein ländliches Schauspiel mit Gesang [L–1778] Singspiel [L–1791] – 1)
Gotha (23 Feb 1776) Court Theater
Short score: Gotha: C. W. Ettinger, 1777 [B 1886]
Excerpts: In *SADdT*: "Selbst die glücklichste der Ehen" (Rondo) 1:30–2, "Hütte, die mich liebreich deckte" 4:43–6
Ms.: D-B mus. ms. 1353. D-Bds autogr. part. 1776. D-Mbs mus. ms. 1183. D-DS mus. ms. 95 (parts). D-SWl (score and parts). US-Bp M.220.11
Ms. excerpts: "Hütte, die mich liebreich deckte" and "Ja, mein Vater! Ja, mein Richter! Ich bein strafbar" D-Mbs mus. ms. 8739, nos. 86–7. Aria "Wer dem Schiffbruch nahe war" in D-HR (parts).

BERGT, CHRISTIAN GOTTLOB AUGUST (1771–1837)

List gegen List
Christoph Friedrich Bretzner (Operette [M] – 1)
Leipzig (12 Sep 1797)
KLA: Leipzig: Breitkopf, [1802]
Ms.: B-Bc ms. 2380. A-Wn (KLA)
    GB-Lbm dates the Breitkopf KLA [1801].

BIANCHI, ANTONIO (1758–after 1817)

Die Insel der Alcina
Carl Alexander Herklots (Oper – 2)
Berlin (16 Feb 1794) National Theater
Ms.: D-SWl

BIEREY, GOTTLOB BENEDICT (1772–1840)

Der Äpfeldieb
Christoph Friedrich Bretzner (Operette [L] – 1)
Leipzig (1793)
    MGG puts the work's première at Breslau in 1809, Graf at Leipzig in 1798. The place and date here are from Stieger.

Die böse Frau
Carl Alexander Herklots (Komisches Original-Singspiel [L] – 2)
Stettin (1792)

Die Ehestandskandidaten [*Die Parodie aus dem Stegreife*]
Johann Christoph Kaffka (Komisches Singspiel [L] – 2)
Leipzig (Feb 1796)

Jery und Bätely
Johann Wolfgang von Goethe (Singspiel [L] – 1)
Leipzig (1795)
    MGG puts the première at Dresden in 1803.

Die Liebe im Lager
unknown (Singspiel – 1)
Leipzig (1792)
  Riemann *OH* places the first performance at Leipzig in 1796 by the Seconda
  Company.

Liebesabentheuer [*Der betrogene Betrüger*; *Wer zuletzt lacht, lacht am besten*]
Gustav Friedrich Wilhelm Grossmann (Komische Oper – 1)
Dresden (Oct 1794)
  MGG places the première at Breslau in 1817.

Der Mädchenmarkt
Carl Alexander Herklots (Singspiel [L] – 2)
Leipzig (1794)
  MGG describes this as a one-act opera first given at Vienna in 1805.

Die offene Fehde
unknown (3 acts)
Leipzig (1794)

Phaedon und Naide [*Der redende Baum*]
Johann Georg Jacobi (Singspiel [L] – 2)
Leipzig (1793)

Der Schlaftrunk
Christoph Friedrich Bretzner (Oper [L] – 2)
Dresden (4 Aug 1797) Seconda Company
KLA excerpts: *Favorit-Gesänge mit Clavierbegleitung aus dem Schlaftrunk von
Bierei* [3 arias], Leipzig: C. F. Lehrmann, n.d. [Exemplar: US-Wc]
  Stieger and *MGG* place the première at Ballenstädt in 1797 (where it was first
  given on 1 December). The date above is from Sonneck.

Der Zauber-Hain [*Das Land der Liebe*]
Th. Berling (Romantisch–komische Oper – 3)
Dresden (8 May 1799) Seconda Company
  Stieger places the première at Ballenstädt in 1799. Our date and place are from
  Sonneck. Riemann *OH* gives the alternate title incorrectly as *Das Band der
  Liebe*.

BIRNBACH, CARL JOSEPH (1751–1805)

Die Fischerweiber in Paris
unknown
Breslau (1790)

Saphire
unknown
Breslau (1788)

BORNHARDT, JOHANN HEINRICH CARL (1774–1840)

Der Eremit auf Formentera
August von Kotzebue (Singspiel [M] Schauspiel mit Gesang [L] – 2)
Brunswick (1797)
KLA: Brunswick: im Musicalischen Magazin auf der Höhe, [1797]
  The KLA is not listed in *RISM*. A copy is at GB-Lbm, which supplies the date
  of publication given here.

Sultan Wampum [*Schah Wampum, Die Wünsche*]
August von Kotzebue (Orientalisches Scherzspiel mit Gesang [L] – 3)
Brunswick (1796)
[KLA: Brunswick; im Musicalischen Magazin auf der Höhe, 1796]
     No copies of the KLA, listed in *QL*, seem to survive. The one *QL* located at
Darmstadt was destroyed in World War II. As with the preceding opera by
Bornhardt, the date and place of the première are possibly those of publication
instead.

BURGMÜLLER, AUGUST FRIEDRICH [JOHANN AUGUST FRANZ] (1766–1824)

Das hätt' ich nicht gedacht!
Christian August Vulpius (Singspiel)
Weimar (1788) Bellomo Troupe
     The place and date are supplied by Riemann *OH*. *ATL* calls the work an
Operette.

CARTELLIERI, CASIMIR ANTONIO (1772–1807)

Die Geisterbeschwörung
Carl Alexander Herklots (Komisches Singspiel [M] – 1 [later 2])
Berlin (18 May 1793) National Theater
KLA excerpt: Romanze: "Ein reicher Junker Sausewind" in *Sammlung vorzüglicher Gesänge aus Opern*, vol. 5 (Berlin: Rellstab, n.d.)
Ms: D-B mus. ms. 3140
     In the ms. an extra number was inserted at the beginning on six folios with the
heading "Zweyter Aufzug [and in another hand:] der Geisterbeschwörung"
which led *QL* to describe the ms. inaccurately as only the second act. The new
number is in fact to be inserted between the old numbers 11 and 12.

DAVANDER (dates unknown)

Julie
F. G. von Nesselrode? (Lustspiel mit Gesang [L] – 3)
Dresden (1781)

DITTERSDORF, CARL DITTERS VON (1739–99)

Don Quixotte der Zweite [*Don Chisciotto*]
Carl Ditters von Dittersdorf (Komisches Singspiel [L] – 2)
Oels (4 Feb 1795) Herzogliches Hoftheater
Ms.: D-Dlb (autograph). US-Wc M 1500 D61D5 (copy of the preceding)
     Krebs claims in *Dittersdorfiana* that this opera was "originally in Italian but
also translated into German" (p. 122).

Das Gespenst mit der Trommel [*Geisterbanner*]
Carl Ditters von Dittersdorf (Deutsches komisches Singspiel [L] – 2)
Oels (16 Aug 1794) Herzogliches Hoftheater
Ms.: A-Wgm (2nd act only). D-Dlb (autograph). D-B mus. ms. 5021
     The Berlin ms. is in West Berlin, not D-Bds as *NG* states.

Gott Mars [*Der eiserne Mann, Der Hauptmann von Bärenzahn, Der Wechsel Gott Mars*]

Carl Ditters von Dittersdorf (Komisches Singspiel [L] – 2)
Oels (30 May 1795) Herzogliches Hoftheater
Ms.: D-Dlb (autograph)
> The opera was produced in a revised version at Oels in 1795 under the alternate title *Der Wechsel Gott Mars*. The autograph at Dresden carries the date 1791.

Die lustigen Weiber von Windsor
Georg C. Römer (Singspiel [L] – 2)
Oels (25 Jun 1796) Herzogliches Hoftheater
Ms.: D-Dlb. US-Wc M 1500 D61L7 (copy of the preceding)
> Krebs, *Dittersdorfiana*, errs in ascribing the text to Herklots. Stieger gives an erroneous date (25 Jun 1798). Riemann *OH* places the première at Vienna in 1796. The place and date given here are from *MGG* and Riedinger.

Der Mädchenmarkt
Carl Alexander Herklots (Singspiel [L] – 3)
Oels (18 Apr 1797) Herzogliches Hoftheater
Ms: D-Dlbs (autograph)
> The same opera was given as an Italian opera buffa in 1798 as *Il mercato delle ragazze*.

Der Schah von Schiras
after August von Kotzebue (Komische Oper – 2)
Oels (15 Sep 1795) Herzogliches Hoftheater
Ms.: D-Dlb (autograph)
> Stieger gives an erroneous date for the première (15 Jul 1795).

Ugolino
Carl Ditters von Dittersdorf? (Tragische Oper – 2)
Oels (11 Jun 1796) Herzogliches Hoftheater
Ms.: D-Dlb (autograph)
> *MGG* follows Riedinger in calling this an "ernsthaftes Singspiel."

DROBISCH, J. F. (*fl.* 1790–3)

Der blinde Ehemann
Johann Friedrich Jünger (Operette [L] – 2)
Lübeck (Oct 1791)

DUNKEL, FRANZ (1769–1845)

Lieb' um Liebe [*Die Flucht nach Asien*]
K. A. Zschiedrich (Romantisch–komische Oper [L] – 2)
Dresden (17 Jun 1796) Seconda Company

EBELL, HEINRICH KARL (1775–1824)

Der Schutzgeist
unknown (4 acts)
Berlin (1798)

Seliko und Berissa [*Die Tugend unter Wilden*]
Kinderling (Singspiel – 4)
Berlin (1799 ?)
> All the above information comes from Riemann *OH*.

EBERS, KARL FRIEDRICH (1770–1836)

Die Blumeninsel [*Die bestrafte Schöne, Die bestrafte Spröde*]
unknown (Oper [M])
Brunswick (1797)
KLA excerpt: Aria of Ruttilio, "Ein Auge, das mir Liebe lacht," no. 22 in *Auswahl der besten Kompositionen*, ed. Johann Heinrich Olbers (Hamburg, n.d.) [exemplar at D-Lr]
Ms.: "Ouverture und Gesänge aus der Oper" (KLA) US-Bp M.225.26, no. 1

Der Eremit auf Formentera
August von Kotzebue (Schauspiel mit Gesang [L] – 2)
Schwerin (1793)
> Stieger gives the place and date as Stralsund 1794. The one supplied here is from the dedication letter in Ebers' cantata *Das Lob des Höchsten* (ms. at D-SWl, see Kade II:371), dated Schwerin, 20 Sep 1794, which begins: "Most gracious Sovereign and Lady! Animated by the high favor, whereby Your Ducal Eminence recently deigned to attend the performance of *Der Eremit auf Formentera*, composed by me in the past year. . . " Later he adds the interesting remark: "*Der Eremit auf Formentera* was one of my first efforts at composition and, with such weak assistance from the local orchestra and the doleful singing of the actors who are here now, could scarcely have received the approbation of your Ducal Eminence."

Der Liebeskompass
unknown (Singspiel)
Brunswick (1797)

EBERWEIN, TRAUGOTT MAXIMILIAN (1775–1831)

Szenen der Vorwelt
unknown (Komische Oper – 1)
Rudolstadt (1799)

EHRENBERG (?–1790)

Die Alpenhütte
unknown
Dessau? (*ca.* 1780)
KLA excerpt: "Adelaide" in *TK* 1781
> The composer may possibly be identical with Georg Carl Claudius, who used the pseudonym Franz Ehrenberg and also set some poems by Reichard, the editor of *TK*. The following item, however, is most probably by the Ehrenberg who Gerber in *NTL* states died young in 1790.

Azakia
Christian Friedrich Schwan (Singspiel [L] – 3)
Dessau (1790)

ESCHERICH, JOHANN CHRISTOPH (?–*ca.* 1794)

Der Kobold
Daniel Heinrich Thomas (Operette – 2)
Stralsund (Nov 1777) Ilgener Company
> *QL* gives the date as 1779.

ESSIGER (dates unknown)

Barbier und Schornsteinfeger
Autenrieth (1 act)
Lübben (1798)

Sultan Wampum [*Die drei Wünsche*]
August von Kotzebue (Orientalisches Scherzspiel mit Gesang [L] – 3)
Lübben (1797)

EULE, CARL DIEDRICH (1776–1827)

Der verliebte Werber
unknown (Oper [L] – 2)
Hamburg (10 Sep 1799) Theater bei der Gänsemarkt
    The ms., according to *MGG*, has been missing since 1945.

FEIGE, JOHANN GOTTLIEB (1748–?)

Der Frühling [*Das Fest der Flora*]
Johann Martin Kellner
Breslau (1775)
    Possibly an occasional piece.

Die Kirmess [*Die Eifersucht auf dem Lande*]
Johann Martin Kellner
Breslau (1775)

FISCHER, KARL LUDWIG (1743–?)

Der bestrafte Hochmuth
unknown (Komische Oper – 1)
Leipzig (22 Dec 1773) Fischer Company
    This is probably identical with a work given at Osnabrück on 8 March 1780 by
    the second Wäser Company, *Der bestrafte Hochmuth, oder Johann der
    Scherenschleifer.*

FLEISCHER, FRIEDRICH GOTTLOB (1722–1806)

Braut, Friseur, Hexe und Advocat in einer Person
unknown (Komische Verkleidungs-Operette – 2)
Berlin (21 Apr 1777) Döbbelins Theater
    Stieger calls this an Oper in one act.

Das Orackel
Christian Fürchtegott Gellert (Operette [M] – 2)
Brunswick (1771)
KLA: Brunswick: Fürstliche Waisehaus-Buchhandlung, 1771 [F 1119]
    Stieger's place and date of the première may be those of publication.

FLIESS, J. B. (*fl.* 1768–98)

Die Regata zu Venedig [*Die Liebe unter den Gondolieren*]
Samuel Gottlieb Bürde (Oper [M] Singspiel [L] – 2)

Berlin (3 Aug 1798) National Theater
Ms.: D-B mus. ms. 6430
   It is not known who revised Bürde's three-act text for Fliess. Stieger gives the
   composer's name as Wilhelm Fliess, *QL* and the ms. as D. J. B. Fliess (but the
   D. stands for "Dr."). The date of the première was the birthday of Friedrich
   Wilhelm III. Fliess's opera was given only twice at Berlin.

FLORSCHÜTZ, EUCHARIUS (1756-1831)

Richter und Gärtnerin
unknown (Operette)
Rostock (1790)
   QL dates the opera 1792.

FRISCH (dates unknown)

Fräulein von Ueberklug und Herr Gleichzu
unknown (Operette - 2)
Brunswick (9 Jan 1769) Kleines Fürstliches Theater

FRISCHMUTH, JOHANN CHRISTIAN (1741-90)

Clarisse [*Das unbekannte Dienstmädchen*]
Johann Christian Bock (Komische Operette [L] - 3)
Berlin (26 May 1775) Kochs Theater
Ms.: D-B mus. ms 6670 (KLA)
   Stieger gives the date as 16 Jun 1775; *Teichmann*, Graf, *QL*, and *MGG* the one
   supplied here. The ms. is dated 1771, which is the year Bock's libretto first
   appeared.

Der Kobold
Daniel Heinrich Thomas (Operette - 2)
unperformed

Die kranke Frau
Daniel Heinrich Thomas (Singspiel - 1)
Berlin (7 Jul 1773) Kochs Theater
   This work is not listed by Graf in his catalogue of Koch's repertory.

Das Monden-Reich
unknown (Operette [L] - 3)
Berlin (1769) Döbbelin Company, Theater Monbijou

GESTEWITZ, FRIEDRICH CHRISTOPH (1753-1805)

Die Liebe ist sinnreich
unknown (Operette - 1)
Dresden (27 Nov 1781)
Excerpts: 2 arias in Hiller's *Arien und Duetten des deutschen Theaters* (Leipzig, 1781)
Ms.: B-Bc ms. 2392
   See *BTC*: 840.

Der Meyerhof
unknown (Operette)

Leipzig (20 Sep 1780)
Excerpt: "Palläste blenden, Thronen glänzen" in *SADdT* 6:28–32.

GRÜGER, JOSEF (?-1814)

Hass und Aussöhung [*Hass und Versöhnung, Die verfolgte und triumphirende Liebe*]
Ernst Ferdinand Rordorf (Schauspiel mit Gesang [L] – 4)
Breslau (1797)
KLA: Glatz: E. F. Rudorf, n.d. [G 4765]
[Score and KLA: Breslau: Adolph Gehr, 1798]
    The Breslau score and KLA have not been traced.

GÜRRLICH, JOSEF AUGUST (1761-1817)

Das Inkognito
Carl Alexander Herklots (Singspiel [L] – 1)
Berlin (9 Nov 1797) National Theater
    MGG places the première on 9 Dec 1797 with a note that the opera had been composed in 1792. The opera was given only three times. The Berlin ms. mentioned in *QL* (D-B mus. ms. 8790) was lost during World War II.

HAACK, FRIEDRICH WILHELM (1760-1827)

Die Geisterinsel
Johann Friedrich Wilhelm Gotter (Singspiel [L] – 3)
Stettin (1798)
    Stieger gives the erroneous première date of 1794.

HALBE, JOHANN AUGUST (dates unknown)

Die Liebe auf der Probe [*Die Liebesprobe*]
Johann August Halbe (Komische Operette [M, L] – 3)
Mitau (1781)
Ms.: D-B mus. ms. 9290.
    The Berlin ms. describes this as "a comic operetta in three acts with retention of Neefe's melodies" and carries the place and date given above. Neefe's music to the nine numbers in d'Arien's *Heinrich und Lyda* is retained in this opera, with the text of the Romanze rewritten, reducing it from fifteen to ten quatrains. An entirely new episode forms the second act of Halbe's opera, and the material of the original is stretched out to fill acts one and three. There are eleven new musical numbers composed by Halbe.

HALTER, WILHELM FERDINAND (?-1806)

Die Kantons-Revision
Ludwig Adolf Franz Joseph von Baczko (Komische Oper [L] – 3)
Königsberg (1792) Ackermanns Schauspielhaus
Excerpts: Aria "Was seufzen! was klagen!" in *MM* 5. Stück (Nov 1793): 142–3, Aria "Unser Glück macht Fröhlichkeit" in *BmZ* 47. Stück (7 Dec 1793): 188
    Stieger gives a première date of 1794, but the two publications listed above make Riemann *OH*'s, given here, more likely.

HANKE, KARL (1750-1803)

Doktor Fausts Leibgürtel
Bernhard Christoph d'Arien (Oper – 1)
Hamburg (1786)
 MGG places the première at Flensburg in 1794 and identifies this as a two-act opera.

Hüon und Amande
Friederike Sophie Seyler (Romantisches Singspiel [L] – 5)
Schleswig (1789)
 MGG's place and date of première (Flensburg, 1794) are incorrect.

Xaphire [*Haphire*]
Bernhard Christoph d'Arien (Grosse Romantische Oper)
Hamburg (1786)
 Place and date of première are from *MGG* and *NG*. Stieger lists Flensburg, 1793.

HATTASCH [HATAŠ], HEINRICH CHRISTOPH (1756-?)

Der Barbier von Bagdad
Wilhelm Christhelf Siegmund Mylius (Singspiel)
Hamburg (after 1780)
 Stieger sets the première *ca*. 1775, but, since Hattasch was not at Hamburg until 1778, *MGG*'s date is to be preferred.

Der ehrliche Schweitzer
Caroline Luise von Klenke (Schauspiel [L] – 2)
Hamburg (1780) Theater bei der Gänsemarkt
[Excerpts: Recitative, aria, rondo, and duet (Hamburg, 1790)]
 The excerpts are mentioned in *MGG*.

Helva und Zeline
unknown (Singspiel)
Hamburg (1795)
Excerpts: Recitative, aria, rondo, and duet (Hamburg: Günther and Böhme, 1796) [H 2349]

HAUSING (dates unknown)

Der Eichenstamm
unknown (Oper)
Stade (Aug 1798)

HELMIG, JOHANN MICHAEL (*fl*. 1770-83)

Der Deserteur
unknown (Singspiel)
Breslau (1772) Theater in der Taschengasse

Das Milchmädchen
unknown (Singspiel)
Breslau (1772) Theater in der Taschengasse

HENSEL, JOHANN DANIEL (*ca.* 1752–?)

Cyrus und Kassandane
Carl Wilhelm Ramler (Singspiel [L, M] – 1)
Halle (1786)
KLA: Halle: Selbstverlag, 1787 [H 5080]

Daphne [*Die Frühlingsfeyer in Arkadien*]
Johann Daniel Hensel (Oper [L] – 3)
Hirschberg (late 1798) concert performance
  Hensel's preface to the printed libretto, dated Hirschberg, February 1799,
  refers to an earlier concert performance of the opera. Stieger gives the preface
  date as the première date, and Riemann *OH* places the first performance at
  Goldberg in 1799.

Die Geisterbeschwörung
Johann Daniel Hensel (Operette [L] – 3)
Hirschberg (1799)

Die Geisterinsel
Johann Daniel Hensel (Singspiel [L] – 4)
Hirschberg (1799)

HILLER, FRIEDRICH ADAM (*ca.* 1767–1812)

Adelstan und Röschen
Johann Friedrich Schink (Trauerspiel [L] – 2)
Güstrow (6 Sep 1792) Theater im Rathause
  Other dates and places of première: *MGG* (Güstrow, 1796), *NG* (Schwerin,
  1796), Riemann *OH* (Schwerin, 1786).

HILLER, JOHANN ADAM (1728–1804)

Der Aerndtekranz
Christian Felix Weisse (Comische Oper [M, L] – 3)
Leipzig (early 1771) Theater am Rannstädter Thor
KLA: Leipzig: J. F. Junius, 1772 [H 5254]
Ms.: D-B mus. ms. 10639. A-Wn ms. 15523. US-Wc M 1500 H65A3 (copy of the
preceding with overture omitted)
  The Viennese ms. is a revision by an unknown editor who tampers a great deal
  with Hiller's orchestration. See also *BTC*: 439–40, 559. Reger's Variationen
  und Fuge über ein lustiges Thema von J. A. Hiller für Orchester, op. 100 (1907)
  are based on "Gehe, guter Peter" from this opera.

Das Denkmal in Arkadien
Christian Felix Weisse (Ländliches Schauspiel für die Jugend mit untermischten
Gesängen [L] – 1)
unperformed (composed *ca.* 1782)

Der Dorfbalbier [*Der Dorfbarbier*]
Christian Felix Weisse (Comische Operette [M] Komische Oper [L] – 2 [earlier 1])
1-act: Leipzig (18 Apr 1771) Theater am Rannstädter Thore
2-act: Leipzig (1 Aug 1771) Theater am Rannstädter Thore
KLA: Leipzig: B. C. Breitkopf & Sohn, 1771 (with *Die Muse*) [H 5255]
Ms.: B-Bc ms. 3505 (KLA)
  See *BTC*: 559. Ten of the arias were set by Hiller's pupil, Christian Gottlob
  Neefe.

Das Grab des Mufti [*Die zwey Geizigen*, *Die beyden Geizigen*]
August Gottlieb Meissner (Komische Oper [L, M] – 2)
Leipzig (17 Jan 1779) Theater am Rannstädter Thore
KLA: Leipzig: Dyck, 1779 [H 5256]. Breslau: Korn, 1781 [H 5257].
Excerpts: In *SADdT*: "Süsses Liebchen, ach, erscheine!" 2:51–3, "Wach auf, geliebter
Schläfer" 4:47–9
Ms. excerpt: Aria of Carl, "Süsses Liebchen, ach, erscheine!" in D-Lr (KLA)
    The première date in Riemann *OH* (1775) is incorrect.

Die Jagd
Christian Felix Weisse (Comische Oper [L, M] – 3)
Weimar (29 Jan 1770) Koch Company
KLA: Leipzig: Breitkopf & Sohn, 1771 [H5258]. 2nd ed. 1772 [H 5259]. 3rd ed. 1776
[H 5260]
Excerpts: *Arien aus der Jagd* (Schleusingen: Müller and Brückner, 1773) [H 5261]. In
SADdT: "Was sind die Menschen nicht für Thoren" 1:53–5 [recomposed for a member
of the Seyler Company, for whom the first version was not deep enough]. In *DOAM*:
"Mein Töffel ist ein Mann für mich," "Wenn ich nur mein Röschen hätte," "Mein
Engelchen, was machst du," "Wie schön war sie," "Du warst zwar sonst ein gutes
Kind," "Schön sind Rosen und Jesmin," pp. 12–19
Mss.: D-B mus. ms. 10638. US-Wc M 1500 H65J3 (copy of the preceding). D-Dlb
(KLA). CH-Zz (parts)
Ms. excerpt: Aria "Du süsser Wohnplatz stiller Freuden!" D-Mbs mus. ms. 8739, no.
41 (KLA)
    See *BTC*: 435, 559. Facsimile edition of the Berlin ms.: *GGO*, vol. 1.

Die Jubelhochzeit [*Das Jubelfest*]
Christian Felix Weisse (Komische Oper [L, M] – 3)
Berlin (5 Apr 1773) Theater in der Behrenstrasse
KLA: Leipzig: J. F. Junius, 1773 [H 5262]
Ms.: D-Dl ms. F/12
    See *BTC*: 559. Neefe wrote a set of keyboard variations on a Romanze from
this opera, "Kunz fand einst einen armen Mann." The Dresden ms., which
belonged to the principal Wäser, includes the song from Weisse's libretto
which Hiller omitted from his printed KLA (act 1, no. 9: "Ich mach' es wie die
grossen Herr'n" for Berthold).

Die kleine Ährenleserinn
Christian Felix Weisse (Operette [M] Lustspiel für Kinder [L] – 1)
no public performance known
KLA: Leipzig: S. L. Crusius, 1778 [H 5263]
Ms.: A-Wn ms. 16175.
    The KLA includes two accompanying violins.

Der Krieg
Christian Felix Welix Weisse and Carl Wilhelm Ramler (Comische Oper [L, M] – 3)
Berlin (17 Aug 1772) Theater in der Behrenstrasse
KLA: Leipzig: B. C. Breitkopf & Sohn, 1773 [H 5264]
    See *BTC*: 559.

Die Liebe auf dem Lande
Christian Felix Weisse (Comische Oper [L, M] – 3)
Leipzig (18 May 1768) Theater am Rannstädter Thore
KLA: Leipzig: B. C. Breitkopf & Sohn, 1769 [H 5265]. 2nd ed. 1770 [H 5266]
Excerpts: In *DOAM*: "Nur für mein Mädchen allein," "Wie wird mir bange," "O wie

sehr liebt mein gutes Hänschen," "So ist denn dies die Liebe," "Ich lieb ihn ja," "Die Liebe die dies Paar entzündet" (Rundgesang), pp. 20–31.
Mss.: D-LEm PM 684 and III 15 17. D-Rtt (KLA)
Ms. excerpt: "Wie wird mir bange!" D-DS 1393/1 (KLA)
    See *BTC*: 436–7, 559.

Lisuart und Dariolette [*Die Frage und die Antwort*]
Daniel Schiebeler (Romantisch–comische Oper [M-KLA–1768] Comische Oper [M-KLA–1769, L-1769–1771–n.d.] Singstück [L-1770–1773] – 2 [later 3])
2-act: Leipzig (25 Nov 1766) Theater am Rannstädter Thore
3-act: Leipzig (7 Jan 1767) Theater am Rannstädter Thore
KLA: Leipzig: B. C. Breitkopf & Sohn, 1768 [H 5267]. 2nd expanded ed. 1769 [H 5268] (both 3-act)
Excerpts: In *WNA*: "Kleine Seelen (o der Schande!)" 1:258–60, Aria: "Bald die Blonde, bald die Braune" 1:265–8. In *Unterhaltungen*: Romanze: "Es war einmal ein Königssohn" 3 (1767): 162, Lied: "Die schöne Morgenröthe" 4 (1767): 1039.
Ms.: B-Bc ms. 2410. D-B mus. ms. 10636. US-Wc M 1500 H65L6 (copy of the preceding). USSR-KAu. D-W. (all 3-act)
Ms. excerpts: Aria: "Die schöne Morgenröthe" D-Mbs mus. ms. 8739, no. 39 (KLA). "Vater vom Entzücken," "Es war einmal ein Königssohn" (Romanze), "Die Prinzessin zu entdecken," "O Bild voll göttlich hoher Reize," "Die schöne Morgenröthe," "Wir fragten uns ohn Unterlass," "Das ganze weibliche Geschlecht," "Der Teufel kam vor vielen Jahren," "Auf ewig würde sie die Meine?" "Frische Lippen, rohe Wangen," "So darf ich dich die Meine nennen?" D-B mus. ms. 106360/2 (KLA)
    See *BTC*: 559. The 1768 edition of the KLA omits the overture.

Lottchen am Hofe [*Lottchen, Das Bauernmägdchen am Hofe*]
Christian Felix Weisse (Comische Oper [L, M] – 3)
Leipzig (24 Apr 1767) Theater am Rannstädter Thore
KLA: Leipzig: B.C. Breitkopf & Sohn, 1769 [H 5269]. 2nd ed. 1770 [H 5270]. 3rd ed. 1776 [H 5271]
Excerpts: Arie: "Lustig zur Arbiet" in *Unterhaltungen* 6 (1768): 152. Aria: "Gürge, nun entsag ich dir" in *WNA* 1:384–6. In *DOAM*: "Lustig zur Arbiet," "O seht doch, seht," "Bald pflück ich mir Rosen," "Gürge, nun entsag ich dir," "Es ist die Mode so," "Ach, ach! sie fliehet," "O macht mir doch von ewger Treu," pp. 32–44
Ms.: D-B mus. ms. 10637. US-Wc M 1500 H65L5 (copy of the preceding) D-Mbs mus. ms. 2806 (KLA) (omits overture and 11 numbers). CH-Zz (parts)
Ms. excerpts: "Schelm, bessre dich!" "Es ist die Mode so" D-DS ms. 1393/1 (KLA)
    See *BTC*: 437–8, 559. The Munich ms. is dated 27 August 1778.

Der lustige Schuster [*Der Teufel ist los*, Part 2]
Christian Felix Weisse (Comische Oper [L, M] – 3)
Leipzig (1766) Koch Company
KLA: Leipzig: J. F. Junius, 1771 [H 5272]
    See *BTC*: 559. Hiller composed only seven arias and a new overture for this revision of Standfuss's comic opera. The 32 numbers still in Standfuss's settings were lightly revised by Hiller in the KLA. Hiller's explanatory preface is reprinted in full by Kade II: 377.

Die Muse
Daniel Schiebeler (Nachspiel [M-KLA] Singstück [M-KLA] Singspiel [M-Ms] Comödie [L] – 1)
Leipzig (3 Oct 1767) Theater am Rannstädter Thore
KLA: Leipzig: B. C. Breitkopf & Sohn, 1771 (with *Der Dorfbalbier*) [H 5255]

Ms.: US-Bp M. 360.16
　　See *BTC*: 588, 836. The KLA designates the opera a "Nachspiel" on its title
　　page, a "Singstück" on the first page of the opera itself.

Poltis [*Das gerettete Troja*]
Gottfried Samuel Brunner and Magister Steinel (Operette [M] Komische Oper [L] – 3)
unperformed
KLA: Leipzig: Schwickert, [1782] [H 5274]. 2nd ed. Leipzig: Georg Emanuel Beer, [*ca.*
1791] [H 5275]
Excerpts: In *SADdT*: "Wenn unser Mund, aus strenger Pflicht" 2:45-8, "Was wollte
der, o Liebe, dich," 2:48-51
Ms. excerpts: "Ich kenne die Pflicht," "Um Spöttern die Freude zu stören," "Ich bin
ihr ergebenster Diener" USSR-KAu (KLA). Aria of Ortyx, "Was wollte der, o Liebe,"
in D-Lr (KLA)

Die verwandelten Weiber [*Der Teufel ist los*, Part 1]
Christian Felix Weisse (Comische Oper [L, M] – 3)
Leipzig (28 May 1766) Theater in Quandt's Court
KLA: Leipzig: J. F. Junius, 1770 [H 5276]
Excerpt: "Ohne Lieb' und ohne Wein" in *Unterhaltungen* 2 (1766): 150
Ms.: D-Mbs mus. ms. 1190 (KLA). USSR-KAu (KLA)
　　See *BTC*: 559. The Munich ms. lacks the overture and presents many variants
　　in the numbers themselves (an aria and a march are omitted, and new settings
　　of the same texts are to be found for eight of the numbers as published in the
　　KLA). The Kaliningrad ms. includes only nos. 1–19 and 24. Stieger places the
　　première at the Theater am Rannstädter Thore, which was not completed until
　　October 1766. Hiller's preface to the KLA is reprinted in full by Kade II:
　　376-7.

HINZE, AUGUST HIMBERT (*fl. ca.* 1797)

Der Eremit auf Formentera
August von Kotzebue (Schauspiel mit Gesang [L] – 2)
Waldenburg in Silesia (8 Jan 1797) Gesellschafts-Bühne
　　Stieger states that this version was in three acts.

Der Spiegelritter
August von Kotzebue (Singspiel [L] – 3)
Waldenburg in Silesia (28 Mar 1797) Gesellschafts-Bühne

HÖNICKE, JOHANN FRIEDRICH (1755-1809)

Die Heyrath aus Liebe
Hermann Ewald Schack (Nachspiel mit Arien und Gesängen [L] – 2)
Gotha (9 Jul 1777) Court Theater

HOLLY, FRANZ ANDREAS [HOLÝ, ONDŘEJ FRANTIŠEK] (*ca.* 1747-83)

Der Bassa von Tunis [*Der Pascha von Tunis, Der Baron von Tunis*]
Karl Franz Henisch (Komische Operette [L] – 1)
Berlin (6 Jan 1774) Theater in der Behrenstrasse
[KLA: Berlin, 1775]
Ms.: B-Bc ms. 2413
　　See *BTC*: 758. The lone copy of the printed KLA mentioned in *QL* (formerly at

D-DS) was destroyed in World War II, and the ms. at D-Dlb mentioned by *QL*
is no longer there.

Das Gärtnermädchen
Johann Carl August Musäus (Komische Oper [L] – 3)
Breslau (1775) Wäser Company

Gelegenheit macht Diebe
Karl Franz Henisch (Operette – 3)
Breslau (1775) Wäser Company

Der Irrwisch
Christoph Friedrich Bretzner (Operette [L] – 3)
Breslau (1779) Wäser Company

Der Kaufmann von Smyrna [*Der Warenhändler von Smyrna, Der Sklavenhändler von Smyrna*]
Christian Friedrich Schwan (Komische Oper [M] Operette [L] – 1)
Berlin (13 Nov 1773) Theater in der Behrenstrasse
KLA: Berlin: C. F. Himburg, 1775 [H 6332]
  Stieger's date of première (20 Mar 1773) is erroneous. *MGG* reproduces a facsimile of the title page of the KLA (vol. 6, cols. 645–6). The Darmstadt ms. mentioned in *QL* was destroyed during World War II. See also *BTC*: 588, 758. As noted in Stieger, the score contains additions by Johann Philipp Kirnberger.

HUNT, KARL (1766–1831)

Das Denkmal in Arkadien
Christian Felix Weisse (Ländliches Schauspiel für die Jugend mit untermischten Gesängen [L] – 1)
Dresden (1791)

HURKA, FRIEDRICH FRANZ (1762–1805)

Das wütende Heer [*Das Mädchen im Thurme*]
Christoph Friedrich Bretzner (Operette [L] – 3)
Schwedt (1788)

KAFFKA, JOHANN CHRISTOPH (1754–1814) [Stage name and pseudonym of JOHANN CHRISTOPH ENGELMANN]

Der Äpfeldieb [*Der Schatzgräber*]
Christoph Friedrich Bretzner (Operette [L] – 1)
Berlin (26 Jun 1780) Döbbelins Theater
Excerpt: Rondo: "Ach, das wahre Glück der Ehen" in *Musikalischer Beytrag für Liebhaber des deutschen Singspiels beym Clavier*, ed. Johann Christoph Kaffka (Breslau: Korn, 1783), pp. 23–6
  Stieger gives the incorrect date of première 20 Jun 1780.

Der blinde Ehemann
Johann Friedrich Jünger (Operette [L] – 2)
Breslau (1788) Wäser Company

Der Guck Kasten [*Das Beste komt zulezt*]
Johann Christoph Kaffka (Komische Operette [L] – 2)
Breslau (1782) Wäser Company

So prellt man alte Füchse
Friedrich Ludwig Wilhelm Meyer, adapted by Johann Christoph Kaffka (Komische Operette [L] – 1)
Breslau (1782) Wäser Company
Stieger lists the number of acts incorrectly as two.

Der Talisman [*Der seltene Spiegel, Die seltsamen Spiegel, Der seltsame Spiegel*]
Christoph Friedrich Bretzner (Romantisch-komische Oper – 3)
Breslau (1789) Wäser Company
Ms.: D-Bhm
MGG states that this opera is in only two acts.

Das wütende Heer [*Das reitende Heer, Das Mädchen im Thurme*]
Christoph Friedrich Bretzner (Operette [L] – 3)
Breslau (Jan 1782) Wäser Company
Ms.: D-Bhm

KALKBRENNER, CHRISTIAN (1755–1806)

Demokrit
C. F. Schröter (Komische Oper [L,M] – 3)
Rheinsberg (1791) Private theater of Prince Heinrich of Prussia
Ms.: D-SWl
Riemann *OH* describes this as a French opera in two acts, given at Rheinsberg in 1792 (where nearly everything was done in French), possibly a subsequent adaptation. The libretto (Schatz 4997) is in German; it mentions the librettist only as the "Verfasser der Grossen Toilette."

KALLENBACH, GEORG ERNST GOTTLIEB (fl. ca. 1780–99)

Ehestandsszenen
unknown (Intermezzo)
Magdeburg (1775) Schauspielhaus

Die Opera buffa
Christoph Friedrich Bretzner (Komisches Singspiel [L] – 2)
Magdeburg (1798) Schauspielhaus

Das Schattenspiel an der Wand
Christoph Friedrich Bretzner (Singspiel [L] – 2)
Magdeburg (1797) Schauspielhaus

Der Schlaftrunk
Christoph Friedrich Bretzner (Komisches Singspiel [L] – 2)
Altona (25 Jun 1799) National Theater
Excerpts: "Liebe, Freundschaft, Kuss und Wein," "Ich sass im Mondenschimmer," "Sanft umstrahlt von Lieb' und Hoffnung" in *Klavierauszüge der Arien und Duetts aus den neuesten beliebtesten Opern*, Part 2 (Halle: Renger, and Magdeburg: Giesecke, n.d.)

KOCH, JOHANN AUGUST CHRISTOPH (fl. ca. 1754–92)

Der Holzhauer [*Die drei Wünsche*]
Johann Joachim Eschenburg (Komische Oper [L] – 1)
Berlin (20 Feb 1774) Theater in der Behrenstrasse

KÖNIG, JOHANN MATTHEUS (dates unknown)

Die Execution
unknown (Singspiel)
Ellrich (1784)

Lilla [*Die Gärtnerin*]
unknown (Lyrisches Schauspiel [M] – 3)
unperformed
KLA: Berlin: Hummel, 1783 [K 1232]
    The aria "Im Grab ist Nacht" in Königs *Lieder mit Melodien. . . Zweite Samm-lung* (Berlin, 1780) is most likely from one of these two operas. The copy of this print at D-SWl carries the ms. notation "Aus einer ungedruckten Operette." Kade (I:450) suggests *Die Execution*, since *Lilla* appeared in print, but this probably occurred after the publication of the collection of songs.

KOPPRASCH, WILHELM (dates unknown)

Einer jagt den Andern
unknown (Singspiel)
Dessau (*ca.* 1795)

KOSPOTH, OTTO CARL ERDMANN FREIHERR VON (1753–1817)

Adrast und Isidore [*Die Serenate*]
Christoph Friedrich Bretzner (Oper [M] Komische Oper [L] – 2)
Berlin (16 Oct 1779) Döbbelins Theater
Excerpts: "Sind wir gleich im Anfang spröde," "Süss ist der Schlaf am Morgen," Romanze: "Es hatte Alexander," "Weiber sind ja keine Engel," "Ach dies Mädchen, welch Entzücken," "Will ich schlummern, will ich schlafen," "Glauben sie mir ohne Schwur" in *Favorit-Gesänge aus den Opern Adrast und Isidore und dem Irrwisch* (Berlin: Rellstab, n.d.) [K 1349]. Rondo: "Sind wir gleich im Anfang spröde" in André, *Lieder und Gesänge*. "Süss ist der Schlaf am Morgen" in *Klavierauszüge der Arien und Duetts aus den neuesten beliebtesten Opern*, Part 2 (Halle: Renger, and Magde-burg: Giesecke, n.d.), pp. 38–44.
Ms.: D-B mus. ms. 11882
    The place and date of première given by Sonneck (Dresden, 22 February 1779, Hoftheater) are those of Friedrich Preu's setting of the same libretto.

Bella und Fernando [*Die Satyre*]
Christian August Vulpius (Operette [L] – 1)
Berlin (1790)

Der Irrwisch [*Endlich hat er sie, Endlich fand er sie*]
Christoph Friedrich Bretzner (Singspiel [L-1784] Operette [L-1787] – 3)
Berlin (2 Oct 1780) Döbbelins Theater
Excerpts: "Irrwischgen tanze mit deinem Glanze," "Schönheit gleicht der jungen Rose," "Liebe hebt zu höhern Freuden," "Göttin der Tugend, hör unser Flehen," "Ach, noch schwank ich halb im Taumel" in *Favorit-Gesänge aud den Opern Adrast und Isidore und dem Irrwisch* (Berlin: Rellstab, n.d.) [K 1349]. In *LAD*: Romanze: "Zu Steffen sprach im Traume" 1:3, "Solch ein Mädchen sah ich nirgends" 2:1
Ms.: D-F
    Pazdírek mentions an "Arie für Tenor" published by Breitkopf.

Karoline [*Die Parforcejagd*]
Carl August Gottlieb Seidel (Operette [L] – 4)
unperformed

Der kluge Jakob
Johann Carl Wezel (Komische Oper [L, M] – 3)
Berlin (26 Feb 1788) National Theater
Ms.: D-B mus. ms. 11880
> *QL* dates the première December 1787. The opera was given only four times at
> Berlin.

Der Mädchenmarkt [*Der Mädchenmarkt zu Ninive*]
Carl Alexander Herklots (Komische Oper [M] Komisches Singspiel [L] – 2)
Hamburg (3 Sep 1793) Theater an der Gänsemarkt
Excerpts: Introduction [overture], Aria: "Verzweiflung tobt in meiner Seele," Duetto:
"Lieb' und Gegenliebe," Recitative and aria: "Die Deinige?. . . Wie oft getäuscht von
einen [*sic*] Schlummerbilde," "Es müsste kein windiges Herrchen," Duetto: "Kund
und zu wissen sey hiermit," "Lautre Wonne füllt mein ganzes Wesen," Chor: "Herzen
ohne Zärtlichkeit, lernet schleunig lieben" in *Ouverture und Gesänge aus der
komischen Oper der Mädchenmarkt* (Leipzig: Breitkopf, [1795]) [K 1350].

KRAUS, BENEDIKT (before 1750–after 1785)

Amors Zufälle
Joseph Bellomo (Operette – 2)
Weimar (1785) Bellomo Company

KRAUSE, CHRISTIAN GOTTFRIED (1719–70)

Der lustige Schulmeister
Christoph Friedrich Nicolai (Singspiel)
Berlin (1766) Schuch Company

KREBS, JOHANN GOTTFRIED (1741–1814)

Crispin und Eliante
unknown (Oper)
Rostock (1776)

LAUBE, ANTON (1718–84)

[As noted in *NG*, the identity of this composer with the Laube who wrote the following operas is not certain.]

Deukalion und Pyrrha [*Die belebte Bildsäule*]
Karl Emil Schubert? (Operette – 2)
Berlin (12 May 1777) Döbbelins Theater

Der italienische Garkoch zu Genua → Josef Schubert

Der Kapellmeister und die Schülerin
Johann Christian Ast (Komische Oper – 2)
Stralsund (Apr 1768) Gilly Company
> Graf and *Teichmann* give as place and date of première a revival at Berlin by
> the Döbbelin Company on 5 May 1777.

Matz und Anna [*Wurst wider Wurst*]
Johann Christian Ast (Komische Farse – 2)
Stralsund (Apr 1768) Gilly Company
    Graf gives as place and date of première a revival at Berlin by the Döbbelin
    Company on 17 Apr 1777.

Pierre und Narciss [*Betrug für Betrug*]
unknown (Komische Oper – 3)
Berlin (10 Apr 1777) Döbbelins Theater
    Graf attributes this score to Anton Zimmermann. Stieger lists the date of
    première incorrectly as 10 Apr 1772.

Der studierte Jäger [*Das Bauernmädchen*]
unknown (Oper – 2)
Berlin (11 Jun 1777) Döbbelins Theater
    Stieger lists the date of première incorrectly as 11 June 1772.

LICHTENSTEIN, KARL AUGUST LUDWIG FREIHERR VON (1767–1845)

Bathmendi
1st version: Ernst Wolfgang Behrisch (Grosse allegorisch–komische Oper – 3)
2nd version: Karl August Ludwig Freiherr von Lichtenstein (Grosse Oper [L] – 2)
1st version: Dessau (26 Dec 1798) Hoftheater
2nd version: Dessau (7 Jul 1799) Hoftheater
KLA excerpt: Duet: "Lasse die Blüthe des Lebens" in *AMZ* 1 (1799) Supplement
No. 10
Ms.: A-Wn (score). A-Wgm (KLA) [2nd version]
Ms. excerpt: "Lasse die Blüthe des Lebens" D-SWl
    Stieger lists the première incorrectly as 16 Dec 1798 and describes it as a two-
    act opera, which is true only of the second version.

Glück und Zufall [*Knall und Fall*]
Karl August Ludwig Freiherr von Lichtenstein (Komische Oper – 2)
Hannover (26 Apr 1793) Grossmann Company
    MGG and Riemann *OH* give *Knall und Fall* (the title Lichtenstein gave to an
    early version of the opera) as the main title. Riemann also claims it was in three
    acts. *QL* puts the première in 1795.

Die steinerne Braut
Karl August Ludwig Freiherr von Lichtenstein (Singspiel [L] – 2)
Dessau (25 Apr 1799) Hoftheater

LÖWE, FRIEDRICH AUGUST LEOPOLD (1777–after 1815)

Rinaldo und Alcina [*Die Insel der Verführung*]
Ludwig Adolf Franz Joseph von Baczko (Oper [M] Komische Oper [L] – 2)
Brunswick (1 Jun 1797)
KLA: Brunswick: Magazin auf der Höhe, [*ca.* 1800]
    The KLA, which is not listed in *RISM*, contains the overture and "Favorit-
    gesänge." An imperfect exemplar is at D-W.

MÜHLE, NIKOLAUS (dates unknown)

Der Äpfeldieb [*Der Schatzgräber*]
Christoph Friedrich Bretzner (Operette [L] – 1)
Danzig (1781) Schauspielhaus

Der Eremit auf Formentera
August von Kotzebue (Schauspiel mit Gesang [L] - 2)
Königsberg (1790)

Fremore und Melime
H. Graf von Spaur (Schauspiel mit Gesang [L] - 3)
Königsberg (1778)

Mit dem Glockenschlag: zwölf! [*Laura*]
Friedrich Julius Heinrich von Soden von Sassanfart (Ernsthafte Operette [L-1781]
Operette [L-1789] - 2)
Mitau (1783)
    The title pages of both librettos state erroneously that the work is in three acts.

Der Schiffbruch
H. Graf von Spaur (Märchen [L] - 4)
Königsberg (1778)

Die schöne Fürstin
August Friedrich Ernst Langbein (Schwank)
Königsberg (1799)

Die Singschule [*Drei Heirathen an einem Tage*]
Ludwig Adolf Franz Joseph von Baczko (Komische Oper [L] - 3)
Königsberg (1794) Ackermanns Theater

MÜLLER, KARL WILHELM (*ca.* 1769-1819)

Don Sylvio von Rosalva [*Der Sieg der Natur über die Schwärmerey*]
Samuel Gottlieb Bürde (Oper [M] Komische Oper [L] - 5)
Berlin (1799)
KLA excerpts: "Ha! mir ihr Bildniss zu entwenden!" "Lieb' und Hoffnung," Finale:
"Den Verlust dir zu vergüten," Recitative and aria: "Du wirst ihn wiedersehen. . . O
Liebe, o Liebe die zum ersten Mahl," "Der Leichtsin weicht den Sorgen," "Was für ein
Saal!" "Find' ich ihr mich gegenüber," "Kamilla kann von Trennung sprechen,"
Romanze: "Nein, nein, ich bin euch Mann dafür!" "Mein Herz soll sich erklären?" in
Favorit-Arien und Gesänge aus der Oper Don Sylvio von Rosalva (Berlin: J. J.
Hummel, [*ca.* 1802])

NEEFE, CHRISTIAN GOTTLOB (1748-98)

Amors Guckkasten
Johann Benjamin Michaelis (Operette [L, M] - 1)
Leipzig (10 May 1772)
KLA: Leipzig: Schwickert, 1772 [N 334]
    See *BTC*: 559. The date of première given here is from *NG*. Stieger gives
    Königsberg, February 1772, Ackermann's Theater (and Sonneck makes this
    August 1772). A modern edition of the KLA, edited by G. von Westermann,
    appeared at Munich in 1922.

Die Apotheke
Johann Jakob Engel (Comische Oper [L, M] - 2)
Berlin (13 Dec 1771) Theater in der Behrenstrasse
KLA: Leipzig: J. F. Junius, 1772 [N 335]
Ms. excerpts: Overture, aria, and Rundgesang (KLA) USSR-KAu
    See *BTC*: 559. The date of première given here is that of Sonneck, *NG* and

Graf. *MGG* gives 13 Nov 1771, Stieger 13 Feb 1771. The KLA, which is dedicated to Hiller, carries the date 1 January 1772. Its dedicatory preface is reprinted in full by Kade II:388

Der Dorfbalbier → Johann Adam Hiller

Der Einspruch [*Die Einsprüche*]
Johann Benjamin Michaelis (Comische Oper [M] Operette [L] – 1 [later 2])
1-act: Leipzig (late 1772) Theater am Rannstädter Thore
2-act: Berlin (16 Oct 1773) Theater in der Behrenstrasse
KLA: Leipzig: Schwickert, 1773 [N 336] (2-act)
Ms.: D-B mus. ms. 16011. B-Bc ms. 2444. D-Mbs mus. ms. 16009. (all 2-act)
See *BTC*: 559, 838–9. As Neefe states in his preface to the KLA, he took a reviewer's advice and changed the drama's name to *Die Einsprüche*, "since in fact not one but two legal protests (Einsprüche) occur in it." This print also includes two arias from Michaelis's libretto *Je unnatürlicher, je besser*. The KLA is in two acts, although the opera was given its première in the one-act version in which Michaelis had written it. Neefe notes a hostility toward one-act operas at Leipzig and relates that an unnamed friend of his altered the libretto, adding two duets ("Wenn er nun nicht hexen kann?" and "Keine Seele lässt sich blicken") around the act division. *MGG* and *NG* give the erroneous date of première 16 October 1772.

Heinrich und Lyda
Bernhard Christoph d'Arien (Drama [M] Scene aus dem menschlichen Leben [L] – 1)
Berlin (26 Mar 1776) Döbbelins Theater
KLA: Naumburg and Zeitz: Heinrich Wilhelm Friedrich Flittner, 1777 [N 337]
Ms.: A-Wn ms. 16147
Ms. excerpts: In D-Mbs mus. ms. 8739: no. 75 "Sey mir gegrüsst, du goldner Morgen," no. 76 "Mit warmer Sorgfalt zog ich dich," no. 77 "Mit seinen Händen pflegt' er dich," no. 79 "Jetzt will ich dir im Traum erscheinen," no. 80 "Ich sah sein innres Leiden," no. 83 "O die Freuden dieses Lebens" (KLA)
See *BTC*:624. The Vienna ms. calls the work "eine Idylle." For an expanded version retaining Neefe's music, see Johann August Halbe, *Die Liebe auf der Probe.*

Zemire und Azor
Moritz August von Thümmel (Komische Oper [L] – 4)
Leipzig (5 Mar 1776) Koberwein Troupe
Ms. excerpt: Aria of Zemire, "Der Blumen Königin" in D-Lr (KLA)
It is sometimes stated that this opera was not given its première until Neefe arrived in the Rhineland. The above date is taken from a handwritten addition to the published libretto (Frankfurt and Leipzig, 1776) found on the title page of a copy at D-B (Mus. Tm 110) [ms. additions shown here in italics]:
Zemire und Azor. Eine komische Oper *in 4 Aufzügen.* Nach dem Französischen des Herrn Marmontel. *übersetzt von Moritz August von Thümmel. Musik von P. G. Neefe* [sic]. *zum ersten Male aufgeführt d. 5 Maerz 1776. von der Koberweinschen Gesellschaft in Leipzig am Namenstage des Chürfesten* [sic] *von Sachsen,* Frankfurth und Leipzig. 1776
The music was subsequently used by G. F. W. Grossmann for his libretto *Was vermag ein Mädchen nicht!* (Brunswick: Schulbuchhandlung, 1789). In his preface Grossmann claims he wrote his play, which has many points of contact with *Zémire et Azor*, in order to make better use of Neefe's music, which French "Modesucht" and German "Kaltsinn" have kept below Grétry's in public favor.

NEUMANN, FRIEDRICH (dates unknown)

Das Mädchen nicht ohne den Ring
unknown (Singspiel)
Altona (1798)

OHLHORST, JOHANN CHRISTIAN (1753–1812)

Adelstan und Röschen
Johann Friedrich Schink (Trauerspiel [L] – 2)
Neustrelitz (1782)

Das Jahresfest
Neumann (Singspiel)
Neustrelitz (1783)

Meister Johannes, der lustige Schuster
Ch. G. Korb (Singspiel – 1)
Neustrelitz (1791)

PHANTY, OTTO CHRISTIAN FRIEDRICH (dates unknown)

Doktor Fausts Zaubergürtel [*Dr. Fausts Leibgürtel*]
Wilhelm Christoph Siegmund Mylius and Johann Friedrich Schink (Singspiel)
Lübeck (1784)

Don Sylvio von Rosalva [*Der Sieg der Natur über die Schwärmerey*]
Samuel Gottlieb Bürde (Komische Oper [L] – 4)
Schleswig (2 Mar 1796) Hoftheater

PREU, FRIEDRICH (dates unknown)

Adrast und Isidore [*Die Serenate*]
Christoph Friedrich Bretzner (Komische Oper [L] – 2)
Dresden (22 Feb 1779) Hoftheater
Ms.: D-B mus. ms. 17920. A-Wn ms. 16154
    See *BTC*:758. Riemann *OH* calls this a "gr[osse] Oper" with the title *Adrast*,
    given at Riga in 1785.

Der Irrwisch [*Endlich fand er sie*]
Christoph Friedrich Bretzner (Operette [L] – 3)
Leipzig (1779) Theater am Rannstädter Thore
    See *BTC*: 758.

REICHARDT, JOHANN FRIEDRICH (1752–1814)

Amors Guckkasten
Johann Benjamin Michaelis (Operette [L, M] – 1)
unperformed (composed in 1772)
KLA: Riga: J. F. Hartknoch, 1773 (with *Hänschen und Gretchen*) [R 805]

Claudine von Villa Bella
Johann Wolfgang von Goethe (Singspiel [L] – 3)
Charlottenburg (29 Jul 1789) Schlosstheater
Ms.: D-B mus. ms. 18213/1. D-Bds mus. ms. 29056 (parts). D-WRdn
Ms. excerpts: "Es erhebt sich eine Stimme," "Wie lieb ich die Schöne" in D-B mus. ms.
18213/5 (the latter also in D-B mus. ms. 18213/6). "Lebet wohl geliebte Bäume" D-B

mus. ms. 18213/10 (KLA). "Wie lieb ich die Schöne" D-LEm (KLA). "Ich habe Lucinden, die Freundin verloren" D-Bds mus. ms. autogr. (Reichardt, J. F.) 40. Romanze: "Liebliches Kind" D-Fmi Not. III R. 1/4 and D-Bds mus. ms. 30324 and 30041 ["Cavatine"] (all three KLA). Rondo: "Lebet wohl geliebte Bäume" in D-Bds mus. ms. 30041 (KLA). Trio: "In dem stillen Mondenscheine" D-Bds mus. ms. 30046

Erwin und Elmire
Johann Wolfgang von Goethe (Singspiel [L, M] – 2)
Berlin (early 1793) benefit concert for Madame Bachmann
KLA: Berlin: Unger, 1791 [not in *RISM*]. Berlin: Neue Berlinische Musikhandlung, [1793] (= *Musik zu Göthe's Werken*, vol. 1) [R 796]
Excerpts: Lied "Sieh mich, Heil'ger, wie ich bin" in *MW* 2:21 (1793): 168 and in *BmZ* 4 (2 Mar 1793): 16. Lied "Ein Veilchen auf der Wiese stand" in *BmZ* 35 (5 Oct 1793): 140 and in *Berlinische Monatsschrift* 4 (1783): 404.
Ms.: D-B mus. ms. 18202. US-Wc M 1500 R285E5 (copy of preceding). D-WRdn
Ms. excerpts: Lied "Ein Veilchen auf der Wiese stand" in D-Bds mus. mss. 38078, 38129, 38133
    Though a setting of Goethe's revised version of the text, Reichardt had already published his setting of "Das Veilchen" in 1783 as an independent song. Pazdírek mentions a KLA of the opera published by Breitkopf.

Die Geisterinsel [*Der Sturm*]
Johann Friedrich Wilhelm Gotter (Singspiel [L, M] – 3)
Berlin (6 Jul 1798) National Theater
KLA: Berlin: Neue berlinische Musikhandlung, [1799] [R 797]. Berlin: Rudolph Werckmeister, [1799] [R 799]. n.p., n.d. [R 798]
Excerpts: "Sterbt auf meiner Maja Grabe," "Hier wo wir geborgen," "Mein Eifer kann dem Schicksal nur erliegen," "Froher Sinn und Herzlichkeit," "Ich sollte hier, getrennt von dir," "Ich küsse dich, o Schleier," "Wären lüsterne Najaden" in *Gesänge im Klavierauszuge aus der Geisterinsel* (Berlin: J. F. Unger, 1798) [R 801]. Act 1 only (Berlin: Trautwein, n.d.). Overture (KLA) (n.p., n.d.) [R 800]. Rondo "Trockne deine Thränen" *AMZ* 1 (1799): Beilage 8. Duet "Ach was ist die Liebe" in *Rellstabs Klavier-Magazin* 3 (1787): 42.
Ms.: D-B mus. ms. 18214. D-Bds mus. ms. 29150 (parts). D-WRdn
Ms. excerpts: "Ach was ist die Liebe für ein süsses Ding" in CH-Bmi (KLA). Rondo "Trockne deine Thränen" D-KNmi. "Ich küsse dich, o Schleier" D-SWl (score) and D-Bds mus. ms. 30062 (KLA). "Sterbt auf meiner Maja Grabe" D-B mus. ms. 18214/5 (KLA). Recitative and aria: "Fernando, darf ich's glauben. . . Trockne deine Thränen" D-HAh (KLA). Overture: D-B mus. ms. 18214/2 (parts). Finales of acts 2 and 3: D-B mus. ms. 18214/3 (parts)
    Teichmann states that the opera was given 58 times at Berlin up to 1825 (Pröpper counts only 55 performances). The Werckmeister KLA uses the plates of the Berlinische Musikhandlung edition, which were prepared by Reichardt himself. In 1799 F. Lauska published eight variations for fortepiano on "Ich küsse dich, o Schleier." Facsimile edition of the West Berlin ms.: *GGO*, vol. 7.

Hänschen und Gretchen
Johann Christian Bock (Operette [L, M] – 1)
unperformed (composed 1772)
KLA: Riga: J. F. Hartknoch, 1773 (with *Amors Guckkasten*) [R 805]
    Stieger dates this work Riga, 1773, apparently from the KLA. Riemann *OH* gives Königsberg 1772. *NG* lists Leipzig, 1772, the place and date of composition. Pröpper concluded that the work was unperformed.

Der Holzhauer [*Die drei Wünsche*]
unknown (Komische Oper [L] - 1)
unperformed (composed *ca.* 1775)
KLA Excerpt: "Wams und Mieder, Haub und Mützen" in *SADdT* 3:43-5.
Ms. excerpt: "Wams und Mieder, Haub und Mützen" in US-Wc M 1517 A2H65, and
D-Lr
    Reichardt mentions this work as available in score in a list of his compositions
    published in *Musikalisches Kunstmagazin* 1 (1782): 207-9. Two other operas
    attributed to him but not listed here are not found in this listing (*Der Bley-*
    decker, Der Hufschmied).

Liebe nur beglückt [*Liebe allein macht glücklich*]
Johann Friedrich Reichardt (Schauspiel mit Zwischenmusick und Gesang [M]
Deutsches Singeschauspiel [L] - 3)
Dessau (autumn 1781) Hoftheater
Ms.: D-B mus. ms. 18214. D-Bds mus. ms. autogr. (Reichardt, J. F.) 4.
Ms. excerpts: Finale "O nur Liebe, Liebe nur beglückt" A-Wn ms. 18529. Aria "O der
seeligen Wonne" D-WRtl. Aria, "Poch nicht zu heftig," in D-Rtt Pr.D. 1789 ff. 19
    Eitner gives an incorrect ms. number for the West Berlin copy of the score
    (18204) in *QL* and further claims incorrectly that the opera was in only two
    acts. Pröpper asserts that no performance of the work is known.

RELLSTAB, JOHANN CARL FRIEDRICH (1759-1813)

Die Apotheke
Johann Jakob Engel (Komische Oper [L] - 2)
Berlin (May 1788)
Excerpts: one in *Clavier-Magazin für Kenner und Liebhaber* (1787), two in *Melodie*
und Harmonie (1788), and five in *Lieder und Gesänge verschiedener Art* (1791)
    NG records that the opera was never performed.

REYMANN, F. G. (dates unknown)

Der Derwisch [*Die Derwische*]
Georg Heinrich Rathje (Operette - 4)
Neustrelitz (1797) Hoftheater
    Riemann places the première at Strelitz in 1783.

RÖLLIG, KARL LEOPOLD (? -1804)

Clarisse [*Das unbekannte Dienstmädchen*]
Johann Christian Bock (Komische Operette [L] - 3)
Hamburg (10 Oct 1771) Theater beim Gänsemarkt
    Litzmann, *Schröder*, dates the première 8 Oct 1771.

ROLLE, JOHANN HEINRICH (1716-85)

Melida
Christoph Joseph Sucro (Singspiel [M] - 3)
Magdeburg (early 1784) concert performance
KLA: Leipzig: Schwickert, 1785 [R 2056]
Ms.: B-Bc ms. 2451. CH-Bu kk VIII 221 (score and parts)
    The Brussels ms. represents a revision of the score by J. C. Fischer in 1787,
    which calls itself "ein Trauerspiel mit Gesang in drey Aufzügen nach Sucro
    und Rolle, für die Bühne bearbeitet von Fischer." Stieger gives the impossibly

early place and date of première as Leipzig, 1775, Theater am Rannstädter
Thore.

Der Sturm [*Die bezauberte Insel*]
Johann Samuel Patzke (Drama mit Gesang – 1)
Berlin (28 Mar 1782) Döbbelins Theater

RUST, FRIEDRICH WILHELM (1739–96)

Der blaue Montag [*Der Schuster ein Moralist*]
Traugott Benjamin Berger (Komische Operette)
Dessau (1777)
>   Stieger lists this as a duodrama. Czach describes it as "mit recht als komische
>   Operette bezeichnet" in his *F. W. Rust*, p. 142. Stieger gives for the première
>   Berlin and Riga, 1778.

SANDER, F. J. SIGISMUND (*ca.* 1760–96)

Don Sylvio von Rosalva [*Der Sieg der Natur über die Schwärmerey*]
Samuel Gottlieb Bürde (Komische Oper [L] – 2)
Oels (17 Jun 1797) Herzogliches Theater

Die Regata zu Venedig [*Die Liebe unter den Gondolieren*]
Samuel Gottlieb Bürde (Oper [L] – 3)
Oels (1796) Herzogliches Theater
>   According to *NTL* this work was composed only for keyboard. Stieger gives
>   Breslau as the place of first performance.

SCHAUM, JOHANN OTTO HEINRICH (*fl.* 1795–1804)

Jery und Bätely
Johann Wolfgang von Goethe (Singspiel [L] – 1)
Oels (1795) Herzogliches Theater

SCHMIDT, JOHANN PHILIPP SAMUEL (1779–1853)

Der Schlaftrunk
Christoph Friedrich Bretzner (Komisches Singspiel [L] – 2)
Königsberg (1797) Interims-Theater

SCHMIEDT, SIEGFRIED (*ca.* 1756–99)

Melida
unknown (Singspiel [M] – 3)
Leipzig (1797) Theater am Rannstädter Thore
Excerpts: Overture, "Hat Mannes Muth und Vestigkeit," "O Hoffnung, Himmels
Tochter," "Empfange mich o heilige Stille," "Auf zu eurem Sternenthrone, Götter!"
"Nie im Ungemach erliegen" in *Ouverture und Gesänge im Klavierauszuge aus dem
Singspiel Melida* (Leipzig: Schmiedt and Rau, [1797]) [S 1754]
>   Pazdírek mentions a KLA issued by Breitkopf as well as the overture in KLA.
>   US-Bp dates the above KLA [1796].

SCHÖNBECK, KARL SIEGMUND (1758–after 1800)

Esther
Friedrich Ernst Jester (Oper – 3)

Königsberg (1793)
Riemann *OH* places the opera at Berlin *ca.* 1775 (and gives the composer incorrectly as Jester).

Der Küster im Stroh
unknown (Singspiel)
Königsberg (1778)

Der Wunderigel
Friedrich Ernst Jester (Comische Operette [M, L] – 1)
Königsberg (early 1793)
KLA: Königsberg: Fr. Nicolovius, [1793] [S 2035]
   Stieger dates the première 30 August 1795, Riemann *OH* gives 1788.

SCHRÖTER, CORONA ELISABETH WILHELMINE (1751–1802)

Die Fischerinn
Johann Wolfgang von Goethe (Singspiel [L] – 1)
Tiefurth an der Ilm (22 Jul 1782) outdoor performance on natural stage
Ms.: D-WRtl sig. nr. 81 (KLA). D-WRdn.

SCHUBERT, JOHANN FRIEDRICH (1770–1811)

Die nächtliche Erscheinung
unknown (Komische Oper – 2)
Stettin (1798)

SCHUBERT, JOSEPH (1757–1837)

Das blaue Ungeheuer [*Die Landplage*]
unknown
Schwedt (1781)

Die Entzauberung
unknown
Schwedt (1781)

Der italienische Garkoch zu Genua [*Der Gasthof zu Genua*]
"von einem Freund des Schauspiels" (Komische Operette – 1)
Berlin (12 Jul 1777) Döbbelins Theater
   Schubert collaborated with Anton Laube on the music to this opera.

Rosalia
Johann Friedrich Schink (Nachspiel mit Arien [L] – 1)
Berlin (8 Mar 1777) Döbbelins Theater

SCHULZ, JOHANN ABRAHAM PETER (1747–1800)

Clarisse [*Das unbekannte Dienstmädchen*]
Johann Christian Bock (Komische Operette [L] – 3)
unperformed in German
Excerpts: "Hans war des alten Hansens Sohn," "Der Landmann hat viel Freude,"
"Dort unter jenem Baum stand ich," "Das ganze Dorf lad' ich mir ein," "Gekränkter
Liebe Schmerzen," "Die stillen Gründe," "Kommt, Schäfchen, kommt herein," "Hier
in der niedern Hütte" in *Lieder im Volkston* (Berlin: George Jakob Decker, 1782),
pp. 46–53, 2nd ed. (1785), pp. 41–9

Ms. excerpts: Nos. 1, 3, 6–8 listed above in D-HR (KLA)
The place and date of première given by Stieger (Berlin, 26 May 1775, Döbbe-lins Theater) are those of Johann Christian Frischmuth's setting. Riemann *OH* notes that Schulz's version was given in French at Rheinsberg in 1783.

SCHUSTER, JOSEPH (1748–1812)

Der Alchymist [*Der Liebesteufel*]
August Gottlieb Meissner (Operette [L] – 1)
Dresden (Mar 1778) Kleines Kurfürstliches Theater
Excerpts: Favoritaria "Glück der Menschheit, mächtge Liebe," (n.p., n.d.) [S 2432]. In *SADdT*: "Glück der Menschheit, mächt'ge Liebe" 4:31–2, "Wie durch meine kleinste Nerven" 4:33–42.
Ms.: D-F. A-Wn ms. 16161. D-Dlb. D-Rp. D-B. D-Mbs mus. mss. 6138 (score) and 1042 (KLA). Us-Wc M 1500 S457A4
Ms. excerpt: "Wie durch meine kleinste Nerven" D-Mbs mus. ms. 13345 (KLA) and USSR-KAu (violin and bass accompaniment)
 See *BTC*: 700. The KLA ms. at Munich (mus. ms. 1042) was prepared by the Darmstadt Capell-Director Georg Sartorius. A new edition of the score, edited by Richard Engländer, appeared at Kassel in 1958. Facsimile edition of the Munich ms.: *GGO*, vol. 5.

Die wüste Insel
August Gottlieb Meissner (Singspiel [L] – 1)
Leipzig (30 Sep 1779) Theater am Rannstädter Thore
KLA excerpt: "Heiliger als tausend Leben" in *SADdT* 5:47–9.
Ms.: A-Wn. D-B (2 copies)
Ms. excerpt: "Heiliger als tausend Leben" USSR-KAu
 See *BTC*: 700, 836.

SCHWANENBERGER, JOHANN GOTTFRIED (*ca.* 1740–1804)

Der Deserteur
unknown (Singspiel)
Brunswick (1784)

SCHWEITZER, ANTON (1735–87)

Alceste
Christoph Martin Wieland (Singspiel [L] – 5)
Weimar (28 May 1773) Seyler Company
KLA/Score: Leipzig: Schwickert, 1774 [S 2476]
KLA: Berlin and Libau: Selbstverlag in Commission bey Lagarde und Friedrich, 1786 [S 2477]
Ms.: D-B mus. ms. 20549 (score and parts). D-Dlb ms. 797c. US-Wc M 1500 S46A5 (copy of preceding). D-Dlb ms. B656 (fragments). D-Ds. A-Wgm. A-Wn ms. 16152. D-LEm. F-Pc.
Ms. excerpts: In D-Mbs mus. ms. 8739: no. 49 "O du! für die ich welcher Ruh und Amors süssem Schmerz entsage," no. 60 "Noch lebt Admet in deinem Herzen," no. 85 "Weine nicht! Du meines Herzens Abgott!" (all KLA). At D-SWl: "O der ist nicht vom Schicksal," "O du, für die ich weicher Ruh und Amors süssem Schmerz entsage" [lacks voice part], "Wem dank ich dies Leben," (all parts). At CH-Zz: Recitative and aria of Admet, "Flieh, geliebter Schatten" (parts)

See *BTC*: 520, 559, 624. The 1774 KLA, prepared by Schweitzer himself, presents some numbers in KLA and some in short sore. The 1786 KLA was edited by "M***." Facsimile edition of the Vienna ms. A-Wn 16152: *GGO*, vol. 3.

Die Dorfgala
Johann Friedrich Wilhelm Gotter (Komische Operette [M] Operette [L-1772] Lustspiel mit Arien und Gesängen [L-1774] Komische Oper [L-1778 (2 acts)] Singspiel [L-1805 (1 act)] – 3 [later 2])
3-act: Weimar (18 May 1772) Seyler Company
2-act: Hamburg (21 Jan 1779) Schröder-Ackermann Company
KLA: Leipzig: Schwickert, 1777 [S 2478]
Excerpt: "Umschmachtet von flatternden Westen" in *TK* 1774
Ms.: D-Bds mus. ms. 20548. D-Dlb. US-Wc M 1500 S46D5 (copy of preceding). D-F
See *BTC*: 559, 585, 624.

Erwin und Elmire
Johann Wolfgang von Goethe (Schauspiel mit Gesang [L] – 2)
unperformed (composed 1775–6)
Excerpt: "Ein Veilchen auf der Wiese stand" in *TK* 1777 [S 2480]
How much of Goethe's first version of this work Schweitzer set is not known. The only mention of a full setting is in a works list in *TK* 1776. Schweitzer mentions only a "Liedlein" in his correspondence with Bertuch in 1775–6 (see Maurer). In April 1776 Seckendorff mentioned that the opera was to be performed "d'après la musique de Schweitzer," but in May Anna Amalia's setting was produced at Weimar (Bode, *Der weimarische Musenhof*, p. 302, n. 2).

Der lustige Schuster
Christian Felix Weisse (Komische Oper – 3)
Celle (21 May 1770) Seyler Company
See *BTC*: 624, 758.

Walmir und Gertraud [*Man kann es ja probieren*]
Johann Benjamin Michaelis (Operette [L] – 3)
unperformed (composed *ca.* 1769)
Excerpts: "Ein arger Poltergeist," "Man überleg' es um und an" in *TK* 1776
This score proved too difficult for the Seyler troupe and was never performed although Maurer and Stieger claim that it was.

Das wütende Heer [*Das Mädchen im Thurme*]
Christoph Friedrich Bretzner (Operette [L] – 3)
unperformed
About all we know of this setting is mention of Schweitzer as composer of the text on the title page of Bretzner's libretto. Maurer does not mention the work, and both Graf and Sonneck place it impossibly early (*ca.* 1772 and 1773–4 respectively, well before Bretzner wrote the libretto around 1779).

SECKENDORFF, KARL SIEGMUND FREIHERR VON (1744–85)

Der Blumenraub
Karl Siegmund Freiherr von Seckendorff (Operette – 2)
Weimar (1784) Bellomo Company

Jery und Bätely
Johann Wolfgang von Goethe (Singspiel [L] – 1)
Weimar (12 Jul 1780) Neues Theater

SEYDELMANN, JOHANN NIKOLAUS FRANZ (1748–1806)

Arsene [*Die schöne Arsene*]
August Gottlieb Meissner (Singspiel [L] – 4)
Dresden (3 Mar 1779) Churfürstliches Kleines Theater
KLA: Leipzig: J. G. I. Breitkopf, 1779 [S 2864]
Ms.: D-Dlb
> See *BTC*: 700, 878–9. Stieger states that the opera was in three acts. This refers only to a concert version, however (Schatz 11748). He gives as date and place of first performance Leipzig [15 April] 1779, but the Bondini Company had presented it earlier at Dresden.

Der Kaufmann von Smyrna
Christian Friedrich Schwan (Operette [L] – 1)
Dresden (1778) Bondini Company
Excerpt: Recitative and aria "Schön war Chlora. . . O! nur einen ihrer Blicke!" in *SADdT* 5:8–20

Der lahme Husar
Friedrich Carl Koch (Comische Oper [L] – 2)
Leipzig (17 Jul 1780) Theater am Rannstädter Thore
Excerpts: In *SADdT*: "Freyheit wallt in meinen Adern" 6:1–7, "Lieber erster Sonnenstrahl" 6:8–12
Ms.: D-Dlb
> See *BTC*: 700, 879–80.

Der Soldat
unknown (Oper – 1)
Gotha (1783) Bellomo Company
> Stieger dates the work 1784. The date here is from *MGG* and *NG*.

SPINDLER, FRANZ STANISLAUS (1763–1819)

Achmet und Zenaide [*Achmet und Zaide*]
unknown (Schauspiel mit Gesang)
Breslau (1796)

Don Quixotte [*Ritter Don Quixotte, Das Abentheuer am Hofe*]
unknown (Oper [L] – 2)
Breslau (1797)

STEGMANN, CARL DAVID (1751–1826)

Clarisse [*Das unbekannte Dienstmädchen*]
Johann Christian Bock (Komische Operette [L] – 3)
Hamburg (Nov 1778) Opernhaus beim Gänsemarkt

Erwin und Elmire
Johann Wolfgang von Goethe (Schauspiel mit Gesang [L] – [2])
Königsberg (1776)
KLA: Leipzig and Königsberg: Auf Kosten des Autors, 1776 [S 4745]
> See *BTC*: 624.

Der Kaufmann von Smyrna
Christian Friedrich Schwan (Komische Operette [M] Singspiel [L-1782] Operette [L-1785] – 1)
1st version: Königsberg (1773) Ackermanns Theater

2nd version: Hamburg (1796)
KLA: Berlin and Königsberg: G. L. Hartung and G. J. Decker, 1773 [S 4749]
Ms.: B-Bc ms. 2464
> See *BTC*: 584, 700. The second version incorporates a new and far more extensive finale.

Das Mündel
Chr. G. Korb (Lustspiel mit Gesängen [L] – 2)
Altona (1783)
> A composer for this opera is not recorded in Sonneck. Riemann *OH* attributes the score to the librettist.

Die Recrouten auf dem Lande
unknown (Komische Oper [L] – 3)
Danzig (1775)
Ms.: D-Dlb ms. 796e (autograph)
> *MGG* states that the opera is in only two acts, but the libretto (Schatz 10041) shows three. Stieger gives for the première Königsberg, 1775, Ackermanns Theater; Riemann *OH* places it at Mitau in 1775. The place and date preferred here are from *MGG*.

Das redende Gemälde
unknown (Comische Oper [M] – 2)
Königsberg (1775)
KLA: Mitau and Hasenboth: J. F. Hinz, 1775 [S 4751]
> See *BTC*: 588. Stieger sets the première at Mitau in 1774. It is perhaps worth noting here that another French-derived opera, *Der Deserteur*, is incorrectly ascribed to Stegmann by almost everyone. The deception arises from the wording of the title page of the published KLA (Leipzig and Königsberg: G. L. Hartung, 1775): "*Der Deserteur*, eine Operette in drey Akten, in deutsche Musik aufs Clavier gesetzt von Carl David Stegmann." Those who bother to look beyond this page will quickly discover that the print contains a keyboard reduction by Stegmann of Monsigny's famous *drame lyrique*. The only change is a substitution of new music for the very difficult fugal first half of the trio "O ciel! quoi tu vas mourir."

Der Triumf der Liebe [*Das kühne Abentheuer, Die Roseninsel* (3-act version)]
Friedrich Ernst Jester (Feen-Oper [M] Singspiel [L] – 4 [later 3])
4-act: Hamburg (27 Feb 1796) Theater beim Gänsemarkt
3-act: Hamburg (24 Nov 1806)
KLA: Königsberg: Friedrich Nicolovius, [1796] [S 4752]
Ms.: D-B mus. ms. 21250
Ms. excerpt: Recitative and aria in D-Dlb ms. 796d
> The text of the three-act version was revised by C. L. Costenoble. Sonneck gives as the date of première for the four-act version 4 April 1796; the one above is from Stieger and *NG*. The ms. excerpt at Dresden is also dated "Hamburg 27. Febr. 1796."

STENGEL, GOTTFRIED (dates unknown)

Amadis der fahrende Ritter von Gallien
Carl Ludwig Giesecke (Oper – 4)
Hamburg (4 Nov 1798)
> The librettist's name is a pseudonym of Johann Georg Metzler.

UBER, CHRISTIAN BENJAMIN (1746-1812)

Clarisse [*Das unbekannte Dienstmädchen*]
Johann Christian Bock (Comische Oper [M] Komische Operette [L] - 3)
Breslau (1771)
KLA: Breslau: Johann Ernst Meyer, 1772 [U 1]
Ms. excerpts: five arias, USSR-KAu
   See *BTC*: 559, 885-6. The KLA also contains Uber's setting of an ode from the
   novel *The History of Miss Fanny Wilkes*, "Dir folgen meine Thränen." The
   letter of dedication (to Uber's brother) and part of the preface are reprinted by
   Kade II:394.

VOLANEK [WOLANEK, WOLLANECK, WOLLANEK], ANTONÍN JOSEF
ALOIS [ANTON] (1761-1817)

Die Ueberraschung
Barchielli (Singspiel - 1)
Leipzig (20 Dec 1797) Theater am Rannstädter Thore

WALTER IGNAZ (1755-1822)

Die böse Frau
Carl Alexander Herklots (Komisches Original-Singspiel [L] - 2)
Hannover (26 Sep 1794) Grossmann Company
Ms.: D-Dlb
   Sonneck gives as place and date of première: Bremen, 3 November 1794,
   Theater an der Bastion beim Osterthore. Those here are from Stieger.

Doktor Faust
Heinrich Gottlieb Schmieder (Original-Oper [L] - 4)
1st version: Bremen (28 Dec 1797)
2nd version: Hannover (8 Jun 1798)
Ms.: D-Bhm (2nd version)

WEBER, BERNHARD ANSELM (1764-1821)

Menöceus [*Die Rettung von Thebe*]
Friedrich Bouterwek (Trauerspiel mit Gesang [L] - 3)
Hannover (1792)

Der Theater-Prinzipal
Carl Alexander Herklots (Lyrische Posse [L] - 1)
Berlin (15 Apr 1796) National Theater
   This short farce, which includes only one singing character, was given only
   once at Berlin.

WEBER, EDMUND KASPAR JOHANN JOSEF MARIA FREIHERR VON
(1766-1828)

Der Transport im Koffer [*Eine glückliche Entwicklung*]
unknown (Singspiel [L] - 3)
Hamburg (30 May 1791) Theater beim Gänsemarkt
   MGG sets the première at Nüremberg on 12 Jul 1792.

WEIMAR, GEORG PETER (1734–1800)

Die Schadenfreude
Christian Felix Weisse (Operette für Kinder [M] Kleines Lustspiel für Kinder mit Liederchen [L] – 1)
Erfurt (1776)
KLA: Leipzig: S. L. Crusius, 1779 [W 552]
   See *BTC*: 668.

WEISFLOG, CHRISTIAN GOTTHILF (1732–1804)

Der Einsiedler
L. (Schauspiel mit Gesang)
no performance known

Die Erbschaft
unknown
Sagan (1776)

Das Erntefest
Christian Gotthilf Weisflog (Singspiel – 1)
Bautzen (1769)
   Riemann *OH* dates this work *ca.* 1767.

Das Frühstück auf der Jagd [*Der neue Richter*]
Christian Gotthilf Weisflog (Ländliches Lustspiel mit Gesang [L] – 2)
Sagan (1772)

Das glückliche Unglück
unknown
Sagan (*ca.* 1780)
   The place and date of first performance are from Riemann *OH*.

Der Schatz
Christian Gotthilf Weisflog (Singspiel – 1)
Sagan (12 Jan 1781)
   Riemann *OH* dates this opera *ca.* 1770.

WESSELY, CARL BERNHARD (1768–1826)

Psyche
Carl Friedrich Müchler (Singspiel [L] – 2)
Berlin (18 Nov 1789) National Theater
Ms.: D-B mus. ms. 23020 (1st act only)
   The opera was given only three times at Berlin.

WITTROCK, G. H. L. (dates unknown)

Die kleine Ährenleserinn
Christian Felix Weisse (Operette [L] – 1)
Lübeck (1787)

WOLF, ERNST WILHELM (1735–92)

Der Abend im Walde
Gottlob Ephraim Heermann (Comische Oper [M] Operette [L] – 2)
Weimar (10 Dec 1773) Schlosstheater in der Wilhelmsburg

KLA: Riga: J. F. Hartknoch, 1775 [W 1774]
> See *BTC*: 559, 875–6. One of the arias in the KLA is printed in full score.

Alceste
Christoph Martin Wieland (Singspiel [L] – 5)
Weimar (1786) Herzogliches Comödienhaus
Ms.: D-WRtl
> *MGG* dates this setting 1780.

Angelica
Christoph Martin Wieland (Singspiel)
Berlin (1788)
> Riemann places the première at Weimar, *ca*. 1790.

Die Dorfdeputirten
Gottlob Ephraim Heermann (Komische Oper [L] – 3)
Weimar (10 Feb 1772) Seyler Company
KLA: Weimar: Carl Ludolf Hoffmann, 1773 [W 1775]
Ms.: D-B mus. ms. 20240
Ms. excerpts: nos. 5 to 8 (KLA) USSR-KAu
> See *BTC*: 559. The mss. of *Die Dorfdeputirten* at Brussels (B-Bc ms. 2496) and Washington (US-Wc M 1500 W84D5, a transcript of the preceding) are Lukas Schubaur's setting of Heermann's libretto, although both libraries ascribe the work to Wolf. Conversely, the Berlin ms. listed above is described as Schubaur's setting. This manuscript, which is unusual among eighteenth-century German opera scores in that it includes Wolf's ballet music to follow the opera itself, is reproduced in facsimile in *GGO*, vol. 2.

Ehrlichkeit und Liebe [*Rechtschaffenheit und Liebe*]
Christian Jakob Wagenseil (Schauspiel mit Gesang [M] Ländliches Schauspiel mit Gesang [L] – 1)
Weimar (1776)
KLA: Dessau: Auf Kosten der Verlagskasse für Gelehrte und Künstler, 1782 [W 1776]. 2nd ed. Leipzig: Gräff, 1794 [W 1777].
Ms.: D-Bds (autograph)
> See *BTC*: 700, 831–2. Stieger gives as place and date of première those of a later production (Gotha, 21 Jul 1779, Court Theater).

Der Eremit auf Formentera
August von Kotzebue (Schauspiel mit Gesang [L-1787] Oper [L-1790] – 2)
Weimar? (1786)
> Stieger gives as the première date that of the Bellomo Company's production at Weimar (26 November 1789), but in the first edition of the libretto (Reval, 1787) Kotzebue writes: "This little play has been set to music by the famous Kapellmeister Wolff and has won applause in Germany on several stages" (p. [5]).

Erwin und Elmire
Johann Wolfgang von Goethe (Schauspiel mit Gesang [L] – [2])
Weimar (1785) Herzogliches Comödienhaus
> *MGG* dates the première 1780.

Das Gärtnermädchen
Karl August Musäus (Comische Oper [M] – 3)
Weimar (1769) Schlosstheater in der Wilhelmsburg
KLA: Weimar: C. L. Hoffmann, 1774 [W 1778]

Ms.: D-Bhm
See *BTC*: 559, 833–4.

Das grosse Loos
Friedrich Johann Justin Bertuch (Komische Oper [L] – 2)
Gotha (2 Sep 1774) Seyler Company
[KLA: Berlin: C. U. Ringmacher, 1776]
Ms.: D-Bds. B-Bc ms. 2495. B-Br (Fétis 2822)
    See *BTC*: 559, 586–7. No copies of the KLA appear to have survived. *MGG*
    puts the première at Weimar in 1774.

Das Rosenfest
Gottlob Ephraim Heermann (Operette [L, M] – 3)
Weimar (4 Sep 1770) Schlosstheater in der Wilhelmsburg
KLA: Berlin: Winter, 1771 [W 1781]. 2nd ed. 1775 [W 1782]
Excerpts: In *DOAM*: "Nein, glaubt mirs nur," "Ihr schöner Blick," "Wir reisen seit
dem zwölften Jahre," "Ihr Mädchen, wollt ihr wenn ihr freyt," pp. 4–11
    See *BTC*: 559, 832–3. *MGG* and *NG* give for the date of première 1772. The
    date given here, that of Prince Karl August's birthday, is from Wilhelm Bode,
    Der weimarische Musenhof. The publisher's letter of dedication in the first
    edition of the KLA is reprinted by Kade II: 397.

Der Schleyer
Christian August Vulpius (Singspiel [L] – 3)
Weimar (1786)
    Sonneck puts the première at Hamburg, 22 May 1788, Theater beim Gän-
    semarkt.

Superba
Carl August Gottfried von Seckendorff (Singspiel – 3)
Weimar (30 Jan 1785)
    The date of première is Duchess Luise's birthday.

Die treuen Köhler
Gottlob Ephraim Heermann (Operette [L, M] – 2)
Weimar (14 Jul 1772) Schlosstheater in der Wilhelmsburg
KLA: Weimar: C. L. Hoffmann, 1774 [W 1779]
Ms.: B-Bc ms. 2494
    See *BTC*: 559, 876–7.

Die Zauberirrungen [*Die Irrthümer der Zauberey*]
Hildebrand Freiherr von Einsiedel (Schauspiel mit Gesang – 2)
Weimar (24 Oct 1785) Hochfürstliches Hoftheater (Bellomo Company)
    The date is Anna Amalia's birthday.

ZELLER, GEORG BERNHARD LEOPOLD (1728–after 1787)

Der ehrliche Räuber
C. G. Korb (Schauspiel mit Gesang [L] – 2)
Neubrandenburg (2 Jul 1787) Herzogliches Schauspielhaus

Part II

The texts of North German opera, 1766–1799

Section A
Texts composed for performance

Der Abend im Walde
Gottlob Ephraim Heermann (based on characters and incidents from Saxon history)
Ernst Wilhelm Wolf (Weimar, 1773)
1. (Operette, 2) [Wolf]
   Weimar: Carl Ludolf Hoffmann, 1774 [Schatz 11075]
2. (Komische Oper, 2)
   Komische Opern (Berlin and Leipzig, 1776), vol. 3, pp. 161–264
BIBL.: *AdB* 27:1 (1775): 154–6; 28:2 (1776): 486–7; 35:1 (1778): 174–7.

[*Das Abentheuer am Hofe* → *Don Quixotte*]

[*Achmet und Zaide* → *Achmet und Zenaide*]

Achmet und Zenaide
unknown
Franz Stanislaus Spindler (Breslau, 1796)

Adelstan und Röschen
Johann Friedrich Schink (based on a ballad by Hölty)
Johann Christian Ohlhorst (Neustrelitz, 1782)
Friedrich Adam Hiller (Güstrow, 1792)
1. (Trauerspiel mit Gesang, [2])
   Berlin: Himburg, 1776
2A. (Trauerspiel, [2]) [Hiller]
   n.p., n.d. [Schatz 4714]
BIBL.: *AdB* 36:2 (1778): 485–6.

Adrast und Isidore, *oder Die Serenate*
Christoph Friedrich Bretzner (after Molière, *Le Sicilien*)
Friedrich Preu (Dresden, 1779)
Otto Carl Erdmann Freiherr von Kospoth (Berlin, 1779)
1. (Komische Oper, 2) [Preu]
   C. F. Bretzner: *Operetten* (Leipzig, 1779), vol. 1, pp. [193]–254 [Schatz 11680, 8462]
2A. (Komische Oper, 2)
   n.p., 1787 [Schatz 5217]
3. (Comische Oper, 2)
   n.p., 1793 [USSR-KAu]
BIBL.: *LTZ* 2 (1779): 695–6, 778–9. *AdB* 41:2 (1780): 457–9. *BTJ* 187–191 [Kospoth].
DB 21:325. *AdT* 5 (1790): 46. *AdM* 1780: 41
   Sonneck prints an excerpt from the preface to no. 1 (p. 36).

[*Die Ährenleserinn* → *Die kleine Ährenleserinn*]

Der Äpfeldieb, *oder Der Schatzgräber*
Christoph Friedrich Bretzner (adapted from a spoken comedy by the author with the same title [1771])
Johann Christoph Kaffka (Berlin, 1780)
Nikolaus Mühle (Danzig, 1781)
Gottlob Benedict Bierey (Leipzig, 1793)
1. (Operette, 1) [Kaffka]
    C. F. Bretzner: *Operetten* (Leipzig, 1779), vol. 1, pp. [255]–298 [Schatz 11680, 4982]
2. (Operette, 1) [Kaffka]
    Leipzig: Carl Friedrich Schneider, 1788 [Schaal 21]
BIBL.: Schmid *C* 294 [186]. *LTZ* 2 (1779): 695–6. *AdB* 41:2 (1780): 457–9. *DB* 21:326. Sonneck prints an excerpt from the preface to no. 1 (p. 41). The spoken version appeared in *Theater der Deutschen*, vol. 14 (Königsberg and Leipzig, 1774), no. 90.

Der Aerndtekranz
Christian Felix Weisse (original)
Johann Adam Hiller (Leipzig, 1771)
1. (Komische Oper, 3)
    Leipzig: Dyckische Buchhandlung, 1771 [Schatz 4718]
2. (Komische Oper, 3)
    [C. F. Weisse:] *Komische Opern* (Leipzig: Dyckische Buchhandlung, 1771), vol. 3, pp. 225–438 [Schaal 22]
3A. (Komische Oper, 3)
    n.p., 1772 [USSR-KAu]
4. (Komische Oper, 3)
    C. F. Weisse: *Komische Opern* (Carlsruhe: Schmieder, 1778), vol. 3, pp. [135]–264 [Schaal 23, US-Wc ML 49 A2W2]
5. (Komische Oper, 3)
    Theater der Deutschen, vol. 11 (Königsberg and Leipzig, 1772), no. 70.
6. (Komische Oper, 3)
    Stuttgart: Christoph Friedrich Cotta, 1779 [Schaal 24]
7A. (Komische Oper, 3)
    Berlin, 1794 [Schaal 25]
BIBL.: Schmid *T* 115–26. *AdB* 17:2 (1772): 564–8, 19:2 (1773): 429–38. Schmid *C* 310–11 [196]. *LTZ* 2 (1779): 632. *KT* 292–4.

[*Der Aerntekranz* → *Der Aerndtekranz*]

Alceste
Christoph Martin Wieland (after Euripides, *Alkestis*)
Anton Schweitzer (Weimar, 1773)
Friedrich Wilhelm Heinrich Benda (Berlin, 1786)
Ernst Wilhelm Wolf (Weimar, 1786)
1. (Singspiel, 5)
    Leipzig: Weidmann, 1773 [*Wolf.* 44]
2. (Singspiel, 5)
    n.p., 1773 [Schatz 9768]
3. (Singspiel, 5)
    Theater der Deutschen, vol. 13 (Königsberg and Leipzig, 1773), no. 82.

4. (Singspiel, 5)
  Munich: Franz Joseph Thuille, 1779 [Schaal 34]
5. (Singspiel, 5) [Schweitzer]
  Wielands Sämmtl. Werke (n.p., n.d.), vol. 26, pp. 1–58 [Schatz 9768a, *Wolf.* 45]
BIBL.: *TM* 1 (1773): 34–72, 223–43; 2 (1773): 306–8; 3 (1773): 299–301; 5 (1774): 366–7 (1774): 396, 1775:3 (July): 63–87, (August): 268–9, 1775:4 (November): 156–73. *AdB* 21:1 (1774): 188–9. Dressler: *Theater-Schule*, 68ff, and 169–95 [reprinted separately as his *Gedanken* (1774)].Schmid *C* 334–5 [212]. Schubart *DC* 1775: 535, 575–6, 720. *DM* 1777:1 (March): 262–76, 1778:1 (March): 263–5. *LTZ* 1 (1778): 230, 248–50; 3 (1780): 760; 4 (1781): 515–17, 574–6. *MdM* 1:1 (1783): 600–1. Schütze 504. Brandes, *Lebensgeschichte*, vol. 2, p. 157.

Der Alchymist, *oder Der Liebesteufel*
August Gottlieb Meissner (after Legrand, *L'Amour diable*)
Johann André (Berlin, 1778)
Joseph Schuster (Dresden, 1778)
1. (Operette, [1])
  Leipzig: Dyckische Buchhandlung, 1778 [Schatz 9742]
2. *Der Liebesteufel* (no desig., 1)
  A. G. Meissner: *Operetten* (Leipzig: Dyckische Buchhandlung, 1778), pp. 1–79 [US-Wc ML 49 A2M3]
3A. (Operette, 1)
  n.p., 1778 [Schatz 177]
4A. (Operette, 1) [Schuster]
  Hamburg: J. M. Michaelsen, 1779 [Schatz 9742a]
5. (no desig., 1) [Schuster]
  Lyrisches Theater der Deutschen (Leipzig: Dyckische Buchhandlung, 1782), vol. 1, no. 4 [D-W Lo 1133]
6A. (Operette, 1) [Schuster]
  n.p., 1805 [USSR-KAu]
7A. *Der Liebesteufel* (Operette, 1)
  n.p., n.d. [D-B Mus. Ta 874]
BIBL.: *LTZ* 1 (1778): 31–2; 5 (1782): 172–3. *AdB* Appendix 25–36 (1778): 2963–4. *DM* 1778:1 (June): 569 [Schuster]. *TJ* 5 (1778): 80; 16 (1780): 60–2. *DB* 26:410–12. *TSS* 298–9.
  Libretto no. 2 is the same as no. 1 with a new title page. In Sonneck the Schatz number of no. 3A is incorrectly given as 1770. No. 5 is the original edition of 1778 with a new title page. The D-B catalogue assigns no. 7A to André, but it is not in exact accord with the score of his setting (D-B mus. ms. 603).

Die Alpenhütte
unknown
Ehrenberg (unperformed)

Der alte Freyer
Johann André (adapted from his comedy of the same name)
Johann André (Berlin, 1775)
1. (Komische Oper, 1) [André]
  Frankfurt am Main: Johann Christian Gebhard, 1775 [Schatz 178]
  Sonneck reprints an excerpt from André's prefatory note (p. 70). André's spoken comedy was printed at Frankfurt by J. G. Garbe in 1772 and reviewed in *AdB* 22 (1774): 220.

[*Alter schützt für Thorheit nicht* → *Kurze Thorheit ist die beste*]

Amadis der fahrende Ritter von Gallien
Carl Ludwig Giesecke (after Wieland, *Der neue Amadis*)
Gottfried Stengel (Hamburg, 1798)

Amors Guckkasten
Johann Benjamin Michaelis (based on a short story by the author)
Christian Gottlob Neefe (Leipzig, 1772)
Johann Friedrich Reichardt (unperformed)
1. (Operette, 1)
   Leipzig: Dyckische Buchhandlung, 1772 [Schatz 7069, Schaal 55]
2. (Operette, 1)
   Theater der Deutschen (Königsberg and Leipzig, 1772), vol. 12, no. 75
3. (no desig., 1) [Reichardt, Neefe]
   Lyrisches Theater der Deutschen (Leipzig: Dyckische Buchhandlung, 1782), vol. 1,
   no. 2 [D-W Lo 1133]
4. (Operette, 1)
   Sämmtliche Werke des Johann Benjamin Michaelis (Vienna: Alberti, 1791), vol. 4,
   pp. 11–58 [*Wolf.* 101]
BIBL.: *AdB* 19:1 (1773): 257:8; 24:1 (1775): 112 [Reichardt]. Schmid *C* 329 [208].
   No. 2 is the original edition of 1772 with a new title page.

Amors Zufälle
Joseph Bellomo (from the Italian)
Benedikt Kraus (Weimar, 1785)

Angelica
Christoph Martin Wieland (after Metastasio, *L'Angelica*)
Ernst Wilhelm Wolf (Berlin, 1788)

Die Apotheke
Johann Jakob Engel
Christian Gottlob Neefe (Berlin, 1771)
Johann Carl Friedrich Rellstab (Berlin, 1788)
1. (Komische Oper, 2)
   Leipzig: Dyckische Buchhandlung, 1772 [Schatz 7070, *Wolf.* 154]
2. (Komische Oper, 2)
   Komische Opern (Berlin and Leipzig, 1775), vol. 2, pp. 113–82 [D-B Mus. T 145]
3. (no desig., 2) [Neefe]
   Lyrisches Theater der Deutschen (Leipzig: Dyckische Buchhandlung, 1782), vol. 1,
   no. 1 [D-W Lo 1133]
BIBL.: Schmid *T* 1–10. *AdB* 19:1 (1773): 256–7; 21:1 (1774): 191. Schmid *C* 311 [196].
   No. 2 omits the dedication and preface found in no. 1. No. 3 is the original edition of 1772 with a new title page. Sonneck prints an excerpt from the preface
   of no. 1 (p. 131).

Arsene
August Gottlieb Meissner (after Favart, *La Belle Arsène* [1773])
Franz Seydelmann (Dresden, 1779)
1. (Singspiel, [4])
   Leipzig: Dyckische Buchhandlung, 1778 [Schatz 9841]
2. (no desig., 4)
   A. G. Meissner: *Operetten* (Leipzig: Dyckische Buchhandlung, 1778) [US-Wc ML
   49 A2M3]

3. (no desig., 4) [Seydelmann]
Lyrisches Theater der Deutschen (Leipzig: Dyckische Buchhandlung, 1782), vol. 2, no. 4 [Schatz 9842, D-W Lo 1133]
4. (Singspiel, 3) [Seydelmann]
n.p., n.d. [Schatz. 11748]
BIBL.: *AdB* Appendices 25–36 (1778): 2963–4. *TSS* 340–1. *MdM* 1:2 (1783): 916.
  Nos. 2 and 3 are the original edition of 1778 with new title pages. Sonneck prints an excerpt from the preface to no. 1 (p. 158). No. 4 is a concert version omitting three of the original numbers and adding a new one; the dialogue is changed to recitative and considerably reduced.

[*Der Authomat* → *Der Liebhaber als Automat*]

[*Das Automat* → *Der Liebhaber als Automat*]

Azakia
Christian Friedrich Schwan
Johann André (Berlin, 1778)
Ehrenberg (Dessau, 1790)
[1. (Singspiel, 3) [Cannabich]
Mannheim: C. F. Schwan, 1778 [Schatz 1573]
BIBL.: *AdB* Appendices 25–36 (1778): 3004. *TJ* 6 (1778): 82. *LTZ* 1 (1778): 224; 2 (1779): 12 [André]. *TSS* 306.

[*Der Balbier von Bagdad* → *Der Barbier von Bagdad*]

Barbier und Schornsteinfeger
Autenrieth
Essiger (Lübben, 1798)

Der Barbier von Bagdad (I)
Johann André (after Palissot de Montenoy)
Johann André (Berlin, 1783)
BIBL.: *LTZ* 6 (1783): 284. *MdM* 1:1 (1783): 593–5.
  André's prose translation of Palissot's one-act comedy appeared at Frankfurt and Leipzig, published by Esslinger, in 1772.

Der Barbier von Bagdad (II)
Wilhelm Christhelf Siegmund Mylius
Heinrich Christoph Hattasch (Hamburg, after 1780)

Der Barbier von Seville, *oder Die vergebliche Vorsicht*
Gustav Friedrich Wilhelm Grossmann (Caron de Beaumarchais, *Le Barbier de Séville*)
Friedrich Ludwig Benda (Leipzig, 1776)
1. (Lustspiel. . . mit untermischten Gesängen, 4)
  Leipzig: Dyckische Buchhandlung, 1784 [Schatz 764, Schaal 186]
2A. (Singspiel, [4])
  Leipzig, 1801 [D-B Mus. Tb 510]
BIBL.: *AdB* 40:? (1780): 487–8. *LTZ* 6 (1783): 403. *BLT* 34–5.
  Sonneck prints an excerpt from the preface to no. 1 (p. 199).

[*Der Baron von Tunis* → *Der Bassa von Tunis*]

Der Bassa von Tunis
Karl Franz Henisch

Franz Andreas Holly (Berlin, 1774)
1. (Komische Operette, 1) [Holly]
    Berlin and Leipzig, 1774 [Schatz 4768]
2A. (Komische Operette, 3)
    n.p., n.d. [D-B Mus. Th 906]
    No. 2A omits two numbers of no. 1, substitutes for one other, and adds eight numbers which comprise all of act two.

Bathmendi
1st version: Ernst Wolfgang Behrisch (after the novella of the same name by Jean-Pierre Claris de Florian [1784])
2nd version: Karl August Ludwig Freiherr von Lichtenstein
Karl August Ludwig Freiherr von Lichtenstein (1st version: Dessau, 1798; 2nd version: Dessau, 1799)
[1. (Grosse Oper, 2) [Lichtenstein]
    Vienna: Joh. Baptist Wallishausser, 1801 [US-PHu]
BIBL.: *AMZ* 1 (1798.9): 239–40; 2 (1799.1800): 53. *JLM* 14 (1799): 82–7, 400–2.
    As noted in *JLM*, Behrisch's original libretto was published at Dessau in 1798 "with dialogue and all the trimmings."

[*Das Bauernmädchen → Der studierte Jäger*]

[*Das Bauernmägdchen am Hofe → Lottchen am Hofe*]

[*Die belebte Bildsäule → Deukalion und Pyrha*]

Bella und Fernando, *oder Die Satire*
Christian August Vulpius
Otto Carl Erdmann Freiherr von Kospoth (Berlin, 1790)
[1. (no desig., 1) [Preu]
    C. A. Vulpius: *Operetten* (Bayreuth, 1790), vol. 1, pp. [111]–176 [Schatz 8463]
BIBL.: *AdB* 101:2 (1791): 402–3; 110:1 (1792): 113. *ALZ* 1797:3:231–2.

Belmont und Constanze, *oder Die Entführung aus dem Serail*
Christoph Friedrich Bretzner
Johann André (Berlin, 1781)
1. (Operette, 3) [André]
    Leipzig: Carl Friedrich Schneider, 1781 [Schatz 183]
2. (Singspiel, 3) [André]
    Brno: Swoboda, 1782 [A-Wn 625.676-B. Th.]
BIBL.: *LTZ* 3 (1780): 672; 4 (1781): 426–8; 5 (1782): 347–9; 6 (1783): 398. *AdB* 49:1 (1782): 127–8. *BTJ* 310–13.

[*Das Beste komt zulezt → Der Guck Kasten*]

Der bestrafte Hochmut
unknown
Karl Ludwig Fischer (Leipzig, 1773)

[*Die bestrafte Schöne → Die Blumeninsel*]

[*Die bestrafte Spröde → Die Blumeninsel*]

[*Der betrogene Betrüger → Der Dorfbalbier*]

[*Der betrogene Betrüger → Liebesabentheuer*]

[*Betrug für Betrug* → *Pierre und Narciss*]

[*Die beyden Geizigen* → *Das Grab des Mufti*]

Die Bezauberten
Johann André (after Madame Favart, *Les Ensorcelés, ou Jeannot et Jeannette* [1757],
itself a parody of Marivaux, *Les Surprises de l'amour*)
Johann André (Berlin 1777)
1. (Komische Oper, 1) [André]
   Berlin: Christian Friedrich Himburg, 1777 [Schatz 184, Schaal 202]
2. *Peter und Hannchen* (Operette, 1) ["Die Musik ist vom Uebersetzer"]
   Frankfurt am Main and Leipzig: Esslingerlische Buchhandlung, 1772
BIBL.: *AdB* Appendices 25–36 (1778): 755.
   The second libretto is cited by Stauder. Its date places it one year before
   André's first performed opera, *Der Töpfer* (Hanau, 1773).

Der blaue Montag
Traugott Benjamin Berger
Friedrich Wilhelm Rust (Dessau, 1778)

Das blaue Ungeheuer
Walter Anton Schwick (presumably after Gozzi's *Il mostro turchino*)
Joseph Schubert (Schwedt, 1781)

Der blinde Ehemann
Johann Friedrich Jünger (adapted from Johann Christian Krüger's spoken comedy of
the same name [1747])
Johann Christoph Kaffka (Breslau, 1788)
J. F. Drobisch (Lübeck, 1791)
1. (Operette, 2)
   Berlin: Friedrich Maurer, 1784 [GB-Lbm]
BIBL.: *AdB* 69:1 (1786): 102. *NTD* 2 (1789): 38–46, 112.

Die Blumeninsel
unknown
Karl Friedrich Ebers (Brunswick, 1797)

Der Blumenraub
Karl Siegmund Freiherr von Seckendorff
Karl Siegmund Freiherr von Seckendorff (Weimar, 1784)

Die böse Frau
Carl Alexander Herklots (original)
Gottlob Benedict Bierey (Stettin, 1792)
Ignaz Walter (Hannover, 1794)
1. (Komisches Original-Singspiel, 2)
   Herklots' Operetten (Berlin, 1793), pp. [297]–392 [Schatz 10858]
BIBL.: *ALZ* 1793:4:92–3.

Braut, Friseur, Hexe und Advocat in einer Person
unknown
Friedrich Gottlob Fleischer (Berlin, 1777)

Brutus
Johann Gottfried von Herder (after Shakespeare, *Julius Caesar*, and Plutarch's
"Brutus")
2nd version: Johann Christian Friedrich Bach (Bückeburg, 1774)

1. (Drama zur Musik, [3]) [Bach] (2nd version)
n.p., 1774
Herder's first version, completed by May 1772, was never published in his life-
time. Bach's setting was performed for him on 3 March 1774 and in response to
this Herder eliminated the opening two scenes and substituted a new one, but
too late to be included in the above print, which was arranged for by Prince
Wilhelm of Bückeburg himself. The first version of the text has been printed by
Bernard Suphan in *Herders Sämmtliche Werke* (Berlin: Weidmann, 1884), vol.
28, pp. 11–27.

Clarisse, *oder Das unbekannte Dienstmädgen*
Johann Christian Bock (adapted from J. F. Marmontel, *La Bergère des alpes* [1755])
Karl Leopold Röllig (Hamburg, 1771)
Christian Benjamin Uber (Breslau, 1771)
Johann Christian Frischmuth (Berlin, 1775)
Carl David Stegmann (Hamburg, 1778)
Johann Abraham Peter Schulz (unperformed in German)
1. (Komische Operette, 3)
J. C. Bock: *Für das Deutsche Theater.* Part I (Leipzig: Christian Gottlob Hilscher,
1770), pp. [1]–144 [GB-Lbm]
2. (Komische Operette, 3)
Leipzig: Christian Gottlob Hilscher, 1772 [Schatz 8856]
BIBL.: *AdB* 18:2 (1773): 412; 23:2 (1775): 530 [Uber]. Schmid *DP* 61–73. Schmid
C 307 [194]. *MdM* 1:1 (1783): 585 [Stegmann]. Schütze 382.
The opera is mentioned by Karl Philipp Moritz in his autobiographical novel
Anton Reiser.

Claudine von Villa Bella
Johann Wolfgang von Goethe
1st version: Johann André (unperformed)
2nd version: Johann Friedrich Reichardt (Berlin, 1789)
1st version:
1. (Schauspiel mit Gesang, [1])
Berlin: August Mylius, 1776 [*Wolf.* 441]
2nd version:
1. (Singspiel, [3])
Leipzig: Georg Joachim Göschen, 1788 [*Wolf.* 442, US-Wc PT 1915 C2 1788]
2. (Singspiel, [3]
Goethe's Schriften (Leipzig: Göschen, 1788), vol. 5, pp. 199–324 [*Wolf.* 443]
3A. (Singspiel, [3])
Berlin, 1789 [Schatz 8640]
4A. (Singspiel, [3])
n.p., n.d. [GB-Lbm]
BIBL.: *ABSS* 3 (1776): 189–90. *AdB* 31:2 (1777): 494–5. *BAZG* 1799:240–4
[Reichardt].

Crispin und Eliante
unknown
Johann Gottfried Krebs (Rostock, 1776)

Cyrus und Kassandane
Carl Wilhelm Ramler
Johann Daniel Hensel (Halle, 1786)

1. (Singspiel, [1])
   Berlinische Monatsschrift 4 (1784): 97–130 [*Wolf.* 510]
2. (Singspiel, [1])
   Karl Wilhelm Ramlers poetische Werke (Berlin: Sandersche Buchhandlung, 1825),
   pt. 2, pp. 84–123 [D-Mbs]

[*Cyrus und Kassandra* → *Cyrus und Kassandane*]

[*Die dankbare Tochter* → *Julie*]

Daphne, oder Die Frühlingsfeier in Arkadien
Johann Daniel Hensel (adapted from C. F. Weisse, *Das Denkmal in Arkadien*)
Johann Daniel Hensel (Hirschberg, 1799)
1. (Oper, [3])
   J. D. Hensel: *Singspiele* (Hirschberg: Wolfgang Pittschiller und Komp., 1799), vol.
   1, pp. 77–116 [Schatz 4635, US-Wc ML 49 A2H3]
   Sonneck prints an excerpt from the preface (pp. 545–6).

Das hätt' ich nicht gedacht!
Christian August Vulpius
August Friedrich Burgmüller (Weimar, 1788)

Demokrit
C. F. Schröter (adapted from Regnard, *Démocrite* [1700])
Christian Kalkbrenner (Rheinsberg, 1791)
1. (Komische Oper, 3) [Kalkbrenner]
   Berlin: Friedrich Maurer, 1791 [Schatz 4997]

Das Denkmal in Arkadien
Christian Felix Weisse (after George Keate, *The Monument in Arcadia* [1773])
Johann Adam Hiller (unperformed)
Karl Hunt (Dresden, 1791)
1. (Ländliches Schauspiel für die Jugend mit untermischten Gesängen, 1) *Der Kinder-
   freund: Ein Wochenblatt* (Leipzig: Siegfried Lebrecht Crusius, 1782) pt. 24, nos.
   321–6 (25 Aug–29 Sep 1781), pp. 117–92
BIBL.: Hiller *L*, p. 314.

Der Derwisch
Rathje
F. G. Reymann (Neustrelitz, 1797)

Der Deserteur
unknown (after J. M. Sedaine, *Le Déserteur* [1767])
Johann Michael Helmig (Breslau, 1772)
Johann Gottfried Schwanenberger (Brunswick, 1784)

Deukalion und Pyrrha
unknown
Anton Laube (Berlin, 1777)

Doktor Faust
Heinrich Gottlieb Schmieder (after Goethe's *Faust* [Part One])
Ignaz Walter (1st version: Bremen, 1797; 2nd version: Hannover, 1798)
1A. (Original-Oper, 4) [Walter] (1st version)
    Bremen: Friedrich Meiers Erben, n.d. [Schatz 10859]

Dr. Fausts Leibgürtel
Bernhard Christoph d'Arien (after Rousseau, *La Ceinture magique*)
Karl Hanke (Hamburg, 1786)

Doktor Fausts Zaubergürtel
Wilhelm Christhelf Siegmund Mylius and Johann Friedrich Schink (after Rousseau,
La Ceinture magique)
Otto Christian Friedrich Phanty (Lübeck, 1784)
1. *Doktor Fausts Leibgürtel* (Posse. . . mit Gesang, 1)
   Gotha: Karl Wilhelm Ettinger, 1781 [D-GOl, Poes. 2700]
BIBL.: Plümicke 334–5.

[*Don Chisciotto* → *Don Quixotte der Zweite*]

Don Quixotte, *oder Das Abentheuer am Hofe*
unknown
Franz Stanislaus Spindler (Breslau, 1797)
1A. (Oper, 2) [Spindler]
    Breslau: Königl. privil. Graffische Stadtbuchdruckerey, 1798 [D-B Mus. Ts 1604]

Don Quixotte der Zweite
Karl Ditters von Dittersdorf (from the Italian)
Karl Ditters von Dittersdorf (Oels, 1795)
1. (Komisches Singspiel, 2)
   Oels: Samuel Gottlieb Ludwig, n.d. [Schatz 2589]
BIBL.: *ALZ* 1796:1:71–2

Don Sylvio von Rosalva, *oder Der Sieg der Natur über die Schwärmerey*
Samuel Gottlieb Bürde (adapted from Wieland's novel *Der Sieg der Natur über die
Schwärmerey oder Die Abentheuer des Don Sylvio von Rosalva* [1764])
Otto Christian Friedrich Phanty (Schleswig, 1796)
F. J. Siegmund Sander (Oels, 1797)
Gottlob Bachmann (Brunswick, 1797)
Karl Wilhelm Müller (Berlin, 1799)
1. (Komische Oper, 5)
   Königsberg: Friedrich Nicolovius, 1795 [Schatz 9371, 8004]
BIBL.: *ALZ* 1797:1:84–5

Der Dorfbalbier
Christian Felix Weisse (after Sedaine, *Blaise le savetier* [1759])
Johann Adam Hiller and Christian Gottlob Neefe (Leipzig, 1771)
1A. *Der Dorfbarbier* (Comische Oper, 2)
    n.p., 1771 [USSR-KAu]
2. (Komische Oper, 2)
   Leipzig: Dyckische Buchhandlung, 1772 [Schatz 4719]
3. (Komische Oper, 2)
   [C. F. Weisse:] *Komische Opern* (Leipzig: Dyckische Buchhandlung, 1772), vol. 2,
   pp. 273–360 [Schaal 336]
4. (Komische Oper, 2)
   Komische Opern (Berlin and Leipzig, 1776), vol. 3, pp. 353–414 [D-B Mus. T 145]
5. (Komische Oper, 2)
   C. F. Weisse: *Komische Opern* (Carlsruhe: Schmieder, 1778), vol. 2, pp. [195]–252
   [Schaal 337, US-Wc ML 49 A2W2]
BIBL.: Schmid *T* 59–60, 136–9. *AdB* 24:2 (1775): 418–19. Neefe, *Lebenslauf*, p. 14.
   Sonneck prints an excerpt from the preface to no. 1 (p. 406).

[*Der Dorfbarbier* → *Der Dorfbalbier*]

Die Dorfdeputirten
Gottlob Ephraim Heermann (after Goldoni's comedy *Il feudatorio* [1752])
Ernst Wilhelm Wolf (Weimar, 1772)
1. (Komische Oper, 3)
    Weimar: Carl Ludolf Hoffmann, 1773 [Schatz 11077]
2. (Komische Oper, 3)
    Komische Opern (Berlin and Leipzig, 1774), vol. 1, pp. 1–152 [D-B Mus. T 145]
3A. (Komische Oper, 3)
    Riga: Gottlob Christian Froelich, n.d. [Schatz 11077a]
BIBL.: *AdB* 23:1 (1774): 250–2. *KT* 299. *AdT* 2 (1788): 95.

Die Dorfgala
Johann Friedrich Wilhelm Gotter
Anton Schweitzer (Weimar, 1772)
1A. (Operette, 2)
    n.p., 1772 [Schaal 341]
2. (Lustspiel. . . mit Arien und Gesängen, 3) [Schweitzer]
    Gotha: Carl Wilhelm Ettinger, 1774 [Schatz 9770, *Wolf.* 590]
3A. (Komische Oper, 2) [Schweitzer]
    Hamburg: J. M. Michaelsen, 1778 [Schatz 9771]
4A. (Singspiel, 1) [Schweitzer]
    Berlin. 1805 [D-B Mus. Ts 1126]
BIBL.: Schmid *C* 344 [218]. *AdB* 25:2 (1775): 499–501, Appendices 25–36 (1778): 874.
LTZ 7 (1784): 37 (1-act).
      In *AdB* 25:2 (1775): 501 the reviewer Biesler points out borrowings from
Shakespeare's *Midsummer Night's Dream*, Voltaire's *Pucelle*, and Horace.

[*Der Dorfjahrmarkt* → *Der Jahrmarkt*]

[*Drei Heirathen an einem Tage* → *Die Singschule*]

[*Die drei Wünsche* → *Der Holzhauer*]

[*Die drey Wünsche* → *Sultan Wampum*]

Die Ehestandskandidaten, *oder Die Parodie aus dem Stegreife*
Johann Christoph Kaffka (adapted from Baczko's *Die Singschule* [q.v.])
Gottlob Benedict Bierey (Leipzig, 1796)
1. (Komisches Singspiel, 2) [Bierey]
    Riga and Leipzig: Nordische Commissionshandlung, 1805 [Schatz 1021]

Ehestandsszenen
unknown
Georg Ernst Gottlieb Kallenbach (Magdeburg, 1795)

Der ehrliche Räuber
Ch. G. Korb
Georg Bernhard Leopold Zeller (Neubrandenburg, 1787)
1. (Schauspiel mit Gesang, 2) [Zeller]
    Neubrandenburg: die Officin des Verfassers, 1785 [Schatz 11164]
    Sonneck prints an excerpt from the preface (p. 425).

Der ehrliche Schweizer
Caroline Luise von Klenke
Heinrich Christoph Hattasch (Hamburg, 1780)

1. (Schauspiel, 2)
   Berlin and Leipzig: George Jacob Decker, 1776 [GB-Lbm]
   The arias are not included in the text itself but printed in an appendix
   (pp. 101–8) as "Willkührliche Arien."

Ehrlichkeit und Liebe
Christian Jacob Wagenseil (two scenes are derived from Gessner's *Erast*)
Ernst Wilhelm Wolf (Weimar, 1776)
1. (Ländliches Schauspiel mit Gesang, 1) [Wolf]
   Gotha: Carl Wilhelm Ettinger, 1779 [D-B Mus. Tw 651]
2A. (Ländliches Schauspiel mit Gesang, [1]) [Wolf]
   Kaufbeuren: Neth, 1781 [Schatz 11078]
BIBL.: *LTZ* 2 (1779): 590–2. *TM* 1779:1 (March): 284; 1780:2 (June): 245; 1782:3
(July): 85. *AdB* 41:2 (1780): 461–2. *AdM* 1780:53
   No. 2A contains three numbers not found in no. 1, including a handwritten
   addition (in Wagenseil's hand) in the Schatz copy – "Wolthat des Lebens" –
   which he describes as "after my composition." Another, "Blühe, liebes Veilchen," carries the footnote: "This little song does not properly belong to the
   piece, but an attempt has been made to work it in owing to its special naïveté
   and its lovely melody." After the text Wagenseil wrote the poet's name,
   [Christian Adolf] Overbeck. The Lied "Was ist Lieb?" found in both librettos
   is taken from the novel *Siegwart*.

Der Eichenstamm
unknown
Hausing (Stade, 1798)

[*Die Eifersucht auf dem Lande* → *Die Kirmess*]

Einer jagt den Andern
unknown
Wilhelm Kopprasch (Dessau, *ca.* 1795)

[*Eines wird doch helfen* → *Eins wird doch helfen*]

Der Einsiedler
L.
Christian Gotthilf Weisflog (no performance known)
   A libretto with this title is listed in Section B of Part II.

Der Einspruch
Johann Benjamin Michaelis
Christian Gottlob Neefe (1st version: Leipzig, 1772; 2nd version: Berlin, 1773)
1. (Operette, 1)
   Leipzig: Dyckische Buchhandlung, 1772 [Schatz 7071]
2. (Operette, 1)
   Operetten von J. B. Michaelis (Leipzig: Dyckische Buchhandlung, 1772). vol. 1, pp.
   55–162 [Schaal 352]
3. (Operette, 1)
   Theater der Deutschen (Königsberg and Leipzig: Johann Jacob Kanter, 1773),
   pt. 13, pp. 249–328 [GB-Lbm]
4. (no desig., 1) [Neefe]
   Lyrisches Theater der Deutschen (Leipzig: Dyckische Buchhandlung, 1782), vol. 1,
   no. 3 [D-W Lo 1133]

5. (Operette, 1)
Sämmtliche Werke des Johann Benjamin Michaelis (Vienna: Alberti, 1791), vol. 4, pp. 59–150 [*Wolf.* 619]
BIBL.: *AdB* 24:1 (1775): 111. Schmid *C* 329 [208].
   Nos. 2 and 4 are the original edition of 1772 with a new title page (and pages renumbered in no. 2). Sonneck prints an excerpt from the preface (pp. 426–7). No. 4 omits the preface.

[*Die Einsprüche* → *Der Einspruch*]

Eins wird doch helfen, *oder Die Werbung aus Liebe*
Johann Daniel Sander (after Le Sage and d'Orneval)
Johann André (Berlin, 1782)
1A. (Komische Oper, 2) [André]
   n.p., 1784
BIBL.: *BTJ* 414–15. *BTML* 255. *LTZ* 7 (1784): 146.

[*Der eiserne Mann* → *Gott Mars*]

Elmine
Carl Wilhelm Freiherr von Drais
Johann André (Berlin, 1782)
1. (Schauspiel mit Gesang, 3)
   Nürnberg: George Peter Monath, 1781 [Schatz 185]
BIBL.: *BTJ* 123–4. *LTZ* 5 (1782): 138–9. *AdB* 49:1 (1782): 127–8. *MdM* 1:1 (1783): 487–8. *TM* 1782:1 (February): 170.

[*Endlich fand er sie* → *Der Irrwisch*]

[*Endlich hat er sie* → *Der Irrwisch*]

[*Die Entführung aus dem Serail* → *Belmont und Constanze*]

Die Entzauberung
unknown
Joseph Schubert (Schwedt, 1781)

Die Erbschaft
unknown
Christian Gotthilf Weisflog (Sagan, 1776)

Der Eremit auf Formentera
August von Kotzebue
Ernst Wilhelm Wolf (Weimar, 1786)
Nikolaus Mühle (Königsberg, 1790)
Karl Ebers (Schwerin, 1793)
August Himbert Hinze (Waldenburg, 1797)
Johann Heinrich Carl Bornhardt (Brunswick, 1797)
1. (Schauspiel mit Gesang, 2)
   Reval: Iversen & Fehmer, 1787 [D-B Mus. Tw 652]
2. (Schauspiel mit Gesang, 2)
   Sammlung der besten und neuesten Schauspiele (Mainz: Sartorius, 1778), vol. 2 [Schaal 375]
3A. (Oper, 2) [Wolf]
   [Regensburg,] 1790 [Schatz 11081]
4. (Schauspiel mit Gesang, 2)
   Deutsche Schaubühne (Augsburg, 1790), vol. 7, pp. 1–76 [GB-Lbm]

5. (Schauspiel mit Gesang, 2)
   Frankfurt and Leipzig, 1794 [*Wolf.* 646]
BIBL.: *JLM* 5 (1790): 115, 142. *AdT* 15 (1795): 80 [Mühle] *ALZ* 1789:1:183–4.
The original edition of the libretto (no. 1) contains a letter of dedication to
Fräulein Maria von Rosen and a preface addressed to the reader. The latter
states that Wolf has already composed the text, and the former mentions that
Kotzebue had written the work two years earlier (in 1785) and that it had been
performed for the first time on the Rosen family's private stage with Maria von
Rosen taking the part of Selima.

Das Erntefest
Christian Gotthilf Weisflog
Christian Gotthilf Weisflog (Bautzen, 1769)

[*Der Erntekranz* → *Der Aerndtekranz*]

Erwin und Elmire
Johann Wolfgang von Goethe (based on a poetic romance in Chapter 8 of Gold-
smith's *The Vicar of Wakefield* [1766])
1st version:
Johann André (Berlin, 1775)
Anton Schweitzer (unperformed)
Duchess Anna Amalia (Weimar, 1776)
Carl David Stegmann (Königsberg, 1776)
Ernst Wilhelm Wolf (Weimar, 1785)
2nd version:
Johann Friedrich Reichardt (Berlin, 1793)
1st version:
1. (Schauspiel mit Gesang, [2])
   Iris 2:3 (March, 1775): 161–224 [*Wolf.* 662]
2. (Schauspiel mit Gesang, [2])
   Frankfurt and Leipzig, 1775 [US-BE]
3. (Schauspiel mit Gesang, [2])
   Frankfurt and Leipzig, 1775 [Schatz 186]
4. (Schauspiel mit Gesang, [2])
   Berlin: Himburg, 1776 [*Wolf.* 663]
5A. (Operette, [2])
   Weimar: [Glüsing], [15 May] 1776
6. (Schauspiel mit Gesang, [2])
   Theater der Deutschen, vol. 17 (Königsberg and Leipzig, 1776), no. 112
7. (Schauspiel mit Gesang, 2)
   Regensburg: mit Breitfeldischen Schriften, n.d. [Schatz 11453]
2nd version:
1. (Singspiel, [2])
   Leipzig: Georg Joachim Göschen, 1788 [*Wolf.* 664, US-Wc PT 1915 E8 1788]
2. (Singspiel, [2])
   Goethe's Schriften (Leipzig: Göschen, 1788), vol. 5, pp. 325–88 [*Wolf.* 665]
3. (Singspiel, [2])
   Berlin, 1793 [D-BNms]
BIBL.: *Iris* 3:3 (June 1775): 238–9; 4:1 (July 1775): 57–9; 7:3 (1776): 697. Schubart *DC*
1775: 615–16; 1776: 599–600 [André]. *TM* 1776:1 (January): 9–10; 1776:2 (May):
197–8; 1798:1 (March): 349 [Reichardt]. *AdB* 31:2 (1777): 493–4. Dressler, *Theater-
Schule*, p. 32. *LTZ* 5 (1782): 137 [André]. *BTJ* 60, 358–9 [André]. *BmZ* 32:125
[Reichardt], 177. *ALZ* 1794:3:774–6 [Reichardt].

No. 1 of the first version includes André's music for the Romanze "Das Veil-chen" and the aria "Ein Schauspiel für Götter" bound in. Nos. 2 and 3 of the first version differ only in that the former has Goethe's name on the title page. No. 3 is in fact an offprint of no. 1, and only fifty copies were issued. For the 2nd version, no. 1 is a separate edition of no. 2.

Esther
Friedrich Ernst Jester
Karl Siegmund Schönbeck (Königsberg, 1793)

Die Execution
unknown
Johann Mattheus König (Ellrich, 1784)

[*Das Fest der Flora* → *Der Frühling*]

Das Findelkind
Christian Felix Weisse
Georg Benda (unperformed)
1. *Unverhoft kömt oft, oder Das Findelkind* (Komische Oper, 1)
   Briefwechsel der Familie des Kinderfreundes (Leipzig: Siegfried Lebrecht Crusius, 1786), pt. 5, pp. 103–234 [GB-Lbm]
BIBL.: *AdB* Appendices 53–86 (1789): 1881–3.

Die Fischerinn
Johann Wolfgang von Goethe
Corona Elisabeth Wilhelmine Schröter (Tiefurth, 1782)
1. (Singspiel, [1])
   [Weimar: Glüsing,] 1782 [Schatz 9696]
2. (Singspiel, [1])
   Litteratur- und Theater-Zeitung 5 (1782): 593–604, 609–19
   No. 1 was printed in 150 copies for the première at the order and expense of Anna Amalia.

Die Fischerweiber in Paris
unknown
Carl Joseph Birnbach (Breslau, 1790)

[*Die Flucht nach Asien* → *Lieb' um Liebe*]

Fräulein von Ueberklug und Herr Gleichzu
unknown
Frisch (Brunswick, 1769)

[*Die Frage und die Antwort* → *Lisuart und Dariolette*]

Fremore und Melime
H. Graf von Spaur
Nikolaus Mühle (Königsberg, 1778)
[1. (Schauspiel mit Gesang, 3) [Michl]
   Frankfurt am Main: mit Andreaeischen Schriften, 1778 [Schatz 6484]
BIBL.: *LTZ* 1 (1778): 155–7, 368. *TSS* 358–9.
   The *TSS* observes that "it takes its plot from a well-known novel."

Der Frühling
Johann Martin Kellner
Johann Gottlieb Feige (Breslau, 1775)

[*Die Frühlingsfeier in Arkadien* → *Daphne*]

Das Frühstück auf der Jagd, *oder Der neue Richter*
Christian Gotthilf Weisflog
Christian Gotthilf Weisflog (Sagan, 1772)
1. (Ländliches Lustspiel mit Gesang, 2)
    Sorau and Leipzig: Erdmann Gotthelf Deinzer, 1785 [Schatz 10983]
BIBL.: *DB* 29:456.
    The libretto describes the work as "principally for school theaters."

[*Die Gärtnerin* → *Lilla*]

Das Gärtnermädchen
Johann Carl August Musäus (based on the French novel *La Jardinière de Vincennes*)
Ernst Wilhelm Wolf (Weimar, 1769)
Franz Andreas Holly (Breslau, 1775)
1A. (Komische Oper, 3) [Wolf]
    n.p., 1769
2. (Komische Oper, 3)
    Weimar: Karl Rudolf Hoffmann, 1771 [Schatz 11079, Schaal 453]
3. (Komische Oper, 3)
    Komische Opern (Berlin and Leipzig, 1775), vol. 2, pp. 1–112 [D-B Mus. T 145]
BIBL.: *UeKS* 89–94. Schmid *C* 281 [178]. *AdB* 33:1 (1778): 168–9. Schmid *T* 140–9.
DBW 3 (1769): 520–1, 525; 4 (1770): 645–7.
    Sonneck prints an excerpt from the preface to no. 2 (pp. 540–1) in which Mus-
äus mentions a corrupt version of his text published at Berlin by a member of
Koch's troupe and complains of the adverse criticism of his libretto by Christian Heinrich Schmid.

[*Geisterbanner* → *Das Gespenst mit der Trommel*]

Die Geisterbeschwörung (I)
Carl Alexander Herklots
Casimir Antonio Cartellieri (Berlin, 1793)
BIBL.: *BmZ* 16:61–2.

Die Geisterbeschwörung (II)
Johann Daniel Hensel
Johann Daniel Hensel (Hirschberg, 1799)
1. (Operette, [3])
    Singspiele von Johann Daniel Hensel (Hirschberg: Wolfgang Pittschiller und
    Komp., 1799), vol. 1, pp. 1–76 [Schatz 4653, US-Wc ML 49 A2H3]

Die Geisterinsel (I)
Johann Friedrich Wilhelm Gotter and Friedrich Hildebrand von Einsiedel (after
Shakespeare, *The Tempest*)
Johann Friedrich Reichardt (Berlin, 1798)
Friedrich Wilhelm Haack (Stettin, 1798)
1. (Singspiel, 3)
    Die Horen 3 (1797), pt. 8, [1]–26 and pt. 9, [1]–78
2A. (Singspiel, 3) [Reichardt]
    Berlin, 1798 [Schatz 8641]
3. (Singspiel, 3)
    F. W. Gotter: *Literarischer Nachlass* (Gotha: J. Perthes, 1802), pp. 419–564
    [GB-Lbm]
BIBL.: *HT* 2:667–72, 730–5. *BAZG* 1798:2, pp. 295–302 [Reichardt]. *AMZ* 1 (1798/9):
16, *Intelligenz-Blatt* 5–6, 2 (1799/1800): 135 [Haack]. *JLM* 14 (1799): 355. *ALZ*
1799:4:84–7 [Reichardt].

Die Geisterinsel (II)
Johann Daniel Hensel (after Gotter, *Die Geisterinsel*; Döring, *Der Sturm*; and
Shakespeare, *The Tempest*)
Johann Daniel Hensel (Hirschberg, 1799)
1. (Singspiel, 4)
   Hirschberg: Wolfgang Pittschiller und Komp., 1799 [Schatz 4637]
   Sonneck prints an excerpt from the preface (p. 546).

Gelegenheit macht Diebe
Karl Franz Henisch
Franz Andreas Holly (Breslau, 1775)

[*Das gerettete Troja* → *Poltis*]

Das Gespenst mit der Trommel
Carl Ditters von Dittersdorf (after Goldoni's opera buffa *Il Conte Caramella* [1751],
itself based on Addison's *The Drummer*)
Carl Ditters von Dittersdorf (Oels, 1794)
1. (Deutsches komisches Singspiel, 2) [Dittersdorf]
   Oels: Samuel Gottlieb Ludwig, n.d. [Schatz 2591, Schaal 463]
   The libretto may also be found in the microfilm series *German Baroque Litera-*
   ture (Yale University, no. 1792) where the text is misattributed to Frau Luise
   Gottsched, who wrote a prose translation of Addison's comedy.
BIBL.: *ALZ* 1796:1:255-6.

[*Eine glückliche Entwicklung* → *Der Transport im Koffer*]

Das glückliche Unglück
unknown
Christian Gotthilf Weisflog (Sagan, *ca.* 1780)

Glück und Zufall
Carl August Ludwig Freiherr von Lichtenstein
Carl August Ludwig Freiherr von Lichtenstein (Hannover, 1793)

Gott Mars, *oder Der eiserne Mann*
Carl Ditters von Dittersdorf
Carl Ditters von Dittersdorf (Oels, 1795)
1. (Komisches Singspiel, 2) [Dittersdorf]
   Oels: Samuel Gottlieb Ludwig, n.d. [Schatz 2592]
BIBL.: *ALZ* 1796:3:511-12.

Das Grab des Mufti, *oder Die zwey Geizigen*
August Gottlieb Meissner (after F. de Falbaire, *Les Deux Avares* [1770])
Gotthilf von Baumgarten (Breslau, 1776)
Johann Adam Hiller (Leipzig, 1779)
1. (Komische Oper, 2)
   Leipzig: Dyckische Buchhandlung, 1776 [Schatz 4720]
2. (no desig., 2)
   A. G. Meissner: *Operetten* (Leipzig: Dyckische Buchhandlung, 1778) [US–Wc ML
   49 A2M3]
BIBL.: *AdB* 30:1 (1777): 239; 46:1 (1781): 184. *LTZ* 3 (1780): 782-3.
   No. 2 is no. 1 with a title page for the collected edition added. Sonneck prints
   an excerpt from the preface to no. 1 (p. 572).

Das grosse Loos
Friedrich Johann Justin Bertuch (after Favart, *Le Coq du village* [1743])
Ernst Wilhelm Wolf (Gotha, 1774)

1. (Komische Oper, 2) [Wolf]
   Weimar: Carl Ludolf Hoffmann, 1774 [Schatz 11080, Schaal 487]
2. (Komische Oper, 2)
   Komische Opern (Berlin and Leipzig, 1776), vol. 3, pp. 265–350 [D-B Mus. T 145]
BIBL.: Schubart *DC* 1774: 478–9. *AdB* 25:2 (1775): 499–501.

Der Guck Kasten, *oder Das Beste komt zulezt*
Johann Christoph Kaffka (after the Italian)
Johann Christoph Kaffka (Breslau, 1782)
1. (Komiche Operette, 2)
   J. C. Kaffka: *Sammlung auserlesener Theaterstücke in die deutsche Bühne bearbeitet* (Breslau, 1784), pp. [73]–126 [Schatz 4984]

Hänschen und Gretchen
Johann Christian Bock (after Sedaine, *Rose et Colas* [1764])
Johann Friedrich Reichardt (unperformed)
BIBL.: Reichardt *BaRM* I:154. *AdB* 24:1 (1775): 112. Schmid *C* 340–1 [215–16].

[*Haphire* → *Xaphire*]

Hass und Aussöhnung, *oder Die verfolgte und triumphirende Liebe*
Ernst Ferdinand Rordorf
Josef Grüger (Breslau, 1797)
1. (Schauspiel mit Gesang, 4)
   Glatz: Ernst Ferdinand Rordorf, 1797 [Schatz 4223]

[*Hass und Versöhnung* → *Hass und Aussöhnung*]

[*Der Hauptmann von Bärenzahn* → *Gott Mars*]

Heinrich und Lyda
Bernhard Christoph d'Arien (a reworking of his prose drama of 1774)
Christian Gottlob Neefe (Berlin, 1776)
1. (Scene aus dem menschlichen Leben, [1])
   Leipzig: Christian Gottlob Hilscher, 1776 [Schatz 7073]
BIBL.: *AdB* 29:2 (1776): 504–5, Appendices 23–56 (1778): 875. *Berlinisches Literarisches Wochenblatt* (1776): 56. *TM* 1776:1 (February): 192. Schubart *DC* 1776:239.

Helva und Zeline
unknown
Heinrich Christoph Hattasch (Hamburg, 1795)

Heyrath aus Liebe
Hermann Ewald Schack
Johann Friedrich Hönicke (Gotha, 1777)
1. (Nachspiel mit Arien und Gesängen, [1])
   Gotha: Carl Wilhelm Ettinger, 1781 [Schatz 4787]
BIBL.: *AdB* 51:2 (1782): 424.

Der Holzhauer, *oder Die drey Wünsche* (I)
unknown (after Castet and Guichard, *Le Bûcheron* [1763])
Johann Friedrich Reichardt (unperformed)

Der Holzhauer, *oder Die drey Wünsche* (II)
Johann Joachim Eschenburg (after Castet and Guichard, *Le Bûcheron* [1763])
Johann August Christoph Koch (Berlin, 1774)
BIBL.: Schmid *C* 340–1 [215–16]

Der Holzhauer, *oder Die drey Wünsche* (III)
Johann Friedrich Wilhelm Gotter and Wulf (after Castet and Guichard, *Le Bûcheron*
[1763])
Georg Benda (Gotha, 1778)
1. (Komische Oper, 1)
    Berlin: Christian Friedrich Himburg, 1772 [Schatz 770a]
2A. (Komische Operette, 1) [Benda]
    Riga: Gottlob Christian Froelich, n.d. [Schatz 770a]
BIBL.: *AdB* 20:1 (1773): 226; 40:1 (1780): 128–30. *LTZ* 3 (1780): 250–1; 4 (1781): 356–7.
Plümicke 276.

Hüon und Amande
Friederike Sophie Seyler (after Wieland's epic poem *Oberon* [1781])
Karl Hanke (Schleswig, 1789)
1. (Romantisches Singspiel, 5)
    Flensburg, Schleswig, and Leipzig: Kortensche Buchhandlung, 1789 [*Wolf.* 881]
BIBL.: *ALZ* 1790:4:317.

Das Inkognito
Carl Alexander Herklots (after St.-Foix, *Julie, ou l'heureuse épreuve* [1746])
Josef August Gürrlich (Berlin, 1797)
1A. (Singspiel, 1)
    Berlin, 1792 [D-B Mus. Tg 1106]
2. (Singspiel, 1)
    Herklots' Operetten (Berlin, 1793), pp. [1]–56 [Schatz 4372a]
BIBL.: *ALZ* 1793:4:92–3.

Die Insel der Alcina
Carl Alexander Herklots (after Bertati, *L'isola di Alcina* [1772])
Antonio Bianchi (Berlin, 1794)

[*Die Insel der Verführung* → *Rinaldo und Alcina*]

[*Die Irrthümer der Zauberei* → *Die Zauberirrungen*]

Der Irrwisch, *oder Endlich fand er sie*
Christoph Friedrich Bretzner
Franz Andreas Holly (Breslau, 1779)
Friedrich Preu (Leipzig, 1779)
Otto Carl Erdmann Freiherr von Kospoth (Berlin, 1780)
1. (Operette, 3) [Preu]
    C. F. Bretzner: *Operetten* (Leipzig, 1779), vol. 1 [Schatz 11680]
2. (Operette, 3)
    Stuttgart: Christoph Gottfried Mäntler, 1779 [Schaal 527]
3. (Operette, 3)
    Stuttgart: Christoph Gottfried Mäntler, 1782 [Schatz 2579]
4A. (Singspiel, 3) [Kospoth]
    n.p., 1784 [US-Wc ML 50.2 I68K6]
5A. (Operette, 3) [Kospoth]
    n.p., 1787 [Schatz 5218]
6. (Operette, 3) [Preu]
    Leipzig: Carl Friedrich Schneider, 1788 [Schatz 8464]
BIBL.: *LTZ* 2 (1779): 695–6; 4 (1781): 111–12, 121; 5 (1782): 713 [Mühle]. *AdB* 41:2
(1780): 457–9; 89:2 (1789): 418. *TM* 1780:2 (June): 244–5. *BTJ* 332–9 [Kospoth]. *KT*
129–35. *DB* 11:172–4. *AdM* 1780:40–1.

Der italienische Garkoch zu Genua
"von einem Freund des Schauspiels"
Anton Laube and Joseph Schubert (Berlin, 1777)

Die Jagd
Christian Felix Weisse (after Collé's spoken comedy *La Partie de chasse de Henri IV.*
and Sedaine's libretto *Le Roi et le fermier,* both based on Robert Dodsley's story "The
Miller and the Maid of Mansfield")
Johann Adam Hiller (Weimar, 1770)
1. (Komische Oper, 3)
   Leipzig: Dyckische Buchhandlung, 1770 [Schatz 4721]
2A. (Komische Oper, 3)
   n.p., 1770 [D-B Mus. Th 700/1]
3. (Komische Oper, 3)
   Leipzig: Dyckische Buchhandlung, 1771 [Schaal 542]
4. (Komische Oper, 3)
   [C. F. Weisse:] *Komische Opern* (Leipzig: Dyckische Buchhandlung, 1771), vol. 3
   [Schaal 543]
5. (Komische Oper, 3)
   Leipzig: Dyckische Buchhandlung, 1772 [D-B Mus. Th 700/3]
6. (Komische Oper, 3)
   Komische Opern (Berlin and Leipzig, 1776), vol. 3, pp. 1–160
7. (Komische Oper, 3)
   C. F. Weisse: *Komische Opern* (Carlsruhe: Schneider, 1778), vol. 3 [Schaal 544,
   US–Wc ML 49 A2W2]
8. (Komische Oper, 3)
   Prague: J. Eman, 1785 [US-BE]
9A. (Komische Oper, 3)
   n.p., 1796 [D-B Mus. Th 700/2]
BIBL.: *AdB* 17:2 (1772): 564–8; 19:2 (1773): 429–38; 35:1 (1778): 177–9. Reichardt,
Ueber die deutsche comische Oper, pp. 24–96. Reichardt *BaRM* I:154–6. *UeKS* 27–32.
Schmid *C* 296–7 [187–8]. Schink *DM* 3:653–63. *DBW* 4 (1770): 212.

Das Jahresfest
Neumann
Johann Christian Ohlhorst (Neustrelitz, 1783)

Der Jahrmarkt
Johann Friedrich Wilhelm Gotter; 2-act version adapted by Johann Jakob Engel
Georg Benda (Gotha, 1775)
1. (Komische Oper, 2)
   F. W. Gotter: *Singspiele* (Leipzig: Dyckische Buchhandlung, 1778), vol. 1, no. 2
   [Schatz 772, *Wolf.* 956, US-Wc ML 50.2 J2B2]
2. (Komisches Singspiel, 1) [Benda]
   Vienna: Logenmeister, 1779 [*Wolf.* 957]
3A. *Der Dorfjahrmarkt* (no desig., [2])
   n.p., 1790 [Schatz 773]
BIBL.: Schmid *C* 356 [225]. *TM* 1775:3 (September): 275–6; 1780:2 (June): 244. *LTZ*
1 (1778): 600–3; 6 (1783): 404. *AdB* 34:1 (1778): 222–4; 74:2 (1787): 438. *TSS* 293.
Brandes, *Lebensgeschichte,* II: 193–4.
   Sonneck prints an excerpt from the notice to the reader in no. 1 as well as a
   translation of the preface to Benda's KLA (pp. 658–9). A manuscript of the
   one-act version of Gotter's libretto is at D-GOl, Chart. B 1474.

Das Jahrmarktsfest zu Plundersweilern
Johann Wolfgang von Goethe
Duchess Anna Amalia (Weimar, 1778)
[1. (Schönbartspiel, [1])
Leipzig and Frankfurt, 1774 [*Wolf.* 958]
[2. (Schönbartspiel, [1]
Goethe's Schriften (Vienna and Leipzig, 1789), vol. 1, pp. 7–66 [*Wolf.* 959]
Anna Amalia set a second and expanded version of this farce, for which no
eighteenth-century libretto is known.

Jery und Bätely
Johann Wolfgang von Goethe
1st version: Karl Siegmund Freiherr von Seckendorff (Weimar, 1780)
2nd version: Johann Otto Heinrich Schaum (Oels, 1795),
Gottlob Benedict Bierey (Leipzig, 1795)
2nd version:
1. (Singspiel, [1])
Leipzig: Georg Joachim Göschen, 1790 [US-Wc PT 1958 J5 1790]
2. (Singspiel, [1])
Leipzig: Georg Joachim Göschen, 1790 [US-Wc PT 1958 J5 1790a]
3. (Singspiel, [1])
Goethe's Schriften (Leipzig: Georg Joachim Göschen, 1790), vol. 7, pp. 161–224
[*Wolf.* 971]
Sonneck notes that nos. 1 and 2 differ only in two slight particulars. Reichardt
also set the second version around 1791, but it was not performed until 1801.

[*Johann Faust* → *Doktor Faust*]

[*Das Jubelfest* → *Die Jubelhochzeit*]

Die Jubelhochzeit
Christian Felix Weisse (original)
Johann Adam Hiller (Berlin, 1773)
1. (Komische Oper, 3)
Leipzig: Dyckische Buchhandlung, 1773 [Schatz 4722]
2. (Komische Oper, 3)
Komische Opern (Berlin and Leipzig, 1774), vol. 1, no. 3 [D-B Mus. T 145]
3. (Komische Oper, 3)
C. F. Weisse: *Lustspiele* (Carlsruhe: Schmieder, 1778), vol. 3, pp. 351–520 [*Wolf.*
976]
BIBL.: *AdB* 22 (1774): 220–2, 241–2. Schmid *C* 334 [211–12]. *TW* 13–15, 97–120.

Julie, *oder Die dankbare Tochter*
F. G. von Nesselrode
Davander (Dresden, 1781)
[1. (Lustspiel mit Gesang, [3]) [Kirzinger]
Regensburg: Montagische Buchhandlung, 1780 [Schatz 5339]
It is not certain that this is the *Julie* which Davander set.

[*Julie und Romeo* → *Romeo und Julie*]

Die Kantons-Revision
Ludwig Adolf Franz Joseph von Baczko
Wilhelm Ferdinand Halter (Königsberg, 1792)

1. (Komische Oper, 3)
   Königsberg: Hartung, 1794 [Schatz 4449]
BIBL.: *MM* 2:53, 84.

Der Kapellmeister und die Schülerin
Johann Christian Ast
Anton Laube (Stralsund, 1768)

Karoline, *oder Die Parforcejagd*
Carl August Gottlieb Seidel
Otto Carl Erdmann Freiherr von Kospoth (unperformed)
1. (Operette, 4)
   n.p., 1781 [US-Wc ML 50.2 K2]

Der Kaufmann von Smyrna
Christian Friedrich Schwan (adapted from his translation [1770] of Chamfort's comedy)
Franz Andreas Holly (Berlin, 1773) [with additions by Kirnberger]
Carl David Stegmann (1st version: Königsberg, 1773; 2nd version: Hamburg, 1796)
Johann Nikolaus Franz Seydelmann (Dresden, 1778)
1. (Operette, 1) [Holly]
    Frankfurt and Leipzig, 1774 [Schatz 4770]
2. (Operette, 1)
    Komische Opern (Berlin and Leipzig, 1775), vol. 2, pp. 353–404 [D-B Mus. T 145]
3A. (Operette, 1) [Stegmann]
    Riga, 1785 [D-B Mus. T 22]
4A. (Singspiel, 1) [Stegmann]
    Hamburg: Johann Matthias Michaelsen, 1792 [Schatz 10040]
BIBL.: *AdB* 24:1 (1775): 112–13; 33:1 (1778): 173 [Holly]. *KT* 219–20 [Stegmann]. *LTZ* 7 (1784): 118. *TfT* 1 (1795): 104.

Die Kirmess
Johann Martin Kellner
Johann Gottlieb Feige (Breslau, 1775)

Die kleine Ährenleserinn
Christian Felix Weisse
Johann Adam Hiller (Leipzig, 1778)
G. H. L. Wittrock (Lübeck, 1787)
1. (Lustspiel für Kinder, 1)
    Der Kinderfreund: Ein Wochenblatt (Leipzig: Siegfried Lebrecht Crusius, 1777), pt. 8, nos. 113–16 (30 Aug–20 Sep 1777), pp. [133]–197
2A. (Operette, [1]) [Wittrock]
    Lübeck, 31 March 1785 [Schatz 11068]
3A. (Operette, 1)
    n.p., n.d. [D-B Mus. Th 699]
BIBL.: *AdB* 40:1 (1780): 127 [Hiller]

Der kluge Jakob
Johann Carl Wezel
Otto Carl Erdmann Freiherr von Kospoth (Berlin, 1788)
1. (Komische Oper, 3)
   Leipzig: Dyckische Buchhandlung, 1787 [Schatz 5219]
2. (Komische Oper, 3)
   J. K. Wezel: *Lustspiele* (Leipzig: Dyckische Buchhandlung, 1787), vol. 4, pp. 1–143
   No. 1 is a separate edition of no. 2.

[*Knall und Fall* → *Glück und Zufall*]

Der Kobold
Daniel Heinrich Thomas
Johann Christian Escherich (Stralsund, 1777)
Johann Christian Frischmuth (unperformed)
BIBL.: *TJ* 9 (1779): 79; 18 (1781): 62–5 [Escherich]. *BTML* 197–8 [Escherich].

Die kranke Frau
Daniel Heinrich Thomas (after Gellert's afterpiece of the same name)
Johann Christian Frischmuth (Berlin, 1773)
BIBL.: *TJ* 9 (1779):79.

Der Krieg
Christian Felix Weisse and Carl Friedrich Ramler (after Goldoni, *La guerra* [1760])
Johann Adam Hiller (Berlin, 1772)
1A. (Lustspiel, 3)
    n.p., 1772 [USSR-KAu]
2. (Komische Oper, 3)
    Leipzig: Adam Friedrich Böhme, 1773 [Schatz 4723]
3. (Komische Oper, 3)
    Komische Opern (Berlin and Leipzig, 1774), vol. 1, no. 2 [D-B Mus. T 145]
4A. (Komische Oper, 3)
    n.p., n.d. [D-B Mus. Th 701]
BIBL.: *AdB* 22 (1774): 241–2.

[*Das kühne Abentheuer* → *Der Triumf der Liebe*]

Der Küster im Stroh
unknown
Karl Siegmund Schönbeck (Königsberg, 1778)

Kurze Thorheit ist die beste
Friedrich Ludwig Wilhelm Meyer (after Molière, *Le Mariage forcé*)
Johann André (Berlin, 1780)
[1A. *Alter schützt für Thorheit nicht* (Komische Oper, 1)
    Hamburg: J. M. Michaelsen, 1781 [Schatz 179]
 2. *Die Reue vor der Hochzeit* (Singspiel, 1)
    Berlin: Friedrich Maurer, 1782 [US-Wc ML 50.2 R44, GB-Lbm]
BIBL.: *LTZ* 3 (1780): 764–8; 4 (1781): 478. *MdM* 1:1 (1783): 91, 556.
    No. 1A corresponds to a version of this work with André's music first given at
Mannheim on 20 June 1779. No. 2 is a revision of the presumably unpublished
version for Berlin; it uses half of the musical texts found in 1A and the ms. of
André's opera (which are in complete accord with each other in all ten of their
musical numbers) and adds fifteen new musical texts.

Der lahme Husar
Friedrich Carl Koch
Johann Nikolaus Franz Seydelmann (Leipzig, 1780)
1. (Comische Oper, 2)
    Dresden and Leipzig: Breitkopfische Buchhandlung, 1784 [Schatz 9845, Schaal 563
    (imperfect)]
BIBL.: *AdB* 66:1 (1786): 79–80.

[*Das Land der Liebe* → *Der Zauber-Hain*]

[*Die Landplage* → *Das blaue Ungeheuer*]

Laura Rosetti
Bernhard Christoph d'Arien
Johann André (Berlin, 1778)
1. (Schauspiel mit Gesang, [3])
   Leipzig: Dyckische Buchhandlung, 1777 [Schatz 188]
2. (no desig., 3) [André]
   Lyrisches Theater der Deutschen (Leipzig: Dyckische Buchhandlung, 1782), vol. 1,
   no. 5 [D-W Lo 1133]
BIBL.: *TJ* 5 (1778): 73–4. *LTZ* 1 (1778): 579–81. *AdB* 36:1 (1778): 130–1; Appendices
25–36 (1778): 3031–2. Schink *DF* 2 (1781): 457–76.
   No. 2 is the original edition of 1777 with a new title page.

[*Liebe allein macht glücklich* → *Liebe nur beglückt*]

Die Liebe auf dem Lande
Christian Felix Weisse (after Favart, *Annette et Lubin* (1762), in acts 1 and 3; after
Anseaume, *La Clochette* (1766) in act 2)
Johann Adam Hiller (Leipzig, 1768)
1A. (Komische Opera, [3])
   Hamburg, 1768 [*Wolf.* 1002]
2. (Komische Oper, 3)
   [C. F. Weisse:] *Komische Opern* (Leipzig: Dyckische Buchhandlung, 1771), vol. 1,
   pp. [145]–304 [Schaal 566]
3A. (Comische Oper, 3)
   n.p., 1771 [USSR-KAu]
4. (Komische Oper, 3)
   Leipzig: Dyckische Buchhandlung, 1776 [Schatz 4724]
5. (Komische Oper, 3)
   C. F. Weisse: *Komische Opern* (Carlsruhe: Schmieder, 1778), vol. 1, pp. [97]–188
   [Schaal 567, US-Wc ML 49 A2W2]
6. (Komische Oper, 3)
   Prague: J. E. Diesbach, 1785 [US-U]
BIBL.: *Unterhaltungen* 6 (1768): 511. *WNA* II:368. *AdB* 13:1 (1770): 84–90. *UeKS*
74–7, Reichardt *BaRM* 11:94–104. Schmid *C* 271–2 [172]. *KT* 72–4, 195–7. *DBW*
2 (1768): 118–23; 3 (1769): 524, 531; 4 (1770): 227.

Die Liebe auf der Probe
Johann August Halbe (an expansion of d'Arien's 1-act *Heinrich und Lyda*, q.v.)
Johann August Halbe (Mitau, 1781) [using melodies by Christian Gottlob Neefe in
Heinrich und Lyda]
1. (Komische Operette, 3)
   Mitau: J. F. Steffenhagen, n.d. [GB-Lbm]
BIBL.: *KT* 220–2.
   The British Library Catalogue dates this print 1787.

Die Liebe im Lager
unknown
Gottlob Benedict Bierey (Leipzig, 1792)

Die Liebe ist sinnreich
unknown
Friedrich Christoph Gestewitz (Dresden, 1781)

Liebe nur beglückt
Johann Friedrich Reichardt
Johann Friedrich Reichardt (Dessau, 1781)

1. (Deutsches Singeschauspiel, 3)
   Berlin: Winters Erben, 1781 [US-Bp]
BIBL.: *MW* IX.

Liebesabentheuer
Gustav Friedrich Wilhelm Grossmann
Gottlob Benedict Bierey (Dresden, 1794)

Der Liebeskompass
unknown
Karl Friedrich Ebers (Brunswick, 1797)

[*Die Liebesprobe* → *Die Liebe auf der Probe*]

[*Der Liebesteufel* → *Der Alchymist*]

[*Die Liebe unter den Gondolieren* → *Die Regata zu Venedig*]

Der Liebhaber als Automat
Johann André (after Cuinet Dorbeil, *L'Amant statue*)
Johann André (Berlin, 1782)
1A. *Der Authomat* (Operette, 1) [André]
   Hamburg: J. M. Michaelsen, 1783 [Schatz 180]
2A. *Das Authomat* (Operette, 1) [André]
   Lübeck: Greenische Schriften, 1784 [Schatz 181]
3A. (Singspiel, 1) [André]
   Hamburg: J. M. Michaelsen, 1787 [D-Bds]
BIBL.: *BTJ* 411–14. *TZD* 105.
   In *BTJ* it is remarked that not all the songs are by the adapter, some are by Herr
   von St* * *, already a famous poet.

Lieb' um Liebe, *oder Die Flucht nach Asien*
K. A. von Zschiedrich (after Giovanni Bertati)
Franz Dunkel (Dresden, 1796)
1. (Romantisch–komische Oper, 2)
   Leipzig: G. J. Göschen, 1797 [D-B Mus. Td 705]

Lilla
unknown
Johann Mattheus König (unperformed)
BIBL.: *MdM* 1:2 (1783): 913.

List gegen List
Christoph Friedrich Bretzner
Christian Gottlob August Bergt (Leipzig, 1797)
   Inasmuch as the opera is through-composed, the complete text is available in
   Bergt's keyboard reduction.

Lisuart und Dariolette, *oder Die Frage und die Antwort*
Daniel Schiebeler (after Favart, *La Fée Urgèle* [1765])
Johann Adam Hiller (2-act version: Leipzig, 1766; 3-act version: Leipzig, 1767)
1. (Operette, 2)
   [Vienna:] Krausischer Buchladen, 1766 [Schatz 4726]
2. (Comische Oper, 3)
   Theater der Deutschen (Berlin, Königsberg, and Leipzig: Johann Jacob Kanter,
   1769), pt. 8, pp. 319–64 [GB-Lbm]

3. (Singstück, 3)
    [Daniel] S[chiebeler]: *Musikalische Gedichte* (Hamburg: Michael Christian Bock, 1770), pp. 15-66 [D-B Mus. Ts 393]
4A. (Comische Oper, 3)
    n.p., 1771 [Schaal 572]
5. (Singstück, 3)
    Riga: Johann Friedrich Hartknoch, 1773 [Schatz 4734]
6A. (no desig., [3]) [Hiller]
    Nüremberg, 24 May 1780 [Schatz 4727]
7. (Comische Oper, 2)
    n.p., n.d. [Schaal 571]
8. (Comische Oper, 3)
    n.p., n.d. [D-B Mus. Th 702]
BIBL.: *WNA* I:219, 253-60, 265-8; II:135-9, 368. *AdB* 10:2 (1769): 180-9; 14:2 (1771): 440-3. *UeKS* 58. Reichardt *BaRM* II:23-39. Hiller *L* 311-13. *DBW* 4 (1770): 184, 218-22.

[*Lottchen* → *Lottchen am Hofe*]

Lottchen am Hofe
Christian Felix Weisse (after Favart, *Ninette à la cour* [1755], itself a parody of Goldoni's *Bertoldo in corte* [1749])
Johann Adam Hiller (Leipzig, 1767)
1. (Komische Oper, 3)
    Leipzig: Dyckische Buchhandlung, 1768 [GB-Lbm]
2. (Komische Oper, 3)
    [C. F. Weisse:] *Komische Opern* (Leipzig: Dyckische Buchhandlung, 1768), vol. 1
3A. *Lottchen, oder Das Bauermägdchen am Hofe* (Comische Opera, 3)
    Altona, 1770 [Schatz 4729]
4. (Komische Oper, 3)
    [C. F. Weisse:] *Komische Opern* (Leipzig: Dyckische Buchhandlung, 1771), vol. 1 [Schaal 574]
5. (Komische Oper, 3)
    Leipzig: Dyckische Buchhandlung, 1776 [Schatz 4728]
6. (Komische Oper, 3)
    C. F. Weisse: *Komische Opern* (Leipzig: Dyckische Buchhandlung, 1777), vol. 1, pp. 1-104
7.· (Komische Oper, 3)
    C. F. Weisse: *Komische Opern* (Carlsruhe: Christian Gottlieb Schmieder, 1778), vol. 1, pp. 1-96 [Schaal 574a, US-Wc ML 49 A2W2]
8A. *Lottchen, oder Das Bauermägdchen am Hofe* (Comische Opera, 3)
    n.p., n.d. [USSR-KAu]
BIBL.: *WNA* I:376-7. *AdB* 13:1 (1770): 84-90. *UeKS* 23-5. Schmid *C* 262-3 [166]. *KT* 232-7. *DBW* 2 (1768): 118-23; 4 (1770): 212-13.

Louise
Friedrich Ernst Jester
Friedrich Ludwig Benda (Königsberg, 1791)
1A. (Oper, 3) [Benda]
    Riga: Julius Conrad Daniel Müller, 1794 [Schatz 765]
BIBL.: *AdT* 7 (1791): 104-8. *BmZ* 11:42.

[*Lukas und Bärbchen* → *Der Jahrmarkt*]

Lukas und Hannchen
Johann Joachim Eschenburg (after Favart, *Annette et Lubin* [1762], and its source,

Marmontel's "histoire véritable" of the same name [1761])
Johann Friedrich Gottlieb Beckmann (Brunswick, 1768)
1. *Hannchen und Lukas* (Operette, 1)
   Unterhaltungen 4 (1767): 828ff.
2. (Operette, [1])
   Brunswick: Fürstliche Waisenhausbuchhandlung, 1768 [Schatz 685]
3. (Operette, [1])
   Hamburg, 1782
BIBL.: *AdB* 11:2 (1770): 1–5.

Die lustigen Weiber von Windsor
Georg C. Römer (after Shakespeare, *The Merry Wives of Windsor*)
Carl Ditters von Dittersdorf (Oels, 1796)
[1. *Die lustigen Weiber* (Singspiel, 4) [Ritter]
   n.p., 1792 [Schatz 8825 (imperfect)]
   Krebs in *Dittersdorfiana* incorrectly states that this libretto is by Herklots. A
   comparison of Dittersdorf's score with Römer's libretto, however, shows that
   he did indeed set this text, which Peter Ritter had composed for Mannheim
   two years earlier. Krebs's assertion is apparently based on a misattribution in
   AMZ 1 (1798/9): *Intelligenz-Blatt*. 19.

Der lustige Schulmeister
Christoph Friedrich Nicolai
Christian Gottfried Krause (Berlin, 1766)
BIBL.: Plümicke 256–7. Schmid *C* 255 [162].

Der lustige Schuster, *oder Der zweite Theil vom Teufel ist los*
Christian Felix Weisse (after Coffey, *The Merry Cobler* [1735])
Johann Standfuss and Johann Adam Hiller (Leipzig, 1766)
Anton Schweitzer (Celle, 1770)
1. (Komische Oper, 3)
   Leipzig: Dyckische Buchhandlung, 1768 [GB-Lbm]
2. (Komische Oper, 3)
   [C. F. Weisse:] *Komische Opern* (Leipzig: Dyckische Buchhandlung, 1772), vol. 2,
   pp. [145]–272 [Schaal 581]
3. (Komische Oper, 3)
   C. F. Weisse: *Komische Opern* (Carlsruhe: Schmieder, 1778), vol. 2, pp. [105]–194
   [Schaal 582, Schatz 4733, US-Wc ML 49 A2W2]
BIBL.: *AdB* 17:2 (1772): 569. Schmid *C* 277 [175] [Hiller], 288 [182] [Schweitzer].
DBW 2 (1768): 416–21; 4 (1770): 643–5.

[*Das Mädgen im Thurme* → *Das wütende Heer*]

Der Mädchenmarkt
Carl Alexander Herklots (after St.-Foix, *La Colonie* [1750])
Otto Carl Erdmann Freiherr von Kospoth (Hamburg, 1793)
Gottlob Benedict Bierey (Leipzig, 1794)
Carl Ditters von Dittersdorf (Oels, 1797)
1. (Komisches Singspiel, 3)
   Herklots' Operetten (Berlin, 1793), vol. 3, pp. [187]–296 [Schatz 3601]
2A. (Singspiel, 2) [Kospoth]
   Hamburg: Joh. Matth. Michaelsens Wittwe, 1793 [Schatz 5220]
BIBL.: *TfT* 1 (1795): 104. Schütze 679 [Kospoth]. *ALZ* 1793:4:92–3.
   No. 2A reduces the musical numbers from 33 to 25.

[*Der Mädchenmarkt zu Ninive* → *Der Mädchenmarkt*]

Das Mädchen nicht ohne den Ring
unknown
Friedrich Neumann (Altona, 1798)

[*Mann kann es ja erproben* → *Walmir und Gertraud*]

[*Mann kann es ja probieren* → *Walmir und Gertraud*]

Mariechen
Friedrich Ernst Jester
Friedrich Ludwig Benda (Königsberg, 1791)
BIBL.: *BmZ* 11:42.

Matz und Anna
Johann Christian Ast
Anton Laube (Stralsund, 1768)
BIBL.: Schütze 346.

Meister Johannes, der lustige Schuster
Ch. G. Korb
Johann Christian Ohlhorst (Neustrelitz, 1791)

Melida (I)
Christoph Joseph Sucro
Johann Heinrich Rolle (Magdeburg, 1784)
BIBL.: *LTZ* 7 (1784): 72. *MdM* 2:1 (1784): 184, 268-70. *ELT* 6 (1787): 403-5.
   Since the opera is through-composed, the complete text is available in Rolle's
   keyboard reduction.

Melida (II)
unknown
Siegfried Schmiedt (Leipzig, 1797)
   Possibly this is a translation of Fenouillot de Falbaire's *Mélide, ou Le
   Navigateur* (1773).

Menöceus, *oder Die Rettung von Thebe*
Friedrich Bouterwek (after an episode in Euripides, *The Phoenicians*)
Bernhard Anselm Weber (Hannover, 1792)
1.   (Trauerspiel mit Gesang, [3])
      Hannover: Schmidtsche Buchhandlung, 1788 [GB-Lbm]
BIBL.: *DB* 21:326-30. *AdB* 94:1 (1790): 122-5.

[*Metz und Anne* → *Matz und Anna*]

Der Meyerhof
unknown (from the Italian [possibly Goldoni, *La cascina* (1756)])
Friedrich Christoph Gestewitz (Leipzig, 1780)
BIBL.: *LTZ* 3 (1780): 831.

Das Milchmädchen
unknown (after Anseaume, *Les Deux Chasseurs et la laitière* [1763])
Johann Michael Helmig (Breslau, 1772)

[*Milmi und Almador* → *Der Spiegelritter*]

Mit dem Glockenschlag: zwölf!
Friedrich Julius Heinrich Soden von Sassanfart
Nikolaus Mühle (Mitau, 1783)

1. (Ernsthafte Operette, 3 [recte 2])
   Ansbach: Haueisen, 1781 [Schatz 6871]
2. *Laura* (Operette, 3 [recte 2])
   J. S. von Sassanfart: *Werke* (Berlin: Maurer, 1789), vol. 2, pp. [257]–314 [Schatz 11459]
   BIBL.: *TZD* 119. *DB* 10:149.

Das Monden-Reich
unknown
Johann Christian Frischmuth (Berlin, 1769)
1. (Operette, 3) [Frischmuth]
   n.p., n.d. [Schatz 3373]
   This libretto is unrelated to Goldoni's *Il mondo della luna*.

Das Mündel
Ch. G. Korb
Carl David Stegmann (Altona, 1783)
1. (Lustspiel mit Gesängen, 2)
   Altona: J. H. S. Hellmann, 1783 [US-Wc ML 50.2 M86]

Die Muse
Daniel Schiebeler
Johann Adam Hiller (Leipzig, 1767)
1. (Comödie, 1)
   [Daniel] S[chiebeler]: *Musikalische Gedichte* (Hamburg: Michael Christian Bock, 1770), pp. 67–84 [D-B Mus. Ts 393]
   BIBL.: *WNA* II:118. *AdB* 14:2 (1771): 443–4.

Die nächtliche Erscheinung
unknown
Johann Friedrich Schubert (Stettin, 1798)

[*Der neue Richter* → *Das Frühstück auf der Jagd*]

Das neue Rosenmädchen
unknown
Diedrich Christian Aumann (Hamburg, 1789)
   The relationship of this text with Favart's *La Rosière de Salency* (1769) is not known.

Die offene Fehde
unknown
Gottlob Benedict Bierey (Leipzig, 1794)

Opera buffa
Christoph Friedrich Bretzner
Georg Ernst Gottlieb Kallenbach (Magdeburg, 1798)
1. (Komisches Singspiel, 2)
   C. F. Bretzner: *Singspiele* (Leipzig, 1796), pp. [95]–218 [Schatz 4999]

Das Orakel
Christian Fürchtegott Gellert (after St.-Foix, *L'Oracle*)
Friedrich Gottlob Fleischer (Brunswick, 1771)
1. (Operette, [2])
   C. F. Gellerts sämmtliche Schriften (Leipzig: M. G. Weidmanns Erben und Reich, und Caspar Fritsch, 1769), pt. 3, pp. [111]–144

2. (Operette, [2])
idem., 1784, pt. 3, pp. [111]–144
BIBL.: *AdB* 22 (1774): 533–4. Reichardt *BaRM* II:51–4. Hiller *L* 300.
No. 2, a "neue, verbesserte Auflage," changes nothing in the text.

Orpheus
Gottfried Ferdinand Lindemann
Friedrich Wilhelm Heinrich Benda (Berlin, 1785)
1. (Singspiel, 3) [Benda]
   n.p., 1784 [D-B Mus. T 23]
2. (Singspiel, 3) [Benda]
   n.p., 1785 [Schatz 766]
3. (Singspiel, 3) [Benda]
   n.p., 1788 [D-B Mus. Tb 505^b]
BIBL.: *STM* 27. *DM* 1778:2 (October): 382–3. *TM* 1785:2 (September): cxlvii–cxlviii; 1787:2 (May): lvii–lviii; 1787:4 (December): clxxix.
   D-B places no. 1 at Hamburg.

[*Orpheus und Euridice* → *Der Tod des Orpheus*]

[*Die Parforcejagd* → *Karoline*]

[*Die Parodie aus dem Stegreife* → *Die Ehestandskandidaten*]

[*Der Pascha von Tunis* → *Der Bassa von Tunis*]

[*Peter und Hannchen* → *Die Bezauberten*]

Phaedon und Naide, *oder Der redende Baum*
Johann Georg Jacobi
Gottlob Benedict Bierey (Leipzig, 1793)
Gottlob Bachmann (Brunswick, 1795)
1. (Singspiel, 2)
   Leipzig: Göschen, 1788
2. (Singspiel, 2)
   J. G. Jacobi: *Theatralische Schriften: Nachtrag zu seinen sämtlichen Werken* (Leipzig: G. J. Göschen, 1792), pp. 1–83 [Schatz 1113]
BIBL.: *TZD* 109–10. *DB* 14:223–4. *AdB* 89:2 (1789): 437. *ALZ* 1793:2:229–31.

Philoktetes
Johann Gottfried von Herder (after Sophocles, *Philoctetes*)
Johann Christian Friedrich Bach (Bückeburg, 1775)
   A modern critical edition is in *Herders Sämmtliche Werke*, ed. Bernhard Suphan, vol. 28 = *Herders Poetische Werke*, ed. Carl Redlich, vol. 4 (Berlin, 1884), pp. 69–78.

Pierre und Narciss
unknown
Anton Laube (Berlin, 1777)

Poltis, *oder Das gerettete Troja*
Steinel and Gottfried Samuel Brunner (prompted by a remark in Pope)
Johann Adam Hiller (unperformed)
1. (Komische Oper, 3)
   Leipzig: Friedrich Gotthold Jacobaeer, 1773 [Schatz 4731, Schaal 726]
BIBL.: *TM* 2 (1773): 199. Schmid *C* 340 [215]. *AdB* 24:1 (1775): 100–1; 111:1 (1792): 116–17.

According to Schmid *C*, Brunner found this play in a spoken version among the papers of "Magister Steinel" (who died in 1764) and added arias to make it a comic opera. The libretto appeared anonymously.

Psyche
Karl Friedrich Müchler
Carl Bernhard Wessely (Berlin, 1789)
1. (Singspiel, 2)
   Berlin: Friedrich Maurer, 1789 [Schatz 10990]
2. (Singspiel, 2)
   Berlin: Friedrich Maurer, 1790 [GB-Lbm]
BIBL.: *AdT* 4 (1789). *JLM* 5 (1790): 115. *AdB* 99:1 (1791): 122–3.

[*Rechtschaffenheit und Liebe* → *Ehrlichkeit und Liebe*]

Die Recrouten auf dem Lande
unknown
Carl David Stegmann (Danzig, 1775)
1. (Komische Oper, 3)
   Wittenberg and Zerbst: Samuel Gottfried Zimmermann, 1781 [Schatz 10041]

[*Der redende Baum* → *Phaedon und Naide*]

[*Das redende Bild* → *Das redende Gemälde*]

Das redende Gemälde
unknown (after Anseaume, *Le Tableau parlant*)
Carl David Stegmann (Königsberg, 1775)
BIBL.: *AdB* 33:1 (1778): 166–7.

Die Regata zu Venedig, *oder Die Liebe unter den Gondolieren*
Samuel Gottlieb Bürde (based on a Venetian novella in a collection of essays by Countess von Rosenberg, after an actual event at the 1784 regatta)
F. J. Sigismund Sander (Oels, 1796) [3-act version]
J. B. Fliess (Berlin, 1798) [2-act version]
1. (Oper, 3)
   Königsberg: Friedrich Nicolovius, 1795 [Schatz 9372]
2A. (Singspiel, 2) [Fliess]
   Berlin, 1798 [Schatz 3247]
BIBL.: *BZG* 1798:2, p. 308. *ALZ* 1796:3:727–8; 1797:1:84–5.
   The two-act version reduces the musical numbers from 25 to 15. Sonneck prints a brief excerpt from the preface to no. 1.

[*Das reitende Heer* → *Das wütende Heer*]

[*Die Rettung von Thebe* → *Menöceus*]

[*Die Reue vor der Hochzeit* → *Kurze Thorheit ist die beste*]

Richter und Gärtnerin
unknown
Eucharius Florschütz (Rostock, 1790)

Rinaldo und Alcina
Ludwig Adolf Franz Joseph von Baczko
Friedrich August Leopold Löwe (Brunswick, 1797)
1. (Komische Oper, 3)
   Königsberg: Hartung, 1794 [Schatz 7770]

[*Ritter Don Quixotte* → *Don Quixotte*]

Romeo und Julie
Johann Friedrich Wilhelm Gotter (after Weisse's tragedy of the same name and Shakespeare, *Romeo and Juliet*)
Georg Benda (Gotha, 1776)
1. (Schauspiel mit Gesang, 3)
   F. W. Gotter: *Singspiele* (Leipzig: Dyckische Buchhandlung, 1779), vol. 1, pp. 3–64 [Schatz 776, *Wolf.* 1414]
2A. (Schauspiel mit Gesang, 3) [Benda]
   Riga, 1784 [D-B Mus. T 24]
3. (Schauspiel mit Gesang, 3)
   Frankfurt and Leipzig, 1785 [D-B Mus. Tb 502/2]
4A. (Schauspiel mit Gesang, 3) [Benda]
   Berlin, 1793 [Schaal 555]
5A. *Julie und Romeo* (Schauspiel mit Gesang, 3) [Benda]
   Berlin, 1796 [Schatz 777]
6A. *Julie und Romeo* (Schauspiel, 3) [Benda]
   Hamburg: J. M. Michaelsen, n.d. [D-B Mus. Tb 520/1]
BIBL.: *TJ* 9 (1779): 67–73; 16 (1780): 52–3. *LTZ* 2 (1779): 436–7; 4 (1781): 346, 365–6. *AdB* 40:1 (1780): 128–30; 72:2 (1787): 388–9. *TM* 1780:2 (June): 244. *BTJ* 459–64. *KT* 171–6, 179–84, 211–12, 248–9. *BmZ* 15:59. *AdT* 6 (1790): 75. *Lyceum der schönen Künste* 1:1 (1797): 132–44.
   Sonneck prints an excerpt from the notice to the reader in no. 1 (p. 950).

Rosalia
Johann Friedrich Schink (after Marmontel, *Silvain*)
Joseph Schubert (Berlin, 1777)
1. (Nachspiel mit Arien, [1])
   Gotha: Carl Wilhelm Ettinger, 1777 [Schatz 9704]
BIBL.: *TJ* 1 (1777): 88. *AdB* 36:2 (1778): 485–6.

Das Rosenfest
Gottlob Ephraim Heermann (after Favart, *La Rosière de Salency* [1769])
Ernst Wilhelm Wolf (Weimar, 1770)
1. (Operette, 3)
   Weimar: Karl Ludolf Hoffmann, 1771 [Schaal 806]
2. (Operette, 3)
   Theater der Deutschen, vol. 12 (Königsberg and Leipzig, 1772), no. 77.
3. (Operette, 3)
   Weimar: Carl Ludolf Hoffmann, 1774 [Schatz 11083]
4. (Operette, 3)
   n.p., 1776 [US-Wc ML 50.2 R75W6]
5A. (Operette, 3)
   Brunswick, 1776 [*Wolf.* 1421]
6A. (Komische Oper, 3) [Wolf]
   n.p., n.d. [USSR-KAu]
BIBL.: Schmid *T* 93–101. Schmid *DP* 48–61. *UeKS* 43–6, 105–7. *AdB* 23:1 (1774): 250–2, Appendices 13–24 (1777): 1152; 35:1 (1778): 177–9. *ABSS* 1 (1776): 30–2. *KT* 161–4. *LTZ* 6 (1783): 729; 7 (1784): 117–18.
   The anonymous *Das Rosenfest zu Salenci* published at Vienna in 1779 is another translation of Favart's libretto.

[*Die Roseninsel* → *Der Triumf der Liebe*]

Saphire
unknown
Carl Josef Birnbach (Breslau, 1788)
    Possibly this is identical with B. C. d'Arien's *Xaphire*, set by Karl Hanke for
    Hamburg in 1786.

[*Die Satire* → *Bella und Fernando*]

[*Schach Wampum* → *Sultan Wampum*]

Die Schadenfreude
Christian Felix Weisse
Georg Peter Weimar (Erfurt, 1776)
Johann André (Berlin, 1778)
1. (Kleines Lustspiel für Kinder mit Liederchen, [1])
    Der Kinderfreund: Ein Wochenblatt (Tübingen, 1778), nos. 71-3 (11-25 November
    1776), pp. [101]-130 [Schatz 10963]

Der Schah von Schiras
unknown (adapted from Kotzebue, *Sultan Wampum*, q.v.)
Carl Ditters von Dittersdorf (Oels, 1795)

Schattenspiel an der Wand
Christoph Friedrich Bretzner
Georg Ernst Gottlieb Kallenbach (Magdeburg, 1797)
1. (Singspiel, 2)
    C. F. Bretzner: *Singspiele* (Leipzig, 1796) [Schatz 5000]
    Sonneck prints an excerpt from the collection's preface (p. 969).

Der Schatz
Christian Gotthilf Weisflog
Christian Gotthilf Weisflog (Sagan, 1781)

[*Der Schatzgräber* → *Der Äpfeldieb*]

Der Schiffbruch
H. Graf von Spaur
Nikolaus Mühle (Königsberg, 1778)
[1. (Märchen, 4) [Kerpen]
    Frankfurt: Andreäische Schriften, 1778 [Schatz 5142]
BIBL.: *LTZ* 1 (1778): 155-7, 446. *TSS* 302. *AdB* 42:1 (1780): 86-9.

Der Schlaftrunk
Christoph Friedrich Bretzner
Gottlob Benedict Bierey (Dresden, 1797)
Johann Philipp Samuel Schmidt (Königsberg, 1797)
Georg Ernst Gottlieb Kallenbach (Altona, 1799)
1. (Komisches Singspiel, 2)
    C. F. Bretzner: *Singspiele* (Leipzig: Friedrich Gotthold Jacobäer, 1796)
2A. (Oper, 2) [Bierey]
    Breslau: Grass und Barth, n.d. [Schatz 1028]
3A. (Komisches Singspiel, 2) [Kallenbach]
    Altona: Gebrüder Meyn, n.d. [Schatz 5001]
BIBL.: *JLM* 5 (1790): 44. *HATLZ* 1 (1799): 422-4.

Der Schleyer
Christian August Vulpius

Ernst Wilhelm Wolf (Weimar, 1786)
1A. (Singspiel, 3) [Wolf]
    Hamburg: Johann Matthias Michaelsen, 1788 [Schatz 11084]
2. (Operette, 3) [Wolf]
    Bayreuth and Leipzig: Johann Andreas Lübeks Erben, 1789 [US-NH]
3. (no desig., [3])
    C. A. Vulpius: *Opern* (Bayreuth and Leipzig, 1790), vol. 1 [Schatz 11084a]
BIBL.:*ELT* 6 (1787): 172. *AdT* 2 (1788): 101. *AdB* 96:2 (1790): 423; 101:2 (1791):
402–3. *ALZ* 1797:3:231–2.
    No. 3 is no. 2 without its title page.

[*Die schöne Arsene* → *Arsene*]

Die schöne Fürstin
August Friedrich Ernst Langbein
Nikolaus Mühle (Königsberg, 1799)

[*Der Schuster ein Moralist* → *Der blaue Montag*]

Der Schutzgeist
unknown
Heinrich Karl Ebell (Berlin, 1798)

Seliko und Berissa
Kinderling
Heinrich Karl Ebell (Berlin, 1799)

[*Der seltene Spiegel* → *Der Talisman*]

[*Die seltsamen Spiegel* → *Der Talisman*]

[*Der seltsame Spiegel* → *Der Talisman*]

[*Der seltsame Spiegel* → *Der Spiegelritter*]

[*Die Serenate* → *Adrast und Isidore*]

[*Der Sieg der Natur über die Schwärmerey* → *Don Sylvio von Rosalva*]

Die Singschule, *oder Drei Heirathen an einem Tage*
Ludwig Adolf Franz Joseph von Baczko
Nikolaus Mühle (Königsberg, 1794)
1. (Komische Oper, 3)
    Königsberg: Hartung, 1794 [Schatz 6872]
BIBL.: *BmZ* 11:42.
    This text was later adapted by Johann Christoph Kaffka as *Die Ehestandskandidaten* (q.v.).

[*Der Sklavenhändler von Smyrna* → *Der Kaufmann von Smyrna*]

Der Soldat
unknown
Johann Nikolaus Franz Seydelmann (Gotha, 1783)
1. (Singspiel, 1)
    Jena: Melchior, 1778
BIBL.: *TSS* 323.

So prellt man alte Füchse
Friedrich Ludwig Wilhelm Meyer, adapted by Johann Christoph Kaffka (after
Molière, *Le Mariage forcé*)

Johann Christoph Kaffka (Breslau, 1782)
1. (Komische Operette, 1) [Kaffka]
    J. C. Kaffka: *Sammlung auserlesener Theater-Stücke, in die deutsche Bühne be-arbeitet* (Breslau: Wilhelm Gottlieb Korn, 1784), pp. [127]–180 [Schatz 4987, GB-Lbm]
    This text is unrelated to another libretto, by Mylius and d'Arien, with the same title (based on another Molière play), listed in Section B of Part II. The present libretto is sometimes incorrectly ascribed to Kaffka and August Gottlieb Meissner.

Der Spiegelritter
August von Kotzebue
August Himbert Hinze (Waldenburg, 1797)
Carl Christian Agthe (Ballenstädt, 1795)
1. (Oper, 3)
    n.p., n.d., pp. [321]–448 [Schatz 10865a]
2. (Oper, 3)
    Theater von August von Kotzebue (Vienna: Mich. Lechner, 1831), vol. 3, pp. [3]–58
BIBL.: *ZTK* 7:129–35.
    Sonneck prints an excerpt from the preface of no. 1 (p. 1026), from an unidentified collected edition of Kotzebue's theatrical works.

Die steinerne Braut
Carl August Ludwig Freiherr von Lichtenstein
Carl August Ludwig Freiherr von Lichtenstein (Dessau, 1799)
1A. (Singspiel, [2]) [Lichtenstein]
    Dessau: H. G. Heybruch, 1799 [Schatz 5599]
BIBL.: *AMZ* 1 (1798/9): 511–14; 2 (1799/1800): 2–5. *JLM* 14 (1799): 251, 401.

Der studierte Jäger
unknown
Anton Laube (Berlin, 1777)

Der Sturm
Johann Samuel Patzke (after Shakespeare, *The Tempest*, with borrowings from Wieland's translation)
Johann Heinrich Rolle (Berlin, 1782)
BIBL.: *BTJ* 222–7. *LTZ* 5 (1782): 329.

[*Der Sturm* → *Die Geisterinsel*]

Sultan Wampum, *oder Die Wünsche*
August von Kotzebue
Johann Heinrich Carl Bornhardt (Brunswick, 1796)
Essiger (Lübben, 1797)
1. (Orientalisches Scherzspiel mit Gesang, 3)
    Deutsche Schaubühne (Augsburg, 1794), vol. 8 [Schatz 10042, GB-Lbm]
2. (Orientalisches Scherzspiel mit Gesang, 3)
    n.p., n.d. [Schatz 11749]
BIBL.: *HT* 2:166–70, 789. *ALZ* 1795:1:405–8.

Superba
Carl August Gottfried von Seckendorff
Ernst Wilhelm Wolf (Weimar, 1785)
1. (Oper)
    Weimar, 1779

2A. (Oper)
Weimar, 1785

Szenen der Vorwelt
unknown
Traugott Maximilian Eberwein (Rudolstadt, 1799)

Der Talisman
Christoph Friedrich Bretzner
Johann Christoph Kaffka (Breslau, 1789)
BIBL.: *NTD* 2 (1789): 112.

Das tartarische Gesetz
Johann Friedrich Wilhelm Gotter (based on an episode in Gozzi, *I pitocchi fortunati* [1764])
Johann André (Berlin, 1779)
1. (Schauspiel mit Gesang, 2)
Leipzig: Dyckische Buchhandlung, 1779 [Schatz 190, *Wolf.* 1549]
BIBL.: *LTZ* 1 (1778): 754–5; 2 (1779): 514–15 [André]. *AdB* 38:1 (1779): 149:50. *TM* 1780:2 (June): 244.

Gotter's libretto was very popular in South Germany, where it was set by Zumsteeg (1780), Eberhard (1780), and d'Antoin (1782). Georg Benda's setting was first given at Mannheim as well (1787).

[*Der Teufel ist los*, Part 1 → *Die verwandelten Weiber*]

[*Der Teufel ist los*, Part 2 → *Der lustige Schuster*]

Der Theater-Prinzipal
Carl Alexander Herklots
Bernhard Anselm Weber (Berlin, 1796)
1. (Lyrische Posse, [1]) [Weber]
Berlin: J. H. Brüder, 1796 [Schaal 898]
2. (Lyrische Posse, [1]) [Weber]
Breslau: Grasses Erben und Barth, n.d. [Schatz 10881]

Der Tod des Orpheus
Johann Georg Jacobi
Gottlob Bachmann (Brunswick, 1798)
1. (Singspiel, 3)
Neues deutsches Museum 1790:2, pp. 863ff.
2. (Singspiel, 3)
J. G. Jacobi: *Theatralische Schriften: Nachtrag zu seinen sämtlichen Werken* (Leipzig: G. J. Göschen, 1792), pp. [85]–162 [Schatz 537]
BIBL.: *ALZ* 1793:2:229–31.

Der Transport im Koffer
unknown
Edmund Kaspar Johann Josef Maria Freiherr von Weber (Hamburg, 1791)
1A. (Singspiel, 3) [Weber]
Hamburg: Johann Matthias Michaelsen, 1791 [Schatz 10916]

Die treuen Köhler
Gottlob Ephraim Heermann (based on an episode and characters from Saxon history)
Ernst Wilhelm Wolf (Weimar, 1772)
1. (Operette, 2)
Weimar: Carl Ludolf Hoffmann, 1773 [Schatz 11085, Schaal 919]

2. (Operette, 2)
    Weimar: Carl Ludolf Hoffmann, 1777 [GB-Lbm]
BIBL.: *TM* 2 (1773): 221. Schubart *DC* 1774:478–9. *AdB* 21:1 (1774): 190; 23:1 (1774): 250–2. Schmid *C* 323 [204].

Der Triumf der Liebe
Friedrich Ernst Jester (revised by C. L. Costenoble in 1806)
Carl David Stegmann (1st version: Hamburg, 1796; 2nd version [as *Die Roseninsel*]: Hamburg, 1806)
1st version:
1A. (Singspiel, 4) [Stegmann]
    Hamburg: Freystatzky und Rabe, 1796 [Schatz 10044]
2nd version:
1A. *Die Roseninsel* (Oper, 3) [Stegmann]
    Hamburg: Friedrich Hermann Nestler, n.d. [Schatz 10045]
BIBL.: *AdT* 18 (1796): 44–5.

[*Die Tugend unter Wilden* → *Seliko und Berissa*]

Die Ueberraschung
Barchielli
Antonín Josef Alois Volanek (Leipzig, 1797)

Ugolino
unknown (after Gerstenberg's tragedy of the same name)
Carl Ditters von Dittersdorf (Oels, 1796)

[*Das unbekannte Dienstmädgen* → *Clarisse*]

[*Die unnöthige Vorsicht* → *Der Barbier von Seville*]

[*Unverhoft kömt oft* → *Das Findelkind*]

[*Die verfolgte und triumphirende Liebe* → *Hass und Aussöhnung*]

[*Die vergebliche Vorsicht* → *Der Barbier von Seville*]

Der verliebte Werber
unknown (adapted from André, *Eins wird doch helfen*, q.v.)
Carl Diedrich Eule (Hamburg, 1799)
1A. (Oper, 2) [Eule]
    Hamburg: Peter Christian Heinrich Rabe, 1799 [Schatz 2961]
BIBL.: *HATLZ* 2 (1799): 307–8, 339–41. *AMZ* 2 (1799/1800): 408.

Die Verlobung
Friedrich Ernst Jester
Friedrich Ludwig Benda (Königsberg, 1789)
BIBL.: *MM* 2:51–3.

Die verwandelten Weiber, *oder Der Teufel ist los*
Christian Felix Weisse (after Coffey, *The Devil to Pay* [1728] and Sedaine's adaptation of the same source, *Le Diable à quatre* [1756])
Johann Standfuss and Johann Adam Hiller (Leipzig, 1766)
1. (Komische Oper, 3)
    [C. F. Weisse:] *Komische Opern* (Leipzig: Dyckische Buchhandlung, 1771), vol. 2 [Schaal 956]

2. (Komische Oper, 3)
   Leipzig: Dyckische Buchhandlung, 1772 [Schatz 4732]
3. (Komische Oper, 3)
   Leipzig: Dyckische Buchhandlung, 1776 [D-B Mus. Th 704]
4. (Komische Oper, 3)
   C. F. Weisse: *Komische Opern* (Carlsruhe: Schmieder, 1778), vol. 2 [Schaal 957, US-Wc ML 49 A2W2]
5A. (Komische Oper, 3) [Standfuss and Hiller]
   Riga: Julius Conrad Daniel Müller, 1794 [Schatz 4732a]
BIBL.: *AdB* 17:2 (1772): 569. *LTZ* 5 (1782): 275. *KT* 116-19. *BTJ* 364-8. Hiller *L*, p. 311. *AdT* 7 (1791): 77. *DBW* 2 (1768): 416-21; 4 (1770): 215-17.

Walder
Johann Friedrich Wilhelm Gotter (after Marmontel, *Silvain*)
Georg Benda (Gotha, 1776)
1A. (Operette, 1) [Benda]
   n.p., 1776 [Schaal 971]
2. (Ländliches Schauspiel mit Gesang, 1) [Benda]
   Gotha: Carl Wilhelm Ettinger, 1778 [Schatz 778]
3A. (Ernsthafte Operette, [1]) [Benda]
   Bamberg, n.d. [D-Mbs]
4A. (Singspiel, 1)
   Hamburg: Johann Matthias Michaelsen, 1791 [D-B Mus. Tb 522]
BIBL.: *MKB* II:230-74. *AdB* Appendices 25-36 (1778): 766-7; 40:1 (1780): 128-30. *LTZ* 5 (1782): 274 [Benda-Grétry]. *DB* 7:102-4. *HT* 1:402-4.
   No. 4A was issued in connection with a production of *Walder* by Schröder at Hamburg using music of both Benda and Grétry (whose setting of *Silvain* [1770] was still very popular there). Five of the numbers are Benda's and six are Grétry's. D-SWl has a ms. part for Vater Dolmon (Kade II:362), on which the opera is called *Walder und Sophie*.

Walmir und Gertraud, *oder Man kann es ja probieren*
Johann Benjamin Michaelis
Anton Schweitzer (unperformed)
1. (Operette, 3)
   [J. B. Michaelis:] *Einzelne Gedichte, Erste Sammlung* (Leipzig: S. L. Crusius, 1769) [D-B Mus. Ts 1130]
2. (Operette, 3)
   Sämtliche Werke des Johann Benjamin Michaelis (Vienna: Schrämbl, 1791), vol. 3, pp. [13]-75 [Schatz 9776, *Wolf.* 1709]
   Sonneck prints a short excerpt from the preface to no. 2 (p. 1150).

[*Der Warenhändler von Smyrna* → *Der Kaufmann von Smyrna*]

[*Der Wechsel Gott Mars* → *Gott Mars*]

[*Die Werbung aus Liebe* → *Eins wird doch helfen*]

[*Wer zuletzt lacht, lacht am besten* → *Liebesabentheuer*]

[*Die Wünsche* → *Sultan Wampum*]

Die wüste Insel
August Gottlieb Meissner (translated from Metastasio, *L'isola disabitata* [1752])
Joseph Schuster (Leipzig, 1779)

1. (Singspiel, [1])
Leipzig: Dyckische Buchhandlung, 1778 [Schatz 9758]
2. (no desig., 1) [Schuster]
Lyrisches Theater der Deutschen (Leipzig: Dyckische Buchhandlung, 1782), vol. 2, no. 3 [D-W Lo 1133]
BIBL.: *LTZ* 1 (1778): 316–17. *TSS* 281–2. *AdB* 42:1 (1780): 86–9.
Sonneck prints an excerpt from Meissner's prefatory note to No. 1 (pp. 1157–8). No. 2 is the original edition of 1778 with a new title page.

Das wütende Heer, *oder Das Mädgen im Thurme*
Christoph Friedrich Bretzner
Anton Schweitzer (unperformed)
Johann André (Berlin, 1780)
Johann Christoph Kaffka (Breslau, 1782)
Friedrich Franz Hurka (Schwedt, 1788)
1. (Operette, 3) [Schweitzer]
C. F. Bretzner: *Operetten* (Leipzig, 1779), vol. 1, pp. [99]–192 [Schatz 11680]
2. (Operette, 3) [Schweitzer]
Leipzig: Carl Friedrich Schneider, 1788 [Schatz 9777]
BIBL.: *LTZ* 2 (1779): 695–6. *DB* 11:172. *TM* 1780:2 (June): 244–5. *AdB* 41:2 (1780): 457–9; 89:1 (1789): 418–19. *AdM* 1780:41.

Der Wunderigel
Friedrich Ernst Jester
Karl Siegmund Schönbeck (Königsberg, 1793)
1. (Komische Operette, 1)
Königsberg, 1793)
BIBL.: *BmZ* 11:42.

[*Wurst wider Wurst → Matz und Anna*]

Xaphire
Bernhard Christoph d'Arien
Karl Hanke (Hamburg, 1786)

Der Zauber-Hain, *oder Das Land der Liebe*
Th. Berling
Gottlob Benedict Bierey (Dresden, 1799)
1A. (Romantisch-komische Oper, 3) [Bierey]
n.p., 1799 [Schatz 1032]
BIBL.: *AMZ* 2 (1799/1800): 134–5.

Die Zauberirrungen
Friedrich Hildebrand von Einsiedel (after Shakespeare, *A Midsummer Night's Dream*) Ernst Wilhelm Wolf (Weimar, 1785)

Zemire und Azor (I)
Moritz August von Thümmel (translated from Marmontel, *Zémire et Azor* [1771])
Christian Gottlob Neefe (Leipzig, 1776)
1. (Komische Oper, [4])
Frankfurt and Leipzig, 1776 [D-B Mus. Tm 110]
BIBL.: *Berlinisches Literarisches Wochenblatt* 1776:1, pp. 177–200. *TK* 1776:191.
On the ms. addition to the title page of the above copy see the entry for this work under Neefe in Part I.

Zemire und Azor (II)
Karl Emil Schubert (arias) and Gotthilf von Baumgarten (dialogue) (after Marmontel, *Zémire et Azor* [1771])
Gotthilf von Baumgarten (Breslau, 1776)
1. (Romantisch–komische Oper, 4)
   Breslau: Johann Friedrich Korn d. Ältere, 1775 [Schatz 658, Schaal 978]
2. (Romantisch–komische Oper, 4)
   K. E. Schubert: *Schauspiele mit Gesang* (Breslau and Leipzig: Chr. Fr. Gutsch, 1779)
BIBL.: *AdM* 1776:80, 1780:41. *AdB* 33:1 (1778): 172. *LTZ* 2 (1779): 511–12.
   In the 1779 edition (no. 2) Schubert "improves" the dialogue that Baumgarten had written for the original edition (no. 1).

[*Die zwey Geizigen* → *Das Grab des Mufti*]

Section B
Unset published librettos

Achills zürnender Schatten
Traugott Benjamin Berger
1. (Tragisches Singspiel, 5)
   Leipzig: Christian Gottlob Hilscher, 1777 [Schatz 11595]
BIBL.: *TJ* 4 (1777). *AdB* Appendices 25–36 (1778): 704.

Agaton und Psiche
Friedrich Christian Schlenkert (taken from Wieland's novel *Agaton*)
1. (Drama mit Gesang, [3])
   Leipzig: Paul Gotthlef Kummer, 1780 [Schatz 11598]
BIBL.: *AdB* 44:1 (1780): 110–11. *AdM* 1781:99.

Die Arzeney der Liebe
unknown
1. (Komische Oper)
   Hamburg: Gleditsch, 1779
BIBL.: *AdB* 44:1 (1780): 111. *AdM* 1781:101.

Der Barbier von Bagdad
Wilhelm Christhelf Siegmund Mylius [dialogue] and Johann Friedrich Schink [arias] (after Palissot)
1. (Schnurre. . . mit Gesang, 1)
   Theater-Journal für Deutschland vom Jahre 1780, pt. 15, pp. 3–40

Die beschleunigte Hochzeit
Traugott Benjamin Berger
1. (Komische Oper, 3)
   Leipzig: Schneider, 1778
BIBL.: *TJ* 5 (1778): 80. *LTZ* 1 (1778): 540. *AdB* Appendices 25–36 (1778): 781–2. *TSS* 313.
   Berger had asked his publisher not to print this work, promising him a new one in its stead, but Schneider published it anyway.

Die dankbare Tochter, *oder Die Einquartierung*
Andreas Gottlieb Hartmann

1. (Lustspiel mit Gesang, 1)
   Budissin: Deinzer, 1780
2. (Ländliches Lustspiel, [1])
   Budissin, 1784
BIBL.: *AdB* 44:1 (1780): 111. *AdM* 1781:99–100.

Diana und Endymion
Friedrich Karl von Strombeck (after Metastasio, *Endimione* [1721])
1. (Singspiel, [2])
   Brunswick: Johann Christoph Meyer, 1795 [Schatz 11604, *Wolf.* 553]

Die Dorfkirmse, *oder Die Politik der Bauern*
unknown
1. (Komische Oper, 4)
   n.p., 1775
BIBL.: *AdB* 31:1 (1777): 207.

Eimsbüttel, *oder Die Johannisnacht*
Johann Friedrich Schütze
1. (Komische Operette, 3)
   Hamburg, 1791

[*Die Einquartierung* → *Die dankbare Tochter*]

Der Einsiedler
L.
1. (Schauspiel mit Gesang, [1])
   Leipzig: Christian Gottlob Hilscher, 1780 [Schatz 11452]
BIBL.: *LTZ* 3 (1780): 479. *AdB* 47:2 (1781): 426. *AdM* 1781:100.
   This is possibly the opera *Der Einsiedler* set by Weisflog.

Erano
August Johann Georg Carl Batsch
1. (Schauspiel mit Gesängen, 3)
   n.p., 1779 [US-Wc ML 50.2 E58]
BIBL.: *LTZ* 3 (1780): 479. *AdM* 1781:101.

Das Familiengelübde
unknown
1. (Theaterstück mit Gesang, 3)
   Hildburghausen, 1786
BIBL.: *ELT* 6 (1787): 334–5.

Frea's Niederfahrt
D. Neubeck (after Sayer, *Dramatic Sketches of the Ancient Northern Mythology*)
1. (Lyrisches Drama, 2)
   Der Neue Teutsche Merkur 1793:1 (April): 337–60

Die Frühlingsnacht
Johann Wolfgang Andreas Schöpfel
1. (Operette, 1)
   Frankfurt and Leipzig: Christian Gottlieb Hertel, 1773 [Schatz 11612]
BIBL.: *AdB* Appendices 13–24 (1777): 435.

Das Hallorenfest
Friedrich Gustav von Schlicht

1. (Singeschauspiel, 3)
   Magdeburg: Scheidhauerscher Verlag, 1783 [US-Wc ML 50.2 H16]

Hannchen Robert
Jakob Matthesius
1. (Operette, 3)
   Gotha: Carl Wilhelm Ettinger, 1779 [Schatz 11615]
BIBL.: *AdM* 1780:53.

Jeder Topf find't seinen Deckel
unknown (based on *Der neue Amadis*)
1. (Comische Operette)
   Magdeburg, 1775
BIBL.: *AdB* 30:1 (1777): 243.

Je unnatürlicher, je besser
Johann Benjamin Michaelis
1. (Komische Oper, 3)
   [J. B. Michaelis:] *Einzelne Gedichte, Erste Sammlung* (Leipzig: S. L. Crusius, 1769), pp. 85ff.
2. (Komische Oper, 3)
   Sämmtliche Werke des Johann Benjamin Michaelis (Vienna: Schrämbl, 1791), vol. 3, pp. 81–205
BIBL.: Schmid *C* 292 [184].
   Neefe included settings of two arias from this opera in his keyboard reduction of Michaelis's *Der Einspruch* (Leipzig, 1773).

[*Die Johannisnacht* → *Eimsbüttel*]

Komala
Friedrich Bouterwek (after Ossian)
1. (Singspiel, [1])
   Deutsches Museum 1788:4 (December): 512–27

[*Die küssende Diana* → *Der vergnügte Traum*]

[*Leidenschaft und Täuschung* → *Rudolph von Mohelli*]

Der Lindwurm
Veit Weber [pseudonym of Georg Philipp Ludwig Leonhard Wächter] ("nach der Englischen Farce: The Dragon of Wantley, verwebert")
1. (Posse mit Gesang, 3)
   Ephemeriden der Litteratur und des Theaters 5 (1787): 177–87, 204–6, 209–222

Lykon und Agle
unknown
1. (Scene aus der alten Welt)
   Leipzig: Hilscher, 1778
BIBL.: *AdB* 42:1 (1780): 86–9.

[*Die Macht der Feen* → *Selim und Zelinde*]

Der Mann von Vierzig in Windeln
unknown
1. (Komische Operette, 4)
   Leipzig: Johann Samuel Hensius und Sohn, 1793 [Schaal 589]
BIBL.: *HT* 2:789.

Der Nachtwandler
Karl Rechlin
1. (Singspiel, 1)
Berlinisches Archiv der Zeit und ihres Geschmacks 1798:1, pp. 457-69

Palaemon
Johann Wolfgang Andreas Schöpfel
1. (Schäferspiel mit Gesängen, 2)
Frankfurt and Leipzig: Christian Gottlieb Hertel, 1774 [Wolf. 1219, US-Wc ML 50.2 P16]
BIBL.: TM 8 (1774): 188-9.
Sonneck summarizes the preface to the libretto (pp. 843-4).

Pandora
Christoph Martin Wieland (after Le Sage, La Boëte de Pandore [1721])
1. (Lustspiel, 2)
Der teutsche Merkur 1779:3 (July): [3]-48

Peter der Grosse, Kayser von Russland
Christian Gottlob Hempel (based on a historical incident)
1. (Musikalisches Drama, 5)
Leipzig: Haug, 1780 [Wolf. 1263]
BIBL.: AdB 43:1 (1780): 138-9.

[Die Politik der Bauern → Die Dorfkirmse]

Pygmalion, oder Die Reformation der Liebe
Carl Alexander Herklots
1. (Lyrisches Drama, 2)
Berlin 1794

Der Rangstreit
Siegmund Immanuel Matthesius
1. (Singspiel)
Chemnitz, 1784
Riemann OH dates this work 1783.

[Die Reformation der Liebe → Pygmalion]

Der Rekrut
Friedrich Gustav Hagemann
1. (Deutsches Schauspiel mit Gesang, 5)
Hamburg: Reuss, 1783
BIBL.: AdB 56:1 (1783): 121.

Rudolph von Mohelli, oder Leidenschaft und Täuschung
unknown
1. (Trauerspiel. . . mit Gesang, 3)
Breslau: Wilhelm Gottlieb Korn, 1789
2. (Trauerspiel. . . mit Gesang, 3)
Deutsche Schaubühne (Augsburg, 1789), vol 5, pp. [209]-312
BIBL.: AdB 97:1 (1780): 161.

Schwarz und weiss
Carl Alexander Herklots (after St.-Foix, L'Île Sauvage [1743])
1. (Singspiel, 2)
C. A. Herklots: Operetten (Berlin, 1793), pp. [57]-176 [Schatz 11649, D-Mbs]
BIBL.: ALZ 1793:4:92-3.

Selim und Zelinde
unknown
1. (Romantisch-komische Oper, 2)
   Breslau and Hirschberg: Korn der Ältere, 1788
BIBL.: *AdB* 89:1 (1789): 85.

Selinde
Johann Heinrich Weismann
1. (Singspiel)
   Rudolstadt, 1783
2. (Singspiel)
   Leipzig, 1786
BIBL.: *AdB* 77:2 (1787): 416–17.

Der Sklav
Carl August Gottlieb Seidel
1. (Schauspiel mit Gesang)
   Berlin, 1783
2. (Schauspiel mit Gesang)
   Olla Potrida 1778:3

So prelt man alte Füchse, *oder Wurst wider Wurst*
Wilhelm Christhelf Siegmund Mylius and Bernhard Christoph d'Arien (a translation
of Molière, *Les Fourberies de Scapin* [1671])
1. (Posse mit Gesängen und Balletten, [3])
   Halle: J. C. Hendel, 1777
BIBL.: Plümicke 333.

Das Testament
unknown
1. (Komische Operette, 1)
   *Zwo komische Operetten von G * * nebst andern Gedichten zum Anhange*
   (Chemnitz: Stössel und Putscher, 1773), pp. [185]–246 [Schatz 11655, *Wolf.* 1577]
BIBL.: *AdB* 24:1 (1775): 99–100.

Theseus auf Kreta
Friedrich Rambach
1. (Lyrisches Drama, [3])
   Leipzig: Johann Ambrosius Barth, 1791 [GB-Lmb]
BIBL.: *AdT* 9 (1792): 126–8. *ALZ* 1792:3:309–12.
   The libretto is prefaced with an interesting note to the reader by Johann
   Joachim Eschenburg and is followed by an extensive appendix by Rambach,
   "Über das dramatisch-lyrische Gedicht" (pp. 135–215).

[*Die Thränen des Wiedersehens* → *Wunna*]

Das Urtheil des Midas
Christoph Martin Wieland (after Lafont, *Le Jugement d'Apollon et de Pan par
Midas* [1721])
1. (Komisches Singspiel, 1)
   Der teutsche Merkur 1775:1 (January): 1–19
2. (Komisches Singspiel, 1)
   C. M. Wielands Sämtliche Werke (Leipzig: Göschen, 1796), vol. 26, pp. 199–227
   [*Wolf.* 1654]
   This text was later set by Hans Hermann (1870–1931).

Der vergnügte Traum, *oder Die küssende Diana*
unknown
1. (Operette, [1])
   Frankfurt and Leipzig: Martin Jacob Bauer, 1769 [GB-Lbm]

Das vornehme Suschen
unknown
1. (Komische Operette, 3)
   *Zwo komische Operetten von G * * nebst andern Gedichten zum Anhange*
   (Chemnitz: Stössel und Putscher, 1773), pp. 1-184 [Schatz 11655, *Wolf.* 1706]
   BIBL.: *AdB* 24:1 (1775): 99-100.
   Sonneck prints an excerpt from the prefatory note (p. 1148). The review cited
   incorrectly links the work with Molière's *Les Precieuses ridicules* (1659); the
   title role here has a mild case of the much graver fashion fever possessing the
   daughter and niece in Molière's one-act play.

Die Wassergeister
Friedrich Hildebrand von Einsiedel
1. (Operette, [1])
   F. H. von Einsiedel: *Neueste vermischte Schriften*, 2 vols. (Dessau, 1783-4),
   vol. 2, pp. 129ff.
   Only the arias are written out in full in this text; the action is described where
   the dialogue is to occur in order to guide the actors' extemporizings.

Wilhelm und Hannchen
Sophie Eleonore von Titzenhofer
1. (Operette, 3)
   Breslau, 1778
   BIBL.: *TJ* 7 (1778): 94. *TSS* 283. *AdB* 42:1 (1780): 86-9.

Wunna, *oder Die Thränen des Wiedersehens*
Ludwig Theobul Kosegarten
1. (Schauspiel mit Gesang)
   n.p., 1780
   BIBL.: *AdB* 46:2 (1781): 433-4. *AdM* 1781:80-1.

[*Wurst wider Wurst* → *So prelt man alte Füchse*]

Part III

Index of librettists

ANDRÉ, JOHANN (1741–99)
Der alte Freyer
André (1775)
Der Barbier von Bagdad
André (1783)
Die Bezauberten
André (1777)
Der Liebhaber als Automat
André (1782)

D'ARIEN, BERNHARD CHRISTOPH (1754–?)
Dr. Fausts Leibgürtel
Hanke (1786)
Heinrich und Lyda
Neefe (1776)
Laura Rosetti
André (1778)
[*So prelt man alte Füchse* → Wilhelm Christhelf Siegmund Mylius]
Xaphire
Hanke (1786)

AST, JOHANN CHRISTIAN (1729–?)
Der Kapellmeister und die Schülerin
Laube (1768)
Matz und Anna
Laube (1768)

AUTENRIETH (dates unknown)
Barbier und Schornsteinfeger
Essiger (1798)

BACZKO, LUDWIG ADOLF FRANZ JOSEPH VON (1756–1823)
Die Kantons-Revision
Halter (1792)
Rinaldo und Alcina
Löwe (1797)
Die Singschule
Mühle (1794)

BARCHIELLI (dates unknown)
Die Ueberraschung
Volanek (1797)

416

Opera buffa
  Kallenbach (1798)
Schattenspiel an der Wand
  Kallenbach (1797)
Der Schlaftrunk
  Bierey (1797) Schmidt (1797) Kallenbach (1799)
Der Talisman
  Kaffka (1789)
Das wütende Heer
  André (1780) Kaffka (1782) Hurka (1788) Schweitzer (unperformed)

BRUNNER, GOTTFRIED SAMUEL (dates unknown)
Poltis [with Steinel]
  Hiller (unperformed)

BÜRDE, SAMUEL GOTTLIEB (1753–1831)
Don Sylvio von Rosalva
  Phanty (1796) Sander (1797) Bachmann (1797) Müller (1799)
Die Regata zu Venedig
  Sander (1796) Fliess (1798)

DITTERSDORF, CARL DITTERS VON (1739–99)
Don Quixotte der Zweite
  Dittersdorf (1795)
Das Gespenst mit der Trommel
  Dittersdorf (1794)
Gott Mars
  Dittersdorf (1795)

DRAIS VON SAUERBRONN, CARL WILHELM LUDWIG FREIHERR VON
(1755–1830)
Elmine
  André (1782)

EINSIEDEL, FRIEDRICH HILDEBRAND FREIHERR VON (1750–1828)
[*Die Geisterinsel* → Johann Friedrich Wilhelm Gotter]
Die Wassergeister
  (publ. 1784)
Die Zauberirrungen
  Wolf (1785)

ENGEL, JOHANN JAKOB (1741–1802)
Die Apotheke
  Neefe (1771) Rellstab (1788)
[*Der Jahrmarkt* → Johann Friedrich Wilhelm Gotter]

ESCHENBURG, JOHANN JOACHIM (1743–1820)
Der Holzhauer
  Koch (1774)
Lukas und Hannchen
  Beckmann (1768)

GELLERT, CHRISTIAN FÜRCHTEGOTT (1715–69)
Das Orakel
  Fleischer (1771)

GIESECKE, CARL LUDWIG [pseud. of Johann Georg Metzler] (1761–1833)
Amadis der fahrende Ritter von Gallien
  Stengel (1798)

GOETHE, JOHANN WOLFGANG VON (1749–1832)
Claudine von Villa Bella
  1st version: André (unperformed)
  2nd version: Reichardt (1789)
Erwin und Elmire
  1st version: André (1775) Anna Amalia (1776) Stegmann (1776) Wolf (1785)
  Schweitzer (unperformed)
  2nd version: Reichardt (1790)
Die Fischerinn
  Schröter (1782)
Das Jahrmarktsfest zu Plundersweilern
  Anna Amalia (1778)
Jery und Bätely
  1st version: Seckendorff (1780)
  2nd version: Bierey (1795) Schaum (1795)

GOTTER, JOHANN FRIEDRICH WILHELM (1746–97)
Die Dorfgala
  Schweitzer (1772)
Die Geisterinsel [with Friedrich Hildebrand von Einsiedel]
  Reichardt (1798) Haack (1798)
Der Holzhauer [with Wulf]
  Benda (1778)
Der Jahrmarkt [2-act version adapted by Johann Jakob Engel]
  Benda (1775)
Romeo und Julie
  Benda (1776)
Das tartarische Gesetz
  André (1779)
Walder
  Benda (1776)

GROSSMANN, GUSTAV FRIEDRICH WILHELM (1746–96)
Der Barbier von Seville
  Benda (1776)
Liebesabentheuer
  Bierey (1794)

HAGEMANN, FRIEDRICH GUSTAV (1760–after 1829)
Der Rekrut
  (publ. 1783)

HALBE, JOHANN AUGUST (1755–?)
Die Liebe auf der Probe
  Halbe (1781)

HARTMANN, ANDREAS GOTTLIEB (1751–87)
Die dankbare Tochter
(publ. 1780)

HEERMANN, GOTTLOB EPHRAIM (1727–1815)
Der Abend im Walde
Wolf (1773)
Die Dorfdeputirten
Wolf (1772)
Das Rosenfest
Wolf (1770)
Die treuen Köhler
Wolf (1772)

HEMPEL, CHRISTIAN GOTTLOB (1748–1824)
Peter der Grosse, Kayser von Russland
(publ. 1780)

HENISCH, CARL FRANZ (1745–?)
Der Bassa von Tunis
Holly (1774)
Gelegenheit macht Diebe
Holly (1775)

HENSEL, JOHANN DANIEL (1757–1839)
Daphne
Hensel (1799)
Die Geisterbeschwörung
Hensel (1799)
Die Geisterinsel
Hensel (1799)

HERDER, JOHANN GOTTFRIED VON (1744–1803)
Brutus
Bach (1774)
Philoktetes
Bach (1775)

HERKLOTS, CARL ALEXANDER (1759–1830)
Die böse Frau
Bierey (1792) Walter (1794)
Die Geisterbeschwörung
Cartellieri (1793)
Das Inkognito
Gürrlich (1797)
Die Insel der Alcina
Bianchi (1794)
Der Mädchenmarkt
Kospoth (1793) Bierey (1794) Dittersdorf (1797)
Pygmalion
(publ. 1794)
Schwarz und weiss
(publ. 1793)

Der Theater-Prinzipal
  Weber (1796)

JACOBI, JOHANN GEORG (1740–1814)
Phaedon und Naide
  Bierey (1793) Bachmann (1795)
Der Tod des Orpheus
  Bachmann (1798)

JESTER, FRIEDRICH ERNST (1743–1822)
Esther
  Schönbeck (1793)
Louise
  Benda (1791)
Mariechen
  Benda (1791)
Der Triumf der Liebe [2nd version revised by C. L. Costenoble]
  Stegmann (1st version: 1796; 2nd version: 1806)
Die Verlobung
  Benda (1789)
Der Wunderigel
  Schönbeck (1793)

JÜNGER, JOHANN FRIEDRICH (1759–97)
Der blinde Ehemann
  Kaffka (1788) Drobisch (1791)

KAFFKA, JOHANN CHRISTOPH (1754–1815)
Die Ehestandskandidaten
  Bierey (1796)
Der Guck Kasten
  Kaffka (1782)
[*So prellt man alte Füchse* → Friedrich Ludwig Wilhelm Meyer]

KELLNER, JOHANN MARTIN (1756–?)
Der Frühling
  Feige (1775)
Die Kirmess
  Feige (1775)

KINDERLING, [JOHANN FRIEDRICH AUGUST? (1743–1807)]
Seliko und Berissa
  Ebell (1799)

KLENKE, CAROLINE LUISE KARSCH VON (1754–1802)
Der ehrliche Schweizer
  Hattasch (1780)

KOCH, FRIEDRICH CARL (*ca.* 1740–97)
Der lahme Husar
  Seydelmann (1780)

KORB, CH. G. (dates unknown)
Der ehrliche Räuber
  Zeller (1787)
Meister Johannes, der lustige Schuster
  Ohlhorst (1791)
Das Mündel
  Stegmann (1783)

KOSEGARTEN, LUDWIG (THEOBUL) GOTTHARD (1758–1818)
Wunna
  (publ. 1780)

KOTZEBUE, AUGUST VON (1761–1819)
Der Eremit auf Formentera
  Wolf (1786) Mühle (1790) Ebers (1793) Hinze (1797) Bornhardt (1797)
Der Spiegelritter
  Agthe (1795) Hinze (1797)
Sultan Wampum
  Bornhardt (1796) Essiger (1797)

LANGBEIN, AUGUST FRIEDRICH ERNST (1757–1835)
Die schöne Fürstin
  Mühle (1799)

LICHTENSTEIN, CARL AUGUST LUDWIG FREIHERR VON (1767–1845)
Bathmendi [2nd version]
  Lichtenstein (1799)
Glück und Zufall
  Lichtenstein (1793)
Die steinerne Braut
  Lichtenstein (1799)

LINDEMANN, GOTTFRIED FERDINAND VON (1744–?)
Orpheus
  Benda (1785)

MATTHESIUS, JACOB (1752–?)
Hannchen Robert
  (publ. 1779)

MATTHESIUS, SIEGMUND IMMANUEL (dates unknown)
Der Rangstreit
  (publ. 1784)

MEISSNER, AUGUST GOTTLIEB (1753–1807)
Der Alchymist
  André (1778) Schuster (1778)
Arsene
  Seydelmann (1779)
Das Grab des Mufti
  Baumgarten (1776) Hiller (1779)
Die wüste Insel
  Schuster (1779)

MEYER, FRIEDRICH LUDWIG WILHELM (1759–1840)
Kurze Thorheit ist die beste
  André (1780)
So prellt man alte Füchse [with Johann Christoph Kaffka]
  Kaffka (1782)

MICHAELIS, JOHANN BENJAMIN (1746–72)
Amors Guckkasten
  Neefe (1772)
Der Einspruch
  Neefe (1-act: 1772, 2-act: 1773)
Je unnatürlicher, je besser!
  (publ. 1769)
Walmir und Gertraud
  Schweitzer (unperformed)

MÜCHLER, KARL FRIEDRICH (1763–1857)
Psyche
  Wessely (1789)

MUSÄUS, JOHANN CARL AUGUST (1735–87)
Das Gärtnermädchen
  Wolf (1769) Holly (1775)

MYLIUS, WILHELM CHRISTHELF SIEGMUND (1754–1827)
Der Barbier von Bagdad [with Johann Friedrich Schink]
  (publ. 1780)
Doktor Fausts Zaubergürtel [with Johann Friedrich Schink]
  Phanty (1784)
So prelt man alte Füchse [with Bernhard Christoph d'Arien]
  (publ. 1777)

NESSELRODE ZU HUGUENBOTT, F. G. VON (dates unknown)
Julie
  Davander (1781)

NEUMANN (dates unknown)
Das Jahresfest
  Ohlhorst (1783)

NICOLAI, CHRISTOPH FRIEDRICH (1733–1811)
Der lustige Schulmeister
  Krause (1766)

PATZKE, JOHANN SAMUEL (1727–87)
Der Sturm
  Rolle (1782)

RAMBACH, FRIEDRICH EBERHARD (1767–1826)
Theseus auf Kreta
  (publ. 1791)

RAMLER, CARL WILHELM (1725-98)
Cyrus und Kassandane
  Hensel (1786)
[*Der Krieg* → Christian Felix Weisse]

RATHJE [RAHTJE], GEORG HEINRICH (dates unknown)
Der Derwisch
  Reymann (1797)

RECHLIN, KARL (dates unknown)
Der Nachtwandler
  (publ. 1798)

REICHARDT, JOHANN FRIEDRICH (1752-1814)
Liebe nur beglückt
  Reichardt (1781)

RÖMER, GEORG C. (1766-1829)
Die lustigen Weiber von Windsor
  Dittersdorf (1796)

RORDORF, ERNST FERDINAND (dates unknown)
Hass und Aussöhnung
  Grüger (1797)

SANDER, JOHANN DANIEL (1759-1825)
Eins wird doch helfen
  André (1782)

SCHACK, HERMANN EWALD (dates unknown)
Heyrath aus Liebe
  Hönicke (1777)

SCHIEBELER, DANIEL (1741-71)
Lisuart und Dariolette
  Hiller (2-act: 1766, 3-act: 1767)
Die Muse
  Hiller (1767)

SCHINK, JOHANN FRIEDRICH (1755-1835)
Adelstan und Röschen
  Ohlhorst (1782) Hiller (1792)
[*Der Barbier von Bagdad* → Wilhelm Christhelf Siegmund Mylius]
[*Doktor Fausts Zaubergürtel* → Wilhelm Christhelf Siegmund Mylius]
Rosalia
  Schubert (1777)

SCHLENKERT, FRIEDRICH CHRISTIAN (1757-1826)
Agaton und Psiche
  (publ. 1780)

SCHLICHT, FRIEDRICH GUSTAV VON (1758–?)
Das Hallorenfest
(publ. 1783)

SCHMIEDER, HEINRICH GOTTLIEB (1763–1828)
Doktor Faust
Walter (1st version: 1797, 2nd version: 1798)

SCHÖPFEL, JOHANN WOLFGANG ANDREAS (1752–?)
Die Frühlingsnacht
(publ. 1773)
Palaemon
(publ. 1774)

SCHRÖTER, C.F. (dates unknown)
Demokrit
Kalkbrenner (1791)

SCHUBERT, KARL EMIL (1741–1803)
Zemire und Azor
Baumgarten (1776)

SCHÜTZE, JOHANN FRIEDRICH (1758–1810)
Eimsbüttel
(publ. 1791)

SCHWAN, CHRISTIAN FRIEDRICH (1733–1815)
Azakia
André (1778) Ehrenberg (1790)
Der Kaufmann von Smyrna
Holly (1773) Stegmann (1st version: 1773, 2nd version: 1796) Seydelmann (177

SCHWICK, WALTER ANTON (dates unknown)
Das blaue Ungeheuer
Schubert (1781)

SECKENDORFF, KARL AUGUST GOTTFRIED FREIHERR VON (1744–85)
Der Blumenraub
Seckendorff (1784)
Superba
Wolf (1785)

SEIDEL, CARL AUGUST GOTTLIEB (1754–1822)
Karoline
Kospoth (unperformed)

SEYLER, FRIEDERIKE SOPHIE (1738–89)
Hüon und Amande
Hanke (1789)

SODEN VON SASSANFART, FREIHERR JULIUS (1754–1831)
Mit dem Glockenschlag: zwölf!
Mühle (1783)

SPAUR, H. GRAF VON (dates unknown)
Fremore und Melime
 Mühle (1778)
Der Schiffbruch
 Mühle (1778)

STEINEL (dates unknown)
[*Poltis* → Gottfried Samuel Brunner]

STROMBECK, FRIEDRICH KARL VON (1771–1848)
Diana und Endymion
 (publ. 1795)

SUCRO, CHRISTOPH JOSEPH (dates unknown)
Melida
 Rolle (1784)

THOMAS, DANIEL HEINRICH (1739–1808)
Der Kobold
 Escherich (1777) Frischmuth (unperformed)
Die kranke Frau
 Frischmuth (1773)

THÜMMEL, MORITZ AUGUST VON (1738–1817)
Zemire und Azor
 Neefe (1776)

TITZENHOFER, SOPHIE ELEONORE VON (1749–1823)
Wilhelm und Hannchen
 (publ. 1778)

VULPIUS, CHRISTIAN AUGUST (1762–1827)
Bella und Fernando
 Kospoth (1790)
Das hätt' ich nicht gedacht!
 Burgmüller (1788)
Der Schleyer
 Wolf (1786)

WAGENSEIL, CHRISTIAN JACOB (1756–1839)
Ehrlichkeit und Liebe
 Wolf (1776)

WEBER, VEIT [pseud. of Georg Philipp Ludwig Leonhard Wächter] (1762–1837)
Der Lindwurm
 (publ. 1787)

WEISFLOG, CHRISTIAN GOTTHILF (1732–?)
Das Erntefest
 Weisflog (1769)
Das Frühstück auf der Jagd
 Weisflog (1772)
Der Schatz
 Weisflog (1781)

WEISMANN, JOHANN HEINRICH (dates unknown)
Selinde
(publ. 1783)

WEISSE, CHRISTIAN FELIX (1726–1804)
Der Ärndtekranz
  Hiller (1771)
Das Denkmal in Arkadien
  Hunt (1791) Hiller (unperformed)
Der Dorfbalbier
  Hiller and Neefe (1771)
Das Findelkind
  Benda (unperformed)
Die Jagd
  Hiller (1770)
Die Jubelhochzeit
  Hiller (1773)
Die kleine Ährenleserinn
  Hiller (1778) Wittrock (1787)
Der Krieg [with Carl Wilhelm Ramler]
  Hiller (1772)
Die Liebe auf dem Lande
  Hiller (1768)
Lottchen am Hofe
  Hiller (1767)
Der lustige Schuster
  Standfuss and Hiller (1766) Schweitzer (1770)
Die Schadenfreude
  Weimar (1776) André (1778)
Die verwandelten Weiber
  Standfuss and Hiller (1766)

WEZEL, JOHANN CARL (1747–1819)
Der kluge Jakob
  Kospoth (1788)

WIELAND, CHRISTOPH MARTIN (1733–1813)
Alceste
  Schweitzer (1773) Benda (1786) Wolf (1786)
Angelica
  Wolf (1788)
Pandora
  (publ. 1779)
Das Urtheil des Midas
  (publ. 1775)

WULF (dates unknown)
[*Der Holzhauer* → Johann Friedrich Wilhelm Gotter]

ZSCHIEDRICH, K. A. VON (dates unknown)
Lieb' um Liebe
  Dunkel (1796)

Selective bibliography

Abert, Hermann. "J. G. Noverre und sein Einfluss auf die dramatische Balletkomposition." *Gesammelte Schriften und Vorträge*, ed. Friedrich Blume. Halle, 1929, pp. 264–86.

Adams, John Quincy. *Memoirs of John Quincy Adams: Comprising Portions of His Diary from 1795 to 1848*. Ed. Charles Francis Adams. Philadelphia, 1874.

Allgemeine Bibliothek für Schauspieler und Schauspielliebhaber. Ed. Christian August von Bertram. Frankfurt and Leipzig, 1776.

Allgemeine deutsche Bibliothek. Ed. Friedrich Nicolai. 118 vols. and 21 vols. suppl. Berlin and Stettin, 1766–96.

Allgemeine musikalische Zeitung. Ed. Friedrich Rochlitz. Vols. 1–2. Leipzig, 1798–1800.

Almanach der deutschen Musen auf dem Jahr. . . Ed. Christian Heinrich Schmid. 10 vols. Leipzig, 1770–9.

Angermüller, Rudolph. "'Les Époux esclaves ou Bastien et Bastienne à Alger'. Zur Stoffgeschichte der 'Entführung aus dem Serail.'" *Mozart-Jahrbuch 1978/9*, pp. 70–88.

Annalen des Theaters. Ed. Christian August von Bertram. 20 vols. Berlin, 1788–97.

[d'Arien, Bernhard Christoph.] *Beyträge zur Litteratur- und Theaterkunde*. Hamburg, 1785.

Bauman, Thomas. "Benda, the Germans, and Simple Recitative." *Journal of the American Musicological Society* 34 (1981): 119–31.

"Music and Drama in Germany: A Traveling Company and its Repertory, 1767–1781." Ph. D. Diss., University of California at Berkeley, 1977.

"Opera *versus* Drama: *Romeo and Juliet* in Eighteenth-Century Germany." *Eighteenth-Century Studies* 11 (1977/8): 186–203.

"Wieland's 'Aufklärungsoper'." *Report of the Twelfth Congress Berkeley 1977, International Musicological Society*. Ed. Daniel Heartz and Bonnie Wade. Kassel, Basel, and London, 1981, pp. 245–9.

ed. *German Opera, 1770–1800*. 22 vols. New York: Garland, 1985 [facsimile series].

Beiträge zum Theater, zur Musik und der unterhaltenden Lektüre überhaupt. Ed. Johann Christian Friedrich Dietz. Stendal, 1785.

Berlinische Musikalische Zeitung historischen und kritischen Inhalts. Ed. Carl Spazier. Berlin, 1794.

Berlinisches Archiv der Zeit und ihres Geschmacks. Ed. Rambach and Fessler. 8 vols. Berlin, 1796–9.

[Bertram, Christian August von.] *Ueber die Kochische Schauspielergesellschaft. Aus Berlin an einen Freund*. Berlin and Leipzig, 1771.

Biedermann, Woldemar Freiherr von. *Goethe und Leipzig: Zur hundertjährigen Wiederkehr des Tags von Goethe's Aufnahme auf Leipzigs Hochschule*. Vol. 1: *Goethe's Leben in Leipzig*. Leipzig, 1865.

Bobrik, Günther E. G. *Wielands Don Sylvio und Oberon auf der deutschen Singspiel-bühne.* Ph. D. Diss, Ludwig-Maximilian University, Munich. Königsberg, 1909.

Bode, Wilhelm. *Die Tonkunst in Goethes Leben.* 2 vols. Berlin, 1912. *Der weimarische Musenhof 1756–1781.* Berlin, 1920.

Bötcher, Elmar. *Goethes Singspiele "Erwin und Elmire" und "Claudine von Villa Bella" und die "opera buffa".* Ph. D. Diss., University of Marburg (partial printing). Marburg, 1911.

Böttiger, Karl August. *Literarische Zustände und Zeitgenossen: in Schildereyen aus Karl Aug. Böttiger's handschriftlichem Nachlasse.* Ed. K. W. Böttiger. 2 vols. Leipzig, 1838.

B[oni]n, [Christian Friedrich] von. *Berliner Theater-Journal für das Jahr 1782.* Berlin, 1783.

Borcherdt, Hans Heinrich. "Die Entstehungsgeschichte von 'Erwin und Elmire'." *Goethe-Jahrbuch* 32 (1911): 73–82.

Born, Gerhard. *Die Gründung des Berliner Nationaltheaters und die Geschichte seines Personals, seines Spielplans und seiner Verwaltung bis zu Döbbelins Abgang (1786–1789).* Ph. D. Diss, Friedrich-Alexander University, Erlangen. Borna-Leipzig, 1934.

Brachvogel, A[delbert] E[mil]. *Geschichte des Königlichen Theaters zu Berlin: Nach Archivalien des Königl. Geh. Staats-Archivs und des Königl. Theaters.* 2 vols. Berlin, 1877.

Brandes, Johann Christian. *Meine Lebensgeschichte.* 3 vols. Berlin, 1799–1800.

Branscombe, Peter. "*Die Zauberflöte*: A Lofty Sequel and Some Lowly Parodies." *Publications of the English Goethe Society* n.s. 48 (1977/8): 1–21.

Braun, Julius W. *Goethe im Urtheile seiner Zeitgenossen: Zeitungskritiken, Berichte, Notizen, Goethe und seine Werke betreffend, aus den Jahren 1773–1786.* Berlin, 1883.

The Breitkopf Thematic Catalogue: The Six Parts and Sixteen Supplements 1762–1787. Ed. Barry S. Brook. New York, 1966.

Brinitzer, Carl. *Die Geschichte des Daniel Ch[odowiecki]: Ein Sittenbild des 18. Jahrhunderts.* Stuttgart, 1973.

Brockt, Johannes. *Ernst Wilhelm Wolf (Leben und Werke): Ein Beitrag zur Musik-geschichte des 18. Jahrhunderts.* Ph. D. Diss., Friedrich-Wilhelm University (partial printing). Striegau, 1927.

[Bumbrey, Carl Wilhelm.] *Briefe über Musikwesen, besonders Cora in Halle.* Qued-linburg, 1781.

Burkhardt, C[arl] A[ugust] H[ugo]. *Goethe und der Komponist Ph. Chr. Kayser.* Leipzig, 1879.

Das Repertoire des Weimarischen Theaters unter Goethes Leitung, 1791–1817. Theatergeschichtliche Forschungen, vol. 1. Hamburg and Leipzig, 1891.

Burney, Charles. *The Present State of Music in Germany, the Netherlands and United Provinces.* 2 vols. London, 1773.

Cahn-Speyer, Rudolf [Simon]. *Franz Seydelmann als dramatischer Komponist.* Ph. D. Diss, Ludwig-Maximilian University, Munich. Leipzig, 1909.

Calmus, Georgy. *Die ersten deutschen Singspiele von Standfuss und Hiller.* Publika-tionen der Internationalen Musik-Gesellschaft, Beihefte, n.s., vol. 6. Leipzig, 1908.

Costenoble, Carl Ludwig. *Carl Ludwig Costenoble's Tagebücher von seiner Jugend bis zur Uebersiedlung nach Wien (1818).* Schriften der Gesellschaft für Theater-geschichte, vols. 18–19. Berlin, 1912.

Czach, Rudolf. *Friedrich Wilhelm Rust.* Ph. D. Diss, Friedrich-Wilhelm University, Berlin. Essen, [1927].

Deetjen, Werner. "Der 'Sturm' als Operntext bearbeitet von Einsiedel und Gotter." *Shakespeare-Jahrbuch* 64 (1928): 77–89.

Dent, Edward J. *Mozart's Operas: A Critical Study.* 2nd ed. London, Oxford, and New York, 1947.

Deutsche Chronik auf das Jahr. . . Ed. Christian Friedrich Daniel Schubart. 4 vols. Augsburg, 1774–7.

Deutsche Operetten im Auszuge mit Musik der besten deutschen Componisten. Erster Theil. [No more publ.] Flensburg, 1776.

Deutsches Museum. Ed. Heinrich Christian Boie and Christian Wilhelm von Dohm. 26 vols. Leipzig, 1776–88.

Devrient, Hans. *Johann Friedrich Schönemann und seine Schauspielergesellschaft: Ein Beitrag zur Theatergeschichte des 18. Jahrhunderts.* Theatergeschichtliche Forschungen, vol. 11. Hamburg and Leipzig, 1895.

Dingelstedt, Franz, ed. *Johann Valentin Teichmanns weiland königl. preussischen Hofrathes ec. Literarischer Nachlass.* Stuttgart, 1863.

Dittersdorf, Karl Ditters von. *Lebensbeschreibung: Seinem Sohne in die Feder diktiert.* Ed. Karl Spazier. Leipzig, 1801.

Dreetz, Albert. *Aus Erfurts Musikgeschichte (1750–1800).* Leipzig, [1932].

Dressler, Ernst Christoph. *Gedanken, die Vorstellung der Alceste, ein deutsches ernsthaftes Singspiel betreffend.* Frankfurt and Leipzig, 1774.

   Theater-Schule für die Deutschen, das Ernsthafte Sing-Schauspiel betreffend. Hannover and Kassel, 1777.

Eitner, Robert. *Biographisch-bibliographisches Quellen-Lexikon der Musiker und Musikgelehrten der christlichen Zeitrechnung bis zur Mitte des 19. Jahrhunderts.* 10 vols. Leipzig, 1898–1904.

Engländer, Richard. "Die Opern Joseph Schusters (1748–1812)." *Zeitschrift für Musikwissenschaft* 10 (1927/8): 257–91.

Ephemeriden der Litteratur und des Theaters. Ed. Christian August von Bertram. 6 vols. Berlin, 1785–7.

Erste [-Sechste] Sammlung der vorzüglichsten, noch ungedruckten Arien und Duetten des deutschen Theaters, von verschiedenen Componisten. Ed. Johann Adam Hiller. Leipzig, 1777–80.

Eximeno [y Pujades], D. Antonio. *Dell'origine e delle regole della musica colla storia del suo progresso, decadenza, e rinnovazione.* Rome, 1774.

Fischer-Lamberg, Hanna. *Der junge Goethe.* 2nd ed. 5 vols. Berlin and New York, 1963–73.

Flaherty, Gloria. *Opera in the Development of German Critical Thought.* Princeton, 1978.

Forkel, Johann Nicolaus, ed. *Musikalisch-Kritische Bibliothek.* 3 vols. Gotha, 1778–9.

Frenzel, Herbert A. *Brandenburg-Preussische Schlosstheater: Spielarte und Spielformen vom 17. bis zum 19. Jahrhundert.* Berlin, 1959.

Fürstenau, Moritz. "Die Theater in Dresden: 1763 bis 1777." *Mittheilungen des Königlich Sächsischen Alterthumsvereins* 25 (1873): 44–78.

Gerber, Ernst Ludwig. *Historisch-Biographisches Lexikon der Tonkünstler.* Leipzig, 1790–2.

   Neues historisch-biographisches Lexikon der Tonkünstler. 4 vols. Leipzig, 1812–14.

Glaser, Adolf. *Geschichte des Theaters zu Braunschweig.* Brunswick, 1861.

Goethe, Johann Wolfgang von. *Gedenkausgabe der Werke, Briefe und Gespräche.* Ed. Ernst Beutler. 24 vols. Zurich, 1949–54.

Goldschmidt, Arthur. *Goethe im Almanach.* Leipzig, 1932.

Graf, Herbert. *Das Repertoire der öffentlichen Opern- und Singspielbühnen in Berlin seit dem Jahre 1771.* Vol. 1 [no more publ.] Berlin, 1934.

[Gruenter, Rainer, ed.] *Das deutsche Singspiel im 18. Jahrhundert: Colloquium der Arbeitsstelle 18. Jahrhundert Gesamthochschule Wuppertal Universität Münster, Amorbach vom 2. bis 4. Oktober 1979.* Beiträge zur Geschichte der Literatur und Kunst des 18. Jahrhunderts, vol. 5. Heidelberg, 1981.

Güttler, Hermann. *Königsbergs Musikkultur im 18. Jahrhundert.* Kassel, [1925].

Hagen, E[rnst] A[ugust]. *Geschichte des Theaters in Preussen, vornämlich der Bühnen in Königsberg und Danzig von ihren ersten Anfängen bis zu den Gastspielen J. Fischer's und L. Devrient's.* Königsberg, 1854.

Hagen, J. J. A. von, ed. *Magazin zur Geschichte des Deutschen Theaters.* Halle, 1773.

Hamburgisch- und Altonaische Theater- und Litteratur-Zeitung. Nebst verschiedenen Nachrichten aus dem Gebiete der Gelehrsamkeit und Kunst. Ed. Friedrich Wilhelm von Schütz. 4 vols. [Hamburg,] 1799–1800.

Heartz, Daniel. "The Creation of the Buffo Finale in Italian Opera." *Proceedings of the Royal Musical Association* 114 (1977/8): 67–78.

"From Garrick to Gluck: The Reform of Theater and Opera in the Mid-Eighteenth Century." *Proceedings of the Royal Musical Association* 94 (1967/8): 111–27.

Herder, Johann Gottfried. *Briefe: Gesamtausgabe 1763–1803.* (In progress.) 7 vols. Weimar, 1977–82.

Hiller, Johann Adam. *Lebensbeschreibungen berühmter Musikgelehrten und Tonkünstler neuerer Zeit.* Vol. 1. Leipzig, 1784.

ed. *Ueber die Musik und deren Wirkungen.* (Annotated trans. of Michel-Paul-Guy de Chabanon: *Observations sur la musique et principalement sur la métaphysique de l'art.* Paris, 1779.) Leipzig, 1781; photo-reprint: Leipzig, 1974.

Hitzig, Wilhelm. "Beiträge zum Weimarer Konzert, 1773–1786." *Der Bär: Jahrbuch von Breitkopf & Härtel auf das Jahr 1925.* Leipzig, 1925, pp. 78–97.

Hodermann, Richard. *Geschichte des Gothaischen Hoftheaters, 1775–1779: Nach den Quellen.* Theatergeschichtliche Forschungen, vol. 9. Hamburg and Leipzig, 1894.

Hoffmann, Carl Julius Adolph. *Die Tonkünstler Schlesiens: Ein Beitrag zur Kunstgeschichte Schlesiens, vom Jahre 960 bis 1830.* Breslau, 1830.

Holtei, Karl von, ed. *Dreihundert Briefe aus zwei Jahrhunderten.* 4 pts. in 2 vols. Hannover, 1872.

Hurrelmann, Bettina. *Jugendliteratur und Bürgerlichkeit: Soziale Erziehung in der Jugendliteratur der Aufklärung am Beispiel von Christian Felix Weisses "Kinderfreund" 1776–1782.* Informationen zur Sprach- und Literaturdidaktik, vol. 5. Paderborn, 1974.

Iris. Ed. Johann Georg Jacobi. 8 vols. Düsseldorf, 1774–5; Berlin, 1776.

Jacobi, Friedrich Heinrich. *Friedrich Heinrich Jacobi's auserlesener Briefwechsel.* 2 vols. Leipzig, 1825–7.

Journal des Luxus und der Moden. Ed. F. J. Bertuch and G. M. Kraus. Vols. 1–14. Weimar, 1786–99.

Kade, Otto. *Die Musikalien-Sammlung des grossherzoglich Mecklenburg-Schweriner Fürstenhauses aus den letzten zwei Jahrhunderten.* 2 vols. Schwerin, 1893.

Kawada, Kyoko. *Studien zu den Singspielen von Johann Adam Hiller (1728–1804).* Ph.D. Diss., Phillips University. Marburg/Lahn, 1969.

Kindermann, Heinz. *Theatergeschichte Europas.* Vol. 4: *Von der Aufklärung zur Romantik* (Part 1). Salzburg, 1961.

Kirby, F[rank] E. "Herder and Opera." *Journal of the American Musicological Society* 15 (1962): 316–29.

Knab, Valentin. "Karl Siegmund von Seckendorff (1774–1785): Ein Beitrag zur Geschichte des deutschen volkstümlichen Liedes und der Musik am Weimarer Hof im 18. Jahrhundert." *60. Jahresbericht des Historischen Vereins für Mittelfranken.* Ansbach, 1914, pp. 17–184.

[Knigge, Adolf Freiherr von.] *Dramaturgische Blätter.* 36 pts. Hannover, 1788–9.

Knoll, Hans. "Friedrich Hildebrand von Einsiedel: Ein Liebhaber der schönen Wissenschaften und Künste." *Zeitschrift des Vereins für Thüringische Geschichte und Altertumskunde,* n.s. 22 (1915): 188–202.

Knop, Leo. *Friedrich Bouterwek als Dramatiker und Romanschriftsteller.* Ph.D. Diss., Greifswald Royal University. Leipzig, 1912.

Koch, Hans-Albrecht. *Das deutsche Singspiel.* Stuttgart, 1974.

"Die Singspiele." *Goethes Dramen: Neue Interpretationen.* Ed. Walter Hinderer. Stuttgart, 1980.

Krogmann, Willy. "Die persönlichen Beziehungen in Goethes Schauspiel mit Gesang 'Claudine von Villa Bella'." *Germanisch-Romanische Monatsschrift* 19 (1931): 348–61.

Leux, Irmgard. *Christian Gottlob Neefe (1748–1798).* Leipzig, 1925.

Lieder, Arien und Duette beym Klavier. Ed. Johann André. 8 pts. in 2 vols. Berlin, 1780–2.

Litteratur- und Theater-Zeitung. Ed. Christian August von Bertram. 7 vols. Berlin, 1778–84.

Litzmann, Berthold. *Friedrich Ludwig Schröder: Ein Beitrag zur deutschen Litteratur- und Theatergeschichte.* 2 vols. Hamburg and Leipizig, 1890–4.

ed. *Schröder und Gotter: Eine Episode aus der deutschen Theatergeschichte: Briefe Friedrich Ludwig Schröders an Friedrich Wilhelm Gotter, 1777 und 1778.* Hamburg and Leipzig, 1887.

Loewenberg, Alfred. *Annals of Opera, 1597–1940.* 2nd ed. Geneva, [1954].

Lorenz, Franz. *Die Musikerfamilie Benda: Georg Anton Benda.* Berlin and New York, 1971.

Lyncker, Karl Freiherr von. *Am Weimarischen Hofe unter Amalien und Karl August.* Ed. Marcè Scheller. (Written between 1837 and 1840.) Berlin, 1912.

Magazin der Musik. Ed. Carl Friedrich Cramer. 2 vols. Hamburg, 1783–4.

Mai, Alfred. *Die Wäser'sche Schauspielergesellschaft in Schlesien (1772–97).* Ph.D. Diss., Silesian Friedrich-Wilhelm University (partial printing). Breslau, 1928.

Mann Michael. "Die feindlichen Brüder." *Germanisch-Romanische Monatsschrift,* n.s., vol. 18 (1968): 225–47.

Martin, Ernst, ed. *Ungedruckte Briefe von und an Johann Georg Jacobi mit einem Abrisse seines Lebens und seiner Dichtung.* Quellen und Forschungen zur Sprach- und Culturgeschichte der germanischen Völker, vol. 2. Strassburg and London, 1874.

Martinsen, Woldemar [Johann Gottlieb]. *Goethes Singspiele im Verhältnis zu den Weissischen Operetten.* Ph.D. Diss., Archducal Hessian Ludewig University (partial printing). Dresden, 1887.

Maurer, Julius. *Anton Schweitzer als dramatischer Komponist.* Publikationen der Internationalen Musikgesellschaft, n.s., vol. 11. Leipzig, 1912.

Meessen, H. J. "*Clavigo* and *Stella* in Goethe's Personal and Dramatic Development." *Goethe Bicentennial Studies.* Ed. H. J. Meessen. Indiana University Publications, Humanities Series, vol. 22. Bloomington, 1950, pp. 153–206.

[Mercier, Louis-Sébastien]. *Du Théâtre, ou nouvelle essai sur l'art dramatique* Amsterdam, 1773.

Meyer, F[riedrich] L[udwig] W[ilhelm]. *Friedrich Ludwig Schröder: Beitrag zur Kunde des Menschen und des Künstlers.* 2 pts. Hamburg, 1819.

Meyer, Günter. *Hallisches Theater im 18. Jahrhundert.* Emsdetten, 1950.

Michtner, Otto. *Das alte Burgtheater als Opernbühne: Von der Einführung des deutschen Singspiels (1778) bis zum Tod Kaiser Leopolds II (1792).* Vienna, 1970.

Minor, Jakob. *Christian Felix Weisse und seine Beziehungen zur deutschen Literatur des achtzehnten Jahrhunderts.* Innsbruck, 1880.

[Mohr, Friedrich Samuel.] *Königsbergisches Theaterjournal fürs Jahr 1782.* Königsberg, [1782].

Münnlich, Richard. "Aus der Musiksammlung der Weimarer Landesbibliothek, besonders dem Nachlass der Anna Amalia." *Aus der Geschichte der Landesbibliothek zu Weimar und ihrer Sammlungen: Festschrift.* Ed. Hermann Blumenthal. *Zeitschrift des Vereins für Thüringische Geschichte,* Supplement 23. Jena, 1941, pp. 168–84.

Musikalisches Monathsschrift. Ed. Johann Friedrich Reichardt. Berlin, 1792.

Musikalisches Real-Zeitung für das Jahr... Ed. Heinrich Philipp Carl Bossler. 3 vols. Speier, 1788–90.

Musikalisches Wochenblatt: Studien für Tonkünstler und Musikfreunde. Eine historisch-kritische Zeitschrift mit neun und dreissig Musikstücken von verschiedenen Meistern fürs Jahr 1792. Ed. F[riedrich Ludwig] Ae[melius] Kunzen and J[ohann] F[riedrich] Reichardt. Berlin, 1793.

Die Musik in Geschichte und Gegenwart. Ed. Friedrich Blume. 16 vols. Kassel and Basel, 1949–79.

Neefe, Christian Gottlob. *Lebenslauf: Von ihm selbst beschrieben, nebst beigefügtem Karackter.* Ed. Walther Engelhardt. Beiträge zur Rheinischen Musikgeschichte, vol. 21. Cologne, 1957.

Neues Theaterjournal für Deutschland. Ed. Wilhelm von Bube. 2 vols. Leipzig, 1788–9.

Der neue Teutsche Merkur vom Jahre... Ed. Christoph Martin Wieland. 10 vols. Weimar, 1790–9.

The New Grove Dictionary of Music and Musicians. Ed. Stanley Sadie. 20 vols. London, 1980.

Orel, Alfred. *Goethe als Operndirektor.* Bregenz, 1949.

Pasqué, Ernst. *Goethe's Theaterleitung in Weimar: In Episoden und Urkunden dargestellt.* 2 vols. Leipzig, 1863.

Pazdírek, Bohumil. *Universal-Handbuch der Musikliteratur Aller Zeiten und Völker: Als Nachschlagewerk und Studienquelle der Welt-Musikliteratur.* 14 vols. Vienna, [ca. 1904–10].

Pies, Eike. *Das Theater in Schleswig, 1618–1839.* Veröffentlichungen der Schleswig-Holsteinischen Universitätsgesellschaft, n.s., no. 53. Kiel, 1970.

Plümicke, C. M. *Entwurf einer Theatergeschichte von Berlin, nebst allgemeinen Bemerkungen über den Geschmack, hiesige Theaterschriftsteller und Behandlung der Kunst, in den verschiedenen Epochen.* Berlin and Stettin, 1781.

Preibisch, Walter. "Quellenstudien zu Mozart's 'Entführung aus dem Serail': Ein Beitrag zu der Geschichte der Türkenoper." *Sammelbände der Internationalen Musik-Gesellschaft* 10 (1908/9): 430–76.

Pröpper, Rolf. *Die Bühnenwerke Johann Friedrich Reichardts (1752–1814).* 2 vols. Bonn, 1965.

Rahlfs, Heinz. *Die Städtischen Bühnen zu Hannover und ihre Vorläufer in wirtschaftlicher und sozialischer Hinsicht.* Wirtschaftswissenschaftliche Gesellschaft zum Studium Niedersachsens E. V., Series B: Researches, vol. 2. Hannover, 1928.

Reclam, Ernst. *Johann Benjamin Michaelis: Sein Leben und seine Werke.* Ph.D. Diss., University of Leipzig. Leipzig, 1904.

Reden-Esbeck, Friedrich Johann Freiherr von. *Caroline Neuber und ihre Zeitgenossen: Ein Beitrag zur deutschen Kultur- und Theatergeschichte.* Leipzig, 1881.

Reichardt, Johann Friedrich. *Briefe eines aufmerksamen Reisenden, die Musik betreffend.* 2 vols. Frankfurt and Leipzig, 1774; Frankfurt and Breslau, 1776.

Musikalisches Kunstmagazin. 2 vols. Berlin, 1782, 1791.

Ueber die deutsche comische Oper: Nebst einem Anhange eines freundschaftlichen Briefe über die musikalische Poesie. Hamburg, 1774.

Répertoire International des Sources Musicales: Einzeldrücke vor 1800. 9 vols. Kassel, 1971–81.

Riedinger, Lothar. "Karl von Dittersdorf als Opernkomponist: Eine stilkritische Untersuchung." *Studien zur Musikwissenschaft* 2 (1914): 212–349.

Riemann, Hugo. *Opern-Handbuch: Repertorium der dramatisch-musikalischen Litteratur.* 2nd ed. Leipzig, [1893].

Rosen, Elisabet. *Revaler Theater-Chronik: Festschrift zur Eröffnung des neuen Schauspielhauses in Reval im September 1910.* Reval, 1910.

Rousseau, J[ean-] J[acques]. *Dictionnaire de musique.* Paris, 1768.

Rubsamen, Walter. "Mr. Seedo, Ballad Opera, and the Singspiel." *Miscellánea en homenaje a Mons. Higinio Anglés.* Barcelona, 1958–61, pp. 775–809.

Rudloff-Hille, Gertrud. "Das Leipziger Theater von 1766." *Maske und Kothurn* 14 (1968): 217–38.

Salmen, Walter. "Herder und Reichardt." *Herder-Studien.* Ed. Walter Wiora. Marburger Ostforschungen, vol. 10. Würzburg, 1960, pp. 95–108.

Schaal, Richard. *Die vor 1801 gedruckten Libretti des Theatermuseums München.* Kassel, 1963. [Also published in *Die Musikforschung* 10–14 (1957–61).]

Schering, Arnold. *Johann Sebastian Bach und das Musikleben Leipzigs im 18. Jahrhundert.* Leipzig, 1941.

Schink, Johann Friedrich. *Dramaturgische Fragmente.* 4 vols. Graz, 1781–2.

Dramaturgische Monate. 4 vols. Schwerin, 1790.

Hamburgische Theaterzeitung. 2 vols. Hamburg, 1792–3.

Schlesinger, Maximilian. *Geschichte des Breslauer Theaters.* 2 vols. Breslau, 1898.

Schletterer, H. M. *Das deutsche Singspiel von seinen Anfängen bis auf die neueste Zeit: Zur Geschichte dramatischer Musik und Poesie in Deutschland.* Vol. 1 (no more publ.) Augsburg, 1863.

Schlösser, Rudolf. *Friedrich Wilhelm Gotter: Sein Leben und seine Werke.* Theatergeschichtliche Forschungen, vol. 10. Hamburg and Leipzig, 1894.

Vom Hamburger Nationaltheater zur Gothaer Hofbühne, 1767–1779: Dreizehn Jahre aus der Entwickelung eines deutschen Theaterspielplans. Theatergeschichtliche Forschungen, vol. 13. Hamburg and Leipzig, 1895.

Schmid, Christian Heinrich. *Chronologie des deutschen Theaters.* Ed. Paul Legband. Schriften der Gesellschaft für Theatergeschichte, vol. 1. Berlin, 1902 (orig. publ. 1775.)

Das Parterr. Erfurt, 1771.

Theater-Chronick. Giessen, 1771.

Schmidt, Erich, ed. *Caroline: Briefe aus der Frühromantik.* 2 vols. Leipzig, 1913.

Schneider, L[ouis]. *Geschichte der Oper und des Königlichen Opernhauses in Berlin.* Berlin, 1852.

Schütze, Johann Friedrich. *Hamburgische Theater-Geschichte.* Hamburg, 1794.

Schulze, Friedrich. *Hundert Jahre Leipziger Stadttheater.* Leipzig, 1917.

Schusky, Renate, ed. *Das deutsche Singspiel im 18. Jahrhundert: Quellen und Zeugnisse zu Ästhetik und Rezeption.* Gesamthochschule Wuppertal, Schriftenreihe Literaturwissenschaft, vol. 12. Bonn, 1980.

Sichardt, Gisela. *Das Weimarer Liebhabertheater unter Goethes Leitung.* Weimar, 1957.

Sievers, Heinrich. *Hannoversche Musikgeschichte: Dokumente, Kritiken und Meinungen.* Vol. 1: *Von den Anfängen bis zu den Befreiungskriegen.* Tutzing, 1979.

Sonneck, Oscar George Theodore. *Catalogue of Opera Librettos Printed Before 1800* [Library of Congress]. 2 vols. Washington, 1914.

Spitta, Philipp. "Die älteste Faust-Oper und Goethe's Stellung zur Musik." *Zur Musik.* Berlin, 1892, pp. 197–234.

Stauder, Wilhelm. "Johann André: Ein Beitrag zur Geschichte des deutschen Sing-spiels." *Archiv für Musikwissenschaft* 1 (1936): 318–60.

Stephanie der Jüngere, [Johann Gottlieb]. "Vorrede." *Sämmtliche Singspiele*. Liegnitz, 1792.

Stieger, Franz. *Opernlexikon*. 11 vols. Tutzing, 1975–83.

Studien für Tonkünstler und Musikfreunde. SEE *Musikalisches Wochenblatt*.

Taschenbuch für Schauspieler und Schauspielliebhaber. Ed. Ulrich Weiss. Offenbach, 1779.

Taschenbuch fürs Theater auf 1798 und 1799. Ed. Heinrich Gottlieb Schmieder. Mainz and Hamburg, 1798.

Der Teutsche Merkur (*Der deutsche Merkur* in vol. 1). Ed. Christoph Martin Wieland. 23 vols. Weimar, 1773–89.

Theater-Journal für Deutschland. Ed. Heinrich August Ottokar Reichard. 22 pts. Gotha, 1777–84.

Theater-Kalender (*Taschenbuch für die Schaubühne auf das Jahr...*). Ed. Heinrich August Ottokar Reichard. 25 vols. Gotha, 1775–1800.

Theater-Zeitung für Deutschland. Ed. Christian August von Bertram. 26 pts. Berlin, 1789.

Theatralisches Wochenblatt von 1774 und 1775. Ed. Johann Christian Bock. 24 pts. Hamburg, 1775.

Thiel, E., and G. Rohr. *Kataloge der Herzog-August-Bibliothek Wolfenbüttel*. Vol. 14: *Libretti: Verzeichnis der bis 1800 erschienenen Textbücher*. Frankfurt am Main, 1970.

Treisch, Margarete. "Goethes Singspiele im Kompositionen seiner Zeitgenossen." *Wissenschaftliche Zeitschrift der Humboldt-Universität zu Berlin: Gesellschafts- und sprachwissenschaftliche Reihe*, no. 4:3 (1953/4): 253–70. (Ph.D. Diss., partial printing.)

Vogel, Julius. *Goethes Leipziger Studentenjahre: Ein Bilderbuch zu Dichtung und Wahrheit als Festgabe zum 150. Geburtstage des Dichters*. Leipzig, 1899.

Wagner, Heinrich Leopold. *Briefe, die Seylerische Schauspieler-Gesellschaft und ihre Vorstellungen zu Frankfurt a. M. betreffend*. Frankfurt am Main, 1777.

Weisse, Christian Felix. *Selbstbiographie*. Ed. Christian Ernst Weisse and Samuel Gottlob Frisch. Leipzig, 1806.

Wenzel, Joachim E. *Geschichte der Hamburger Oper 1678–1978*. Brunswick, [1978].

Werner, Richard Maria, ed. *Gallerie von Teutschen Schauspielern und Schauspiel-erinnen nebst Johann Friedrich Schinks Zusätzen und Berichtigungen*. Schriften der Gesellschaft für Theatergeschichte, vol. 13. Berlin, 1910.

Wilmanns, Wilhelm. "Ueber Goethe's Erwin und Elmire." *Goethe-Jahrbuch* 2 (1881): 146–67.

Wöchentliche Nachrichten und Anmerkungen, die Musik betreffend. Ed. Johann Adam Hiller. 4 vols. Leipzig, 1766–70.

Wolf, Ernst Wilhelm. *Auch eine Reise aber nur eine kleine musikalische in den Monaten Junius, Julius und August 1782*. Weimar, 1784.

Wustmann, Gustav. *Quellen zur Geschichte Leipzigs: Veröffentlichungen aus dem Archiv und der Bibliothek der Stadt Leipzig*. 2 vols. Leipzig, 1889–95.

Zeitung für Theater und andere schöne Künste. Ed. Heinrich Gottlieb Schmieder. 9 vols. [Mannheim,] 1793–7.

Zelter, [Karl Friedrich]. "Ausstellung einer Szene aus dem musikalischen Drama *Romeo und Julie*, von Georg Benda." *Lyceum der schönen Künste* 1:1 (1797): 132–44.

INDEX

The following index excludes the Catalogue of North German operas appended to the present study (pages 323–427) and the tables found in the eight chapters. A number in italics indicates a musical example from the opera cited. An asterisk after a page reference denotes an illustration. Opera titles are listed under their composers and librettists, and not independently except for anonymous works. Theatrical companies are also not listed separately but included in the page references to their principal's name or else listed under the sponsoring city or court.

52,190

ML
1729
.B38
1985

Bauman, Thomas,
1948-

North German opera
in the age of
Goethe

ML
1729
.B38
1985

Bauman, Thomas,
1948-

52,190

North German opera
in the age of
Goethe

DATE	BORROWER'S NAME	
Nov. 19/92	K Weatherington	884 m
25. Feb 94	Linda Kristensen Box 227 M P	

© THE BAKER & TAYLOR CO.